The Great Cryptogram: Francis Bacon's Cipher In The So-called Shakespeare Plays, Volume 1...

Ignatius Donnelly

Nabu Public Domain Reprints:

You are holding a reproduction of an original work published before 1923 that is in the public domain in the United States of America, and possibly other countries. You may freely copy and distribute this work as no entity (individual or corporate) has a copyright on the body of the work. This book may contain prior copyright references, and library stamps (as most of these works were scanned from library copies). These have been scanned and retained as part of the historical artifact.

This book may have occasional imperfections such as missing or blurred pages, poor pictures, errant marks, etc. that were either part of the original artifact, or were introduced by the scanning process. We believe this work is culturally important, and despite the imperfections, have elected to bring it back into print as part of our continuing commitment to the preservation of printed works worldwide. We appreciate your understanding of the imperfections in the preservation process, and hope you enjoy this valuable book.

THE GREAT CRYPTOGRAM:
FRANCIS BACON'S CIPHER In The SO-CALLED SHAKESPEARE PLAYS.

By IGNATIUS DONNELLY, Author of "Atlantis: The Antediluvian World," and "Ragnarök: The Age of Fire and Gravel."

> "And now I will vnclaspe a Secret booke
> And to your quicke conceyuing Difcontents
> Ile reade you Matter, deepe and dangerous,
> As full of perill and aduenturous Spirit,
> As to oerwalke a Current, roaring loud,
> On the vnftedfaft footing of a Speare."
> *1st Henry IV, Act I, Sc. 3.*

VOL. I.

London
Sampson Low, Marston, Searle & Rivington, L^{td}
St Dunstan's House, Fetter Lane.
1888.

Republished 1972
Scholarly Press, Inc., 22929 Industrial Drive East
St. Clair Shores, Michigan 48080
THE PENNSYLVANIA STATE UNIVERSITY
COMMONWEALTH CAMPUS LIBRARIES

Library of Congress Catalog Card Number: 76-108476
ISBN 0-403-00419-5

INTRODUCTION.

THE question may be asked by some, Why divide your book into two parts, an argument and a demonstration? If the Cipher is conclusive, why is any discussion of probabilities necessary?

In answer to this I would state that, for a long time before I conceived the idea of the possibility of there being a Cipher in the Shakespeare Plays, I had been at work collecting proofs, from many sources, to establish the fact that FRANCIS BACON was the real author of those great works. Much of the material so amassed is new and curious, and well worthy of preservation. While the Cipher will be able to stand alone, these facts will throw many valuable side-lights upon the story told therein.

Moreover, that part of the book called "PARALLELISMS" will, I hope, be interesting to scholars, even after BACON's authorship of the Plays is universally acknowledged, as showing how the same great mind unconsciously cast itself forth in parallel lines, in prose and poetry, in the two greatest sets of writings in the world.

And I trust the essays on the geography, the politics, the religion and the purposes of the Plays will possess an interest apart from the question of authorship.

I have tried to establish every statement I have made by abundant testimony, and to give due credit to each author from whom I have borrowed.

For the shortcomings of the work I shall have to ask the indulgence of the reader. It was written in the midst of many interruptions and distractions; and it lacks that perfection which ampler leisure might possibly have given it.

As to the actuality of the Cipher there can be but one conclusion. A long, continuous narrative, running through many pages, detailing historical events in a perfectly symmetrical, rhetorical, grammatical manner, and *always growing out of the same numbers, employed in the same way, and counting from the same, or similar, starting-points, cannot be otherwise than a pre-arranged arithmetical cipher.*

Let those who would deny this proposition produce a single page of a connected story, eliminated, by an arithmetical rule, from any other work; in fact, let them find five words that will cohere, by accident, in due order, in any publication, where they were not first placed with intent and aforethought. I have never yet been able to find even three such. Regularity does not grow out of chaos. There can be no intellectual order without preëxisting intellectual purpose. The fruits of mind can only be found where mind is or has been.

It may be thought, by some, that I speak with too much severity of Shakspere and his family; but it must be remembered that I am battling against the great high walls of public prejudice and intrenched error. "Fate," it is said, "obeys the downright striker." I trust my earnestness will not be mistaken for maliciousness.

In the concluding chapters I have tried to do justice to the memory of FRANCIS BACON, and to the great minds that first announced to the world his claim to the authorship of the Plays. I feel that it is a noble privilege to thus assist in lifting the burden of injustice from the shoulders of long-suffering merit.

The key here turned, for the first time, in the secret wards of the Cipher, will yet unlock a vast history, nearly as great in bulk as the Plays themselves, and tell a mighty story of one of the greatest and most momentous eras of human history, illuminated by the most gifted human being that ever dwelt upon the earth.

I conclude by invoking, in behalf of my book, the kindly judgment and good-will of all men. I. D.

THE TABLE OF CONTENTS.

BOOK I.—THE ARGUMENT.

PART I.

WILLIAM SHAKSPERE DID NOT WRITE THE PLAYS.

CHAPTER I.—THE LEARNING OF THE PLAYS,	13
II.—SHAKSPERE'S EDUCATION,	27
III.—SHAKSPERE'S REAL CHARACTER,	44
IV.—THE LOST MANUSCRIPTS AND LIBRARY,	73
V.—THE AUTHOR OF THE PLAYS A LAWYER,	108

PART II.

FRANCIS BACON THE REAL AUTHOR OF THE PLAYS.

CHAPTER I.—FRANCIS BACON A POET,	121
II.—THE AUTHOR OF THE PLAYS A PHILOSOPHER	149
III.—THE GEOGRAPHY OF THE PLAYS,	161
IV.—THE POLITICS OF THE PLAYS,	173
V.—THE RELIGION OF THE PLAYS,	196
VI.—THE PURPOSES OF THE PLAYS,	212
VII.—THE REASONS FOR CONCEALMENT,	246
VIII.—CORROBORATING CIRCUMSTANCES,	259

PART III.

PARALLELISMS.

CHAPTER I.—IDENTICAL EXPRESSIONS,	295
II.—IDENTICAL METAPHORS,	335
III.—IDENTICAL OPINIONS,	370
IV.—IDENTICAL QUOTATIONS,	397
V.—IDENTICAL STUDIES,	411
VI.—IDENTICAL ERRORS,	437
VII.—IDENTICAL USE OF UNUSUAL WORDS,	444
VIII.—IDENTITIES OF CHARACTER,	460
IX.—IDENTITIES OF STYLE,	461

ILLUSTRATIONS IN VOL. I.

FRANCIS BACON—THE TRUE SHAKESPEARE. After the portrait by Van Somer - - - - - - - *Frontispiece*.

WILLIAM SHAKSPERE. *Fac-simile* of the celebrated Droeshout portrait in the 1623 Folio - - - - - - - 64

BEN JONSON. After the portrait by Oliver - - - - 96

GORHAMBURY. Bacon's residence - - - - - 160

SIR ROBERT CECIL - - - - - - - 193

BOOK I.
·THE ARGUMENT·

"Nay, pray you come;
Or if thou wilt hold further argument,
Do it in notes."
Much Ado about Nothing, II, 3.

PART I.

WILLIAM SHAKSPERE DID NOT WRITE THE PLAYS.

CHAPTER I.

THE LEARNING REVEALED IN THE SHAKESPEARE WRITINGS.

> "From his cradle
> He was a scholar, and a ripe and good one."
> *Henry VIII.*, iv. 2.

IT was formerly the universal belief, entertained even among the critical, that the writings which go by the name of *William Shakespeare* were the work of an untaught, unlearned man.

Addison compared Shakspere[1] to the agate in the ring of Pyrrhus, which had the figure of Apollo and the nine Muses pictured in the veins of the stone by the hand of Nature, without any assistance from Art.

Voltaire regarded him as a "drunken savage."

Pope speaks of him as "a man of no education."

Richard Grant White says Shakspere was regarded, even down to the time of Pope, as "this bewitching but untutored and half-savage child of nature."

He was looked upon as a rustic-bred bard who sang as the birds sing — a greater Burns, who, as Milton says, "warbled his native wood-notes wild."

This view was in accordance with the declaration of Ben Jonson that he possessed "small Latin and less Greek," and the state-

---

[1] Wherever reference is had in these pages to the man of Stratford the name will be spelled, as he spelled it in his will, *Shakspere*. Wherever the reference is to the Plays, or to the real author of the Plays, the name will be spelled *Shakespeare*, for that was the name on the title-pages of quartos and folios.

ment of old Fuller, in his *Worthies*, in 1622, that "his learning was very little."

Fuller says:

Plautus was never any scholar, as doubtless our Shakespeare, if alive, would confess himself.

Leonard Digges says:

>The patterne of all wit,
>*Art without Art* unparaleld as yet.
>Next Nature onely helpt him, for looke thorow
>This whole booke, thou shalt find he doth not borrow
>One phrase from Greekes, nor Latines imitate,
>Nor once from vulgar languages translate.

Rev. John Ward, Vicar of Stratford, writing forty-seven years after Shakspere's death, and speaking the traditions of Stratford, says:

I have heard that Mr Shakespeare was a natural wit, *without any art at all.*

Seventy odd years after Shakspere's death, Bentham, in his *State of the English Schools and Churches*, says:

William Shakespeare was born at Stratford, in Warwickshire; his learning was very little, and therefore it is more a matter for wonder that he should be a very excellent poet.[1]

But in the last fifty years this view is completely changed. The critical world is now substantially agreed that the man who wrote the plays was one of the most learned men of the world, not only in that learning which comes from observation and reflection, but in book-lore, ancient and modern, and in the knowledge of many languages.

I. HIS CLASSICAL LEARNING.

Grant White admits:

He had as much learning as he had occasion to use, and even more.[2]

It was at one time believed that the writer of the plays was unable to read any of the Latin or Greek authors in the original tongues, and that he depended altogether upon translations; but such, it is now proved, was not the case.

The Comedy of Errors, which is little more than a reproduction of the *Menoechmi* of Plautus, first appeared at certain

[1] Chap. 19.   [2] White, *Life and Genius of Shakespeare*, p. 50.

Christmas revels given by Bacon and his fellow lawyers, at Gray's Inn, in 1594; while, says Halliwell, "the *Menoechmi* of Plautus was not translated into English, or rather no English translation of it was printed, before 1595."

"The greater part of the story of *Timon* was taken from the untranslated Greek of Lucian."[1]

"Shakespeare's plays," says White,[2] "show forty per cent of Romance or Latin words, which is probably a larger proportion than is now used by our best writers; certainly larger than is heard from those who speak their mother tongue with spontaneous, idiomatic correctness."

We find in *Twelfth Night* these lines:

> Like the Egyptian thief, at point of death,
> Kill what I love.[3]

This is an allusion to a story from Heliodorus' *Æthiopics*. I do not know of any English translation of it in the time of Shakspere.

Holmes says:

> The writer was a classical scholar. Rowe found traces in him of the *Electra* of Sophocles; Colman, of Ovid; Pope, of Dares Phrygius, and other Greek authors; Farmer, of Horace and Virgil; Malone, of Lucretius, Statius, Catullus, Seneca, Sophocles, and Euripides; Stevens, of Plautus; Knight, of the *Antigone* of Sophocles; and White, of the *Alcestis* of Euripides.[4]

White says:

> His very frequent use of Latin derivatives in their radical sense shows a somewhat thoughtful and observant study of that language.[5]

White further says:

> Where, even in Plutarch's pages, are the aristocratic republican tone and the tough muscularity of mind, which characterized the Romans, so embodied as in Shakespeare's Roman plays? Where, even in Homer's song, the subtle wisdom of the crafty Ulysses, the sullen selfishness and conscious martial might of broad Achilles; the blundering courage of thick-headed Ajax; or the mingled gallantry and foppery of Paris, so vividly portrayed as in *Troilus and Cressida*?[6]

Knight says:

> The marvelous accuracy, the real, substantial learning, of the three Roman plays of Shakespeare present the most complete evidence to our minds that they were the result of a profound study of the whole range of Roman history, including the nicer details of Roman manners, not in those days to be acquired in a compendious form, but to be brought out by diligent reading alone.[7]

---

[1] Holmes, *Authorship of Shakespeare*, p. 57.
[2] *Life and Genius of Shakespeare*, p. 226.
[3] Act v, scene 1.
[4] *Authorship of Shakespeare*, p. 57.
[5] *Life and Genius of Shakespeare*, p. 31.
[6] Ibid., p. 257.
[7] Knight's *Shak. Biography*, p. 528.

And again:

> In his Roman plays he appears co-existent with his wonderful characters, and *to have read all the obscure pages of Roman history with a clearer eye than philosopher or historian*. When he employs Latinisms in the construction of his sentences, and *even in the creation of new words*, he does so with singular facility and unerring correctness.[1]

Appleton Morgan says:

> In *Antony and Cleopatra*, Charmian suggests a game of billiards. But this is not, as is supposed, an anachronism, for *the human encyclopedia* who wrote that sentence appears to have known — what very few people know nowadays — that the game of billiards is older than Cleopatra.[2]

Whately[3] describes Shakespeare as possessed of "an amazing genius which could pervade all nature at a glance, and to whom nothing within the limits of the universe appears to be unknown."

A recent writer says, speaking of the resemblance between the *Eumenides* of Æschylus and the *Hamlet* of Shakespeare:

> The plot is so similar that we should certainly have credited the English poet with copying it, if he could have read Greek.... The common elements are indeed remarkable. Orestes and Hamlet have both to avenge a beloved father who has fallen a victim to the guilty passion of an unfaithful wife; in each case the adulterer has ascended the throne; and a claim of higher than mere mortal authority demands his punishment; for the permitted return of Hamlet's father from the world beyond the grave may be set beside the command of Apollo to Orestes to become the executive of the wrath of Heaven.[4]

Knight[5] sees evidence that Shakespeare was a close student of the works of Plato.

Alexander Schmidt, in his lexicon, under the word *Adonis*, quotes the following lines from Shakespeare:

> Thy promises are like Adonis' gardens,
> That one day bloomed and fruitful were the next.[6]

Upon which Schmidt comments:

> Perhaps confounded with the garden of King Alcinous in the *Odyssey*.[7]

Richard Grant White says:

> No mention of any such garden in the classic writings of Greece and Rome is known to scholars.

But the writer of the plays, who, we are told, was no scholar, had penetrated more deeply into the classic writings than his learned critics; and a recent commentator, James D. Butler, has found out the source of this allusion. He says:

---

[1] Knight's *Shak. Biography*, p. 528.
[2] *Some Shak. Commentators*, p. 35.
[3] *Shak. Myth.*, p. 82.
[4] Julia Wedgewood.
[5] Knight's *Shak.*, note 6, act v, *Merchant of Venice*.
[6] *1st Henry VI.*, i, 6.
[7] vii, 117-126.

This couplet must have been suggested by Plato. (*Phaedrus*, p. 276.) The translation is Jowett's — that I may not be suspected of warping the original to fit my theory:

Would a husbandman, said Socrates, who is a man of sense, take the seeds, which he values and which he wishes to be fruitful, and in sober earnest plant them during the heat of summer, in some garden of Adonis, that he may rejoice when he sees them in eight days appearing in beauty? Would he not do that, if at all, to please the spectators at a festival? But the seeds about which he is in earnest he sows in fitting soil, and practices husbandry, and is satisfied if in eight months they arrive at perfection.[1]

Here we clearly have the original of the disputed passage:

> Thy promises are like Adonis' gardens,
> That one day bloomed and fruitful were the next.

Judge Holmes[2] finds the original of the expression, "the mind's eye," in Plato, who uses precisely the same phrase. He also thinks the passage of Plato, —

While begetting and rearing children, and handing in succession from some to others life like a torch, and even paying, according to law, worship to the gods, —

gave the hint for the following lines in *Measure for Measure:*

> Heaven doth with us as we with torches do,
> Not light them for ourselves.

He also finds in Plato the original of Lear's phrase, "this same learned Theban."

Knight thinks the expression, —

> Were she as rough
> As the swelling Adriatic seas,[3] —

was without doubt taken from Horace,[4] "*of whose odes there was no translation in the sixteenth century.*"

The grand lines in *Macbeth,* —

> And all our yesterdays have *lighted* fools
> The way to dusty death. Out, out, *brief candle!* —

are traced to Catullus. I give the translation of another:

> *Soles occidere et redire possunt,*
> *Nobis, cum semel occidit brevis lux,*
> *Nox est perpetuo una dormienda.*

> (The *lights* of heaven go out and return.
> When once our *brief candle* goes out,
> One night is to be perpetually slept.)

That beautiful thought in *Hamlet,* —

> And from her unpolluted flesh
> May violets spring,[5] —

---

[1] *Shakespeariana*, May, 1886, p. 230.
[2] *Authorship of Shakespeare*, p. 396.
[3] *Taming of the Shrew*, i, 2.
[4] Ode xix, book iii.
[5] Act v, scene 1.

seems to have had its original in the lines of Persius:

> *Nunc levior cippus non imprimit ossa,*
> *Laudat posteritas, nunc non è manibus illis,*
> *Nunc non è tumulo fortunataque favilla*
> *Nascuntur violæ?*[1] —

which has been translated:

> Will a less tomb, composed of smaller stones,
> Press with less weight upon the under bones?
> Posterity may praise them, why, what though?
> Can yet their manes such a gift bestow
> As to make violets from their ashes grow?

W. O. Follett (Sandusky, Ohio), in his pamphlet, *Addendum to Who Wrote Shakespeare*, quotes[2] a remark of the brothers Langhorne in the preface to their translation of the *Lives of Plutarch*, to this effect:

> It is said by those who are not willing to allow Shakspere much learning, that he availed himself of the last mentioned translation [of Plutarch, by Thomas North]. But they seem to forget that, in order to support their arguments of this kind, it is necessary for them to prove that Plato, too, was translated into English at the same time; for the celebrated soliloquy, "To be or not to be," is taken almost verbatim from that philosopher; yet we have never found that Plato was translated in those times.

Mrs. Pott has shown in her great work[3] that very many of the Latin quotations found in Francis Bacon's sheets of notes and memoranda, preserved in the British Museum, and called his *Promus of Formularies and Elegancies*, are either transferred bodily to the plays or worked over in new forms. It follows, therefore, that the writer of the Plays must have read the authors from whom Bacon culled these sentences, or have had access to Bacon's manuscript notes, or that he was Bacon himself.

In the *Promus* notes we find the proverb, "*Diluculo surgere saluberrimum.*"

Sir Toby Belch says to Sir Andrew Aguecheek:

Approach, Sir Andrew; not to be a-bed after midnight is to be up betimes, and *diluculo surgere*, thou knowest.[4]

Again:

Qui dissimulat liber non est. (He who dissembles is not free.)[5]

In Shakespeare we have:

> The dissembler is a slave.[6]

[1] Sat. i.
[2] Page 7.
[3] *Promus*, pp. 31–38.
[4] *Twelfth Night*, ii, 3.
[5] *Promus* notes, folio 83 C.
[6] *Pericles*, i, 1.

Again, in the *Promus* notes, we have:

Divitiæ impedimenta virtutis. (The baggage of virtue.)

Bacon says:

I cannot call riches better than the baggage of virtue.

Shakespeare says:

> If thou art rich, thou'rt poor;
> For, like an ass whose back with ingots bows,
> Thou bearest thy heavy riches but a journey,
> Till death unloads thee.[1]

Again:

Mors et fugacem persequitur virum. (Death pursues even the man that flies from him.)

Shakespeare has:

> Away! for death doth hold us in pursuit.[2]

And again:

Mors omnia solvit. (Death dissolves all things.)

Shakespeare has:

> Let heaven *dissolve* my life.[3]

And again:

Hoc solum scio, quod nihil scio. (This only I know, that I know nothing.)

Shakespeare has:

> The wise man knows himself to be a fool.[4]

Again:

Tela honoris tenerior. (The stuff of which honor is made is rather tender.)

Shakespeare has:

> The tender honor of a maid.[5]

Again:

Tranquillo qui libet gubernator.—Eras. Ad. 4496. (Any one can be a pilot in fine weather.)

Shakespeare says:

> Nay, mother,
> Where is your ancient courage? You were used
> To say, extremity was the trier of spirits;
> That common chances common men could bear;
> That when the sea was calm all boats alike
> Showed mastership in floating.[6]

---

[1] *Measure for Measure*, iii, 1.
[2] *3d Henry VI.*, ii, 5.
[3] *Antony and Cleopatra*, iii, 2.
[4] *As You Like It*, v, 1.
[5] *All's Well that Ends Well*, iii, 5.
[6] *Coriolanus*, iv, 1.

Again:

In aliquibus manetur quia non datur regressus. (In some [places] one has to remain because there is no getting back.)[1]

And in Shakespeare we find:

> I am in blood
> Stepped in so far, that, should I wade no more,
> Returning were as easy as go o'er.[2]

Again:

Frigus adurit. (Cold parches.)

And Shakespeare says:

> Frost itself as actively doth burn.[3]

Again:

Anosce teipsim. (Know thyself.)

Shakespeare has:

> Mistress, know yourself.[4]
> He knows nothing who knows not himself.[5]
> That fool knows not himself.[6]

I could cite many other similar instances, but these will doubtless be sufficient to satisfy the reader.

II. HIS KNOWLEDGE OF THE MODERN LANGUAGES.

It furthermore now appears that the writer of the Plays was versed in the languages and literature of France, Italy, and even Spain; while he had some familiarity with the annals and tongues of Northern Europe.

As to the French, whole pages of the Plays are written in that language.[7]

His knowledge of Italian is clearly proved.

The story of *Othello* was taken from the Italian of Cinthio's *Il Capitano Moro*, of which no translation is known to have existed; the tale of *Cymbeline* was drawn from an Italian novel of Boccaccio, not known to have been translated into English, and the like is true of other plays.[8]

Richard Grant White[9] conclusively proves that the writer of *Othello* had read the *Orlando Furioso* in the original Italian; that the very words are borrowed as well as the thought; and that the

---

[1] *Promus* notes, No. 1361.
[2] *Macbeth*, iii, 4.
[3] *Hamlet*, iii, 4.
[4] *As You Like It*, iv, 1.
[5] *All's Well that Ends Well*, ii, 4.
[6] *Troilus and Cressida*, ii, 1.
[7] *Henry V.*
[8] Holmes, *Authorship of Shakespeare*, p. 58.
[9] *Life and Genius of Shakespeare*, p. 35.

author adhered to the expressions in the Italian where the only translation then in existence had departed from them. The same high authority also shows that in the famous passage, "Who steals my purse steals trash," etc., the writer of *Othello* borrowed from the *Orlando Innamorato* of Berni, "of which poem *to this day there is no English version.*"

The plot of the comedy of *Twelfth Night; or, What You Will*, is drawn from two Italian comedies, both having the same title, *Gl' Inganni* (The Cheats), both published before the date of Shakespeare's play, and which Shakespeare must have read in the original Italian, as there were, I believe, no English translations of them.

The Two Gentlemen of Verona is supposed to have been written several years before 1598, the year when Bartholomew Yonge's translation of the *Diana* of Jorge de Montemayor was published in England; and Halliwell believes that there are similarities between Shakespeare's play and Montemayor's romance "too minute to be accidental." If this is the case we must conclude that Shakespeare either read some translation of the romance in manuscript before 1598, or else that he read it in the original. Says Halliwell:

> The absolute origin of the entire plot has possibly to be discovered in some Italian novel. The error in the first folio of *Padua* for *Milan*, in act ii, scene 5, has perhaps to be referred to some scene in the original novel. Tieck mentions an old German play founded on a tale similar to *The Two Gentlemen of Verona;* but it has not yet been made accessible to English students, and we have no means of ascertaining how far the resemblance extends.

It further appears that Shakespeare found the original of *The Merchant of Venice* in an untranslated Italian novel. Mr. Collier says:

> In the novel *Il Pecorone* of Giovanni Fiorentino, the lender of the money (under very similar circumstances, and the wants of the Christian borrower arising out of nearly the same events) is a Jew; and there also we have the
>
> > equal pound
> > Of your fair flesh, to be cut off and taken
> > In what part of your body pleaseth me.
>
> The words in the Italian are "*ch'el Giudeo gli potesse levare una libra di carne d'addosso di qualumque luogo e' volesse,*" which are so nearly like those of Shakespeare as to lead us to believe that he followed here some literal translation of the novel in *Il Pecorone*. None such has, however, reached our time, and the version we have printed at the foot of the Italian was made and published in 1765.[1]

Mrs. Pott, in her great work, calls attention to the following

---

[1] *Introduction to the Adventures of Gianetta*, Shakespeare's Library, part 1, vol. 1, p. 315.

Italian proverb, and the parallel passage in *Lear*. No one can doubt that the former suggested the latter:

> *Non far ciò che tu puoi;*
> *Non spender ciò che tu hai;*
> *Non creder ciò che tu odi;*
> *Non dir ciò che tu sai.*[1]

> (Do less than thou canst;
> Spend less than thou hast;
> Believe less than thou hearest;
> Say less than thou knowest.)

While in Shakespeare we have:

> Have more than thou showest,
> Speak more than thou knowest,
> Lend less than thou owest,
> Ride more than thou goest,
> Learn more than thou trowest.[2]

And, again, the same author calls attention to the following Italian proverb and parallel passage:

Il savio fa della necessità virtù. (The wise man makes a virtue of necessity.)[3]

Shakespeare says:

Are you content to make a virtue of necessity?[4]

The same author calls attention to numerous instances where the author of the Plays borrowed from Spanish proverbs. I select one of the most striking:

Desque naci lloré ye cada dia nace porque. (When I was born I cried, and every day shows why.)

Shakespeare has:

> When we are born we cry, that we are come
> To this great stage of fools.[5]

In *Love's Labor Lost*[6] we find the author quoting part of an Italian proverb:

> *Vinegia, Vinegia,*
> *Chi non ti vede ei non ti pregia.*

The proverb is:

> *Venetia, Venetia, chi non ti vede, non ti pregia,*
> *Ma chi t' ha troppo veduto ti dispregia.*

The plot of *Hamlet* was taken from Saxo Grammaticus, the Danish historian, of whom, says Whately, writing in 1748, "no

---

[1] *Promus*, p. 524.
[2] *Lear*, i, 6.
[3] *Promus*, p. 525.
[4] *Two Gentlemen of Verona*, iv, 1.
[5] *Lear*, iv, 6.
[6] Act iv, scene 2.

translation hath yet been made."[1] So that it would appear the author of *Hamlet* must have read the Danish chronicle in the original tongue.

Dr. Herman Brunnhofer, Dr. Benno Tschischwitz (in his *Shakespeare Forschungen*) and Rev. Bowechier Wrey Savile[2] all unite in believing that the writer of *Hamlet* was familiar with the works of Giordano Bruno, who visited England, 1583 to 1586; and that the words of Hamlet,[3] "If the sun breed maggots in a dead dog, being a god kissing carrion," etc., are taken from Bruno's *Spaccio della Bestia Trionfante*. Furthermore, that the author of *Hamlet* was familiar with "the atomic theory" of the ancients. And the Rev. Bowechier Wrey Savile says:

Inasmuch as neither Bruno's *Spaccio*, nor the fragments of Parmenides' poem, *On Nature*, which have come down to us, were known in an English dress at the beginning of the seventeenth century (Toland's translation of Bruno's *Spaccio* did not appear until 1713), it would seem to show that the author of *Hamlet* must have been acquainted with both Greek and Italian, as was the case with the learned Francis Bacon.

III. A Scholar Even in His Youth.

The evidences of scholarship mark the earliest as well as the latest works of the great poet; in fact, they are more observable in the works of his youth than in those of middle life. Even the writers who have least doubt as to the Shaksperean authorship of the Plays admit this fact.

White says the early plays show "A mind fresh from academic studies."[4]

Speaking of the early plays, Prof. Dowden finds among their characteristics:

Frequency of classical allusions, frequency of puns and conceits, wit and imagery drawn out in detail to the point of exhaustion. . . . In *Love's Labor Lost* the arrangement is too geometrical; the groupings are artificial, not organic or vital.

Coleridge was of opinion that

A young author's first work almost always bespeaks his recent pursuits.

And, hence, he concludes that

The habits of William Shakespeare had been scholastic and those of a student.

The scholarship of the writer of the Plays and his familiarity with the Latin language are also shown in the use of odd and

---

[1] *An Inquiry into the Learning of Shakespeare.*   [3] Act ii, scene 1.
[2] *Shakespeariana*, Oct., 1884, p. 312.   [4] White, *Shakespeare's Genius*, p. 257.

extraordinary words, many of them coined by himself, and such as would not naturally occur to an untaught genius, familiar with no language but his own. I give a few specimens:

Rubrous, *Twelfth Night*, i, 4.
Pendulous, *King Lear*, iii, 4.
Abortive, *Richard III.*, i, 2.
Cautelous, *Julius Cæsar*, ii, 1.
Cautel, *Hamlet*, i, 3.
Deracinate, *Troilus and Cressida*, i, 3; *Henry V.*, v, 2.
Surcease, *Macbeth*, i, 7.
Recordation, *2d Henry IV.*, ii, 3.
Enwheel, *Othello*, ii, 1.
Armipotent, *All's Well That Ends Well*, iv, 3.
Evitate, *Merry Wives of Windsor*, v, 5.
Imbost, *Antony and Cleopatra*, iv, 3.
Disnatured, *King Lear*, i, 4. [ii, 1.
Inaidable, *All's Well That Ends Well*,
Unsuppressive, *Julius Cæsar*, ii, 1.
Oppugnancy, *Troilus and Cressida*, i, 3.
Enskied, *Measure for Measure*, i, 5.
Legerity, *Henry V.*, iv, 1.
Propinquity, *King Lear*, i, 1.
Credent, *Hamlet*, i, 3.
Sluggardised, *The Two Gentlemen of Verona*, i, 1.

Knight says, speaking of the word *expedient*:[1]

Expedient. The word properly means, "that disengages itself from all entanglements." To set at liberty the *foot* which was held fast is *exped-ire.* Shakspere always uses this word in strict accordance with its derivation, *as, in truth, he does most words that may be called learned.*[2]

Knight[3] also notes the fact that he uses the word *reduce* in the Latin sense, "to bring back."

IV: HIS UNIVERSAL LEARNING.

The range of his studies was not confined to antique tongues and foreign languages. He must have read all the books of travel which grew out of that age of sea-voyages and explorations.

Dr. Brinton[4] points out that the idea of Ariel having been pegged in the knotty entrails of an oak until freed by Prospero was borrowed from the mythology of the Yurucares, a South American tribe of Indians, in which the first men were confined in the heart of an enormous bole, until the god Tiri let them out by cleaving it in twain. He further claims that Caliban is undoubtedly the word *Carib*, often spelt Caribani and Calibani in olden writers; and his "dam's god, *Setebos*," was the supreme deity of the Patagonians, when first visited by Magellan.

In *The Merchant of Venice* we read:

Bring them, I pray thee, with imagined speed,
Unto the *tranect*, to the common ferry.[5]

[1] *King John*, ii, 1. [2] *Knight's Shak.*, i History, p. 24. [3] *Richard III.*, v, 4.
[4] *Myths of the New World*, p. 240, note. [5] Act iii, scene 5.

Of this word Knight says:

> No other example is found of the use of this word in English, and yet there is little doubt that the word is correct. *Tranare* and *trainare* are interpreted by Florio not only as *to draw*, which is the common acceptation, but as *to pass or swim over*. Thus the *tranect* was most probably the tow-boat of the ferry.[1]

In *King John* we have:

> Now, by my life, this day grows wondrous hot;
> Some *airy* devil hovers in the sky,
> And pours down mischief.[2]

Collier changed *airy* to *fiery*, "which, we may be sure," he says, "was the word of the poet." But Knight turns to Burton and shows that he described "aerial spirits or devils, who keep most quarter in the air, and cause many tempests, thunder and lightning," etc. And he also referred to the fact that "Paul to the Ephesians called them forms of the *air*." Knight adds:

> Shakspere knew this curious learning from the schoolmen, but the correctors knew nothing about it.

We have another instance, in the following, where the great poet knew a good deal more than his commentators.

In *Romeo and Juliet* he says:

> Are you at leisure, holy Father, now;
> Or shall I come to you at evening mass?[3]

Upon this Richard Grant White says:

> If he became a member of the Church of Rome it must have been after he wrote *Romeo and Juliet*, in which he speaks of "evening mass;" for the humblest member of that church knows that there is no mass at vespers.[4]

But we have the authority of the learned Cardinal Bona that the name *mass* was given to the morning and evening prayers of the Christian soldiers. Salvazzio states that the name was given to the lectures or lessons in matins. In the "Rule of St. Aurelian" it is stated that at Christmas and on the Epiphany six masses are to be read at matins, from the prophet Isaiah, and six from the gospel; whilst on the festivals of martyrs the first mass is to be read from the acts of the martyrs. In his rule for nuns the same holy Bishop tells them that, as the nights are long, they may recite three masses at the lectern. As the female sex could n. act as priests, it is plain that the word *mass* was formerly the

---

[1] Knight's *Shak. Com.*, p. 240.
[2] Act iii, scene 2.
[3] Act iv, scene 1.
[4] *Life and Genius of Shak.*, p. 187.

synonym for prayers, and did not mean, as nowadays, exclusively the great sacrifice of the church; and therefore "evening mass" simply means the evening service. In fact, as Bishop Clifford shows, the word *mass* or, as it was written in Anglo-Saxon, *masse*, came to be regarded as the synonym for *feast;* hence, *Candlemas, lammas, Michaelmas,* etc., are the feast of candles, the feast of loaves, the feast of St. Michael, etc. "Moreover, *mass* being the chief religious service of the Catholic Church, the word came to be used in the sense of church service in general. *Evening-mass* means evening service or vespers."

What a curious reaching-out for facts, in a day barren of encyclopædias, is shown in these lines:

Adrian. Widow Dido, said you? You make me study of that: she was of Carthage, not of Tunis.
Gonzalo. This Tunis, sir, *was* Carthage.
Adrian. Carthage?
Gonzalo. I assure you, Carthage.[1]

V. Our Conclusion.

We commence our argument, therefore, with this proposition: The author of the Plays, whoever he may have been, was unquestionably a profound scholar and most laborious student. He had read in their own tongues all the great, and some of the obscure writers of antiquity; he was familiar with the languages of the principal nations of Europe; his mind had compassed all the learning of his time and of preceding ages; he had pored over the pages of French and Italian novelists; he had read the philosophical utterances of the great thinkers of Greece and Rome; and he had closely considered the narrations of the explorers who were just laying bare the secrets of new islands and continents. It has been justly said that the Plays could not have been written without a library, and cannot, to-day, be studied without one. To their proper elucidation the learning of the whole world is necessary. Goethe says of the writer of the Plays: "He drew a sponge over the table of human knowledge."

We pass, then, to the question, Did William Shakspere possess such a vast mass of information?—could he have possessed it?

[1] *Tempest*, ii, 2.

CHAPTER II.

THE EDUCATION OF WILLIAM SHAKSPERE.

Touchstone. Art thou learned?
William. No, sir.
Touchstone. Then learn this of me: to have is to have.
As You Like It, v, i.

IT must not be forgotten that the world of three hundred years ago was a very different world from that of to-day.

A young man, at the present time, can receive in the backwoods of the United States, or Canada, or in the towns of Australia, an education which Cambridge and Oxford could not have afforded to the noblemen of England in the sixteenth century. That tremendous educator, the daily press, had then no existence. Now it comes to almost every door, bringing not only the news of the whole world, but an abstract of the entire literary and scientific knowledge of the age.

I. ENGLAND IN THE SIXTEENTH CENTURY.

Three hundred years ago the English-speaking population of the world was confined almost altogether to the island of Great Britain, and the refinement and culture of the island scarcely extended beyond a few towns and the universities. London was the great center, not only of politics, but of literature and courtly manners. The agricultural population and the yeomanry of the smaller towns were steeped to the lips in ignorance, rude and barbarous in their manners, and brutal in their modes of life.

They did not even speak the same language. Goadby tells us that, when the militia met from the different counties to organize resistance to the invasion of the Spaniards,

> It was hard to catch the words of command, so pronounced were the different dialects.[1]

Simpson says:

> If cattle-driving was to be interpreted as levying war, all England at harvest tide was in a state of warfare. The disputes about tithes and boundaries were

---

[1] Goadby, *England of Shak.*, p. 83.

then usually settled by bands of armed men, and the records of the Star-Chamber swarm with such cases.[1]

The cots or dwellings of the humble classes in Shakspere's time were, as the haughty Spaniard wrote, in the reign of Elizabeth's sister, built "of sticks and dirt."

"People," says Richard Grant White, "corresponding in position to those whose means and tastes would now insure them as much comfort in their homes as a king has in his palace, and even simple elegance beside, then lived in houses which in their best estate would seem at the present day rude, cheerless and confined, to any man not bred in poverty."[2]

II. STRATFORD IN THE TIME OF SHAKSPERE.

The lives of the people were coarse, barren and filthy.

Thorold Rogers says:

In the absence of all winter roots and herbs, beyond a few onions, a diet of salted provisions, extending over so long a period, would be sure to engender disease; . . . and, as a matter of fact, scurvy and leprosy, the invariable results of an unwholesome diet, *were endemic*, the latter malignant and infectious in medieval England. The virulence of these diseases, due in the first instance to unwholesome food, was aggravated by *the inconceivably filthy habits of the people*.[3]

Richard Grant White says:

Stratford then contained about fifteen hundred inhabitants, who dwelt chiefly in thatched cottages, which straggled over the ground, too near together for rural beauty, too far apart to seem snug and neighborly; and scattered through the gardens and orchards around the best of these were neglected stables, cow-yards and sheep-cotes. Many of the meaner houses were *without chimneys or glazed windows*. The streets were cumbered with logs and blocks, and foul with offal, mud, muck-heaps and reeking stable refuse, the accumulation of which the town ordinances and the infliction of fines could not prevent *even before the doors of the better sort of people*. The very first we hear of John Shakespeare himself, in 1552, is that he and a certain Humphrey Reynolds and Adrian Quiney "*fecerunt sterquinarium*," in the quarter called Henley Street, against the order of the court; for which dirty piece of business they were "*in misericordia*," as they well deserved. But the next year John Shakespeare and Adrian Quiney repeated the unsavory offense, and this time in company with the bailiff himself.[4]

Halliwell-Phillipps says:

The sanitary condition of the thoroughfares of Stratford-on-Avon was, to our present notions, simply terrible. Under-surface drainage of every kind was then an unknown art in the district. There was a far greater amount of moisture in the land than would now be thought possible, and streamlets of water-power suffi-

---

[1] *School of Shak.*, vol. i, p. 60.
[2] *Life and Genius of Shak.*, p. 17.
[3] *Work and Wages*, Thorold Rogers, p. 96.
[4] *Life and Genius of Shak.*, p. 21.

cient for the operation of corn-mills meandered through the town. This general humidity intensified the evils arising from the want of scavengers, or other effective appliances for the preservation of cleanliness. House-slops were recklessly thrown into ill-kept channels that lined the sides of unmetaled roads; pigs and geese too often reveled in the puddles and ruts, while here and there were small middens, ever in the course of accumulation, the receptacles of offal and of every species of nastiness. A regulation for the removal of these collections to certain specified localities, interspersed through the borough and known as common dung-hills, appears to have been the extent of the interference that the authorities ventured or cared to exercise in such matters. Sometimes when the nuisance was thought to be sufficiently flagrant, they made a raid on those inhabitants who had suffered their refuse to accumulate largely in the highways. On one of these occasions, in April, 1552, John Shakespeare was fined the sum of twelve pence for having amassed what was no doubt a conspicuous *sterquinarium* before his house in Henley Street, and under these unsavory circumstances does the history of the poet's father commence in the records of England. It is sad to be compelled to admit that there was little excuse for his negligence, *one of the public stores of filth being within a stone's throw of his residence.*[1]

The people of Stratford were densely ignorant. At the time of Shakspere's birth, only six aldermen of the town, out of nineteen, could write their names; and of the thirteen who could not read or write, Shakspere's father, John Shakspere, was one.

Knight says:

We were reluctant to yield our assent to Malone's assertion that Shakspere's father had a mark to himself. The marks are not distinctly affixed to each name in this document. But subsequent discoveries establish the fact that he used two marks — one something like an open pair of compasses, the other the common cross.[2]

III. SHAKSPERE'S FAMILY TOTALLY UNEDUCATED.

Shakspere's whole family were illiterate. He was the first of his race we know of who was able to read and write. His father and mother, grandfathers and grandmothers, aunts and cousins — all signed their names, on the few occasions when they were obliged to sign them, with crosses. His daughter Judith could not read or write. The whole population around him were in the same condition.

The highest authority upon these questions says:

Exclusive of Bibles, church services, psalters and educational manuals, there were certainly not more than two or three dozen books, if so many, in the whole town.

The copy of the black-letter English History, so often depicted as well thumbed by Shakespeare, in his father's parlor, never existed out of the imagination.[3]

[1] *Outlines Life of Shak.*, p. 18. [2] *Knight's Shak. Biography*, p. 17.
[3] Halliwell-Phillipps, *Life of Shak.*, p. 42.

Goadby says:

The common people were densely ignorant. They had to pick up their mother tongue as best they could. *The first English grammar was not published until 1586.* [This was after Shakspere had finished his education.] It is evident that much schooling was impossible, for the necessary books did not exist. *The horn-book for teaching the alphabet would almost exhaust the resources of any common day schools that might exist in the towns and villages.* LITTLE IF ANY ENGLISH WAS TAUGHT EVEN IN THE LOWER CLASSES OF THE GRAMMAR SCHOOLS.[1]

Prof. Thorold Rogers says:

Sometimes perhaps, in the days after the Reformation, a more than ordinarily opulent ecclesiastic, having no family ties, would train up some clever rustic child, teach him and help him on to the university. But, as a rule, since that event, *there was no educated person in the parish beyond the parson,* and he had the anxieties of a narrow fortune and a numerous family.[2]

The Rev. John Shaw, who was temporary chaplain in a village in Lancashire in 1644, tells of an old man of sixty years of age, whose whole knowledge of Jesus Christ had been derived from a miracle play. "'Oh, sir,' said he, 'I think I heard of that man you speak of once in a play at Kendall called *Corpus Christi Play* where there was a man on a tree and blood ran down.'"

IV. THE UNIVERSITIES OF THAT DAY.

Even the universities were not such schools as the name would to-day imply.

The state of education was almost as unsettled as that of religion. The Universities of Cambridge and Oxford were thronged with poor scholars, and eminent professors taught in the schools and colleges. But the Reformation had made sad havoc with their buildings and libraries, and the spirit of amusement had affected their studies.[3]

The students turned much more readily to dissipation than to literature. In the year 1570, the scholars of Trinity College, Cambridge, consumed 2,250 barrels of beer![4]

The knowledge of Greek had sensibly declined, but Latin was still cultivated with considerable success.[5]

The number of scholars of the university fit for schoolmasters was small. "Whereas they make one scholar they marre ten," averred Peacham, who describes one specimen as whipping his boys on a cold morning "for no other purpose than to get himself a heate."[6]

The country swarmed to such an extent with scholars of the universities, who made a living as beggars, that Parliament had to interfere against the nuisance. By the act of 14th Elizabeth, "all

---

[1] Goadby, *England of Shak.*, p. 101. [3] Goadby, *England*, p. 97. [5] Ibid., p. 97.
[2] Rogers, *Work and Wages*, p. 85. [4] Ibid., p. 73. [6] Ibid., p. 99.

scholars of the Universities of Oxford or Cambridge that go about begging, not being authorized under the seal of said universities," are declared "vagabonds," and punishable as such.

V. "A Bookless Neighborhood."

If this was the condition of the two great "twins of learning," sole centers of light in the darkness of a barbarous age, we can readily conceive what must have been the means of public education in the dirty little hamlet of Stratford, with its fifteen hundred untaught souls, its two hundred and fifty householders, and its illiterate officials.

It was, as Halliwell-Phillipps has called it, "a bookless neighborhood."

We have the inventory of the personal property of Robert Arden, Shakspere's mother's father, and the inventory of the personal property of Agnes Arden, his widow, and the will of the same Agnes Arden, and any number of other wills, but in them all, in the midst of a plentiful array of "oxenne," "kyne," "sheepe," "pigges," "basons," "chafyng dyches," "toweles and dyepers," "shettes," "frying panes," "gredyerenes," "barrelles," "hansaws," "knedyng troghs," "poringers," "sawcers," "pott-hookes," and "linkes," we do not find reference to a single book, not even to a family Bible or a prayer-book. Everything speaks of a rude, coarse and unintellectual people. Here is an extract from the will of Agnes Arden, Shakspere's grandmother:

I geve to the said Jhon Hill my best platter of the best sort, and my best platter of the second sorte, and j poringer, one sawcer and one best candlesticke. And I also give to the said Jhon one paire of sheetes. I give to the said Jhon my second pot, my best pan, . . . and one cow with the white rump.

"One John Shakspeare, of Budbrook, near Warwick, considered it a sufficient mark of respect to his father-in-law to leave him 'his best boots.'"[1]

VI. A Gross Improbability.

It would indeed be a miracle if out of this vulgar, dirty, illiterate family came the greatest genius, the profoundest thinker, the broadest scholar that has adorned the annals of the human race. It is possible. It is scarcely probable.

[1] *Outlines Life of Shak.*, p. 183.

Professor Grant Allen, writing in the *Science Monthly* of March, 1882 (p. 591), and speaking of the life of Sir Charles Lyell, says:

Whence did he come? What conditions went to beget him? From what stocks were his qualities derived, and why? These are the questions that must henceforth always be first asked when we have to deal with the life of any great man. For we have now learned that a great man is no unaccountable accident, no chance result of a toss-up on the part of nature, but simply the highest outcome and final efflorescence of many long ancestral lines, converging at last toward a single happy combination.

Herbert Spencer says:

If you assume that two European parents may produce a negro child, or that from woolly-haired prognathous Papuans may come a fair, straight-haired infant of Caucasian type, you may assume that the advent of the great man can occur anywhere and under any circumstances. If, disregarding these accumulated results of experience which current proverbs and the generalizations of psychologists alike express, you suppose that a Newton might be born in a Hottentot family; that a Milton might spring up among the Andamanese; that a Howard or a Clarkson might have Fiji parents: then you may proceed with facility to explain social progress as caused by the actions of the great man. But if all biological science, enforcing all popular belief, convinces you that by no possibility will an Aristotle come from a father and mother with facial angles of fifty degrees; and that out of a tribe of cannibals, whose chorus in preparation for a feast of human flesh is a kind of rhythmical roaring, there is not the remotest chance of a Beethoven arising: then you must admit that the genesis of the great man depends on the long series of complex influences which has produced the race in which he appears, and the social state into which that race has slowly grown.

And it is to this social state, to this squalid village, that the great thinker of the human race, after association, as we are told, with courts and wits and scholars and princes, returned in middle life. He left intellectual London, which was then the center of mental activity, and the seat of whatever learning and refinement were to be found in England, not to seek the peace of rural landscapes and breathe the sweet perfumes of gardens and hedge-rows, but to sit down contentedly in the midst of pig-sties, and to inhale the malarial odors from reeking streets and stinking ditches. To show that this is no exaggeration, let me state a few facts.

Henry Smith, of Stratford, in 1605, is notified to "plucke downe his pigges cote, which is built nere the chapple wall, and the house of office there." And John Sadler, miller, is fined for bringing feed and feeding his hogs in "chapple lane." In 1613 John Rogers, the vicar, erected a pig-sty immediately opposite the back court of Shakspere's residence. For one hundred and fifty years after Shakspere's death, Chapel Ditch, which *lay next to the New Place*

Garden, "was a receptacle for all manner of filth that any person chose to put there."[1] It was four or five feet wide and filled for a foot deep with flowing filth. More than one hundred years after Shakspere's death, to-wit, in 1734, the Court Leet of Stratford presented Joseph Sawbridge, in Henley Street, "for not carring in his muck before his door."[2]

The houses were thatched with reeds.[3]

The streets were narrow, irregular and without sidewalks; full of refuse, and lively with pigs, poultry and ravenous birds.[4]

The highways were "foule, long and cumbersome."[5] Good bridges were so rare that in some cases they were ascribed to the devil. There was no mail service except between London and a few principal points. The postage upon a letter from Lynn to London was 26s. 8d., equal in value to about $30 of our money to-day. The stage wagons moved at the rate of two miles an hour. Places twelve miles apart were then practically farther removed than towns would now be one hundred miles apart. There was little or no intercourse among the common people. Men lived and died where they were born.

There were no carriages. The Queen imported a Dutch coach in 1564, the sight of which "put both man and horse in amazement," remarks Taylor, the water poet. "Some said it was a great crab-shell, brought out of China, and some imagined it to be one of the pagan temples, in which the cannibals adored the devil." There were few chimneys; dining-room and kitchen were all one; "each one made his fire against the reredrosse in the hall where he dined and dressed his meat," says Harrison. The beds were of straw, with wooden bolsters (like the Chinese); the people ate out of wooden platters with wooden spoons. The churches were without pews and full of fleas.[6]

VII. THE ENGLISH PEOPLE IN THE SIXTEENTH CENTURY.

The people were fierce, jovial, rude, hearty, brutal and pugnacious. They were great eaters of beef and drinkers of beer. We find them accurately described in the Plays:

---

[1] *Outlines Life of Shak.*, p. 429.
[2] Ibid., p. 205.
[3] Goadby's *England of Shak.*, p. 16.
[4] Ibid.
[5] Ibid.
[6] Ibid., p. 75.

The men do sympathise with the mastiffs, in robustious and rough coming-on, leaving their wits with their wives; and then give them great meals of beef, and iron and steel, they will eat like wolves and fight like devils.[1]

They lived out of doors; they had few books, and, of course, no newspapers. Their favorite amusements were bear-baitings, bull-baitings, cock-fights, dog-fights, foot-ball and "rough-and-tumble fighting."[2] The cock, having crowed when Peter denied his Master, was regarded as the devil's bird, and many clergymen enjoined cock-throwing, or throwing of sticks at cocks, as a pious exercise and agreeable to God.

There were few vegetables upon the tables, and these were largely imported from Holland. The leaves of the turnip were used as a salad. Vegetables were regarded as medicines. No forks were used until 1611, when the custom was imported from Italy. Tea came into England in 1610, and coffee in 1652. Beer or wine was used with all meals. Men and women went to the taverns and drank together.

The speech of the country people was a barbarous jargon: we have some specimens of it in the Plays.

Take, for instance, the following from *Lear:*

Stewart. Let go his own.
Edgar. Chill not go, zir,
Without vurther 'casion. . .
Let poor volke passe: and chud ha' bin zwaggerd out of my life, 'twould not ha' bin zo long as 'tis, by a vortnight. . . . Keepe out of che vor'ye or ice try whither your Costard or my Ballow be the harder; chill be plaine with you.[3]

VIII. A Country School in Shakspere's Time.

Halliwell-Phillipps says, speaking of Shakspere's education in "the horn-book and the A, B, C":

There were few persons at that time at Stratford-on-Avon capable of initiating him even into these preparatory accomplishments.[4]

What manner of school was it in which he received all the education ever imparted to him?

The following is Roger Ascham's description of schools and schoolmasters in his day, as quoted by Appleton Morgan, in a newspaper article:

It is pitie that commonly more care is had, yea, and that among verie wise men, to find out rather a cunnynge man for their horse, than a cunnynge man for

---

[1] *Henry V.*, iii, 7.
[2] *Goadby's England*, p. 69.
[3] Act iv, scene 6.
[4] Halliwell-Phillipps, *Outlines Life of Shak.*, p. 24.

their children.[1] . . . The master mostly being as ignorant as the child, what to say properly and fitly to the matter.[2] They for the most part so behave themselves that their very name is hateful to the scholar, who trembleth at their coming-in, rejoiceth at their absence, and looketh him returned in the face as his deadly enemy.

Mr. Morgan continues:

To the charges of undue severity, says Drake, "we must add the accusation of immorality and buffoonery. They were put on the stage along with the zany and pantaloon, to be laughed at."[3]

As to school books, or other implements of instruction, except the following, viz. (to cite them in the order in which they were prized and employed): First, the birch rod; second, the church catechism; third, the horn-book or criss-cross row. Drake says,[4] the thirty-ninth injunction of Elizabeth enacted that every grammar school "shall teach the grammar set forth by King Henry the VIII., of noble memory, and continued in the reign of Edward the VI., and none other." This was the Lily's Latin Grammar, and its study appears to have constituted the difference between a "school" and a "grammar school." Drake adds, "There was, however, another book which we may almost confidently affirm young Shakspere to have studied under the tuition of the master of the free grammar school at Stratford, the production of one Ockland, a panegyric on the characters and government of the reign of Elizabeth and her ministers, which was enjoined by authority to be read in every grammar school." Another text-book which may have been extant was the one referred to by Ascham as follows: "I have formerly seen Mr. Horman's book, who was a master of Eton school. The book itself could be of no great use, for, as I remember, it was only a collection of single sentences without order or method, put into Latin." But the rod was for long years the principal instructor. Peter Mason, a pupil of Nicholas Udal, master of Eton, says he used to receive fifty-three lashes in the course of one Latin exercise. At that temple of learning, and from Dr. Busby's time downward, the authorities agree in giving it the foremost place in English curriculums.

In *The Compleat Gentleman*, edition of 1634, the author says a country school teacher "by no entreaty would teach any scholar further than his (the scholar's) father had learned before him; as, if he had but only learned to read English, the son, though he went with him seven years, should go no further. His reason was that they would otherwise prove saucy rogues and control their fathers. Yet these are they that have our hopeful gentry under their charge."

Nay, in 1771, when Shakspere had been dead a century and a half, things were about as he left them. John Britton, who attended the provincial grammar school of Kingston, St. Nicholas parish, in Wilts, about 1771-80, says that he was taught the "criss-cross row," imparted by the learned pedagogue as follows:

Teacher — "Commether Billy Chubb, an' breng the horren book. Ge ma the vester in the wendow, you Pat Came. What! be a sleepid? I'll wake ye! Now, Billy, there's a good bway; ston still there, an' mind what I da za ta ye, an' whan I da point na! Criss-cross girta little A, B, C. That's right, Billy; you'll zoon larn criss-cross row; you'll zoon averg it, Bobby Jiffry! You'll zoon be a sco...ard! A's a purty chubby bwoy, Lord love en!"

[1] *Works*, Bennett's edition, p. 212.
[2] Ibid., p. 12.
[3] *Shak. and His Times*, vol. i, p. 97.
[4] Ibid., p. 26.

IX. English not Taught in the Schools of That Day.

And it is very doubtful, as we have seen, whether English was taught at all in that Stratford school. It certainly was not in most of the grammar schools of England at that time. Even White is forced to admit this. He says:

> For book instruction there was the free grammar school of Stratford, well endowed by Thomas Jolyffe, in the reign of Edward IV., where, unless it differed from all others of its kind, he could have learned Latin and some Greek. Some English, too; *but not much, for English was held in scorn by the scholars of those days, and long after.*[1]

It will readily be conceded that in such a town, among such a people, and with such a school, Shakspere could have learned but little, and that little of the rudest kind. And to this conclusion even so stout a Shaksperean as Richard Grant White is driven. He says, in a recent number of the *Atlantic* magazine:

> Shakespeare was the son of a Warwickshire peasant, or very inferior yeoman, by the daughter of a well-to-do farmer. Both his father and mother were so ignorant that they signed with a mark instead of writing their names. Few of their friends could write theirs. Shakespeare probably had a little instruction in Latin in the Stratford grammar school. When, at twenty-two years of age, he fled from Stratford to London, we may be sure that he had never seen half a dozen books other than his horn-book, his Latin accidence and a Bible. Probably there were not half a dozen others in all Stratford. The notion that he was once an attorney's clerk is blown to pieces.

Where, then, did he acquire the vast learning demonstrated by the Plays?

X. Shakspere's Youthful Habits.

There can be no doubt that the child is father to the man. While little Francis Bacon's youthful associates were enjoying their game of ball, the future philosopher was at the end of a tunnel experimenting in echoes. Pope "lisped in numbers, for the numbers came." At nine years of age Charles Dickens (a sort of lesser Shakespeare) knew all about *Falstaff*, and the robbery at Gad's Hill, and had established the hope in his heart that he might some day own the handsome house in that place in which he afterward resided. It was his habit to creep away to a garret in his father's house, and there, enraptured, pore over the pages of *Roderick Random*, *Peregrine Pickle*, *Humphrey Clinker*, *Tom Jones*, *The Arabian Nights*,

---

[1] *Life and Genius of Shak.*, p. 30.

The Vicar of Wakefield, and *Robinson Crusoe*. Dr. Glennie tells us of Byron, that in his boyhood "his reading in history and poetry was far beyond the usual standard of his age. . . . He was a great reader and admirer of the Old Testament, and had read it through and through before he was eight years old." At fifteen years of age Robert Burns had read *The Spectator*, Pope's works, some of Shakespeare's plays, Locke's *Essay on the Human Understanding*, Allan Ramsay's works, and a number of religious books, and "had studied the English grammar and gained some knowledge of the French."

Genius is a powerful predisposition, so strong that it overrules a man's whole life, from boyhood to the grave. The greatness of a mind is in proportion to its receptivity, its capacity to assimilate a vast mass of food; it is an intellectual stomach that eliminates not muscle but thought. Its power holds a due relation to its greed — it is an eternal and insatiable hunger. In itself it is but an instrument. It can work only upon external material.

The writer of the Plays recognizes this truth. He says, speaking of Cardinal Wolsey:

> *From his cradle*
> He was a scholar, and a ripe and good one,
> Exceeding wise, fair-spoken and persuading.[1]

The commentators have tried to alter the punctuation of this sentence. They have asked, "How could he be 'a scholar from his cradle'?" What the poet meant was that the extraordinary capacity to receive impressions and acquire knowledge, which constitutes the basis of the education of the infant, continued with unabated force all through the life of the great churchman. The retention of this youthful impressibility of the mind is one of the essentials of greatness.

And again the poet says:

> This morning, like the spirit of a youth
> That means to be of note, *begins betimes*.[2]

How did William Shakspere, the Stratford-on-Avon boy, "begin betimes"?

In his fourteenth year it is supposed he left school; but there is really no proof that he ever attended school for an hour.

---

[1] *Henry VIII.*, iv. 2.   [2] *Antony and Cleopatra*, iv. 2.

White expresses the opinion that "William Shakespeare was obliged to leave school early and earn his living."

At sixteen, tradition says, he was apprenticed to a butcher.

Aubrey says:

> I have been told heretofore by some of the neighbors that when he was a boy he exercised his father's trade; but when he killed a calf he would doe it in a *high* style and make a speech.

Rowe, speaking for Betterton, says, "Upon his leaving school he seems to have given entirely into that way of living which his father proposed to him," that of a dealer in wool.

Neither the pursuit of butcher or wool-dealer could have been very favorable to the acquisition of knowledge in a rude age and a "bookless neighborhood."

But perhaps the boy was of a very studious nature and his industry eked out the poor materials available? Let us see:

There is a tradition of his youth setting forth that in the neighboring village of Bidford there was a society—not a literary society, not a debating club like that of which Robert Burns was a member—but a brutal crew calling themselves "The Bidford Topers," whose boast was that they could drink more beer than the "topers" of any of the adjoining intellectual villages. They challenged Stratford, and among the gallant young men who accepted the challenge was William Shakspere. The "Bidford topers" were too many for the Stratford "topers," and the latter attempted to walk home again, but were so besotted that their legs gave out, and they spent the night by the roadside under a large crab-tree, which stands to this day and is known as "Shakspere's crab." As the imagination sees him, stretched sodden and senseless, beneath the crab-tree, we may apply to him the words of the real Shakespeare:

> O monstrous beast!—how like a swine he lies.[1]

The first appearance of the father is connected with a filth-heap. The first recorded act of the son is this spirituelle contest.

The next incident in the life of Shakspere occurred when he was nineteen years old. This was his marriage to a girl of twenty-seven, that is to say, eight years older than himself. Six months after the marriage their first child was born.

[1] *Taming of the Shrew.*

But perhaps, after this inauspicious match, he settled down and devoted himself to study? Not at all.

The Reverend William Fulman, an antiquary, who died in 1688, bequeathed his manuscript biographical memoranda to the Reverend Richard Davies, rector of Sapperton, in Gloucestershire, and archdeacon of Lichfield, who died in 1708. To a note of Fulman's, which barely records Shakspere's birth, death and occupation, Davies made brief additions, the principal of which is that William Shakspere was "much given to all unluckinesse in stealing venison and rabbits, particularly from Sir Lucy, *who had him oft whipt* and sometimes imprisoned, and at last made him fly his native county, to his great advancement."

The man who wrote this was probably born within little more than twenty-five years after Shakspere's death. The tradition comes to us also from other sources.

The same story is told by Rowe, on the authority of Betterton, who went down to Stratford to collect materials for a life of Shakspere. Rowe says:

> He had, by a misfortune common enough to young fellows, fallen into ill company, and amongst them some, that made a frequent practice of deer-stealing, engaged him more than once in robbing a park that belonged to Sir Thomas Lucy, of Charlecote, near Stratford. For this he was prosecuted by that gentleman, as he thought, somewhat too severely, and in order to revenge that ill-usage he made a ballad upon him. And although this, probably the first essay of his poetry, be lost, yet it is said to have been so very bitter that it redoubled the prosecution against him to that degree that he was obliged to leave his business and family in Warwickshire for some time and shelter himself in London.

A pretended specimen of the ballad has come down to us, a rude and vulgar thing:

> A parliament member, a justice of peace,
> At home a poor scare-crow, at London an asse.
> If lowsie is Lucy, as some volke miscalle it,
> Then Lucy is lowsie whatever befall it.
>   He thinks himself great,
>   Yet an ass is his state;
> We allow by his ears but with asses to mate.
> If Lucy is lowsie as some volke miscalle it,
> Sing lowsie Lucy whatever befall it.

And touching this Sir Thomas Lucy, Richard Grant White, after visiting Stratford and Charlecote, speaks as follows:

This was a truly kindly nature, we may almost say a noble soul. I am with Sir Thomas in this matter, and if Shakespeare suffered any discipline at his hands, I believe that he deserved it.[1]

XI. Shakspere Goes to London.

He proceeded to London "somewhere about 1586 or 1587," say his biographers. His twin children, Hamnet and Judith, had been born in February, 1585.

We can readily conceive his condition. His father was bankrupt; his own family rapidly increasing — his wife had just been delivered of twins; his home was dirty, bookless and miserable; his companions degraded; his pursuits low; he had been whipped and imprisoned, and he fled, probably penniless, to the great city. As his admirer, Richard Grant White, says, "we may be sure he had never seen half a dozen books other than his horn-book, his Latin accidence, and a Bible." There is indeed no certainty that he had ever seen even the last work, for neither father nor mother could read or write, and had no use for, and do not seem to have possessed, a Bible.

Says Halliwell-Phillipps:

> Removed prematurely from school; residing with illiterate relatives in a bookless neighborhood; thrown into the midst of occupations adverse to scholastic progress, it is difficult to believe that when he left Stratford he was not *all but destitute of polished accomplishments.*[2]

To London fled all the adventurers, vagabonds and paupers of the realm. They gathered around the play-houses. These were rude structures, open to the heavens — sometimes the roofless yard of a tavern served as the theater, and a rough scaffold as the stage. Here the ruffians, the thieves, the vagabonds, the apprentices, the pimps and the prostitutes assembled — a stormy, dirty, quarrelsome multitude. Here William Shakspere came. He was, we will concede, bright, keen and active, intent on getting ahead in the world, fond of money, but poor as poverty and ignorant as barbarism. What could he do?

XII. He Becomes a Horse-holder.

He took to the first thing that presented itself, holding horses at the door of the play-house for the young gentlemen who came to witness the performance. And this, tradition assures us, he did.

[1] *England Without and Within*, p. 514. [2] Halliwell-Phillipps, *Outlines Life of Shak.*, p. 63.

He proved trustworthy, and the youthful aristocrats would call, we are told, for Will Shakspere to hold their horses. Then his business faculty came into play, and he organized a band of assistants, who were known then, and long afterward, as "Shakspere's boys." Gradually he worked his way among the actors.

XIII. He Becomes a Call-boy, and then an Actor.

Betterton heard that "he was received into the company at first in a very mean rank;" and the octogenarian parish clerk of Stratford told Dowdall, in 1693, that he "was received into the playhouse as a serviture"—that is, as a servant, a supernumerary, or "supe." Tradition says he was the prompter's call-boy, his duty being to call the actors when it was time for them to go upon the stage. In time he rose a step higher: he became an actor. He never was a great actor, but performed, we are told, insignificant parts. "He seems," says White, "never to have risen high in this profession. The Ghost in *Hamlet*, and old Adam in *As You Like It*, were the utmost of his achievements in this direction."

It must have taken him some time, say a year or two at the very least, to work up from being a vagabond horse-holder to the career of a regular actor. We will see, when we come to discuss the chronology of the Plays, that they began to appear almost as soon as he reached London, if not before, although Shakspere's name was not connected with them for some years thereafter. And the earliest plays, as we shall see, were the most scholarly, breathing the very atmosphere of the academy.

XIV. No Tradition Refers to Him as a Student or Scholar.

There was certainly nothing in his new surroundings in London akin to Greek, Latin, French, Italian, Spanish and Danish studies; there was nothing akin to medical, musical and philosophical researches.

And assuredly his life in Stratford, reckless, improvident, dissipated, degraded, does not represent the studious youth who, in some garret, would pore over the great masters, and fill his mind with information, and his soul with high aspirations. There is r. a single tradition which points to any such element in his character.

Aubrey asserts that, from the time of leaving school until his departure for Warwickshire, Shakspere was a schoolmaster. We have seen that it did not require a very extensive stock of learning to constitute a schoolmaster in that age; but even this, the only tradition of his life which points to anything even akin to scholarly accomplishments, must be abandoned.

Lord Campbell says:

> Unfortunately, however, the pedagogical theory is not only quite unsupported by evidence, but it is not consistent with established facts. From the registration of the baptism of Shakespeare's children, and other well authenticated circumstances, we know that he continued to dwell in Stratford, or the immediate neighborhood, till he became a citizen of London: there was no other school in Stratford except the endowed grammar school, where he had been a pupil; of this he certainly never was master, for the unbroken succession of masters from the reign of Edward VI. till the reign of James I. is of record; . . . and there is no trace of there having been any usher employed in this school.[1]

Only a miracle of studiousness could have acquired, in a few years, upon a basis of total ignorance and bad habits, the culture and refinement manifested in the earliest plays; and but a few years elapsed between the time when he fled scourged from Stratford and the time when the Plays began to appear, in his name, in London. But plays, now believed to have been written by the same hand that wrote the Shakespeare Plays, were on the boards *before he left Stratford.* The twins, Judith and Hamnet, were born in February, 1585, Shakspere being then not yet twenty-one years of age, and we will see hereafter that *Hamlet* appeared for the first time in 1585 or 1587. If he had shown, anywhere in his career, such a trait of immense industry and scholarly research, some tradition would have reached us concerning it. We have traditions that he was the father of another man's supposed son (Sir William Davenant); and we are told of a licentious amour in which he outwitted Burbage; and we hear of *wet-*combats in a tavern; but not one word comes down to us of books, or study, or industry, or art.

XV. The "Venus and Adonis."

"The first heir of his invention," he tells us, was "the *Venus and Adonis,*" published in 1593; and many think that this means that he wrote it before any of the plays, and even before he left Stratford.

Richard Grant White says:

> In any case, we may be sure that the poem [*Venus and Adonis*] was written some years before it was printed; and it may have been brought by the young poet

---

[1] *Shakespeare's Legal Acquirements,* p. 19.

from Stratford in manuscript, and read by a select circle, according to the custom of the time, before it was published.

But here is a difficulty that presents itself: the people of Warwickshire did not speak the English of the London court, but a *patois* almost as different from it as the Lowland Scotch of Burns is to-day different from the English of Westminster.

To give the reader some idea of the kind of language used by Shakspere during his youth, and by all the uneducated people of his county, I select, at random, a few words from the Warwickshire dialect:

Tageous, troublesome;	Fameled, starving;
Kiver, a butter tub;	Brévet, to snuff, to sniff;
Grinsard, the turf;	Unked, solitary;
Slammocks, untidy;	Roomthy, spacious;
He's teddin, he's shaking up hay;	Mulled, sleepy;
He do fash hisself, he troubles himself;	Glir, to slide;
Cob, thick;	Work, a row, a quarrel;
Gidding, thoughtless;	Whittaw, a saddler;
Jackbonnial, a tadpole;	Still, respectable;
Cade, tame;	Her's childing, she is with child;
A' done worritin me, stop teasing me;	A' form, properly;
Let's gaig no', let's take a swing;	Yawrups, stupid;
Franzy, passionate; etc.	

Let any one read the *Venus and Adonis*, and he will find it written in the purest and most cultured English of the age, without a word in it of this Warwickshire *patois*.

Halliwell-Phillipps says:

It is extremely improbable that an epic so highly finished, and so completely devoid of *patois*, could have been produced under the circumstances of his then domestic surroundings.[1]

In fact, if we except the doggerel libel on Sir Thomas Lucy, with its "volke" (and the authenticity of even this is denied by the commentators), Shakspere never wrote a line impregnated with the dialect of the people among whom he lived from childhood to manhood. All attempts to show the peculiar phraseology of Warwickshire in his writings have failed. A few words have been found that were used in Warwickshire, but investigation has shown that they were also used in the dialects of other portions of England.

White says:

As long as two hundred years after that time the county of each member of Parliament was betrayed by his tongue; but then the speech of the cultivated

[1] *Outlines Life of Shak.*, p. 71.

people of Middlesex and vicinity had become for all England the undisputed standard. Northumberland, or Cornwall, or Lancashire, might have produced Shakespeare's mind; but had he lived in any one of these counties, or in another, like them remote in speech as in locality from London, and written for his rural neighbors instead of the audiences of the Blackfriars and the Globe, the music of his poetry would have been lost in sounds uncouth and barbarous to the general ear, and the edge of his fine utterance would have been turned upon the stony roughness of his rustic phraseology.[1]

White seems to forget that the jargon of Warwickshire was well nigh as uncouth and barbarous as that of Northumberland or Cornwall.

Appleton Morgan says:

Now, even if, in Stratford, the lad had mastered all the Latin and Greek extant, this poem, dedicated to Southampton, coming from his pen, is a mystery, if not a miracle. The genius of Robert Burns found its expression in the *idiom* of his father and his mother, in the dialect he heard around him, and into which he was born. When *he* came to London and tried to warble in urban English, his genius dwindled into formal commonplace. But William Shakespeare, a peasant, born in the heart of Warwickshire, without schooling or practice, pours forth the purest and most sumptuous of English, unmixed with the faintest trace of that Warwickshire *patois* that his neighbors and coetaneans spoke — the language of his own fireside.[2]

And Shakespeare prefaced the *Venus and Adonis* with a Latin quotation from the *Amores* of Ovid. Halliwell-Phillipps, an earnest Shaksperean, says:

It is hardly possible that the *Amores* of Ovid, whence he derived his earliest motto, could have been one of his school books.[3]

No man can doubt that the *Venus and Adonis* was the work of a scholar in whom the intellectual faculties vastly preponderated over the animal. Coleridge notices —

The utter aloofness of the poet's own feelings from those of which he is at once the painter and the analyst.

Says Dowden:

The subjects of these poems did not possess him and compel him to render them into art. The poet sat himself down before each to accomplish an exhaustive study of it.

Hazlitt says:

These poems appear to us like a couple of ice houses. They are about as hard, as glittering and as cold.

It is not possible for the human mind to bring these beautiful poems, written in such perfect English, so cold, so passionless, so

---

[1] *Life and Genius of Shak.*, p. 202. [2] *The Shakespeare Myth*, p. 41.
[3] *Outlines Life of Shak.*, p. 63.

cultured, so philosophical, so scholastic, into connection with the first inventions of the boy we have seen lying out drunk in the fields, poaching, rioting, whipped, imprisoned, and writing vulgar doggerel, below the standard of the most ordinary intellect. Compare for one instant:

> A Parliament member, a justice of peace,
> At home a poor scare-crow, at London an asse.
> He thinks himself great, yet an ass is his state,
> Condemned for his ears with asses to mate.

with—

> Oh, what a sight it was wistly to view
> How she came stealing to the wayward boy!
> To note the fighting conflict of her hue!
> How white and red each other did destroy!
> But now her cheek was pale, and by and by
> It flashed forth fire, as lightning from the sky.[1]

Can any one believe that these two passages were born in the same soul and fashioned in the same mind?

A rough but strong genius, coming even out of barbarian training, but thrown into daily contact with dramatic entertainments, might have begun to imitate the works he was familiar with; might gradually have drifted into play-making. But here we learn that the first heir of his invention was an ambitious attempt at a literary performance based on a classical fable, and redolent of the air of the court and the schools. It is incomprehensible.

Even Hallam, years ago, was struck by the incongruity between Shakspere's life and works. He says:

> If we are not yet come to question his [Shakespeare's] unity, as we do that of "the blind old man of Scio's rocky isle"—(an improvement in critical acuteness doubtless reserved for a distant posterity), we as little feel the power of identifying the young man who came up from Stratford, was afterwards an indifferent player in a London theater, and retired to his native place in middle life, with the author of *Macbeth* and *Lear*.[2]

Emerson says:

> Read the antique documents extricated, analyzed and compared, by the assiduous Dyce and Collier; and now read one of those skiey sentences—aerolites—which seem to have fallen out of heaven, . . . and tell me if they match.[3]
>
> . . . The Egyptian verdict of the Shakesperean societies comes to mind, that he was a jovial actor and manager. I cannot marry this fact to his verse. Other admirable men have led lives in some sort of keeping with their thought; but this man in wide contrast. . . . This man of men, he who gave the science of mind a new and larger subject than had ever existed, and planted the standard of humanity

---

[1] *Venus and Adonis*. [2] *Introduction to Literature of Europe*. [3] *Rep. Men*, p. 205.

ity some furlongs forward in chaos — it must ever go into the world's history, that the best poet led an obscure and profane life, using his genius for the public amusement.[1]

Such a proposition cannot be accepted by any sane man.

Francis Bacon seems to have had these plays in his mind's eye when he said:

If the sow with her snout should happen to imprint the letter *A* upon the ground, wouldst thou therefore imagine that she could write out a whole tragedy as one letter?[2]

---

[1] *Representative Men*, p. 215.   [2] *Interpretation of Nature*.

CHAPTER III.

THE REAL CHARACTER OF WILLIAM SHAKSPERE.

> What a thrice-double ass
> Was I, to take this drunkard for a god,
> And worship this dull fool.
> *Tempest*, v, 1.

WE have seen that the Plays must have been written by a scholar, a man of wide and various learning.

We have seen that William Shakspere, of Stratford-on-Avon, could not have acquired such learning in his native village, and that his pursuits and associates in London were not favorable to its acquisition there; and that there is no evidence from tradition or history, or by the existence of any books or papers, or letters, that he was of a studious turn of mind, or in anywise scholarly. We have further seen that the families of his father and mother were, and had been for generations, without exception, rude and bookless.

Now let us put together all the facts in our possession, and try to get at some estimate of the true character of the man himself.

He was doubtless, as tradition says, "the best of that family." His career shows that he was adventurous, and what we call in America "smart." His financial success demonstrates this fact. He had probably a good deal of mother wit and practical good sense. It is not impossible that he may have been able to string together barbaric rhymes, some of which have come down to us. But conceding all this, and a vast gulf still separates him from the colossal intellect made manifest in the Plays.

I. SHAKSPERE WAS A USURER.

The probabilities are that he was a usurer.

Richard Grant White (and it is a pleasure to quote against Shakspere so earnest a Shaksperean — one who declares that every man who believes Bacon wrote the Plays attributed to Shakspere should be committed at once to a mad-house) — Richard Grant White says:

The following passage, in a tract called *Ratsei's Ghost, or the Second Part of his Mad Prankes and Robberies,* of which only one copy is known to exist, plainly refers, first to Burbadge and *next to Shakespeare.* This book is without date, but is believed to have been printed before 1606. Gamaliel Ratsei, who speaks, is a highwayman, who has paid some strollers forty shillings for playing for him, and afterwards robbed them of their fee.[1]

The passage is as follows:

And for you, sirrah (says he to the chiefest of them), thou hast a good presence upon a stage, methinks thou darkenest thy merit by playing in the country; get thee to London, for if one man were dead they will have much need of such as thou art. There would be none, in my opinion, fitter than thyself to play his parts; my conceit is such of thee that I durst venture all the money in my purse on thy head to play Hamlet with him for a wager. There thou shalt learn to be frugal (for players were never so thrifty as they are now about London), and *to feed upon all men;* to let none feed upon thee; *to make thy hand a stranger to thy pocket;* thy heart slow to perform thy tongue's promise; and when thou feelest thy purse well lined, *buy thee some place of lordship in the country;* that growing weary of playing thy money may there *bring thee to dignity and reputation;* then thou needest care for no man; *no, not for them that before made thee proud with speaking* THEIR *words on the stage.*

Sir, I thank you (quoth the player) for this good council. I promise you I will make use of it, for I have heard, indeed, of some that have *gone to London very meanly,* and have come in time to be exceeding wealthy.

This curious tract proves several things:

The Shakspereans agree that Ratsei, in the latter part of the extract quoted, referred unquestionably to Shakspere. Ratsei, or the writer of the tract, doubtless expressed the popular opinion when he described Shakspere as a thrifty, money-making, uncharitable, cold-hearted man, "feeding upon all men," to-wit, by lending money at usurious rates of interest, for there is nothing else to which the words can apply. There can be no question that he refers to Shakspere. *He* was an actor; *he* came to London "very meanly;" *he* was not born there; *he* "lined his purse;" *he* had "grown exceeding wealthy;" *he* "bought a place of lordship in the country," where he lived "in dignity and reputation." And doubtless Ratsei spoke but the popular report when he said that some others "made him proud with speaking *their* words on the stage."

Let us see if there is anything that confirms Ratsei's estimate of Shakspere's character. Richard Grant White says:

The fact is somewhat striking in the life of a great poet that the only letter directly addressed to Shakespeare, which is known to exist, is one which asks for a loan of £30.[2]

---

[1] *Life and Genius of Shakespeare*, p. 164.   [2] Ibid., p. 123.

There is another letter extant from Master Abraham Sturley, 1595, to a friend in London, in reference to Shakspere lending "some monei *on some od yarde land* or other att Shottri or neare about us." And there is still another letter, dated November 4, 1598, from Abraham Sturley to Richard Quiney, in which we are told that our "countriman Mr. Wm. Shak. would *procure us monei*, wc. I will like of." And these, be it remembered, are all the letters extant addressed to, or referring to, Shakspere

In 1598 he loaned Richard Quiney, of Stratford, £30 upon proper security.[1]

In 1600 he brought action against John Clayton, *in London*, for £7, and got judgment in his favor.

He also sued Philip Rogers, at Stratford, for two shillings *loaned*.

In August, 1608, he prosecuted John Addenbroke to recover a debt of £6, and then sued his surety, Hornby.

His lawyer, Thomas Greene, lived in his house.[2]

Halliwell-Phillips says:

The precepts, as appears from memoranda in the originals, were issued by the poet's solicitor, Thomas Greene, who was then residing, *under some unknown conditions*, at New Place.[3]

We, of course, only hear of those transactions in which the debtor did not pay, and the loans became matters of court record. We hear nothing of the more numerous instances where the money was repaid without suit. But even these scraps of fact show that he carried on the business of money-lending *both in London and at Stratford*. He kept an attorney in his house, probably for the better facility of collecting the money due him.

No wonder Richard Grant White said, when such facts as these came to light, voicing the disappointment of his heart:

These stories grate upon our feelings. . . . The pursuit of an impoverished man, for the sake of imprisoning him and depriving him, both of the power of paying his debt and supporting himself and his family, is an incident in Shakespeare's life which it requires the utmost allowance and consideration for the practice of the time and country to enable us to contemplate with equanimity — satisfaction is impossible. The biographer of Shakespeare must record these facts, because the literary antiquaries have unearthed and brought them forward as new particul of the life of Shakespeare. We hunger, and we receive these husks; we open our mouths for food, and we break our teeth against these stones."[4]

---

[1] Halliwell-Phillipps, *Outlines Life of Shak.*, p. 105. [2] Ibid., p. 147.
[3] Ibid., p. 149. [4] *Life and Genius of Shak.*, p. 146.

Is it possible that the man who described usurers as "bawds between gold and want;" who drew, for all time, the typical and dreadful character of Shylock; who wrote:—

> I can compare our rich misers to nothing so fitly as to a whale, that plays and tumbles, driving the poor fry before him, and at last devours them at a mouthful. Such whales I have heard of on land, who never leave gaping till they have swallowed up a whole parish, church, steeple, bells and all.[1]—

could, as described by White, have pursued the wretched to jail, and by his purchase of the tithes of Stratford have threatened "the whole parish, church, steeple, bells and all"?

II. He Carried on Brewing in New Place.

Let us pass to another fact.

It is very probable that the alleged author of *Hamlet* carried on the business of brewing beer in his residence at New Place.

He sued Philip Rogers in 1604, so the court records tell us, for several bushels of "malt" sold him at various times, between March 27th and the end of May of that year, amounting in all to the value of £1 15s. 10d.

> Malt is barley or other grain steeped in water until it germinates, and then dried in a kiln to evolve the saccharine principle. It is used in brewing.[2]

The business of beer-making was not unusual among his townsmen.

> George Perrye, besides his glover's trade, useth buying and selling of woll [wool] and yorn [yarn] and *making of malt*.[3]

> Robert Butler, besides his glover's occupation, usethe *makinge of malt*.[4]

> Rychard Castell, Rother Market, useth his glover's occupation, *his wiffe uttereth weeklye by bruynge* [brewing] 1j strikes of malte.[5]

And we read of a Mr. Persons who for a "longe tyme used makinge of mallte and bruyinge [brewing] to sell in his howse."[6]

There is, of course, nothing dishonorable in this humble occupation; but it is a little surprising that a man who in the Plays never refers to tradesmen without a sneer, or to the common people except as "mechanic slaves" "that made the air unwholesome" throwing up "their stinking greasy caps," a "common cry of curs," or "the clusters," "the mutable, the rank-scented many," or "the beastly plebeians;" and whose sympathies seem to have been always

---

[1] *Pericles*, ii. 1.
[2] *Webster's Dictionary*.
[3] MS. dated 1595.
[4] Ibid.
[5] Ibid.
[6] Ibid.

with the aristocracy, should convert the finest house in Stratford, built by Sir Hugh Clopton, into a brewery, and employ himself peddling out malt to his neighbors, and suing them when they did not pay promptly.

Think of the author of *Hamlet* and *Lear* brewing beer! Verily, "the dust of Alexander may come to stop the bung-hole of a beer-barrel."

III. SHAKSPERE'S HOSPITALITY.

And taken in connection with this sale of malt there is another curious fact that throws some light upon the character of the man and the household.

In the Chamberlain's accounts of Stratford[1] we find a charge, in 1614, for "on quart of sack and on quart of clarett wine geven to a preacher at the New Place," Shakspere's house. What manner of man must he have been *who would require the town to pay for the wine he furnished his guests?* And we may be sure the town would not have paid for it unless first asked to do so. And the money was accepted by Shakspere, or it would not stand charged in the accounts of the town. And this was but two years before Shakspere's death, when he was in possession of an immense income. Did ever any rich man, with the smallest instincts of a gentleman, do a deed like this? Would even the poorest of the poor do it? It was, in fact, a species of "going on the county" for help, — a partial pauperism.

IV. HE ATTEMPTS TO ENTER THE RANKS OF THE GENTRY BY FALSE REPRESENTATIONS.

Some one has said: "To be accounted a gentleman was the chief desire of Shakspere's life."

Did he pursue this ambition, honorable enough in itself, in an honorable manner?

In October, 1596, Shakspere, the actor, applied to the College of Arms for a grant of coat-armor to his father, John Shakspere. At this time Shakspere was beginning to make money. He bought New Place, Stratford, in 1597. His profession as a "vassal actor" prevented any hope of having a grant of arms made

---

[1] White, *Life and Genius of Shak.*, p. 176.

directly to himself, and so he applied in the name of his father, who not long before had been in prison, or hiding from the Sheriff.

White would have us believe that the coat-of-arms was granted; but the latest and most complete authority on the subject, Halliwell-Phillipps, says it was not:

> Toward the close of the year 1599, a renewed attempt was made by the poet to obtain a grant of coat-armor to his father. It was now proposed to impale the arms of Shakespeare with those of Arden, and on each occasion *ridiculous statements were made respecting the claims of the two families. Both were really descended from obscure country yeomen*, but the heralds made out that the predecessors of John Shakespeare were rewarded by the Crown for distinguished services, and that his wife's ancestors were entitled to armorial bearings. *Although the poet's relatives, at a later date, assumed his right to the coat* suggested for his father in 1596, *it does not appear that either of the proposed grants was ratified by the college*, and certainly nothing more is heard of the Arden impalement.[1]

The application was made on the ground that John Shakspere's "parent and late antecessor, for his faithful and approved service to the late most prudent prince, King Henry VII., of famous memory, was advanced and rewarded with lands and tenements given to him in those parts of Warwickshire, ... and that the said John had married the daughter and one of the heirs of Robert Arden, of Wilmecote."

Now, these statements, as Halliwell-Phillipps says, *were plainly false*.

John Shakspere's ancestors had *not* been advanced by King Henry VII.; and they had *not* received lands in Warwickshire; and his mother was *not* the daughter of one of the heirs of Robert Arden, of Wilmecote, *gentleman*. They had been landless peasants for generations; and John Shakspere was an illiterate farm-hand, hired by Robert Arden, a plain farmer, as illiterate as himself, to work by the month or year.

And William Shakspere, who made this application, knew perfectly well that all these representations were falsehoods. He was trying to crawl up the battlements of respectability on a ladder of lies—plain, palpable, notorious, ridiculous lies—lies that involved the title to real property and the records of his county.

Would that grand and noble soul who really wrote the Plays seek to be made a *gentleman* by such means?

But the falsifications did not end here.

---

[1] *Outlines*, p. 87.

"The delay of three years," says Richard Grant White, "in granting these arms, must have been caused by some opposition to the grant; the motto given with them, *Non sans droict* (not without right), itself seems to assert a claim against a denial."

Doubtless the Lucys, and other respectable families of the neighborhood, protested against the play-actor forcing himself into their ranks by false pretenses.

If the reader who is curious in such matters will turn to the two drafts of the application for the coat-of-arms, that of 1596, on page 573 of Halliwell-Phillipps' *Outlines*, and that of 1599, on page 589 of the same work, and examine the interlineations that were made from time to time, and which are indicated by italics, he will see how the applicant was driven from falsehood to falsehood, to meet the objections made against his claim of gentility. In the first application it was stated that it was John Shakspere's "parents and late antecessors" who rendered valiant service to King Henry VII. and were rewarded by him. This was not deemed sufficiently explicit, and so it was interlined that the said John had "married Mary, daughter and one of the heirs of Robert Arden, of Wilmecote, in the said county, *gent.*" But in the proposed grant of 1599 it is stated that it was John Shakspere's *great*-grandfather who rendered these invaluable services to King Henry VII., and, being driven to particulars, we are now told that this grandfather was "advanced and rewarded *with landes and tenementes given to him in those partes of Warwickshire, where they have continued by some descents in good reputacion and credit.*"

This is wholesale lying. There were no such lands, and they had not descended by some descents in the family.

But this is not all. Finding his application opposed, the fertile Shakspere falls back on a new falsehood, and declares that a coat-of-arms had already been given his father twenty years before.

And he also produced this, his aunciert cote-of-arms, heretofore assigned to him whilst he was her Majestie's officer and baylefe of that town.

And White tells us that upon the margin of the draft of 1596, John Shakspere

Sheweth a patent thereof under Clarence Cook's hands in paper, twenty years past.[1]

---

[1] *Life and Genius of Shakespeare*, p. 118.

But this patent can no more be found than the land which Henry VII. granted to John Shakspere's great-grandfather for his approved and faithful services.

The whole thing was a series of lies and forgeries, a tissue of fraud from beginning to end;—and William Shakspere had no more title to his coat-of-arms than he has to the great dramas which bear his name.

And living in New Place, brewing beer, selling malt and suing his neighbors, the Shakspere family assumed to use this coat-of-arms, *never granted to them,* and to set up for "gentry," in the midst of the people who knew the hollowness of their pretensions.

And the same man, we are told, who was so anxious for this kind of a promotion to the ranks of gentlemen, wrote as follows:

Fool. Prithee, nuncle, tell me whether a madman be a gentleman or a yeoman.
Lear. A king, a king!
Fool. No, he's a yeoman, that has a gentleman to his son; for he's a mad yeoman that sees his son a gentleman before him.[1]

And that the same man mocked at new-made gentility, in the scene where the clown and the old shepherd were suddenly elevated to rank by the king of Bohemia:

Shepherd. Come, boy; I am past more children, but thy sons and daughters will all be gentlemen born.
Clown (to Autolycus). You are well met, sir; you denied to fight with me this other day because I was no gentleman born. See you these clothes? . . .
Autolycus. I know you are now, sir, a gentleman born.
Clown. Ay, and have been so any time these four hours.
Shepherd. And so have I, boy.
Clown. So you have. But I was a gentleman born before my father; for the king's son took me by the hand and called me brother: . . . and so we wept: and these were the first gentleman-like tears that ever we shed.[2]

And that the same man wrote:

By the Lord, Horatio, these three years I have taken note of it: the age is grown so picked that the toe of the peasant comes so near the heel of the courtier that he galls his kibe.[3]

And this is the man, we are told, who also wrote:

              Let none presume
To wear an undeservèd dignity.
Oh, that estates, degrees and offices
Were not derived corruptly! and that clear honor
Were purchased by the merit of the wearer!
How many then should cover that stand bare:

---

[1] *Lear,* iii, 6.   [2] *Winter's Tale,* v, 3.   [3] *Hamlet,* v, 1.

> How many be commanded that command;
> How much low peasantry would then be gleaned
> From the true seed of honor; and how much honor
> Picked from the chaff and ruin of the times
> To be new-varnish'd.[1]

Is there any man who loves the memory of the real Shakespeare — gentle, thoughtful, learned, humane, benevolent, with a mind loftier and wider than was ever before conferred on a child of earth — who can believe that he would be guilty of such practices, even to obtain a shabby gentility in the dirty little village of Stratford?

All this may not perhaps strike an American with its full force.

In this country every well-dressed, well-behaved man is a *gentleman*. But in England in the sixteenth century it meant a great deal more. It signified a man of *gentle blood*. A great and impassable gulf lay between "the quality," "the gentry," the hereditary upper class, and the common herd who toiled for a living. It required all the power of Christianity to faintly enforce the idea that they were made by the same God and were of one flesh. The distinction, in the England of 1596, between the yeoman and the gentleman, was almost as wide as the difference to-day in America between the white man and the black man; and the mulatto who would try to pass himself off as a white man, and would support his claim by lies and forgeries, will give us some conception of the nature of this attempt made by William Shakspere in 1596.

V. The House in Which he Was Born.

As to this I will simply quote what Richard Grant White says of it:

> My heart sank within me as I looked around upon the rude, mean dwelling-place of him who had filled the world with the splendor of his imaginings. It is called a house, and any building intended for a dwelling-place is a house; but the interior of this one is hardly that of a rustic cottage; it is almost that of a *hovel* — poverty-stricken, squalid, kennel-like. A house so cheerless and comfortless I had not seen in rural England. The poorest, meanest farm-house that I had ever entered in New England or on Long Island was a more cheerful habitation. And amid these sordid surroundings William Shakespeare grew to early manhood! A thought of stately Charlecote, the home of the Lucys, who were but simple country gentlemen; and then for the first time I knew and felt from how low a condition of

[1] *Merchant of Venice*, ii, 9.

life Shakespeare had arisen. For his family were not reduced to this; they had risen to it. This was John Shakespeare's home *in the days of his brief prosperity*, and, when I compared it with my memory of Charlecote, I knew that Shakespeare himself must have felt what a sham was the pretension of gentry set up for his father, when the coat-of-arms was asked and obtained by the actor's money from the Heralds' College — that coat-of-arms which Shakespeare prized because it made him "a gentleman" by birth! This it was, even more than the squalid appearance of the place, that saddened me. For I felt that Shakespeare himself must have known how well founded was the protest of the gentlemen who complained that Clarencieux had made the man who lived in that house a gentleman of coat-armor.[1]

VI. HIS NAME.

The very name, *Shakspere*, was in that day considered the quintessence of vulgarity. My friend William D. O'Connor, the author of *Hamlet's Note Book*, calls my attention to a recent number of *The London Academy*, in which a Mr. Lupton proves that in Elizabeth's time the name *Shakspere* was considered vile, just as *Ramsbottom*, or *Snooks*, or *Hogsflesh* would be with us; and men who had it got it changed by legislation. Mr. Lupton gives one case where a man called *Shakspere* had his name altered by law to *Saunders*.

VII. HE COMBINES WITH OTHERS TO OPPRESS AND IMPOVERISH THE PEOPLE.

But there is one other feature of Shakspere's biography which throws light upon his character.

From remote antiquity in England the lower classes possessed certain rights of common in tracts of land. Prof. Thorold Rogers says:

The arable land of the manor was generally communal, *i.e.*, each of the tenants possessed a certain number of furrows in a common field, the several divisions being separated by balks of unplowed ground, on which the grass was suffered to grow. The system, which was almost universal in the thirteenth century, has survived in certain districts up to living memory.[2]

This able writer shows that the condition of labor steadily improved in England up to the reign of Henry VIII., and from that period it steadily declined to recent times. He makes this remarkable statement in the preface to his work:

I have attempted to show that the pauperism and the degradation of the English laborer were the result of a series of acts of Parliament and acts of government, which were designed or adopted *with the express purpose of compelling the*

---

[1] *England Without and Within*, p. 526. [2] *Work and Wages*, p. 88.

laborer to work at the lowest rate of wages possible, and which succeeded at last in effecting their purpose.[1]

Among these acts were those giving the Courts of Quarter Sessions the right to fix the wages of laborers; and, hence, as Prof. Rogers shows, while the inflowing gold and silver of Mexico and Peru were swelling the value of all forms of property in England, the value of labor did not rise in proportion; and the common people fell into that awful era of poverty, wretchedness, degradation, crime, and Newgate-hanging by wholesale which mark the reigns of Henry VIII. and his children.

As part of the same scheme of oppression of the humble citizens by those who wielded the power of government, a system of inclosures of common lands by the landlords, without any compensation to the tenants, was inaugurated, and aided greatly to swell the general misery.

The benevolent soul of Francis Bacon took part against this oppression. In his *History of Henry VII.* he said:

Another statute was made of singular policy for the population apparently, and (if it be thoroughly considered) for the soldiery and military forces of the realm. Inclosures at that time began to be more frequent, whereby arable land (which could not be manured without people and families) was turned into pasture, which was easily rid by a few herdsmen; and tenancies for years, lives and at will (whereupon much of the yeomanry lived) were turned into demesnes. . . . The ordinance was that, That all houses of husbandry that were used with twenty acres of ground and upward should be maintained and kept up forever, together with a competent proportion of land to be used and occupied with them, and in no wise to be severed from them. . . . This did wonderfully concern the might and mannerhood of the kingdom, to have farms as it were of a standard sufficient to maintain an able body out of penury.

In 1597 Francis Bacon, then a member of Parliament, made a speech, of which we have a very meager report:

Mr. Bacon made a motion against depopulation of towns and houses of husbandry, and for the maintenance of husbandry and tillage. And to this purpose he brought in two bills, as he termed it, not drawn with a polished pen, but with a polished heart. . . . And though it may be thought ill and very prejudicial to lords that have enclosed great grounds, and pulled down even whole towns, and converted them to sheep pastures, yet, considering the increase of the people, and the benefit of the commonwealth, I doubt not but every man will deem the revival of former moth-eaten laws in this point a praiseworthy thing. For in matters of policy ill is not to be thought ill, which bringeth forth good. For enclosure of grounds brings depopulation, which brings forth first, idleness; secondly, decay of tillage; thirdly, subversion of homes, and decrease of charity and charge to the

---

[1] *Work and Wages*, Preface, p. 6.

poor's maintenance; fourthly, the impoverishing the state of the realm. . . . And I should be sorry to see within this kingdom that piece of Ovid's verse prove true, *Jam seges est ubi Troja fuit;* so in England, instead of a whole town full of people, none but green fields, but a shepherd and a dog. The eye of experience is the sure eye, but the eye of wisdom is the quick-sighted eye; and by experience we daily see, *Nemo putat illud videri turpe quod sibi sit quæstuosum.* And therefore almost there is no conscience made in destroying the savour of our life, bread I mean, for *Panis sapor vitæ.* And therefore a sharp and vigorous law had need be made against *these viperous natures* who fulfill the proverb, *Si non posse quod vult, velle tamen quod potest.*[1]

Hepworth Dixon says:

The decay of tillage, the increase of sheep and deer are for the yeoman class, and for the country of which they are the thew and sinew, dark events. . . . He [Bacon] makes a wide and sweeping study of this question of Pasturage *versus* Tillage, of Deer *versus* Men, which convinces him of the cruelty and peril of depopulating hamlets for the benefit of a few great lords. This study will produce, when Parliament meets again, a memorable debate and an extraordinary change of law.[2]

Bacon's bills became laws, after a fierce and bitter contest with the peers; they are in the statute book of England, 39 Elizabeth, 1 and 2. They saved the English yeomanry from being reduced to the present condition of the Irish peasantry.

They provide that no more land shall be cleared without special license; and that all land turned into pasture since the Queen's accession, no less a period than forty years, shall be taken from the deer and sheep within eighteen months, and restored to the yeoman and the plow.[3]

These great, radical and sweeping measures should endear Bacon's memory to every Englishman, and to every lover of his kind, the world over. They saved England from depopulation. They laid the foundation for the greatness of the nation. They furnished the great middle class who fought and won at Waterloo. And what a broad, noble, far-sighted philanthropy do they evidence! Here, indeed, "distribution did undo excess" that "each man" might "have enough." Here, indeed, was the greed of the few arrested for the benefit of the many.

While broad-minded and humane men took this view of the policy of enclosures, let us see how William Shakspere regarded it. I quote from Halliwell-Phillipps' *Outlines:*

In the autumn of the year 1614 there was great excitement at Stratford-on-Avon respecting an attempted enclosure of a large portion of the neighboring *common-field*—not commons, as so many biographers have inadvertently stated. The

---

[1] *Life and Works of Francis Bacon,* Spedding, Ellis and Heath, vol. iii. p. 81.
[2] *Personal History of Lord Bacon,* p. 87. [3] Ibid., p. 105.

design was resisted by the corporation under the natural impression that, if it were realized, both the number of agricultural employés and the value of the tithes would be seriously diminished. There is no doubt that this would have been the case, and, as might be expected, William Combe, the squire of Welcombe, who originated the movement, encountered a determined, and, in the end, a successful opposition. He spared, however, no exertions to accomplish the object, and, in many instances, if we may believe contemporary allegations, tormented the poor and coaxed the rich into an acquiescence with his views.[1]

Here was an opportunity for the pretended author of the Plays to show the stuff that was in him. Did he stand forward as—

> The village Hampden who, with dauntless breast,
> The little tyrant of his fields withstood?

Did he pour forth an impassioned defense of popular rights, whose eloquence would have forever ended all question as to the authorship of the Plays? It is claimed that he had written:

> Take physic, pomp;
> Expose thyself to feel what wretches feel;
> That thou mayst shake the superflux to them,
> And show the heavens more just.[2]

And again:

> I love not to see wretchedness o'ercharged,
> And duty in his service perishing.[3]

This is in the very spirit of Bacon's defense of the common people against those "viperous natures" that had "pulled down whole towns," or, as he expresses it in *Pericles*, had "swallowed up a whole parish, church, steeple, bells and all."

See how touchingly the writer of the Plays makes the insubstantial spirit, Ariel, non-human in its nature, sympathetic with the sufferings of man; and Prospero (the image of the author) says, even in the midst of the remembrance of his wrongs:

> Hast thou, which art but air, a touch, a feeling
> Of their afflictions, and shall not I, myself,
> *One of their kind, that relish all as sharply,*
> Fashioned as they, be kindlier moved than thou art?
> Though with their high wrongs I am struck to the quick,
> Yet with my nobler reason 'gainst my fury
> Do I take part.[4]

Was William Shakspere of Stratford-on-Avon,—himself one of the common people, "fashioned as they,"—kindly "moved by their

---

[1] *Outlines Life of Shak.*, p. 197.
[2] *Lear*, iii, 4.
[3] *A Midsummer Night's Dream*, v, 1.
[4] *Tempest*, v, 1.

afflictions;" and did he throw his wealth and influence into the scale in their defense? Not at all.

Knight says:

> The enclosure would probably have improved his property, and especially have increased the value of the tithes, of the moiety of which he held a lease. The corporation of Stratford were opposed to the inclosure. They held that it would be injurious to the poorer inhabitants, *who were then deeply suffering from the desolation of the fire.*[1]

Let us resume Halliwell-Phillipps narrative of the transaction:

> It appears most probable that Shakespeare was one of the latter who were so influenced, and that, *amongst perhaps other inducements*, he was allured to the unpopular side by Combe's agent, one Replingham, guaranteeing him from prospective loss. However that may be, *it is certain that the poet was in favor of the enclosures*, for, on December 23d, the corporation addressed a letter of remonstrance to him on the subject, and another on the same day to a Mr. Mainwaring. The latter, *who had been practically bribed by some land arrangements at Welcombe*, undertook to protect the interests of Shakespeare, so there can be no doubt that *the three parties were acting in unison.*[2]

Observe how tenderly the Shakspereans touch the wretched record of their hero. Mr. Mainwaring "was practically bribed by some land arrangements," but Mr. Shakspere, acting in concert with Mainwaring and Combe, under agreements of indemnification, was not bribed at all.

And that this agreement contemplated driving the people off the land and pauperizing them, is plain from the terms of the instrument, for Replingham contracts to indemnify *Shackespeare* for any loss he may sustain in his tithes "by reason of any inclosure or *decay of tillage there ment and intended by the said William Replingham.*"

Three greedy cormorants combine to rob the people of their ancient rights, and cause a decay of tillage, and one of the three is the man who is supposed to have possessed the greatest mind and most benevolent heart of his age; a heart so benevolent toward the poor and suffering that he anticipated the broadest claims put forth by the communists of to-day:

> Here, take this purse, you whom the heaven's plagues
> Have humbled to all strokes: that I am wretched
> Makes thee the happier:— Heavens, deal so still!
> Let the superfluous and lust-dieted man,
> That slaves your ordinance, that will not see
> Because he does not feel, feel your power quickly;

[1] Knight's *Shak. Biography*, p. 528.   [2] *Outlines*, p. 168.

> *So distribution should undo excess,*
> *And each man have enough.*[1]

Do we not see in this attempt of Shakspere to rob the poor of their rights, at the very time they had been impoverished by a great fire, the same man described by Ratsei — the thrifty play-actor, that fed on all men and permitted none to feed on him; who made his hand a stranger to his pocket, and his heart slow to perform his tongue's promise?

And all for what? To add a few acres more to his estate; a few pounds more to his fortune, on which, as he fondly hoped, through the heirs of his eldest daughter, he was to found a *family* which should wear that fictitious coat-of-arms, based on those lands which the King never conferred, for services which were never rendered, and glorified by the immortal plays which he never wrote.

Was this the spirit of the real author of the plays? No, no; listen to him:

> Tell her my love, more noble than the world,
> Prizes not quantity of dirty lands.[2]

And again he says:

Dost know this water-fly? . . . 'tis a vice to know him. He hath much land and fertile; let a beast be lord of beasts, and his crib shall stand at the king's mess. 'Tis a chough; but, as I say, spacious in the possession of dirt.[3]

This fellow might be in 's time a great buyer of land, with his statutes, his recognizances, his fines, his double vouchers, his recoveries; is this the fine of his fines, and the recovery of his recoveries, to have his fine pate full of fine dirt?[4]

And again:

Hamlet. Is not parchment made of sheep-skins?
Horatio. Ay, my lord, and of calf-skins, too.
Hamlet. They are sheep and calves which seek out assurances in that.

The real Shakespeare — Francis Bacon — said, "My mind turns on other wheels than profit." He regarded money as valuable only for the uses to which he put it, "the betterment of the state of man;" he had no faculty to grasp money, especially from the poor and oppressed; and as a consequence he died, leaving behind him a bankrupt estate and the greatest memory in human history.

Is it possible that the true Shakespeare could have taken such pains, as the Stratford man did, to entail his real-estate upon one

---

[1] *Lear*, iv, 1. [2] *Twelfth Night*, ii, 4. [3] *Hamlet*, v, 2. [4] *Hamlet*, v, 1.

of his children and her heirs, and forget totally to mention in his will that grander, that immortal estate of the mind which his genius had created, inconceivably more valuable than his "spacious possessions of dirt"?

VIII. His Treatment of his Father's Memory.

Let us pass to one other incident in the career of the Shakspere of Stratford.

We have seen that he strove to have his father made a gentleman. It will therefore scarcely be believed that, with an income equal to $25,000 per year of our money, he left that same father, and his mother, and his son Hamnet — his only son — without even the humblest monument to mark their last resting-place.

Richard Grant White says:

> Shakespeare seems to have set up no stone to tell us where his mother or father lay, and the same is true as to his son Hamnet.[1]

It appears that he inherited some property from his father, certainly enough to pay for a headstone to mark the everlasting resting-place of the father of the richest man in Stratford — the father of the man who was "in judgment a Nestor, in genius a Socrates, in art a Maro!"

And they would have us believe that he was the same man who wrote:

> I'll sweeten thy sad grave. Thou shalt not lack
> The flower that's like thy face, pale primrose; nor
> The azured hare-bell, like thy veins; no, nor
> The leaf of eglantine, whom not to slander,
> Out-sweetened not thy breath: the robin would
> With charitable bill (O bill, *sore-shaming*
> *Those rich-left heirs that let their fathers lie*
> *Without a monument!*) bring thee all this.[2]

IX. His Daughter Judith.

But let us go a step farther, and ask ourselves, what kind of a family was it that inhabited New Place during the latter years of Shakspere's life?

We have seen that the poet's father, mother and relatives generally were grossly ignorant; that they could not even write their own names, or read the Lord's Prayer in their native

---

[1] *Life and Genius of Shak.*, p. 144. [2] *Cymbeline*, iv, 2.

tongue; and that they did not possess even a Bible in their households.

But we now come face to face with a most astounding fact.

Shakspere had but two children who lived to maturity, his daughters Susanna and Judith, *and Judith could not read or write!*

Here is a copy of the mark with which the daughter of Shakspere signed her name. It appears as that of an attesting witness to a conveyance in 1611, she being then twenty-seven years of age.

Think of it! The daughter of William Shakspere, the daughter of the greatest intellect of his age, or of all ages, the profound scholar, the master of Latin, Greek, Italian, French, Spanish, Danish, the philosopher, the scientist, the politician, the statesman, the physician, the musician, signs her name with a curley-queue like a Pottawatomie Indian. And this girl was twenty-seven years old, and no idiot; she was subsequently married to one of the leading citizens of the town, Thomas Quiney, vintner. She was raised in the same town wherein was the same free-school in which, we are assured, Shakspere received that magnificent education which is manifested in the Plays.

Imagine William E. Gladstone, or Herbert Spencer, dwelling in the same house with a daughter, in the full possession of all her faculties, who signed her name with a pot-hook. Imagine the father and daughter meeting every day and looking at each other! And yet neither of these really great men is to be mentioned in the same breath with the immortal genius who produced the Plays.

With what divine anathemas did the real Shakespeare scourge ignorance!

He says:

Ignorance is the curse of God.[1]

And again:

The common curse of mankind, folly and *ignorance*, be thine in great revenue! Heaven bless thee from a tutor and discipline come not near thee.[2]

And again:

There is no darkness but ignorance.[3]

He pelts it with adjectives:

Barbarous ignorance.[4]

---

[1] *2d Henry VI.*, iv, 7.
[2] *Troilus and Cressida*, ii, 3.
[3] *Twelfth Night*, iv, 2.
[4] *King John*, iv, 2.

>   Dull, unfeeling ignorance.[1]
>   Gross and miserable ignorance.[2]
>   Thou monster, ignorance.[3]
>   Short-armed ignorance.[4]

Again, we read:
>   I held it ever,
> Virtue and cunning [knowledge] were endowments greater
> Than nobleness and riches; careless heirs
> May the two latter darken and expend;
> But immortality attends the former,
> Making a man a god.[5]

And he found—
>   More content in course of true delight
> Than to be thirsty after tottering honor,
> Or tie my treasure up in silken bags,
> To please the fool and death.[6]

Can it be conceived that the man who wrote these things would try, by false representations, to secure a coat-of-arms for his family, and seek by every means in his power to grasp the shillings and pence of his poorer neighbors, and at the same time leave one of his children in "barbarous, barren, gross and miserable ignorance"?

With an income, as we have shown, equal to $25,000 yearly of our money; with the country swarming with graduates of Oxford and Cambridge, begging for bread and ready to act as tutors; living in a quiet, rural neighborhood, where there were few things to distract attention, William Shakspere permitted his daughter to attain the ripe age of twenty-seven years, unable to read the immortal quartos which had made her father famous and wealthy. We will not — we cannot — believe it.

X. Some of the Educated Women of that Age.

But it may be said that it was the fault of the age.

It must be remembered, however, that the writer of the Plays was an exceptional man. He possessed a mind of vast and endless activity, which ranged into every department of human thought; he eagerly absorbed all learning.

Such another natural scholar we find in Sir Anthony Cook, tutor to King Edward IV., grandfather of Francis Bacon and Robert Cecil.

---

[1] *Richard II.*, i, 3. [3] *Love's Labor Lost*, iv, 2. [5] *Pericles*, iii, 2.
[2] *2d Henry IV.*, iv, 2. [4] *Troilus and Cressida*, ii, 3. [6] *Ibid.*

WILLIAM SHAKSPERE.

FRANCIS BACON'S MASK.

Fac-simile of the Frontispiece in the Folio of 1623.

Facing this portrait in the Folio are presented Ben Jonson's famous lines:

This Figure, that thou here seest put
It was for gentle Shakespeare cut;
Wherein the Graver had a strife
With nature, to out-doo the life:
O, could he but have drawn his wit
As well in brasse, as he hath hit
His face, the Print would then surpasse
All that was ever writ in brasse.
But since he cannot, Reader, looke
Not on his Picture, but his Booke.

Like Shakspere of Stratford, his family consisted of girls, and he was not by any means as wealthy as Shakspere. Did he leave his daughters to sign their names with hieroglyphics? No.

Macaulay says:

> Katherine, who became Lady Killigrew, wrote Latin hexameters and pentameters which would appear with credit in the *Musæ Etonenses*. Mildred, the wife of Lord Burleigh, was described by Roger Ascham as the best Greek scholar among the young women of England, Lady Jane Grey always excepted. Anne, the mother of Francis Bacon, was distinguished both as a linguist and a theologian. She corresponded in Greek with Bishop Jewell, and translated his *Apologia* from the Latin so correctly that neither he nor Archbishop Parker could suggest a single alteration. She also translated a series of sermons on fate and free will from the Tuscan of Bernardo Ochino.[1]

They were not alone. There were learned and scholarly women in England in those days, and many of them, as there have been in all ages since.

Macaulay says:

> The fair pupils of Ascham and Aylmer who compared, over their embroidery, the styles of Isocrates and Lysias, and who, while the horns were sounding and the dogs in full cry, sat in the lonely oriel with eyes riveted to that immortal page which tells how meekly and bravely the first great martyr of intellectual liberty took the cup from his weeping jailer.[2]

It is not surprising that William Shakspere, poacher, fugitive, vagabond, actor, manager, brewer, money-lender, land-grabber, should permit one of his two children to grow up in gross ignorance, but it is beyond the compass of the human mind to believe that the author of *Hamlet* and *Lear* could have done so. He indicates in one of his plays how a child should be trained. Speaking of King Leonatus, in *Cymbeline*, he says:

> Put him to all the learnings that his time
> Could make him receiver of; which he took
> As we do air, fast as 'twas ministered, and
> In his spring became a harvest.[3]

If Judith had been the child of the author of the Plays, and had "something of Shakespeare in her," she would have resented and struggled out of her shameful condition; her mind would have sought the light as the young oak forces its way upward through the brush-wood of the forest. She would have replied to her neglectful father as Portia did:

---

[1] Macaulay's *Essays, Bacon*, p. 246.   [2] Ibid., p. 247.   [3] *Cymbeline*, i, 1.

> But the full sum of me
> Is sum of nothing, which to term in gross
> Is an unlessoned girl, unschooled, unpracticed;
> Happy in this, she is not yet so old
> But she may learn; happier than this,
> She is not bred so dull but she can learn;
> Happiest of all, is, that her gentle spirit
> Commits itself to yours to be directed,
> As from her lord, her governor, her king.[1]

But if she was the natural outcome of ages of ignorance, developed in a coarse and rude state of society, and the daughter of a cold-blooded man, who had no instinct but to make money, we can readily understand how, in the midst of wealth, and under the shadow of the school-house, she grew up so grossly ignorant.

XI. SHAKSPERE'S FAMILY.

There seems to have been something wrong about the whole breed.

In 1613, Shakspere being yet alive, Dr. Hall, his son-in-law, husband of his daughter Susanna, brought suit in the ecclesiastical court against one John Lane, for reporting that his wife "had the runninge of the raynes, and had bin naught with Rafe Smith and John Palmer." Halliwell-Phillipps says:

> The case was heard at Worcester on July the 15th, 1613, and appears to have been *conducted somewhat mysteriously*, the deposition of Robert Whatcot, the poet's intimate friend, being the only evidence recorded, and *throwing no substantial light on the merits of the dispute.*[2]

Nevertheless, the defendant was excommunicated.

This being the case of the oldest daughter, the other, the pot-hook heiress, does not seem to have been above suspicion. Judith's marriage with Thomas Quiney was a mysterious and hurried one. Phillipps says:

> There appears to have been some reason for accelerating this event, for they were married without a license, and were summoned a few weeks afterward to the ecclesiastical court at Worcester to atone for the offense.[3]

Ignorance, viciousness, vulgarity and false pretenses seem to have taken possession of New Place.

Not a glimpse of anything that might tell a different story escapes the ravages of time.

---

[1] *Merchant of Venice*, iii, 2.   [2] *Outlines Life of Shak.*, p. 166.
[3] Halliwell-Phillipps, *Outlines Life of Shak.*, p. 182.

Appleton Morgan says:

> It is simply impossible to turn one's researches into any channel that leads into the vicinity of Stratford without noticing the fact that the Shakspere family left in the neighborhood where it flourished one unmistakable trace, familiar in all cases of vulgar and illiterate families, namely, the fact that they never knew or cared, or made an effort to know, of what vowels or consonants their own name was composed, or even to prepare the skeleton of its pronunciation. They answered — and made their marks — indifferently to *Saxpir*, or *Chaksper*, or to any other of the thirty forms given by Mr. Grant White, or the fifty-five forms which another gentleman has been able to collect.[1]

Even the very tombs of the different members of the family present different renderings of the name. Under the bust it is Shakspeare, while he signed the will as Shakspere; over the grave of Susanna it is Shakspere; over the other members of the family it is Shakespeare.

In short, the name was nothing. They

>Answered to " Hi!"
>Or any loud cry.

XII. The Origin of the Name.

We have been taught to believe that the name was *Shakespeare*, and it has been suggested that this was a reminiscence of that "late antecessor" who rendered such valuable services to the late King Henry VII.; that he shook a speare in defense of the King so potently that he was ever after known as *Shake-speare*. It is in this way the name is printed in all the publications put forth in Shakspere's lifetime. But it is no less certain that this name is another imposture. There never was a "shake" to it; and possibly never a "speare." The name was *Shak-speare*, or *speer*, or *spur*, or *pierre*, the first syllable rhyming to *back* and not to *bake*. *Shake-speare* was doubtless an invention of the man who assumed the name at a later date as a mask, and he wanted something that would "heroically sound." The fictitious *speare* passed to the fraudulent coat-of-arms.

In the bond given to enable William to marry, he is called "William *Shagspere*." In the bill of complaint of 1589 of John Shakspere in connection with the Wilmecote property, his son is alluded to as "William Shackespere." The father signs his cross to a deed to Robert Webb, in which he is described as " John Shax-

[1] *The Shakespeare Myth*, p. 160.

pere;" and his mother makes her mark as "Marye Shaksper." His father is mentioned in the will of John Webbe, in 1573, as "John Schackspere." In 1567 he is alluded to in the town records as "Mr. Shakspyr," and when elected high bailiff, in 1568, he is referred to as "Mr. John Shakysper." The only letter extant addressed to Shakspere was written October 25, 1598, by Richard Quiney, his townsman, and it is addressed to "Mr. Wm. Shackespere." In 1504–5 he is referred to in the court record as "Shaxberd." In 1508 he is referred to in the corporation records of Stratford as selling them a load of stone: "Paid to Mr. Shaxpere for on lod of ston x d." In his will the attorney writes it "Schackspeare," and the man himself signed his name Shakspere.

Hallam says:

The poet and his family spelt their name Shakspere, and to this spelling there are no exceptions in his own autographs.

The name is spelled by his townsman, Master Abraham Sturley, in 1599, *Shak*spere, and in 1598 he alludes to him as "Mr. William Shak." And when he himself petitioned the court in chancery in 1612, in reference to his tithes, he described himself as "William Schackspeare."

White says:

In the irregular, phonographic spelling of antiquity, the name appears sometimes as *Chacksper* and *Shaxpur*. It is possible that *Shakespeare* is a corruption of some name of a more peaceful meaning, and therefore perhaps of humbler derivation.[1]

It has been suggested, and with a good deal of probability, that the original name was Jacques-Pierre, pronounced Chackspere, or Shaks-pere.

The French *Jacques* (James) seems, by some mutation, to have been transformed in England into "a nickname or diminutive for John."[2]

Thus it may be that the original progenitor of this grandiloquent, martial cognomen, which "doth like himself heroically sound," may have been, in the first instance, a peasant without a family name, and known as plain Jack-Peter.

[1] White, *Life and Genius of Shak.*, p. 5.
[2] See Webster's *Unabridged Dictionary*, p. 712, the word *Jack*.

XIII. His Humiliation.

Despite his wealth, his position in his native town could not have been a very pleasant one. In 1602, and again in 1612, the very year in which we are told Shakspere returned to Stratford to spend the rest of his life, the most stringent measures were taken by the corporation to prevent the performance of plays. The pursuit in which he had made his money was thus stamped by his fellow townsmen as something shameful and degrading. Even this dirty little village repudiated it. The neighboring aristocracy must have turned up their noses and laughed long and loud at the plebeian's son setting up a coat-of-arms. By profession he was, by the statutes of his country, a "vagabond," and had, in the past, only escaped arrest as such by entering himself as a servitor, or servant, to some nobleman.

The vagabond, according to the statutes, was to "be stripped naked, from the middle upwards, and to be whipped until his body was bloody, and to be sent from parish to parish, the next straight way, to the place of his birth."[1]

He was buried in the chancel of the church, not as recognition of his greatness, but because that locality was "the legal and customary burial-place for the owners of the tithes."[2]

XIV. His Handwriting.

The very signature of Shakspere has provoked discussion. The fact that the will as originally drawn read, "witness my seal," and that the "seal" was erased and "hand" written in, has been cited to prove that the lawyer who drew the will believed that the testator could not read or write. In an article in *The Quarterly Review* in 1871, we read:

> If Shakspere's handwriting was at all like his signature, it was by no means easy to decipher. If we may speak dogmatically upon such slender proofs as we now possess, he learnt to write after the old German text-hand then in use at the grammar school of Stratford. It was in this respect fifty years behindhand, as any one may see by comparing Shakspere's signature with that of Sir Thomas Lucy, Lord Bacon, or John Lilly. *The wonder is how with such a hand he could have written so much.*

Mr. William Henry Burr, of Washington, D. C., has written an interesting pamphlet, to prove that Shakspere could not read or write, but simply traced his name from a copy set him; and that,

---

[1] Knight's *Illust. Shaks.*, *Trag.*, l, p. 442.   [2] *Outlines Life of Shak.*, p. 171.

as the copy furnished him at different times was written by different hands, there is a great difference in the shape of the letters composing his name.

Certain it is his autographs do not look like the work of a scholarly man. The following cut is a representation of all the signatures known, beyond question, to have been written by Shakspere:

The first is from Malone's *fac-simile* of a mortgage deed which has been lost; the second is from a conveyance in the possession of the corporation of London; the other three are from the three sheets of paper constituting his will.

Compare the foregoing scrawls with the clear and scholarly writing of Ben Jonson, affixed in 1604–5 to a copy of his *Mask of Blackness*, and now preserved in the British Museum:

Or compare them with the handwriting of the famous and popular John Lyly, the author of *Euphues*, written about 1580:

Or compare them with the following signature of Francis Bacon:

Or compare them with the signature of the famous Inigo Jones, who assisted in getting up the scenery and contrivances for masks at court:

XV. His Death.

Let us pass to another point.

We saw that the first recorded fact in reference to the Stratford boy was a drunken bout in which he lost consciousness, and lay out in the fields all night. The history of his life terminates with a similar event.

Halliwell-Phillipps thus gives the tradition:

It is recorded that the party was a jovial one, and, according to a somewhat late but apparently reliable tradition, when the great dramatist was returning to New Place in the evening, he had taken more wine *than was conducive to pedestrian accuracy*. Shortly or immediately afterwards, he was seized by the lamentable fever which terminated fatally on Friday, April 23. The cause of the malady, then attributed to undue festivity, would now be readily discernible in the wretched sanitary conditions surrounding his residence. If truth, and not romance, is to be invoked, were there the woodbine and the sweet honeysuckle within reach of the poet's death-bed, their fragrance would have been neutralized by their vicinity to middens, fetid water-courses, mud-walls and piggeries.[1]

[1] Halliwell-Phillipps, *Outlines Life of Shak.*, p. 170.

And from such a cause, and in the midst of such surroundings, we are told, died the greatest man of his race; leaving behind him not a single tradition or memorial that points to learning, culture, refinement, generosity, elevation of soul or love of humanity.

If he be in truth the author of the Plays, then indeed is it one of the most inexplicable marvels in the history of mankind. As Emerson says, "I cannot marry the facts to his verse."

CHAPTER IV.

THE LOST LIBRARY AND MANUSCRIPTS.

> Come, and take choice of all my library,
> And so beguile thy sorrow.
> *Titus Andronicus, iv, 1.*

THE whole life of Shakspere is shrouded in mystery. Richard Grant White says:

> We do not know positively the date of Shakespeare's birth, or the house in which he first saw the light, or a single act of his life from the day of his baptism to the month of his obscure and suspicious marriage. We are equally ignorant of the date of that event, and of all else that befell him from its occurrence until we find him in London; and when he went there we are not sure, or when he finally returned to Stratford. . . . Hardly a word that he spoke has reached us, and not a familiar line from his hand, or the record of one interview at which he was present.[1]

And, again, the same writer says:

> From early manhood to maturity he lived and labored and throve in the chief city of a prosperous and peaceful country, at a period of high intellectual and moral development. His life was passed before the public in days when the pen recorded scandal in the diary, and when the press, though the daily newspaper did not yet exist, teemed with personality. Yet of Dante, driven in haughty wretchedness from city to city, and singing his immortal hate of his pursuers as he fled, we know more than we do of Shakespeare, the paucity of whose personal memorials is so extreme that he has shared with the almost mythical Homer the fortune of having the works which made his name immortal pronounced medleys, in the composition of which he was but indirectly and partially concerned.[2]

Hallam says:

> Of William Shakespeare it may be truly said we know scarcely anything. . . . While I laud the labors of Mr. Collier, Mr. Hunter and other collectors of such crumbs, I am not sure that we should not venerate Shakespeare as much if they had left him undisturbed in his obscurity. To be told that he played a trick on a brother player in a licentious amour, or that he died of a drunken frolic, does not exactly inform us of the man who wrote *Lear*. If there was a Shakespeare of earth there was also one of heaven, and it is of him that we desire to know something.[3]

This is certainly extraordinary.

It was an age of great men.

---

[1] White, *Life and Genius of Shak.*, p. 4. [2] Ibid., p. 1. [3] *Introduction to Literature of Europe.*

Richard Grant White says:

Unlike Dante, unlike Milton, unlike Goethe, unlike the great poets and tragedians of Greece and Rome, Shakespeare left no trace upon the political, or even the social life of his era. Of his eminent countrymen, Raleigh, Sidney, Spenser, Bacon, Cecil, Walsingham, Coke, Camden, Hooker, Drake, Hobbes, Inigo Jones, Herbert of Cherbury, Laud, Pym, Hampden, Selden, Walton, Wotton and Donne may be properly reckoned as his contemporaries; and yet there is no proof whatever that he was personally known to either of these men, or to any others of less note among the statesmen, scholars, soldiers and artists of his day, except the few of his fellow craftsmen whose acquaintance with him has been heretofore mentioned.[1]

It was an age of pamphlets. Priests, politicians and players all vented their grievances, or set forth their views, in pamphlets, but in none of these is there one word from or about Shakspere.

1. WHERE ARE HIS LETTERS?

It was an age of correspondence. The letters which have come down to us from that period would fill a large library, but in no one of them is there any reference to Shakspere.

The man of Stratford passed through the world without leaving the slightest mark upon the politics or the society of his teeming and active age.

Emerson says:

If it need wit to know wit, according to the proverb, Shakespeare's time should be capable of recognizing it. Sir Henry Wotton was born four years after Shakespeare, and died twenty-three years after him, and I find among his correspondents and acquaintances the following persons: Theodore Beza, Isaac Casaubon, Sir Philip Sidney, the Earl of Essex, Lord Bacon, Sir Walter Raleigh, John Milton, Sir Henry Vane, Isaac Walton, Dr. Donne, Abraham Cowley, Bellarmine, Charles Cotton, John Pym, John Hales, Kepler, Vieta, Albericus Gentilis, Paul Sarpi, Arminius — with all of whom exists some token of his having communicated, without enumerating many others whom doubtless he (Wotton) saw — Shakspeare, Spenser, Jonson, Beaumont, Massinger, two Herberts, Marlowe, Chapman and the rest. Since the constellation of great men who appeared in Greece in the time of Pericles, there was never any such society; yet their genius failed them to find out the best head in the universe. Our poet's mask was impenetrable.[2]

We read in a sonnet attributed to his pen that he highly valued Spenser; and we find Spenser, it is claimed, alluding to the author of the Plays; the dedications of the *Venus and Adonis* and the *Rape of Lucrece* are supposed to imply close social relationship with the Earl of Southampton; we are told Elizabeth conversed with him and King James wrote him a letter; we have pictures of him sur-

[1] *Life and Genius of Shak.*, p. 185.   [2] *Representative Men*, p. 200.

rounded by a circle of friends, consisting of the wisest and wittiest of the age; and yet there has been found *no scrap of writing from him or to him;* no record of any dinner or festival at which he met any of his associates. In the greatest age of English literature the greatest man of his species lives in London for nearly thirty years, and no man takes any note of his presence.

Contrast the little we know of Shakspere with the great deal we know of his contemporary Ben Jonson. We are acquainted somewhat with the career even of Ben's father; we know that Ben attended school in London, and was afterward at Cambridge;—there is no evidence that Shakspere ever was a day at school in his life. We know that Jonson enlisted and served as a young man in the wars in the Low Countries. Shakspere's biography, from the time he left Stratford, in 1585-7, until he appears in London as a writer of plays, is an utter blank, except the legend that he held horses at the door of the theater. We know all about Jonson's return home; his marriage; his duel with Gabriel Spencer. We are certain of the date of the first representation of each of his plays; there is a whole volume of matter touching the quarrels between himself and other writers. He published his own works in 1616, and received a pension from James I. We have letters extant describing the suppers he gave, his manners, weaknesses, appearance, etc.

But with Shakspere all this is different. Where are the letters he must have received during the thirty years he was in London, if he was the man of active mind given out by the Plays? If he had received but ten a year, they would make a considerable volume, and what a world of light they would throw upon his pursuits and character.

But two letters are extant—those to which I have already referred: one addressed to him soliciting a loan of money; another addressed to a third party, in which he is referred to in the same connection; but there is not one word as to studies, or art, or literature, or politics, or science, or religion; and yet the mind that wrote the Plays embraced all these subjects, and had thought profoundly on all of them. He loved the art of poetry passionately; he speaks of "the elegance, facility and golden cadence of poetry;"[1]

[1] *Love's Labor Lost*, iv, 2.

he aspired to a " muse of fire that would ascend the highest heaven of invention;" he struggled for perfection. Had he no intercourse with the poets of his time? Was there no mutual coming-together of men of kindred tastes and pursuits?

Is it not most extraordinary that he should leave behind him this vast body of plays, the glory and the wonder of which fills the world, and not a scrap of paper except five signatures, three of which were affixed to his will, and the others to some legal documents?

On the one side we have the Plays — vast, voluminous, immortal; covering and ranging through every department of human thought. These are the works of *Shake-speare*.

On the other hand, these five signatures are the sum total of the life-labors of *Shak-spere* which have come down to us.

In these rude, illiterate scrawls we stand face to face with the man of Stratford. What an abyss separates them from the majestic, the god-like Plays?

It is a curious fact that all the writings were put forth in the name of *Shakespeare*, very often printed with a hyphen, as I have given it above, *Shake-speare;* while in every one of the five cases where the man's signature has come down to us, he spells his name *Shakspere*.

In this work, wherever I allude to the mythical writer, I designate him as *Shakespeare;* whenever I refer to the man of Stratford, I give him the name he gave himself — *Shakspere*.

The history of mankind will be searched in vain for another instance where a great man uniformly spelled his name one way on the title-pages of his works, and another way in the important legal documents which he was called upon to sign. Can such a fact be explained?

But passing from this theme we come to another question:

II. Where are his Books?

We have seen that the author of the Plays was a man of large learning; that he had read and studied Homer, Plato, Heliodorus, Sophocles, Euripides, Dares Phrygius, Horace, Virgil, Lucretius, Statius, Catullus, Seneca, Ovid, Plautus, Plutarch, Boccaccio, Berni and an innumerable array of French novelists and Spanish and

Danish writers. The books which have left their traces in the Plays would of themselves have constituted a large library.

What became of them?

There were no public libraries in that day to which the student could resort. The man who wrote the Plays must have gathered around him a vast literary store, commensurate with his own intellectual activity.

Did William Shakspere, of Stratford-on-Avon, possess such a library?

If he did, there is not the slightest reference to it in his will.

The man who wrote the Plays would have loved his library; he would have remembered it in his last hours. He could not have forgotten Montaigne, Holinshed, Plutarch, Ovid, Plato, Horace, the French and Italian romances, to remember his "brod silver and gilt bole," his "sword," his "wearing apparel," and his "second best bed with the furniture."

The man of Stratford forgot Homer and Plato, but his mind dwelt lovingly, at the edge of the grave, on his old breeches and the second-hand bed-clothes.

Compare his will with that of one who was his contemporary, Robert Burton, the author of *The Anatomy of Melancholy*. I quote a few items from it.

After leaving certain sums of money to Christ Church, Oxford, *to buy books with*, and to Brasennose Library, he says:

> If I have any books the University Library hath not, let them take them. If I have any books our own library hath not, let them take them. I give to Mrs. Fell all my English Books of Husbandry one excepted. . . . To Mrs. Iles my Gerard's *Herbal*. To Mrs. Morris my *Country Farm*, translated out of French, 4, and all my English Physick Books to Mr. Whistler, the Recorder of Oxford. . . . To all my fellow students, Mrs. of Arts, a book in Folio or two apiece. . . . To Master Morris my *Atlas Geografer* and *Ortelius Theatrum Mond*. . . . To Doctor Iles, his son, *Student Salauntch on Paurrhelia* and Lucian's Works in 4 tomes. If any books be left let my executors dispose of them with all such Books as are written with my own hands, and half my *Melancholy* copy, for Crips hath the other half.

This will was made in 1639, twenty-three years after Shakspere's death, and shows how a scholar tenderly remembers his library when he comes to bid farewell to the earth.

The inventory of Shakspere's personal property has never been found. Halliwell-Phillipps says:

If the inventory ever comes to light, it can hardly fail to be of surpassing interest, especially if it contains a list of the books preserved at New Place. *These must have been very limited in number, for there is no allusion to such luxuries in the will.* Anything like a private library, even of the smallest dimensions, was then of the rarest occurrence, and that Shakespeare ever owned one, at any time of his life, *is exceedingly improbable*.[1]

But surely the man who could write as follows could not have lived without his books:

Sir, he hath never fed of the dainties that are bred in a book; . . . his intellect is not replenished; he is only an animal; only sensible in the duller parts.[2]

There is no evidence that Shakspere possessed a single book. It was supposed for some time that the world had a copy of a work from his library, the *Essays of Montaigne*, but it is now conceded that the signature on the title-leaf is a forgery. The very forgery showed the instinctive feeling which possessed intelligent men that the author of *Hamlet* must have owned a library, and would have lovingly inscribed his name in his favorite books.

III. WHERE IS THE DÉBRIS OF HIS WORK-SHOP.

It was an age of commonplace-books.

Halliwell-Phillipps calls the era of Shakspere "those days of commonplace-books."

Shakespeare himself presented a commonplace-book to some friend, and wrote this sonnet, probably on the fly-leaf:

> Thy glass will show thee how thy beauties wear,
>   Thy dial how thy precious moments waste;
> The *vacant leaves* thy mind's imprint will bear,
>   And of *this book* this learning mayst thou taste.
> The wrinkles which thy glass will truly show
>   Of mouthéd graves will give thee memory;
> Thou by the dial's shady stealth mayst know
>   Time's thievish progress to eternity.
> Look, *what thy memory cannot contain,*
>   *Commit to these waste blanks,* and thou shalt find
> These children nursed, delivered from thy brain
>   *To take a new acquaintance of thy mind.*
>   These offices, so oft as thou wilt look,
>   Shall profit thee, and much enrich thy book.[3]

That distinguished scholar, Prof. Thomas Davidson, expresses the opinion that this word *offices* may be identical with the *Promus* of Bacon, some leaves of which are now in the British Museum.

---

[1] Halliwell-Phillipps, *Outlines Life of Shak.*, p. 186. [2] *Love's Labor Lost*, iv, 2.
[3] Sonnet lxxvii.

The sonnet describes just such a commonplace-book as Bacon's *Promus* is; and Prof. Davidson adds:

> *Promus* is the Latin for *offices*, that is, *larder*. *Offices* here has always seemed a strange word. Its significance appears to have been overlooked. The German translations omit it.

The real author of the Plays was a laborious student; we will see hereafter how he wrote and re-wrote his works. This sonnet shows that he must have kept commonplace-books, in which he noted down the thoughts and facts which he feared his memory could not contain, to subsequently "enrich his book" with them. With such habits he must have accumulated during his life-time a vast mass of material, the *débris*, the chips of the work-shop, hewn off in shaping the stately statues of his thought.

What became of them?

IV. WHERE ARE THE ORIGINAL COPIES OF THE PLAYS?

Let the reader write off one page of any one of the Shakespeare Plays, and he can then form some conception of the huge mass of manuscripts which must have been in the hands of the author. But as there is evidence that some of the Plays were re-written more than once, and "enlarged to as much again," there must have been, in the hands of the author, not only these original or imperfect manuscript copies, but the final ones as well. Moreover, there had been seventy-two quarto editions of the Plays. These, even if imperfect and pirated, as it is claimed, were

> His children, nursed, delivered of his brain;

and if the Stratford man was really the father of the Plays, and believed that

> Not marble,
> Nor the gilded monuments of princes,
> Should outlive this powerful rhyme,

what would be more natural than that he should take with him to Stratford copies of these quarto editions? Can we conceive of a great writer withdrawing to his country residence, to live out the remainder of his life, without a single copy of the works which had given him wealth, fame and standing as a gentleman?

And if he possessed such books, commonplace-books and manuscripts, why did he not,

> Dying, mention them within his will,

as the real author says the Roman citizen would a hair from the head of the dead Cæsar? For all the dust of all the Cæsars would not compare in interest for mankind with these original manuscripts and note-books; and the man who wrote the Plays knew it, and announced it with sublime audacity:

> But thy eternal summer shall not fade,
>   Nor lose possession of that fair thou owest;
> Nor shall Death brag thou wanderest in his shade,
>   When in *eternal lines* to time thou goest.
>   *So long as men can breathe or eyes can see,*
>   *So long lives this, and this gives life to thee.*

Appleton Morgan says:

More than a century and a half of vigorous and exhaustive research, bounded only by the limits of Great Britain, have failed to unearth a single scrap of memoranda or manuscript notes in William Shakespeare's handwriting, as preparation for any one or any portion of these plays or poems.

But it will be said that this utter disappearance of the original copies, note-books, memoranda, letters, quarto editions and library is due to the destruction and waste of years.

> Time hath, my lord, a wallet at his back,
> Wherein he puts alms for oblivion.

But certain things are to be remembered.

It must be remembered that Shakspere was the one great man of his race and blood. He had lifted his family from obscurity to fame, from poverty to wealth, from the condition of yeomanry to that of pretended gentry; all their claims to consideration rested upon him; and this greatness he had achieved for them not by the sword, or in trade, but by his intellectual genius. Hence, they represented him, in his monument, with pen in hand, in the act of writing; hence, they placed below the monument a declaration in Latin that he was, "In judgment, a Nestor — in genius, a Socrates — in art, a Maro," and an English inscription which says that

> All that he hath writ
> Leaves living art but page to serve his wit.

His daughter Susanna was buried with these lines upon her tomb:

> Witty above her sex, but that's not all,
> Wise to salvation was good Mistress Hall;
> Something of Shakespeare was in that, but this
> Wholly of him with whom she's now in bliss.

His genius was more or less the subject of comment even while he lived and soon after his death.

We are told in the preface to the quarto edition of *Troilus and Cressida*, published in 1609, that Shakespeare's Plays are equal to the best comedy in *Terence* or *Plautus*.

And, believe this that when he is gone and his Comedies out of sale, you will scramble for them, and set up a new English Inquisition.

In 1662, forty-six years after his death, and eight years before the death of his grand-daughter Elizabeth, wife of Sir John Barnard, the vicar of Stratford proceeded to note down the traditions about him.

How comes it, then, that this family — thus made great by the genius of one man, by his *literary* genius; conscious of his greatness; aware that the world was interested in the details of his character and history — should have preserved no scrap of his writing; no manuscript copy of any of his works; no quarto edition of the Plays; no copy of the great Folio of 1623; no book that had formed part of his library; no communication addressed to him by any one on any subject; no incident or anecdote that would have illustrated his character and genius? They had become people of some note; they lived in the great house of the town. One son-in-law was a physician, who had preserved a written record of the diseases that came under his observation; his grand-daughter Elizabeth, in 1643, entertained Queen Henrietta Maria, wife of King Charles, the reigning monarch, and daughter of the great King Henry IV. of France. The Queen remained in Shakspere's house, New Place, for three weeks, on her progress to join King Charles at Oxford. The Plays of Shakespeare were the delight of King Charles' court. We are assured by Dryden that Shakespeare was greatly popular with "the last King's court" — that of King James — and that Sir John Suckling, and the greater part of the courtiers, rated him "our Shakespeare," far above Ben Jonson, "even when his (Jonson's) reputation was at the highest."

Could it be possible that the Queen and courtiers would find themselves in the house of the author of *Hamlet* and *The Merry Wives of Windsor*, and yet ask no questions about him? And if they did, what more natural than for his grand-daughter to produce the relics she possessed of the great man — the letter of compliment which King James, the King's father, had written him, as tradition affirms. Kings' letters were not found on every bush in Stratford. And such memorials, once presented to the inspection of the curious, would never again be forgotten.

Would not a sweet and gentle and cultured nature have left behind him, in the bosom of his family, a multitude of pleasant anecdotes, redolent of the wit and humor that sparkle in the Plays? And, once uttered, the world would never permit them to die.

> No accent of the Holy Ghost
> The heedless world has ever lost.

We are told, by Oldys, that when his brother, in his latter years, visited London, he was beset with questions by the actors touching his illustrious relative, held by them in the highest veneration; but he could tell them nothing. Would not similar questions be propounded to his family? His nephew, the son of his sister, was an actor in London for years, but he, too, seems to have had nothing to tell. We know that Leonard Digges, seven years after his death, refers to the "Stratford monument." Interest in him was active.

Dr. Hall's diary of the patients he visited, and the diary of lawyer Green, Shakspere's cousin, concerning his petty law business, are both extant, and are pored over by rapturous students; but where are Shakspere's diary and note-books?

Neither is there any reason why his personal effects should disappear through carelessness. Dr. Hall was a man of education. He must have known the value of Shakspere's papers. His own and his father-in-law's personal property continued in the hands of Shakspere's heirs *down to the beginning of the present century*, having passed by will from Lady Barnard in 1670 to the heirs of Joan Hart, Shakspere's sister. This was long after the great Garrick Jubilee had been held at Stratford, and long after the world had grown intensely curious about everything that concerned its most famous man. Surely the memorials of one who was believed by his heirs to be the rival of Socrates in genius and of Maro in art would not be permitted to be destroyed by a family of even ordinary intelligence. See how the papers of Bacon — of Bacon who left no children, and probably an unfaithful wife — have come down to us: the MSS. of his books; great piles of letters, written, most of them, not when he was Lord Chancellor, but when he was plain Master

Francis Bacon. Even his commonplace-books have found their way into the British Museum, and the very scraps of paper upon which his amanuensis tried his pen. Remember how Spedding found the original packages of the private letters of Lord Burleigh, just as they were tied up by the great Lord Treasurer's own hand, never opened or disturbed for nigh three hundred years!

In the British Museum they have the original manuscript copies of religious plays written in the reign of Henry VI., two hundred years before the time of Shakspere; but that marvelous collection has not a line of any of the plays written by the author of *Lear* and *Hamlet*.

V. THE MONEY VALUE OF THE PLAYS.

Nothing is clearer than that Shakspere was a money-getting man. He achieved a very large fortune in a pursuit in which most men died paupers. He had a keen eye to profit. He was ready to sue his neighbor for a few shillings loaned. I have shown that he must have carried on the business of brewing in New Place. He entered into a conspiracy to wrest the right of common from the poor people of the town, for his own profit.

Now, the Plays represented certain values; not alone their value on the stage, but the profits which came from their publication. They were popular.

Appleton Morgan says:

> Although constantly pirated during his lifetime, it is impossible to discover that anybody, or any legal representative of anybody, named Shakespeare, ever set up any claim to proprietorship in any of these works — works which beyond any literary production of that age were (as their repeatedly being subjects of piracy and of registration on the Stationers' books proves them to have been) of the largest market value.

Why should the man who sued his neighbors for petty sums like two shillings pass by, in his will, these sources of emolument?

But it may be said he had already sold the plays and poems to others. This answer might suffice as to those already printed, but there were seventeen plays that never saw the light until they appeared in the Folio edition of 1623, published seven years after his death. He must have owned these. Why did he make no provision in his will for their publication — if not for glory, for gain? It may be said that *John Heminge* and *Henry Cundell*, who appear to have put forth the Folio of 1623, are mentioned in his will, and that they acted therein as his literary executors. But they are not named as executors. His sole executors are Dr. John Hall, his son-in-law, and Susanna, his daughter, with Thomas Russell, Esq., and Francis Collins, gent., as overseers. None of these parties appear to have had any connection with the great Folio. It was a large and costly work, and, even though eventually profitable, must have required the advance of a large sum to print it. Where did this money come from? Is it probable that a couple of poor actors, like Heminge and Condell, would have undertaken such an outlay and risk while the children of Shakspere were alive and exceedingly wealthy? I do not suppose that a work of the magnitude of the Folio of 1623 could have been printed for a less sum than the equivalent of $5,000 of our money. But at the back of the Folio we find this entry:

Printed at the charges of W. Jaggard, Ed. Blount, I. Smithweeke and W. Aspley, 1623.

On the title-page we read:

Printed by Isaac Jaggard and Ed. Blount, 1623.

So that it appears that three men, W. Jaggard, I. Smithweeke and W. Aspley, paid the expenses of the publication, while only one man, Ed. Blount, was concerned in printing and expense both.

So that it appears that neither Heminge and Condell, nor Dr. John Hall, nor Shakspere's daughter Susanna, nor Thomas Russell, nor Francis Collins, nor anybody else who represented Shakspere's blood or estate, had anything to do with the expense of publishing the complete edition of Shakespeare's Plays, including seventeen that had never before been printed.

VI. A Mysterious Matter.

But there is still another curious feature of this mysterious business.

I quote again from Appleton Morgan:

It is not remarkable, perhaps, that we find no copyright entries on the Stationers' books in the name of Jonson, Marlowe, or other of the contemporary poets and dramatists, for these were continually in straitened circumstances. But, William Shakespeare being an exceedingly wealthy and independent gentleman (if, besides, one of the largest owners of literary property of his time), it is remarkable that the only legal method of securing literary matter, and putting it in shape to alienate, was never taken by him, or in his name. The silence of his will as to any literary property whatever is explained by the commentators by supposing that Shakespeare sold all his plays to the Globe or other theaters on retiring, and that the Globe Theater was destroyed by fire. If so, let it be shown from *the only place where the legal transfer could have been made*—the books of the Stationers' Company, which were not destroyed by fire, but are still extant.

Other commentators—equally oblivious of such trifling obstacles as the laws of England—urge that, being unmentioned in the will, the Plays went by course of probate to Dr. Hall, the executor.

But even more, in that case, certain entries and transfers at Stationers' Hall would have been necessary. Moreover, the copyright, being not by statute, was perpetual, and could not have lapsed. In the preface to their first folio Heminge and Condell announced that all other copies of Shakespeare's plays are "stolen and surreptitious." But on consulting the Stationers' books it appears that the quarto editions were mostly regularly copyrighted according to law, *whereas the first folio was not*. Nor were the plays already copyrighted *ever transferred to Heminge and Condell or to their publishers*.

What legal rights in England ever centered in this great first folio, except as to the plays which appeared therein for the first time (which Blount and Jaggard did copyright), must always remain a mystery. If "stolen and surreptitious copies" existed, therefore, they were the folio, not the quarto copies.

And again, in another publication, Mr. Morgan says:

Heminge and Condell asserted, in 1623, that all the editions of the plays called Shakespeare, except their own, were "stolen and surreptitious copies." If the laws of England in those days are of the slightest consequence in this investigation, it must appear that it was actually these very men, Heminge and Condell, and not the other publishers, who were utterers of "stolen and surreptitious copies." For, whereas all other printers of Shakespeare's plays observed the laws and entered them for copyright, Heminge and Condell appear never to have heard of any legal obligations of the sort. Unless they stole them, it certainly passes man's understanding to conceive how they got hold of them. For, whatever property could be legally alienated in those days without a record, literary property certainly could not be so alienated. *The record of alienation could have been made in but one place, and it was never made there.*

It may be said that Heminge and Condell, being merely play-actors, were unfamiliar with the copyright system and law, and, hence, failed to properly enter the work. But Heminge and Condell, it appears by the first Folio itself, were not the men who put their money into the venture, but Messrs. "W. Jaggard, Ed. Blount, I. Smithweeke and W. Aspley." Why did *they* not secure a title to the work in which they were venturing $5,000? They were business men, not actors.

As the Folio of 1623 declares that the previous quarto editions were "stolen and surreptitious copies" of the Plays, "maimed and deformed by the frauds and stealths of injurious impostors that exposed them," and that *they* now present them "cured and perfect of their limbs, and all the rest, absolute in their numbers as he conceived them," etc., it follows that in 1623 Heminge and Condell must have had the original manuscripts in the handwriting of "the poet." And they assert this:

> And what he thought he uttered with that easiness that we have scarce received a blot in his papers.

Now, as Heminge and Condell possessed Shakspere's original copies in 1623, they could not have been burned in the Globe Theater in 1613.

A very large box would be required to contain them. What became of these fairly written, unblotted manuscripts? Did his "pious fellowes," who so loved the memory of their associate that they compiled and published in huge and costly folio his completed works, care nothing for these memorials, in the very handwriting of him whom Ben Jonson pronounced, in the same volume and edition, the

> Soul of the age,
> The applause, delight, the wonder of our stage;

who "was not for an age, but for all time," and in comparison with whom "all that insolent Greece or haughty Rome" had produced was as nothing?

Those manuscripts have never been found, never been heard of; no tradition refers to them; no scrap, rag, remnant or fragment of them survives.

Why did not the men who so eagerly questioned his brother, and who, we are told, so carefully preserved the Chandos portrait, secure some part of these invaluable documents, which would to-day be worth many times their weight in gold?

VII. ANOTHER MYSTERY.

But another mystery attaches to these manuscripts.

The first appearance of *Troilus and Cressida* was in quarto form in 1609, and the book contains a very curious preface, in which we are told that the play had never been played, "never clapper-clawed with the palms of the vulgar," "never sullied with the smoky breath of the multitude," and we find also this remarkable statement:

> And believe this, that when he is gone and his *comedies* out of sale, you will scramble for them and set up a new English Inquisition. Take this for a warning and at the peril of your pleasures' loss and judgments refuse not, nor like this the less for not being sullied with the smoky breath of the multitude; but thank for-

tune for the 'scape it hath made among you, *since by the grand possessors' wills I believe you should have prayed for them rather than been prayed.*

Here two remarkable facts present themselves:

1. That Shakspere, who was supposed to have written his plays for the stage, for the profit to be drawn from their representation to the swarming multitudes, writes a play which never is acted, but printed, so that any other company of players may present it. And this play is one of the profoundest productions of his great genius, full of utterances upon statecraft that are a million miles above the heads of the rag-tag-and-bobtail who "thunder at the play-house and fight for bitten apples."[1]

2. That the original copies of this play and his other comedies — some or all of them — have passed out of his hands, and are now possessed by some grand persons not named. For, note the language: The writer of the preface speaks of Shakespeare's "comedies" in the plural; then of the particular comedy of *Troilus and Cressida;* then of the "'scape *it* hath made amongst you," that is, its escape out of the "grand possessors'" hands, who were unwilling to have it "'scape." In other words, we are told that these "grand possessors' wills" were opposed to letting *them* — the comedies — be published.

Charles Knight says:

It is difficult to understand this clearly, but we learn that the copy *had an escape from some powerful possessors*. It appears to us that these *possessors* were powerful enough to prevent a single copy of any one of the plays which Shakspere produced in his "noon of fame," with the exception of the *Troilus and Cressida* and *Lear*, being printed till after his death; and that between his death, in 1616, and the publication of the Folio, in 1623, *they continued the exercise of their power*, so as to allow only one edition of one play which had not been printed in his lifetime (*Othello*) to appear. The clear deduction from this statement of facts is, that the original publication of the fourteen plays published in Shakspere's lifetime was, with the exceptions we have pointed out, authorized *by some power having the right to prevent the publication;* that, after 1603, till the publication of the Folio, that right was not infringed or contested, except in three instances.[2]

Knight thinks that these "grand possessors" were Shakspere's fellow actors, to whom he had assigned the Plays; but this difficulty presents itself: Would the man who wrote the preface to the *Troilus and Cressida* of 1609, and who evidently looked with contempt upon the players and the play-house, and who boasts that

[1] *Henry VIII.*, v, 3.   [2] *Shak., History*, vol. i, p. 314.

the play in question had never been "clapper-clawed with the palms of the vulgar," or "sullied with the smoky breath of the multitude"—would he speak of the actors who made their humble living before this vulgar multitude, the "vassal actors," the "legal vagabonds," as "grand possessors"? Do not the words imply some persons of higher social standing?

And then comes this further difficulty: If the actors owned *Troilus and Cressida*, why would they not have played it, and gotten all the pennies and shillings out of it possible? Or why, if written by an actor for actors, should it have been written so transcendently above the heads of the multitude that it could not be acted? And why, if it was worth anything as a play, would the actors have allowed it to "'scape" into the hands of a publisher who sends it forth with a sneer at the audiences who frequent their places of amusement. And why, if they owned all the plays, does not their ownership appear somewhere on the books of copyright? And why, if they owned them, would they destroy their own monopoly by publishing them in folio in 1623, thus throwing open the doors to all the players of the world to act them? And why would they not even copyright the book when they did so publish it? And why, if they did so publish it, does it appear, by the book itself, that they were not at the charge of publishing it, but that it was sent forth at the cost of four men, not actors, therein named?

Thus, in whatever direction we penetrate into this subject, inexplicable mysteries meet us face to face.

VIII. Pregnant Questions.

Why should the wealthy Shakspere permit the Plays, written while he was wealthy, to pass into the hands of certain "grand possessors"? And if these men were not actors, but bought the Plays of Shakspere, why should they make no attempt, during twenty years, to get their money back by publishing them? And could they have procured them of the money-making Shakspere, if he wrote them, without paying for them? And what business would "grand" men, not actors, not publishers, not speculators for profit, have with the Plays anyway? And why should they stand guard over them and keep them from the public for twenty years, and then put them all out at once, and not copyright them, thus making them a present to the public? And when they did publish them, why should they place the papers in the hands of two play-actors, Heminge and Condell, who pretend that they are putting them forth out of love for the memory of that good fellow, Will Shakspere? Were not Heminge and Condell a mere mask and cover for the "grand possessors" of the unblotted manuscripts?

And if the man who sued Philip Rogers for £1 19s. 10d. for malt sold, and for two shillings money loaned, had any ownership in any of these plays, can we believe he would not have enforced it to the uttermost farthing? Would not he and his (for they were all litigious) have chased the stray shillings that came from their publication, through court after court, and thus placed the question of authorship forever beyond question?

We are forced to conclude:

1. Shakspere did not own the Plays and never had owned them.

2. They were in the hands of and owned by some "grand" person or persons.

3. This "grand" person or persons cared nothing for the interests of the players and made them public property; therefore, Heminge and Condell did not represent the players.

4. This "grand" person or persons cared nothing for the money to be derived from their sale, and took out no copyright, but presented them freely to the world; and this was not in the interest of Shakspere's heirs, if he had any claim to them.

5. And this "grand" person or persons cared nothing for the money to be made out of them, or he or they would, in the period of twenty years, between 1603 and 1623, have printed and reprinted them in quarto form, and made a profit out of them.

But there is another striking fact in connection with the question of the manuscripts.

IX. ANOTHER MYSTERY.

The whole publication of the Folio of 1623 is based on a fraudulent statement.

Heminge and Condell, in their preface, addressed "to the great variety of readers," say:

It had bene a thing, we confesse, worthy to have been wished that the author himself had lived to have set forth, and overseen his own writings. But since it hath bin ordained otherwise, and he by death departed from that right, we pray you do not envy his friends the office of their care and paine to have collected and publish'd them; and so to have publish'd them as where (before) you were abus'd with diverse stolne and surreptitious copies, maimed and deformed by the frauds and stealthes of injurious impostors, that exposed them, even those are now offered to your view cur'd and perfect of their limbs, and all the rest, absolute in their numbers, as he conceived them. Who, as he was a happie imitator of nature, was a most gentle expresser of it. His mind and his hand went together. And what he thought he uttered with that easiness that we have scarce received from him a blot in his papers.

And on the title-page of the Folio we read: "Mr. William Shakespeare's Comedies, Histories and Tragedies. Published *according to the true originall copies.*" We have also a list of "the principal actors in all these plays," prefaced by these words:

The works of William Shakespeare, containing all his Comedies, Histories and Tragedies: *Truely set forth according to their first originall.*

Here we find four things asserted:

1. That the Folio was printed from the original copies.
2. That Heminge and Condell had "collected" these copies and published them in the Folio.
3. That the quarto editions were "stolne and surreptitious copies, maimed and deformed."
4. That what Shakespeare wrote was poured from him, as if by inspiration, so that he made no corrections, and "never blotted a line," as Ben Jonson said.

These statements are met by the following facts:

I. Some of the finest thoughts and expressions, distinctively Shakespearean, and preëminently so, are found in the quarto editions, *and not in the Folio.*

For instance, in the play of *Hamlet*, nearly all of scene iv, act 4, is found in the quarto and not in the Folio. In the quarto copy we find the following passages:

> What is a man,
> If his chief good and market of his time
> Be but to sleep and feed? A beast, no more.
> Sure he that made us with such large discourse,
> Looking before and after, gave us not
> That capability and god-like reason
> To fust in us unused.

And again:

> Rightly to be great
> Is, not to stir without great argument,
> But greatly to find quarrel in a straw,
> When honor's at the stake.

No one can doubt that these passages came from the mind we are accustomed to call Shakespeare. Hundreds of other admirable sentences can be quoted which appear in the quartos, but not in the Folio. It follows, then, that Heminge and Condell did not have "the true original copies," or they would have contained these passages. It follows, also, that there must have been some reason why portions of the quarto text were omitted from the Folio. It follows, also, that, in some respects, the "stolne and surreptitious" copies of the quarto are more correct than the Folio, and that but for the quartos we would have lost some of the finest gems of thought and expression which go by the name of Shakespeare.

II. The statement that Shakespeare worked without art, that he improvised his great productions, that there was scarce "a blot in his papers," in the sense that he made no corrections, is not only incompatible with what we know of all great works of art, but is contradicted on the next page but one of the Folio, by Ben Jonson, in his introductory verses.

He says:

> Yet must I not give Nature all. Thy Art,
> My gentle Shakespeare, must enjoy a part.
> For though the Poet's matter Nature be,
> His Art doth give the fashion. And that he
> Who casts to write a living line must sweat
> (Such as thine are) and strike the second heat
> Upon the Muse's anvile; turn the same
> (And himself with it) that he thinks to frame,
> Or for the laurel he may gain a scorne;
> For a good Poet's made, as well as borne.
> *And such wert thou.* Look how the father's face
> Lives in his issue; even so the race
> Of Shakespeare's mind and manners brightly shines
> In his well-torned and true-filed lines.

Here, then, we have the two play-actors, and friends of Shakespeare, Heminge and Condell, squarely contradicted by another friend and play-actor, Ben Jonson. One asserts that Shakespeare wrote without art; the other, that he sweat over his "true-filed lines" and turned them time and again on the "Muse's anvile."

Several of the plays exist in two forms:—first, a brief form, suitable for acting; secondly, an enlarged form, double the size of the former. This is true of *Romeo and Juliet*, *Henry V.*, *The Merry Wives of Windsor* and *Hamlet*.

For instance, the first edition of *Henry V.* contains 1,800 lines; the enlarged edition has 3,500 lines. Knight says:

> In this elaboration the old materials are very carefully used up; but they are so thoroughly refitted and dovetailed with what is new, that the operation can only be compared to the work of a skillful architect, who, having an ancient mansion to enlarge and beautify, with a strict regard to its original character, preserves every feature of the structure, under other combinations, with such marvelous skill, that no unity of principle is violated, and the whole has the effect of a restoration in which the new and the old are undistinguishable.[1]

Knight gives a specimen of this work, taken from the quarto *Henry V.* of 1608 and the Folio of 1623. We print in the second column, in italics, those parts of the text derived from the quarto, and which reappear in the Folio:

QUARTO 1608.	FOLIO 1623.
King. Sure we thank you; and, good my lord, proceed	*King.* Sure, we thank you. My learned lord, I pray you to *proceed* And justly and religiously unfold
Why the law Salique, which they have in France,	*Why the law Salique, that they have in France,*
Or should or should not stop us in our claim:	*Or should or should not bar us in our claim.*
And God forbid, my wise and learned lord,	*And God forbid, my* dear *and* faithful *lord,*
That you should fashion, frame or wrest the same.	*That you should fashion, wrest or* bow your reading,
For God doth know how many now in health	Or nicely charge your understanding soul
Shall drop their blood, in approbation	With opening titles miscreate, whose right.
Of what your reverence shall incite us to.	Suits not in native colors with the truth.
Therefore, take heed how you impawn our person;	*For God doth know how many now in health*
How you awake the sleeping sword of war:	*Shall drop their blood, in approbation*
We charge you in the name of God take heed.	*Of what your reverence shall incite us to:*
After this conjuration speak, my lord;	*Therefore, take heed how you impawn our person;*
And we will judge, note and believe in heart	*How you awake the sleeping sword of war;*

[1] Charles Knight, *Pict. Shak.*, *Histories*, vol. i, p. 310.

That what you speak is washed as pure As sin in baptism.	*We charge you in the name of God take heed.* For never two such kingdoms did contend Without much fall of blood, whose guiltless drops Are every one a woe, a sore complaint, 'Gainst him whose wrongs give edge unto the swords That make such waste in brief mortality. Under *this conjuration speak, my lord;* *And we will* hear, *note and believe in heart,* *That what you speak is,* in your conscience, *washed* *As pure as sin* with *baptism*.

Now Heminge and Condell claim, in the Folio, that the play of *Henry V.* was printed from the "true original" copy, and that it came from the mind of Shakspere without a blot; while here is proof conclusive that it was not printed from the first original copy; and that it did not come, heaven-born, from the soul of the creator; but that the writer, whoever he might be, was certainly a man of vast industry and immense adroitness, nimbleness and subtlety of mind.

False in one thing, false in all. Heminge and Condell did not have the author's original manuscripts, with all the interlineations and corrections, before them to print from, but a fair copy from some other pen. They do not seem to have known that there was that 1608 edition of the play. In fact, they do not even seem to know how to spell their own names. At the end of the introduction, from which I have quoted, they sign themselves, "John Heminge" and "Henrie Condell," while in the list of actors, published by themselves, they appear as "John Hemmings" and "Henry Condell;" and Shakspere calls them, in his will, "John Hemynge" and "Henry Cundell."

If the play-actor editors thus falsified the truth, or were themselves the victims of an imposition, what confidence is to be placed in any other statement they make? What assurance have we that they had collected the original manuscript copies; that they ever saw them; in short, that they were the work of Shakspere or in his handwriting? What assurance have we that the whole introduction and dedication to which their names are appended were not written by some one else, and that they were but a mask for those "grand possessors" who, seven years before Shakspere's death, owned the play of *Troilus and Cressida?*

In fact, a skeptical mind can see, even in the verses which face the portrait of Shakspere in the Folio of 1623, the undercurrent of a double meaning. They commence:

> The figure that thou here seest put,
> It was for gentle Shakespeare cut.

Is the word *gentle* here, a covert allusion to Shakspere's ridiculous and fraudulent pretensions to "gentle" blood, and to that bogus coat-of-arms which we are told he had engraved in stone over the door of New Place in Stratford?

> Wherein the graver had a strife [1]
> With Nature to out-doo the life.

No one can look at that picture and suppose that B. I. (Ben Jonson) was serious in this compliment to the artist.

Appleton Morgan says.

In this picture the head of the subject is represented as rising out of an horizontal plane of collar appalling to behold. The hair is straight, combed down the sides of the face and bunched over the ears, the forehead is disproportionately high; the top of the head, bald; the face has the wooden expression familiar in the Scotchmen and Indians used as signs for tobacconists' shops, accompanied by an idiotic stare that would be but a sorry advertisement for the humblest establishment in that trade.

If this picture "out-does the life," what sort of a creature must the original have been?

> O, could he but have drawn his wit
> As well in brass as he hath hit
> His face, the print would then surpass
> All that was ever writ in brass.

This thought of "drawing his wit" is singularly enough taken from an inscription around another portrait — not that of Shakspere, but of Francis Bacon. On the margin of a miniature of Bacon, painted by Hilliard in 1578, when he was in his eighteenth year, are found these words, "the natural ejaculation, probably," says Spedding, "of the artist's own emotion" *Si tabula daretur digna, animum mallem* — if one could but paint his mind![2]

---

[1] *The Shak. Myth*, p. 95.   [2] *Life and Works of Bacon*, Spedding, Ellis, etc., vol. ., p. 7.

Let us read again those lines:

> O, could he but have drawn his wit
> As well in *brass* as he hath hit
> His face, the print would then surpass
> All that was ever writ—*in brass!*

That is to say, his wit drawn *in brass* would surpass, *in brass*, all that was ever written. Is not this another way of intimating that only a brazen-faced man, like Shakspere, would have had the impudence to claim the authorship of plays which were not written by him?

And that this is not a forced construction we can see by turning to the Plays, where we will find the words *brass* and *brazen* used in the same sense as equivalents for impudence.

> Can any face of *brass* hold longer out?[1]
> Well said, *brazen*-face.[2]
> A *brazen*-faced valet.[3]

It seems to me there is even a double meaning to some of the introductory verses of the Folio of 1623, signed Ben Jonson. The verses are inscribed—

> To the memory of my beloved—the Author—Mr. William Shakespeare—and—*what he hath left us.*

What does this mean: "what he hath left us"? Does it mean his works? How could Ben Jonson inscribe verses to the *memory* of works—plays? We speak of the memory of persons, not of productions; of that which has passed away and perished, not of that which is but beginning to live; not of the

> Soul of the age!
> The applause! delight! the wonder of our stage!

In the same volume, on the next page, we are told,

> For though his line of life went soon about,
> *The life yet of his lines will never out.*

Could Ben Jonson inscribe his verses to the *memory* of works which, he assures us in the same breath, were not "for an age, but for all time"? Can you erect a memorial monument over immortal life?

What did William Shakspere leave behind him that held any connection with the Plays? Was it the real author—Francis Bacon?

---

[1] *Love's Labor Lost*, v, 2.   [2] *Merry Wives of Windsor*, iv, 2.   [3] *Lear*, ii, 2.

And this thought seems to pervade the verses. Jonson says:

> *Thou art alive still*—while thy book doth live.

And again:

> Sweet Swan of Avon! what a sight it were
> To see thee in our waters *yet appear*,
> And make those flights upon the banks of Thames,
> That so did take Eliza and our James.

That is to say, Ben Jonson expresses to the dead Shakspere the hope that he would reappear and make some more dramatic "flights"—that is, write some more plays. Such a wish would be absurd, if applied to the dead man, but would be very significant, if the writer knew that the real author was still alive and capable of new flights. And the closing words of the verses sound like an adjuration to Bacon to resume his pen:

> *Shine forth*, thou Starre of Poets, and with rage
> Or influence chide or *cheer* the drooping stage,
> Which, since thy flight from thence, hath mourned like night,
> And despaires day, but for thy volumes' light.

The play-houses had the manuscript copies of the Plays, and had been regularly acting them; it needed not, therefore, the publication of the Folio in 1623 to enable the poet to shine forth.

If the "drooping stage" "mourned like night," it was not for the Plays which appear in the Folio, for it possessed them; it had been acting them for twenty years; but it was because the supply of *new* plays had given out. Hugh Holland says on the next page:

> Dry'd is that vein, dry'd is the Thespian spring.

How comes it, then, that Ben Jonson expresses the hope that the author would reappear, and write new plays, and cheer the drooping stage, and shine forth again, if he referred to the man whose mouldering relics had been lying in the Stratford church for seven years?

X. Ben Jonson's Testimony.

It must not be forgotten that Ben Jonson was in the employment of Francis Bacon; he was one of his "good pens;" he helped him to translate his philosophical works into Latin. If there was a secret in connection with the authorship of the Plays, Ben Jonson, as Bacon's friend, as play-actor and play-writer, doubtless knew it. And it is very significant that at different periods, far apart, he employed precisely the same words in describing the genius of

Hos ego versiculos feci.
Ben: Jonson.

William Shakspere and the genius of Francis Bacon. In these verses, from which I have been quoting, he says, speaking ostensibly of Shakspere:

> Or when thy socks were on,
> Leave thee alone, for the comparison
> Of all that *insolent Greece or haughty Rome*
> Sent forth, or since did from their ashes come.

Jonson died in 1637. His memoranda, entitled *Ben Jonson's Discoveries*, were printed in 1640. One of these refers to the eminent men of his own and the preceding era. After speaking of Sir Thomas More, the Earl of Surrey, Challoner, the elder Wyatt, Sir Nicholas Bacon, Sir Philip Sydney, the Earl of Essex and Sir Walter Raleigh, he says:

> Lord Egerton, a grave and great orator, and best when he was provoked; but his learned and able but unfortunate successor (Sir Francis Bacon) *is he that hath filled up all numbers*, and performed that in our tongue which may be compared or preferred either *to insolent Greece or haughty Rome*.

What a significant statement is this!

Francis Bacon had "filled up all numbers." That is to say, he had compassed all forms of poetical composition. Webster defines "numbers" thus:

> That which is regulated by count; poetic measure, as divisions of time or number of syllables; hence, poetry, verse — chiefly used in the plural.
> I lisped in *numbers*, for the *numbers* came.—*Pope*.
> Yet should the muses bid my *numbers* roll.—*Pope*.

In *Love's Labor Lost*, Longaville says, speaking of some love verses he had written:

> I fear these stubborn lines lack power to move;
> O sweet Maria, empress of my love,
> These *numbers* will I tear, and write in *prose*.[1]

But when Ben Jonson, who had helped translate some of Bacon's prose works, comes to sum up the elements of his patron's greatness, he passes by his claims as a philosopher, a scholar, a lawyer, an orator and a statesman; and the one thing that stands out vividly before his mind's eye, that looms up above all other considerations, is that Francis Bacon is a *poet* — a great poet — a poet who has written in all measures, "has filled up all numbers" — the sonnet, the madrigal, rhyming verse, blank verse. And what had he written? Was it the translation of a few psalms in his old

---

[1] Act iv, scene 3.

age, the only specimens of his poetry that have come down to us, in his acknowledged works? No; it was something great, something overwhelming; something that is to be "compared or preferred either to insolent Greece or haughty Rome."

And what was it that "insolent Greece and haughty Rome" had accomplished to which these "numbers" of Bacon could be preferred? We turn to Jonson's verses in the Shakespeare Folio and we read:

> And though thou hadst small Latine and less Greek,
> From thence to honor thee I would not seeke
> For names, but call forth thundering Æschilus,
> Euripides and Sophocles to us,
> Paccuvius, Accius, him of Cordova dead,
> To life again, to hear thy buskin tread,
> And shake a stage; or, when thy socks were on,
> Leave thee alone, for the comparison
> Of all that *insolent Greece or haughty Rome*
> Sent forth, or since did from their ashes come.

The "numbers" of Bacon are to be compared or preferred either to insolent Greece or haughty Rome — that is to say, to the best poetical compositions of those nations. And when Ben Jonson uses this expression we learn, from the verses in the Folio, what kind of Greek and Roman literary work he had in his mind; it was not the writings of Homer or Virgil, but of Æschylus, Euripides, Sophocles, etc. — that is to say, the *dramatic writers.* Is it not extraordinary that Jonson should not only assert that Bacon had produced poetical compositions that would challenge comparison with the best works of Greece and Rome, but that he should use the same adjectives, and in the same order, that he had used in the Folio verses, viz.: *insolent Greece and haughty Rome?* It was not haughty Greece and insolent Rome, or powerful Rome and able Greece, or any other concatenation of words; but he employs precisely the same phrases in precisely the same order. How comes it that when his mind was dwelling on the great poetical and secret works of Bacon — for they must have been secret — he reverted to the very expressions he had used years before in reference to the Shakespeare Plays?

And it is upon Ben Jonson's testimony that the claims of William Shakspere, of Stratford, to the authorship of the Plays, principally rest.

If the Plays are not Shakspere's then the whole make-up of the Folio of 1623 is a fraud, and the dedication and the introduction are probably both from the pen of Bacon.

Mr. J. T. Cobb calls attention to a striking parallelism between a passage in the dedication of the Folio and an expression of Bacon:

Country hands reach forthe milk, cream and *fruits*, or what they have.[1]

Bacon writes to Villiers:

And now, because I am in the country, I will send you some of *my country fruits*, which with me are good meditations, which when I am in the city are choked with business.[2]

And in the " discourse touching the plantation in Ireland," he asks his majesty to accept *"the like poor field-fruits."*

We can even imagine that in the line,

And though thou hadst small Latine and less Greek,

Ben Jonson has his jest at the man who had employed him to write these verses. For Jonson, it will be remembered, was an accurate classical scholar, while Bacon was not. The latter was like Montaigne, who declared he could never thoroughly acquire any language but his own. Dr. Abbott, head master of the City of London school, in his introduction to Mrs. Pott's great work,[3] refers to "several errors which will make Latin and Greek scholars feel uneasy. For these in part Bacon himself, or Bacon's amanuensis, is responsible; and many of the apparent Latin solecisms or mis-spellings arise . . . from the manuscripts of the *Promus*." He adds in a foot-note:

I understand that it is the opinion of Mr. Maude Thompson, of the British Museum manuscript department, that all entries, except some of the French proverbs, are in Bacon's handwriting; so that no amanuensis can bear the blame of the numerous errors in the Latin quotations.

How "rare old Ben" must have enjoyed whacking Bacon over Shakespeare's shoulders, in verses written at the request of Bacon!

XI. A Greater Question.

When the crushing blow of shame and humiliation fell upon Francis Bacon in 1621, and he expected to die under it, he hurriedly drew a short will. It does not much exceed in length one page of Spedding's book, and yet in this brief document he found time to say:

---

[1] *Dedication*, Folio 1623.   [2] Montagu, iii, p. 20.   [3] *Promus*, p. 13.

My compositions unpublished, or the fragments of them, I require my servant Harris to deliver to my brother Constable, to the end that if any of these be fit, in his judgment, to be published, he may accordingly dispose of them. And in particular I wish the Elogium I wrote, *In felicem memoriam Reginæ Elizabethæ*, may be published. And to my brother Constable I give all my books; and to my servant Harris for this his service and care fifty pieces in gold, pursed up.

He disposed of all his real property in five lines, for the payment of his debts.

And when Bacon came to draw his last will and testament,[1] he devoted a large part of it to the preservation of his writings. He says:

For my name and memory, I leave it to men's charitable speeches, and to foreign nations, and the next ages. But as to the *durable part of my memory, which consisteth of my works and writings*, I desire my executors, and especially Sir John Constable, and my very good friend Mr. Bosvile, to take care that of all my writings, both of English and of Latin, there may be books fair bound and placed in the King's library, and in the library of the University of Cambridge, and in the library of Trinity College, where myself was bred, and in the library of the University of Oxonford, and in the library of my lord of Canterbury, and in the library of Eaton.

Then he bequeaths his register books of orations and letters to the Bishop of Lincoln; and he further directs his executors to "take into their hands all my papers whatsoever, which are either in cabinets, boxes or presses, and them to seal up until they may at their leisure peruse them."

We are asked to believe that William Shakspere was, necessarily, as the author of the Plays, a man of vast learning, the owner of many books, and that he left behind him, unpublished at the time of his death, such marvelous and mighty works as *The Tempest, Macbeth, Julius Cæsar, Timon of Athens, Coriolanus, Henry VIII.* and many more; and that, while he carefully bequeathed his old clothes and disposed of his second-best bed, he made no provision for the publication of his works, "*the durable part of his memory.*"

Is it reasonable? Is it probable? Is it not grossly improbable? What man capable of writing *Macbeth* and *Julius Cæsar*, and knowing their value to mankind — knowing that they lay in his house, in some "cabinet, box or press," probably in but one manuscript copy each, and that they might perish in the hands of his illiterate family and "bookless" neighbors — would, while carefully remembering

[1] *Life and Works*, vol. vii, p. 539.

so much of the litter and refuse of the world, have died and made no provision for their publication?

But it may be said he did not own them; he may have sold them. It seems not, for Heminge and Condell, in their introduction to the first Folio, say that they received the original copies which they published from Shakespeare himself:

And what he thought he uttered with that easiness that we have scarce *received from him* a blot in his papers.

And again:

It has been a thing, we confess, worthy to have been wished, that the author himself had lived to have set forth and overseen his own writings.

What right would he have had to set them forth if they belonged to some one else?

But since it hath been ordained otherwise, and he by death departed from that right, we pray you do not envy his friends the office of their care.

If this introduction means anything, it means that Shakspere owned these Plays; that he would have had the right to publish them if death had not interfered; that his friends and fellow-actors, Heminge and Condell, had, "to keep the memory of so worthy a friend and fellow alive as was our Shakespeare," assumed the task of publishing them; that they had received the original manuscripts from him — that is, from his family — free from blot, and that they published from them, as all the quarto copies were "stolne and surreptitious, maimed and deformed by the frauds and stealthes of injurious impostors."

And yet these Plays, which belonged to Shakspere's wealthy family, as the heirs of the author, which were printed by his "fellows" to sell to make money—for they say in their introduction:

The fate of all books depends upon your capacities: and not of your heads alone but of your purses. . . . Read and censure. Do so, but buy first.

—these Plays were not published or paid for by Shakspere's family, but, as the Folio itself tells us, were

Printed at the charges of W. Jaggard, Ed. Blount, I. Smithweeke, and W. Aspley, 1623.

CHAPTER V.

THE WRITER OF THE PLAYS A LAWYER.

Why may that not be the skull of a lawyer?
Hamlet, v, 1.

NOTHING is more conclusively established than that the author of the Plays was a lawyer.

Several works have been written in England and America to demonstrate this. I quote a few extracts:

Franklin Fiske Heard says:

The Comedy of Errors shows that Shakespeare was very familiar with some of the most refined of the principles of the science of special pleading, a science which contains the quintessence of the law. . . . In the second part of *Henry IV.*, act v, scene 5, Pistol uses the term *absque hoc*, which is technical in the last degree. This was a species of traverse, used by special pleaders when the record was in Latin, known by the denomination of a *special traverse*. The subtlety of its texture, and the total dearth of explanation in all the reports and treatises extant in the time of Shakespeare with respect to its principle, seem to justify the conclusion that *he must have attained a knowledge of it from actual practice*.[1]

Senator Davis says:

We seem to have here something more than a sciolist's temerity of indulgence in the terms of an unfamiliar art. *No legal solecisms will be found.* The abstrusest elements of the common law are impressed into a disciplined service with every evidence of the right and knowledge of commanding. Over and over again, where such knowledge is unexampled in writers unlearned in the law, Shakespeare appears in perfect possession of it. In the law of real property, its rules of tenure and descents, its entails, its fines and recoveries, and their vouchers and double vouchers; in the procedure of the courts, the method of bringing suits and of arrests; the nature of actions, the rules of pleading, the law of escapes and of contempt of court; in the principles of evidence, both technical and philosophical; in the distinction between the temporal and spiritual tribunals; in the law of attainder and forfeiture; in the requisites of a valid marriage; in the presumption of legitimacy; in the learning of the law of prerogative; in the inalienable character of the crown, this mastership appears with surprising authority.[2]

And again the same writer says:

I know of no writer who has so impressed into his service the terms of any science or art. They come from the mouth of every personage: from the Queen; from the child; from the merry wives of Windsor; from the Egyptian fervor of Cleopatra; from the lovesick Paphian goddess; from violated Lucrece; from Lear;

---

[1] *Shakespeare as a Lawyer*, pp. 43, 48. [2] *The Law in Shakespeare*, p. 4.

Hamlet and Othello; from Shakespeare himself, soliloquizing in his sonnets; from Dogberry and Prospero; from riotous Falstaff and melancholy Jacques. Shakespeare utters them at all times as standard coin, no matter when or in what mint stamped. These emblems of his industry are woven into his style like the bees into the imperial purple of Napoleon's coronation robes.[1]

Lord Chief Justice Campbell sees the clearest evidences in the Plays that the writer was learned in the law. I quote a few of his expressions:

These jests cannot be supposed to arise from anything in the laws or customs of Syracuse; but they show the author to be *very familiar with some of the most abstruse proceedings in English jurisprudence*.[2]

Quoting the description of the arrest of Dromio in *The Comedy of Errors*, he says:

Here we have a most circumstantial and graphic account of an English arrest on *mesne process* ["before judgment"] in an action on *the case*.[3]

In act iii, scene 1 (of *As You Like It*) *a deep technical knowledge of the law is displayed*.[4]

It is likewise remarkable that Cleomenes and Dion (*The Winter's Tale*, Act iii, scene 2), the messenger who brought back the response from the oracle of Delphi, to be given in evidence, are sworn to the genuineness of the document they produce almost in the very words now used by the Lord Chancellor when an officer presents at the bar of the House of Lords the copy of a record of a court of justice:

> You here shall swear. . . .
> That you, Cleomenes and Dion, have
> Been both at Delphos; and from thence have brought
> The sealed-up oracle, by the hand delivered
> Of great Apollo's priest; and that since then
> You have not dared to break the holy seal
> Nor read the secrets in't.[5]

And again, Lord Chief Justice Campbell says:

We find in several of the Histories Shakespeare's fondness for law terms; and it is still more remarkable that *whenever he indulges this propensity he uniformly lays down good law*.[6]

While novelists and dramatists are constantly making mistakes as to the law of marriage, of wills and of inheritance, to Shakespeare's law, lavishly as he propounds it, there can neither be demurrer, nor bill of exception, nor writ of error.[7]

If Lord Eldon could be supposed to have written the play, I do not see how he would be chargeable with having forgotten any of his law while writing it.[8]

The indictment in which Lord Say was arraigned, in act iv, scene 7 (*2d Henry VI.*), seems *drawn by no inexperienced hand*. . . . How acquired I know not, but it is quite certain that the drawer of this indictment must have had some acquaintance with *The Crown Circuit Companion*, and must have had *a full and accurate*

---

[1] *The Law in Shak.*, p. 51.   [3] Ibid., p. 39.   [5] Ibid., p. 60.   [7] Ibid., p. 108.
[2] *Shak. Legal Acquirements*, p. 38.   [4] Ibid., p. 42.   [6] Ibid., p. 61.   [8] Ibid., p. 73.

knowledge of that rather obscure and intricate subject—"Felony and Benefit of Clergy."[1]

Speaking of Gloster's language in *Lear*,[2] Lord Campbell says:

In forensic discussions respecting legitimacy the question is put, whether the individual whose *status* is to be determined is "capable," *i.e.*, capable of inheriting; but it is only a lawyer who could express the idea of legitimizing a natural son by simply saying:

>   I'll work the means
> To make him *capable*.

Speaking of *Hamlet*, his Lordship says:

Earlier in the play[3] Marcellus inquires what was the cause of the warlike preparations in Denmark:

> And why such daily cast of brazen cannon,
> And foreign mart for implements of war?
> Why such impress of shipwrights, whose sore task
> Doth not divide the Sunday from the week?

Such confidence has there been in Shakespeare's accuracy that this passage has been quoted, both by text-writers and by judges on the bench, as an authority upon the legality of the *press-gang*, and upon the debated question whether *shipwrights* as well as common seamen are liable to be pressed into the service of the royal navy.[4]

Lord Campbell quotes sonnet xlvi, of which he says:

I need not go farther than this sonnet, which is so *intensely legal in its language and imagery that without a considerable knowledge of English forensic procedure it cannot be fully understood*.

SONNET XLVI.

> Mine Eye and Heart are at a mortal war
>   How to divide the conquest of thy sight;
> Mine Eye my Heart thy picture's sight would bar,
>   My Heart mine Eye the freedom of that right.
> My Heart doth plead that thou in him dost lie
>   (A closet never pierced with crystal eyes),
> But the Defendant doth that plea deny,
>   And says in him thy fair appearance lies.
> To 'cide this title is impaneled
>   A quest of Thoughts, all tenants of the Heart;
> And by their verdict is determined
>   The clear Eye's moiety, and the dear Heart's part;
>   As thus: mine Eyes' due is thine outward part,
>   And my Heart's right, thine inward love of heart.

One is reminded, in reading this, of Brownell's humorous lines:

THE LAWYER'S INVOCATION TO SPRING.

> Whereas on certain boughs and sprays
>   Now divers birds are heard to sing;
> And sundry flowers their heads upraise,
>   Hail to the coming on of spring!

---

[1] *Shak. Legal Acquirements*, p. 75.
[2] Act ii, scene 1.
[3] *Hamlet*, i, 1.
[4] *Shak. Legal Acquirements*, p. 83.

> The songs of those said birds arouse
>   The memory of our youthful hours,
> As green as those said sprays and boughs,
>   As fresh and sweet as those said flowers.
>
> The birds aforesaid — happy pairs ! —
>   Love, 'mid the aforesaid boughs, inshrines
> In freehold nests; themselves their heirs,
>   Administrators and assigns.
>
> Oh, busiest term of Cupid's court,
>   Where tender plaintiffs actions bring;
> Season of frolic and of sport,
>   Hail — as aforesaid — coming spring !

Lord Campbell says:

In *Antony and Cleopatra*,[1] Lepidus, in trying to palliate the bad qualities and misdeeds of Antony, uses the language of a conveyancer's chambers in Lincoln's Inn:

> His faults, in him, seem as the spots of heaven,
> More fiery by night's blackness; *hereditary*
> Rather than *purchased*.

That is to say, they are taken by *descent*, not by *purchase*. *Lay gents* (viz., all except lawyers) understand by *purchase* buying for a sum of money, called the price, but lawyers consider that *purchase* is opposed to *descent;* that all things come to the owner either by *descent* or by *purchase*, and that whatever does not come through operation of law by *descent* is *purchased*, although it may be the free gift of a donor. Thus, if land be devised by will to A in fee, he takes by purchase; or to B for life, remainder to A and his heirs (B being a stranger to A), A takes by *purchase;* but upon the death of A, his eldest son would take by *descent*.[2]

Appleton Morgan says:

But most wonderful of all is the dialogue in the graveyard scene.

In the quarto the two grave-diggers are wondering whether Ophelia, having committed suicide, is to be buried in consecrated ground, instead of at a cross-road with a stake driven through her body, and clumsily allude to the probability that, having been of noble birth, a pretext will be found to avoid the law.

It happens that in the first volume of Plowden's Reports there is a case (Hales vs. Petit, I. Pl. 253) of which the facts bore a wonderful resemblance to the story of Ophelia.

Sir James Hales was a judge of the Common Pleas, who had prominently concerned himself in opposing the succession of Mary the Bloody. When Mary ascended the throne, he expected decapitation, and was actually imprisoned, but by some influence released. His brain, however, became affected by his vicissitudes, and he finally committed suicide by throwing himself into a water-course. Suicide was felony, and his estates became escheated to the crown. The crown in turn granted them to one Petit. But Lady Hales, instructed that the escheat might be attacked, brought ejectment against Petit, the crown tenant. The point was as to whether the forfeiture could be considered as having taken place in the lifetime of Sir James; for, if not, the plaintiff took the estate by survivorship. In other words, could Sir James be visited with the penalty for plunging into a

---

[1] Act 1, scene 4.   [2] *Shak. Legal Acquirements*, p. 94.

stream of water? For that was all he did actually do. The suicide was only the result of his act, and can a man die during his life? Precisely the point in Ophelia's case as to her burial in consecrated ground. If Ophelia only threw herself into the water, she was only a suicide by consequence, *non constat* that she proposed to die in the aforesaid water. So the case was argued, and the debate of the momentous questions—whether a man who commits suicide dies during his own life or only begins to die; whether he drowns himself, or only goes into the water; whether going into water is a felony, or only part of a felony, and whether a subject can be attainted and his lands escheated for only part of a felony—is so rich in serious absurdity, and the grave-diggers' dialogue over Ophelia's proposed interment in holy ground so literal a travesty, that the humor of the dialogue— entirely the unconscious humor of the learned counsel in Hales *vs.* Petit—can hardly be anything but proof that, admitting William Shakespeare to have written that graveyard scene, William Shakespeare was a practicing lawyer.

Especially since it is to be remembered that *Plowden's report was then, as it is to-day, accessible in Norman Latin law jargon and black-letter type, utterly unintelligible to anybody but an expert antiquarian, and utterly uninviting to anybody.* Law Norman or law Latin was just as unattractive to laymen in Elizabeth's day as it is to lawyers in ours; if possible, more so.

The decision in Hales *vs.* Petit—on account of the standing of parties-plaintiff—might have been town-talk for a day or two; but that the wearying, and, to us, ridiculous dialectics of the argument and decision were town-talk, seems the suggestion of a very simple or of a very bold ignorance as to town life and manners.

Besides, nobody sets the composition of *Hamlet* earlier than Nash's mention of "whole *Hamlets*" in 1587 or 1589—and every commentator of standing puts it about ten years later. That the hair-splitting of a handful of counsel would remain town-talk for twenty-five or thirty-six years is preposterous to suppose. Reference to the arguments in that case could only have been had from Plowden's report.

My friend Senator Davis[1] points out another curious fact, viz.: that a comparison of the *Hamlet* of the quarto of 1603, with the Folio of 1623, shows that part of the text was re-written, to make it more correct in a legal point of view. In the quarto we read:

> Who by a sealed compact, well ratified by law
> And heraldrie, did forfeit with his life all those
> His lands, which he stood seized of, to the conqueror,
> Against the which a moiety competent
> Was gaged by our king.

But to state this in legal form there is appended, when *Hamlet* comes to be printed in the Folio:

> —which had returned
> To the inheritance of Fortinbras
> Had he bin Vanquisher, as by the same cov'nant
> The carriage of the article designed,
> His fell to *Hamlet*.[2]

[1] *The Law in Shakespeare.*   [2] *Hamlet*, i, 1.

What poet, not a lawyer, would have stated the agreement in such legal phraseology; and what poet, not a lawyer, would have subsequently added the lines given, to show the *consideration* moving to Fortinbras for the contract? And this for the benefit of such an audience as commonly frequented the Globe!

Richard Grant White says:

No dramatist of the time, not even Beaumont, who was a younger son of a judge of the Common Pleas, and who, after studying in the inns of court, abandoned law for the drama, used legal phrases with Shakespeare's readiness and exactness. And the significance of this fact is heightened by another, that it is only to the language of the law that he exhibits this inclination. The phrases peculiar to other occupations serve him on rare occasions by way of description, comparison or illustration, generally when something in the scene suggests them; but legal phrases *flow from his pen as part of his vocabulary and parcel of his thought.* The word *purchase*, for instance, which in ordinary use meant, as now it means, to acquire by giving value, applies in law to all legal modes of obtaining property, except inheritance or descent. And in this peculiar sense the word occurs five times in Shakespeare's thirty-four plays, but only in a single passage in the fifty-four plays of Beaumont and Fletcher. And in the first scene of the *Midsummer Night's Dream* the father of Hermia begs the ancient privilege of Athens, that he may dispose of his daughter either to Demetrius or to death,

> According to our law
> Immediately provided in that case.

He pleads the statute; and the words run off his tongue in heroic verse, as if he was reading them from a paper.

As the courts of law in Shakespeare's time occupied public attention much more than they do now, it has been suggested that it was in attendance upon them that he picked up his legal vocabulary. But this supposition not only fails to account for Shakespeare's peculiar freedom and exactness in the use of that phraseology — it does not even place him in the way of learning those terms, his use of which is most remarkable, which are not such as he would have heard at ordinary proceedings at *nisi prius*, but such as refer to the tenure or transfer of real property — "fine and recovery," "statutes merchant," "purchase," "indenture," "tenure," "double voucher," "fee simple," "fee farm," "remainder," "reversion," "forfeiture," etc. This conveyancer's jargon could not have been picked up by hanging around the courts of law in London 250 years ago, when suits as to the title to real property were comparatively so rare. And besides, Shakespeare uses his law just as freely in his early plays, written in his first London years, as in those produced at a later period. Just as exactly, too; for the correctness and propriety with which these terms are introduced have compelled the admiration of a chief justice and a lord chancellor.[1]

And again Mr. White says:

Genius, although it reveals general truth and facilitates all acquirement, does not impart facts or acquaintance with general terms; how then can we account for the fact that, in an age when it was the common practice for young lawyers to write plays, one playwright left upon his plays a stronger, a sharper legal stamp than

---

[1] R. G. White, *Life and Genius of Shak.*, p. 74.

appears upon those of any of his contemporaries, and that the characters of this stamp are those of the complicated law of real property.[1]

And the same man who wrote this, and who still believed the deer-stealer wrote the Plays, said, shortly before his death, in the *Atlantic Magazine:*

The notion that he was once an attorney's clerk is blown to pieces.

The first to suggest that Shakspere might, at some time, have been a lawyer's clerk, was Malone, who, in 1790, said:

His knowledge of legal terms is not merely such as might be acquired by the casual observation of even his all-comprehending mind; it has the appearance of *technical* skill, and he is so fond of displaying it on all occasions, that I suspect he was early initiated in at least the forms of law, and was employed, while he yet remained at Stratford, in the office of some country attorney, who was at the same time a petty conveyancer, and perhaps also the seneschal of some manor court.

But even Lord Chief Justice Campbell, who, as we have seen, asserts that the writer of the Plays was familiar with the abstrusest parts of the law, is forced to abandon this theory. He says, writing to J. Payne Collier, who favored the law-clerk theory:

Resuming the judge, however, I must lay down that your opponents are not called upon to prove a negative, and that the *onus probandi* rests upon you. You must likewise remember that you require us implicitly to believe a fact, which, were it true, positive and irrefragable evidence, in Shakespeare's own handwriting, might have been forthcoming to establish it. Not having been actually enrolled as an attorney, neither the records of the local court at Stratford, nor of the superior courts at Westminster, would present his name, as being concerned in any suits as an attorney; but it might have been reasonably expected that there would have been deeds or wills witnessed by him still extant; and, *after a very diligent search, none such can be discovered.* Nor can this consideration be disregarded, that between Nash's Epistle, in the end of the sixteenth century, and Chalmers' suggestion, more than two hundred years afterwards, there is no hint, by his foes or his friends, of Shakespeare having consumed pens, paper, ink and pounce in an attorney's office at Stratford.[2]

The Nash Epistle here referred to was an "Epistle to the Gentlemen Students of the Two Universities, by Thomas Nash," prefixed to the first edition of Robert Green's *Menaphon*, published, according to the title-page, in 1589. In it Nash says:

It is a common practice now-a-days, amongst a sort of shifting companions that run through every art and thrive by none, to leave the trade of *noverint*, whereto they were born, and busy themselves with the endeavors of art, that could scarcely Latinize their neck verse if they should have need; yet English Seneca, read by candle-light, yields many good sentences, as *Blood is a beggar*, and so forth; and if you entreat him fair, in a frosty morning, he will afford you whole *Hamlets;* I should say handfuls of tragical speeches.

[1] *Life and Genius of Shak.*, p. 76.   [2] *Shak. Legal Acquirements*, p. 110.

This epistle has been cited to prove that Shakspere was a lawyer. In Elizabeth's reign deeds were in the Latin tongue; and all deeds poll, and many other papers, began with the words: "NOVERINT *universi per presentes*"—"Be it known to all men by these presents;"—and hence the business of an attorney was known as "the trade of *noverint*."

But here are the difficulties that attend this matter: In the first place Nash charges that the party he has in view, "the shifting companion" who could afford whole *Hamlets*, was not only a lawyer, but *born a lawyer;*—"the trade of noverint *whereto they were born*." In other words, that the party who wrote *Hamlet* had *inherited* the trade of lawyer. We say of one "he was born a gentleman," and we mean, thereby, that his father before him was a gentleman. Now, it is within the possibilities that Shakespeare might have studied for a few months, or a year or two, in some lawyer's office, but assuredly his father was not a lawyer; he could not even write his own name; he was a glover, wool-dealer or butcher. But the description applies precisely to Bacon, whose father had been an eminent lawyer, and who was therefore born a *noverint*.

But there is another mystery about this Nash Epistle.

It is universally conceded, by all the biographers and commentators, that Shakespeare did not begin to write for the stage until 1592. Our highest and most recent authority, J. O. Halliwell-Phillipps,[1] fixes the date of the appearance of Shakespeare's first play as the third of March, 1592, when *Henry VI.* was put on the boards for the first time; and this same Nash tells us that between March 3d, 1592, and the beginning of July, it had been witnessed by "ten thousand spectators at least." And yet we are asked to believe that when Nash, in 1589, or, as some will have it, in 1587, wrote his epistle, and mocked at some lawyer who had written *Hamlet*, he referred to the butcher's apprentice, who did not commence to write until three or five years subsequently!

And there are not wanting proofs, as we will see hereafter, that *Hamlet* appeared in 1585, the very year Shakspere's wife was delivered of the twins, Hamnet and Judith; the very year probably, when Shakspere, aged twenty-one, whipped, scourged and imprisoned for poaching, fled from Stratford to London.

[1] *Outlines of the Life of Shak.*, p. 64.

We can conceive the possibility of a rude and ignorant peasant-boy coming to London, and, conscious of his defects and possessing great powers, applying himself with superhuman industry to study and self-cultivation; but we will find that *Hamlet*, that most thoughtful and scholarly production, was on the boards in 1587, if not in 1585; and *Venus and Adonis*, the "first heir of his invention," must have antedated even this.

Richard Grant White says:

> It has most unaccountably been assumed that this passage [in Nash's Epistle] refers to Shakespeare.... That Shakespeare had written this tragedy in 1586, when he was but twenty-two years old, is improbable to the verge of impossibility.[1]

Halliwell-Phillipps says:

> The preceding notices may fairly authorize us to infer that the ancient play of *Hamlet* was written either by an attorney or an attorney's clerk.[2]

The Shakspereans, to avoid the logical conclusions that flow from this Epistle of Nash, are forced to suggest that there must have been an older play of *Hamlet*, written by some one else—"the ancient *Hamlet*," to which Halliwell-Phillipps alludes. But there is no evidence that any other playwright wrote a play of *Hamlet*. It is not probable.

The essence of a new play is its novelty. We find Augustine Phillips, one of the members of Shakspere's company, objecting to playing *Richard II.*, in 1600, for the entertainment of the followers of Essex, because it was an old play, and would not draw an audience, and thereupon Sir Gilly Merrick pays him forty shillings extra to induce him to present it.

The name of a new play has sometimes as much to do with its success as the name of a new novel. Is it probable that a playwright, having written a new play and desirous to draw a crowd and make money, would affix to it the name of some old play, written by some one else, which had been on the boards for ten years or more, and had been worn threadbare? Fancy Dickens publishing a new novel and calling it *Roderick Random*. Or Boucicault bringing out a new drama under the name of *Othello*. The theory is absurd.

We have now two forms of the play of *Hamlet*, published within a year of each other, both with Shakespeare's name on the title-

---

[1] *Life and Genius of Shak.*, p. 71.   [2] *Outlines Life of Shak.*, p. 170.

page; and one is the crude, first form of the play, and the other is its perfected form, "enlarged to almost twice as much again." Is this first form "the ancient *Hamlet*" to which Nash alluded in 1589? or is it the successor of some still earlier edition? Bacon said of himself: "I never alter but I add." He re-wrote his *Essays*, we are told, thirty times. Says his chaplain, Rawley:

> I have myself at least twelve copies of his *Instauration*, revised year after year, one after another, and every year altered and amended in the frame thereof, till at last it came to that model in which it was committed to the press, as many living creatures do lick their young ones till they bring them to the strength of their limbs.

Why is it not probable that the young *noverint*, "born a lawyer," Francis Bacon, of age in 1582, may, in 1585, when twenty-three years of age, having been "put to all the learning that his time could make him master of," have written a play for the stage, called *Hamlet*, at a time when William Shakspere, three years his junior in age, and fifty years his junior in opportunities, was lying drunk under the crab-tree, or howling under the whips of the beadles?

Hamlet, then, was written by a lawyer; and Shakspere never was a lawyer.

This fact must also not be forgotten, that the knowledge of the law shown in the Plays is not such as could be acquired during a few months spent in a lawyer's office in the youth of the poet, and which would constitute such a species of learning as might be recalled upon questioning. It is evident that the man who wrote the Plays was a thorough lawyer, a learned lawyer, a lawyer steeped in and impregnated with the associations of his profession, and who bubbled over with its language whenever he opened his mouth. For he did not use law terms only when speaking upon legal subjects: the phraseology of the courts rose to his lips even in describing love scenes. He makes the fair Maria, in *Love's Labor Lost*, pun upon a subtle distinction of the law:

> *Boyet.* So you grant pasture for me.
>   *Offering to kiss her.*
> *Maria.* Not so, gentle beast:
> My lips are no *common* though *several* they be.
> *Boyet.* Belonging to whom?
> *Maria.*   To my fortunes and me.[1]

[1] Act II, scene 1.

Grant White gives this explanation:

Maria's meaning and her first pun are plain enough; the second has been hitherto explained by the statement that the several or severall in England was a part of the common, set apart for some particular person or purpose, and that the town bull had equal rights of pasture in common and several. It seems to me, however, that we have here another exhibition of Shakespeare's familiarity with the law, and that the allusion is to tenancy in common by several (*i.e.*, divided, distinct) title. Thus: "Tenants in Common are they which have Lands or Tenements in Fee-simple, fee-taile, or for terme of life, &c., and they have such Lands or Tenements by severall Titles and not by a joynt Title, and none of them know by this his severall, but they ought by the Law to occupie these Lands or Tenements in common and *pro indiviso*, to take the profits in common."[1] . . . Maria's lips were several, as being two, and (as she says in the next line) as belonging in common to her fortunes and to herself, but they were no common pasturage.[2]

There was no propriety in placing puns on law phrases in the mouth of a young lady, and still less in representing a French lady as familiar with English laws and customs as to the pasturage of the town-bull. These phrases found their way to the fair lips of Maria because the author was brimming full of legal phraseology.

Take another instance. We read of —

> A *contract* of *eternal bond* of love,
> *Confirmed* by *mutual joinder* of your *hands*,
> *Attested* by the holy close of lips,
> Strengthened by *interchangement* of your rings;
> And all the ceremony of this *compact*
> *Sealed* in my function by my *testimony*.[3]

To be so saturated with the law the writer must have been in daily practice of the law, and in hourly converse with men of the same profession. He did not seek these legal phrases; they burst from him involuntarily and on all occasions.

Gerald Massey well says:

The worst of it, for the theory of his having been an attorney's clerk, is that it will not account for his insight into law. His knowledge is not office-sweepings, but ripe fruits, mature, *as though he had spent his life in their growth*.[4]

But it is said that a really learned lawyer could not have written the Plays, because the law put forth in the great trial scene of *The Merchant of Venice* is not good law.

Lord Chief Justice Campbell, however, reviews the proceedings in the case, and declares that "the trial is duly conducted according to the strict forms of legal procedure. . . . Antonio is made to

---

[1] Co. Litt., lib. iii, cap. 4, sec. 292.
[2] *Shakespeare*, vol. iii, p. 453.
[3] *Twelfth Night*, v, 1.
[4] *Shakespeare's Sonnets*, p. 504.

confess that Shylock is entitled to the pound of flesh ... according to *the rigid strictness of the common law of England.*"

It is claimed that Shylock could not enforce the penalty of his bond, but was entitled only to the sum loaned and legal interest; and that Antonio should have applied for an injunction to restrain Shylock from cutting off the pound of flesh.

Imagine the play so reformed. The audience are looking forward with feelings of delight to the great trial scene, with its marvelous alternations of hope and despair; with Portia's immortal appeal for mercy while the Jew whets his knife; and anticipating the final triumph of virtue and the overthrow of cruelty. The curtain rolls up, and a dapper lawyer's-clerk steps forward to the footlights to inform the expectant audience that Antonio has procured an injunction, with proper sureties, from the Court of Equity, and that they will find the whole thing duly set forth in the next number of the *Law Reporter!*

In the first place, it is absurd to try a Venetian lawsuit by the antique and barbarous code of England.

In the next place, it is not clear that, even by the rules of the Court of Equity of England, Antonio could have been relieved of the penalty without good cause shown.

> There seems to be a distinction taken in equity between penalties and forfeitures. . . In the latter, although compensation can be made, relief is not always given.[1]

In the case of Antonio, the pound of flesh was to be *forfeited*.

> If you repay me not on such a day,
> In such a place, such sum or sums as are
> Expressed in the condition, let the *forfeit*
> Be nominated for an equal pound
> Of your fair flesh.[2]

And in the court scene Shylock says:

> My deeds upon my head! I crave the law,
> The penalty and *forfeit* of my bond.[3]

And Portia says:

> Why, this bond is *forfeit*.

Certain it is, Bacon, a thorough lawyer, did not understand that *he* could escape the penalty of a bond, even under the laws of Eng-

---

[1] 3 Daniel's *Cham. Plead. and Prac.*, p. 1946: 2 Story's *Equity Jur.*, § 1321, etc.
[2] Act I, scene 3.
[3] Act iv, scene 1.

land, by simply paying the debt and interest. In July, 1603, he was arrested at the suit of a Jew (the original probably of Shylock), and thrown into a sponging-house, and we have his letter to his cousin Robert, Lord Cecil, Secretary of State, begging him to use his power to prevent his creditors from "taking any part of the penalty [of his bond] but principal, interest and costs."

The Judge says:

> There is no power in Venice
> Can alter a decree established.
> *'Twill be recorded for a precedent,*
> And many an error by the same example
> Will rush into the state.

Before a writ of error can be taken from Portia's ruling, it must be shown by some *precedent*, or "decree established," of the Venetian chancery, that Antonio had the right to avoid the forfeiture by tendering the amount received and simple interest; and as no such man as Shylock ever lived, and no such case as that in question was ever tried, it will puzzle the critics to know just how far back to go to establish the *priority* of such a decision.

Again, the point is made that, if Shylock was entitled to his pound of flesh, he was entitled to the blood that would necessarily flow in cutting it; upon the principle, it is said, that if I own a piece of land I have the right to a necessary roadway over another man's land to reach it. True. But in case I can only reach my land by committing murder (for that was what Shylock was undertaking), my lesser property right must be subordinated to the greater natural right of the other man to his life.

But all this reasoning, if it be intended to show that the writer of the play was but partially learned in the law, must give way to the fact that *Shylock* vs. *Antonio* is a dramatic representation, for popular entertainment, and not a veritable law-suit. The plot of *The Merchant of Venice* was taken from the Italian romance *Il Pecorone*, of Giovanni Fiorentino, written in 1378; and there we have the decision of the judge, that the Jew must cut a precise pound of flesh, neither more nor less, and that, if he draw a drop of Christian blood in so doing, he must die for it.

It would be absurd to suppose that a dramatic writer, even though a lawyer, would be obliged to leave out these striking incidents, and substitute a tamer something, in accordance with that barbarous jumble of justice and injustice called law in England.

But the question after all is to be decided by Venetian, not English precedents. The scene is laid in Venice.

John T. Doyle, Esq., of California, writes a letter to Lawrence Barrett, Esq., the celebrated actor, which has been published in the *Overland Monthly*, in which he discusses "The Case of Shylock." He says:

> The trial scene in *The Merchant of Venice* has, however, always seemed inconsistent with his [Bacon's] supposed legal learning, for the proceedings in it are such as never could have occurred in any court administering English law. Lord Campbell, in his letter to Payne Collyer, has attempted to gloss over the difficulty, but to all common lawyers the attempt is a failure. Save in the fact that the scene presents a plaintiff, a defendant and a judge—characters essential to litigation under any system of procedure—there is no resemblance in the proceedings on the stage to anything that could possibly occur in an English court, or any court administering English law. No jury is impaneled to determine the facts, no witnesses called by either side; on the contrary, when the court opens, the duke who presides is already fully informed of the facts, and has even communicated them, in writing, to Bellario, a learned doctor of Padua, and invited him to come and render judgment in the case.

Mr. Doyle then proceeds to give his experience of a lawsuit he had in the Spanish-American republic of Nicaragua in 1851-2. After describing the verbal summons he received from the *alguasil* to the *alcalde* in his court, Mr. Doyle says:

> Proceedings of some sort were going on at the moment, but the *alcalde* suspended them, received me very courteously, and directed some one present to go and call Don Dolores Bermudez, the plaintiff, into court. The substance of Mr. Bermudez' complaint against the company was then stated to me, and I was asked for my answer to it. I sent for my counsel, and the company's defense was stated orally. The contract out of which the controversy arose was produced, and perhaps a witness or two examined, and some oral discussion followed; those details I forget, for there was nothing in them that struck me as strange. There was, in fact, little, if any, dispute about the facts of the case, the real controversy being as to the company's liability and its extent. We were finally informed that on a given day we should be expected to attend again, when the judge would be prepared with his decision.
>
> At the appointed time we attended accordingly, and the judge read a paper in which all the facts were stated, at the conclusion of which he announced to us that he proposed to submit the question of law involved to Don Buenaventura Silva, a practicing lawyer of Granada, as a "jurisconsult," unless some competent objections were made to him. I learned then that I could challenge the proposed jurisconsult for consanguinity, affinity or favor, just as we challenge a juror. I knew of no cause of challenge against him; my counsel said he was an unexceptionable person; and so he was chosen, and the case was referred to him. Some days after, he returned the papers to the *alcalde* with his opinion, which was in my favor, and the plaintiff's case was dismissed.

In the course of the same afternoon, or next day, I received an intimation that Don Buenaventura expected from me a gratification — the name in that country for what we call a gratuity — and I think the sum of $200 was named. This did not harmonize with my crude notions of the administration of justice, and I asked for explanations. They were given in the stereotyped form used to explain every other anomaly in that queer country, *"Costumbre del pais."* I thought it a custom more honored in the breach than the observance.

Here we find that the writer of the Plays followed, in all probability, the exact course of procedure usual in Venice, and in all countries subject to the civil law. We even have, as in Portia's case, the expectation that the judge should be rewarded with a gratuity.

The only difference between the writer of the Plays and his critics is, that he knew what he was talking about, and they did not.

My friend Senator Davis, of Minnesota, as a crowning proof that Francis Bacon did not write the Plays, says:

. . . Again, Bacon was actively engaged in the court of chancery many years before he became Lord Chancellor. It was then that the memorable war of jurisdiction was waged between Ellesmere and Coke — and yet there is not in Shakespeare a single phrase, word or application of any principle peculiar to the chancery.[1]

To this my friend John A. Wilstach, Esq., the learned translator of Virgil,[2] and an eminent lawyer, says in a letter addressed to me:

In the English courts, ancient and modern — as even laymen know — the practice at common law and in chancery were and are severed, although the barriers between the two are now, by the gradual adoption of chancery rules in common law practice, largely broken down. In the time of Bacon and Shakespeare the division was distinct: the common-law lawyer was not a chancery practitioner; the chancery practitioner was not a practitioner in the courts of common law. But the general language of both branches of the profession was necessarily (for in history and method they intertwined), if even superficially, known to the followers of both, and the probability is that a practitioner of the one would easily use the current verbiage of the other; indeed it would be strange if either should hold away from the other. A Lord Coke, in the wide scope of literature, would relax his common-law exclusiveness and enlarge the narrow circuit of his professional prepossessions. A Lord Bacon, a student or a judge in chancery, would delight to turn aside from the roses and lilies of equity — some of them exotic plants — and become, for the time, a gratified wanderer in an historic common of pasture, among the butterflies and bees of an indigenous jurisprudence. Hence my suggestion, opposed to that of the learned jurist, is, that this very scope and freedom of law in literature is what the writer of the Shakespeare Plays has given himself. And I find in the rambling pasture of the common law, according to his own outgivings, he has met, besides its attractive features, other and repelling ones — thorns, quagmires and serpents. I find that, on a close examination of

---

[1] *Law in Shakespeare.* [2] Boston: Houghton, Mifflin & Co. 1884.

the Shakespeare Plays, the averment of the learned jurist as to the want of chancery features therein is not proven. I find that there *are* passages wherein, in the most evident manner, chancery principles and the equity practice are recognized and extolled; and, further yet, that among passages tolerant or praiseful of the common law are also found passages wherein *its* principles and practice are held up to derision and even to scorn. And while it is true that phrases are not proofs, but only grounds whence inferences may be drawn, yet the citations I shall offer will be of as high a grade as those which are offered to support the propositions which I contest. Nor is the argument weakened in its application to the Baconian question by the establishment of the fact that the participation in the production of the Shakespeare Plays on the part of Bacon was the work of his *early* manhood. Coleridge well formulates the general experience when he says that "a young author's first work almost always bespeaks his recent pursuit."

He is, at this early age, too, more conversant with the literature of his art; is more recently from the books and sometimes is observed to carry a head inflated with pride in that branch of the profession which his bent of mind has led him to favor. First let me recall some of those passages wherein derision and censure are visited upon the common law — the "biting" severity of its principles, the "hideous" deformity of its practice.

The most superficial reader of these dramas will need no reminder of the satires conveyed in the conversation of Justices Dogberry and Shallow, Constable Elbow and the clowns in *Twelfth Night*, and the more dignified broadsides of Wolsey and Queen Katharine, and Hamlet and Portia, and their interlocutors. As my reading goes, puerility, pedantry, corruption and chicanery, in legal practice, have found in all literature no denunciations so severe, no ridicule so effective.

In *1st Henry IV.*, i, 2, the derision takes, in the mouth of Falstaff, the form of " the rusty curb of old Father Antic, the Law," the metaphor being that of a superannuated clown who, with rusty methods, methods old and lacking polish, cheats the people out of the attainment of their cherished desires.

> When law can do no right,
> Let it be lawful that law bar no wrong.[1]
>
> Since law itself is perfect wrong,
> How can the law forbid my tongue to curse?[2]
>
> The state of law is bond-slave to the law.[3]
>
> But in these nice, sharp quillets of the law, etc.[4]
>
> The laws, your curb and whip, in their rough power,
> Have checked theft.[5]
>
> The bloody book of law, etc.[6]
>
> Crack the lawyer's voice,
> That he may nevermore false title plead.[7]
>
> My head to my good man's hat,
> These oaths and laws will prove an idle scorn.[8]

Parolles, the lawyer in *All's Well that Ends Well*, uses contemptuously the legal machinery applicable to English estates in describing how Dumain would convey away a title in fee-simple to his salvation; and, with the same contemptuous reference to the same machinery, Mrs. Page describes the devil's titles to Falstaff.

Now let us take up the praises of chancery.

---

[1] *King John*, iii, 1.   [2] *Ibid.*, iii, 1.   [3] *Richard II.*, ii, 1.
[4] *1st Henry VI.*, ii, 4.   [5] *Timon of Athens*, iv, 2.   [6] *Othello*, iii, 1.
[7] *Timon of Athens*, v, 3.   [8] *Love's Labor Lost*, i, 1.

And, first, I cite a passage which the learned jurist himself quotes. My italics will indicate my impression that, in his bent for common law, he has failed to give emphasis to the most important feature of the passage.

> In the corrupted currents of this world
> Offense's gilded hand may shove by justice,
> And oft 'tis seen the wicked prize itself
> Buys out the law: but 'tis not so above;
> There is no shuffling, *there the action lies
> In his true nature, and we ourselves compell'd
> Even to the teeth and forehead of our faults,
> To give in evidence*.[1]

And, to pass to others:

> Ah, gracious lord, these days are dangerous;
> *Virtue* is choked with foul ambition,
> And *charity* chased hence by rancor's hand,
> Fell subornation is predominant,
> And *equity* exiled your highness' land.[2]

What a trinity is here: Virtue, Charity, Equity! Opposed, too, to the hellish trio of ambition, rancor and subornation.

A larger definition of equity jurisprudence could not well be had than that it is "strong authority looking into the blots and stains of right."

> *King John.* From whom hast thou this great commission,
> To draw mine answer from thine articles?
>
> *King Philip.* From that supernal judge that stirs good thoughts
> In any breast of *strong authority,
> To look into the blots and stains of right.*
> That judge hath made me guardian to this boy:
> Under whose warrant I impeach thy wrong,
> And by whose help I mean to chastise it.

This passage is also cited by the learned jurist, but it is only to remark upon the words *warrant* and *impeach*. It contains, as I have observed, the very definition of chancery jurisprudence, and besides employs terms technical in chancery practice, *commission articles* and *answer*.

Themes which, in an especial manner, engage the intellect and the heart of the student and practitioner of chancery principles are "Charity," "Mercy," "Conscience."

In contrast with the evasions and chicanery which are, in the Shakespeare Plays and elsewhere, the reproach of the practice at common law, chancery decides from considerations of what is right and just between man and man, *ex æquo et bono*. Chancery jurisdiction enters the breast of the party himself, and there sets up its forum in his conscience. The interrogatories authorized by the chancery practice arraign and search that conscience, and, upon an oath binding upon it, "compel" the reluctant litigant, "even to the teeth and forehead of his faults, to give in evidence."

> Every man's conscience is a thousand swords.[3]
> My conscience hath a thousand several tongues.[4]
> The worm of conscience still begnaw thy soul![5]
>
> Well, believe this,
> No ceremony that to great ones 'longs
> Not the king's crown, nor the deputed sword,
> The marshal's truncheon, nor *the judge's robe*,
> Becomes them with one-half so good a grace
> As *mercy* does.[6]

[1] *Hamlet*, iii. 3.   [3] *Richard III.*, v, 2.   [5] Ibid., i, 3.
[2] *2nd Henry VI.*, iii, 1.   [4] Ibid., v, 3.   [6] *Measure for Measure*, ii, 2.

> The quality of mercy is not strained;
> . . . .
> It is an attribute to God himself;
> And earthly power doth then show likest God's,
> When mercy seasons justice.[1]

In addition to these citations, touching Shakespeare's use of the terms of the equity courts, I would quote the following from Judge Holmes:

Indeed, it is clear that Portia's knowledge extended even to chancery practice, and continued to the end of the piece:

> *Portia.* Let us go in
> And charge us there upon int'rogatories,
> And we will answer all things faithfully.[2]

The terms of chancery practice, *charges, interrogatories* and *answer*, are dragged in by the heels despite the protests of the refractory meter.

But passing from this point, I will add a few more extracts which bespeak the lawyer:

Sir, for a *quart d'écu* he will sell the fee-simple of his salvation, the inheritance of it; and cut the entail for all remainder.[3]

And again:

If the devil have him not in fee-simple, with fine and recovery, he will never, I think, in the way of waste, attempt us again.[4]

And again:

Time stays still with lawyers in the vacation; for they sleep between term and term.[5]

Judge Holmes says:[6]

Mr. Rushton cites the statute 16 Richard II., which was leveled against the Pope's usurpations of sovereignty in England, and enacted that "if any do bring any translation, process, sentence of excommunication, bulls, instruments, etc., within the realm, or receive them, *they shall be put out of the King's protection, and their lands, tenements, goods and chattels forfeited to the King,*" and compares it with the speech of Suffolk in the play of *Henry VIII.*, thus:

> *Suff.* Lord Cardinal, the King's further pleasure is,
> Because all those things you have done of late
> By your power legatine within this kingdom,
> Fall into the compass of a præmunire,
> That therefore such a writ be sued against you:
> *To forfeit all your goods, lands, tenements,
> Chattels and whatsoever, and to be
> Out of the King's protection.* This is my charge.[7]

---

[1] *Merchant of Venice*, iv, 1.
[2] *Authorship of Shak.*, 3d ed., p. 637.
[3] *All's Well that Ends Well*, iv, 3.
[4] *Merry Wives of Windsor*, iv, 2.
[5] *As You Like It*, iii, 2.
[6] *Authorship of Shak.*, 3d ed., p. 630.
[7] *Henry VIII.*, iii, 2.

It is manifest here, as Mr. Rushton thinks, that the author of the Plays was exactly acquainted with the very language of this old statute.

This, then, is the syllogism which faces the Shakspereans:

1. The man who wrote the Plays was a lawyer.
2. William Shakspere was not a lawyer.
3. Therefore, William Shakspere did not write the Plays.

But if they shift their ground, and fall back upon the *supposition* that Shakspere might have been a lawyer's clerk during his pre-London residence in Stratford, they encounter these difficulties:

1. There is not the slightest proof of this fact; and if it was true, proof could not fail to be forthcoming.
2. There is not a scrap of tradition that points to it.
3. Granting it to be possible, it would not explain away the difficulty. It would not have been sufficient for Shakspere to have passed a few months in a lawyer's office in Stratford in his youth. The man who wrote the Plays must have lived and breathed in an atmosphere of the law, which so completely filled his whole being that he could not speak of war or of peace, of business or of love, of sorrow or of pleasure, without scintillating forth legal expressions; and these he placed indifferently in the mouths of young and old, learned and unlearned, Greeks, Romans, Italians, Frenchmen, Scotchmen and Englishmen.

Having, as I hope, demonstrated to the satisfaction of my readers that William Shakspere could not have written the Plays which go abroad in his name, we come to the second branch of my argument, to-wit: that FRANCIS BACON, of St. Albans, son of Queen Elizabeth's Lord Keeper, Nicholas Bacon, was their real author.

PART II.

FRANCIS BACON THE AUTHOR OF THE PLAYS.

CHAPTER I.

FRANCIS BACON WAS A POET.

<blockquote>
Mount, eagle, to thy palace crystalline.
Cymbeline, v, 4.
</blockquote>

WE come now to an important branch of this inquiry.

It will be said: Granted that Francis Bacon possessed a great and mighty genius; granted that he was master of the vast learning revealed in the Plays; granted that he had the laborious industry necessary for their preparation; granted that they reveal a character and disposition, political, social and religious views, studies and investigations, identical with his own; granted that we are able to marshal a vast array of parallel thoughts, beliefs, expressions and even errors: the great question still remains, Was Francis Bacon a poet? Did he possess the imagination, the fancy, the sense of the beautiful — in other words, the divine faculty, the fine phrensy, the capacity to "give to airy nothing a local habitation and a name"? Was he not merely a philosopher, a dry and patient investigator of nature, a student of things, not words; of the useful, not the beautiful?

I. THE UNIVERSAL MIND.

Ralph Waldo Emerson grasped the whole answer to this question when he said: "The true poet and the true philosopher are one." The complete mind (and we are reminded of Ulysses' application of the word to Achilles, "thou great and *complete* man") enfolds in its orb all the realms of thought; it perceives not alone the nature of things, but the subtle light of beauty which irradiates them; it is able not only to trace the roots of facts into the dead, dull, material earth, but to follow the plant as it rises into the air and find in the flower thoughts too deep for tears. The purpose of things, the wherefore of things and the glory of things are all one to the God who made them, and to the great broad brain to which He has given power enough to comprehend them. But such minds are rare. Science tells us that the capacity of memory underlies those portions of the brain that perceive, but only a small share of them, and that if you excise a part of the brain, but not all of any particular department, the surrounding territory, which theretofore lay dormant, will now develop the faculty which was formerly exercised by the part removed. So it would seem that in all brains there is the capacity for universal intelligence, but there is lacking some power which forces it into action. The intellect lies like a mass of coals, heated, alive, but dormant; it needs the blow-pipe of genius to oxygenate and bring it to a white heat; and it rarely happens, in the history of mankind, that the whole brain is equally active, and the whole broad temple of the soul lighted up in every part. The world is full of men whose minds glow in spots. The hereditary blood-force, or power of nutrition, or purpose of God, or whatever it may be, is directed to a section of the intelligence, and it blazes forth in music, or poetry, or painting, or philosophy, or action, or oratory. And the world, as it cannot always behold the full orb of the sun, is delighted to look upon these stars, points of intense brilliancy, glorious with a fraction of the universal fire.

II. JOHANN WOLFGANG VON GOETHE.

But occasionally there is born into the world a sun-like soul, the orb of whose brain, as Bacon says, "is concentric with the universe."

One of these was Johann Wolfgang von Goethe, the great spirit of German literature. Like Bacon, he sprang from the common people; but, like him, not directly from them. His father was an imperial councilor, his mother was the daughter of the chief magistrate of the city. Like Bacon, he was thoroughly educated. Like him, his intellectual activity manifested itself in his early years. "Before he was ten years of age he wrote several languages, meditated poems, invented stories and had considerable familiarity with works of art." He began to write verse while yet at college. He associated with actors, free-thinkers and jovial companions. When twenty-three years of age he published his first play, *Götz von Berlichingen;* two years later he wrote *The Sorrows of Werther*, and *Clavigo*, a drama. He also projected a drama on Mohammed and another on Prometheus, and began to revolve in his mind his greatest work, *Faust*. At the same time, while he was astonishing the world with his poetical and dramatic genius, he was engaged in a profound study of natural science. When forty-three years of age, he published his *Beiträge sur Optik*, and his *Farbenlehre*, in the latter of which he questioned the correctness of the Newtonian theory of colors. "He wrote also on the metamorphosis of plants, and on topics of comparative anatomy. In all these he displayed remarkable penetration and sagacity, and his remarks on the morphology of plants are now reckoned among the earlier enunciations of the theory of evolution." *Faust* was not finished until he was fifty-six years old.

We see here, as in the case of Bacon, a vivacious, active youth, full of emotion and poetry; the dramatic faculty forcing itself out in great dramas; wide learning; some capacity for affairs of state (he was privy councilor of legation at the court of the Duke of Saxe-Weimar); and, running through all, profound studies in philosophy and natural science. Goethe was always in easy circumstances. We have only to imagine him living in poverty, forced to maintain appearances, and yet to earn his living by his pen, with no avenue open to him but the play-house, and we have all the conditions, with added genius and philanthropic purposes, to make Bacon.

If the poetical works of Goethe had been published anonymously, or in the name of some friend, it would have been difficult to persuade the world, in after years, that the philosopher and the poet were one.

III. HAD BACON THE POETIC TEMPERAMENT?

First, let us inquire whether Bacon possessed the poetic temperament.

Bacon says:

For myself, I found that I was fitted for nothing so well as for the study of truth; as having a mind *nimble and versatile* enough to catch the resemblances of things.[1]

But, it may be asked, had he that fine sensibility which accompanies genius; did he possess those delicate chords from which time and chance and nature draw their most exquisite melodies — those chords which, as Burns says,

     Vibrate sweetest pleasure,

and

    Thrill the deepest notes of woe?

The answer is plain.

Macaulay speaks of Bacon's mind as

The most exquisitely constructed intellect that has ever been bestowed on any of the children of men.[2]

Montagu says

His imagination was fruitful and vivid. He was of a temperament *of the most delicate sensibility:* so excitable as to be affected by the slightest alterations in the atmosphere.[3]

And remember that neither Macaulay nor Montagu dreamed of the possibility of Bacon being the author of the Shakespeare Plays.

Emerson calls the writer of the Plays, as revealed therein, "the most susceptible of human beings."

Bacon's chaplain and biographer, Dr. Rawley, says:

It may seem the moon had some principal place in the figure of his nativity, for the moon was never in her passion or eclipsed but he was surprised with a sudden fit of fainting; and that though he observed not nor took any previous knowledge of the eclipse thereof; and as soon as the eclipse ceased he was restored to his former strength again.

IV. Was he a Lover of Poetry?

Many things might be quoted from his writings to show his love of poetry and his profound study of it. He says it "elevates the mind from the dungeon of the body to the enjoying of its own divine essence."

He even contemplated the improvement of poetry by the invention of new measures or meters. He says:

---

[1] Preface to *The Interpretation of Nature*.   [2] *Essays*, Bacon, p. 263.
[3] Montagu's *Life of Bacon*.

> For though men with learned tongues do tie themselves to the ancient measures, yet in modern languages it seemeth to me as free to make new measures of verses as of dances; for a dance is a measured pace, as a verse is a measured speech.[1]

The basis of Bacon's mind was the imagination. This is the eye of the soul. By it the spirit sees into the relations of objects. This it is gives penetration, for it surveys things as the eagle does — from above. And this is Bacon's metaphor. He says:

> Some writings have more of the *eagle* in them than others.[2]

It was this descending sight, commanding the whole landscape, that enabled him to make all knowledge his province, and out of this vast scope of view grew his philosophy. It was but a higher poetry. Montaigne says:

> Philosophy is no other than a falsified poesic. . . . Plato is but a poet unript. All superhuman sciences make use of the poetic style.

V. THE CHARACTER OF BACON'S MIND.

Alfred H. Welsh says of Bacon:

> *He belongs to the realm of the imagination*, of eloquence, of history, of jurisprudence, of ethics, of metaphysics; the investigation of the powers and operations of the human mind. His writings have the gravity of prose, *with the fervor and vividness of poetry*. . . . Shakespeare, with greater variety, contains no more vigorous or expressive condensations.

Edmund Burke says:

> Who is there that, hearing the name of Bacon, does not instantly recognize everything of genius the most profound, of literature the most extensive, of discovery the most penetrating, of observation of human life the most distinguishing and refined?

Macaulay says:

> The poetical faculty was powerful in Bacon's mind, but not, like his wit, so powerful as occasionally to usurp the place of his reason, and to tyrannize over the whole man. No imagination was ever at once so strong and so thoroughly subjugated. It never stirred but at a signal from good sense; it stopped at the first check of good sense. Yet, though disciplined to such obedience, it gave noble proofs of its vigor. In truth, much of Bacon's life was passed in a visionary world, amidst things as strange as any that are described in the Arabian tales.[3]

Montagu says:

> His mind, like the sun, had both light and agility; it knew no rest but in motion, no quiet but in activity; it did not so properly apprehend as irradiate the object. . . . His understanding could almost pierce into future contingents, his

---

[1] *Advancement of Learning*, book ii.   [2] Ibid.   [3] *Essays, Bacon*, p. 285.

conjectures improving even to prophecy; he saw consequences yet dormant in their principles, and effects yet unborn in the womb of their causes.[1]

Macaulay speaks of his

Compactness of expression and richness of fancy.[2]

Addison said of his prayer, composed in the midst of his afflictions, in 1621:

For elevation of thought and greatness of expression, it seems rather the devotion of an angel than a man.[3]

Fowler says:

His utterances are not infrequently marked with a grandeur and solemnity of tone, a majesty of diction, which renders it impossible to forget, and difficult even to criticise them. . . . There is no author, unless it be Shakespeare, who is so easily remembered or so frequently quoted. . . . The terse and burning words issuing from the lips of an irresistible commander.[4]

R. W. Church speaks of

The bright torch of his incorrigible imaginativeness.[5] . . . He was a genius second only to Shakespeare. . . . He liked to enter into the humors of a court; to devote *brilliant imagination* and *affluence of invention* to devising a pageant which should throw all others into the shade.[6]

That he was master of the dramatic faculty will be made plain to any one who reads that interesting dialogue entitled *An Advertisement Touching an Holy War*, and observes the skill with which the conversation is carried on, and the separate characters of the parties maintained.

VI. DID BACON CLAIM TO BE A POET?

Let us next ask ourselves this question: Did Bacon *claim* to be a poet?

Certainly. We have among his acknowledged works a series of translations, the Psalms of David, made in his old age, and composed upon a sick-bed.

Mr. Spedding says of these translations:

It has been usual to speak of them as a ridiculous failure; a censure in which I cannot concur. . . . I should myself infer from this sample that Bacon had all the natural faculties which a poet wants: a fine ear for meter, a fine feeling for imaginative effect in words, and a vein of poetic passion. . . . The thought could not well be fitted with imagery, words and rhythm more apt and imaginative; and there is a tenderness of expression which comes manifestly out of a heart in sensitive sympathy with nature. The heroic couplet could hardly do its work better in

---

[1] Montagu's *Life of Bacon*. [3] Fowler's *Bacon*, p. 57. [5] *Francis Bacon*, p. 208.
[2] *Essays, Bacon*, p. 249. [4] Ibid., p. 208. [6] Ibid., p. 214.

the hands of Dryden. The truth is that Bacon was not without the fine phrensy of the poet.[1]

I quote a few passages from these Psalms, selected at random:

> There do the stately ships plough up the floods;
> The greater navies look like walking woods.

This reminds us of the walking wood in *Macbeth:*

> As I did stand my watch upon the hill,
> I looked toward Birnam, and, anon, methought,
> The wood began to move.[2]

He speaks of

> The sappy cedars, tall like stately towers.

Again:

> The vales their hollow bosoms opened plain,
> The streams ran trembling down the vales again.

He speaks of the birds —

> Stroking the gentle air with pleasant notes.

He describes life as

> This bubble light, this vapor of our breath.

He says:

> So that, with present griefs and future fears,
> Our eyes burst forth into a stream of tears.

Again:

> Why should there be such turmoil and such strife,
> To spin in length this feeble line of life?

It must be remembered, in extenuation of any defects in these translations, that they were the work of sickness and old age, when his powers were shrunken. They were written in his sixty-fifth year — one year before his death. We will see that they are not equal in scope and vigor even to his prose writings. He himself noted this difference between youth and age.

He says:

> There is a youth in thoughts as well as in age; and yet the invention of young men is more lively than that of old, and *imaginations stream into their minds better*, and as it were *more divinely*.[3]

VII. THE EXALTATIONS OF GENIUS.

Neither can we judge what great things genius can do in the blessed moments of its highest exaltation by the beggarly dregs of daily life. Lord Byron said, in a letter to Tom Moore:

---

[1] *Works*, vii, 269.   [2] *Macbeth*, v, 4.   [3] Essay *Of Youth and Age*.

A man's poetry has no more to do with the every-day individual than the inspiration with the Pythoness, when removed from the tripod.

Richard Grant White ridicules "the great inherent absurdity — the unlikeness of Bacon's mind and style to those of the writer of the Plays," to which William D. O'Connor well replies:

> Of all fudge ever written this is the sheerest. Methinks I see a critic with his sagacious right eye fixed upon the long loping alexandrines of Richelieu, and his sagacious left eye fixed upon Richelieu's *Maxims of State*, oracularly deciding from the unlikeness of mind and style that the great Cardinal could not have written the tragi-comedy of *Mirame!* Could he inform us (I will offer the most favorable instance possible) what likeness of "mind and style" he could detect between Sir William Blackstone's charming verses, *A Lawyer's Farewell to his Muse*, and the same Sir William Blackstone's *Commentaries?* What likeness of "mind and style" could he establish between the famous treatise by Grotius, on *The Rights of Peace and War*, and the stately tragedy by Grotius entitled *Adam in Exile?* Where is the identity of "mind and style" between Sir Walter Raleigh's dry-as-dust *Cabinet Council* and Sir Walter Raleigh's magnificent and ringing poem, *The Soul's Errand?* What likeness of "mind and style" could he find between Coleridge's *Aids to Reflection* and the unearthly melody and magian imagery of Coleridge's *Kubla Khan?* What likeness of "mind and style" exists between the exquisite riant grace, lightness and Watteau-color of Milton's *Allegro*, the gracious andante movement and sweet cloistral imagery of Milton's *Penserosa*, and the *Tetrachordon*, or the *Areopagitica* of the same John Milton? Are the solemn, rolling harmonies of *Paradise Lost* one in "mind and style" with the trip-hammer crash of the reply to Salmasius by Cromwell's Latin secretary? Could the most astute reviewer discover likeness of "mind and style" between *Peregrine Pickle* or *Roderick Random* and the noble and majestic passion of the *Ode to Independence?* —
>
> > Thy spirit, Independence, let me share,
> > Lord of the lion-heart and eagle-eye!
> > Thy steps I'll follow with my bosom bare,
> > Nor heed the storm that howls along the sky.[1]

VIII. BACON'S COURT MASK.

Let us go a step farther and prove that Bacon wrote verse, and mastered the difficulties of rhythm and rhyme, in other productions besides the translation of a few psalms.

Messrs. Spedding and Dixon brought to light, in their researches, two fragments of a court mask which is believed to be unquestionably Bacon's, and in it, as an oracle, occur these verses, spoken of a blind Indian boy. The queen, of course, is Elizabeth:

> Seated between the Old World and the New,
> A land there is no other land may touch,
> Where reigns a queen in peace and honor true;
> Stories or fables do describe no such.

---

[1] *Hamlet's Note Book*, p. 56, Houghton, Mifflin & Co., Boston and New York.

> Never did Atlas such a burden bear,
>   As she in holding up the world opprest;
> Supplying with her virtue everywhere
>   Weakness of friends, errors of servants best.
> No nation breeds a warmer blood for war,
>   And yet she calms them by her majesty;
> No age hath ever wits refined so far,
>   And yet she calms them by her policy:
>   To her thy son must make his sacrifice
>   If he will have the *morning of his eyes*.

Certainly this exhibits full possession of the powers requisite in metrical composition, while the closing expression for restoration from blindness, "the morning of his eyes," is eminently poetical.

IX. OTHER VERSES BY BACON.

There are also some other verses which go under the name of Bacon. They are worthy of the pen that wrote Shakespeare:

Mr. Spedding publishes, in his great edition of *Bacon's Works*,[1] a poem, which he calls "a remarkable performance." It is a paraphrase of a Greek epigram, attributed by some to Poseidippus, by others to Plato, the comic poet, and by others to Crates, the cynic. In 1629, only three years after Bacon's death, Thomas Farnaby, a contemporary and scholar, published a collection of Greek epigrams. After giving the epigram in question, with its Latin translation on the opposite page, he adds: "*Huc elegantem V. C. L. Domini Verulamii παρωδίαν adjicere adlubuit;*" and then prints the English lines below (the only English in the book), with a translation of his own opposite in rhyming Greek. A copy of the English lines was also found among Sir Henry Wotton's papers, with the name *Francis Lord Bacon* at the bottom. Spedding says, "Farnaby's evidence is direct and strong," and he expresses the opinion that the internal evidence is in favor of the poem being the work of Bacon. Spedding says:

> The English lines which follow are not meant for a translation, and can hardly be called a paraphrase. They are rather another poem on the same subject and with the same sentiment; and though the topics are mostly the same, the treatment of them is very different. The merit of the original consists almost entirely in its compactness; there being no special felicity in the expression, or music in the meter. In the English, compactness is not aimed at, and a tone of plaintive melody is imparted, which is due chiefly to the metrical arrangement, and has something very pathetic in it to the ear.

[1] Vol. xiv, p. 115, Boston ed.

> The world's a bubble, and the life of man
>   Less than a span;
> In his conception wretched, from the womb
>   So to the tomb;
> Cursed from his cradle and brought up to years
>   With cares and fears:
> Who, then, to frail mortality shall trust,
> But limns the water, or but writes in dust.
> Yet, whilst with sorrow here we live opprest,
>   What life is best?
> Courts are but only superficial schools,
>   To dandle fools;
> The rural parts are turned into a den
>   Of savage men;
> And where's the city from foul vice so free
> But may be termed the worst of all the three?
> Domestic cares afflict the husband's bed,
>   Or pains his head.
> Those that live single take it for a curse,
>   Or do things worse.
> Some would have children; those that have them moan,
>   Or wish them gone.
> What is it, then, to have or have no wife,
> But single thraldom or a double strife?
> Our own affections still at home to please
>   Is a disease:
> To cross the seas to any foreign soil,
>   Perils and toil.
> Wars with their noise affright us; when they cease,
>   We're worse in peace
> What then remains, but that we still should cry
> Not to be born, or, being born, to die?

I differ with Mr. Spedding. These verses are exceedingly terse and compact. They exhibit a complete mastery over rhythm and rhyme. Those two lines,—

> Who then to frail mortality shall trust,
> But limns the water, or but writes in dust,—

are worthy of any writer in the language. We are reminded of the pathetic utterance of poor Keats, who requested that his friends should place upon his tomb the words:

> Here lies one whose name was writ in water.

Mr. Spedding also gives us[1] the following lines, inferior to the above, found in a volume of manuscript collections now in the British Museum:

[1] Vol. xiv, p. 114.

VERSES MADE BY MR. FRANCIS BACON.

The man of life upright, whose guiltless heart is free
From all dishonest deeds and thoughts of vanity;
The man whose silent days in harmless joys are spent,
Whom hopes cannot delude, nor fortune discontent:
That man needs neither towers, nor armor for defense
Nor secret vaults to fly from thunder's violence;
He only can behold with unaffrighted eyes
The horrors of the deep and terrors of the skies;
Thus scorning all the care that Fate or Fortune brings,
He makes the Heaven his book, his wisdom heavenly things;
Good thoughts his only friends, his life a well-spent age,
The earth his sober inn,—a quiet pilgrimage.

Mrs. Pott[1] quotes a poem entitled *The Retired Courtier*, from Dowland's *First Book of Songs,* published 1600; and she gives many very good reasons for believing that it was from the pen of Bacon. Certain it is that the verses are of extraordinary excellence, and were claimed by no one else, and they afford numerous parallels with the Plays:

THE RETIRED COURTIER.

I.

His golden locks hath Time to silver turned;
  O time too swift! O swiftness never ceasing!
His youth 'gainst time and age hath ever spurned,
  But spurned in vain; youth waneth by increasing.
Beauty, strength, youth, are flowers but fading seen,
Duty, faith, love, are roots, and ever green.

II.

His helmet now shall make a hive for bees,
  And lovers' sonnets turn to holy psalms.
A man-at-arms must now serve on his knees,
  And feed on prayers which are age's alms;
But though from court to cottage he depart,
His saint is sure of his unspotted heart.

III.

And when he saddest sits in homely cell,
  He'll teach his swains this carol for a song:
Blest be the hearts that wish my sovereign well!
  Curst be the soul that thinks her any wrong!
Goddess, allow this aged man his right,
To be your beadsman now that was your knight.

What a beautiful and poetical conception is that:

His helmet now shall make a hive for bees.

---

[1] *Promus*, appendix D, p. 528.

If Bacon did not write this, who was the unknown poet to whom it can be ascribed?

says the poem.
>His saint is sure of his *unspotted heart*,

says Shakespeare.[1]
>A pure, *unspotted heart*,

>Allow this aged man his right
>To *be your beadsman* now.

Says Bacon to Lord Burleigh (1597):
>I will still *be your beadsman*.

X. Bacon's Concealed Writings.

Let us next inquire: Were these extracts all of Bacon's poetical works? Is there any evidence that he was the author of any *concealed* writings?

Yes. Mrs. Pott says:

>There are times noted by Mr. Spedding when Bacon wrote with closed doors and when the subject of his studies is doubtful; and there is one long vacation of which the same careful biographer remarks that he cannot tell what work the indefatigable student produced during those months, for that he knows of none whose date corresponds with the period. Perhaps it was at such a time Bacon took recreation in the form in which he recommended it to others, not by idleness, but by bending the bow in an opposite direction; for he says: "I have found now twice, upon amendment of my fortunes, disposition to melancholy and distaste, especially the same happening against the long vacation, when company failed and business both." The same distaste to what he in a letter calls the "dead vacation" is seen in *As You Like It*, act iii, scene 2:
>>Who stays it [time] still withal?
>>With lawyers in the vacation.

Bacon says in a letter to Tobie Matthew:

>I have sent you some copies of my book of the *Advancement*, which you desired; and a little work *of my recreation*, which you desired not. My *Instauration* I reserve for conference; it sleeps not. Those works of the *alphabet* are in my opinion of less use to you where you now are than at Paris. [1607-9.]

Mr. Spedding cannot guess what those works of the *alphabet* may have been, unless they referred to Bacon's experiments at cipher-writing.

When he has become *Sir* Francis, Bacon writes to Tobie Matthew:

>I send my desire to you in this letter that you will *take care not to leave the writing which I left with you last with any man so long that he may be able to take a copy of it*.

And that this was evidently some composition of his own appears by the fact that he asks his friend's criticism upon it, and to

---
[1] *1st Henry VI.*, v, 4.

"point out where I do perhaps *indormiscere*, or where I do *indulgere genio;* or where, in fine, I give any manner of disadvantage to myself."

Does this mean that he fears he will reveal himself by his style?

Again, he writes to the same friend:

> You conceive aright, that in this and the other, you have commission to impart and communicate them to others, according to your discretion; *other matters I write not of.*[1]

What was the meaning of all this mystery?

Bacon refers to some unnamed work which he sends to his friend as "a work of his recreation." And in *The Advancement of Learning*[2] he says:

> As for poesy, it is rather a pleasure or play of the imagination than a work or duty thereof.

And in *Macbeth* we have:

> The labor we delight in physics pain.[3]

And in *Antony and Cleopatra* we have:

> The business that we love, we rise betimes
> And go to it with delight.[4]

Bacon in his *Apology* says:

> It happened, a little before that time, that her Majesty had a purpose to dine at Twickenham Park, at which time I had (although I *profess* not to be a poet) prepared a sonnet directly tending and alluding to draw on her Majesty's reconcilement to my Lord, which I remember I also showed to a great person.

Mr. William Thompson[5] calls attention to the fact that this sonnet has never been found among Bacon's papers, or elsewhere, and suggests that this is one of the sonnets that go under the name of Shakespeare.

When James I., after the death of Elizabeth, was about to come to England, to assume the crown, Master John Davis, afterward Sir John Davis, the poet and courtier, went to meet him, whereupon Bacon sent after him this significant letter:

Master Davis:
> Though you went on the sudden, yet you could not go before you had spoken with yourself to the purpose which I will now write. And, therefore, I know it shall be altogether needless, save that I meant to show you that I was not asleep.

---

[1] Letter to Tobie Matthew, 1609. [2] Book ii. [3] Act ii, scene 3. [4] Act iv, scene 4.
[5] *The Renascene Drama; or, History Made Visible.* By William Thompson, F.R.C F.L.S. Melbourne, 1880.

Briefly, I commend myself to your love and the well-using of my name, as well in repressing and answering for me, if there be any biting or nibbling at it, in that place; as by imprinting a good conceit and opinion of me, chiefly in the King (of whose favor I make myself comfortable assurance), and otherwise in that court. And, not only so, but generally to perform to me all the good offices which the vivacity of your wit can suggest to your mind, to be performed to one with whose affection you have so great sympathy, and in whose fortune you have so great interest. *So desiring you to be good to all concealed poets*, I continue, etc.

This letter is very significant. It is addressed to a poet; it anticipates that there will be "biting and nibbling" at his good name; it begs the friendly services of Davis; and it concludes by asking him to be good "*to all concealed poets.*" This plainly refers to himself. The whole context shows it. We know that Bacon was a poet. Here he admits that he is a *concealed* poet. That is to say, that he was the author of poetical writings which he does not acknowledge—"which go about in others' names."

This pregnant admission half proves my case; for if the "concealed" poetical writings were not the Shakespeare Plays, what were they? Are there any other poetical writings in that age whose authorship is questioned? If so, what are they?

And we have another proof of this in a letter of Sir Tobie Matthew to Bacon, which, being addressed to him as the Viscount St. Albans, must necessarily have been written subsequent to the 27th January, 1621, when his Lordship was invested with that title. Judge Holmes says:

It appears to be in answer to a letter from Lord Bacon, dated "the 9th of April" (year not given), accompanying some great and noble token of his "Lordship's favor," which was in all probability a newly printed book; for Bacon, as we know from the letters, was in the habit of sending to Mr. Matthew a copy of his books as they were published.... Neither is there anything in the way of the supposition that this date may actually have been the 9th of April, 1623; and there was no publication of any work of Bacon, during that spring, which he would be sending to Mr. Matthew unless it were precisely this Folio of 1623.[1]

The postscript is as follows:

P. S. The most prodigious wit that ever I knew of my nation, and of this side of the sea, *is of your Lordship's name*, THOUGH HE BE KNOWN BY ANOTHER.

If we suppose that "the great and noble token" was the Shakespeare Folio of 1623, we can understand this. If Tobie Matthew, Bacon's intimate friend and correspondent, his "other self" as he calls him, to whom he wrote about the mysterious works of the

---

[1] *Authorship of Shak.*, p. 172.

alphabet, and to whom he sent "the works of his recreation" (not to be left where any one could take a copy of them) — if Tobie Matthew knew that "the great and noble token" was written by "the concealed poet," Bacon, and if he desired, as part of his thanks, to compliment him upon the mighty genius manifested in it, what is more natural than that he should allude to the hidden secret in the way he does? He says, in effect, writing from abroad: "Thanks for the Folio. Your Lordship is the greatest wit of our nation, and of this side of the sea (that is, in all Europe), though your noblest work is published under another name."

In another letter Tobie Matthew writes him:

> I shall give you "*Measure for Measure.*"

He was familiar with the Plays of Shakespeare. After Shakespeare's death, he wrote a letter, in which he refers to Falstaff as the author of a speech which he quotes. And in 1598 he writes to Dudley Carleton, again quoting from Falstaff: "Well, honour pricks them on, and the world thinckes that honour will quickly prick them off againe."

That there were concealed poets in London among the gentlemen scholars, and the lawyers in the inns of court, we know in another way: In Webb's *Discourse of Poetry*, published in 1586, after enumerating the writers of the day, Whetstone, Munday, etc., he adds:

> I am humbly to desire pardon of the learned company of *gentlemen scholars* and students of the universities and *inns of court*, if I omit their several commendations in this place, which I know a great number of them have worthily deserved, *in many rare devices and singular inventions of poetry;* for neither hath it been my good hap to have seen all which I have heard of, neither is my abiding in such place where I can with facility get knowledge of their works.[1]

In Spenser's *Teares of the Muses*, printed in 1591, there is a passage beginning:

> And he the man whom Nature's self had made
> To mock her selfe and Truth to imitate,
> With kindly counter under mimic shade,
> Our pleasant Willy, ah, is dead of late!

This has been held to refer to Shakspere, chiefly, it would seem, because of the name Willy. "But," says Richard Grant White,[2] "'Willy,' like 'shepherd,' was not uncommonly used merely to mean a poet, and was distinctly applied to Sir Philip

---

[1] Knight, *Shak. Biography*, p. 328. [2] *Life and Genius of Shak.*, p. 95.

Sidney, in an eclogue preserved in Davidson's *Poetical Rhapsody*, published in 1602. And *The Teares of the Muses* had certainly been written before 1590, when Shakspere could not have arisen to the position assigned, by the first poet of the age, to the subject of this passage, and probably before 1580, when Shakspere was a boy of sixteen at Stratford."

And if these lines referred to Shakspere, what is meant by the words, "with kindly counter under mimic shade"? Certainly Shakspere never appeared under any mimic shade or disguise; while, if the lines referred to Bacon, old enough even in 1580 to be a poet and a friend of Spenser, there might be an allusion here to his use of some play-actor's name as a disguise for his productions, just as we find him in the sonnets referring to himself as

> Keeping invention in a *noted weed*
> Till *every word does almost speak my name.*

But I shall discuss this matter more at length hereafter.

And Bacon, in a prayer made while Lord Chancellor, refers to the same weed or disguise:

The state and bread of the poor and oppressed have been precious in mine eyes; I have hated all cruelty and hardness of heart. I have, *though in a despised weed*, procured the good of all men.

We will see hereafter that the purpose of the Plays was the good of all men.

And we find in the following sentence proof that Bacon used the word *weed* to signify a disguise:

This fellow, when Perkin took sanctuary, chose rather to take a holy habit than a holy place, and clad himself like a hermit, and in that *weed* wandered about the country until he was discovered and taken.[1]

We find many evidences that Bacon's pursuits were poetical. He writes to the Earl of Essex on one occasion:

Desiring your good Lordship, nevertheless, not to conceive out of this my diligence in soliciting this matter, that I am either much in appetite or much in hope. For, as for appetite, *the waters of Parnassus* are not like the waters of the Spa, that give a stomach, but rather they quench appetite and desires.

And when, after Essex was released from confinement in 1600, Bacon wrote him a congratulatory letter, Essex replied, evidently somewhat angry at him, as follows:

[1] *History of Henry VII.*

I can neither expound nor censure your late actions, being ignorant of them all save one, and having directed my sight inward only to examine myself. . . . I am a stranger to all *poetical conceits*, or else *I should say somewhat of your poetical example*.[1]

And we have many proofs that Bacon was engaged in some studies which absorbed him to the exclusion of law and politics.

He says:

I do confess, since I was of any understanding, my mind hath, in effect, been absent from that I have done, and in absence errors are committed, which I do willingly acknowledge; and amongst the rest this great one which led the rest: that knowing myself by inward calling to be fitter to hold a book than to play a part, I have led my life in civil causes, for which I was not very fit by nature, and more unfit *by the preoccupation of my mind*.[2]

And he makes this apology for the failure of his life:

This I speak to posterity, not out of ostentation, but because I judge it may somewhat import the dignity of learning, to have a man *born for letters* rather than anything else, who should by a certain fatality, and against the bent of his own genius, be compelled into active life.[3]

XI. THE IMAGINATION REVEALED IN BACON'S ACKNOWLEDGED WRITINGS.

But, after all, the best evidence of the fact that Bacon possessed the imagination, the fancy and the wit necessary for the production of the Plays, must be found in his acknowledged writings.

I assert, first, that he had all the fancy, vivacity and sprightliness of mind necessary for the task.

Let me give a few proofs of this. He says:

Extreme self-lovers will set a man's house on fire, though it were but to roast their eggs.[4]

Money is like muck, not good unless it be spread.[5]

You have built an ark to save learning from deluge.[6]

He calls the great conquerors of history "the troublers of the world;" he speaks of "the tempest of human life."

He says:

A full heart is like a full pen; it can hardly make any distinguished work.[7]

He says:

For as statues and pictures are dumb histories, so histories are speaking pictures.[8]

---

[1] Letter from Essex to Bacon, 1600.
[2] Letter to Sir Thomas Bodley.
[3] *Advancement of Learning*, viii, 3.
[4] *Coll. Sens.*
[5] Essay *Of Seditions*.
[6] Letter to Sir Thomas Bodley.
[7] Letter to the King.
[8] Letter to the Chancellor.

In so grave and abstract a matter as the dedication of *The Arguments of Law*, he says:

For the reasons of municipal laws, severed from the grounds of nature, manners and policy, are like wall-flowers, which, though they grow high upon the crests of states, yet have no deep roots.

How figurative, how poetical is this! Not only the municipal laws are compared to wall-flowers, but they grow upon the *crests* of states!

He says also:

Fame hath swift swings, especially that which hath black feathers.[1]

Meaning, by black feathers, slanders.

He also says:

For, though your Lordship's fortunes be above the thunder and storms of inferior regions, yet, nevertheless, to hear the wind and not to feel it, will make one sleep the better.[2]

He says:

Myself have ridden at anchor all your Grace's absence, and my cables are now quite worn.[3]

We also find this:

The great labor was to get entrance into the business; but now the portcullis is drawn up.[4]

He says:

Hereupon presently came forth swarms and volleys of libels, which are the gusts of liberty of speech restrained, and the females of sedition, containing bitter invectives and slanders.[5]

Again:

I shall perhaps, before my death, have rendered the age a light unto posterity, by kindling this new torch amid the darkness of philosophy.[6]

Again:

Time, like a river, hath brought down all that was light and inflated, and hath sunk what was weighty and solid.[7]

Again:

I ask for a full pardon, that I may *die out of a cloud*.[8]

Again:

As for gestures, they are as transitory hieroglyphics.[9]

---

[1] Letter to Sir George Villiers, 1615.
[2] Letter to Buckingham, April, 1623.
[3] Letter to Buckingham, October 12, 1623.
[4] Letter to Buckingham, 1619.
[5] *History of Henry VII.*
[6] Letter to King James.
[7] Preface to *Great Instauration*.
[8] Letter to Buckingham, November 25, 1623.
[9] *Advancement of Learning*, book ii.

He says:

> Words are the footsteps and prints of reason.[1]

Again:

Hope is a leaf-joy, which may be beaten out to a great extension, like gold.[2]

Again:

The reason of this omission I suppose to be that hidden rock whereupon both this and many other barks of knowledge have been cast away.[3]

Again he speaks of

The Georgics of the mind, concerning the husbandry and tillage thereof.[4]

Again:

> Such men are, as it were, the very suitors and lovers of fables.[5]

This reminds us of Shakespeare:

> The very beadle to a humorous sigh.[6]

Speaking of the then recent voyages in which the earth was circumnavigated, he uses this poetical expression:

Memorable voyages, after the manner of heaven, about the globe of the earth.[7]

Did ever grave geographer use such a simile as this?

He says:

Industrious persons . . . do save and recover somewhat from the deluge of time.[8]

Also:

Remnants of history which have casually escaped the shipwreck of time.[9]

Again:

Times answerable, like waters after a tempest, full of working and swelling.[10]

He says:

The corrupter sort of politicians . . . thrust themselves into the center of the world, as if all lines should meet in them and their fortunes; never caring, in all tempests, what becomes of the ship of state, so they may *save themselves in the cock-boat of their own fortune*.[11]

Again:

> Virtue is like a rich stone, best plain set.[12]

He says:

If a man be gracious and courteous to strangers, it shows he is a citizen of the world, and that his heart is no island cut off from other lands, but a continent that joins to them.[13]

---

[1] *Advancement of Learning*, book ii.
[2] *History of Life and Death*.
[3] *Advancement of Learning*, book ii.
[4] Ibid.
[5] *Novum Organum*, book ii.
[6] *Love's Labor Lost*, iii, 1.
[7] *Advancement of Learning*, book ii.
[8] Ibid.
[9] Ibid.
[10] Ibid., book ii.
[11] Ibid., book i.
[12] Essay *Of Beauty*.
[13] Essay *Of Goodness*.

He says:

It is sport to see a bold fellow out of countenance, for that puts his face into a most shrunken and wooden posture.[1]

Again:

Suspicions among thoughts are like bats among birds — they ever fly by twilight.[2]

Again:

Some men's behavior is like a verse, wherein every syllable is measured.[3]

He says:

Certainly there be whose fortunes are like Homer's verses, that have a slide and an easiness more than the verses of other poets.[4]

Speaking of those studies that come home to the hearts of men, or, to use his phrase, "their business and bosoms," he says:

So men generally take well knowledges that are drenched in flesh and blood.[5]

He says:

Duty, though my state lie buried in the sands, and my favors be cast upon the waters, and my honors be committed to the wind, yet standeth surely built upon the rock, and hath been, and ever shall be, unforced and unattempted.[6]

Speaking of the Perkin Warbeck conspiracy, Bacon says:

After such time . . . she began to cast with herself *from what coast this blazing star should first appear*, and at what time it must be *upon the horizon* of Ireland, for there had been the like *meteor strong* influence before. The time of the *apparition* to be when the King should be engaged into a war with France.[7]

Again he says:

Honor that is gained and broken upon another hath the quickest reflection, *like diamonds cut with facets*.[8]

Again:

In fame of learning the flight will be slow without some feathers of ostentation.[9]

Again:

Pope Alexander . . . was desirous to trouble the waters in Italy, that he might fish the better; casting the net not out of St. Peter's, but out of Borgia's bark.[10]

He uses this expression:

Their preposterous, fantastic and hypothetical philosophies which have led experience captive.[11]

---

[1] *Essay Of Goodness.*
[2] *Essay Of Suspicion.*
[3] *Essay Of Praise.*
[4] *Essay Of Fortune.*
[5] *Advancement of Learning*, book ii.
[6] Letter written in Essex' name to the Queen, 1600.
[7] *History of Henry VII.*
[8] *Essay Of Honor and Reputation.*
[9] *Essay Of Vain Glory.*
[10] *History of Henry VII.*
[11] *Novum Organum.*

Speaking again of the Perkin Warbeck conspiracy, he expresses it in this most figurative manner:

> At this time the King began to be haunted with spirits, by the magic and curious arts of the Lady Margaret, who raised up the ghost of Richard, Duke of York, second son to King Edward the Fourth, to walk and vex the King.[1]

Again:

> Every giddy-headed humor keeps, in a manner, revel-rout in false religions.[2]

Again:

> It is the extremity of evil when mercy is not suffered to have commerce with misery.[3]

When he would say that the circumstances were favorable for the inauguration of the Perkin Warbeck conspiracy, he puts it thus:

> Now did the sign reign, and the constellation was come, under which Perkin should appear.[4]

[We find the Duke telling Viola:

> I know thy *constellation* is right apt
> For this affair.[5]]

And again:

> But all this upon the French King's part was but a trick, the better to bow King Henry to peace. And therefore upon the first grain of incense that was sacrificed upon the altar of peace, at Bololgn, Perkin was smoked away.[6]

When Bacon would say that King Henry VII. used his wars as a means and excuse to fill his treasury, he expresses it in this picturesque fashion:

> His wars were always to him as a mine of treasure of a strange kind of ore; iron at the top and gold and silver at the bottom.[7]

Again he says:

> And Perkin, *for a perfume before him* as he went, caused to be published a proclamation.[8]

Again:

> So certainly, if a man meditate much upon the universal frame of nature, the earth with men upon it (the divineness of souls except) will not seem much other than an ant-hill, where, as some ants carry corn, and some carry their young, and some go empty, and all — to and fro — a little heap of dust.[9]

He uses this expression after his downfall:

> Here I live upon the sword-point of a sharp air.[10]

---

[1] *History of Henry VII.*
[2] *Wisdom of the Ancients — Dionysius.*
[3] Ibid. — *Diomedes.*
[4] *History of Henry VII.*
[5] *Twelfth Night*, i, 4.
[6] *History of Henry VII.*
[7] Ibid.
[8] Ibid.
[9] *Advancement of Learning*, book i.
[10] Petition to the House of Lords.

Alluding to Perkin Warbeck, he says:

But it was ordained that this winding-ivy of a Plantagenet should kill the true tree itself.[1]

Again:

It was a race often dipped in their own blood.[2]

Speaking of the crowds of rabble who followed Perkin Warbeck after his capture, to mock and deride him, Bacon uses this poetical figure:

They flocked about him as he went along: that one might know afar off where the owl was by the flight of birds.[3]

After his downfall he writes:

I desire to do, for the little time God shall send me life, like the merchants of London, which, when they give over trade, lay out their money upon land. So being freed from civil business, I lay forth my poor talent upon those things which may be perpetual.[4]

Again:

And as in the tides of people once up, there want not commonly stirring winds to make them more rough.[5]

Speaking of Henry VII., after he had overcome the rebellions of Simnell and Warbeck, Bacon says:

This year also, though the King was no more haunted with sprites, for that by the sprinkling, partly of blood, and partly of water, he had chased them away.[6]

Again he says:

As if one were to employ himself poring over the dissection of the dead carcass of nature, rather than to set himself to ascertain the powers and properties of living nature.[7]

He says:

Nothing appears omitted for preparing the senses to inform the understanding, and we shall no longer dance, as it were, within the narrow circles of the enchanter, but extend our march around the confines of the world itself.[8]

Again:

A fellow that thinks with his magistrality and goosequill to give laws and menages to crowns and scepters.[9]

This is rather a long list of examples to prove that Bacon possessed in a preëminent degree fancy, vivacity and imagination, but I feel that no man can say his time is wasted in reading such a catalogue of gems.

---

[1] *History of Henry VII.*
[2] Ibid.
[3] Ibid.
[4] Letter to the King, Oct. 8, 1621.
[5] *History of Henry VII.*
[6] Ibid.
[7] *Nature of Things.*
[8] *Exper. History.*
[9] Charge against Talbot.

XII. Had he the Higher Genius?

We come now to another question. Granted that he had these humbler qualities of a vivacious mind, did he possess the loftier features of the imagination, those touches where heart and soul and sense of melody are fused together as in the great Plays?

Undoubtedly an affirmative answer must be given to this question. But as in the doings of daily life he was, as Byron says, "off the tripod," it is only when he is, as Prospero has it, "touched to the quick," by some great emotion, that he forgets the philosophical and political restraints he has imposed upon himself, and pours forth his heart in words. One of these occasions was his downfall, in utter disgrace, fined, imprisoned, exiled from the court. In his petition to the House of Lords he cries out from the depths of his soul:

> I am old, weak, ruined, in want, a very subject of pity.

We seem to hear the voice of Lear:

> A poor, infirm, weak and despised old man.[1]

And, still speaking of himself, he continues with this noble thought:

> It may be you will do posterity good, if out of the carcass of dead and rotten greatness, as out of Samson's lion, there may be honey gathered for the use of future times.[2]

What a noble, what a splendid image is this! How the metaphor is interwoven, Shakespeare-wise, not as a distinct comparison, but into the entire body of the thought. He is appealing for mercy, for time to finish his great works; he is himself already "dead and rotten greatness," but withal majestic greatness; he is Samson's lion, but in the carcass the bees have made their hive and hoarded honey for posterity. And what a soul! That in the hour of ruin and humiliation, sacrificed, as I believe, to save a dishonest King and a degraded favorite, he could still love humanity and look forward to its welfare.

Could that expression have come from any other source than the mind that wrote Shakespeare? The image was not unfamiliar to the writer of the Plays:

> 'Tis seldom when the bee doth leave her comb
> In the dead carrion.[3]

---

[1] *Lear*, iii, 2.   [2] Petition to the House of Lords.   [3] *2d Henry IV.*, iv, 4.

Take another instance. Bacon speaks of

The ocean, the solitary handmaid of eternity.[1]

If that thought was found in the Plays, would it not be on the tongues of all men as a magnificent image?

And what poetry is there in this?

But men must learn that in this theater of man's life it is reserved only for God and the angels to be lookers-on.[2]

If Shakespeare had written a prose essay, should we not expect him to speak something after this fashion?

But the images of men's wits and knowledges remain in books, exempted from the wrong of time and capable of perpetual renovation. Neither are they fitly to be called images, because they generate still and cast their seeds in the minds of others, provoking and causing infinite actions and opinions in succeeding ages; so that if the invention of the ship was thought so noble, which carrieth riches and commodities from place to place and consociateth the most remote regions in participation of their fruits, how much more are letters to be magnified, which, as ships, pass through the vast seas of time and make ages so distant to participate of the wisdom, illuminations and inventions, the one of the other.[3]

How poetical is the following:

Her royal clemency which as a sovereign and precious balm continually distilleth from her fair hands, and falleth into the wounds of many that have incurred the offense of the law.[4]

Again we have:

Sure I am that the treasure that cometh from you to her Majesty is but as a vapor which riseth from the earth and gathereth into a cloud and stayeth not there long, but upon the same earth it falleth again. It is like a sweet odor of honor and reputation to our nation throughout the world.[5]

We are reminded of Portia's:

> The quality of mercy is not strained,
> It droppeth like the gentle rain from heaven
> Upon the place beneath.[6]

And also of the following:

> The heavens rain odors on you.[7]

How beautiful is this expression of Bacon:

A crowd is not company, and faces are but a gallery of pictures, and talk but a tinkling cymbal where there is no love.[8]

---

[1] *The Nature of Things.*
[2] *Advancement of Learning*, book ii.
[3] Ibid., book i.
[4] Discourse in Praise of the Queen; *Life and Works*, vol. i, p. 129.
[5] Bacon's Speech in Parliament, 1597-8, vol. ii, p. 86.
[6] *Merchant of Venice*, iv, 1.
[7] *Twelfth Night*, iii, 1.
[8] Essay *Of Friendship.*

How figurative is this:

The King slept out the sobs of his subjects until he was awakened with the thunderbolt of a Parliament.[1]

What poet has written in prose anything more poetical than this?

The unfortunate destinies of hopeful young men, who, like the sons of Aurora, puffed up with the glittering show of vanity and ostentation, attempt actions above their strength. . . . For among all the disasters that can happen to mortals, there is none so lamentable, and so powerful to move compassion, as *the flower of virtue cropped with too sudden a mischance.* . . . Lamentation and mourning *flutter around their obsequies like those funereal birds.*[2]

How fine is this expression:

He took, as it were, the picture of words from the life of reason.[3]

There is a rhythm in this:

Bred in the cells of gross and solitary monks.[4]

How poetical is his conception when he speaks[5] of the preparation for the grand Armada and the Spanish invasion of England, as being "*like the travail of an elephant.*" And again, when he speaks of one of the Popes, who, by his labors, prevented the Mohammedanizing of the white race, as one who had "*put a ring in the snout of the Ottoman boar,*" whereby he was prevented from rooting up and ravaging the fair field of Europe. The words draw a picture for us which the memory cannot forget.

What a command of language does he exhibit! Take these sentences:

Words that come from wasted spirits and an oppressed mind are more safe in being deposited in a noble construction.[6]

Neither doth the wind, as far as it carrieth a voice, with a motion thereof, confound any of the *delicate and figurative articulations of the air,* in variety of words.[7]

Who taught the bee to sail through such a vast *sea of air?*[8]

The first of these expeditions invasive was achieved with great felicity, ravished a strong and famous port in the lap and bosom of their high countries.[9]

Whilst I live, my affection to do you service shall remain quick under the ashes of my fortune.[10]

He speaks of Catiline as —

A very fury of lust and blood.[11]

---

[1] Report of Spanish Grievances.
[2] *Wisdom of the Ancients—Memnon.*
[3] *Advancement of Learning,* book i.
[4] Ibid., book ii.
[5] *In Praise of the Queen.*
[6] His Submission to Parliament.
[7] *Natural History,* cent. ii, §125.
[8] *Advancement of Learning,* book ii.
[9] Bacon's Speech in Parliament, 39 Eliz. (1597). *Life and Works,* ii, 88.
[10] Letter to Earl of Bristol.
[11] *Advancement of Learning,* book ii.

Take these sentences:

Religion sweetly touched with eloquence.[1]

The admirable and exquisite subtility of nature.[2]

Have you never seen a fly in amber more beautifully entombed than an Egyptian monarch?

When it has at last been clearly seen what results are to be expected from the nature of things and the nature of the mind, we consider that we shall have prepared and adorned a nuptial couch for the mind and the universe, the Divine Goodness being our bridesmaid.

The blustering affection of a wild and naked people.[3]

Sweet, ravishing music. . . .
The melody and delicate touch of an instrument.[4]

But these blossoms of unripe marriages were but friendly wishes and the airs of loving entertainments.[5]

To dig up the sepulchers of buried and forgotten impositions.[6]

But the King did much to overcast his fortunes, which proved for many years together full of broken seas, tides and tempests.[7]

Neither was the song of the sirens plain and single, but consisting of such a variety of melodious tunes, so fitting and delighting the ears that heard them, as that it ravished and betrayed all passengers.[8]

We might make a book of such citations.

Mr. John H. Stotsenburg, of New Albany, Indiana, has put together, in a newspaper article, a number of extracts from Bacon, and arranged them as if they were blank verse. I give a few of these. It is surprising to observe how much, in this shape, they resemble the poetry of the Shakespeare Plays, and how readily they would deceive an ordinary reader:

> Truth may come, perhaps,
> To a pearl's value that shows best by day,
> But rise it will not to a diamond's price
> That showeth always best in varied lights.
>
> Yet it is not death man fears,
> But only the stroke of death.
>
> Virtue walks not in the highway
> Though she go heavenward.
>
> Why should we love our fetters, though of gold?
>
> When resting in security, man is dead;
> His soul is buried within him
> And his good angel either forsakes his guard or sleeps.

---

[1] *Advancement of Learning*, book i.
[2] *Novum Organum*, book ii.
[3] *History of Henry VII.*
[4] *Wisdom of the Ancients.*
[5] *History of Henry VII.*
[6] Speech in Parliament, 39 Elizabeth, 1597.
[7] *History of Henry VII.*
[8] *Wisdom of the Ancients — Sirens.*

>There is nothing under heaven
>To which the heart can lean, save a true friend.
>
>Why mourn, then, for the end which must be
>Or spend one wish to have a minute added
>To the uncertain date which marks our years?
>Death exempts not man from being,
>But marks an alteration only.
>He is a guest unwelcome and importunate
>And he will not, must not be said nay.
>Death arrives gracious only
>To such as sit in darkness
>Or lie heavy-burdened with grief and irons.
>To the poor Christian that sits slave-bound
>In the galleys;
>To despairful widows, pensive pensioners and deposed kings;
>To them whose fortune runneth backward
>And whose spirits mutiny:
>Unto such death is a redeemer,
>And the grave a place of retiredness and rest.
>These wait upon the shore, and waft to him
>To draw near, wishing to see his star
>That they may be led to him,
>And wooing the remorseless sisters
>To wind down the watch of life
>And break them off before the hour.
>
>It is as natural to die
>As to be born.

In many of these there are scarcely any changes, except in arranging them as blank verse instead of the form of prose; and they have been taken as prose simply because Bacon so first wrote them.

No man, I think, can have followed me thus far in this argument without conceding that Bacon was a poet. If a poet, "the greatest of mankind" would be the greatest poet of mankind. Whatever such a mind strove to accomplish would be of the highest. Nothing commonplace could dwell in such a temple.

We must admit that he possessed everything needed for the preparation of the Shakespeare Plays. Learning, industry, ambition for immortality; command of language in all its heights and depths; the power of compressing thought into condensed sentences; wit, fancy, imagination, feeling and the temperament of genius.

XIII. His Wit.

But it will be said, Was he not lacking in the sense of humor?

By no means. It was the defect of his public speeches that his wit led him aside from the path of dignity. Ben Jonson says his oratory was "nobly censorious when he could spare or pass by a jest." Sir Robert Naunton says, "He was abundantly facetious, which took much with the Queen." The Queen said, "He hath a great wit." "I wish your Lordship a good Easter," says the Spanish Jew, Gondomar, about to cross the Channel. "I wish you a good Pass-over," replied Bacon. Queen Elizabeth asked Bacon whether he had found anything that smacked of treason in a certain book. "No," said Bacon, "but I have found much felony." "How is that?" asked the Queen. "The author," said Bacon "has stolen many of his conceits from Cornelius Tacitus."

In the midst even of his miseries, after his downfall, he writes (1625) to the Duke of Buckingham:

> I marvel that your Grace should think to pull down the monarchy of Spain without my good help. *Your Grace will give me leave to be merry, however the world goeth with me.*

I have just quoted Macaulay's declaration that Bacon's sense of wit and humor was so powerful that it oftentimes usurped the place of reason and tyrannized over the whole man.

We find in the author of the Shakespeare Plays the same inability to restrain his wit.

Says Carlyle:

> In no point does Shakespeare exaggerate but only in laughter. Fiery objurgations, words that pierce and burn, are to be found in Shakespeare; yet he is always in measure here, never what Johnson would remark as a specially "good hater." But his laughter seems to pour from him in floods. . . . Not at mere weakness, at misery or poverty, never.

CHAPTER II

THE WRITER OF THE PLAYS A PHILOSOPHER.

> First, let me talk with this philosopher.
> *Lear, iii, 4.*

IN the attempt to establish identity I have shown that Bacon was a poet as well as a philosopher. I shall now try to establish that the writer of the Plays was a philosopher as well as a poet. In this way we will come very near getting the two heads under one hat.

The poet is not necessarily a philosopher; the philosopher is not necessarily a poet. One may be possessed of marvelous imaginative powers, with but a small share of the reasoning faculty. Another may penetrate into the secrets of nature with a brain as dry as grave-dust.

The crude belief about Shakespeare is that he was an inspired plow-boy, a native genius, a Cornish diamond, without polishing; a poet, and nothing but a poet. I propose to show that his mind was as broad as it was lofty; that he was a philosopher, and more than that, a *natural* philosopher; and more than that, that he held precisely the same views which Bacon held.

Let us see what some of the great thinkers have had to say upon this subject:

Carlyle makes this most significant speech:

> There is an *understanding* manifested in the construction of Shakespeare's Plays equal to that in Bacon's *Novum Organum*.

Hazlitt has struck upon the same pregnant comparison:

> The wisdom displayed in Shakespeare was equal in profoundness to the great Lord Bacon's *Novum Organum*.

Coleridge said:

> He was not only a great poet, but a great philosopher.

Richard Grant White calls him

> The greatest philosopher and the worldly-wisest man of modern times.

Says Emerson:

> He was inconceivably wise. The others conceivably.[1]

Barry Cornwall says:

> He was not a mere poet in the vulgar sense of the term. . . . On the contrary, he was a man eminently acute, logical and philosophical. His reasoning faculty was on a par with his imagination and pervaded all his works completely.[2]

Landor calls Shakespeare

> The *wisest* of men, as well as the greatest of poets.

Pope calls Bacon

> The *wisest* of mankind.

Jeffrey says of Shakespeare:

> He was more full of wisdom and sagacity than all the moralists and satirists that ever lived.

Coleridge says:

> Shakespeare's judgment equaled, if it did not surpass, his creative faculty.

Dr. Johnson says:

> From his works may be collected a system of civil and economical prudence.

Swinburne calls Shakespeare:

> *The wisest and mightiest mind* that ever was informed with the spirit or genius of creative poetry.

Richard Grant White says of Shakespeare:

> He was the most observant of men.

On the other hand, Edmund Burke said of Bacon:

> He possessed the most distinguished and refined observation of human life.

Alfred H. Welsh says of Bacon:

> Never was observation at once more recondite, better-natured and more carefully sifted.

Surely these two men, if we can call them such, ran in closely parallel lines.

And it must be remembered that these witnesses are not advocates of the Baconian authorship of the Plays. Many of them never heard of it.

I. Bacon's Philosophy.

But there are two kinds of philosophy — the transcendental and the practical. Naturally, the first has most relation to the imagination; the latter tends to drag down the mind to the base details

---

[1] *Representative Men*, p. 209. [2] Preface to *Works of Ben Jonson*.

of life. The mind must be peculiarly constructed that can at the same time grapple with the earth and soar in the clouds. It was the striking peculiarity of Bacon's system of philosophy that it tended to make great things little and little things great.

It was the reverse of that old-time philosophy to which Shakespeare sneeringly alluded when he said:

> We have our philosophical persons, to make modern and familiar things supernatural and causeless.[1]

Says Macaulay:

> Some people may think the object of the Baconian philosophy a low object.[2]

And again he observes:

> This persuasion that nothing can be too insignificant for the attention of the wisest which is not too insignificant to give pleasure or pain to the meanest, is the essential spirit of the Baconian philosophy.[3]

Bacon cared nothing for the grand abstrusenesses: he labored for the "betterment of men's bread and wine"—the improvement of the condition of mankind in their worldly estate. This was the gospel he preached. Like Socrates, he "dragged down philosophy from the clouds." He said:

> The evil, however, has been wonderfully increased by an opinion, or inveterate conceit, which is both vainglorious and prejudicial, namely, that the dignity of the human mind is lowered by long and frequent intercourse with experiments and particulars, which are the objects of sense and confined to matter, especially since such matters are *mean* subjects for meditation.[4]

And again, in his *Experimental Natural History*, he says:

> We briefly urge as a precept, that there be admitted into this (natural) history: 1. The most common matters, such as one might think it superfluous to insert, from their being well known; 2. Base, illiberal and filthy matters, and also those which are trifling and puerile, . . . nor ought their worth to be measured by their intrinsic value, but by their application to other points and their influence on philosophy.

And again:

> This was a false estimation that it should be a diminution to the mind of man to be much conversant in experiences and particulars, subject to sense and bound in matter, and which are laborious to search, ignoble to meditate, harsh to deliver, illiberal to practice, infinite as is supposed in number, and noways accommodate to the glory of arts.[5]

And, strange to say, when we turn to Shakespeare we find embalmed in poetry, where one would think there would be the

---

[1] *All's Well that Ends Well*, ii, 3. [3] Ibid., p. 272. [5] *Filum Labyrinthi.*
[2] *Essay Bacon*, p. 278. [4] *Novum Organum*, book i.

least chance to find it, and with which it would seem to have no natural kindred or coherence, this novel philosophy.

Shakespeare says:

> Some kinds of *baseness*
> Are nobly undergone, and most poor *matters*
> Point to rich ends.[1]

And again:

> Nature, what things there are,
> Most *abject in regard and dear in use!*
> What things again most dear in the esteem
> And poor in worth![2]

This is the very doctrine taught by Bacon, which I have just quoted:

Base, illiberal and filthy *matters*, and also those which are trifling and puerile, . . . nor ought their worth to be measured by their intrinsic value, but by their application to other points and their influence on philosophy.

Why did not Bacon quote that sentence from the *Tempest?*

> Some kinds of *baseness*
> Are nobly undergone, and most poor *matters*
> Point to rich ends.

No wonder Birch is reminded of Bacon when he reads Shakespeare. He says:

Glendower is very angry at the incredulity of Hotspur, and reiterates again and again the signs that he thought marked him extraordinary. Hotspur not only replies with badinage, but ascribes, *with Baconian induction*, all that Glendower thought miraculous and providential to nature and the earth.[3]

Dowden describes the philosophy of Shakespeare in words that fully fit the philosophy of Bacon. He says:

The noble positivism of Shakespeare. . . . Energy, *devotion to the fact*, self-government, tolerance, . . . an indifference to externals in comparison with that which is of the invisible life, and a resolution to judge of all things *from a purely human standpoint.*[4]

The same writer says:

The Elizabethan drama is essentially mundane. To it all that is upon this earth is real, and it does not concern itself greatly about the reality of other things. Of heaven or hell it has no power to sing. It finds such and such facts here and now, and does not invent or discover supernatural causes to explain these facts.[5]

Richard Grant White says:

For although of all poets he is most profoundly psychological, as well as most fanciful and most imaginative, yet with him philosophy, fancy and imagination

---

[1] *Tempest*, iii, 1. [3] Birch, *Philos. and Relig. of Shak.*, p. 138. [5] Ibid., p. 23.
[2] *Troilus and Cressida*, iii, 3. [4] Dowden, *Shak. Mind and Art*, p. 34.

are penetrated with the spirit of that unwritten law of reason which we speak of as if it were a faculty — common sense. *His philosophy is practical and his poetical views are fused with philosophy and poetry.* He is withal the sage and the oracle of this world. . . . There is in him the constant presence and rule of reason in his most exalted flights.[1]

Jeffrey says:

When the object requires it he is always keen and *worldly* and *practical*, and yet, without changing his hand or stopping his course, he scatters around him as he goes all sounds and shapes of sweetness.

It needs no further argument to demonstrate:
1. That the writer of the Plays was a philosopher.
2. That he was a practical philosopher.

I shall now go farther, and seek to show that, like Bacon, he was a *natural philosopher*, a student of nature, a materialist.

Bacon says:

Divine omnipotence was required to create anything out of nothing, so also is that omnipotence to make anything lapse into nothing.[2]

The writer of the Plays had grasped the same thought:

O anything of nothing first created.[3]

Bacon says:

Nothing proceeds from nothing.[4]

Shakespeare says:

Nothing will come of nothing.[5]

Nothing can be made out of nothing.[6]

We see the natural philosopher also in those reflections as to the indestructibility of matter and its transmutations in these verses:

Full fadom five thy father lies;
Of his bones are coral made;
These are pearls that were his eyes:
Nothing of him that doth fade,
But doth suffer a sea-change
Into something rich and strange.[7]

Hamlet's meditations run in the same practical direction. He perceives that the matter of which Alexander was composed was indestructible:

Alexander died, Alexander was buried, Alexander returned to dust; the dust is earth, of earth we make loam, and why of that loam (whereto he was converted) might they not stop a beer barrel?

---

[1] *Life and Genius of Shak.*, p. 293. [3] *Romeo and Juliet*, i, 1. [5] *Lear*, i, 1.
[2] *Thoughts on the Nature of Things.* [4] *Novum Organum*, book ii. [6] Ibid., i, 4.
[7] *Tempest*, i, 2.

> Illustrious Cæsar, dead and turn'd to clay,
> Might stop a hole to keep the wind away.

And when we turn again to Bacon we find him considering how

All things pass through an appointed circuit and succession of transformations. . . . All things change; nothing really perishes.[1]

And again Bacon says:

For there is nothing in nature more true . . . than that nothing is reduced to nothing.[2]

Henry IV. delivers what Birch calls "an episode proper to a geological inquirer, and savoring of the theory of the materialist with regard to the natural and not providential alteration of the globe," when he says:

> O Heaven! that one might read the book of fate
> And see the revolution of the times;
> Make mountains level, and the continent
> (Weary of solid firmness) melt itself
> Into the sea! and other times to see
> The beachy girdle of the ocean,
> Too wide for Neptune's hips; how chances, mocks
> And changes fill the cup of alteration
> With divers liquors.[3]

Birch adds:

When he returns to politics, and makes them a consequence, as it were, of the preceding philosophical reflections, we do not see the connection, except in that *materialistic* view of things, and *necessitarian way of thinking*, in which Shakespeare frequently indulges, and which involved all alike, physical and human effects, *in the causes and operations of nature*. We either see the unavoidable tendency of Shakespeare's mind to drag in some of his own thoughts at the expense of situation or probability, or we must admit them so mixed up in his philosophy as not to be divided.[4]

We find the man of Stratford (if we are to believe he wrote the Plays), while failing to teach his daughter to read and write, urging that the *sciences* should be taught in England!

> Even so our houses, and ourselves, and children,
> Have lost, or do not learn, for want of time,
> The *sciences* that should become our country.[5]

We see the natural philosopher also in Shakespeare's reflections in *Measure for Measure:*

> Thou art not thyself;
> For thou exist'st on many a thousand grains
> That issue out of dust.[6]

---

[1] *Thoughts on the Nature of Things.*
[2] *Novum Organum*, book ii.
[3] *Henry IV.*, iii, 1.
[4] Birch, *Philosophy and Religion of Shak.*, p. 249.
[5] *Henry V.*, v, 2.
[6] Act iii, scene 1.

Here we find the same mind, that traced the transmutations of the dust of Alexander and Cæsar, following, in reverse order, the path of matter from the inorganic dust into the organic plant, thence into fruit or grain, thence into the body, blood and brain of man. Man is not himself; he is simply a congeries of atoms, brought together by a power beyond himself.

And Shakespeare says:

It is as easy to count atomies as to resolve the propositions of a lover.[1]

The natural philosopher is shown also in that wise and merciful reflection:

> For the poor beetle that we tread upon
> In corporal sufferance finds as great a pang
> As when a giant dies.[2]

And we turn to Bacon, and we find him indulging in a similar thought:

But all violence to the organization of animals is accompanied with a sense of pain, according to their different kinds and peculiar natures, owing to that sentient essence which pervades their frames.[3]

Observe the careful student of nature also in this:

> Many for many virtues excellent,
> None but for some, and yet all different.
> O, mickle is the powerful grace that lies
> In herbs, plants, stones and their true qualities:
> For naught so vile that on the earth doth live,
> But to the earth some special good doth give;
> Nor aught so good, but, strained from that fair use,
> Revolts from true birth, stumbling on abuse.[4]

Here, again, we see the Baconian idea that the humble things of earth, even the vilest, have their noble purposes and uses.

And the same study of plants is found in the following:

> Checks and disasters
> Grow in the veins of actions highest reared;
> As knots, by the conflux of meeting sap,
> Infect the sound pine, and divert his grain
> Tortive and errant from his course and growth.[5]

And in the very direction of Bacon's curious investigations into life is this reference to the common belief of the time, that a horse-hair, left in the water, turns into a living thing:

---

[1] *As You Like It*, iii, 2.
[2] *Measure for Measure*, iii, 1.
[3] *The Nature of Things.*
[4] *Romeo and Juliet*, ii, 3.
[5] *Troilus and Cressida*, i, 3.

> Much is breeding
> Which, like the courser's hair, hath yet but life,
> And not a serpent's poison.[1]

It has even been noted by others that in that famous description of the hair, "standing on end like quills upon the fretful porcupine," the writer hints at the fact that the quills of that animal are really modified hairs.[2]

And when Lady Macbeth says:

> I know
> How tender 'tis to love the babe that milks me:
> I would, while it was smiling in my face,
> Have plucked my nipple from his *boneless* gums
> And dashed the brains out, had I so sworn,
> As you have done to this[3]—

we perceive that the writer had thought it out that the teeth are but modified bones.

The student of natural phenomena is also shown in these sentences:

> Poor soul, the center of my sinful earth.[4]

> Can I go forward when my heart is here?
> Turn back, dull earth, and find thy center out![5]

> I will find
> Where truth is hid, though it were hid, indeed,
> Within the center.[6]

While Bacon, seeming to anticipate the Newtonian speculations, says:

Heavy and ponderous bodies tend toward the center of the earth by their peculiar formation. . . . Solid bodies are borne toward the center of the earth.[7]

And here we perceive that the poet and the play-writer had even considered the force of the sun's heat in producing agitations of the atmosphere.

He says:

> Which shipmen do the hurricano call,
> Constringed in mass by the almighty sun.[8]

Bacon observed that

All kind of heat dilates and extends the air, . . . which produces this breeze as the sun goes forward, . . . and thence thunders and lightnings and storms.[9]

---

[1] *Antony and Cleopatra.*
[2] *American Cyclopedia*, vol. viii, p. 384.
[3] *Macbeth*, i, 7.
[4] Sonnet cxlvi.
[5] *Romeo and Juliet*, ii, 1.
[6] *Hamlet*, ii, 2.
[7] *Novum Organum*, book ii.
[8] *Troilus and Cressida*, v, 2.
[9] *Author. of Shak.*, p. 310.

And Judge Holmes calls attention to the following parallel thought in Shakespeare:

> As whence the sun 'gins his reflection,
> Ship-wrecking storms and direful thunders break.[1]

And that all-powerful preponderance of the sun in the affairs of the planet, which modern science has established, was realized by the author of the Plays, when he speaks, in the foregoing, of "the almighty sun," "constringing" the air and producing the hurricane. It is no wonder that Richard Grant White exclaims:

> The entire range of human knowledge must be laid under contribution to illustrate his writings.[2]

And the natural philosopher is shown in the question of Lear (for Shakespeare's lunatics ask many questions that wise men cannot answer):

> Canst tell how an oyster makes his shell?[3]

In his *Natural History*, we find Bacon occupying himself with kindred thoughts. He discusses the casting-off of the shell of the lobster, crab, cra-fish, the snail, the tortoise, etc., and the making of a new shell:

> The cause of the casting of the skin and shell should seem to be the great quantity of matter that is in those creatures that is fit to *make* skin or *shell*.[4]

And again says Lear:

> First let me talk with this philosopher:
> What is the cause of thunder?[5]

And Bacon had considered this question also. He says:

> We see that among the Greeks those who first disclosed the natural *causes of thunder* and storms, to the yet untrained ears of man, were condemned as guilty of impiety towards the gods.[6]

Shakespeare says:

> And do but see his vice;
> 'Tis to his virtue a just equinox,
> The one as long as the other.[7]

In this we have another observation of a natural phenomenon. And here is another:

> Know you not
> The fire, that mounts the liquor till it run o'er,
> In seeming to augment it, wastes it.[8]

---

[1] *Macbeth*, i, 1.
[2] *Shak. Genius*, p. 252.
[3] *Lear*, i, 5.
[4] *Century* viii, § 732.
[5] *Lear*, iii, 4.
[6] *Novum Organum*, book i.
[7] *Othello*, ii, 3.
[8] *Henry VIII.*, i, 1

The poet had also studied the causes of malaria. He says:

> All the infections that the sun sucks up
> From bogs, fens, flats, on Prosper fall, and make him
> By inch-meal a disease.[1]

And again:
> Infect her beauty,
> Yon fen-sucked fogs, drawn by the powerful sun,
> To fall and blast her pride.[2]

And in the following the natural philosopher is clearly apparent:

> The sun's a thief, and with his great attraction
> Robs the vast sea; the moon's an arrant thief,
> And her pale fire she snatches from the sun.
> The sea's a thief, whose liquid surge resolves
> The moon into salt tears; the earth's a thief
> That feeds and breeds by a composture stolen
> From general excrement.[3]

I shall hereafter show, in the chapter on "Identical Comparisons," that both Bacon and Shakespeare compared man to a species of deputy God, a lesser Providence, with a power over nature that approximated in kind, but not in degree, to the creative power of the Almighty. He says in one place:

For in things artificial nature takes orders from man and works under his authority; without man such things would never have been made. But by the help and ministry of man a new force of bodies, another universe, or theater of things, comes into view.

And in Shakespeare we have the following kindred reflections:

> *Perdita.*   For I have heard it said,
> There is an art which, in their piedness, shares
> With great creating nature.
>
> *Pol.*   Say there be;
> Yet nature is made better by no mean,
> But nature makes that mean; so o'er that art
> Which you say adds to nature, is an art
> That nature makes. You see, sweet maid, we marry
> A gentler scion to the wildest stock,
> And make conceive a bark of baser kind
> By bud of nobler race: this is an art
> Which does mend nature, change it rather, but
> The art itself is nature.[4]

---

[1] *Tempest*, ii, 2.   [2] *Lear*, ii, 4.   [3] *Titus Andronicus*, iv, 3.   [4] *Winter's Tale*, iv, 3.

And again:

> 'Tis often seen
> Adoption strives with nature; and choice breeds
> A native slip to us from foreign seeds.[1]

And we have a glimpse in the following of the doctrine that nature abhors a vacuum.

> The air, which, *but for vacancy*,
> Had gone to gaze on Cleopatra, too,
> And made a gap in nature.[2]

And here we find them, again, thinking the same thought, based on the same observation. Bacon says:

As for the inequality of the pressure of the parts, it appeareth manifestly in this, that if you take a body of stone or iron, and another of wood, of the same magnitude and shape, and throw them with equal force, you cannot possibly throw the wood so far as the stone or the iron.[3]

And we find the same thought in Shakespeare:

> The thing that's heavy in itself,
> Upon enforcement flies with greatest speed.[4]

And here is a remarkable parallelism. Shakespeare says:

> There lives within the very flame of love
> A kind of wick, or snuff, that will abate it.[5]

Bacon says:

Take an arrow and hold it in flame for the space of ten pulses, and when it cometh forth you shall find those parts of the arrow which were on the outside of the flame more burned, blackened, and turned almost to a coal, whereas that in the midst of the flame will be as if the fire had scarce touched it. This . . . showeth manifestly that flame burneth more violently towards the sides than in the midst.[6]

And here is another equally striking. Bacon says:

Besides snow hath in it a secret warmth; as the monk proved out of the text "*Qui dat nivem sicut lanam, gelu sicut cineres spargit.*" Whereby he did infer that snow did warm like wool, and frost did fret like ashes.[7]

Shakespeare says:

> Since frost itself as actively doth burn.[8]

Bacon anticipated the discovery of the power of one mind over another which we call mesmerism; and we find in Shakespeare Ariel saying to the shipwrecked men:

> If you could hurt,
> Your swords are now too massy for your strengths,
> And *will not be uplifted.*[9]

---

[1] *All's Well that Ends Well*, i, 3.
[2] *Antony and Cleopatra*, ii, 2.
[3] *Natural History*, § 791.
[4] *2d Henry IV.*, i, 1.
[5] *Hamlet*, iv, 7.
[6] *Natural History*, § 32.
[7] *Natural History*, § 788.
[8] *Hamlet*, iii, 4.
[9] *Tempest*, iii, 3.

I conclude this chapter with the following citations, each of which shows the profound natural philosopher:

> That man, how dearly ever parted,
> How much in having, or without or in,
> Cannot make boast to have that which he hath,
> Nor feels not what he owes, but by reflection;
> As when his virtues *shining upon others*
> *Heat them, and they retort that heat again*
> *To the first giver.*[1]

Again:

> The beauty that is borne here in the face,
> The bearer knows not, but commends itself
> To others' eyes; nor doth the eye itself,
> That most pure spirit of sense, behold itself,
> Not going from itself.[2]

Again:

> No man is the lord of any thing,
> Though in and of him there be much consisting,
> Till he communicate his parts to others.[3]

Again:

> Heaven doth with us as we with torches do,
> Not light them for ourselves; for if our virtues
> Did not go forth of us, 'twere all alike
> As if we had them not. Spirits are not finely touched
> But to fine issues, nor Nature never lends
> The smallest scruple of her excellence,
> But, like a thrifty goddess, she determines
> Herself the glory of a creditor,
> Both thanks and use.[4]

[1] *Troilus and Cressida*, iii, 3. [2] Ibid. [3] Ibid. [4] *Measure for Measure*, i, 1

GORHAMBURY.

1. A. D. 1821.   2. A. D. 1795.   3. A. D. 1568.

CHAPTER III.

THE GEOGRAPHY OF THE PLAYS.

Dear earth! I do salute thee with my hand.
Richard II., iii, 2.

GENIUS, though its branches reach to the heavens and cover the continents, yet has its roots in the earth; and its leaves, its fruit, its flowers, its texture and its fibers, bespeak the soil in which it was nurtured. Hence in the writings of every great master we find more or less association with the scenes in which his youth and manhood were passed — reflections, as it were, on the camera of the imagination of those landscapes with which destiny had surrounded him.

In the work of the peasant-poet, Robert Burns, we cannot separate his writings from the localities in which he lived. Take away

> "Bonnie Doon;"
> "Auld Alloway's witch-haunted kirk;"
> "Ye banks and braes and streams around,
> The castle of Montgomery;"
> "Auld Ayr, which ne er a town surpasses
> For honest men and bonny lasses;"
> "Sweet Afton,
> Atuld its green braes,"

and the thousand and one other references to localities with which his life was associated, and there is very little left which bears the impress of his genius.

If we turn to Byron, we find the same thing to be true. We have his "Elegy on Newstead Abbey;" his poem "On Leaving Newstead Abbey;" his lines on "Lachin y Gair" in the Highlands, where "my footsteps in infancy wandered;" his verses upon "Movren of Snow;" his "Lines written beneath an Elm in the Churchyard of Harrow on the Hill;" his verses "On Revisiting Harrow," and his poem addressed "To an Oak at Newstead;" while "Childe Harold" is full of allusions to scenes with which his life-history was associated.

I. Stratford-on-Avon is not Named in the Plays.

The same is true, to a greater or less extent, of all great writers who deal with the emotions of the human heart.

In view of these things it will scarcely be believed that in all the voluminous writings of Shakespeare there is not a single allusion to Stratford, or to the river Avon. His failure to remember the dirty little town of his birth might be excused, but it would seem most natural that in some place, in some way, in drama or sonnet or fugitive poem, he should remember the beautiful and romantic river, along whose banks he had wandered so often in his youth, and whose natural beauties must have entered deeply into his soul, if he was indeed the poet who wrote the Plays. He does, it is true, refer to Stony-Stratford,[1] a village in the County of Bucks, and this makes the omission of his own Stratford of Warwickshire the more surprising.

II. St. Albans Referred to Many Times.

On the other hand, we find repeated references to St. Albans, Bacon's home, a village of not much more consequence, so far as numbers were concerned, than Stratford.

Falstaff says:

There's but a shirt and a half in all my company; . . . and the shirt, to say the truth, stolen from my host of *Saint Albans*.[2]

In the *2d Henry IV.* we have this reference:

Prince Henry. This Doll Tear-sheet should be some road.
Poins. I warrant you, as common as the road between *Saint Albans* and London.[3]

In *The Contention between the Two Famous Houses of York and Lancaster*, which is conceded to be the original form of some of the Shakespeare Plays, we have:

> For now the King is riding to *Saint Albans*.[4]

> My lord, I pray you let me go post unto the King,
> Unto *Saint Albans*, to tell this news.[5]

> Come, uncle Gloster, now let's have our horse,
> For we will to *Saint Albans* presently.[6]

In the same scene (in *The Contention*), of the miracle at *Saint Albans*:

---

[1] *Richard III.*, ii, 4.
[2] *1st Henry IV.*, iv, 3.
[3] *2d Henry IV.*, ii, 2.
[4] *1st Part of Contention*, i, 2.
[5] *Ibid.*, ii, 3.
[6] *Ibid.*

> Come, my lords, this night we'll lodge in *Saint Albans*¹

In the play of *Richard III.* we have this allusion to Bacon's country seat:

> Was not your husband
> In Margaret's battle at *Saint Albans* slain?²

We have numerous references to St. Albans in the *2d Henry VI*.

> *Messenger.* My Lord Protector, 'tis his Highness' pleasure
> You do prepare to ride unto *Saint Albans*.³

And again:

> *Duchess.* It is enough; I'll think upon the questions
> When from *Saint Albans* we do make return.⁴

And again:

> *York.* The King is now in progress toward *Saint Albans*.⁵

III. THREE SCENES IN THE PLAYS LAID AT ST. ALBANS

Scene 1, act ii, *2d Henry VI.*, *is laid at Saint Albans*; scene 2 act v, of the same is *also laid at Saint Albans*; scene 3, act v, is laid in *Fields, near Saint Albans*.

Note the following:

> Forsooth, a blind man at *Saint Alban's* shrine,
> Within this half-hour hath received his sight.⁶

Again

> Enter the Mayor of *Saint Albans*.

Again.

> Being called
> A hundred times an oftener, in my sleep
> By good *Saint Alban*.⁷

Again:

Glos. Yet thou seest not well.
Simpcox. Yes, master, clear as day; I thank God and *Saint Alban*.⁸

Again:

Gloster. My lord, *Saint Alban* here hath done a miracle.⁹

Gloster. My masters of *Saint Albans*, have you not beadles in your town?¹⁰

And again:

> For underneath an alehouse' paltry sign,
> The castle in *Saint Albans*, Somerset
> Hath made the wizard famous in his death.¹¹

---

¹ *1st Contention*, ii, 1.   ⁴ *2d Henry VI.*, i, 2.   ⁷ Ibid., ii, 1.   ¹⁰ Ibid., ii, 1
² *Richard III.*, i, 3.   ⁵ Ibid., i, 3.   ⁸ Ibid., ii, 1.   ¹¹ *2d Henry VI.*, v
³ *2d Henry VI.*, i, 2.   ⁶ Ibid., ii, 1.   ⁹ Ibid., ii, 1.

> Now by my hand, lords, 'twas a glorious day,
> *Saint Albans'* battle, won by famous York,
> Shall be eternized in all age to come.[1]

In the *3d Henry VI.* we find St. Albans referred to as follows:

> Marched toward *Saint Albans* to intercept the Queen.[2]

Again:

> Short tale to make — we at *Saint Albans* met.[3]

Again:

> When you and I met at *Saint Albans* last.[4]

Again:

> Brother of Gloster, at *Saint Albans'* field
> This lady's husband, Sir John Grey, was slain.[5]

Here is St. Albans referred to in the Shakespeare Plays twenty-three times, and Stratford not once!

Is not this extraordinary? What tie connected the Stratford man with the little village of Hertfordshire, that he should drag it into his writings so often?

We are told that he loved the village of Stratford, and returned, when rich and famous, to end his days there. We have glowing pictures, in the books of the enthusiastic commentators, of his wanderings along the banks of the lovely Avon. Why did he utterly blot them both out of his writings?

IV. WARWICKSHIRE IGNORED IN THE PLAYS.

But he ignored the county of Warwickshire — his own beautiful county of Warwickshire — in like fashion.

Michael Drayton, poet and dramatist, a contemporary of Shakspere, was, like him, born in Warwickshire, but he did not forget his native shire. He thus invocates the place of his birth:

> My native country, then, which so brave spirits hath bred,
> If there be virtues yet remaining in thy earth,
> Or any good of thine thou bred'st into my birth,
> Accept it as thine own, whilst now I sing of thee,
> Of all thy later brood th' unworthiest though I be.

The county of Warwickshire is only referred to once in the Plays (*1st Henry IV.*, iv, 2), and "the lord of Warwickshire" is mentioned twice. The only reference that I know of to localities in Warwickshire is in the introduction to *The Taming of the Shrew*, where *Wincot* is named. It is assumed that this is Wilmecote, three

---

[1] *3d Henry VI.*, v, 2. [2] *3d Henry VI.*, ii, 1. [3] Ibid. [4] Ibid., ii, 2. [5] Ibid., iii, 3.

miles distant from Stratford-on-Avon. But of this there is no certainty.

There is a Woncot mentioned in *2d Henry IV.*—

> William Visor of Woncott;[1]—

and so eager have the Shakspereans been to sustain the Warwickshire origin of the Plays that they have converted this into *Wincot*. As, however, Master Robert Shallow, Esquire, dwelt in Gloucestershire—

> [Ile through Gloucestershire, and there will I visit Master Robert Shallow Esquire,]—

and William Visor was one of his tenants or underlings, this Woncot could not have been Wincot, near Stratford, in Warwickshire.

V. St. Albans the Central Point of the Historical Plays.

Mrs. Pott has pointed out how much of the action of the Shakespeare Plays finds its turning-point and center in St. Albans:

> To any one who sees in it one of the inciting causes for the composition of the historical plays called Shakespeare's, and especially the second part of *Henry VI.* and *Richard III.*, St. Albans and its neighborhood are in the highest degree suggestive and instructive. Gorhambury was one of the boyish homes of Francis Bacon. When, at the age of nineteen, he was recalled from his gay life at the court of the French embassador on account of the sudden death of his father, it was to Gorhambury that he retired with his widowed mother. Thus he found himself on the very scene of the main events which form the plot of the second part of *Henry VI.* . . . The play culminates in the great battle of St. Albans, which took place in a field about one and a half miles from Gorhambury. As a boy, Francis must have heard the battle described by old men whose fathers may even have witnessed it. He must frequently have passed "the alehouse' paltry sign" beneath which Somerset was killed by Richard Plantagenet (*2d Henry VI.*, v, 2). He must have trodden the Key Field where the battle was fought, and in which the last scene of the play is laid. It was a scene not likely to be forgotten. The Lancastrians lost five thousand men, including the detested Duke of Somerset and other nobles, and the poor, weak King, Henry VI., was taken prisoner by the Yorkists. Considering the mildness and moderation which was invariably exercised by the Duke of York, and the violent and bloodthirsty course pursued by Queen Margaret, it is no wonder that this, the first Yorkist victory of the Wars of the Roses, should be kept green on the spot where it took place.
>
> > 'Twas a glorious day.
> > Saint Albans' battle, won by famous York,
> > Shall be eternis'd in all age to come.
>
> Before entering the abbey, let the visitor glance around. To the north of the town stands the old church of St. Peter, and in its graveyard lie the bodies of many of those who were slain in the great battles between the rival houses of York and Lancaster. To the left is Bernard's heath, the scene of the second battle of St.

---
[1] Act v, scene 1.

Albans, where the Yorkist army was defeated, as related in *3d Henry VI.*, ii, 1. In the distance may be seen Hatfield house, the noble residence of the Marquis of Salisbury, but formerly the property of William of Hatfield, second son of Edward III. (*2d Henry VI.*, ii, 2). Within a short distance is King's Langley, the birthplace and burial place of the "famous Edmund Langley, Duke of York" (*1st Henry VI.*, ii, 5), and, as we are further told, "fifth son" of Edward III. (*2d Henry VI.*, ii, 2). On the east of the town lay Key Field, the arena of the first battle of St. Albans. Across it may be seen the ancient manor-house, formerly inhabited by Humphrey, Duke of Gloucester. To the right is Sopwell nunnery, where Henry VIII. married Anne Boleyn. The history of the monastery to which the abbey was attached is intimately associated with English history. To go back no farther than the fourteenth century, there Edward I. held his court; there Edward II. was a frequent visitor; thither, after the battle of Poictiers, Edward III. and the Black Prince brought the French King captive. After the insurrection of Wat Tyler and Jack Straw, Richard II. and his Chief Justice came in person and tried the rioters. A conspiracy to dethrone Richard began at the dinner table of the Abbot, when Gloucester and the Prior of Westminster were his guests. This Gloucester was "Thomas of Woodstock," described in *2d Henry VI.*, ii, 2, as "the sixth son of Edward the Third." At a subsequent meeting of members of the conspiracy, the Duke of Gloucester, "Henry of Hereford, Lancaster and Derby" (*Richard II.*, i, 3), the Earl Marshal (ibid.), Scroop, Archbishop of Canterbury (*Richard II.*, iii, 2), the Abbot of St. Albans and the Prior of Westminster (*Richard II.*, iv, 1) were present, and the perpetual imprisonment of the King was agreed upon. In the play of *Richard II.* every name mentioned in the old manuscript which records this meeting is included, except one — namely, the Abbot of St. Albans; and yet in the old records priority over Westminster is always given to him. It is conjectured that the omission was intentional, and that the author did not wish by frequent repetition to give prominence to a name which would draw attention to the neighborhood of his own home. At the monastery of St. Albans rested the body of John, Duke of Lancaster (*1st Henry IV.*, vol. 4), on the way to London for interment. His son Henry, afterward Cardinal Beaufort (*1st Henry VI.*, i, 3, etc.), performed the exequies. Richard II. lodged at St. Albans on his way to the Tower, whence, having been forced to resign his throne to Bolingbroke, he was taken to Pomfret, imprisoned and murdered. Meanwhile, the resignation of the King being read in the House, the Bishop of Carlisle arose from his seat and stoutly defended the cause of the King. Upon this the Duke of Lancaster commanded that they should seize the Bishop and carry him off to prison at St. Albans. He was afterward brought before Parliament as a prisoner, but the King, to gratify the pontiff, bestowed on him the living of Tottenham. These events are faithfully rendered or alluded to in the Plays, the only notable omission being, as before, any single allusion to the Abbot of St. Albans (See *Richard II.*, vol. vi, 22–29).

Passing over many similar points of interest, let us enter the Abbey church by its door on the south side. There the visitor finds himself close to the shrine erected over the bones of the martyred saint. To this shrine, after the defeat of the Lancastrians, at the first battle of St. Albans, the miserable King, having been discovered at the house of a tanner, was conducted, previous to his removal as a prisoner to London. In the shrine is seen the niche in which handkerchiefs and other garments used to be put, in order that the miraculous powers attributed to the saint should be imparted to the sick and diseased who prayed at his shrine, and thereby hangs a tale. Close by the shrine is the tomb of good Duke Humphrey of Gloucester, who plays such a prominent part in *Henry VI.* The inscription on his tomb is not such as most persons might expect to find as an epitaph on the proud and pugnacious, but popular warrior. No hint is conveyed of his struggles with the Duke of Burgundy, or of his warlike contests for the possession of Holland and Brabant. Three points are noted concerning him: That he was protector to Henry VI.; that he "exposed the impostor who pretended to have been born blind," and that he founded a school of divinity at Oxford. The story of the pretended blind man is the subject of *2d Henry VI.*, ii, 8, where it is introduced with much detail. Sir Thomas More quoted the incident as an instance of Duke Humphrey's acuteness of judgment, but the circumstance which seems to connect the epitaph not only with the play, but with Francis Bacon himself, is that it was not written immediately after the death of the Duke, but tardily, as the inscription hints, and it is believed to be the composition of John Westerham, head-master of the St. Albans grammar school in 1625 — namely, during the lifetime of Bacon, and at a date when Gorhambury was his residence. A phrase in the inscription applies to Margaret of Anjou, Henry's "proud, insulting queen," whose tomb, with her device of "Marguerites," or daisies, is not far from the shrine of St. Alban. It was by the intrigues of Margaret and her partisans that Duke Humphrey was arrested at Bury. The following night he was found dead in his bed — slain, as some old writers record, by the hand of Pole, Duke of Suffolk. (*2d Henry VI.*, iii, 1; 223-281, ii, 1, 1-202.) Not far from these tombs are two more of peculiar interest to students of Shakespeare. One is the resting-place of Sir Anthony de Grey, grandson of Henry Percy, Earl of Northumberland. The inscription says that he married "the fourth sister to our sovraine lady, the queen;" that is, Elizabeth Woodville, queen of Edward IV. She had been formerly married.

> At St. Albans' field
> This lady's husband, Sir John Grey, was slain,
> His lands then seized on by the conqueror.[1]

Her suit to Edward to restore her confiscated property, and her subsequent marriage with him, form a prominent portion of the plot of the third part of *Henry VI*.

Last, but not least, let us not overlook the mausoleum of "the Nevils' noble race," the family of the great Earl of Warwick, the "king-maker." In *2d Henry IV.*, v, 2, Warwick swears by his

> Father's badge, old Nevil's crest,
> The rampant bear chained to the ragged staff.

The passage is vividly brought to the mind by the sight of a row of rampant bears, each chained to his ragged staff, and surmounting the monument erected over the grave of that great family of warriors.

In fact, St. Albans seems to be the very center from which the eye surveys, circling around it, the grand panorama of the historical Plays; while far away to the north lies the dirty little village of Stratford-on-Avon, holding not the slightest relation with anything in those Plays, save the one fact that the man who is said to have written them dwelt there.

[1] *3d Henry VI.*, iii, 2.

VI. York Place.

There was one other spot in England tenderly associated in Bacon's heart with loving memories; that was the royal palace of "York Place," in London, in which he was born. In the day of his success he purchased it, and it was at last, after his downfall, torn from his reluctant grasp by the base Buckingham. Bacon says of it:

> York House is the house wherein my father died, and where I first breathed, and there will I yield my last breath, if so please God.[1]

We turn to the play of *Henry VIII.*, and we find York Place *depicted as the scene where Cardinal Wolsey entertains the King and his companions*, masked as shepherds, with "good company, good wine, good welcome."

And farther on in the play we find it again referred to, and something of its history given:

> *3d Gentleman.*   So she parted,
> And with the same full state paced back again
> To *Yorke-Place*, where the feast is held.
> *1st Gentleman.* You must no more call it *Yorke-Place*, that's past;
> For since the Cardinal fell that title's lost;
> 'Tis now the King's, and called White-hall.
> *3d Gentleman.*   I know it;
> But 'tis so lately altered, that the old name
> Is fresh about me.[2]

How lovingly the author of the Plays dwells on the history of the place!

VII. Kent.

Bacon's father was born in Chislehurst; and we find many touches in the Plays which show that the writer, while he had not one good word to say for Warwickshire, turned lovingly to Kent and her people. He makes the double-dealing Say remark:

> *Say.* You men of Kent.
> *Dick.* What say you, Kent?
> *Say.* Nothing but this: 'tis *bona terra, mala gens.* . . .
> Kent, in the Commentaries Cæsar writ,
> Is termed the civil'st place of all this isle:
> Sweet is the country, because full of riches;
> The people liberal, valiant, active, wealthy.[3]

---

[1] Letter to the Duke of Lenox, 1621.   [2] *Henry VIII.*, iv, 1.   [3] *2d Henry VI.*, iv, 7.

What made the Warwickshire man forget his own county and remember Cæsar's praise of Kent? What tie bound William Shakspere to Kent?

And again, in another play, he comes back to this theme:

> The Kentishmen will willingly rise.
> In them I trust: for they are soldiers,
> Witty, courteous, liberal, full of spirit.[1]

The first scene of act iv of *2d Henry VI.* is laid upon the sea-shore of Kent.

It is in Kent that much of the scene of the play of *King Lear* is laid. Here we have that famous cliff of Dover, to the brow of which Edgar leads Gloucester:

> Come on, sir:
> Here's the place; stand still: how fearful
> And dizzy 'tis to cast one's eyes so low.
> The crows and choughs that wing the midway air
> Shew scarce so gross as beetles. Half way down
> Hangs one that gathers samphire: dreadful trade:
> Methinks he seems no bigger than his head.
> The fishermen that walked upon the beach
> Appear like mice: and yon tall anchoring bark
> Diminished to her cocke; her cocke a buoy
> Almost too small for sight.

"Jack Cade, the clothier," who proposed to dress the commonwealth and put new nap upon it, was a Kentishman. The insurrection was a Kentish outbreak. The play of *2d Henry VI.* largely turns upon this famous rebellion.

Many of the towns of Kent are referred to in the Plays, and Goodwin Sands appears even in the Italian play of *The Merchant of Venice*, as the scene of the loss of one of Antonio's ships.

VIII. THE WRITER OF THE PLAYS HAD VISITED SCOTLAND.

There is some reason to believe that the author of *Macbeth* visited Scotland. The chronicler Holinshead narrates that Macbeth and Banquo, before they met the witches, "went sporting by the way together without other company, passing through the woods and fields, when suddenly, in the midst of a laund, there met them three women in strange and wild apparel." "This description," says Knight, "presents to us the idea of a pleasant and

---

[1] *2d Henry VI.*, i, 3.

fertile place." But the poet makes the meeting with the witches "on the blasted heath." Knight tells us that "the country around Forres is wild moorland. . . . We thus see that, whether Macbeth met the weird sisters to the east or west of Forres, there was in each place that desolation which was best fitted for such an event, and not the woods and fields and launds of the chronicler."

This departure from Holinshead's narrative would strongly indicate that the poet had actually visited the scene of the play.

Again, it is claimed that the disposal of the portal "at the south entry" of the castle of Inverness is strictly in accordance with the facts, and could not have been derived from the chronicle. Even the pronunciation of Dunsináne, with the accent on the last syllable, is shown to have been in accordance with the custom of the peasantry.

Macbeth was evidently written after the accession of James I., and we find that Bacon paid a visit to King James before he came to London and probably while he was still in Scotland. In Spedding's *Life and Letters*[1] we find a letter from Bacon to the Earl of Northumberland, without date, referring to this visit. Spedding says:

> Meanwhile the news which Bacon received from his friends in the *Scotch court* appears to have been favorable: sufficiently so, at least, to encourage him to seek a personal interview with the King. I cannot find the exact date, but it will be seen from the next letter that, before the King arrived in London, he had gone to meet him, carrying a dispatch from the Earl of Northumberland; and that he had been admitted to his presence.

The letter speaks as follows:

It may please your good Lordship:
> I would not have lost this journey, and yet I have not that for which I went. For I have had no private conference to any purpose with the King; and no more hath almost any other English. For the speech his Majesty admitteth with some noblemen is rather matter of grace than of business. With the attorney he spake, being urged by the Treasurer of Scotland, but yet no more than needs must. . . .

I would infer that this interview was held in Scotland. The fact that the Treasurer of Scotland was present and that the English could not obtain private audience with the King would indicate this.

[1] Volume iii, p. 76.

IX. THE WRITER OF THE PLAYS HAD BEEN IN ITALY.

There are many reasons to believe that the writer of the Plays had visited Italy. In a note upon the passage,

> Unto the tranect to the common ferry
> Which trades to Venice,[1]

Knight remarks:

> If Shakspere had been at Venice (which, from the extraordinary keeping of the play, appears the most natural supposition), he must surely have had some situation in his eye for Belmont. There is a common ferry at two places — Fusina and Mestre.

In the same play the poet says:

> This night methinks is but the daylight sick.
> It looks a little paler; 'tis a day
> Such as the day is when the sun is hid.[2]

Whereupon Knight says:

> The light of the moon and stars (in Italy) is almost as yellow as the sunlight in England. . . . Two hours after sunset, on the night of a new moon, we have seen so far over the lagunes that the night seemed only a paler day — "a little paler."

Mr. Brown, the author of *Shakespeare's Autobiographical Plays*, strenuously maintained the opinion that Shakespeare must have visited Italy:

> His descriptions of Italian scenes and manners are more minute and accurate than if he had derived his information wholly from books.

Mr. Knight, speaking of *The Taming of the Shrew*, says:

> It is difficult for those who have explored the city [of Padua] to resist the persuasion that the poet himself had been one of the travelers who had come from afar to look upon its seats of learning, if not to partake of its "ingenious studies." There is a pure Paduan atmosphere hanging about this play.

Bacon, it is known, visited France, and it is believed he traveled in Italy.

X. THE WRITER OF THE PLAYS HAD BEEN AT SEA.

One other point, and I pass from this branch of the subject.
Richard Grant White says:

> Of all negative facts in regard to his life, none, perhaps, is surer than that *he never was at sea;* yet in *Henry VIII.*, describing the outburst of admiration and loyalty of the multitude at sight of Anne Bullen, he says, as if he had spent his life on shipboard:
>
> > Such a noise arose
> > As the shrouds make at sea in a stiff tempest;
> > As loud, and to as many tunes.[3]

---

[1] *Merchant of Venice*, iii, 4. [2] Act v, scene 1. [3] *Life and Genius of Shakespeare*, p. 259.

More than this, we are told that this man, who had never been at sea, wrote the play of *The Tempest*, which contains a very accurate description of the management of a vessel in a storm.

The second Lord Mulgrave gives, in Boswell's edition, a communication showing that

> Shakespeare's technical knowledge of seamanship must have been the result of the most accurate personal observation, or, what is perhaps more difficult, of the power of combining and applying the information derived from others.

But no books had then been published on the subject. Dr. Johnson says:

> His naval dialogue is, perhaps, the first example of sailor's language exhibited on the stage.

Lord Mulgrave continues:

> The succession of events is strictly observed in the natural progress of the distress described; the expedients adopted are the most proper that could be devised for a chance of safety. . . . The words of command are strictly proper. . . . He has shown a knowledge of the new improvements, as well as the doubtful points of seamanship.

Capt. Glascock, R. N., says:

> The Boatswain, in *The Tempest*, delivers himself in the true vernacular of the forecastle.

All this would, indeed, be most extraordinary in a man who had never been at sea. Bacon, on the other hand, we know to have made two voyages to France; we know how close and accurate were his powers of observation; and in *The Natural History of the Winds*[1] he gives, at great length, a description of the masts and sails of a vessel, with the dimensions of each sail, the mode of handling them, and the necessary measures to be taken in a storm.

XI. Conclusions.

It seems, then, to my mind, most clear, that there is not a single passage in the Plays which unquestionably points to any locality associated with the life of the man of Stratford, while, on the other hand, there are numerous allusions to scenes identified with the biography of Bacon; and, more than this, that the place of Bacon's birth and the place of his residence are both made the subjects of scenes in the Plays, and nearly all the historical Plays turn about St. Albans as a common center.

The geography of the Plays would all indicate that Francis Bacon wrote them.

[1] Section 29.

CHAPTER IV.

THE POLITICS OF THE PLAYS.

> I love the people,
> But do not like to stage me to their eyes;
> Though it do well, I do not relish well
> Their loud applause, and *aves* vehement,
> Nor do I think the man of safe discretion
> That does affect it.
> *Measure for Measure*, I, I.

WE know what ought to have been the politics of William Shakspere, of Stratford

He came of generations of peasants; he belonged to the class which was at the bottom of the social scale. If he were a true man, with a burning love of justice, he would have sympathized with his kind. Like Burns, he would have poured forth his soul in protests against the inequalities and injustice of society; he would have asserted the great doctrine of the brotherhood of man; he would have anticipated that noble utterance:

> The rank is but the guinea's stamp,
> The man's the gold for a' that.

If he painted, as the writer of the Plays did, an insurrection of the peasants, *of his own class*, he would have set forth their cause in the most attractive light, instead of burlesquing them. Such a genius as is revealed in the Plays, if he really came from the common people and was filled with their spirit, would have prefigured that great social revolution which broke out twenty years after his death, and which brought a king's head to the block. We should have had, on every page, passages breathing love of equality, of liberty; and other passages of the mockery of the aristocracy that would have burned like fire. He would have anticipated Pym, Hampden and Milton.

A man of an ignorant, a low, a base mind may refuse to sympathize with his own caste, because it is oppressed and downtrodden, and put himself in posture of cringe and conciliation to those whose whips descend upon his shoulders; but a really great and noble soul, a really broad and comprehensive mind, never would dissociate himself from his brethren in the hour of their affliction. No nobler soul, no broader mind ever existed than that revealed in the Plays. Do the utterances of the writer of those Plays indicate that he came of the common people? Not at all.

I. The Writer of the Plays was an Aristocrat.

Appleton Morgan says:

He was a constitutional aristocrat who believed in the established order of things, and wasted not a word of all his splendid eulogy upon any human right not in his day already guaranteed by charters or by thrones.

Swinburne says:

With him the people once risen in revolt, for any just or unjust cause, is always the mob, the unwashed rabble, the swinish multitude.[1]

And again:

For the drovers, who guide and misguide at will the turbulent flocks of their mutinous cattle, his store of bitter words is inexhaustible; it is a treasure-house of obloquy which can never be drained dry.[2]

Walt Whitman says:

Shakespeare is incarnated, uncompromising feudalism in literature.[3]

Richard Grant White says:

He always represents the laborer and the artisan in a degraded position, and often makes his ignorance and his uncouthness the butt of ridicule.[4]

Dowden says:

Shakspere is not democratic. When the people are seen in masses in his Plays they are nearly always shown as factious, fickle and irrational.[5]

Walter Bagehot says:

Shakespeare had two predominant feelings in his mind. First, the feeling of loyalty to the ancient polity of this country, not because it was good, but because it existed. The second peculiar tenet is a disbelief in the middle classes. We fear he had no opinion of traders. You will generally find that when "a citizen" is mentioned he does or says something absurd. . . . The author of *Coriolanus* never believed in a mob, *and did something towards preventing anybody else from doing so.*

We turn to Bacon and we find that he entertained precisely the same feelings.

Dean Church says:

Bacon had no sympathy with popular wants and claims; of popularity, of all that was called popular, he had the deepest suspicion and dislike; the opinions and

---

[1] Swinburne, *Study of Shak.*, p. 54.
[2] Ibid., p. 54.
[3] *Democratic Vistas*, p. 81.
[4] White's *Genius of Shak.*, p. 298.
[5] *Shak. Mind and Art*, p. 284.

the judgment of average men he despised, as a thinker, a politician and a courtier; the "malignity of the people" he thought great. "I do not love," he said, "the word *people*." But he had a high idea of what was worthy of a king.

II. HE DESPISED THE CLASS TO WHICH SHAKSPERE BELONGED.

Shakespeare calls the laboring people:

Mechanic slaves.[1]

The fool multitude that choose by show,
Not learning, more than the fond eye doth teach.[2]

The inundation of mistempered humor.[3]

The rude *multitude*.[4]

The multitude of hinds and peasants.[5]

The *base* vulgar.[6]

O *base* and obscure vulgar.[7]

Base peasants.[8]

A habitation giddy and unsure
Hath he that buildeth on the vulgar heart.[9]

A sort of vagabonds, rascals and run-aways,
A scum of Bretagnes, and base lackey peasants.[10]

The blunt monster with uncounted heads,
The still discordant, wavering multitude.[11]

We shall see hereafter that nearly every one of the Shakespeare Plays was written to inculcate some special moral argument; to preach a lesson to the people that might advantage them. *Coriolanus* seems to have been written to create a wall and barrier of public opinion against that movement towards popular government which not long after his death plunged England into a long and bloody civil war. The whole argument of the play is the unfitness of a mob to govern a state. Hence all through the play we find such expressions as these:

The plebeian multitude.[12]

You common cry of curs.[13]

The mutable, rank-scented many.[14]

You are they
That made the air unwholesome, when you cast
Your stinking, greasy caps, in hooting at
Coriolanus' exile.[15]

[1] *Antony and Cleopatra*, v, 2.
[2] *Merchant of Venice*, ii, 9.
[3] *King John*, v, 1.
[4] *2d Henry VI.*, iii, 2.
[5] Ibid., iv, 4.
[6] *Love's Labor Lost*, i, 2.
[7] Ibid., iv, 1.
[8] *2d Henry VI.*, iv, 8.
[9] *2d Henry IV.*, i, 3.
[10] *Richard III.*, v, 3.
[11] *2d Henry IV.*, Ind.
[12] *Coriolanus*, ii, 1.
[13] Ibid., iii, 3.
[14] Ibid., iv, 6.
[15] *Coriolanus*, iv, 6.

Again he alludes to the plebeians as "those measles" whose contact would "tetter" him.

III. HE DESPISES TRADESMEN OF ALL KINDS.

But this contempt of the writer of the Plays was not confined to the mob. It extended to all trades-people. He says:

Let me have no lying; it becomes none but tradesmen.[1]

We turn to Bacon, and we find him referring to the common people as a *scum*. The same word is used in Shakespeare. Bacon speaks of

The vulgar, to whom nothing moderate is grateful.[2]

This is the same thought we find in Shakespeare:

> What would you have, you curs,
> That like nor peace nor war?[3]

> Who deserves greatness,
> Deserves your hate; and your affections are
> A sick man's appetite, who desires most that
> Which would increase his evil.[4]

Again Bacon says:

The ignorant and rude multitude.[5]

If fame be from the common people, it is commonly false and naught.[6]

This is very much the thought expressed in Shakespeare:

> The fool multitude that choose by show,
> Not learning, more than the fond eye doth teach.[7]

And also in

> He's loved of the distracted multitude,
> Who like not in their judgments, but their eyes.[8]

Bacon says:

For in all times, in the opinion of the multitude, witches and old women and impostors have had a competition with physicians.[9]

And again he says:

The envious and *malignant* disposition of the vulgar, for when fortune's favorites and great potentates come to ruin, then do the common people rejoice, setting, as it were, a crown upon the head of revenge.[10]

---

[1] *Winter's Tale*, iv, 3.
[2] *Wisdom of the Ancients — Diomedes.*
[3] *Coriolanus*, i, 1.
[4] *Ibid.*, i, 1.
[5] *Wisdom of the Ancients.*
[6] *Essay Of Praise.*
[7] *Merchant of Venice*, ii, 9.
[8] *Hamlet*, iv, 3.
[9] *Advancement of Learning*, book ii.
[10] *Wisdom of the Ancients — Nemesis.*

And again he says:

> The nature of the vulgar, always swollen and *malignant*, still broaching new scandals against superiors; . . . the same natural disposition of the people still leaning to the viler sort, being impatient of peace and tranquillity.[1]

Says Shakespeare:

> That like not peace nor war.[2]

And Bacon says again:

> He would never endure that the *base multitude* should frustrate the authority of Parliament.[3]

See how the same words are employed by both. Bacon says:

> The *base multitude.*

Shakespeare says:

> The rude *multitude*—the *base* vulgar.[4]

And the word *malignant* is a favorite with both. Shakespeare says:

> Thou liest, *malignant* thing!
>
> *Malignant* death.[5]
>
> A *malignant* and turbaned Turk.[6]

Bacon says:

> The envious and *malignant* disposition.
>
> The vulgar always *swollen* and *malignant*.

Shakespeare says:

> The *swollen* surge.[7]
>
> Such *swollen* and hot discourse.[8]

But it must be remembered that Bacon was brought up as an aristocrat—connected by blood with the greatest men of the kingdom; born in a royal palace, York Place; son of Elizabeth's Lord Chancellor. And it must not be forgotten that the populace of London of that day had but lately emerged from barbarism; they were untaught in habits of self-government; worshiping the court, sycophantic to everything above them; unlettered, rude, and barbarous; and were, indeed, very different from the populace of the civilized world to-day. They doubtless deserved much of the unlimited contempt which Bacon showered upon them.

---

[1] *Wisdom of the Ancients.*
[2] *Coriolanus*, i, 1.
[3] *History of Henry VII.*
[4] *Tempest*, i, 2.
[5] *Richard III.*, ii, 2.
[6] *Othello*, v, 2.
[7] *Tempest*, ii, 1.
[8] *Troilus and Cressida*, ii, 3.

IV. HE WAS AT THE SAME TIME A PHILANTHROPIST.

But while the writer of the Plays feared the mob and despised the trades-people, with the inborn contempt of an aristocrat, he had a broad philanthropy which took in the whole human family, and his heart went out with infinite pity to the wretched and the suffering.

Swinburne says:

In *Lear* we have evidence of a sympathy with the mass of social misery more wide and deep and direct and bitter and tender than Shakespeare has shown elsewhere. . . . A poet of revolution he is not, as none of his country in that generation could have been; but as surely as the author of *Julius Cæsar* has approved himself in the best and highest sense of the word at least potentially a republican, so surely has the author of *King Lear* avowed himself, in the only good and rational sense of the word, a spiritual if not a political democrat and socialist.[1]

While Bacon's intellect would have revolted from such a hell-dance of the furies as the French Reign of Terror, whose excesses were not due to anything inherent in self-government, but to the degeneration of mankind, caused by ages of royal despotism; and while he abominated the acrid bigotry of the men of his own age, with whom liberty meant the right to burn those who differed from them: his sympathies were nevertheless upon the side of an orderly, well-regulated, intelligent freedom, and strongly upon the side of everything that would lift man out of his miseries.

Says Swinburne:

Brutus is the very noblest figure of a typical and ideal republican in all the literature of the world.[2]

Bacon was ready to stand up against the whole power of Queen Elizabeth, and, as a member of Parliament, defended the rights of that great body, even to the detriment of his own fortunes; but he did not believe, as he says in his *History of Henry VII.*, that "the base multitude should control Parliament" any more than the Queen. And he gives us the same sentiment in *Coriolanus*. Menenius Agrippa, after telling the incensed Roman populace the fable of *The Belly and the Members*, draws this moral:

> The senators of Rome are this good belly,
> And you the mutinous members. . . .
>   You shall find
> No public benefit which you receive
> But it proceeds, or comes, *from them to you*,
> And no way from yourselves.[3]

---

[1] Swinburne, *A Study of Shak.*, p. 175.   [2] Ibid., p. 159.   [3] *Coriolanus*, i, 1.

And he teaches us an immortal lesson in *Troilus and Cressida:*

> Then everything includes itself in *power*,
> Power into will, will into appetite:
> And appetite, an *universal wolf*.
> So doubly seconded with will and power,
> Must make perforce an universal prey,
> And last, eat up itself.

And in *Hamlet* he says:

> By the Lord, Horatio, these three years I have taken notice of it; the age is grown so picked, that the toe of the peasant comes so near the heel of the courtier that he galls his kibe.[1]

Here we have one of Bacon's premonitions of the coming tempest which so soon broke over England; or, as he expresses it in *Richard III.:*

> Before the days of change, still it is so;
> By a divine instinct, men's minds mistrust
> Ensuing danger; as, by proof, we see
> The water swell before a boisterous storm.[2]

And again:

> And in such indexes, although small pricks
> To their subsequent volumes, there is seen
> The baby figure of the giant mass
> Of things to come at large.[3]

Here, then, was indeed a strange compound:—an aristocrat that despised the mob and the work-people, but who, nevertheless, loved liberty; who admired the free oligarchy of Rome, and hated the plebeians who asked for the same liberty their masters enjoyed; and who, while despising the populace, grieved over their miseries and would have relieved them. We read in *Lear:*

> Take physic, pomp;
> Expose thyself to feel what wretches feel:
> *So may'st thou shake the superflux to them,*
> *And show the heavens more just.*

And again:

> Heavens, deal so still!
> Let the superfluous and lust-dieted man,
> That slaves your ordinance, that will not see
> Because he does not feel, feel your power quickly;
> *So distribution should undo excess,*
> *And each man have enough.*

And we turn to Bacon, and we find that through his whole life the one great controlling thought which directed all his labors was

---

[1] *Hamlet*, v, 1. [2] *Richard III.*, ii, 3. [3] *Troilus and Cressida*, i, 3.

a belief that God had created him to help his fellow-men to greater comfort and happiness.

He says:

Believing that I was born for the service of mankind, and regarding the care of the commonwealth as a kind of common property, which, like the air and water, belongs to everybody, I set myself to consider in what way *mankind might be best served*.[1]

Again he says:

This work, which is for the bettering of men's bread and wine, which are the characters of temporal blessings and sacraments of eternal, I hope, by God's holy providence, may be ripened by Cæsar's star.[2]

Again he says:

The state and bread of the poor and oppressed have been precious in mine eyes: I have hated all cruelty and hardness of heart.[3]

And in one of his prayers he says:

To God the Father, God the Word, God the Holy Ghost, I address my most humble and ardent prayers, that, *mindful of the miseries of man*, and of this pilgrimage of life, of which the days are few and evil, they would open up yet new sources of refreshment from the fountains of good *for the alleviation of our sorrows*[4]

He also says that any man who "kindleth a light in nature," by new thoughts or studies, "seems to me to be a propagator of the empire of man over the universe, *a defender of liberty, a conqueror of necessities.*"[5]

It would be indeed strange if two men in the same age should hold precisely the same political views, with all these peculiar shadings and modifications. It would be indeed strange if the butcher's apprentice of Stratford should be filled with the most aristocratic prejudices against the common people; if the "vassal actor," who was legally a vagabond, and liable to the stocks and to branding and imprisonment, unless he practiced his degraded calling under the shadow of some nobleman's name, should bubble over with contempt for the tradesmen who were socially his superiors. And it would be still stranger if this butcher's apprentice, while cringing to a class he did not belong to, and insulting the class he did belong to, would be so filled with pity for the wretchedness of the many, that he was ready to advocate a redis-

---

[1] Preface to *The Interpretation of Nature*.
[2] Letter to the King.
[3] Prayer while Lord Chancellor.
[4] *The Masculine Birth of Time*.
[5] *The Interpretation of Nature*.

tribution of the goods of the world, so that each man might have enough!

V. THE WRITER OF THE PLAYS BELONGED, LIKE BACON, TO THE ESSEX FACTION.

But we go a step farther. While we find this complete identity between the views of Bacon and the writer of the Plays as to the generalities of political thought, we will see that they both belonged to the same political faction in the state.

It is well known that Bacon was an adherent of the Essex party and opposed to the party of his uncle Burleigh, who had suppressed him all through the reign of Elizabeth. These two factions divided the politics of the latter portion of Elizabeth's reign. The first gathered to itself all the discontented elements of the kingdom, the *young men*, the able, the adventurous, who flocked to Essex as to the cave of Adullam. They were in favor of brilliant courses, of wars, of adventures; as opposed to "the canker of a calm world and a long peace," advocated by the great Lord Treasurer. Bacon was undoubtedly for years the brains of this party.

The writer of the Plays belonged to this party also. He was a member of the Lord Chamberlain's company of actors. The Lord Chamberlain's theater represented the aristocratic side of public questions; the Lord Admiral's company (Henslowe's) the plebeian side: the one was patronized by *the young bloods*, the gallants; the other by the tradesmen and 'prentices. It was a time when, in the words of Simpson,

> The civil and military elements were pleading for precedence at the national bar: the one advocating age and wisdom in council and industry and obedience in the nation; the other crying out for youthful counsel, a dashing policy, a military organization and an offensive war. The one was the party of the Cecils, the other that of the Earl of Essex.[1]

Rümelin argues that

> Shakespeare wrote for the *jeunesse dorée* of the Elizabethan theater, and that he already saw the Royalist and Roundhead parties in process of formation, and was opposed to the Puritan *bourgeoisie*. Shakespeare was a pure Royalist, and an adherent of the purest water to the court party and the nobles.

The relations of Shakespeare to Essex, as manifested in the Plays, were as close as those of Bacon. Simpson says of the play

[1] *School of Shak.*, vol. I, p. 155.

of Sir Thomas Stuckley, which he believes to have been an early work of Shakspere:

> The play is a glorification of Stuckley as an idol of the military or Essex party, *to which Shakspere is known to have leant.* . . . The character of Lord Sycophant, contained therein, is a stinging satire on Essex' (Shakspere's hero and patron) great enemy, Lord Cobham.[1]

Speaking of the Plays which appeared at Shakspere's theater, Simpson says:

> When we regard them as a whole, those of the Lord Chamberlain's company are characterized by common sense, moderation, naturalness, and the absence of bombast, and by a great artistic liberty of form, of matter and of criticism; at the same time they favor *liberty in politics and toleration in religion,* and are consistently *opposed to the Cecilian ideal in policy,* while they as consistently *favor that school to which Essex is attached.*[2]

And it must not be forgotten that these striking admissions are made by one who had not a doubt that Shakspere was Shakespeare.

When we turn to the Plays we find a distinct attempt to glorify Essex. Camden says:

> About the end of March (1599) the Earl of Essex set forward for Ireland, and was accompanied out of London with a fine appearance of nobility and gentry, and the most cheerful huzzas of the common people.

Essex returned to London on the 28th of September of the same year; and in the meantime appeared the play of *Henry V.,* and in the chorus of the fifth act we have these words:

> But now behold,
> In the quick forge and working-house of thought,
> How London doth pour out her citizens!
> The mayor and all his brethren, in best sort —
> Like to the senators of antique Rome,
> With the plebeians swarming at their heels —
> Go forth and fetch their conquering Cæsar in:
> As, by a lower but by loving likelihood,
> Were now the general of our gracious empress,
> (As in good time he may), from Ireland coming,
> Bringing rebellion broachèd on his sword,
> How many would the peaceful city quit
> To welcome him?

The play of *2d Henry IV.* and that of *Henry V.* constitute a deification of military greatness; and the representation of that splendid English victory, Agincourt — the Waterloo of the olden age — was meant to fire the blood of the London audiences with admira-

[1] *School of Shak.,* vol. i, p. 10. [2] *Ibid.,* vol. i, p. 29.

tion for that spirit of military adventure of which Essex was the type and representative.

Neither must it be forgotten that it was Southampton, the bosom friend of Essex, who shared with him in his conspiracy to seize the person of the Queen, and who nearly shared the block with him, remaining in the Tower until after the death of Elizabeth. And it was to Southampton that Shakespeare dedicated *Venus and Adonis* and *The Rape of Lucrece*. Bacon was the intimate friend and correspondent of Southampton; they were both members of the law-school of Gray's Inn, and Shakespeare dedicated his poems to him.

VI. THE WRITER OF THE PLAYS, LIKE BACON, HATED COKE.

If there was any one man whom, above all others, Bacon despised and disliked it was that great but brutal lawyer, Coke. And in the Plays we find a distinct reference to Coke:

Sir Toby. Go write it in a martial hand, be curst and brief; . . . taunt him with the license of ink: if thou *thou'st* him some thrice it shall not be amiss. . . . Let there be gall enough in thy ink though thou write with a goose pen, no matter.[1]

Theobald and Knight, and all the other commentators, agree that this is an allusion to Coke's virulent speech against Sir Walter Raleigh, on the trial for treason. The Attorney-General exclaimed to Sir Walter:

All he did was by thy instigation, *thou* viper; for I *thou* thee, *thou* traitor.

Here is the *thou* thrice used. Theobald says it shows Shakespeare's "detestation of Coke."

Let us pass to another consideration.

VII. THE WRITER OF THE PLAYS, LIKE BACON, DISLIKED LORD COBHAM.

Lord Cobham was one of the chief enemies of Essex. Spedding says:

About the same time another quarrel arose upon the appointment of the wardenship of the Cinque Ports, vacant by the death of Lord Cobham, whose eldest son, an enemy of the Earl, was one of the competitors. Essex wished Sir Robert Sydney to have the place, but, finding the Queen resolute in favor of the new Lord Cobham, and "seeing he is likely to carry it away, I mean (said the Earl) resolutely to stand for it myself against him. . . . My Lord Treasurer is come to court, and

[1] *Twelfth Night*, iii, 1.

we sat in council this afternoon in his chamber. I made it known unto them that I had just cause to hate the Lord Cobham, for his villainous dealing and abusing of me; that he hath been my chief persecutor most unjustly; that in him there is no worth."[1]

This was in the year 1597.

And when we turn to the Plays we find that the writer sought to cover the family of Lord Cobham with disgrace and ridicule.

Halliwell-Phillipps says:

The first part of *Henry IV.*, the appearance of which on the stage may be confidently assigned to *the spring of the year 1597*, was followed immediately, or a few months afterward, by the composition of the second part. It is recorded that both these plays were very favorably received by Elizabeth; the Queen especially relishing the character of Falstaff, and they were most probably amongst the dramas represented before that sovereign in the Christmas holidays of 1597-8. At this time, or then very recently, the renowned hero of the Boar's Head Tavern had been introduced as Sir John Oldcastle, but the Queen ordered Shakespeare to alter the name of the character. This step was taken in consequence of the representations of *some member or members of the Cobham family*, who had taken offense at *their illustrious ancestor, Sir John Oldcastle, Lord Cobham, the Protestant martyr, being disparagingly introduced on the stage;* and, accordingly, in or before the February of the following year, Falstaff took the place of Oldcastle, the former being probably one of the few names invented by Shakespeare. . . . The subject, however, was viewed by the Cobhams in a very serious light. This is clearly shown, not merely by the action taken by the Queen, but by the anxiety exhibited by Shakespeare, in the Epilogue to the second part, to place the matter beyond all doubt, by the explicit declaration that there was in Falstaff no kind of association, satirical or otherwise, with the martyr Oldcastle.[2]

The language of the Epilogue is:

One word more, I beseech you. If you be not too much cloyed with fat meat, our humble author will continue the story, with Sir John in it, and make you merry with fair Katharine of France, where, for anything I know, Falstaff shall die of a sweat, unless already he be killed with your hard opinions; *for Oldcastle died a martyr, and this is not the man.*

And yet, there seems to have been a purpose, despite this retraction, to affix the stigma of Falstaff's disreputable career to the ancestor of the Cobham family; for in the first part of *Henry IV.* we find this expression:

Falstaff. Thou say'st true, lad. And is not my hostess of the tavern a most sweet wench?
Prince Henry. As the honey of Hybla, my old lad of the Castle.[3]

Says Knight, as a foot-note upon this sentence:

The passage in the text has given rise to the notion that Sir John Oldcastle was pointed at in the character of Falstaff.

---

[1] *Letters and Life*, vol. ii, p. 48. [2] *Outlines Life of Shak.*, p. 98. [3] Act ii, scene 2.

Oldys remarks:

Upon whom does the horsing of a dead corpse on Falstaff's back reflect? Whose honor suffers, in his being forced, by the unexpected surprise of his armed plunderers, to surrender his treasure? Whose policy is impeached by his creeping into a bucking basket to avoid the storms of a jealous husband?

Fuller says, in his *Church History:*

Stage-poets have themselves been very bold with, and others very merry at, the memory of Sir John Oldcastle, whom they have fancied a boon companion, a jovial royster, and a coward to boot. The best is, Sir John Falstaff hath relieved the memory of Sir John Oldcastle, and of late is substituted buffoon in his place.

It seems to me, there can be no doubt that the author of the Plays disliked the Cobham family, and sought to degrade them, by bringing their ancestor on the stage, in the guise of a disreputable, thieving, cowardly old rascal, who is thumped, beaten and cast into the Thames "like a litter of blind puppies." And even when compelled by the Queen to change the name of the character, the writer of the Plays puts into the mouth of Prince Hal the expression, "My old lad of the castle," to intimate to the multitude that Falstaff was still, despite his change of name, Sir John Oldcastle, the ancestor of the enemy of Bacon's great friend and patron, the Earl of Essex.

VIII. THE WRITER OF THE PLAYS WAS HOSTILE TO QUEEN ELIZABETH.

Let us turn to another point.

We have seen that the writer of the Plays was, by his family traditions and alliances, and his political surroundings, a Protestant. Being such, it would follow that he would be an admirer of Elizabeth, the representative and bulwark of Protestantism in England and on the continent. But we find that, for some reason, this Protestant did not love Elizabeth; and although he sugars her over with compliments in *Henry VIII.*, just as Bacon did in his letters, and probably in his sonnets, yet there was beneath this fair show of flattery a purpose to deal her most deadly blows.

If the divorce of Henry VIII. was based on vicious and adulterous motives, the marriage of the King with Anne Boleyn was discreditable, to say the least. And remembering this we find that the play represents Anne as a frivolous person to whom the King was drawn by his passions.

We read:

> *Suffolk.* How is the King employed?
> *Chamberlain.* I left him private,
> Full of sad thoughts and troubles.
> *Norfolk.* What's the cause?
> *Chamberlain.* It seems, the marriage with his brother's wife
> Has crept too near his conscience.
> *Suffolk.* *No, his conscience*
> *Has crept too near another lady.*
> *Norfolk.* 'Tis so;
> This is the Cardinal's doing.[1]

Birch says:

The scene between the Old Lady and Anne Boleyn seems introduced to make people laugh at the hypocrisy and Protestant conscience of Anne, mixed up with the indecency abjured in the prologue.[2]

The Old Lady says:

> And so would you
> For all this spice of your hypocrisy:
> You that have so fair parts of woman on you,
> Have too a woman's heart; which ever yet
> Affected eminence, wealth, sovereignty;
> Which, to say sooth, are blessings; and which gifts,
> (Saving your mincing), the capacity
> Of your soft cheveril conscience would receive
> If you might please to stretch it.[3]

Knight argues that the play could not have been produced during the reign of Elizabeth. He says:

The memory of Henry VIII., perhaps, was not cherished by her with any deep affection; but would she, who in her dying hour is reported to have said, "My seat has been the seat of kings," allow the frailties, and even the peculiarities of her father, to be made a public spectacle? Would she have borne that his passion for her mother should have been put forward in the strongest way by the poet — that is, in the sequence of the dramatic action — as the impelling motive for the divorce from Katharine? Would she have endured that her father . . . should be represented in the depth of his hypocrisy gloating over his projected divorce with

> But *conscience, conscience,* —
> O! 'tis a tender place, and I must leave her?

Would she have been pleased with the jests of the Old Lady to Anne, upon her approaching elevation — her title — her "thousand pound a year" — and all to be instantly succeeded by the trial-scene — that magnificent exhibition of the purity, the constancy, the fortitude, the grandeur of soul, the self-possession of the "most poor woman and a stranger" that her mother had supplanted?

---

[1] Act ii, scene 2.   [2] *Philosophy and Religion of Shak.*, p. 346.   [3] *Henry VIII.*, ii, 3.

Nothing could be grander than the light in which Katharine is set. Henry himself says:

> Thou art, alone,
> (If thy rare qualities, sweet gentleness,
> Thy meekness saint-like, wife-like government—
> Obeying in commanding—and thy parts
> Sovereign and pious else, could speak thee out),
> The queen of earthly queens.[1]

Anne is made to say of her

> Here's the pang that pinches:
> His highness having lived so long with her; and she
> So good a lady, that no tongue could ever
> Pronounce dishonor of her—by my life
> She never knew harm-doing . . . after this process
> To give her the avaunt! *it is a pity
> Would move a monster*.[2]

And then we have that scene, declared by Dr. Johnson to be the grandest Shakespeare ever wrote, in which angels come upon the stage, and, in the midst of heavenly music, crown Katharine with a garland of saintship, the angelic visitors bowing to her:

> *Katharine.* Saw you not, even now, a blessed troupe
> Invite me to a banquet, whose bright faces
> Cast thousand beams upon me like the sun?
> They promised me eternal happiness,
> And brought me garlands, Griffith, which I feel
> I am not worthy yet to wear; I shall
> Assuredly.[3]

In the epilogue Shakespeare says:

> I fear
> All the expected good we're like to hear
> For this play at this time, is only in
> The merciful construction of good women,
> *For such a one we showed them.*

Upon this Birch says:

This was honest in Shakespeare. He did not put the success of the play upon the flattery of the great or of Protestant prejudices, but upon the exhibition of one good woman, of the opposite party, a Roman Catholic, a Spaniard, and the mother of bloody Mary.

In fact, Shakespeare, strange to say, introduces into the play high praise of this same "bloody Mary," long after she was dead and her sect powerless. He puts it in the mouth of Queen Kath-

[1] *Henry VIII.*, ii, 4. [2] Ibid., ii, 3. [3] Act iv, scene 2.

arine, who, telling Capucius the contents of her last letter to the King, says:

> In which I have commended to his goodness
> The model of our chaste loves, his young daughter:
> The dews of heaven fall thick in blessings on her!
> Beseeching him to give her virtuous breeding;
> (She is young *and of a noble, modest nature;*
> I hope she will deserve well); and a little
> To love her for her mother's sake, that loved him
> Heaven knows how dearly.

The words of praise of Mary are not found in the letter which Katharine actually sent to the King: *they are an interpolation of the poet!*

If Henry put away his true wife, not for any real scruples of conscience, but simply from an unbridled, lustful desire to possess the young and beautiful but frivolous Anne; and if to reach this end he overrode the limitations of the church to which he belonged, then, indeed, Elizabeth was little more than the bastard which her enemies gave her out. A play written to make a saint of Katharine, and a sensual brute of Henry, could certainly bring only shame and disgrace to Anne and her daughter.

What motive could the man of Stratford have to thus contrive debasement for Elizabeth's memory? Why should he follow her beyond the grave for revenge? What wrongs had she inflicted on him? He came to London a poor outcast; during her reign he had risen to wealth and respectability. If tradition is to be believed, she had noticed and honored him. What grievance could he carry away with him to Stratford? Why should it be noticed by contemporaries that when Elizabeth died the muse of Shakespeare breathed not one mournful note of divine praise over her tomb? Chettle, in his *England's Mourning Garment*, thus reproaches Shakespeare that his verse had not bewailed his own and England's loss:

> Nor doth the silver-tongued Melicert
> Drop from his honied muse one sable tear,
> To mourn her death that gracèd his desert,
> And to his lines opened her royal eare.
> Shepherd, remember our Elizabeth,
> And sing her rape, done by the Tarquin, Death.

But as soon as the Tarquin Death had taken Elizabeth, Shakespeare proceeded to show that she was conceived in lust and born in injustice; that her father was a powerful and hypocritical brute; her mother an ambitious worldling; and that the woman she had supplanted was a saint, who passed, upon the wings of cherishing angels, directly to the portals of eternal bliss.

And it will be noted that, although Bacon wrote an essay called *The Felicities of Queen Elizabeth*, it was rather, as its name implies, a description of the happy circumstances that conjoined to make her reign great and prosperous, than a eulogy of her character as admirable or beautiful. He mentions the fact that she

> Was very willing to be courted, wooed and to have sonnets made in her commendation, and that she continued this longer than was decent for her years.

And he says, in anticipation of such a criticism as I make:

> Now, if any man shall allege that against me, which was once said to Cæsar, "we see what we may admire, but we would fain see what we could commend;" certainly, for my part, I hold true admiration to be the highest degree of commendation.

But he did not commend her.

And if we turn to the career of Bacon, we shall find that he had ample cause to hate Elizabeth.

Macaulay says:

> To her it was owing that, while younger men, not superior to him in extraction, and far inferior to him in every kind of personal merit, were filling the highest offices of the state, adding manor to manor, rearing palace after palace, he was lying at a sponging-house for a debt of three hundred pounds.[1]

So long as Elizabeth lived, Bacon was systematically repressed and kept in the most pitiful poverty. The base old woman, knowing his condition, would see him embarrass himself still further with costly gifts, given her on her birthdays, and rewarded him with empty honors that could not keep bread in his mouth, or the constable from his door. Beneath the poor man's placid exterior of philosophical self-control, there was a very volcano of wrath and hate ready to burst forth.

Dean Church says:

> But she still refused him promotion. He was without an official position in the Queen's service, and he never was allowed to have it.[2]

And again:

> Burleigh had been strangely niggardly in what he did to help his brilliant nephew. . . . . . But it is plain that he [his son] early made up his mind to keep

[1] *Macaulay's Essays*, Bacon, p. 254. [2] *Bacon*, p. 52.

Bacon in the background. . . . Nothing can account for Bacon's strange failure for so long a time to reach his due place in the public service, but the secret hostility, whatever may be the cause, of Cecil.[1]

This adverse influence kept Bacon in poverty and out of place as long as Cecil lived, which was for some years after the death of Elizabeth. Bacon writes to the King upon Cecil's death a letter of which Dean Church says:

Bacon was in a bitter mood, and the letter reveals, for the first time, what was really in Bacon's heart about " the great subject and great servant," of whom he had just written so respectfully, and with whom he had been so closely connected for most of his life. The fierceness which had been gathering for years of neglect and hindrance, under that placid and patient exterior, broke out.[2]

How savagely does Bacon's pent-up wrath burst from him when writing to King James about his cousin's death:

I protest to God, though I be not superstitious, when I saw your Majesty's book against Vorstius and Arminius, and noted your zeal to deliver the majesty of God from the vain and indign comprehensions of heresy and degenerate philosophy, as you had by your pen formerly endeavored to deliver kings from the usurpations of Rome, *perculsit illico animum* that God would set shortly upon you *some visible favor, and let me not live if I thought not of the taking away of that man.*[3]

The Cecils ruled Elizabeth, and we may judge from this passionate outburst how deeply and bitterly, for many years, Bacon hated the Virgin Queen and her advisers; how much more bitterly and deeply because his wretched poverty had constrained him to cringe and fawn upon the objects of his contempt and wrath. He expressed his own inmost feelings when he put into the mouth of Hamlet as the strongest of provocations to suicide:

> The law's delay,
> *The insolence of office, and the spurns
> That patient merit of the unworthy takes.*

How bitterly does he break forth in *Lear:*

> Behold the great image of authority ! *A dog's obeyed in office !*

And again, in *Measure for Measure:*

> Man, proud man,
> Drest in a little brief authority,
>   . . . Like an angry ape,
> Plays such fantastic tricks before high heaven,
> As make the angels weep.

---

[1] Ibid., p. 59.   [2] Ibid., p. 90.   [3] Letter to the King, 1612.

And we seem to hear the cry of his own long disappointed heart in the words of Wolsey:

> O, how wretched
> Is that poor man, that hangs on princes' favors!
> There is, between that smile he would aspire to,
> That sweet aspect of princes, and their ruin,
> More pangs and fears than wars or women have.

And Hamlet, his *alter ego*, expresses the self-loathing with which he contemplated the abasements of genius to power:

> No; let the candied tongue lick absurd pomp,
> And crook the pregnant hinges of the knee,
> Where thrift may follow fawning.

These words never came from the smooth surface of a prosperous life: they were the bitter outgrowth of a turbulent and suffering heart. When you would find words that sting like adders — expletives of immortal wrath and hate — you must seek them in the depths of an outraged soul.

What was there in the life of the Stratford man to justify such expressions? He had his bogus coat-of-arms to make him respectable; he owned the great house of Stratford, and could brew beer in it, and sue his neighbors, to his heart's content. He fled away from the ambitions of the court to the odorous muck-heaps and the pyramidal dung-hills of Stratford; and if any grief settled upon his soul he could (as tradition tells us) get drunk for three days at a time to assuage it.

IX. RICHARD III. REPRESENTED ROBERT CECIL.

There is another very significant fact.

The arch-enemy of Bacon and of Essex was Sir Robert Cecil, Bacon's first cousin, the child of his mother's sister. He was the chief means of eventually bringing Essex' head to the block. We have just seen how intensely Bacon hated him, and with what good reason.

He was a man of extraordinary mental power, derived, in part, from the same stock (the stock of Sir Anthony Cook, tutor to King Edward IV.) from which Bacon had inherited much of his ability. But, in his case, the blood of Sir Anthony had been crossed by the shrewd, cunning, foxy, cold-blooded, selfish, persistent stock of his father, Sir William Burleigh, Elizabeth's Lord Treasurer; and hence, instead of a great poet and philosopher, as in Bacon's case, the outcome was a statesman and courtier of extraordinary keenness and ability, and a very sleuth-hound of dissembling persistency and cunning.

He had the upper hand of Bacon, and he kept it. He sat on his neck as long as he lived. Even after the death of Elizabeth and the coming-in of the new King, he held that mighty genius in the mire. He seemed to have possessed some secret concerning Bacon, discreditable to him, which he imparted to King James, and this hindered his advancement after the death of the Queen, notwithstanding the fact that Bacon had belonged to the faction which, prior to Elizabeth's death, was in favor of James as her successor. This is intimated by Dean Church; he says:

> Cecil had, indeed, but little claim on Bacon's gratitude; he had spoken him fair in public, and no doubt in secret distrusted and thwarted him. But to the last Bacon did not choose to acknowledge this. *Had James disclosed something of his dead servant* [Cecil], *who left some strange secrets behind him, which showed his hostility to Bacon?*[1]

Was it for this that Bacon rejoiced over his death? Was the secret an intimation to King James that Bacon was the real author of the Plays that went about in the name of Shakespeare? Whatever it was, there was something potent enough to suppress Bacon and hold him down, even for some time after Cecil's death.

Dean Church says:

> He was still kept out of the inner circle of the council, but from the moment of Salisbury's [Cecil's] death, he became a much more important person. He still sued for advancement, and still met with disappointment; the "mean men" still rose above him. . . . But Bacon's hand and counsel appear more and more in important matters.[2]

Now it is known that Cecil was a man of infirm health, and that *he was a hump-back*.

We turn to the Shakespeare Plays, and we ask: What is the most awful character, the most absolutely repulsive and detestable character, the character without a single redeeming, or beautifying, or humanizing trait, in all the range of the Plays? And the answer is: The crook-backed monster, Richard III.

Richard III. was a satire on Bacon's cousin, Robert Cecil.

To make the character more dreadful, the poet has drawn it in colors even darker than historical truth would justify.

---

[1] *Bacon*, p. 92.   [2] *Ibid.*, p. 93.

Like Cecil, Richard is able, shrewd, masterful, unscrupulous, ambitious; determined, rightly or wrongly, to rule the kingdom. Like Cecil, he can crawl and cringe and dissemble, when it is necessary, and rule with a rod of iron when he possesses the power

Here we have a portrait of Cecil.

SIR ROBERT CECIL.

Was the expression of that face in Bacon's mind when he wrote those lines, which I have just quoted?

> Man, proud man,
> Drest in a little brief authority,
> . . . *like an angry ape*,
> Plays such fantastic tricks before high heaven
> As makes the angels weep.

. The expression of Cecil's countenance is, to my mind, actually ape-like.

The man who has about him any personal deformity never ceases to be conscious of it. Byron could not forget his club-foot. What a terrible revenge it was when Bacon, under the disguise of the irresponsible play-actor, Shakspere, set on the boards of the Curtain Theater the all-powerful courtier and minister, Sir Robert Cecil, in the character of that other hump-back, the bloody and loathsome Duke of Gloster? How the adherents of Essex must have whispered it among the multitude, as the crippled Duke, with his hump upon his shoulder, came upon the stage—"That's Cecil!" And how they must have applied Richard's words of self-description to another?

> I that am curtailed of this fair proportion,
> Cheated of feature by dissembling nature,
> Deformed, unfinished, sent before my time
> Into this breathing world, scarce half made up,
> And that so lamely and unfashionable
> That dogs bark at me as I halt by them—
> Why I, in this weak piping time of peace,
> Have no delight to pass away the time,
> Unless to spy my shadow in the sun,
> And descant on mine own deformity.
> And therefore, since I cannot prove a lover
> To entertain these fair, well-spoken days,
> I am determined to prove a villain,
> And hate the idle pleasures of these days.

And these last lines express the very thought with which Bacon opens his essay *On Deformity*.

> Deformed persons are commonly even with nature; for as nature hath done ill by them, so do they by nature, being for the most part (as the Scripture saith) "void of natural affection;" and so they have their revenge of nature.

And we seem to see the finger of Bacon pointing towards his cousin, in these words:

> Whoever hath any thing fixed in his person that doth induce contempt, hath also a perpetual spur in himself to rescue and deliver himself from scorn; therefore all deformed persons are extreme bold, first, as in their own defense, as being exposed to scorn, but in process of time by a general habit. Also it stirreth in them industry, and especially of this kind, to watch and observe the weaknesses of others, that they may have somewhat to repay. Again, in their superiors it quencheth jealousy towards them, as persons that they think they may at pleasure despise; and it layeth their competitors and emulators asleep, as never believing they should be in possibility of advancement till they see them in possession, so that upon the matter, in a great wit, deformity is an advantage to rising.

Speaking of the death of Cecil, Hepworth Dixon says:

> And when Cecil passes to his rest, a new edition of the *Essays*, under cover of a treatise on Deformity, paints in true and bold lines, but without one harsh touch, the genius of the man.... Every one knows the portrait; yet no one can pronounce this picture of a small, shrewd man of the world, a clerk in soul, without a spark of fire, a dart of generosity in his nature, unfair or even unkind.[1]

One can conceive how bitterly the dissembling, self-controlled Cecil must have writhed under the knowledge that the Essex party, in the Essex theater, occupied by the Essex company of actors, and filled daily with the adherents of Essex, had placed him on the

---

[1] *Personal History of Lord Bacon*, pp. 193, 204.

boards, with all his deformity upon his back, and made him the object of the ribald laughter of the swarming multitude, "the scum" of London. As we will find hereafter Queen Elizabeth saying, "Know ye not I am Richard the Second?" so we may conceive Cecil saying to the Queen: "Know ye not that I am Richard the Third?"

And if he knew, or shrewdly suspected, that his cousin, Francis Bacon, was the real author of the Plays, and the man who had so terribly mocked his physical defects, we can understand why he used all his powers, as long as he lived, to hold him down; and, as Church suspects, even blackened him in the King's esteem, so that his revenge might transcend the limits of his own frail life. And we can understand the exultation of Bacon when, at last, death loosened from his throat the fangs of his powerful and unforgiving adversary.

In conclusion and recapitulation I would say that I find the political identities between Bacon and the writer of the Plays to be as follows:

Both were aristocrats.

Both despised the mob.

Both contemned tradesmen.

Both loved liberty.

Both loved feudalism.

Both pitied the miseries of the people.

Both desired the welfare of the people.

Both foresaw and dreaded an uprising of the lower classes.

Both belonged to the military party.

Both hated Lord Cobham.

Both were adherents of Essex.

Both tried to popularize Essex.

Both were friends of Southampton.

Both hated Coke.

Both, although Protestant, had some strong antipathy against Queen Elizabeth.

Both refused to eulogize her character after death.

Both, though aristocratic were out of power and bitter against those in authority.

Both hated Robert Cecil.

Surely, surely, we are getting the two heads under one hat — and that the hat of the great philosopher of Verulam.

CHAPTER V.

THE RELIGION OF THE PLAYS.

> I sometimes do believe, and sometimes do not.
> *As You Like It*, v, 4.

THE religious world of Elizabeth was divided into two great and antagonistic sects: Catholics and Protestants; and the latter were, in turn, separated into the followers of the state religion and various forms of dissent.

Religion in that day was an earnest, palpable reality: society was set against itself in hostile classes; politics, place, government, legislation—all hinged upon religion. In this age of doubt and indifference, we can hardly realize the feelings of a people to whom the next world was as real as this world, and who were ready to die agonizing deaths, in the flames of Smithfield, for their convictions upon questions of theology.

We are told that William Shakspere of Stratford died a Catholic. We have this upon the authority of Rev. Mr. Davies, who says, writing after 1688, "he died a Papist." Upon the question of the politics of a great man, the leader of either one of the political parties of his neighborhood is likely to be well informed; it is in the line of his interests and thoughts. Upon the question of the religion of the one great man of Stratford, we may trust the testimony of the clergyman of the parish. He could hardly be mistaken. There can be little doubt that William Shakspere of Stratford-on-Avon died a Catholic.

But of what religion was the man who wrote the Plays?

This question has provoked very considerable discussion. He has been claimed alike by Protestants and Catholics.

To my mind it is very clear that the writer of the Plays was a Protestant. And this is the view of Dowden. He says:

> Shakespeare has been proved to belong to each communion to the satisfaction of contending theological zealots.... But, tolerant as his spirit is, it is certain that the spirit of Protestantism animates and breathes through his writings.[1]

What are the proofs?

---
[1] Dowden, *Shak. Mind and Art*, p. 33.

I. He is Opposed to the Papal Supremacy.

The play of *King John* turns largely upon the question of patriotic resistance to the temporal power of the Pope; and this is not a necessary incident of the events of the time, for the poet, to point his moral, antedates the great quarrel between John and the Pope by six years.

He represents King John, upon Ascension Day, yielding up his crown to Pandulph, the Pope's legate, and receiving it back, with these words:

> Take again
> From this, my hand, as holding of the Pope,
> Your sovereign greatness and authority.[1]

In scene 3 of act iii, he makes Pandulph demand of the King why he keeps Stephen Langton, Archbishop of Canterbury, out of his see; and King John replies:

> What earthly name to interrogatories
> Can task the free breath of a sacred king?
> Thou canst not, Cardinal, devise a name
> So slight, unworthy and ridiculous,
> To charge me to an answer, as the Pope.
> Tell him this tale; and from the mouth of England
> Add this much more: That no Italian priest
> Shall tithe or toll in our dominions;
> But as we under heaven are supreme head,
> So under him, that great supremacy,
> Where we do reign, we will alone uphold,
> Without the assistance of a mortal hand:
> So tell the Pope; all reverence set apart,
> To him and his usurped authority.
>
> *King Philip.* Brother of England, you blaspheme in this.
>
> *King John.* Though you, and all the kings of Christendom,
> Are led so grossly by this meddling priest,
> Dreading the curse that money may buy out;
> And, by the merit of vile gold, dross, dust,
> Purchase corrupted pardon of a man,
> Who, in that sale, sells pardon from himself;
> Though you, and all the rest, so grossly led,
> This juggling witchcraft with revenue cherish;
> Yet I, alone, alone do me oppose,
> Against the Pope, and count his friends my foes.

It is scarcely to be believed that a Catholic could have written these lines.

---
[1] *King John*, v. 1.

And it must be remembered that King John is depicted in the play as a most despicable creature; and his eventual submission of the liberties of the crown and the country, to the domination of a foreign power, is represented as one of the chief ingredients in making up his shameful character.

It is needless to say that Bacon had very strong views upon this question of the Pope's sovereignty over England. He says in the *Charge against Talbot:*

> Nay all princes of both religions, for it is a common cause, do stand, at this day [in peril], by the spreading and enforcing of this furious and pernicious opinion of the Pope's temporal power.

II. HE HONORED AND RESPECTED CRANMER.

But it is in the play of *Henry VIII.* that the religious leanings of the writer are most clearly manifested.

It is to be remembered that it was in this reign that Protestantism was established in England, and the man who above all others was instrumental in bringing about the great change was Thomas Cranmer, the first Protestant Archbishop of Canterbury. He, above all other men, was hated by the Catholics. He it was who had sanctioned the divorce of Henry from Katharine; he it was who had delivered the crown to Anne upon the coronation; he had supported the suppression of the monasteries; he had persecuted the Catholic prelates and people, sending numbers to the stake; and when the Catholics returned to power, under Mary, one of the first acts of the government was to burn him alive opposite Baliol College. It is impossible that a Catholic writer of the next reign could have gone out of his way to defend and praise Cranmer, to represent him as a good and holy man, and even as an inspired prophet. And yet all this we find in the play of *Henry VIII.;* the play is, in fact, in large part, an apotheosis of Cranmer.

In act fifth we find the King sending for him. He assures him that he is his friend, but that grave charges have been made against him, and that he must go before the council for trial, and he gives him his ring, to be used in an appeal, in case the council find him guilty. The King says:

> Look, the good man weeps!
> He's honest on mine honor. God's blest mother!
> I swear he is true-hearted; and a soul
> None better in my kingdom.

The council proceed to place Cranmer under arrest, with intent to send him to the Tower, when he exhibits the King's ring and makes his appeal. The King enters frowning, rebukes the persecutors of Cranmer, and says to him:

> Good man, sit down. Now let me see the proudest,
> He that dares most, but wag his finger at thee. . . .
> Was it discretion, lords, to let this man,
> This good man (few of you deserve that title),
> This honest man, wait like a lousy foot-boy
> At chamber-door? . . .
> Well, well, my lords, respect him.
> Take him and use him well, he's worthy of it.
> I will say thus much for him, if a prince
> May be beholden to a subject, I
> Am, for his love and service, so to him.

All this has no necessary coherence with the plot of the play, but is dragged in to the filling up of two scenes.

And, in the last scene of the play, Cranmer baptizes the Princess Elizabeth, and is inspired by Heaven to prophesy:

> Let me speak, sir,
> For Heaven now bids me.

And he proceeds to foretell her future long life and greatness. He says:

> In her days, every man shall eat in safety,
> Under his own vine, what he plants; and sing
> The merry songs of peace to all his neighbors;
> *God shall be truly known.*

It is not conceivable that one who was a Catholic, who regarded with disapproval the establishment of the new religion, and who looked upon Cranmer as an arch-heretic, worthy of the stake and of hell, could have written such scenes, when there was nothing in the plot of the play itself which required it.

The passages in the play which relate to Cranmer are drawn from Fox's *Book of Martyrs*, and the prose version is followed almost literally in the drama; but, strange to say, there is in the historical work no place wherein the King speaks of Cranmer as a "good" man. All this is *interpolated by the dramatist*. We have in the play:

> Good man, sit down.
> This good man.
> This honest man.
> Good man, those joyful tears show thy true heart. Etc.

There is not in Fox's narrative one word of indorsement, by the King, of Cranmer's goodness or honesty.

A Catholic writing a play based on Protestant histories might have followed the text, even against his own prejudices, but it is not to be believed that he would alter the text, and inject words of compliment of a man who held the relations to the Catholics of England that Cranmer did.

We cannot help but believe that the man who did this was a Protestant, educated to believe that the Reformation was right and necessary, and that Cranmer was a good and holy man, the inspired instrument of Heaven in a great work.

The family of Bacon was Protestant. They rose out of the ranks, on the wave of the Reformation. His father was an officer of Henry VIII.; his grandfather was tutor to the Protestant King Edward. During the reign of Mary, the Bacons lived in retirement; they conformed to the Catholic Church and heard mass daily; but, upon the coming in of Elizabeth, they emerged from their hiding-place, and Bacon's father and uncle, Burleigh, were at the head of the Protestant party of England during the rest of their lives. All the traditions of the family clustered around the Reformation. They faithfully believed that "God was truly known" in the religion of Elizabeth, and they were as violently opposed to the Papal supremacy as King John or the Bastard.

It is a curious fact that Bacon alludes, in his prose works, to the reign of Elizabeth, in words very similar to those placed in the mouth of Cranmer. He says:

> This part of the island never had forty-five years of better times. . . . For if there be considered of the one side *the truth of religion established*, the constant *peace and security*, the good administration of justice, etc.[1]

III. THE WRITER OF THE PLAYS WAS TOLERANT OF CATHOLICITY.

But how does it come to pass that in the face of such evidence it has been claimed that the writer of the Plays was a Catholic?

Because, in an age of violent religious hatreds, when the Catholics were helpless, suspected and persecuted, the author of the Plays never uttered a word, however pleasing it might be to the court and the time-serving multitude, to fan the flame of animosity

---

[1] *Advancement of Learning*, book i.

against the Catholics. On the other hand, whenever a Catholic priest is introduced on the scene, he is represented as honest, benevolent and venerable.

"His friars," says one of his commentators, "are all wise, holy and in every respect estimable men. Instance Friar Lawrence, in *Romeo and Juliet*, and the friar in *Much Ado About Nothing*."

When we turn to the writings of Bacon, we find the same broad spirit of religious liberality, as contradistinguished from the bigotry of the age.

Bacon's mind was too great to be illiberal. Bigotry is a burst of strong light, through the crevice of a narrow mind, lighting only one face of its object and throwing all the rest into hideous and grotesque shadows. Bacon's mind, like the sun in the tropics, illuminated all sides of the object upon which it shone, with a comprehensive and vivifying light.

Macaulay says of him:

In what he wrote on church government, he showed, as far as he dared, a tolerant and charitable spirit. . . . He was in power at the time of the Synod of Dort, and must for months have been deafened with talk about election, reprobation and final perseverance. Yet we do not remember a line in his works from which it can be inferred that he was either a Calvinist or an Armenian.[1]

Speaking of Shakespeare, White says:

Nowhere does he show leaning toward any form of church government, or toward any theological tenet or dogma. No church can claim him.[2]

Bacon looked with pity upon the differences that distracted the religious world of his time. He says, speaking of a conspiracy against the crown, organized by Catholics:

Thirdly, the great calamity it bringeth upon Papists themselves, of which the more moderate sort, as men misled, *are to be pitied*.

Again he says:

A man that is of judgment and understanding shall sometimes hear ignorant men differ, and know well within himself that those which so differ mean one thing, and yet they themselves would never agree. And if it came to pass in that distance of judgment which is between man and man, shall we not think that God above, that knows the heart, doth not discern that frail men, in some of their contradictions, intend the same thing, and accepteth of both.[3]

He turned with abhorrence from the burnings of men for conscience' sake. He said:

[1] *Essays, Bacon.* p. 280.   [2] *Life and Genius of Shak.*, p. 188.   [3] Essay *Of Unity in Religion*.

We may not take up the third sword, which is Mahomet's sword, or like unto it, that is, to propagate religion by wars, or by *sanguinary persecutions to force consciences;* . . . much less to authorize conspiracies and rebellions; to put the sword into the people's hands, and the like, tending to the subversion of all government.[1]

And we find the same sentiment in Shakespeare:

> It is an heretic that makes the fire,
> Not she which burns in it.[2]

IV. THE WRITER OF THE PLAYS DISLIKED THE PURITANS.

In both writers we find a profound dislike of the Puritans.

"Shakespeare," says one of his commentators, "never omits an opportunity of ridiculing the Puritan sect."

He says:

There is but one Puritan among them, and he sings songs to hornpipes.[3]

Sir Andrew Aguecheek says:

I would as lief be a Brownist as a politician.[4]

And again:

Though honesty be no Puritan, yet it will do no hurt.[5]

The mocking Falstaff tells the Chief Justice that he lost his voice "singing of anthems."

Says one commentator:

In the introduction of Sir Oliver Mar-text our poet indulges in a sly hit against the Puritan and itinerant ministers, whom he appears to have regarded with aversion.

The play of *Measure for Measure* is an attempt to burlesque the virtue-loving principles of the Puritans; and in the cross-gartered Malvolio of *Twelfth Night* we have the

> Sharp, cross-gartered man,
> Whom their loud laugh may nickname Puritan.

And the immortal question,

> Dost thou think because thou art virtuous there shall be no more cakes and ale?

is universally accepted as a sneer at the asceticism of that grave sect.

Wherever Shakespeare introduces a Dissenting preacher he makes him an ignoramus or a mountebank.

---

[1] Essay *Of Unity in Religion.* [3] Ibid., iv, 2. [5] *All's Well that Ends Well,* i, 3.
[2] *Winter's Tale,* ii, 3. [4] *Twelfth Night,* iii, 2.

Similar views we find in Bacon. He says:

> For as the temporal sword is to be drawn with great circumspection in cases of religion, so it is a thing monstrous to put it into the hands of the common people; *let that be left unto the Anabaptists and other furies.*[1]

In another place he says:

> Besides the Roman Catholics, there is a generation of sectaries, the Anabaptists, Brownists and others of their kinds; they have been several times very busy in this kingdom under the color of zeal for reformation of religion; the King your master knows their disposition very well; a small touch will put him in mind of them; he had experience of them in Scotland. I hope he will beware of them in England; a little countenance or connivancy sets them on fire.[2]

And, like Shakespeare, he ridicules the manners of the Puritans. He says:

> There is a master of scoffing that in his catalogue of books of a feigned library sets down this title of a book, *The Morris-Dance of the Heretics;* for, indeed, every sect of them hath a diverse posture, or cringe, by themselves, which cannot but move derision in worldlings and depraved politics, who are apt to contemn holy things.[3]

Bacon looked with the profoundest apprehension upon the growing numbers and power of that grave, sour, serious sect, with its strong anti-royal tendencies and its anti-social feelings. "They love no plays, as you do, Anthony." They threatened, in his view, by their malignant intolerance, the very existence of civilization. He says:

> Nor am I discouraged from it because I see signs in the times of the decline and overthrow of that knowledge and erudition which is now in use. . . . But the civil wars which may be expected, I think (judging from certain fashions which have come in of late), to spread through many countries, together with the malignity of sects, . . . seem to portend for literature and the sciences a tempest not less fatal, and one against which the printing-office will be no effectual security.[4]

He clearly foresaw the coming revolution which broke out, not long after his death, under the lead of Cromwell. He wrote the King, when he had been overthrown by the agitations in Parliament, that —

> Those who strike at your Chancellor will yet strike at your crown. . . . I wish that, as I am the first, so I may be the last of sacrifices in your times.

Wise as he was, he could not see beyond the tempest which he felt was coming, but he feared that the literature of England would perish in the storm; and he was of course unable to do justice to

---

[1] Essay *Of Unity in Religion.*
[2] Advice to George Villiers.
[3] Essay *Of Unity in Religion.*
[4] Preface to *Interpretation of Nature.*

the real merits of the sect to whom England owes so much of Parliamentary liberty and moral greatness.

His premonitions of the immediate effects of the religious revolution were well founded. Birch says:

> The Bacons and the Shakespeares, the philosophers and scoffers, as well as the Papists, were extinguished by the Puritans. The theater gave way to the pulpit, the actor and dramatist to the preacher. The philosophical and political school of infidelity had no chance against the fanaticism of Cromwell, at the head of the religious spirit of the age.[1]

V. THE WRITER OF THE PLAYS A FREE-THINKER.

But there was a deeper reason for the indifference of the real author of the Plays to the passions and quarrels of Catholics and Protestants. It was this: he did not believe in the doctrines of the Christian religion. This fact has not escaped the notice of commentators.

Swinburne says:

> That Shakespeare was in the genuine sense — that is, in the best and highest and widest meaning of the term — a free-thinker, this otherwise practically and avowedly superfluous effusion of all inmost thought appears to me to supply full and sufficient evidence for the conviction of every candid and rational man.[2]

Dowden says:

> Thus all through the play he wanders between materialism and spiritualism, between belief in immortality and disbelief, between reliance upon Providence and a bowing under fate. In presence of the ghost, a sense of his own spiritual existence and the immortal life of the soul grows strong within him. In presence of a spirit he is himself a spirit:
>
> > I do not set my life at a pin's fee;
> > And for my soul, what can it do to that,
> > Being a thing immortal as itself?
>
> When left to his private thoughts, he wavers uncertainly to and fro; death is a sleep — a sleep, it may be, troubled with dreams. In the graveyard, in the presence of human dust, the base affinities of our bodily nature prove irresistibly attractive to the curiosity of Hamlet's imagination; and he cannot choose but pursue the history of human dust through all its series of hideous metamorphoses.[3]

West says:

> Though there is no reason to think that there was any paganism in Shakespeare's creed, yet we cannot help feeling that the spirit of his art is in many respects pagan. In his great tragedies he traces the workings of noble or lovely human characters on to the point — and no farther — where they disappear into the darkness of death, and ends with a look *back*, never on toward anything beyond.[4]

---

[1] *Philosophy and Religion of Shak.*, p. 9.
[2] *A Study of Shak.*, p. 165.
[3] *Shak. Mind and Art*, p. 118.
[4] E. B. West, *Browning as a Preacher*, Dark Blue Magazine, Oct. and Nov., 1871.

He seems to have been a fatalist. Take these passages as proof:

> But, O vain boast!
> Who can control his fate?[1]

> Our wills and fates do so contrary run,
> That our devices still are overthrown;
> Our thoughts are ours, their ends none of our own.[2]

> Whom destiny
> That hath to instrument this lower world
> And what is in it.[3]

> All unavoided is the doom of destiny.[4]

> 'Tis destiny unshunnable, like death.[5]

But apart from this predestinarian bent there does not seem to be in the Plays any theological preference or purpose. All the plays which preceded the Shakespearean era were of a religious character—they were miracle plays, or moralities, in which Judas and the devil and the several vices shone conspicuously. Some of these plays continued, side by side with the Shakespeare Plays, down to the end of the sixteenth century, and into the beginning of the seventeenth. In Lupton's "moral and pitiful comedy," *All for Money*, the catastrophe represents Judas "like a damned soul in black, painted with flames of fire and a fearful visard, followed by Dives, 'with such like apparel as Judas hath,' while Damnation (another of the *dramatis personæ*), pursuing them, drives them before him, and they pass away, 'making a pitiful noise,' into perdition."

The mouth of hell, painted to represent flames of fire, was a very common scene at the back of the stage.

Birch says:

What a transition to the Plays of Shakespeare, while these miracle and moral plays were fresh in the recollection of the people, and might still be seen. These supernatural, historical and allegorical personages superseded by *a material and philosophical explanation of things!*[6]

VI. The Causes of Infidelity in that Age.

The "malignity of sects" drove many men to infidelity. They saw in religion only monstrous and cruel forces, which lighted horrible fires in the midst of great cities, and filled the air with the stench of burning flesh and the shrieks of the dying victims. They

---

[1] *Othello*, v, 2.　　[3] *Tempest*, iv, 3.　　[5] *Othello*, iii, 3.
[2] *Hamlet*, iii, 2.　　[4] *Richard III.*, iv, 4.　　[6] Birch, *Philosophy and Religion of Shak.*, p. 11.

held religion to account for those excesses of fanaticism in a semi-barbarous age, and they doubted the existence of a God who could permit such horrors. They were ready to exclaim with Macduff, when told that "the hell-kite," Macbeth, had killed all his family, "all his pretty ones," at one fell swoop:

> Did heaven look on,
> And would not take their part?

They came to conceive of God as a cruel monster who relished the sufferings of his creatures. Shakespeare puts this thought into the mouth of Lear:

> As flies to wanton boys are we to the gods:
> They kill us for their sport.[1]

Mankind could only *endure* this divine injustice:

> Arming myself with patience,
> To stay the providence of some high powers
> That govern us below.[2]

But, whatever conclusions men might reach on these questions, it was perilous to express them. The stake and the scaffold awaited the skeptical. If their thoughts were to reach the light it must be through the mouths of madmen, like Lear or Hamlet; and to fall, as Bacon said, like *seeds*, that, by their growth in the minds of generations to come, would mitigate the wrath of sects and prepare the way for an age of toleration.

Birch says:

The spectacle of Brownists, among the Protestants, and of Papists, suffering capital punishment for opinion's sake, alternately presented to the eyes of the public, would create a party hostile to all religion; whilst an occasional atheist burnt would teach the irreligious to keep their opinions to themselves, or caution them in administering infidelity as "medicinable."[3]

However strongly we may be convinced of the great and fundamental truths of religion, it must be conceded that freedom of conscience and governmental toleration are largely the outgrowth of unbelief and indifference.

In an age that realized, without doubt or question, that life was but a tortured hour between two eternities; a thread of time across a boundless abyss; that hell and heaven lay so close up to this breathing world that a step would, in an instant, carry us over the shadowy line into an ocean of flame or a paradise of endless de-

---

[1] *Lear*, iv, 1.   [2] *Julius Cæsar*, v, 1.   [3] Birch, *Philosophy and Religion of Shak.*, p. 8.

lights, it followed, as a logical sequence, that it was an act of the greatest kindness and humanity to force the skeptical, by any torture inflicted upon them during this temporary and wretched existence, to avoid an eternal hell and obtain an eternal heaven. But so soon as doubt began to enter the minds of men; so soon as they said to one another, "Perchance these things may not be exactly as we have been taught; perchance the other world may be but a dream of hope; perchance this existence is all there is of it," the fervor of fanaticism commenced to abate. Not absolutely positive in their own minds as to spiritual things, they were ready to make some allowance for the doubts of others. Thus unbelief tamed the fervor even of those who still believed, and modified, in time, public opinion and public law.

But in Bacon's era every thoughtful soul that loved his fellow-man, and sought to advance his material welfare, would instinctively turn away from a system of belief which produced such holocausts of martyrs, and covered the face of the earth with such cruel and bloody wars.

I have no doubt that Bacon in his youth was a total disbeliever in Christianity. He himself said:

A little philosophy inclineth man's mind to atheism, but depth in philosophy bringeth men's minds about to religion.

There was found among his writings a curious essay, called *The Characters of a Believing Christian, in Paradoxes and Seeming Contradictions.* It is a wholesale burlesque of Christianity, so cunningly put together that it may be read as a commendation of Christians.

I give a few extracts:

1. A Christian is one that believes things his reason cannot comprehend; he hopes for things which neither he nor any man alive ever saw; he labors for that which he knoweth he shall never obtain; yet, in the issue, his belief appears not to be false; his hopes make him not ashamed; his labor is not in vain.

2. He believes three to be one and one to be three; a father not to be elder than his son; a son to be equal with his father, and one proceeding from both to be equal with both; he believing three persons in one nature and two natures in one person. . . .

11. . . . He knoweth if he please men he cannot be the servant of Christ, yet for Christ's sake he pleaseth all men in all things. He is a peace-maker, yet is a continual fighter, and an irreconcilable enemy.

18. . . . He professeth he can do nothing, yet as truly professeth he can do all things; he knoweth that flesh and blood cannot inherit the kingdom of God, yet believeth he shall go to heaven, both body and soul.

20. ... He knoweth he shall not be saved by or for his good works, yet he doth all the good works he can.

21. ... He believes beforehand that God hath purposed what he shall be and that nothing can make him alter his purpose; yet prays and endeavors as if he would force God to save him forever.

24. ... He is often tossed and shaken, yet is as Mount Zion; he is a serpent and a dove, a lamb and a lion, a reed and a cedar. He is sometimes so troubled that he thinks nothing to be true in religion, yet if he did think so he could not at all be troubled.

We turn to Shakespeare and we find in *Richard II.* a similar unbelieving playing upon seeming contradictions in Christianity. It reads like a continuation of the foregoing put into blank verse. Richard is in prison. He says:

> I have been studying how to compare
> This prison, where I live, unto the world:
> And, for because the world is populous,
> And here is not a creature but myself
> I cannot do it: yet I'll hammer 't out.
> My braine, I'll prove the female to my soul,
> My soul, the Father: and these two beget
> A generation of still breeding thoughts;
> And these same thoughts people this little world,
> In humors, like the people of this world,
> For no thought is contented. The better sort,
> As thoughts of things divine, are intermixt
> With scruples, *and do set the Faith itself*
> *Against the Faith:*
> As thus — " Come, little ones;" and then again,
> " It is as hard to come as for a camel
> To thread the postern of a needle's eye."[1]

No one can doubt that these thoughts, showing the same irreligious belief, and the same subtle way of propounding it, came from the same mind. And observe the covert sarcasm of this, among many similar utterances of Bacon:

For those bloody quarrels for religion were unknown to the ancients, the heathen gods not having so much as a touch of that jealousy which is an attribute of the true God.[2]

Through all the Shakespeare Plays we find the poet, by the mouths of all sorts of people, representing death as the end of all things. Macbeth says:

> Duncan is in his grave;
> After life's fitful fever, he *sleeps* well;
> Treason has done his worst; nor steel, nor poison,
> Malice domestic, foreign levy, *nothing*
> Can touch him further.

[1] *Richard II.*, v, 5. [2] *Wisdom of the Ancients — Diomedes.*

Titus Andronicus thus speaks of the grave:

> Here lurks no treason, here no envy swells;
> Here grow no damnéd grudges, here no storms;
> No noise, *but silence and eternal sleep*.

In the sonnets, Shakespeare speaks of

> Death's *dateless* night.

We are also told in the sonnets that we leave "this vile world" "with vilest worms to dwell." In *The Tempest* we are reminded that "our little life is rounded by a sleep"; that is to say, we are surrounded on all sides by total oblivion and nothingness. Iachimo sees in sleep only "the ape of death."

The Duke says, in *Measure for Measure:*

> Thy best of rest is sleep,
> And that thou oft provok'st, yet grossly fear'st
> *Thy death, which is no more.*

Dr. Johnson says:

I cannot, without indignation, find Shakespeare saying that death is only sleep, lengthening out his exhortation by a sentence which in the friar is impious, in the reasoner is foolish, and in the poet trite and vulgar.

In the same play the writer mocks at the idea of an immortal soul:

> But man, proud man!
> Drest in a little brief authority,
> *Most ignorant of what he's most assured,*
> *His glassy essence,* like an angry ape,
> Plays such fantastic tricks before high heaven,
> As make the angels weep.[1]

In this same play of *Measure for Measure*, while he gives us the pagan conception of the future of the soul, he directly slaps in the face the Christian belief in hell. Speaking of death, he says:

> The delighted spirit
> To bathe in fiery floods, or to reside
> In thrilling regions of thick-ribbed ice;
> To be imprisoned in the viewless winds,
> And blown with restless violence round about
> The pendant world; or to be worse than worst
> *Of those, that lawless and incertain thoughts*
> *Imagine howling!*[2]

This is not the language of one who believed that God had said: "Depart from me, ye accursed, into everlasting fire!"

---

[1] *Measure for Measure*, ii, 2.   [2] Ibid., iii, 1.

And, we find the mocking Falstaff talking, in a jesting fashion, about the "primrose way to the *everlasting bonfire!*"

No wonder Birch says, speaking of *Measure for Measure:*

There are passages of infidelity in this play that staggered Warburton, made Johnson indignant, and confounded Coleridge and Knight [1]

VII. CONCLUSIONS.

Thus, then, I decipher the religion of the Plays:

1. They were written by a man of Protestant training, who believed in the political changes brought about by Cranmer and the Reformation. Such a man was Bacon.

2. They were written by one who was opposed to the temporal power of the Pope in England. As I have shown, this was Bacon's feeling.

3. They were written by one who, while a Protestant in politics, did not feel bitterly toward the Catholics, and had no desire to mock or persecute them. We have seen that Bacon advocated the most liberal treatment of the followers of the old faith; he was opposed to the marriage of the clergy; he labored for the unity of all Christians.

4. They were written by one whom the world in that age would have called "an infidel." Such a man, we have reason to believe, was Bacon.

I shall not say that as he advanced in life his views did not change, and that depth of philosophy did not, to use his own phrase, "bring his mind about to religion," even to the belief in the great tenets of Christianity. Certain it is that no man ever possessed a profounder realization of the existence of God in the universe. How sublime, how unanswerable is his expression:

I would rather believe all the fables in the *Talmud* and the *Koran* than that this universal frame is without a mind!

Being himself a mighty *spirit*, he saw through "the muddy vesture of decay" which darkly hems in ruder minds, and beheld the shadowy outlines of that tremendous Spirit of which he was himself, with all created things, but an expression.

He believed that God not only was, but was all-powerful, and all-merciful; and that he had it in his everlasting purposes to

[1] *Philosophy and Religion of Shak.*, p. 353.

lift up man to a state of perfection and happiness on earth; and (as I have shown) he believed that he had created him — even him, Francis Bacon — as an instrument to that end; and to accomplish that end he toiled and labored almost from the cradle to the grave.

He was — in the great sense of the words — a priest and prophet of God, filled with the divine impulses of good. If he erred in his conceptions of truth, who shall stand between the Maker and his great child, and take either to account?

We breathe an air rendered sweeter by his genius; we live in a world made brighter by his philosophy; his contributions to the mental as well as to the material happiness of mankind have been simply incalculable. Let us, then, thank God that he sent him to us on this earth; let us draw tenderly the mantle of charity over his weaknesses, if any such are disclosed by the unpitying hand of history; let us exult that one has been born among the children of men who has removed, on every side for a thousand miles, the posts that experience had set up as the limitations of human capacity.

CHAPTER VI.

THE PURPOSES OF THE PLAYS.

> I have, though in a despised weed, procured the good of all men.
> —*Bacon.*

THE first question asked by every thoughtful mind, touching the things of sense, is: Who made this marvelous world? The second is: *Why* did He make it?

The purpose of the thing must always be greater than the thing itself: it encloses, permeates and maintains it. The result is but a small part of the preëxistent intention. All things must stand or fall by their purposes, and every great work must necessarily be the outgrowth of a great purpose.

Were these wonderful, these oceanic Shakespeare Plays the unconscious outpourings of an untutored genius, uttered with no more method than the song of a bird; or were they the production of a wise, thoughtful and profound man, who wrote them with certain well-defined objects in view?

I. BACON'S AIMS AND OBJECTS.

We are first to ask ourselves, If Francis Bacon wrote the Plays, what were the purposes of his life? For, as the Plays constitute a great part of his life-work, the purposes of his life must envelop and pervade them.

No man ever lived upon earth who possessed nobler aims than Francis Bacon. He stands at the portal of the opening civilization of modern times, a sublime figure — his heart full of love for man, his busy brain teeming with devices for the benefit of man; with uplifted hands praying God to bless his work, the most far-extending human work ever set afoot on the planet.

He says:

> I am a servant of posterity; for these things require some ages for the ripening of them.[1]

[1] Letter to Father Fulgentio, the Venetian.

Again he says, speaking of himself:

Always desiring, with extreme fervency (such as we are confident God puts into the minds of men), to have that which was never yet attempted, now to be not attempted in vain, to-wit: to release men out of their necessities and miseries.[1]

Again he says:

This work [the *Novum Organum*] is for the bettering of men's bread and wine, which are the characters of temporal blessings and sacraments of eternal.[2]

Macaulay says:

The end which Bacon purposed to himself was the multiplying of human enjoyments and the mitigating of human sufferings. . . . This was the object of his speculations in every department of science — in natural philosophy, in legislation, in politics, in morals.[3]

And, knowing the greatness of God and the littleness of man, he prays the source of all goodness for aid:

God, the maker, preserver and renewer of the universe, guide and protect this work, both in its ascent to his own glory, and in its descent to the good of man, through his good will toward man, by his only begotten son, God with us.[4]

And, speaking of his own philosophy, he says:

I am thus persuaded because of its *infinite usefulness*; for which reason it may be ascribed to divine encouragement.[5]

He speaks of himself as "a servant of God." He seems to have had some thought of founding, not a new religion, but a new system of philosophy, which should do for the improvement of man's condition in this world what religion strove to do for the improvement of his condition in the next world.

And Birch says of Shakespeare:

He had a system, which may be drawn from his works, which he contrasts with the notions of mankind taken from Revelation, and which he represents as doing what revelation and a future state purpose to do for the benefit of mankind, and which he thinks sufficient to supply its place.[6]

In his prayer, written at the time of his downfall, Bacon says:

Remember, O Lord, how thy servant hath walked before thee, remember what I have *first* sought, and what hath been principal in mine intentions. . . . The state and bread of the poor and oppressed have been precious in mine eyes: I have hated all cruelty and hardness of heart; I have, *though in a despised weed*, procured the good of all men.[7]

How did he "at *first*" (that is to say in his youth) seek and procure the good of all men? And what was the *"despised weed"*?

---

[1] *Exper. History.*
[2] Letter to King James, October 19, 1620.
[3] *Essays, Bacon*, p. 370.
[4] *Exper. History.*
[5] Letter to Father Fulgentio.
[6] *Philosophy and Religion of Shak.*, p. 10.
[7] *Life and Works*, Spedding, etc., vol. vii, p. 229.

II. Did he Regard the Drama as a Possible Instrumentality for Good?

Do we find any indications that Bacon, with this intent in his heart to benefit mankind, regarded the stage as a possible instrumentality to that end? That it was capable of being so used — in fact *was* so used — there can be no doubt. Simpson says:

> During its palmy days the English stage was the most important instrument for making opinions heard, its literature the most popular literature of the age, and on that account it was used by the greatest writers for making their comments on public doings and public persons. As an American critic says, "it was newspaper, magazine, novel — all in one."[1]

A recent English writer, W. F. C. Wigston, says:

> Sir Philip Sidney, in his *Defense of Poesy*, maintains that the old philosophers disguised or embodied their entire cosmogonies in their poetry, as, for example, Thales, Empedocles, Parmenides, Pythagoras, and Phocyclides, *who were poets and philosophers at once*.[2]

But did Bacon entertain any such views? Unquestionably. He says:

> Dramatic Poesy is as *History made visible;* for it represents actions as if they were present, whereas History represents them as past. Parabolical Poesy is typical History, by which *ideas that are objects of the intellect are represented in forms that are objects of the sense.* . . .
>
> Dramatic Poesy, which has the theater for its world, *would be of excellent use if well directed.* For the stage is capable of no small *influence*, both of discipline and of corruption. Now, of corruptions in this kind we have enough; but the discipline has, in our times, been plainly neglected. And though in modern states play-acting is esteemed but as a toy, except when it is too satirical and biting; yet *among the ancients it was used as a means of educating men's minds to virtue.* Nay, it has been regarded by learned men and great philosophers *as a kind of musician's bow by which men's minds may be played upon*. And certainly it is true, and one of the great secrets of nature, that the minds of men are more open to impressions and affections when many are gathered together than when they are alone.[3]

The reader will note some suggestive phrases in the above: "dramatic poesy, which has the theater for its world." We are reminded of Shakespeare's "All the world's a stage." "A kind of musician's bow, by which men's minds may be played upon." This recalls to us *Hamlet's:*

> Why, do you think that I am easier to *be played on than a pipe?* Call me what instrument you will, though you can fret me, you cannot *play upon me.*[4]

---

[1] *School of Shak.*, vol. i, p. xviii.
[2] *A New Study of Shak.*, p. 42.
[3] *De Augmentis*, book ii, chap. 13.
[4] *Hamlet*, iii, 2.

III. WAS HE ASSOCIATED WITH PLAYS AND PLAYERS?

But it may be said: These are the utterances of a philosopher who contemplates these things with an aloofness, and Bacon may have taken no interest in play-houses or plays.

Let us see.

His loving and religious mother, writing of her sons, Anthony and Francis, in 1594, says:

> I trust they will not mum, nor mask, nor sinfully revel.[1]

In 1594 his brother Anthony had removed from Gray's Inn to a house in Bishopsgate Street, "much to his mother's distress," says Spedding, "who feared the neighborhood of the Bull Inn, where plays and interludes were acted."[2]

Bacon took part in the preparation of many plays and masks, for the entertainment of the court, some of which were *acted by Shakspere's company of players*.

The Queen seemed to have some suspicion of Bacon being a poet or writer of plays. The Earl of Essex writes him, May 18, 1594 — the Earl then urging Bacon for some law office in the gift of the crown:

> And she did acknowledge you had a great wit, and an excellent gift of speech, and much other good learning. But in law she rather thought you could make show to the uttermost of your knowledge, than that you were deep.[3]

And Bacon himself acknowledges that his mind is diverted from his legal studies to some contemplations of a different sort, and more agreeable to his nature. He says, in a letter to Essex:

> Your Lordship shall in this beg my life of the Queen; for I see well the bar will be my bier.

And he writes to his uncle, Lord Burleigh, in 1594:

> To speak plainly, though perhaps vainly, I do not think that the ordinary practice of the law will be admitted for a good account of the poor talent that God hath given me.[4]

Montagu says:

> Forced by the narrowness of his fortune into business, conscious of his own powers, aware of the peculiar quality of his mind, and disliking his pursuits, his heart was often in his study, while he lent his person to the robes of office.[5]

---

[1] Spedding's *Life and Letters*, vol. i, p. 326.
[2] *Life and Works*, vol. i, p. 314.
[3] *Life and Works*, Spedding, vol. i, p. 297.
[4] Letter to Burleigh, 1594.
[5] Montagu, *Life and Works*, vol. i, p. 117.

If, then, it is conceded that Bacon had great purposes for the benefit of mankind, purposes to be achieved by him, not by the sword or by the powers which flow from high positions, but by the pen, by working on "the minds of men;" and if it is conceded, as it must be, that he recognized the stage as an instrumentality that could be made of great force for that end, by which the minds of men could "be played upon;" and if it is conceded that he was the author of masks and the getter-up of other dramatic representations; and that his mind was not devoted to the dry details of his profession; and if it is conceded, as I think it must be, that he had the genius, the imagination, the wit and the industry to have prepared the Shakespeare Plays, what is there to negative the conclusion that he did so prepare them?

And does he not seem to be pointing at the stage, in these words, when, speaking of the obstructions to the reception of truth caused by the ignorance and bigotry of the age, he says, in *The Masculine Birth of Time:*

"And what," you will say, "is this legitimate method? Have done with artifice and circumlocution; show me the naked truth of your design, that I may be able to form a judgment for myself." I would, my dearest son, that matters were in such a state with you as to render this possible. Do you suppose that, when all the entrances and passages to the mind of all men are infested and obstructed with the darkest idols, and these seated and burned in, as it were, into their substance, that clear and smooth places can be found for receiving the true and natural rays of objects? A *new process* must be instituted by which to *insinuate ourselves into minds* so entirely obstructed. For, as the delusions of the insane are removed by art and ingenuity, but aggravated by opposition, so must we *adapt ourselves to the universal insanity.*

And again he says:

So men generally taste well knowledges that are *drenched in flesh and blood*, civil history, morality, policy about which men's affections, praises, fortunes do turn and are conversant.[1]

He not only discusses in his philosophical works dramatic literature and the influence of the stage, but he urges *in the translation* of the second book of the *Advancement of Learning* (but not in the English copy), "that the *art of acting* (*actio theatralis*) should be made a part of the education of youth."[2] "The Jesuits," he says, "do not despise it;" and he thinks they are right, for, "though it

---

[1] *Advancement of Learning*, book ii. [2] *Works of Bacon*, vol. vi. p. 307.

be of ill repute as a profession, yet as a part of discipline it is of excellent use."

Spedding adds:

In Bacon's time, when masks acted by young gentlemen of the universities or inns of court were the favorite entertainment of princes, these things were probably better attended to than they are now.

And Bacon seemed to feel that there ought to be some great writings to show the affections and passions of mankind. He says:

And here again I find it strange that Aristotle should have written divers volumes of ethics and never handled the affections, which is the principal subject thereof. . . . But the poets and writers of histories are the best doctors of this knowledge: where we may find painted forth, with great life, how affections are kindled and incited, and how pacified and refrained; and how again contained from act and further degree; how they disclose themselves; how they work; how they vary; how they gather and fortify; how they are inwrapped, one within another, and how they do fight and encounter one with another, and other like particulars.[1]

And Barry Cornwall says, as if in echo of these sentiments:

If Bacon educated the reason, Shakespeare educated the heart.

The one work was the complement of the other, and both came out of the same great mind. They were flowers growing from the stalk of the same tremendous purpose.

IV. HIS POVERTY.

But the reader may be fencing the truth out of his mind with the thought that Bacon was a rich man's son, and had not the incentive to literary labor. Richard Grant White puts this argument in the following form. Speaking of the humble, not to say vile, circumstances which surrounded Shakspere in his youth, he says:

If Shakespeare had been born at Charlecote, he would probably have had a seat in Parliament, not improbably a peerage; but we should have had no plays, only a few formal poems and sonnets, most likely, and possibly some essays, with all of Bacon's wisdom, set forth in a style more splendid than Bacon's, but hardly so incisive.

It is curious how the critical mind can hardly think of Shakespeare without being reminded of Bacon.

But was Bacon above the reach of poverty? Was he above the necessity of striving to eke out his income with his pen? No. Hepworth Dixon says:

---

[1] *Advancement of Learning*, book ii.

Lady Anne and her sons are poor. Anthony, the loving and beloved, with whom Francis had been bred at Cambridge and in France, has now come home. . . . The two young fellows have little money and expensive ways. . . . Lady Anne starves herself at Gorhambury that she may send to Gray's Inn ale from the cellar, pigeons from her dove-cote, fowls from her farm-yard — gifts which she seasons with a good deal of motherly love, and not a little of her best motherly advice.[1]

In 1612 Bacon writes King James:

My good old mistress [Queen Elizabeth] was wont to call me her watch-candle, because it pleased her to say I did continually burn (and yet she *suffered me to waste almost to nothing*), so I much more owe like duty to your Majesty.[2]

In a letter to Villiers, Bacon says:

Countenance, encourage and advance able men. *For in the time of the Cecils, the father and son, able men were by design and of purpose suppressed.*

The same story runs through all the years during which the Shakespeare Plays were written. Spedding says:

Michaelmas term [1593] passed, and still no solicitor appointed. Meanwhile, the burden of debt and the difficulty of obtaining necessary supplies was daily increasing. Anthony's correspondence during this autumn is full of urgent applications to various friends for loans of money, and the following memorandum shows that much of his own necessity arose from his anxiety to supply the necessities of his brother.[3]

Here Mr. Spedding inserts the memorandum, showing £5 loaned Francis September 12, 1593; £1 loaned him October 23, 1593; £5 loaned him November 19, 1593, with other loans of £10, £20 and £100.

Falstaff expressed Bacon's own experience when he said:

I can get no remedy against this consumption of the purse: borrowing only lingers and lingers it out, but the disease is incurable.[4]

In the year 1594 Bacon describes himself, in a letter, as "*poor and sick, working for bread.*"

In 1597 it is the same story. Spedding says:

Bacon's fortunes are still as they were, only with this difference: that as the calls on his income are increasing, in the shape of interest for borrowed money, the income itself is diminishing through the sale of lands and leases.[5]

His grief and perplexity are so great that he cries out in a letter to his uncle, the Lord Treasurer, written in that year:

I stand indifferent whether God call me or her Majesty.

---

[1] *Personal History of Lord Bacon*, p. 32.
[2] Letter to King James, May 31, 1612.
[3] Spedding, *Life and Works*, vol. i, p. 321.
[4] *2d Henry IV.*, i, 2.
[5] Spedding, *Life and Works*, vol. ii, p. 53.

In 1598 he is arrested for debt by Sympson, the goldsmith; in 1603 he is again in trouble and petitions the Secretary, Cecil, to intercede and prevent his creditors taking more than the principal of his bond, for, he adds, "a Jew can take no more."

He was constantly annoyed and pestered by his creditors. He writes Mr. Michael Hicks, January 21, 1600, that he proposes to clear himself from "the discontent, speech or danger of others" of his creditors. "Some of my debts, of *most clamor and importunity*, I have paid."

Again he says: "I do use to pay my debts *in time*"—not in money.

July 3, 1603, he writes his cousin Robert, Lord Cecil:

> I shall not be able to pay the money within the time by your Lordship undertaken, which was a fortnight. Nay, money I find so hard to come by at this time, as I thought to have become an humble suitor to your Honor to have sustained me, ... with taking up three hundred pounds till I can put away some land.

He hopes, by selling off "the skirts of my living in Hertfordshire," to have enough left to yield him three hundred pounds per annum income.

V. THE PROFIT OF PLAY-WRITING.

The price paid for a new play was from £5 to £20. This, reduced to dollars, is $25 to $100. But money, it is agreed, possessed a purchasing power then equal to twelve times what it has now; so that Bacon, for writing a new play, would receive what would be the equivalent of from $300 to $1,200 to-day. But in addition to this the author was entitled to all the receipts taken in, above expenses, on the second or third day of the play,[1] and this, in the case of a successful play, might be a considerable sum. And probably in the case of plays as popular as were the Shakespeare Plays, special arrangements were made as to the division of the profits. It was doubtless from dividing with Bacon these sums that Shakspere acquired his large fortune.

Such sums as these to a man who was borrowing one pound at a time from his necessitous brother, Anthony, and who was more than once arrested and put in sponging-houses for debt, were a matter of no small moment.

---

[1] See Collier's *Annals of the Stage*, vol. iii, pp. 224, 229, 230, etc.

He seems, from a letter to Essex, to have had some secret means of making money. He says:

> For means I value that most: and the rather because *I am purposed not to follow the practice of the law;* . . . and my reason is only because it drinketh too much time, *which I have dedicated to better purposes.* But, even for that point of estate and means, I partly lean to Thales' opinion, "*that a philosopher may be rich if he will.*"

This is very significant. Even Spedding perceives the traces of a mystery. He says:

> So enormous were the results which Bacon anticipated from such a renovation of philosophy as he had conceived the possibility of, that the reluctance which he felt to devote his life to the ordinary practice of a lawyer cannot be wondered at. It is easier to understand why he was resolved not to do that, than *what other plan he had to clear himself of the difficulties which were accumulating upon him, and to obtain means of living and working.* . . . What course he betook himself to at the crisis at which he had now arrived, I cannot positively say. I do not find any letter of his which can be probably assigned to the winter of 1596; nor have I met among his brother's papers anything which indicates *what he was about.* . . . I presume, however, that he betook himself to his studies.[1]

In the last years of the sixteenth century and the first of the seventeenth Bacon seems to have given up all hope of rising to office in the state. He was under some cloud. He says:

> My ambition is quenched. . . . My ambition now I shall only put upon my pen, whereby I shall be able to maintain memory and merit of the times succeeding.[2]

He was hopeless; he was powerless; he was poor. He had felt

> The whips and scorns of time,
> The oppressor's wrong, the poor man's contumely,
> . . . the law's delay,
> The insolence of office, and the spurns
> That patient merit of the unworthy takes.

He wrote to the Queen that he had suffered

> The contempt of the contemptible, that measure a man by his estate.[3]

What could he make money at? There was no great novel-reading public, as at present. There were no newspapers to employ ready and able pens. There was little sale for the weightier works of literature. There was but one avenue open to him — the play-house.

Did he combine the more sordid and pressing necessity for money with those great, kindly, benevolent purposes toward man-

---

[1] Spedding, *Works of Bacon — Letters and Life*, vol. ii, p. 1.
[2] Letter to R. Cecil, July 3, 1603.
[3] Letter to the Queen, 1599-1600 — *Life and Works*, vol. ii, p. 166.

VI. Great Moral Lessons.

In the first place, the Plays are great sermons against great evils. They are moral epics.

What lesson does *Macbeth* leave upon the mind? It teaches every man who reads it, or sees it acted, the horrors of an unscrupulous ambition. It depicts, in the first place, a brave soldier and patriot, defending his country at the risk of his life. Then it shows the agents of evil approaching and suggesting dark thoughts to his brain. Then it shows us, as Bacon says, speaking of the passions as delineated by the poets and writers of histories:

> Painted forth, with great life, how affections (passions) are kindled and incited; and how pacified and refrained; and how again contained from act and further degree; how they disclose themselves; how they work; how they vary; how they gather and fortify; how they are inwrapped one within another; and how they do fight and encounter one with another.

All this is revealed in *Macbeth*. We see the seed of ambition taking root; we see it "disclosed;" we see self-love and the sense of right warring with each other. We see his fiendish wife driving him forward to crime against the promptings of his better nature. It depicts, with unexampled dramatic power, a cruel and treacherous murder. Then it shows how crime begets the necessity for crime:

> To be thus is nothing,
> But to be safely thus.

It shows one horror treading fast upon another's heels: the usurper troubled with the horrible dreams that "shake him nightly;" the mind of the ambitious woman giving way under the strain her terrible will had put upon it, until we see her seeking peace in suicide; while Macbeth falls at last, overthrown and slaughtered.

Have all the pulpits of all the preachers given out a more terrible exposition and arraignment of ambition? Think of the uncountable millions who, in the past three hundred years, have witnessed this play! Think of the illimitable numbers who will behold it during the next thousand years!

What an awful picture of the workings of a guilty conscience is that exhibited when Macbeth sees, even at the festal board, the blood-boltered Banquo rising up and regarding him with glaring and soulless eyes. And how like the pitiful cry of a lost soul is this utterance?

> I have lived long enough: my way of life
> Is fallen into the sear, the yellow leaf:
> And that which should accompany old age,
> As honor, love, obedience, troops of friends,
> I must not look to have; but, in their stead,
> Curses, not loud but deep, mouth-honor, breath
> Which the poor heart would fain deny, and dare not.

Call the roll of all your pulpit orators! Where is there one that has ever preached such a sermon as that? Where is there one that has ever had such an audience — such an unending succession of million-large audiences — as this man, who, in a "despised weed, sought the good of all men"?

And, remember, that it was not the virtuous alone, the church-goers, the elect, who came to hear this marvelous sermon, but the high, the low; the educated, the ignorant; the young, the old; the good, the vicious; the titled lord, the poor 'prentice; the high-born dame, the wretched waste and wreck of womankind.

A sermon preached almost nightly for nigh three hundred years! Not preached with robe or gown, or any pretense of virtue, but in those living pictures, "that history made visible," of the mighty philanthropist. Not coming with the ostentation and parade of holiness, with swinging censer and rolling organ, but conveyed into the minds of the audience insensibly, insinuated into them, through the instrumentality of a lot of poor players. Precisely as we have seen Bacon suggesting that, by "a new process," truth should be *insinuated* into minds obstructed and infested — a process "*drenched in flesh and blood*," as surely Macbeth is; a process that the ancients used to "educate men's minds to virtue;" by which the minds of men might be "played upon," as if with a "musician's bow," with the greater force because (as he had observed a thousand times in the Curtain Theater) the minds of men are more acted upon when they are gathered in numbers than when alone.

VII. INGRATITUDE.

Turn to *Lear*. What is its text? Ingratitude. Another mighty sermon.

The grand old man who gave all, with his heart in it. The viciousness of two women; the nobleness of a third — for the gentle heart of the poet would not allow him to paint mankind altogether bad; he saw always "the soul of goodness in things evil." And mark the moral of the story. The overthrow of the wicked, who yet drag down the good and noble in their downfall.

VIII. JEALOUSY AND INTEMPERANCE.

Turn to *Othello*. What is the text here? The evils of jealousy and the power for wrong of one altogether iniquitous. The overthrow of a noble nature by falsehood; the destruction of a pure and gentle woman to satisfy the motiveless hate of a villain. And there is within this another moral. The play is a grand plea for temperance, expressed with jewels of thought set in arabesques of speech. Can all the reformers match that expression:

> O thou invisible spirit of wine! If thou hast no name to be known by, let us call thee devil!

The plot of the play turns largely on Cassio's drunkenness; for it is Desdemona's intercession for poor Cassio that arouses Othello's suspicions. And how pitiful are Cassio's exclamations:

> Oh, that men should put an enemy in their mouths to steal away their brains! that we should, with joy, pleasance, revel and applause, transform ourselves *into beasts*. . . . To be now a sensible man, by and by a fool, and presently *a beast!* O strange! Every inordinate cup is unblessed, and the ingredient is a devil.

It is impossible to sum up a stronger appeal in behalf of a temperate use of the good things of this world than these words contain. And, remember, they were written, not in the nineteenth century, but in an age of universal drunkenness, practiced by both men and women; and uttered at first to audiences nine-tenths of whom probably had more ale and sack in them than was good for them, even while they witnessed the play.

And we find the great teacher always preaching the same lesson of temperance to the people, and in much the same phrases. He says:

> When he is best, he is little worse than a man; and when he is worst he is little better than a beast.[1]

And again he says:

> A howling monster; a drunken monster.[2]

---

[1] *Merry Wives of Windsor*, i, 2.   [2] *Tempest*, iii, 2.

And in the introduction to *The Taming of the Shrew*, his Lordship, looking at the drunken Christopher Sly, says:

> Oh, monstrous beast! how like a swine he lies.

IX. TIMON OF ATHENS.

In this play, the moral is the baseness of sycophants and mammon-worshipers. Its bitterness and wrath came from Bacon's own oppressed heart, in the day of his calamities; when he had felt all "the contempt of the contemptible, who measure a man by his estate."

Mr. Hallam says:

> There seems to have been a period of Shakespeare's life when his heart was ill at ease, and ill content with the world or his own conscience; the memory of hours mis-spent, the pang of affection misplaced or unrequited, the experience of man's worser nature, which intercourse with ill-chosen associates by choice or circumstance peculiarly teaches;—these, as they sank down into the depths of his great mind, seem not only to have inspired into it the conception of *Lear* and *Timon*, but that of one primary character, the censurer of mankind.[1]

X. SHYLOCK THE USURER.

In 1594 Bacon was the victim of a Jew money-lender. In 1595 appeared *The Merchant of Venice*, in which, says Mrs. Pott:

> Shylock immortalizes the hard Jew who persecuted Bacon; and Antonius the generous brother Anthony who sacrificed himself and taxed his credit in order to relieve Francis. Antonio in *Twelfth Night* is of the same generous character.

And it will be observed that both Bacon and the writer of the Plays were opposed to usury.

Says Bacon:

> It is against nature for money to *breed* money.[2]

And again he speaks of

> The devouring trade of usury.[3]

While in Shakespeare we have the conversation between Shylock and Antonio, the former justifying the taking of interest on money by the case of Jacob, who "grazed his uncle Laban's sheep" and took "all the yearlings which were streaked and pied." Says Antonio:

> Was this inserted to make interest good?
> Or is your gold and silver ewes and rams?
> *Shylock.* I cannot tell. I make it *breed* as fast.

---

[1] *Literature of Europe*, vol. iii, p. 508. [2] *Essay Of Usury.* [3] *Essay Of Seditions.*

And again we have the same idea of money *breeding* money, used by Bacon, repeated in this conversation. Antonio says:

> I am as like to call thee so again,
> To spit on thee again, to spurn thee, too.
> If thou wilt lend this money, lend it not
> As to thy friends; for when did friendship take
> A *breed* of barren metal from his friend?

And it will be remembered that the whole play turns on the subject of usury. The provocation which Antonio first gave Shylock was that—

> He lends out money gratis, and brings down
> The rate of usance here with us in Venice.

And again:

> Signior Antonio, many a time and oft
> In the Rialto you have rated me
> About my monies and my usances.

The purpose of the play was to stigmatize the selfishness manifested in the taking of excessive interest; which is, indeed, to the poor debtor, many a time the cutting-out of the very heart. And hence the mighty genius has, in the name of Shylock, created a synonym for usurer, and has made in the Jew money-lender the most terrible picture of greed, inhumanity and wickedness in all literature.

Bacon saw the necessity for borrowing and lending, and hence of moderate compensation for the use of money. But he pointed out, in his essay *Of Usury*, the great evils which resulted from the practice. He contended that if the owners of money could not lend it out, they would have to employ it themselves in business; and hence, instead of the "lazy trade of usury," there would be enterprises of all kinds, and employment for labor, and increased revenues to the kingdom. And his profound wisdom was shown in this utterance:

> It [usury] bringeth the treasures of a realm or state into a few hands; for the usurer being at certainties, and others at uncertainties, at the end of the game most of the money will be in his box; and ever a state flourisheth most when wealth is more equally spread.

XI. Mobocracy.

The moral of *Coriolanus* is that the untutored multitude, as it existed in Bacon's day, the mere mob, was not capable of self-government. The play was written, probably, because of the many indications which Bacon saw that "the foot of the peasant was treading close on the kibe of the courtier," as Hamlet says; and that a religious war, accompanied by an uprising of the lower classes, was at hand, which would, as he feared, sweep away all learning and civility in a deluge of blood. The deluge came shortly after his death, but the greatness and self-control of the English race saved it from ultimate anarchy. At the same time Bacon, in his delineation of the patriot Brutus, showed that he was not adverse to a republican government of intelligent citizens.

XII. The Deficiencies of the Man of Thought.

Hamlet is autobiographical. It is Bacon himself. It is the man of thought, the philosopher, the poet, placed in the midst of the necessities of a rude age.

Bacon said:

I am better fitted to hold a book than to play a part.

He is overweighted with the thought-producing faculty: in his case the cerebrum overbalances the cerebellum. He laments in his old age that, being adapted to contemplation and study, his fortune forced him into parts for which he was not fitted. He makes this his apology to posterity:

This I speak to posterity, not out of ostentation, but because I judge it may somewhat import the dignity of learning, to have a man *born for letters rather than anything else*, who should, by a certain fatality, and against the bent of his own genius, *be compelled into active life*.[1]

This is Hamlet. He comes in with book in hand, speculating where he should act. He is "holding a book" where he should "play a part."

Schlegel says of *Hamlet*:

The whole is intended to show that a calculating consideration, which exhausts all the relations and possible consequences of a deed, must cripple the power of acting.

Coleridge says of *Hamlet*:

We see a great, an enormous intellectual activity, and a proportionate aversion to real action consequent upon it.

Dowden says:

When the play opens he has reached the age of thirty years — the age, it has been said, when the ideality of youth ought to become one with and inform the practical tendencies of manhood — and he has received culture of every kind

---

[1] *Advancement of Learning*, book viii, p. 3.

except the culture of active life. He has slipped on into years of full manhood still a haunter of the university, a student of philosophies, an amateur in art, a ponderer on the things of life and death, who has never formed a resolution or executed a deed.

These descriptions fit Bacon's case precisely. His ambition drags him into the midst of the activities of the court; his natural predisposition carries him away to St. Albans or Twickenham Park, to indulge in his secret "contemplations;" and to compose the "works of his recreation" and "the works of the alphabet." He was, as it were, two men bound in one. He aspired to rule England and to give a new philosophy to mankind. He would rival Cecil and Aristotle at the same time.

And this play seems to be autobiographical in another sense. Hamlet was robbed of his rights by a relative — his uncle. He "lacked advancement." Bacon, who might naturally hope to rise to a place in Elizabeth's court similar to that held by his father, "lacks advancement;" and it is his uncle Burleigh and his uncle's son who hold him down. Hamlet is a philosopher. So is Bacon. Hamlet writes verses to Ophelia. Bacon is a poet. Hamlet writes a play, or part of one, for the stage. So, we assert, did Bacon. Hamlet puts forth the play as the work of another. So, we think, did Bacon. Hamlet cries out:

> The play's the thing
> Wherewith I'll catch the conscience of the King.

And it is our theory that Bacon sought with his plays to catch the conscience of mankind. Hamlet has one true, trusted friend, Horatio, to whom he opens the secrets of his heart, and to whom he utters a magnificent essay on friendship. Bacon has another such trusted friend, Sir Tobie Matthew, to whom he opened *his* heart, and for whom, we are told, he wrote his prose essay *Of Friendship*. Hamlet is supposed to be crazy. Bacon is charged by his enemies with being a little daft — with having "a bee in his head" — and each herein, perhaps, illustrates the old truth, that

> Great minds to madness are quite close allied,
> And thin partitions do the bounds divide.

XIII. THE TEMPEST.

The great drama of *The Tempest* contains another personal story. This has, in part, been perceived by others. Mr. Campbell says:

The Tempest has a sort of sacredness as the last work of a mighty workman. Shakespeare, as if conscious that it would be his last, and as if inspired *to typify himself*, has made his hero a natural, a dignified and benevolent magician, who could conjure up spirits from the vasty deep, and command supernatural agency by the most seemingly natural and simple means. . . . Here Shakespeare himself is Prospero, or *rather the superior genius who commands both Prospero and Ariel.* But the time was approaching when the potent sorcerer was to break his staff, and bury it fathoms in the ocean,

> Deeper than did ever plummet sound.[1]

What is the plot of the play?

Prospero was born to greatness, was a "prince of power."

Bacon was born in the royal palace of York Place, and expected to inherit the greatness of his father, Elizabeth's Lord Chancellor. "Bacon," says Hepworth Dixon,[2] "seemed born to power."

Prospero was cast down from his high place. So was Bacon. Who did it? His uncle Burleigh. And in *The Tempest*, as in *Hamlet*, an uncle is the evil genius of the play. Prospero says to his daughter Miranda:

> Thy false uncle — . . .
> Being once perfected how to grant suits,
> How to deny them; whom to advance, and whom
> To trash for over-topping — new created
> The creatures that were mine, I say, or changed them,
> Or else new formed them; having both the key
> Of officer and office, set all hearts i' th' state
> To what tune pleased his ear.

This might be taken to describe, very aptly, the kind of arts by which Bacon's uncle, Burleigh, reached and held power. Bacon wrote to King James:

> In the time of Elizabeth the Cecils purposely oppressed all men of ability.

And why did Prospero lose power? Because he was a student. He neglected the arts of statecraft and politics, and devoted himself to nobler pursuits. He says:

> I, thus neglecting worldly ends, all dedicated
> To closeness and the bettering of my mind.
> . . . . me, poor man! my library
> Was dukedom large enough!

"The bettering of my mind" is very Baconian. But where have we the slightest evidence that the man of Stratford ever strove to improve his mind?

And the labors of Prospero were devoted to the liberal arts and to *secret* studies. So were Bacon's. Prospero says:

---
[1] Knight's *Shakespeare*, introductory notice to *Tempest*.
[2] *Personal History of Lord Bacon*, p. 7.

> And Prospero, the prime duke, being so reputed
> In dignity; and for the liberal arts
> Without a parallel; those being all my study,
> The government I cast upon my brother,
> And to my state grew stranger, being transported
> And rapt in *secret* studies.

What happened? Prospero was dethroned, and with his little daughter, Miranda, was seized upon:

> In few, they hurried us aboard a bark;
> Bore us some leagues to sea, where they prepared
> A rotten carcase of a butt, not rigged,
> Nor tackle, sail, nor mast; the very rats
> Instinctively had quit it.

This was the rotten butt of Bacon's fortunes, when they were at their lowest; when his friends deserted him, like the rats, and when he wrote *Timon of Athens*.

Miranda asks:
> How came we ashore?

Prospero replies:
> By Providence divine
> Some food we had, and some fresh water, that
> A noble Neapolitan, Gonzalo,
> Out of his charity, (who being then appointed
> Master of this design), did give us, with
> Rich garments, linens, stuffs and necessaries
> Which since have steaded much; so of his gentleness,
> Knowing I loved my books, he furnished me,
> From mine own library, with volumes that
> I prize above my dukedom.

How fully is all this in accord with the character of Francis Bacon:—the man who had "taken all knowledge for his province;" the "concealed poet;" the philanthropist; the student; the lover of books! How little is it in accordance with what we know of Shakspere, who does not seem to have possessed a library, or a single book—not even a quarto copy of one of the Plays.

But who was Miranda?

The name signifies *wonderful things*. Does it mean these wonderful Plays? She was Bacon's child—the offspring of his brain. And we find, as I have shown, in sonnet lxxvii these lines, evidently written in the front of a commonplace-book:

> Look what thy memory cannot contain,
> Commit to these waste blanks, and thou shalt find
> *Those children nursed, delivered from thy brain,*
> To take a new acquaintance of thy mind.

Was Miranda the wonderful product of Bacon's brain—the child of the concealed poet?

When Ferdinand sees Miranda, he plays upon the name:

> My prime request,
> Which I do last pronounce, is, O! *you wonder!*
> If you be maid or no?

And it will be noted that Miranda was in existence before Prospero's downfall; and the Plays had begun to appear in Bacon's youth and before his reverses.

And we are further told that when Prospero and his daughter were carried to the island, the love he bore Miranda was the one thing that preserved him from destruction:

> *Miranda.* Alack! what trouble
> Was I then to you?
> *Prospero.* O! a cherubin
> Thou wast that did preserve me! Thou didst smile,
> Infusèd with a fortitude from heaven,
> When I have decked the sea with drops full salt,
> Under my burthen groaned; which raised in me
> An undergoing stomach, to bear up
> Against what should ensue.

That is to say, in the days of Bacon's miseries, his love for divine poetry saved him from utter dejection and wretchedness. And in some large sense, therefore, his troubles were well for him; and for ourselves, for without them we should not have the Plays. And hence we read:

> *Miranda.* O, the Heavens!
> What foul play had we, that we came from thence?
> Or blessed was't we did?
> *Prospero.* Both, both, my girl;
> By foul play, as thou sayst, were we heaved thence;
> But blessedly holp hither.

And the leisure of the retirement to which Bacon was driven enabled him to perfect the Plays, whereas success would have absorbed him in the trivialities of court life. And so Prospero says to Miranda:

> Sit still, and hear the last of our sea-sorrow.
> Here in this island we arrived; and here
> Have I, thy schoolmaster, made thee more profit
> Than other princes can, that have more time
> For vainer hours, and tutors not so careful.

And on the island is Ariel. Who is Ariel? It is a tricksy spirit, a singer of sweet songs, "which give delight and hurt not;"

a maker of delicious music; a secretive spirit, given much to hiding in invisibility while it achieves wondrous external results. It is Prospero's instrumentality in his magic; his servant. And withal it is humane, gentle and loving, like the soul of the benevolent philosopher himself. If Pro-*sper-o* is Shake-*sper*, or, as Campbell says, "the superior genius who commands both Prospero and Ariel," then Ariel is the genius of poetry, the constructive intellectual power of the drama-maker, which he found pegged in the knotty entrails of an oak, uttering the harsh, discordant sounds of the old moralities, until he released it and gave it wings and power. And, like the maker of the Plays, it sings sweet songs, of which Ferdinand says:

> This is no mortal business, nor no sound
> That the earth owns.

And, like the poet, it creates masks to work upon the senses of its audience — it is a play-maker.

And there is one other inhabitant of the island — Caliban —

> A freckled whelp, hag-born.

Who is Caliban? Is he the real Shakspere? He claims the ownership of the island. Was the island the stage, — the playhouse, — to which Bacon had recourse for the means of life, when his fortune failed him; to which he came in the rotten butt of his fortunes, with his child Miranda, — the early plays?

Shakspere, be it remembered, was at the play-house before Bacon came to it. Prospero found Caliban on the island. Caliban claimed the ownership of it. He says, "This island's mine."

> When thou camest first,
> Thou strok'dst me, and made much of me;
> Would give me water with berries in't; and teach me how
> To name the bigger light, and how the less,
> That burn by day and night; and then I loved thee,
> And showed thee all the qualities of the isle,
> The fresh springs, brine springs, barren place and fertile.

That is to say, Shakspere gave Bacon the use of his knowledge of the stage and play-acting, and showed him the fertile places from which money could be extracted.

And do these lines represent Bacon's opinion of Shakspere?

> Abhorred slave,
> Which any print of goodness will not take,
> Being capable of all ill! I pitied thee,
> Took pains to make thee speak, taught thee each hour

> One thing or other: when thou didst not, savage,
> Know thine own meaning, but would gabble like
> A thing most brutish, I endowed thy purposes
> *With words that made them known.*

And again he says — and it will be remembered Shakspere was alive when *The Tempest* was written:

> A devil, a born devil, on whose nature
> Nurture can never stick; on whom my pains,
> Humanly taken, all, all lost, quite lost:
> And as, with age, his body uglier grows,
> So his mind cankers.

Prospero has lost his kingdom. He has had the leisure in the solitude of his "full poor *cell*" to bring *Miranda* to the perfection of mature beauty. The Plays are finished.

[Bacon, after his downfall, in 1623, applied for the place of Provost of Eaton; he says, "it was a pretty *cell* for my fortune."]

When Miranda was grown to womanhood an accident threw Prospero's enemies in his power. A most propitious star shone upon his fortunes. His enemies were upon the sea near him. With the help of Ariel he raised a mighty *tempest* and shipwrecked those who had deprived him of his kingdom, and brought them wretched and half-drowned to his feet. He had always wished to leave the island and recover his kingdom; and, his enemies being in his power, he forced them to restore him to his rights.

Is there anything in Bacon's life which parallels this story? There is.

Bacon, like Prospero, had been cast down. He desired to rise again in the state. And there came a time when he brought his enemies to his feet, in the midst of a tempest of the state, which he probably helped to create. And this very word *tempest*, so applied, is a favorite one with Bacon. He said, at the time of his downfall:

> When I enter into myself, I find not the materials for such a *tempest* as is now come upon me.

In June, 1606, Francis Bacon was out of place and without influence with the court, but he wielded great power in Parliament, of which he was a member, as a noble orator and born ruler of men. He had hoped that this influence would have secured him preferment in the state. He was disappointed. Hepworth Dixon shows that, upon the death of Sir Francis Gawdy and Coke's promotion to the bench, Bacon expected to be made Attorney-General. But his malign cousin, Cecil, again defeated his just and reasonable hopes; and the great man, after all his years of patient waiting, had to step aside once more to make place for some small creature.

But there is trouble in the land. King James of Scotland came down to rule England, and hordes of his countrymen came with, or followed after him, to improve their fortunes in the fat land of which their countryman was monarch. King James desired Parliament to pass the bill of Union, to unite the Scots and English on terms of equality. His heart was set on this measure. But the English disliked the Scots.

Hepworth Dixon says:

> Under such crosses the bill on Union fares but ill. Fuller, the bilious representative of London, flies at the Scots. The Scots in London are in the highest degree unpopular. Lax in morals and in taste, they will take the highest place at table, they will drink out of anybody's can, they will kiss the hostess, or her buxom maid, without saying "by your leave."[1]

We have reason to think that Ariel is at work, invisibly, behind the scenes raising the Tempest. Dixon continues:

> Brawls fret the taverns which they haunt; *pasquins hiss against them from the stage*. . . . *Three great poets, Jonson, Chapman and Marston, go to jail for a harmless jest against these Scots.* Such acts of rigor make the name of Union hateful to the public ear.

Let Hepworth Dixon tell the rest of the story:

> When Parliament meets in November to discuss the bill on Union, Bacon stands back. The King has chosen his attorney; let the new attorney fight the King's battle. The adversaries to be met are bold and many. . . . Beyond the Tweed, too, people are mutinous *to the point of war*, for the countrymen of Andrew Melville begin to suspect the King of a design against the Kirk. . . . Melville is clapped into the Tower. . . . Hobart (the new Attorney-General) goes to the wall. James now sees that the battle is not to the weak, nor the race to the slow. Bacon has only to hold his tongue and make his terms.[2]

Prospero has only to wait for the Tempest to wash his enemies to his feet.

> Alarmed lest the bill of Union may be rejected by an overwhelming vote, Cecil suddenly adjourns the House. He must get strength. . . . Pressed on all sides, here by the Lord Chancellor, there by a mutinous House of Commons, Cecil at length yields to his cousin's claim; Sir John Doderidge bows his neck, and when Parliament meets, after the Christmas holidays, Bacon holds in his pocket a written engagement for the Solicitor's place.

[1] *Personal History of Lord Bacon*, p. 184.   [2] Ibid., p. 183.

The Tempest is past; the Duke of Milan has recovered his kingdom; the poor scholar leaves his cell, at forty-six years of age, and steps into a place worth £6,000 a year, or $30,000 of our money, equal to probably $300,000 per annum to-day. There is no longer any necessity for the magician to remain upon his poor desert island, with Caliban, and write plays for a living. He dismisses Ariel. *The Plays cease to appear.*

But Prospero, when he leaves the island, takes Miranda with him. She will be well cared for. We will see hereafter that "the works of the alphabet" will be "set in a frame," at heavy cost, and wedded to immortality.

The triumphant statesman *leaves Caliban in possession of the island!* He has crawled out from his temporary shelter:

> I hid me under the dead moon-calf's gaberdine, for fear of the storm.

He will devote the remainder of his life to statecraft and philosophy. He will write no more poetry,

> For at his age
> The hey-day in the blood is tame, it's humble
> And waits upon the judgment.

But Prospero will not be idle. Like Bacon, he has great projects in his head. He says:

> Welcome, sir;
> This cell's my court; here have I few attendants
> And subjects none abroad: pray you, look in.
> My dukedom since you have given me again,
> I will requite you with as good a thing;
> At least *bring forth a wonder to content ye*,
> As much as me my dukedom.

That is to say, relieved of the necessities of life, possessed of power and fortune, he will give the world the *Novum Organum*, the new philosophy, which is to revolutionize the earth and lift up mankind.

And yet, turning, as he does, to these mighty works of his mature years, he cannot part, without a sigh, from the labors of his youth; from the sweet and gentle spirit of the imagination — his "chick," his genius, his "delicate Ariel":

> Why, that's my dainty Ariel: *I shall miss thee;*
> But yet thou shalt have freedom.

And then, casting his eyes backward, he exults over his mighty work:

> Graves, at my command,
> Have waked their sleepers; op'd, and let them forth
> By my so potent art.

Indeed, a long and mighty procession! Lear, Titus Andronicus, Coriolanus, Julius Cæsar, Brutus, Cassius, Marc Antony, Cleopatra, Augustus Cæsar, Timon of Athens, Cymbeline, Alcibiades, Pericles, Macbeth, Duncan, Hamlet, King John, Arthur, Richard II., John of Gaunt, Henry IV., Hotspur, Henry V., Henry VI., Richard III., Clarence, Henry VIII., Wolsey, Cranmer, Queen Katharine, and Anne Boleyn.

> But this rough magic
> I here abjure: and, when I have required
> Some heavenly music (which even now I do)—

[that is to say, he retains his magic power a little longer to write one more play, this farewell drama, *The Tempest*]—

> To work mine end upon their senses that
> This airy charm is for, I'll break my staff,
> Bury it certain fathoms in the earth,
> And, deeper than did ever plummet sound
> I'll drown my book.

What does this mean? Certainly that the magician had ended his work; that his rough magic was no longer necessary; that he would no longer call up the mighty dead from their graves. And he dismisses even the poor players through whom he has wrought his charm; they also are but spirits, to do his bidding:

> *Our revels now are ended:* these our *actors*,
> As I foretold you, were all spirits, and
> Are melted into air, into thin air:
> And, like the baseless fabric of this vision,
> The cloud-capped towers, the gorgeous palaces,
> The solemn temples, the great globe itself,
> Yea, all which it inherit, shall dissolve;
> And like this insubstantial pageant faded,
> Leave not a rack behind. We are such stuff
> As dreams are made on, and our little life
> Is rounded with a sleep.

And this play of *The Tempest* is placed at the very beginning of the great Folio of 1623, as an introduction to the other mighty Plays.

And if this be not the true explanation of this play, where are we to find it? If Pro-*sper* is Shake-*sper* (as seems to be conceded), or the one *for* (*pro*) whom Shake-*sper* stood, what is the meaning of his "abjuring his magic," giving up his work and "drowning his book?" And what is that "wonder" he—the man of Stratford—is to bring forth after he has drowned his book:—something more wonderful than Miranda—(the *wonderful things*)—and with which the dismissed Ariel is to have nothing to do? And why should Shakspere drown his book and retire to Stratford, and write no more plays, thus abjuring his magic? Do you imagine that the man who would sue a neighbor for two shillings loaned; or who would sell a load of stone to the town for ten pence; or who would charge his guest's wine-bill to the parish, would, if he had the capacity to produce an unlimited succession of *Hamlets*, *Lears* and *Macbeths*, worth thousands of pounds, have drowned his book, and gone home and brewed beer and sucked his thumbs for several years, until drunkenness and death came to his relief?

And is there any likeness between the princely, benevolent and magnanimous character of Prospero and that of the man of Stratford?

XIV. KINGCRAFT.

Bacon believed in a monarchy, but in a constitutional monarchy, restrained by a liberty-loving aristocracy, with justice and fair play for the humbler classes.

He, however, was utterly opposed to all royal despotism. He showed, as the leader of the people in the House of Commons, that he was ready to use the power of Parliament to restrain the unlimited arrogance of the crown. He saw that one great obstacle to liberty was the popular idea of the divine right of kings. We can hardly appreciate to-day the full force of that sentiment as it then existed. Hence, in the Plays, he labors to reduce the king to the level of other men, or below it. He represents John as a cowardly knave, a truckler to a foreign power, a would-be murderer, and an altogether worthless creature. Richard II. is little better—a frivolous, weak-witted, corrupt, sordid, dishonest fool.

He puts into his mouth the old-time opinion of the heaven-delegated powers of a king:

> Not all the water of the rough, rude sea
> Can wash the balm from an anointed king:
> The breath of worldly men cannot depose
> The deputy elected by the Lord:

> For every man that Bolingbroke hath press'd,
> To lift shrewd steel against our golden crown,
> Heaven for his Richard hath in heavenly pay
> A glorious angel! then, if angels fight,
> Weak men must fall, for Heaven still guards the right!

And then the poet proceeds to show that this is all nonsense: that the "breath of worldly men" can, and that it in fact does depose him; and that not an angel stirs in all the vasty courts of heaven to defend his cause.

And then he perforates the whole theory still further by making the King himself exclaim:

> Let's choose executors and talk of wills;
> And yet not so; for what can we bequeath
> Save our deposèd bodies to the ground?
> Our lands, our lives and all are Bolingbroke's,
> And nothing can we call our own but death;
> And that small model of the barren earth,
> Which serves as paste and cover to our bones.
> For Heaven's sake let us sit upon the ground,
> And tell sad stories of the death of kings:
> How some have been depos'd, some slain in war,
> Some haunted by the ghosts they have depos'd;
> Some poison'd by their wives, some sleeping killed,
> All murder'd. For within the hollow crown
> That rounds the mortal temples of a king,
> Death keeps his court; and there the antic sits,
> Scoffing his state, and grinning at his pomp;
> Allowing him a breath, a little scene,
> To monarchize, be fear'd, and kill with looks;
> Infusing him with self and vain conceit;
> As if this flesh, which walls about our life,
> Were brass impregnable: and humored thus,
> Comes at the last, and, with a little pin,
> Bores through his castle walls, and,—farewell, king!
> Cover your heads, and mock not flesh and blood
> With solemn reverence; throw away respect,
> Tradition, form and ceremonious duty,
> For you have but mistook me all this while:
> I live with bread like you, feel want, taste grief,
> Need friends. Subjected thus,
> How can you say to me—I am a king!

Surely this must have sounded strangely in the ears of a London audience of the sixteenth century, who had been taught to regard the king as anointed of Heaven and the actual viceregent of God on earth, whose very touch was capable of working miracles in the cure of disease, possessing therein a power exercised on earth aforetime only by the Savior and his saints. And the play concludes with *the murder of Richard.*

And then comes Henry IV., usurper, murderer; and the poet makes him frankly confess his villainy:

> Come hither, Harry, sit thou by my bed;
> And hear, I think, the very latest counsel
> That ever I shall breathe. Heaven knows, my son,
> By what by-paths and indirect, crooked ways
> I met this crown.

And yet he lives to a ripe old age, and establishes a dynasty on the corner-stone of the murder of Richard II.

And we have the same lesson of contempt for kings taught in *Lear:*

> They told me I was everything. But when the rain came to wet me once, and the wind to make me chatter; when the thunder would not peace at my bidding, there I found them, there I smelt them out.[1]

And in *The Tempest* we have this expression:

> What care these roarers for the name of king?[2]

Is not the moral plain:—that kings are nothing more than men; that Heaven did not ordain them, and does not protect them; and that a king has no right to hold his place any longer than he behaves himself?

His son, Henry V., is the best of the lot—he is the hero-king; but even he rises out of a shameful youth; he is the associate of the most degraded; the companion of profligate men and women, of highwaymen and pick-pockets. And even in his mouth the poet puts the same declaration of the hollowness of royal pretensions. King Henry V. says, while in disguise:

> I think the King is but a man as I am; the violet smells to him as it doth to me; the element shews to him as it doth to me; all his senses have but human conditions; his ceremonies laid by, in his nakedness he appears but a man.[3]

We turn to Henry VI., and we find him a shallow, empty imbecile, below the measure even of contempt.

In Richard III. we have a horrible monster; a wild beast; a liar, perjurer, murderer; a remorseless, bloody, man-eating tiger of the jungles.

---

[1] *Lear*, iv. 6. [2] *Tempest*, i. 1. [3] *Henry V.*, iv. 1.

In Henry VIII. we have a king divorcing a sainted angel, as we are told, under the plea of conscience, to marry a frivolous woman, in obedience to the incitements of sensual passion.

And this is the whole catalogue of royal representatives brought on the stage by Shakespeare!

And these Plays educated the English people, and prepared the way for the day when Charles I. was brought to trial and the scaffold.

If Bacon intended to strike deadly blows at the idea of divine right, and irresponsible royal authority, in England, certainly he accomplished his object in these "Histories" of English kings. It may be that the Reform he had intended graduated into the Revolution which he had not intended. He could not foresee Cromwell and the Independents; and yet, that storm being past, England is enjoying the results of his purposes, in its wise constitutional monarchy: — the spirit of liberty wedded to the conservative forms of antiquity.

XV. Teaching History.

But there is another motive in these Plays. They are teachers of history. It is probable that the series of historical dramas began with William the Conqueror, for we find Shakspere, in an obscene anecdote, which tradition records, referring to himself as William the Conqueror, and to Burbadge as Richard III. Then we have Shakespeare's *King John*. In Marlowe we have the play of *Edward II*. Among the doubtful plays ascribed to the pen of Shakespeare is the play of *Edward III*. Then follows *Richard II.*; then, in due and consecutive order, *Henry IV.*, first and second parts; then *Henry V.*; then *Henry VI.*, first, second and third parts; then *Richard III.*; there is no play of Henry VII. (*but Bacon writes a history of Henry VII.*, taking up the story just where the play of *Richard III.* leaves it); then the series of plays ends with *Henry VIII.*, and the cipher narrative probably gives us the whole history of the reign of Elizabeth.

All these plays tended to make history familiar to the common people, and we find testimony to that effect in the writings of the day.

XVI. Patriotism.

But there is another purpose transparently revealed in the Plays. It was to infuse the people with a sense of devotion to their native land. Speaking of national patriotism, Swinburne says:

> Assuredly, no poet ever had more than he (Shakespeare); not even the king of men and poets who fought at Marathon and sang at Salamis; much less had any or has any one of our own, from Milton on to Campbell and from Campbell to Tennyson. In the mightiest chorus of *King Henry V.* we hear the pealing ring of the same great English trumpet that was yet to sound over the battle of the Baltic.[1]

And the same writer speaks of

> The national side of Shakespeare's genius, the heroic vein of patriotism that runs, like a thread of living fire, through the world-wide range of his omnipresent spirit.[2]

We turn to Bacon, and we find the same great patriotic inspirations. His mind took in all mankind, but the love of his heart centered on England. His thoughts were bent to increase her glory and add to her security from foreign foes. To do this he saw that it was necessary to keep up the military spirit of the people. He says:

> But above all, for empire and greatness, it importeth most that a nation do profess arms as their principal honor, study and occupation. . . . No nation which doth not directly profess arms may look to have greatness fall into their mouths; and, on the other side, it is a most certain oracle of time that those nations that continue long in that profession (as the Romans and Turks principally have done) do wonders; and those that have professed arms but for an age have, notwithstanding, commonly attained that greatness in that age which maintaineth them long after, when the profession and exercise of arms hath grown to decay.[3]

And again he says:

> Walled towns, stored arsenals and armories, goodly races of horse, chariots of war, elephants, ordnance, artillery and the like; all this but a sheep in a lion's skin, except the *breed* and disposition of the people be stout and war-like.[4]

We turn to Shakespeare, and we find him referring to Englishmen as

> Feared for their *breed* and famous by their birth.

Here is the whole sentence. How exultantly does he depict his own country — "that little body with a mighty heart," as he calls it elsewhere:

> This royal throne of kings, this sceptered isle,
> This earth of majesty, this seat of Mars,
> This other Eden, demi-paradise,
> This fortress built by Nature for herself

---

[1] Swinburne, *Study of Shak.*, p. 113.
[2] Ibid., p. 73.
[3] Essay xxix, *The True Greatness of Kingdoms.*
[4] Ibid.

> Against infection and the hand of war;
> This happy *breed of men*, this little world,
> This precious stone set in the silver sea,
> Which serves it in the office of a wall,
> Or as a moat defensive to a house,
> Against the envy of less happier lands;
> This blessed plot, this earth, this realm, this England,
> This teeming womb of royal kings,
> Fear'd for their *breed* and famous by their birth,
> Renownèd for their deeds as far from home
> (For Christian service and true chivalry),
> As is the sepulcher in stubborn Jewry
> Of the world's ransom, blessed Mary's son;
> This land of such dear souls, this dear, dear land,
> Dear for her reputation through the world.[1]

And again he speaks of England as

> Hedged in with the main,
> That water-walled bulwark, still secure
> And confident from foreign purposes.[2]

And again he says:

> Let us be back'd with God, and with the seas,
> Which he has given for fence impregnable.[3]

And again he says:

> Which stands
> As Neptune's park, ribbed and paled in
> With rocks unscalable and roaring waters.[4]

And again:

> Britain is
> A world by itself.[5]

And again:

> I' the world's volume,
> Our Britain is as of it, but not in it;
> In a great pool, a swan's nest.[6]

And, while Shakespeare alludes to the sea as England's "water-walled bulwark," Bacon speaks of ships as the "walls" of England. And he says:

To be master of the sea is an abridgment of a monarchy.[7]

And he further says:

No man can by care-taking (as the Scripture saith) "add a cubit to his stature" in this little model of a man's body, but in the great fame of kingdoms and commonwealths it is in the power of princes, or estates, to add amplitude and greatness to their kingdoms; for by introducing such ordinances, constitutions and customs as we have now touched, *they may sow greatness to their posterity and succession;* but these things are commonly not observed, but left to take their chance.[8]

---

[1] *Richard II.*, ii, 1.
[2] *King John*, ii, 1.
[3] *3d Henry VI.*, iv, 1.
[4] *Cymbeline*, iii, 1.
[5] Ibid., iii, 1.
[6] Ibid., iii, 4.
[7] Essay, *True Greatness of Kingdoms*.
[8] Ibid.

And was he not, in these appeals to national heroism, "*sowing greatness to posterity,*" and helping to create, or maintain, that warlike "breed" which has since carried the banners of conquest over a great part of the earth's surface? One can imagine how the eyes of those swarming audiences at the Fortune and the Curtain must have snapped with delight at the pictures of English valor on the field of Agincourt, as depicted in *Henry V.;* or at the representation of that tremendous soldier Talbot, in *Henry VI.*, dying like a lion at bay, with his noble boy by his side. How the 'prentices must have roared! How the mob must have raved! How even the gentlemen must have drawn deep breaths of patriotic inspiration from such scenes! Imagine the London of to-day going wild over the work of some great genius, depicting, in the midst of splendid poetry, Wellington and Nelson!

But there are many other purposes revealed in these Plays.

XVII. Dueling.

The writer of the Plays was opposed to the practice of dueling.

One commentator (H. T.), in a note to the play of *Twelfth Night*, says:

> It was the plainly evident intention of Shakespeare, in this play, to place the practice of dueling in a ridiculous light. Dueling was in high fashion at this period — a perfect rage for it existed, and a man was distinguished or valued in the select circles of society in proportion to his skill and courage in this savage and murderous practice. Our poet well knew the power of ridicule often exceeded that of the law, and in the combat between the valiant Sir Andrew Aguecheek and the disguised Viola, he has placed the custom in an eminently absurd situation. Mr. Chalmers supposes that his attention was drawn to it by an edict of James I., issued in the year 1613. From his remarks we quote the following:

> In *Twelfth Night* Shakespeare tried to effect by ridicule what the state was unable to perform by legislation. The duels which were so incorrigibly frequent in that age were thrown into a ridiculous light by the affair between Viola and Sir Andrew Aguecheek. *Sir Francis Bacon* had lamented, in the House of Commons, on the 3d of March, 1609-10, the great difficulty of redressing the evil of duels, owing to the corruption of man's nature. King James tried to effect what the Parliament had despaired of effecting, and in 1613 he issued "An edict and censure against private combats," which was conceived with great vigor, and expressed with decisive force; but whether with the help of Bacon or not I am unable to ascertain.

There can be no question that the *Proposition for the Repressing of Singular Combats or Duels*, in 1613, came from the hand of Bacon. We find it given as his in Spedding's *Life and Works*.[1] He proposed to exclude all duelists from the King's presence, because

---

[1] Vol. iv., p. 397.

"there is no good spirit but will think himself in darkness, if he be debarred . . . of access and approach to the sovereign." He also proposed a prosecution in the Star Chamber, and a heavy, irremissible fine. A proclamation to this effect was issued by the King. We also have the "charge of Sir Francis Bacon, Knight, His Majesty's Attorney-General, touching duels, upon an information in the Star Chamber against Priest and Wright." After commenting on his regret that the offenders were not greater personages, Bacon says:

> Nay, I should think, my lords, that men of birth and quality will leave the practice, when it begins to be vilified, and come so low as to barbers, surgeons and butchers, and such base mechanical persons.

In the course of the charge he says:

> It is a miserable effect when young men, full of towardness and hope, such as the poets call *auroræ filii*, sons of the morning, in whom the comfort and expectations of their friends consisteth, shall be cast away and destroyed in such a vain manner. . . . So as your lordships see what a desperate evil this is; it troubleth peace, it disfurnisheth war, it bringeth calamity upon private men, peril upon the state, and contempt upon the law.

And in this charge we find Bacon using the same sort of argument used by Shakespeare in *Othello*.

Bacon says:

> There was a combat of this kind performed by two persons of quality of the Turks, wherein one of them was slain; the other party was convented before the council of *Bassaes*. The manner of the reprehension was in these words:
>
> How durst you undertake to fight one with the other? Are there not Christians enough to kill? Did you not know that whether of you should be slain, the loss would be the great Seigneour's?

The writer of Shakespeare evidently had this incident in his mind, and had also knowledge of the fact that the Turks did not permit duels, when he put into the mouth of Othello these words:

> Why, how now, ho! from whence ariseth this?
> Are we turned Turks, and to ourselves do that
> Which Heaven hath forbid the Ottomites?
> For Christian shame! put by this barbarous brawl![1]

Bacon secured the conviction of Priest and Wright, and prepared a decree of the Star Chamber, which was ordered read in every shire in the kingdom.

And we find the same idea and beliefs in Shakespeare which are contained in this decree. He says:

---
[1] *Othello*, ii, 3.

> If wrongs be evil, and enforce us kill,
> What folly 'tis to hazard life for ill![1]

And again:

> Your words have took such pains, as if they labored
> To bring manslaughter into form, set quarreling
> Upon the head of valor; which, indeed,
> Is valor misbegot, and came into the world
> When sects and factions were but newly born.[2]

XVIII. Other Purposes.

I might go on and give many other instances to show that the purposes revealed in the Plays are the same which governed Francis Bacon. I might point to Bacon's disapprobation of superstition, his essay on the subject, and the very effective way in which one kind of superstition is ridiculed in the case of the pretended blind man at St. Albans, in the play of *Henry VI.*, exposed by the shrewdness of the Duke Humphrey.

I might further note that Bacon wrote an essay against popular prophecies; and Knight notes[3] that the Fool in *Lear* ridicules these things, as in:

> Then comes the time, who lives to see 't,
> When going shall be used with feet.[4]

Says Knight:

> Nor was the introduction of such a mock prophecy mere idle buffoonery. There can be no question, from the statutes that were directed against these stimulants to popular credulity, that they were considered of importance in Shakespeare's day. Bacon's essay *Of Prophecies* shows that the philosopher gravely denounced what our poet pleasantly ridiculed.

I might show how, in *Love's Labor Lost*, the absurd fashions of language then prevalent among the fastidious at court were mocked at and ridiculed in the very spirit of Bacon. I might note the fact that Bacon expressed his disapprobation of tobacco, and that no reference is had to it in all the Plays, although it is abundantly referred to in the writings of Ben Jonson and other dramatists of the period. I might refer to Bacon's disapprobation of the superstition connected with wedding-rings, and to the fact that no wedding-ring is ever referred to in the Plays. These are little things in themselves, but they are cumulative as matters of evidence.

---

[1] *Titus Andronicus*, iii, 5. [2] Ibid. [3] Notes of act iii of *Lear*, p. 440. [4] Act iii, scene 2.

In conclusion, I would call attention to the fact that nowhere in the Plays is vice or wickedness made admirable. Even in the case of old Sir John Falstaff, whose wit was as keen, sententious and profound as Bacon's own Essays; even in his case we see him, in the close of *2d Henry IV.*, humiliated, disgraced and sent to prison; while the Chief Justice, representing the majesty of law and civilization, is lifted up from fear and danger to the greatest heights of dignity and honor. The old knight "dies of a sweat," and every one of his associates comes to a dishonored and shameful death.

Lamartine says:

It is as a moralist that Shakespeare excels. . . . His works cannot fail to elevate the mind by the purity of the morals they inculcate. They breathe so strong a belief in virtue, so steady an adherence to good principles, united to such a vigorous tone of honor as testifies to the author's excellence as a moralist; nay, as a Christian.

And everywhere in the Plays we see the cultured citizen of the schools and colleges striving to elevate and civilize a rude and barbarous age. The heart of the philosopher and philanthropist penetrates through wit and poetry and dramatic incident, in every act and scene from *The Tempest* to *Cymbeline*.

CHAPTER VII.

THE REASONS FOR CONCEALMENT.

> Some dear cause
> Will in concealment wrap me up awhile.
> When I am known aright, you shall not grieve
> Lending me this acquaintance.
> *Lear, iv, 3.*

IF Bacon wrote the Plays, why did he not acknowledge them? This is the question that will be asked by many.

I. BACON'S SOCIAL POSITION.

What was Francis Bacon in social position? He was an aristocrat of the aristocrats. His grandfather had been the tutor of the King. His father had been for twenty years Lord Keeper of the Seal under Elizabeth. His uncle Burleigh was Lord Treasurer of the kingdom. His cousin Robert was Lord Secretary, and afterward became the Earl of Salisbury. He also "claims close cousinry with Elizabeth and Anne Russell (daughters of Lord John Russell) and with the witty and licentious race of Killigrews, and with the future statesman and diplomatist Sir Edward Hoby."[1]

Francis aspired to be, like his father, Lord Chancellor of the kingdom. Says Hepworth Dixon:

> Bacon seemed born to power. His kinsmen filled the highest posts. The sovereign liked him, for he had the bloom of cheek, the flame of wit, the weight of sense, which the great Queen sought in men who stood about her throne. His powers were ever ready, ever equal. Masters of eloquence and epigram praised him as one of them, or one above them, in their peculiar arts. Jonson tells us he commanded when he spoke, and had his judges pleased or angry at his will. Raleigh tells us he combined the most rare of gifts, for while Cecil could talk and not write, Howard write and not talk, he alone could both talk and write. Nor were these gifts all flash and foam. If no one at the court could match his tongue of fire, so no one in the House of Commons could breast him in the race of work. He put the dunce to flight, the drudge to shame. If he soared high above rivals in his most passionate play of speech, he never met a rival in the dull, dry task of ordinary toil. Raleigh, Hyde and Cecil had small chance against him in debate; in committee Yelverton and Coke had none. . . .

[1] Hepworth Dixon, *Personal History of Lord Bacon*, p. 16.

He sought place, never man with more persistent haste; for his big brain beat with a victorious consciousness of parts; he hungered, as for food to rule and bless mankind. . , . While men of far lower birth and claims got posts and honors, solicitorships, judgeships, embassies, portfolios, how came this strong man to pass the age of forty-six without gaining power or place?[1]

And remember, good reader, that it is precisely during this period, before Bacon was forty-six, and while, as I have shown, he was "poor and working for bread," that the Shakespeare Plays were produced; and that after he obtained place and wealth they ceased to appear; although Shakspere was still living in Stratford and continued to live there for ten years to come. Why was it that the fountain of Shakespeare's song closed as soon as Bacon's necessities ended?

II. THE LAWYERS THEN THE PLAY-WRITERS.

Bacon took to the law. He was born to it. It was the only avenue open to him. Richard Grant White says — and, remember, he is no "Baconian":

There was no regular army in Elizabeth's time; and the younger sons of gentlemen not rich, and of well-to-do yeomen, flocked to the church and to the bar and as the former had ceased to be a stepping-stone to power and wealth, while the latter was gaining in that regard, most of these young men became attorneys or barristers. But then, as now, the early years of professional life were seasons of sharp trial and bitter disappointment. Necessity pressed sorely or pleasure wooed resistlessly; and the slender purse wasted rapidly away while the young lawyer awaited the employment that did not come. He knew then, as now he knows, the heart-sickness that waits on hope deferred; nay, he felt, as now he sometimes feels, the tooth of hunger gnawing through the principles and firm resolves that partition a life of honor and self-respect from one darkened by conscious loss of rectitude, if not by open shame Happy (yet, it may be, O unhappy) he who now in such a strait can wield the pen of a ready writer! For the press, perchance, may afford him a support which, though temporary and precarious, will hold him up until he can stand upon more stable ground. But in the reigns of Good Queen Bess and Gentle Jamie there was no press. There was, however, an incessant demand for new plays. Play-going was the chief intellectual recreation of that day for all classes, high and low. It is not extravagant to say that there were then more new plays produced in London in one month than there are now in both Great Britain and Ireland in a whole year. To play-writing, therefore, the needy and gifted young lawyer turned his hand at that day as he does now to journalism.

III. THE LAW-COURTS AND THE PLAYS. "THE MISFORTUNES OF ARTHUR."

And the connection between the lawyers and the players was, in some sense, a close one. It was the custom for the great law-schools to furnish dramatic representations for the entertainment

---

[1] Hepworth Dixon, *Personal History of Lord Bacon.*

of the court and the nobility. Shakespeare's *Comedy of Errors*, as I have shown, made its first appearance, not on the stage of the Curtain or the Fortune theater, but in an entertainment given by the students of Gray's Inn (Bacon's law-school); and Shakespeare's comedy of *Twelfth Night* was first acted before the "benchers" of the Middle Temple, who employed professional players to act before them every year. We know these facts, as to the two plays named, almost by accident. How many more of the so-called Shakespeare Plays first saw the light on the boards of those law students, at their great entertainments, we do not know.[1]

We find in *Dodsley's Old Plays* a play called *The Misfortunes of Arthur*. The title-leaf says:

Certaine Devises and Shews presented to her Majestie by the Gentlemen of Graye's-Inne, at her Highnesse Court in Greenewich, the twenty-eighth day of February, in the thirtieth year of her Majestie's most happy Raigne. At London. Printed by Robert Robinson. 1587.[2]

Mr. Collier wrote a preface to it, in which he says:

It appears that eight persons, members of the Society of Gray's Inn, were engaged in the production of *The Misfortunes of Arthur*, for the entertainment of Queen Elizabeth, at Greenwich, on the 28th day of February, 1587-8, viz.: Thomas Hughes, the author of the whole body of the tragedy; William Fullbecke, who wrote two speeches substituted on the representation and appended to the old printed copy; Nicholas Trotte, who furnished the introduction; Francis Flower, who penned choruses for the first and second acts; Christopher Yelverton, *Francis Bacon*, and John Lancaster, who devised the dumb-show, then usually accompanying such performances; and a person of the name of Penruddock, who, assisted by Flower and Lancaster, directed the proceedings at court. Regarding Hughes and Trotte no information has survived. . . . The "Maister Francis Bacon" spoken of at the conclusion of the piece was, of course, no other than (the great) Bacon; and it is a new feature in his biography, though not, perhaps, very prominent nor important, *that he was so nearly concerned in the preparation of a play at court*. In February, 1587-8, he had just commenced his twenty-eighth year. . . .

The Misfortunes of Arthur is a dramatic composition only known to exist in the Garrick Collection. Judging from internal evidence, it seems to have been *printed with unusual care, under the superintendence of the principal author*. . . . The mere rarity of this unique drama would not have recommended it to our notice; but it is not likely that such a man as Bacon would have lent his aid to the production of a piece which was not intrinsically good; and, *unless we much mistake, there is a richer and nobler vein of poetry running through it than is to be found in any previous work of the kind*. . . . It forms a sort of connecting link between such pieces of unimpassioned formality as *Ferrex and Porrex*, and rule-rejecting historical plays, as Shakespeare found them and left them.

---

[1] Halliwell-Phillipps, *Outlines Life of Shak.*, p. 128. [2] Hazlitt, vol. iv, p. 240.

I will discuss this play and its merits at more length hereafter, and will make but one or two observations upon it at this time.

1. It does not seem to me probable, if eight young lawyers were preparing a play for the court, and one of them was Francis Bacon, with his ready pen and unlimited command of language, that he would confine himself to "the dumb-show." It will be remembered that he wrote the words of certain masks that were acted before the court.

And if it be true that this youthful performance reveals poetry of a higher order than anything that had preceded, is it more natural to suppose it the product of the mightiest genius of his age, who was, by his own confession, "a concealed poet," or the work of one Thomas Hughes, who never, in the remainder of his life, produced anything worth remembering? And we will see, hereafter, that the poetry of this play is most strikingly Shakespearean.

2. Collier says he knows nothing of Thomas Hughes and Nicholas Trotte. Can Thomas Hughes, the companion of Bacon in Gray's Inn, and his co-laborer in preparing this play, be the same Hughes referred to in that line in one of the Shakespeare sonnets which has so perplexed the commentators —

> A man in hue, all hues in his controlling; —

and which has been supposed by many to refer to some man of the name of Hughes?

3. As to the identity of Nicholas Trotte there can be no question. He is the same Nicholas Trotte with whom Bacon carried on a long correspondence on the subject of money loaned by him to Bacon at divers and sundry times.

But this is not the place to discuss the play of *The Misfortunes of Arthur*. I refer to it now only to show how naturally Bacon might drift into writing for the stage. As:

1. Bacon is poor and in need of money.

2. Bacon assists in getting up a play for his law-school, Gray's Inn, if he does not write the greater part of it.

3. *The Comedy of Errors* appears at Gray's Inn for the first time, acted by Shakspere's company.

4. It was customary for impecunious lawyers in that age to turn an honest penny by writing for the stage.

Here, then, we have the man, the ability, the necessity, the custom, the opportunity. Bacon and Shakspere both on the boards of Gray's Inn at the same time — one directing, the other acting.

If *The Misfortunes of Arthur* was really Bacon's work, and if it was a success on the stage, how natural that he should go farther in the same direction. Poetry is, as Bacon tells us, a "lust of the earth" — a something that springs up from the mind like the rank growths of vegetation from the ground; it is, as Shakespeare says:

> A gum which oozes
> From whence 'tis nourished.

We see a picture of the *poet* at this age in the description of Hepworth Dixon; it is not a description of a philosopher:

Like the ways of all deep dreamers, his habits are odd, and vex Lady Anne's affectionate and methodical heart. The boy sits up late at night, drinks his ale-posset to make him sleep, starts out of bed ere it is light, or, may be, as the whimsy takes him, lolls and dreams till noon, musing, says the good lady, with loving pity, on — she knows not what![1]

IV. Why he Seeks a Disguise.

But if the poetical, the dramatical, the creative instinct is upon him, shall he venture to put forth the plays he produces in his own name? No: there are many reasons say him nay. In the first place, he knows they are youthful and immature performances. In the second place, it will grieve his good, pious mother to know that he doth "mum and mask and sinfully revel." In the third place, the reputation of a poet will not materially assist him up those long, steep stairs that lead to the seat his great father occupied. And, therefore, so he says, "I *profess not* to be a poet." Therefore will he put forth his attempts in the name of Thomas Hughes, or any other friend; or of Marlowe, or of Shakspere, or of any other convenient mask. Hath he it not in his mind to be a great reformer; to reconstruct the laws of the kingdom, and to recast the philosophy of mankind, hurling down Aristotle and the schoolmen from their disputatious pedestals, and erecting a system that shall make men better because happier, and happier because wiser in the knowledge of the nature which surrounds them? Poetry is but a "work of his recreation" — a something he cannot help but yield to,

---

[1] *Personal History of Lord Bacon*, p. 35.

but of which he is half-ashamed. He will write it because he is forced to sing, as the bird sings; because his soul is full; because he is obeying the purpose for which he was created. But publish his productions? No. And therefore he "professes" *not* to be a poet.

And, moreover, he is naturally given to secretiveness. There was a strong tendency in the man to subterranean methods. We find him writing letters in the name of Essex and in the name of his brother Anthony. He went so far, in a letter written by him, in the name of his brother, to Essex, to refer back to himself as follows (the letter and Essex's reply, *also written by him*, being intended for the Queen's eye):

And to this purpose I do assure your Lordship that my brother, Francis Bacon, who is too wise (I think) to be abused, and too honest to abuse, though he be more reserved in all particulars than is needful, yet, etc.

And we positively know, from his letter to Sir John Davies, in which he speaks of himself as "a concealed poet,' that he was the author of poetical compositions, of some kind, which he did not acknowledge, and which must certainly have gone about in the names of other men. And he says himself that, with a purpose to help Essex regain the good graces of the Queen, he wrote a sonnet which he passed off upon the Queen as the work of Essex.

We remember that Walter Scott resorted to a similar system of secretiveness. After he had established for himself a reputation as a successful poet, he made up his mind to venture upon the composition of prose romances; and fearing that a failure in the new field of effort might compromise his character as a man of genius, already established by his poems, he put forth his first novel, *Waverly*, without any name on the title-page; and then issued a series of novels as by "the author of *Waverly*." And in his day there were books written to show by parallel thoughts and expressions that Scott was really the author of those romances, just as books are now written on the Bacon-Shakespeare question.

And who does not remember that the author of *The Letters of Junius* died and made no sign of confession?

Bacon doubtless found a great advantage in writing thus under a mask. The man who sets forth his thoughts in his own name knows that the public will constantly strive to connect his utterances with his personal character: to trace home his opinions to his personal history and circumstances; and he is therefore necessarily always on his guard not to say anything, even in a work of fiction, that he would not be willing to father as part of his own natural reflections.

Richard Grant White says:

> Shakespeare's freedom in the use of words was but a part of that conscious irresponsibility to critical rule which had such an important influence upon the development of his whole dramatic style. To the workings of his genius under this entire unconsciousness of restraint we owe the grandest and the most delicate beauties of his poetry, his poignant expressions of emotion, and his richest and subtlest passages of humor. For the superiority of his work is just in proportion to his carelessness of literary criticism. . . . His plays were mere entertainments for the general public, written not to be read, but to be spoken; written as business, just as Rogers wrote money circulars, or as Bryant writes leading articles. This freedom was suited to the unparalleled richness and spontaneousness of his thought, of which it was, in fact, partly the result, and itself partly the condition.[1]

The Anatomy of Melancholy was first published, not in the name of the alleged author, Robert Burton, but under the *nom de plume* of "Democritus, Junior," and in the address to the reader the author says:

> Gentle reader, I presume thou wilt be very inquisitive to know what antic or personate actor this is that so insolently intrudes upon this common theater, to the world's view, arrogating another man's name. . . . I would not willingly be known. . . . 'Tis for no such respect I shroud myself under his name; but *in an unknown habit to assume a little more liberty and freedom of speech.*

We will see hereafter that there are strong reasons for believing that Francis Bacon wrote *The Anatomy of Melancholy*, and that in these words we have his own explanation of one of the many reasons for his many disguises.

V. Low State of the Dramatic Art.

But there was another reason why an ambitious young aristocrat, and lawyer, and would-be Lord-Chancellor, should hesitate to avow that he was a writer of plays.

Halliwell-Phillipps says:

> It must be borne in mind that actors occupied an inferior position in society, and that even the vocation of a dramatic writer *was considered scarcely respectable.*[2]

The first theater ever erected in England, or, so far as I am aware, in any country, in modern times, was built in London in

---

[1] *Life and Genius of Shak.*, p. 200. [2] *Halliwell-Phillipps, Outlines Life of Shak.*, p. 6.

1575 — five years before Bacon returned from the court of France, and six years before he reached the age of twenty-one years. The man and the instrumentality came together. A writer upon the subject says:

> The public authorities, more especially those who were inclined to Puritanism, exerted themselves in every possible way to repress the performance of plays and interludes. They fined and imprisoned the players, even stocked them, and harassed and restrained them to the utmost of their ability. . . . In 1575 the players were interdicted from the practice of their art (or rather their calling, for it was not yet an art), within the limits of the city.

The legal status of actors was the lowest in the country.

The act of 14th Elizabeth, "for the punishment of vagabonds," included under that name "all fencers, bearwards, *common players in interludes*, and minstrels, not belonging to any baron of this realm."

They traveled the country on foot, with packs on their backs, and were fed in the "buttery" of the great houses they visited.

I quote:

> Thus in Greene's *Never Too Late*, in the interview between the player and Robert (*i.e.*, Greene), on the latter asking how the player proposed to mend Robert's fortune:
>
> "Why, easily," quoth he, "and greatly to your benefit; for men of my profession get by scholars their whole living."
>
> "What is your profession?" said Roberto.
>
> "Truly, sir," said he, "I am a player."
>
> "A player!" quoth Roberto; "I took you rather for a gentleman of great living; for if by outward habit men should be answered [judged], I tell you, you would be taken for a *substantial man*."
>
> "So am I, where I dwell," quoth the player, "reported able at my proper cost to build a wind-mill."
>
> He then proceeds to say that at his outset in life he was fain to carry his "playing fardel," that is, his bundle of stage properties, "a foot back;" but now his show of "playing apparel" would sell for more than £200. In the end he offers to engage Greene to write plays for him, "for which you will be well paid, if you will take the pains."

If the actors did not engage themselves as the servants of some great man, as "the Lord Chamberlain's servants," or "the Lord Admiral's servants," or "the Earl of Worcester's servants," they were liable under the law, as Edgar says in *Lear*,[1] to be "whipped from tything to tything, and stocked, punished and imprisoned;" for by the statute of 39 Elizabeth (1597) and 1st of James I. (1604), as I have shown, the vagabond's punishment was to be "stripped naked from the middle upward, and to be whipped until his body

[1] Act iii, scene 4.

was bloody, and to be sent from parish to parish the next straight way to the place of his birth."

Halliwell-Phillipps says:

Actors were regarded at court in the light of menials, and classed by the public with jugglers and buffoons:[1]

The play-houses were inconceivably low and rude. The Lord Mayor of London, in 1597, describes the theaters as:

Ordinary places for vagrant persons, maisterless men, thieves, horse-stealers, whoremongers, cozeners, cony-catchers, contrivers of treason, and other idele and dangerous persons.[2]

Taine says of Shakspere:

He was a comedian, one of "His Majesty's poor players"—a sad trade, degraded in all ages by the contrasts and the falsehoods which it allows: still more degraded then by the brutalities of the crowd, who not seldom would stone the actors; and by the severities of the magistrates, who would sometimes condemn them to lose their ears.[3]

Edmund Gayton says, describing the play-houses:

If it be on a holiday, when sailors, watermen, shoemakers, butchers and apprentices are at leisure, then it is good policy to amaze those violent spirits with some tearing tragedy, full of fights and skirmishes, as *The Guelphs and Ghibelines*, *Greeks and Trojans*, or *The Three London Apprentices*, which commonly ends in six acts, the spectators frequently mounting the stage and making a more bloody catastrophe among themselves than the players did. I have known, upon one of these festivals, . . . where the players have been appointed, notwithstanding their bills to the contrary, to act what the major part of the company had a mind to; sometimes *Tamburlane*, sometimes *Jugurth*, sometimes *The Jew of Malta*, and sometimes parts of all these; and at last, none of the three taking, they were forced to undress, and put off their tragic habits, and conclude the day with *The Merry Milkmaid*. And unless this were done, and the popular humor satisfied, as sometimes it so fortuned that the players were refractory, the benches, the tiles, the laths, the stones, oranges, apples, nuts flew about-most liberally; and as there were mechanics of all professions, who fell every one to his own trade, and dissolved an house in an instant and made a ruin of a stately fabric.[4]

Taine thus describes the play-houses of Shakspere's time:

Great and rude contrivances, awkward in their construction, barbarous in their appointments; but a fervid imagination supplied all that they lacked, and hardy bodies endured all inconveniences without difficulty. On a dirty site, on the banks of the Thames, rose the principal theater, the Globe, a sort of hexagonal tower, surrounded by a muddy ditch, on which was hoisted a red flag. The common people could enter as well as the rich; there were six-penny, two-penny, even

---

[1] *Outlines Life of Shak.*, p. 296. [2] *City of London MS. Outlines*, p. 214.
[3] *History of English Literature*, book ii, chap. iv, p. 203.
[4] *Festivous Notes on Don Quixote*, 1654, p. 271.

penny seats; but they could not see it without money. If it rained, and it often rains in London, the people in the pit — butchers, mercers, bakers, sailors, apprentices — received the streaming rain upon their heads. I suppose they did not trouble themselves about it; it was not so long since they began to pave the streets of London, and when men, like these, have had experience of sewers and puddles, they are not afraid of catching cold.

While waiting for the piece, they amuse themselves after their fashion, drink beer, crack nuts, eat fruits, howl, and now and then resort to their fists; they have been known to fall upon the actors, and turn the theater upside down. At other times, when they were dissatisfied, they went to the tavern, *to give the poet a hiding, or toss him in a blanket.* . . . When the beer took effect, there was a great upturned barrel in the pit, a peculiar receptacle for general use. The smell rises, and then comes the cry, "Burn the juniper!" They burn some in a plate on the stage, and the heavy smoke fills the air. Certainly the folk there assembled could scarcely get disgusted at anything, and cannot have had sensitive noses. In the time of Rabelais there was not much cleanliness to speak of. Remember that they were hardly out of the Middle Ages, and that in the Middle Ages man lived on a dung-hill.

Above them, *on the stage*, were the spectators able to pay a shilling, the elegant people, the gentlefolk. These were sheltered from the rain, and, if they chose to pay an extra shilling, could have a stool. To this were reduced the prerogatives of rank and the devices of comfort; it often happened that there were not stools enough; then they lie down on the ground; this was not a time to be dainty. They play cards, smoke, insult the pit, who give it them back without stinting, and throw apples at them into the bargain.

The reader can readily conceive that the man must indeed have been exceedingly ambitious of fame who would have insisted on asserting his title to the authorship of plays acted in such theaters before such audiences. Imagine that aristocratic young gentleman, Francis Bacon, born in the royal palace of York Place; an ex-attaché of the English legation at the French court; the son of a Lord Chancellor; the nephew of a Lord Treasurer; the offspring of the virtuous, pious and learned Lady Anne Bacon; with his head full of great plans for the reformation of philosophy, law and government; and with his eye fixed on the chair his father had occupied for twenty years: — imagine him, I say, insisting that his name should appear on the play-bills as the poet who wrote *Mucedorus, Tamburlane, The Jew of Malta, Titus Andronicus, Fair Em, Sir John Oldcastle*, or *The Merry Devil of Edmonton!* Imagine the drunken, howling mob of Calibans hunting through Gray's Inn to find the son of the Lord Chancellor, in the midst of his noble friends, to whip him, or toss him in a blanket, because, forsooth, his last play had not pleased their royal fancies!

VI. Sharing in the Profits of the Play-House.

But suppose behind all this there was another and a more terrible consideration.

Suppose this young nobleman had eked out his miserable income *by writing plays to sell to the theaters.* Suppose it was known that he had his "second" and "third nights;" that he put into his pocket the sweaty pennies of that stinking mob of hoodlums, sailors, 'prentices, thieves, rowdies and prostitutes; and that he had used the funds so obtained to enable him to keep up his standing with my Lord of Southampton, and my Earl of Essex, and their associates, as a gentleman among gentlemen. Think of it!

And this in England, three hundred years ago, when the line of caste was almost as deep and black between the gentlemen and "the mutable, rank-scented many," as it is to-day in India between the Brahmin and the Pariah. Why, to this hour, I am told, there is an almost impassable gulf between the nobleman and the tradesman of great Britain. Then, as Burton says in *The Anatomy of Melancholy,* "idleness was the mark of nobility." To earn money in any kind of trade was despicable. To have earned it by sharing in the pennies and shillings taken in at the door, or on the stage of the play-house, would have been utterly damnable in any gentleman. It would have involved a loss of social position worse than death. One will have to read Thackeray's story of *Miss Shum's Husband* to find a parallel for it.

VII. Political Considerations.

But we have seen that the hiring of actors of Shakspere's company to perform the play of *Richard II.,* by the followers of the Earl of Essex, the day before the attempt to "rase the city" and seize the person of the Queen (even as Monmouth seized the person of Richard II.), and compel a deposition by like means, was one of the counts in the indictment against Essex, which cost him his head. In other words, the intent of the play was treasonable, and was so understood at the time. "Know you not," said Queen Elizabeth, "that *I* am Richard II.?" And I have shown good reason to believe that all the historical Plays, to say nothing of *Julius Cæsar,* were written with intent to popularize rebellion against tyrants.

"The poor player," Will Shakspere, might have written such plays solely for the pence and shillings there were in them, for he had nothing to do with politics: — he was a legal vagabond, a "vassal actor," a social outcast; but if Francis Bacon, the able and ambitious Francis Bacon, the rival of Cecil, the friend of Southampton and Essex; the lawyer, politician, member of Parliament, courtier belonging to the party that desired to bring in the Scotch King and drive the aged Queen from the throne — if *he* had acknowledged the authorship of the Plays, the inference would have been irresistible in the mind of the court, that these horrible burlesques and travesties of royalty were written with malice and settled intent to bring monarchy into contempt and justify the aristocracy in revolution.

VIII. ANOTHER REASON.

But it must be further remembered that while Bacon lived the Shakespeare Plays were not esteemed as they are now. Then they were simply successful dramas; they drew great audiences; they filled the pockets of manager and actors. Leonard Digges, in the verses prefixed to the edition of 1640, says that when Jonson's "Fox and Subtle Alchymist"

> Have scarce defrayed the sea-coal fire
> And door-keepers: when, let but Falstaff come,
> Hal, Poins, the rest — you scarce shall have room,
> All is so pestered: let but Beatrice
> And Benedick be seen, lo! in a trice
> *The cock-pit, galleries, boxes, all are full,*
> To hear Malvolio, that cross-gartered gull.

There was no man in that age, except the author of them, who rated the Shakespeare Plays at their true value. They were admired for "the facetious grace of the writing," but the world had not yet advanced far enough in culture and civilization to recognize them as the great store-houses of the world's thought. Hence there was not then the same incentive to acknowledge them that there would be to-day.

IX. STILL ANOTHER REASON.

If Francis Bacon had died full of years and honors, I can conceive how, from the height of preëminent success, he might have fronted the prejudices of the age, and acknowledged these children of his brain.

But the last years of his life were years of dishonor. He had been cast down from the place of Lord Chancellor for bribery, for selling justice for money. He had been sentenced to prison; he held his liberty by the King's grace. He was denied access to the court. He was a ruined man, "a very subject of pity," as he says himself.

For a man thus living under a cloud to have said, "In my youth I wrote plays for the stage; I wrote them for money; I used Shakspere as a mask; I divided with him the money taken in at the gate of the play-houses from the scum and refuse of London," would only have invited upon his head greater ignominy and disgrace. He had a wife; he had relatives, a proud and aristocratic breed. He sought to be the Aristotle of a new philosophy. Such an avowal would have smirched the *Novum Organum* and the *Advancement of Learning;* it would have blotted and blurred the bright and dancing light of that torch which he had kindled for posterity. He would have had to explain his, no doubt countless, denials made years before, that he had had anything to do with the Plays.

And why should he acknowledge them? He left his fame and good name to his "own countrymen after some time be past;" he believed the cipher, which he had so laboriously inserted in the Plays, would be found out. He would obtain all the glory for his name in that distant future when he would not hear the reproaches of caste; when, as pure spirit, he might look down from space, and see the winged-goodness which he had created, passing, on pinions of persistent purpose, through all the world, from generation to generation. In that age, when his body was dust; when cousins and kin were ashes; when Shakspere had moldered into nothingness, beneath the protection of his own barbarous curse; when not a trace could be found of the bones of Elizabeth or James, or even of the stones of the Curtain or the Blackfriars: then, in a new world, a brighter world, a greater world, a better world,—to which his own age would be but as a faint and perturbed remembrance,—he would be married anew to his immortal works. He would live again, triumphant, over Burleigh and Cecil, over Coke and Buckingham; over parasites and courtiers, over tricksters and panderers:—the magnificent victory of genius over power; of mind over time. And so living, he would live forever.

CHAPTER VIII.

CORROBORATING CIRCUMSTANCES.

> Lapped in proof,
> Confronted him with self-comparisons.
> *Macbeth*, i, 2.

WE sometimes call, in law, an instrument between two parties an *indenture*. Why? Because it was once the custom to write a deed or contract in duplicate, on a long sheet of paper or parchment, and then cut them apart upon an irregular or indented line. If, thereafter, any dispute arose as to whether one was the equivalent of the other, the edges, where they were divided, were put together to see if they precisely matched. If they did not, it followed that some fraud had somewhere been practiced.

Truth, in like manner, is serrated, and its indentations fit into all other truth. If two alleged truths do not thus dovetail into each other, along the line where they approximate, then one of them is not the truth, but an error or a fraud.

Let us see, therefore, if, upon a multitude of minor points, the allegation that Francis Bacon wrote the Shakespeare Plays fits its indentations — its teeth — precisely into what we know of Bacon and Shakspere.

In treating these questions, I shall necessarily have to be as brief as possible.

I. THE QUESTION OF TIME.

Does the biography of Bacon accord with the chronology of the Plays?

Bacon was born in York House, or Palace, on the Strand, January 22, 1561. William Shakspere was born at Stratford-on-Avon, April 23, 1564. Bacon died in the spring of 1626. Shakspere in the spring of 1616. The lives of the two men were therefore parallel; but Bacon was three years the elder, and survived Shakspere ten years.

Bacon's mental activity began at an early age. He was studying the nature of echoes at a time when other children are playing.

At twelve he outstripped his home tutors and was sent to join his brother Anthony, two years his senior, at Trinity College, Cambridge. At eighteen Hilliard paints his portrait and inscribes upon it, "if one could but paint his mind." We will hereafter see reasons to believe that there is extant a whole body of compositions written before he was twenty-one years of age. At about twenty he summarizes the political condition of Europe with the hand of a statesman.

II. PLAYS BEFORE SHAKSPERE COMES TO LONDON.

The Plays antedate the time of the coming of Shakspere to London, which it is generally agreed was in 1587.

That high authority, Richard Simpson, in his *School of Shakespeare*,[1] in his article, "The Early Authorship of Shakespeare'"[2] and in *Notes and Queries*,[3] shows that the Shakespeare Plays *commenced to appear in 1585!* That is to say, *while Shakspere was still living in Stratford*—in the year the twins were born! We are therefore to believe that in that "bookless neighborhood" the butcher's apprentice was, between his whippings, writing plays for the stage! Here are miracles indeed.

In 1585 Robert Greene both registered and published his *Planetomachia*, and in this work he denounces "some avaricious player, . . . who, not content with his own province [of acting], should dare to intrude into the field of authorship, which ought to belong solely to the professed scholars"—like Greene himself. And from that time forward Greene continued to gibe at this same somebody, who was writing plays for the stage. He speaks of "gentlemen poets" in 1588, who set "the end of scholarism in an English blank verse; . . . it is the humor of a *novice* that tickles them with self-love."

Thomas Nash says, in an epistle prefixed to Greene's *Arcadia*, published, according to Mr. Dyce, in 1587:

It is a common practice, now-a-days, amongst a sort of shifting companions, that run through every art and thrive at none, *to leave the trade of noverint* [lawyer], *whereto they were born*, and busy themselves with the endeavors of art, that could scarcely Latinize their neck-verse, if they should have need. Yet English Seneca, read by candle-light, yields many good sentences, as "blood is a beggar," and so forth; and if you entreat him fair, in a frosty morning, he will afford you whole *Hamlets*, I should say handfuls, of tragical speeches.

[1] Vol. ii, p. 342. [2] *North British Review*, vol. lii. [3] 4th series, vol. viii.

Here it appears that in 1587, the very year when Shakspere came to London, and while he was probably holding horses at the front door of the theater, the play of *Hamlet*, Shakespeare's own play of *Hamlet*, was being acted; and was believed by other playwrights to have been composed by some lawyer, who was born a lawyer.

And did not Nash's words, "if you entreat him fair of a frosty morning," allude to that early morning scene "of a frosty morning," where Hamlet meets the Ghost, for the first time, on the platform of the castle:

> *Hamlet.* The air bites shrewdly; it is very cold.
> *Horatio.* It is a nipping and an eager air.

But this lawyer, who was born a lawyer, to whom allusion is made by Nash, so far from being a mere horse-holder, was something of a scholar, for Nash continues:

> But . . . what's that will last always? Seneca let blood line by line and page by page, at length must die to our stage, which makes his [Seneca's] famished followers . . . leap into a new occupation and *translate two-penny pamphlets from the Italian* without any knowledge even of its articles.[1]

We have seen that several of the so-called Shakespeare comedies were founded on untranslated Italian novels. Will the men who argue that Shakspere stood at the door of the play-house and held horses, and at the same time wrote the magnificent and scholarly periods of *Hamlet*, go farther and ask us to believe that the butcher's apprentice, the deer-stealer, the beer-guzzler, "oft-whipped and imprisoned," had, in the filthy, bookless village of Stratford, acquired even an imperfect knowledge of the Italian?

But Nash goes farther. He says:

> Sundry OTHER *sweet gentlemen* I do know, that we [sic] have *vaunted their pens in private-devices* and *tricked up a company of taffaty fools with their feathers*, whose beauty, if our poets had not pecked, with the supply of their perriwigs, they might have anticked it until this time, up and down the country with *The King of Fairies* and dined every day at the pease-poridge ordinary with *Delfrigius*.

What does all this mean? Why, that there were poets who were not actors, "sweet *gentlemen*" (and that word meant a good deal in 1587), who had written "private devices," as we know Bacon to have written "masks" for private entertainments; and these *gentlemen* were rich enough to have furnished out a company

---

[1] *School of Shak.*, vol. II, p. 358.

of actors with feathers and periwigs, to take part in these private theatricals; and if the "gentlemen" had not pecked (objected?) the players would have anticked it, that is, played in this finery, all over the country.

Hamlet says to Horatio, after he has written the play and had it acted and thereby "touched the conscience of the King:"

> Would not this, sir, and a forest of *feathers* (if the rest of my fortunes turn Turk with me), with two provincial roses on my ragged shoes, get me a fellowship in a cry of players?

And three years after Nash wrote the above, Robert Greene refers to Shakspere as the only "*Shake-scene* in the country," and as "an upstart crow beautified with our *feathers*."

III. A Pretended Play-Writer who Cannot Write English.

Simpson believes that *Fair Em* was written by Shakspere in 1587.

In 1587 Greene wrote his *Farewell to Folly*, published in 1591, in which he criticises the play of *Fair Em* and positively states that it was written by some gentleman of position, who put it forth in the name of a play-actor who was almost wholly uneducated. He says:

> Others will flout and over-read every line with a frump, and say 'tis scurvy, when they themselves are such scabbed lads that they are like to die of the *fasion*;[1] but if they come to write or publish anything in print, it is either distilled out of ballads, or borrowed of theological poets, which, for *their calling and gravity being loth to have any profane pamphlets pass under their hand*, get some other Batillus to *set his name to their verses*. Thus is the ass made proud by this underhand brokery. And he *that cannot write true English without the help of clerks of parish churches*, will needs make himself the father of interludes. O, 'tis a jolly matter when a man hath a familiar style, and can endite a whole year and not be beholding to art! But to bring Scripture to prove anything he says, and kill it dead with the text in a trifling subject of love, I tell you is no small piece of cunning. As, for example, two lovers on the stage arguing one another of unkindness, his mistress runs over him with this canonical sentence, "A man's conscience is a thousand witnesses;" and her knight again excuseth himself with that saying of the apostle, "Love covereth a multitude of sins."[2]

The two lines here quoted are from *Fair Em:*

> Thy conscience is a thousand witnesses.[3]
>
> Yet love, that covers multitude of sins.[4]

---

[1] A disease of horses, like glanders.
[2] *School of Shak.*, chap. xi, p. 377.
[3] Sc. xvii, l. 1308.
[4] Ibid., l. 1271.

What does this prove? That it was the belief of Greene, who was himself a playwright, that *Fair Em* was not written by the man in whose name it was put forth, but by some one of "calling and gravity," who had made use of another as a mask. And that this latter person was an ignorant man, who could not write true English without the help of the clerks of parish churches. But Simpson and many others are satisfied that *Fair Em* was written by the same mind which produced the Shakespeare Plays! But as the *Farewell to Folly* was written in 1587, and it is generally conceded that Shakspere did not commence to write until 1592, five years afterward, and as Shakspere was in 1587 hanging about the play-house either as a horse-holder or a "servitor," these words could not apply to him. We will see reason hereafter to conclude that they applied to Marlowe. But if they did apply to Shakspere, then we have the significant fact, as Simpson says,

That Greene here pretends that Shakespeare could not have written the play himself; it was written by some theological poet, and fathered by him.

And Simpson, be it remembered, is no Baconian. It has been urged, as a strong point in favor of William Shakspere's authorship of the Plays, that his right to them was never questioned during his lifetime. If he wrote plays in 1587, then Greene *did* question the reality of his authorship, and boldly charged that he was an ignorant man, and the cover for some one else. If he did not write plays before 1592,—and a series of plays appeared between 1585 and 1592 which the highest critics contend were produced by the same mind which created the Shakespeare Plays,—then the whole series could not have been produced by the man of Stratford-on-Avon; and if the first of the series of identical works was not written by him, the last of the series could not have been. The advocates of Shakspere can take either horn of the dilemma they please.

Simpson thus sums up Greene's conclusions about Shakspere:

That he appropriated and refurbished other men's plays; that he was a lack-latin, who had no acquaintance with any foreign language, except, perhaps, French, and lived from the translator's trencher, and such like. Throughout we see *Greene's determination not to recognise Shakspere as a man capable of doing anything by himself.* At first, Greene simply fathers some composition of his upon "two gentlemen poets," because he, in Greene's opinion, was *incapable of writing anything.* Then as to *Fair Em*, it is either distilled out of ballads, or it is written by some theological poet, who is ashamed to set his own name to it. It could not have been written by one who *cannot write English without the aid of a parish clerk.* Then, at last, Greene owns that his rival might have written a speech or two, might have interpreted for the puppets, have indited a moral, or might be even capable of penning *The Windmill— The Miller's Daughter*—without help, so I interpret the words before quoted, "reputed able at my proper cost to build a windmill," but Greene *will not own that the man is capable of having really done that which passes for his.*

And it seems to me the words, "reputed able at my proper cost to build a windmill," do not refer to the play, but to the wealth of the player.

IV. HE WRITES FOR OTHER COMPANIES BESIDES SHAKSPERE'S.

We turn now to another curious fact, quite incompatible with the theory that the man of Stratford wrote the Plays.

What do we know of him? That when he fled to London he acted at first, as tradition tells us, as a horse-holder, and was then admitted to the play-house as a servant. And the tradition of his being a horse-holder is curiously confirmed by the fact that when Greene alludes to him as "the only Shake-scene in the country," he advises his fellow-playwrights to prepare no more dramas for the actors, because of the predominance of that "Johannes-factotum," Shake-scene, and adds:

Seek you better masters; for it is a pity men of such rare wits should be subject to the pleasure of such rude *grooms.*

Certainly the man who had been recently taking charge of horses might very properly be referred to as a *groom.*

But here we stumble upon another difficulty. Not only did plays which are now attributed to Shakspere make their appearance on the London stage while he was still living in Stratford, whipped and persecuted by Sir Thomas Lucy, and subsequently, while he was acting as *groom* for the visitors to the play-house, but at this very time, we are told, he not only supplied his own theater with plays, but, with extraordinary fecundity, he *furnished plays to every company of actors in London!* Tradition tells us that during his early years in the great city he was "received into the play-house as a serviture." Is it possible that while so employed—a servant, a menial, a call-boy—in one company, he could furnish plays to other and rival companies? Would his profits not have lifted him above the necessity of acting as groom or call-boy? Simpson says:

Other prominent companies were those of the Earl of Sussex (1589), the Earl of Worcester (1590), and the Earl of Pembroke (1592). *For all these Shakspere can be shown to have written during the first part of his career.* According to the well-known epistle annexed to Greene's *Groatsworth of Wit*, Shakspere, by 1592, had become so absolute a *Johannes factotum*, for the actors of the day *generally*, that the man who considered himself the chief of the scholastic school of dramatists not only determined for his own part to abandon play-writing, but urged his companions to do the same. . . . It is clear that *before 1592* Shakspere must have been prodigiously active, and that plays wholly or partly from his pen must have been in the possession of many of the actors and companies. For the fruits of this activity *we are not to look in his recognized works*. Those, with few exceptions, *are the plays he wrote for the Lord Chamberlain's men.* . . . There are two kinds of Shaksperean remains which may be recorded, or rather assigned, to their real original author, by the critic and historian. First, the dramas prior to 1592, *which are not included in his works;* and secondly, the dramas over the production of which he presided, or with which he was connected as editor, reviser or adviser.[1]

And again Simpson says:

The recognized works of Shakspere contain scarcely any plays but those which he produced for the Lord Chamberlain's or King's company of actors. But in 1592 Greene tells us he had almost a monopoly of dramatic production, and had made himself necessary, *not to one company, but to the players in general.* It may be proved that he wrote for the Lord Strange's men, and for those of the Earl of Pembroke and the Earl of Sussex.[2]

But while this distinguished scholar tells us that Shakspere was "prodigiously active prior to 1592," and supplied all the different companies with plays, we turn to the other commentators and biographers, and they unite in assuring us that Shakspere did not appear as an author until 1592! Halliwell-Phillipps fixes the exact date as March 3d, 1592, when a new drama was brought out by Lord Strange's servants, to-wit, *Henry VI.*, "in all probability his earliest complete dramatic work."

Here, then, is our dilemma:

1. It is proved that Shakespeare did not begin to write until 1592.

2. It is proved that there is a whole body of compositions written by the mind which we call Shakespeare, and which were acted on the stage before 1592.

3. It is proved that Shakspere was a servant in or about one play-house.

4. It is proved that while so engaged he furnished plays to rival play-houses.

---

[1] *School of Shak.*, vol. i, p. 20 — Introduction. [2] Ibid., vol. i, p. 8.

Is all this conceivable? Would the proprietor of one theater permit his *servant* to give to other theaters the means of drawing the crowd from his own doors and the shillings from his own pocket?

V. The Plays Cease to Appear Long before Shakspere's Death.

The poet Dryden stated, in 1680, that *Othello* was Shakespeare's last play.

Dryden was born only fifteen years after Shakspere's death. He was himself a play-writer; a frequenter of play-houses; the associate of actors; he wrote the statement quoted only sixty-four years after Shakspere died; he doubtless spoke the tradition common among the actors of London.

Now, it is well known that *Othello* was in existence in 1605, eleven years before Shakspere's death. Malone says, "*We know* it was acted in 1604."

Knight says:

Mr. Peter Cunningham confirms this, by having found an entry in the *Revels at Court* of a performance of *Othello* in 1604.[1]

We can conceive that it may have been the last of the great Shakespearean tragedies, *The Tempest* being the last of the comedies.

Certain it is, however, that the Plays ceased to appear about the time Bacon rose to high and lucrative employment in the state, and several years before the death of their putative author.

All the Plays seem to have originated in that period of time during which Bacon was poor and unemployed. Take even those which are conceded to belong to Shakespeare's "later period."

Halliwell-Phillipps says:

Macbeth, in some form, had been introduced on the English stage as early as 1600, for Kempe, the actor, in his "Nine Daies' Wonder performed in a Daunce from London to Norwich," alludes to a play of *Macdoel*, or *Macdobeth*, or *Macsomewhat*, for I am sure a *Mac* it was, though I never had the maw to see it.[2]

Hamlet, we have seen, first appeared, probably in some imperfect form, in 1585. *Lear* was acted before King James at Whitehall in the year 1606.

Halliwell-Phillipps says:

The four years and a half that intervened between the performance of *The Tempest* in 1611, and the author's death, could not have been one of his periods of

---

[1] Knight, introd. notice *Othello*. [2] Halliwell-Phillipps, *Outlines Life of Shak.*, p. 291.

great literary activity. So many of his plays are known to have been in existence at the former date, it follows that there are only six which could by any possibility have been written after that time; and it is not likely that the whole of those belong to so late an era. These facts lead irresistibly to the conclusion that the poet abandoned literary occupation a considerable period before his decease.[1]

Knight says:

But when the days of pleasure arrived, is it reasonable to believe that the greatest of intellects would suddenly sink to the condition of an every-day man — cherishing no high plans for the future, looking back with no desire to equal and excel the work of the past? At the period of life when Chaucer began to write the *Canterbury Tales*, Shakspere, according to his biographers, was suddenly and utterly to cease to write. We cannot believe it. Is there a parallel case in the career of any great artist who had won for himself competence and fame?[2]

Here, therefore, is another inexplicable fact: Not only did Shakspere, as we are told, write plays for the London stage before he went to London; but after he had returned to Stratford, with ample leisure and the incentive to make money, the man who sued his neighbor for a few shillings, for malt sold, and who was, we are asked to believe, the most fecund of human intelligences, remained idly in his native village, writing nothing, doing nothing. Was there ever heard, before or since, of such a vast and laborious and creative mind, retiring thus into itself, into nothingness, — and locking the door and throwing away the key, — and vegetating, for from five to ten years, amid muck-heaps and filthy ditches? Would the author of *Lear* and *Hamlet* — the profound, the scholarly philosopher — be capable of such mental suicide; such death in life; such absorption of brain in flesh; such crawling into the innermost recesses of self-oblivion? Five or ten years of nothingness! Not a play; not a letter; not a syllable; nothing but three ignorant-looking signatures to a will, which appears to have been drawn by a lawyer who thought the testator could not write his name.

VI. The Sonnets.

And in the so-called "Shakespeare Sonnets" we find a whole congeries of mysteries. The critical world has racked all its brains to determine who W. H. was — "the onlie begetter of these insuing sonnets;" and how any other man could "beget" them if they were Shakespeare's. Some one speaks of that collection of sonnets,

---

[1] Halliwell-Phillipps, *Outlines Life of Shak.*, p. 155.   [2] Knight's *Shak. Biography*, p. 525.

published in 1609, as "one of the most singular volumes ever issued form the press." Let us point at a few of its singularities:

Sonnet lxxvi says:

> Why is my verse so barren of new pride?
>   So far from variation or quick change?
> Why, with the time, do I not glance aside
>   To new-found methods and to compounds strange?
> Why write I still all one, ever the same,
>   *And keep invention in a noted weed,*
> *That every word doth almost tell my name,*
>   *Showing their birth and where they did proceed?*

What is the meaning of this? Clearly that the writer was hidden in a *weed*, a disguise; and we have already seen that Bacon employed the word *weed* to signify a disguise. But it is more than a disguise — it is a *noted* disguise. Surely the name *Shakespeare* was noted enough. And the writer, covered by this disguise, fears that every word he writes doth betray him; — doth "almost tell his name," their birth and where they came from. This is all very remarkable if Shakspere *was* Shakespeare. Then there was no *weed*, no disguise and no danger of the secret authorship being revealed.

But we find Francis Bacon as I have shown, also referring to a *weed*.

> The state and bread of the poor and oppressed have been precious in mine eyes. I have hated all cruelty and hardness of heart. I have, *though in a despised weed*, procured the good of all men.

Marvelous, indeed, is it to find Shakespeare's sonnets referring to "a noted *weed*," and Bacon referring to "a despised *weed*"! — that is to say, Shakespeare admits that the writer has kept invention in a disguise; and Bacon claims that he himself, under a disguise, has procured the good of all men; and that this disguise was a *despised* one, as the name of a play-actor like Shakspere would necessarily be.

But there is another incompatibility in these sonnets with the belief that William Shakspere wrote them. In Sonnet cx we read:

> Alas, 'tis true, I have gone here and there,
>   And made myself a motley to the view,
> Gor'd mine own thoughts, sold cheap what is most dear.

And in the next sonnet we have:

> O, for my sake do you with fortune chide,
>   The guilty goddess of my harmful deeds,
> That did not better for my life provide
>   Than public means, which public manners breeds.
> Thence comes it that *my name receives a brand*,
>   And almost thence my nature is subdued
> To what it works in, like the dyer's hand.

These lines have been interpreted to "refer to the bitter feeling of personal degradation allowed by Shakespeare to result from his connection with the stage."

But Halliwell-Phillipps says:

Is it conceivable that a man who encouraged a sentiment of this nature, one which must have been accompanied with a distaste and contempt for his profession, would have remained an actor years and years after any real necessity for such a course had expired? By the spring of 1602 at the latest, if not previously, he had acquired a secure and definite competence, independently of his emoluments as a dramatist, and yet eight years afterward, in 1610, he is discovered playing in company with Burbadge and Heminge at the Blackfriars Theater.[1]

It is impossible that so transcendent a genius — a statesman, a historian, a lawyer, a philosopher, a linguist, a courtier, a natural aristocrat; holding the "many-headed mob" and "the base mechanical fellows" in absolute contempt; with wealth enough to free him from the pinch of poverty — should have remained, almost to the very last, a "vassal actor," liable to be pelted with decayed vegetables, or tossed in a blanket, and ranked in legal estimation with vagabonds and prostitutes. It is impossible that he should have continued for so many years to have acted subordinate parts of ghosts and old men, in unroofed enclosures, amid the foul exhalations of a mob, which could only be covered by the burning of juniper branches. Surely such a man, in such an age of unrest, when humble but ambitious adventurers rose to high places, would have carved out for himself some nobler position in life; or would, at least, have left behind him some evidence that he tried to do so.

Neither can we conceive how one who commenced life as a peasant, and worked at the trade of a butcher, and who had fled to London to escape public whipping and imprisonment, could feel that his name "received a brand" by associating with Burbadge and Nathaniel Field and the other actors. Was it not, in

---

[1] *Outlines Life of Shak.*, p. 110.

every sense, an elevation for him? And if he felt ashamed of his connection with the stage, why did he, in his last act on earth, the drawing of his will, refer to his "fellows," Heminge and Condell, and leave them presents of rings?

But all this feeling of humiliation here pictured would be most natural to Francis Bacon. The guilty goddess of his harmful deeds had, indeed, not provided him the necessaries of life, and he had been forced to have recourse to "public means," to-wit, play-writing; and thereby his name had been "branded," and his nature had been degraded to the level of the actors.

We turn now to another point.

VII. THE EARLY MARKS OF AGE.

There are many evidences that the person who wrote the sonnets began to show the marks of age at an early period. The 138th sonnet was published in 1599, in *The Passionate Pilgrim*, when William Shakspere was thirty-five years of age; and yet in it the writer speaks of himself as old:

> Although she knows my days are past the best . . .
> And wherefore say not I, that I am old?
> O, love's best habit is in seeming trust,
> And age in love loves not to have years told.

And again he says in the 22d sonnet:

> My glass shall not persuade me I am old,
> So long as youth and thou are of one date.

Again, in the 62d sonnet, he speaks of himself as

> Bated and chopped with tanned antiquity.

And in the 73d sonnet he says:

> That time of year thou may'st in me behold
> When yellow leaves, or none, or few, do hang
> Upon those boughs which shake against the cold,
> Bare, ruined choirs, where late the sweet birds sang.

Now, all this would be unusual language for a man of thirty-five to apply to himself; but it agrees well with what we know of Francis Bacon in this respect.

John Campbell says:

The marks of age were prematurely impressed upon him.

He writes to his uncle Burleigh in 1591:

I am now somewhat ancient; one and thirty years is a great deal of sand in the hour-glass.[1]

And again he says, about the same time:

I would be sorry she [the Queen] should estrange in my last years, for so I account them reckoning by health, not by age.[2]

VIII. THE WRITER'S LIFE THREATENED.

Then there is another passage in the sonnets which does not, so far as we know, fit into the career of the wealthy burgher of Stratford, but accords admirably with an incident in the life of Bacon. In the 74th sonnet we read:

> But be contented: when that fell arrest
>   Without all bail shall carry me away,
> My life hath in this line some interest,
>   Which for memorial still with thee shall stay. . . .
> The earth can have but earth, which is his due:
>   My spirit is thine, the better part of me:
> So then thou hast but lost the dregs of life,
>   The prey of worms, my body being dead;
> *The coward conquest of a wretch's knife,*
>   Too base of thee to be remembered.

And again in the 90th sonnet we read:

> Then hate me if thou wilt, if ever now;
>   *Now while the world is bent my deeds to cross,*
> *Join with the spite of fortune,* make me bow
>   And do not drop in for an after-loss:
>   Ah! do not, when my heart hath scaped this sorrow,
>   Come in the rearward of a conquered woe.

It seems to me the explanation of these lines is to be found in the fact that, after the downfall of Essex, Bacon was bitterly hated and denounced by the adherents of the Earl, and his life was even in danger from their rage. He writes to Queen Elizabeth in 1599:

My life has been threatened and my name libeled, which I count an honor.[3]

Again he says to Cecil:

As for any violence to be offered to me, wherewith my friends tell me I am threatened, I thank God I have the privy coat of a good conscience.

He also wrote to Lord Howard:

For my part I have deserved better than to have my name objected to envy or my life to a ruffian's violence.

---

[1] Letter to Burleigh.   [2] Letter to Sir Robert Cecil.
[3] Letter to Queen Elizabeth, 1599 — *Life and Works*, vol. ii, p. 160.

IX. A Period of Gloom.

We find, too, in the sonnets, reference to a period of gloom in the life of the writer that is not to be explained by anything we know of in the history of William Shakspere. He had all the world could give him; he had wealth, the finest house in Stratford, lands, tithes, and malt to sell; to say nothing of that bogus coat-of-arms which assured him gentility. But the writer of the sonnets (see sonnet xxxvii) speaks of himself as unfortunate, as "made lame by fortune's dearest spite," as "lame, poor and despised." He is overwhelmed with some great shame:

> *When in disgrace with fortune and men's eyes,*
>   I all alone beweep my outcast state,
> And trouble deaf Heaven with my bootless cries,
>   And look upon myself and *curse my fate*.[1]

And the writer had experienced some great disappointment He says:

> Full many a glorious morning have I seen
>   Flatter the mountain tops with sovereign eye,
> Kissing with golden face the meadows green,
>   Gilding pale streams with heavenly alchemy:
> Anon permit the basest cloud to ride,
>   With ugly rack on his celestial face,
> And from the forlorn world his visage hide,
>   Stealing unseen to west with this disgrace;
> *Even so my sun one early morn did shine,*
>   *With all triumphant splendor on my brow;*
> *But out! alack! he was but one hour mine,*
>   *The region cloud hath masked him from me now.*[2]

And the writer is utterly cast down with his disappointment. He cries out in sonnet lxvi:

> Tired of all these, for restful death I cry,
>   As to behold *desert* a *beggar born*,
> And needy *nothing* trimmed in jollity,
>   And purest faith unhappily forsworn,
> And gilded honor shamefully misplaced,
>   And maiden virtue rudely strumpeted,
> And right perfection wrongfully disgraced,
>   And *strength by limping sway disabled,*
> *And art made tongue-tied by authority,*
>   And folly (doctor-like) controlling skill,
> And simple truth miscalled simplicity,
>   And *captive Good attending captain Ill*—
>   Tired with all these, from these I would be gone,
>   Save that to die I leave my love alone.

[1] *Sonnet* xxix.   [2] *Sonnet* xxxiii.

All these words seem to me to fit into Bacon's case. He was in disgrace with fortune and men's eyes. He writes to Essex in 1594:

> And I must confess this very delay has gone so near me as it hath almost overthrown my health. . . . I cannot but conclude that no man ever read a more exquisite disgrace.[1]

He proposed to travel abroad; he hopes her Majesty will not force him

> To pine here with melancholy, for though mine heart be good, yet mine eyes will be sore. . . . I am not an impudent man that would face out a disgrace.[2]

The bright morning sun of hope had ceased to shine upon his brow. He "lacked advancement," like Hamlet; he had been over-ridden by the Queen. He despaired. He writes: "I care not whether God or her Majesty call me." In the sonnet he says:

> Tired of all these, for restful death I cry.

And the grounds of his lamentation are those a courtier might entertain, but scarcely a play-actor. He beholds "desert" a beggar. Surely this was not Shakspere's case. He sees nothingness elevated to power; strength swayed by limping weakness; himself with all his greatness overruled by the cripple Cecil. He sees the state and religion tying the tongue of art and shutting the mouth of free thought. He sees evil triumphant in the world; "captive Good attending captain Ill." And may not the "maiden virtue rudely strumpeted" be a reflection on her of whom so many scandals were whispered; who, it was said, had kept Leicester's bed-chamber next to her own; who had for so many years suppressed Bacon, and for whom, on her death, "the honey-tongued Melicert" dropped not one pitying tear.

X. An Incomprehensible Fact.

Francis Bacon was greedy for knowledge. He ranged the whole amphitheater of human learning. From Greece, from Rome, from Italy, from France, from Spain, from the early English writers, he gathered facts and thoughts. He had his *Promus*, his commonplace-book, so to speak, of "formularies and *elegancies*" of speech. His acknowledged writings teem with quotations from the poets. And yet not once does he refer to William Shakspere or

---

[1] Letter to Essex, March 30, 1594. [2] Letter to Essex.

the Shakespeare writings! The man of Stratford acted in one of the Plays which go by his name, and on the same night, in the same place, was presented a "mask" written by Bacon. We thus have the two men under the same roof, at the same time, engaged in the same kind of work. Shakespeare, the play-writer, and Bacon, the mask-writer, thus rub elbows; but neither seems to have known the other.

Landor says:

Bacon little knew or suspected that there was then existing (the only one that ever did exist) his superior in intellectual power.

Bacon was ravaging all time and searching the face of the whole earth for gems of thought and expression, and here in these Plays was a veritable Golconda of jewels, under his very nose, and he seems not to have known it.

XI. BACON'S LOVE OF PLAYS.

But it may be said that Shakspere moved in a lower sphere of thought, beneath the notice of the great philosopher. This cannot be true; for we have seen that Bacon certainly wrote "masks," which were a kind of smaller plays, and that he united with seven other young lawyers of Gray's Inn to prepare a veritable stage-play, *The Misfortunes of Arthur;* but, more than that, he was very fond of theatricals.

Mrs. Pott says, speaking of the year 1594:

The Calvinistic strictness of Lady Anne Bacon's principles receive a severe shock from the repeated and open proofs which Francis gives of his taste for stage performances. Anthony, about this time, leaves his brother and goes to live in Bishopsgate Street, near "Bull" Inn, where ten or twelve of the "Shakespeare" Plays were acted. Lady Anne "trusts that they will not mum, nor mask, nor sinfully revel at Gray's Inn."

Bacon's acknowledged writings overflow with expressions showing how much his thoughts ran on play-houses and stage-plays. I quote a few expressions, at random, to prove this:

Therefore we see that there be certain "pantomimi" that will represent the voices of players of interludes so to life, as if you see them not you would think they were those players themselves.[1]

Alluding to "the prompter," or "book-holder," as he was then called, Bacon says of himself:

---

[1] *Natural History*, § 240.

Knowing myself to be fitter to hold a book than to play a part.[1]

Speaking of Essex' successes, he says:

Neither do I judge the whole play by the first act.[2]

He writes Lord Burleigh that

There are a dozen young gentlemen of Gray's Inn, that . . . will be ready to furnish a mask, wishing it were in their power to perform it according to their minds.

In the *De Augmentis* he speaks of "*the play-books of philosophical systems*" and "the play-books of this *philosophical theater.*"[3]

He calls the world of art "a universe or *theater* of things."[4]

Speaking of the priest Simonds instructing Simnell to personate Lord Edward Plantagenet, Bacon says:

This priest, being utterly unacquainted with the true person, should think it possible to instruct his *player* either in gesture or fashions. . . . None could *hold the book* so well to prompt and instruct this *stage play* as he could. . . . He thought good, after the manner of *scenes in stage plays and masks*, to show it afar off.[5]

Referring to the degradation of the royal pretender, Lambert Simnell, to a position in the kitchen of the King, Bacon says:

So that in a kind of "matticina" of human force, he turned a broach who had worn a crown; whereas fortune does not commonly bring in a *comedy or farce after a tragedy*.[6]

Speaking of Warbeck's conspiracy, Bacon says:

It was one of the longest plays of that kind that hath been in memory.[7]

And here I group together several similar expressions:

Therefore, now, *like the end of a play*, a great many came upon the stage at once.[8]

He [Perkin Warbeck] had contrived with himself *a vast and tragical plot*.[9]

I have given the rule where a man cannot fitly *play his own part*, if he have not a friend he may *quit the stage*.[10]

But men must know that in *this theater of man's life*, it is reserved only for God and the angels to be lookers-on.[11]

As if they would make you like a king in a play, who, when one would think he standeth in great majesty and felicity, is *troubled to say his part*.[12]

With which speech he put the army into an infinite fury and uproar, whereas truth was he had no brother; neither was there any such matter, but he *played it merely as if he had been upon the stage*.[13]

Those friends whom I accounted no *stage friends*, but private friends.[14]

---

[1] Letter to Sir Thomas Bodley.
[2] Letter to Essex, Oct. 4, 1596.
[3] lxi, lxii.
[4] *History of Henry VII.*
[5] Ibid.
[6] Ibid.
[7] Ibid.
[8] Ibid.
[9] Ibid.
[10] Essay *Of Friendship.*
[11] *Advancement of Learning*, book ii.
[12] *Gesta Grayorum — Life and Works*, vol. i, p. 339.
[13] *Advancement of Learning*, book ii.
[14] Letter to Tobie Matthew.

> All that would be but a *play upon the stage*, if justice went not on in the right course.[1]

> Zeno and Socrates . . . placed felicity in virtue; . . . the Cyrenaics and Epicureans placed it in pleasure, and made virtue (as it is used in some *comedies of errors*, wherein the mistress and maid change habits) to be but as a servant.[2]

> We regard all the systems of philosophy hitherto received or imagined as so many *plays* brought out and performed, creating fictitious and *theatrical worlds*.[3]

> The plot of this our theater resembles those of the poetical, where the plots which are invented for the stage are more consistent, elegant and pleasurable than those taken from real history.[4]

I might continue these examples indefinitely, for Bacon's whole writings bubble and sparkle with comparisons drawn from plays, play-houses and actors; and yet, marvelous to relate, he never notices the existence of the greatest dramatic writings the world had ever known, which he must have witnessed on the stage a thousand times. He takes Ben Jonson into his house as an amanuensis, but the mightiest mind of all time, if Shakspere was Shakespeare, he never notices, even when he is uttering thoughts and preaching a philosophy identical with his own! How can all this be explained?

Mrs. Pott calls attention to the following:

> Beaumont and Fletcher dedicated to Bacon the mask which was designed to celebrate the marriage of the Count Palatine with the Princess Elizabeth, February 14, 1612–13. The dedication of this mask begins with an acknowledgment that Bacon, with the gentlemen of Gray's Inn, and the Inner Temple, had "spared no pains nor travail in the setting forth, ordering and furnishing of this mask . . . and you, Sir Francis Bacon, especially, as you did then by your countenance and loving affection advance it, so let your good word grace it, which is able to add value to the greatest and least matters." "On Tuesday," says Chamberlain, writing on the 18th of February, 1612–13," it came to Gray's Inn and the Inner Temple's turn to come with their mask, *whereof Sir Francis Bacon was the chief contriver.*" (*Court and Times of James I.*, vol. i, p. 227; see Spedding, vol. iv, p. 344.)[5]

And we find Bacon writing an essay on *Masques*, in which he gave directions as to scenery, music, colors and trappings, and even speaks of the necessity of sweet odors "to drown the steam and heat" of the audience!

And he philosophizes, as I have shown, upon the drama, its usefulness, its purposes for good, its characteristics; and describes how, in a play, the different passions may be represented, and how

---

[1] Letter to Buckingham, 1619.
[2] *Advancement of Learning*, book ii.
[3] *Novum Organum*.
[4] Ibid.
[5] *Did Francis Bacon Write "Shakespeare"?* part i, p. 8.

the growth and development of any special feeling or passion may be shown; and Macaulay writes (as if it were a foot-note to the passage) this in reference to the Shakespeare Plays:

> In a piece which may be read in three hours, we see a character gradually unfold all its recesses to us; we see it change with the change of circumstances. The petulant youth rises into the politic and war-like sovereign. The profuse and courteous philanthropist soars into a hater and scorner of his kind. The tyrant is altered by the chastisement of affliction into a pensive moralist.

And this student of the drama, this frequenter of the play-houses, this writer of plays and masks, this sovereign and penetrating intellect could not perceive that there stood at his elbow, (the associate, "the fellow" of his clerk, Jonson) the vastest genius the human race had ever produced! This philosopher of prose could not recognize the philosopher of poetry; this writer of prose histories did not know the writer of dramatical histories; this writer of sonnets, this "concealed poet," this "greatest wit" of the world (although known by another name), took no notice of that other mighty intellect, splendid wit and sweet poet, who acted on the boards of his own law school of Gray's Inn! It is incomprehensible. It is incredible.

And, be it further remembered, Shakespeare dedicated both the *Venus and Adonis* and *The Rape of Lucrece* to the Earl of Southampton, and the Earl was Bacon's particular friend and associate, and *a member of his law school of Gray's Inn;* and yet, while Shakespeare dedicates his poems to the Earl, he seems not to have known his friend and fellow, Francis Bacon. On the other hand, in the fact that Southampton was a student in Gray's Inn, we see the reason why the Shakespeare poems were inscribed to him, under the cover of the play-actor's name.

I have faith enough in the magnanimity of mind of Francis Bacon to believe that if he had really found, in humble life, a man of the extraordinary genius revealed in the Shakespeare Plays (supposing for an instant that they were not Bacon's work), he would have stooped down and taken him by the hand; he would have introduced him to his friends; he would have quoted from him in his writings, and we should have found among his papers numbers of letters to and from him. Their lives would have impinged on each other; they would have discussed poetry and philosophy in speech and in correspondence. Bacon would have visited Stratford, and Shakspere St. Albans. "Poets," said Ben Jonson, "are rarer births than kings;" and the man who wrote the Plays was the king of poets. Was Francis Bacon—"the wisest of mankind"—so blind or so shallow as to be unaware of the greatness of the Shakespeare Plays? Who will believe it?

XII. CERTAIN INCOMPATIBILITIES WITH SHAKSPERE.

Let me touch passingly on some passages in the Plays which it would seem that the man of Stratford could not have written.

Who can believe that William Shakspere, whose father followed the trade of a butcher, and who was himself, as tradition assures us, apprenticed to the same humble calling, could have written these lines in speaking of Wolsey?

> This *butcher's cur* is venom-mouthed, and I
> Have not the power to muzzle him; therefore best
> Not wake him in his slumber. A beggar's book
> Outworths a noble's blood.[1]

Richard Grant White says:

> Shakespeare's works are full of passages, to write which, if he had loved his wife and honored her, would have been gall and wormwood to his soul; nay, which, if he had loved and honored her, he could not have written. The nature of the subject forbids the marshaling of this terrible array; but did the "flax-wench" whom he uses for the most degrading of comparisons (*Winter's Tale*, i, 2) do more, "before her troth-plight," than the woman who bore his name and whom his children called mother?[2]

But Grant White fails to see that it is not a question as to whether Shakspere loved and honored his wife or not. Even if he had not loved and honored her, he would, if a sensitive and high-spirited man, for his own sake and the sake of his family, have avoided the subject as if it carried the contagion of a pestilence.

Again we are told, in all the biographies, that Shakspere was cruelly persecuted and punished by Sir Thomas Lucy, and "forced to fly the country," and that for revenge he wrote a bitter ballad against the Knight; and that subsequently, in *The Merry Wives of Windsor*, he made Sir Thomas the object of his ridicule in the character of Justice Shallow. But if this be true, why did the writer of the Plays in the *1st Henry VI.* bring upon the stage the ancestor of this same Sir Thomas Lucy, Sir William Lucy, and

---

[1] *Henry VIII.*, i, 1.   [2] *Life and Genius of Shak.*, p. 51.

paint him in honorable colors as a brave soldier and true patriot for the admiration of the public and posterity? But the son of Shakspere's Lucy, Sir Thomas Lucy, was the intimate friend and correspondent of Francis Bacon.

XIII. Shakspere was Falstaff.

But there follows another question. It is evident that Justice Shallow was intended to personate Sir Thomas Lucy, and the play of *The Merry Wives of Windsor* opens with an allusion to the stealing of his deer. I quote the beginning of the act:

Shallow. Sir Hugh, persuade me not; I will make a Star Chamber matter of it; if he were twenty Sir John Falstaffs, he shall not abuse Robert Shallow, Esquire. . . .

Slender. . . . They may give the dozen white *luces* in their coat.

The coat-of-arms of the Lucy family was three *luces*, and from this the name was derived. So that herein it is placed beyond question that Justice Shallow is intended to represent Sir Thomas Lucy. This is conceded by all the commentators. It is also conceded that the deer which in this scene Sir John Falstaff is alleged to have killed were the same deer which Shakspere had slain in his youth.

Shallow. It is a riot. . . .
Page. I am glad to see your worships well; I thank you for my venison, Master Shallow.
Shallow. Master Page, I am glad to see you; much good do it your good heart. I wished your venison better; *it was ill killed*. . . .

Enter Falstaff.
Falstaff. Now Master Shallow; you'll complain of me to the King?
Shallow. Knight, you have beaten my men, killed my deer and broken open my lodge.
Falstaff. But not kissed your keeper's daughter.

Therefore it follows that if Shallow was Sir Thomas Lucy, and if the deer that were killed were the deer Shakspere killed, then *Shakspere was Falstaff!*

And if Shakspere wrote the Plays, he deliberately represented himself in the character of Falstaff. And what was the character of Falstaff as delineated in that very play? It was that of a gross, sensual, sordid old liar and thief. The whole play turns on his sensuality united to sordidness. He makes love to Page's wife because "the report goes she has all the rule of her husband's purse; he hath a legion of angels." And Falstaff is also represented as sharing in the thefts of his followers, as witness the following dialogue:

> *Falstaff.* I will not lend thee a penny.
> *Pistol.* Why, then, the world's mine oyster,
> Which I with sword will open.
> *Falstaff.* Not a penny. I have been content, sir, you should lay my countenance to pawn; I have grated upon my good friends for three reprieves for you and your coach-fellow, Nym; or else you had looked through the grate like a geminy of baboons. I am damned in hell for swearing to gentlemen, my friends, you were good soldiers and tall fellows: and when Mistress Bridget lost the handle of her fan, I took 't upon mine honor thou hadst it not.
> *Pistol.* Didst not thou share? Hadst thou not fifteen pence?
> *Falstaff.* Reason, you rogue, reason: think'st thou I'll endanger my soul *gratis*?

Is it conceivable that the great man, the scholar, the philosopher, the tender-souled, ambitious, sensitive man who wrote the sonnets would deliberately represent himself as *Falstaff?*

But if some one else wrote the Plays, then this whole scene concerning the deer-stealing contains, probably, a cipher narrative of the early life of Shakspere; for it is in the same play, as we shall see hereafter, that we find the cipher words *William, Shakes, peere,* and *Francisco Bacon.* And when we read the obscene anecdotes which tradition has delivered down to us, touching Shakspere's sensuality and mother-wit, and then look at the gross face represented in the monument in the Stratford church, we can realize that William Shakspere may have been the original of Falstaff, and that it was not by accident he was represented as having killed the deer of that Justice Shallow who had the twelve white *luces* on his coat-of-arms.

Richard Grant White, earnest anti-Baconian as he is, says of that bust:

The monument is ugly; the staring, painted, figure-head-like bust hideous.[1]

It is the face of Falstaff.

XIV. A Curious Fact.

I proceed now to call the attention of the reader to a curious fact, revealed by a study of the copies of legal documents found in Halliwell-Phillipps' *Outlines of the Life of Shakespeare.*

Shakspere purchased a house and lot in London, on the 10th day of March, 1612, "within the precinct of the late Black Fryers."

---
[1] *England Without and Within,* p. 921.

It has puzzled his biographers to tell what he wanted this property for. All his other purchases were in Stratford or vicinity. He did not need it for a home, for before this time he had retired to Stratford to live in his great house, New Place; and in the deed of purchase of the Blackfriars property he is described as " of Stratford-on-Avon, gentleman." The house and lot were close to the Blackfriars Theater, and property was falling in the neighborhood because of that proximity. Shakspere rented it to one John Robinson.

But there are three curious features in connection with this purchase:

1. Shakspere, although very rich at the time, did not pay down all the purchase-money, but left £60 standing upon mortgage, which was not extinguished until after his death.

2. Shakspere bought the property from Henry Walker, minstrel, for £140, while Walker in 1604 had bought it for £100. This represented an increase equal to $2,400 to-day. And yet we find the people of that vicinity petitioning in 1618–19 to have the theater closed, because of the great injury it did to property-holders around it.

3. Walker's grantor was Matthew BACON, of *Gray's Inn*, in the county of Middlesex, gentleman, and included in the purchase was the following:

And also all that plott of ground on the west side of the same tenement, which was lately inclosed with boordes, on two sides thereof, by *Anne* BACON, *widow*, so farre and in such sorte as the same was inclosed by the said *Anne* BACON and not otherwise.

Was this "Anne Bacon, widow," the mother of Francis Bacon? Her name was Anne. And who was Matthew Bacon, of Gray's Inn? Was he one of Francis Bacon's family? And is it not strange to find the names of *Bacon* and *Shakspere* coming together thus in a business transaction? And does it not look as if Shakspere had paid a debt to some one by buying a piece of property for $2,400 more than it was worth, and giving a mortgage for £60, equal to $3,600 of our money at the present time?

XV. THE NORTHUMBERLAND HOUSE MANUSCRIPT.

There is one other instance where the name of Shakspere is found associated with that of Francis Bacon.

In 1867 there was discovered in the library of Northumberland House, in London, a remarkable MS., containing copies of several papers written by Francis Bacon. It was found in a box of old papers which had long remained undisturbed. There is a title-page, which embraces a *table of contents* of the volume, and this contains not only the names of writings unquestionably Bacon's, but also the names of plays which are supposed to have been written by Shakespeare. But only part of the manuscript volume remains, and the portions lost embrace the following pieces enumerated on the title-leaf:

> *Orations at Graie's Inns revells*
> .... *Queen's Mask* ....
>   *By Mr. Frauncis Bacon*
> *Essaies by the same author.*
> *Richard the Second.*
> *Richard the Third.*
> *Asmund and Cornelia.*
> *Isle of Dogs frmnt.*
>   *By Thomas Nashe, inferior places.*[1]

How comes it that the Shakespeare plays, *Richard II.* and *Richard III.*, should be mixed up in a volume of Bacon's manuscripts with his own letters and essays and a mask written by him in 1592? Judge Holmes says:

> And then, the blank space at the side and between the titles is scribbled all over with various words, letters, phrases and scraps of verse in English and Latin, as if the copyist were merely trying his pen, and writing down whatever first came into his head. Among these scribblings, beside the name of Francis Bacon several times, *the name of William Shakespeare is written eight or nine times over.* A line from *The Rape of Lucrece* is written thus: "Revealing day through every crannie peeps and," the writer taking *peeps* from the next couplet instead of *spies.* Three others are *Anthony comfrt. and consort* and *honorificabilitudino* and *plaies* [plays]. . . . The word *honorificabilitudino* is not found in any dictionary that I know of, but in *Love's Labor's Lost.*[2]

Costard, the clown, bandying Latin with the tall schoolmaster and curate (who "had been at a great feast of languages and stolen the scraps"), exclaims:

> Oh! they have lived long on the alms-basket of words. I marvel thy master hath not eaten thee for a word, for thou art not so long by the head as *honorificabilitudinatibus.*[3]

Let those who are disposed to study this discovery turn to Judge Holmes' work. It is sufficient for me to note here, that in a collection of Bacon's papers, made undoubtedly by his aman-

---

[1] Holmes' *Authorship of Shakespeare*, vol. ii, p. 658, ed. 1886.   [2] Ibid., 658-60.
[2] Act v, scene 1.

uensis, plays that are recognized to be Shakespeare's are embraced; and the name of Francis Bacon and the name of *William Shakspeare* (spelled as it was spelled in the published quartos, but not as the man himself spelled it) are scribbled all over this manuscript collection, and at the same time sentences and words are quoted from the Shakespeare Plays and Poems.

And, while we find this association of the two names in Bacon's library and private papers, there is not one word in his published writings or his correspondence to show that he knew that such a being as William Shakspere ever existed.

"'Tis strange; 'tis passing strange."

XVI. ANOTHER SINGULAR FACT.

Edmund Spenser visited London in 1590, and in 1591 he published his poem, *The Tears of the Muses*, in which Thalia, the muse of poetry, laments that a change has come over the playhouses; that

> The sweet delights of *learning's treasure*,
>   That wont with comic sock to beautify
> The painted theaters, and fill with pleasure
>   The listeners' eyes and ears with melody,

are "all gone."

> And all that goodly glee
> Which wont to be the glory of gay wits,
> Is laid a-bed;

and in lieu thereof "ugly barbarism and brutish ignorance" fill the stage,

> And with vain joys the vulgar entertain.

> Instead thereof scoffing Scurrility
>   And scornful Folly with Contempt is crept,
> Rolling in rhymes of shameless ribaldry
>   Without regard or due decorum kept.

And Spenser laments that the author, who formerly delighted with "goodly glee" and "*learning's* treasure," has withdrawn — is temporarily dead.

> And he, the man whom Nature's self had made
>   To mock herself and Truth to imitate,
> With kindly counter under mimic shade,
>   Our pleasant Willy, ah! is dead of late;
>   With whom all joy and jolly merriment
>   Is also deaded and in dolor drent.

But that this was not an actual death, but simply a retirement from the degenerate stage, is shown in the next verse but one:

> But that same gentle spirit from whose pen
> Large streams of honey and sweet nectar flow.
> Scorning the boldness of such base-born men
> Which dare their follies forth so rashly throw,
> Doth rather choose to sit in idle cell
> Than so himself to mockery to sell.

It is conceded by all the commentators that these lines refer to the writer of the Shakespeare Plays: there was no one else to whom they could refer. But there are many points in which they are incompatible with the young man William Shakspere, of Stratford.

In the first place, they throw back the date of his labors, as I have shown in a former instance, long anterior to the year 1592, at which time it is conceded Shakespeare first began to write for the stage. In 1590, the writer referred to by Spenser had not only written one, but many plays; and had had possession of the stage long enough to give it a cast and character, until driven out by the rage for vulgar satires and personal abuse. White says:

> The *Tears of the Muses* had certainly been written before 1590, when Shakespeare could not have risen to the position assigned by the first poet of the age to the subject of this passage; and probably in 1580, when Shakespeare was a boy of sixteen, in Stratford.

In the next place, the man referred to by Spenser was a *gentleman*. The word *gentle* in these lines is clearly contradistinguished from *base-born*.

> That same *gentle* spirit . . .
> Scorning the folly of such *base-born* men.

No one will pretend that the Stratford fugitive was in 1590 "a gentleman."

Shakspere, we are told, produced his dramas to make money; "for gain, not glory, he winged his roving flight." Young, poor, just risen from the rank of horse-holder or call-boy, if not actually occupying it, it is not likely he could have resisted the clamors of his fellows for productions suitable to the degraded taste of the hour. But the man referred to by Spenser was a gentleman, a man of "learning," a man of refinement, and he

> Rather chose to sit in idle cell
> Than so himself to mockery to sell.

The comparison of the poet to the refined student in his "cell" is a very inapplicable one to apply to an actor, be he Marlowe or Shakspere, daily appearing on the boards in humble characters, and helping to present to vulgar audiences the very obscenities and scurrilities of which Spenser complained.

Again, if we examine that often-quoted verse:

> And he, the man whom Nature's self had made
> To mock herself and Truth to imitate,
> *With kindly counter, under mimic shade*,
> Our pleasant Willy, ah! is dead of late.

The word *counter* is not known to our dictionaries in any sense that is consonant with the meaning of these lines. I take it to be a poetical abbreviation of "counterfeit," and this view is confirmed by the further statement that this gentle-born playwright, who despised the base-born play-makers, imitated truth under a *shade* or disguise; and this disguise was a *mimic* one, to-wit, that of a *mime* — an actor.

The name *Willy* in that day, as I have shown heretofore, was generally applied to all poets.

XVII. Another Extraordinary Fact.

It is sometimes said: How can you undertake to deny Shakspere the honor of his own writings, when the Plays were printed during his life-time with his name on the title-page of each and every one of them?

This is a mistake. According to the list of editions printed in Halliwell-Phillipps' *Outlines of the Life of Shakespeare*, p. 533 (and there is no better authority), it seems that the name of *Shakespeare* did not appear upon the title-page of any of the Plays until 1598. The *Venus and Adonis* and *Rape of Lucrece* contained, it is true, dedicatory letters signed by Shakespeare; but the first play, *Titus Andronicus*, published in 1594, was without his name; the *First Part of the Contention of the two Houses of Yorke and Lancaster*, published in 1594; the *Tragedy of Richard, Duke of Yorke*, published in 1595; *Romeo and Juliet*, published in 1597; *Richard II.*, published in 1597, and *Richard III.*, printed in 1597, were all without the name of Shakspere or any one else upon the title-page. It was not until the publication of *Love's Labor Lost*, in *1598*, that we find him set forth as having any connection with the play; and he does not then claim to be the author of it. The title-page reads:

> As it was presented before her Highness this last Christmas. *Newly corrected and augmented by W. Shakespere.*

In the same year the tragedy of *Richard II.* is published, and the name of "William Shake-speare" appears as the author.

It thus appears that during the six years from 1592 to 1598 eight editions of plays which now go by the name of Shakespeare were published without his name or any other name upon the title-page.

In other words, not only did the Shakespeare Plays commence to appear while Shakspere was still in Stratford, and were captivating the town while the author was holding horses or acting as call-boy; but for six years after the Plays which are distinctively known as his, and which are embraced in the Folio of 1623, had won great fame and profit on the stage, they were published in numerous quarto editions without his name or any other name on the title-page. This is mystery on mystery's head accumulate.

XVIII. WHEN WERE THE PLAYS WRITTEN?

But it will be argued by some that Francis Bacon had not the time to write the Shakespeare Plays; that he was too busy with politics, philosophy, law and statesmanship; that there was no time in his life when these productions could have been produced; and that it is absurd to think that he could act as Lord Chancellor and write plays for the stage at the same time.

In the first place, it must be remembered that Francis Bacon was a man of extraordinary and phenomenal industry. One has but to look at the twenty volumes of his acknowledged writings to concede this. In illustration of his industry, we are told that he re-wrote his Essays *thirty times!* His chaplain and biographer, Dr. Rawley, says:

> I myself have seen at the least *twelve* copies of the *Instauration* [meaning, says Spedding,[1] the *Novum Organum*], revised year by year, one after another, and every year altered and amended in the frame thereof, till at last it came to that model in which it was committed to the press; as many living creatures do lick their young ones, till they bring them to the strength of their limbs. . . . He would suffer no moment of time to slip from him without some present improvement.

[1] *Works*, vol. i, p. 47, Boston ed.

As the *Novum Organum* embraces about three hundred and fifty octavo pages of the Boston edition, the reader can conceive the labor required to re-write this twelve times. Let these things be remembered when we come to consider the vastly laborious cipher-story written into the Plays.

But an examination of Bacon's biography will show that he had ample leisure to have written the Plays.

In the spring of 1579, Bacon, then eighteen years of age, returned from Paris, in consequence of the death of his father. He resided for a year or more at St. Albans. In 1581, then twenty years old, he "begins to keep terms at Gray's Inn." In 1582 he is called to the bar. For three years we know nothing of what he is doing. In 1585 he writes a sketch of his philosophy, entitled *The Greatest Birth of Time*, which, it is supposed, was afterwards broadened out into *The Advancement of Learning*. In 1585 the *Contention between the two Houses of York and Lancaster* is supposed to have appeared. In 1586 he is made a bencher. He is "*in umbra* and not in public or frequent action." "His seclusion is commented on." In this year, according to Malone, *The Taming of the Shrew*, *The Two Gentlemen of Verona* and *Love's Labor Lost* appear, probably in imperfect forms, like the first of those thirty copies of the Essays. In 1587 (the year Shakspere is supposed to have come to London), Bacon helps in getting up a play, for the Gray's Inn revels, called *The Misfortunes of Arthur*. He also assists in some masks to be played before Elizabeth. Here certainly we have the leisure, the disposition and the kindred employment. In 1588 he becomes a member of Parliament for Liverpool. He writes a short paper called an *Advertisement Touching the Controversies of the Church*. To this year Dr. Delius attributes *Venus and Adonis* and Mr. Furnival *Love's Labor Lost.* Shakspere is, at this time, either holding horses at the door of the play-house or acting as call-boy, or in some other subordinate capacity about the play-house. In 1589–90 Bacon puts forth a letter to Walsingham, on *The Government and the Papists*. No one can tell what he is working at; and yet, knowing his industry and energy, we may be sure he is not idle; for in the next year he writes to his uncle Burleigh:

I account my ordinary course of study and meditation to be more painful than most parts of action are.

And again he says in the same letter:

> If your Lordship will not carry me on, . . . I will sell the inheritance I have and purchase some lease of quick revenue, or some office of gain, that shall be executed by deputy, and so give over all care of service and become some sorry *book-maker*, or a true pioneer in that mine of truth which, Anaxagoras said, lay so deep.

In 1591 the Queen visits him at his brother's place at Twickenham, and he *writes a sonnet in her honor*.

Mrs. Pott says:

> To 1591 is attributed *1st Henry VI.*, of which the scene is laid in the same provinces of France which formed Bacon's sole experience of that country. Also *The Two Gentlemen of Verona* (probably in its present form), which reflects Anthony's sojourn in Italy. Henceforth the "Shakespeare" Comedies continue to exhibit the combined influence of Anthony's letters from abroad, with Francis' studies in Gray's Inn.[1]

This *1st Henry VI.* is the play referred to by Halliwell-Phillipps, as acted for the first time March 3, 1592, and as *the first of the Shakespeare Plays*.

In 1592 Francis is in debt, borrowing one pound at a time, and cast into a sponging-house by a "hard" Jew or Lombard on account of a bond. His brother, Anthony, comes to his relief. Soon after appears *The Merchant of Venice*, in which Antonio relieves Bassanio. Does this last name contain a hint of Bacon, after the anagrammatic fashion of the times?

Dr. Delius attributes *Romeo and Juliet* to this date.

In 1593 Bacon composes for some festive occasion a device, or mask, called *A Conference of Pleasure*.

During all these years Bacon lives very much retired. He says, in 1594, he is "poor and sick and *working for bread*." What at? He says, at another time, "The bar will be my bier." He writes his uncle Burleigh in 1595:

> It is true, my life hath been so private as I have no means to do your Lordship service.

The *Venus and Adonis* appears in 1593, with a dedication from William Shakespeare to the Earl of Southampton, Bacon's fellow in Gray's Inn. When the fortunes of Bacon and Southampton afterward separate, because of Southampton's connection with the Essex treason, the poem is re-published *without the dedication*.

---

[1] *Did Francis Bacon Write Shakespeare?* p. 14.

In 1594 Lady Anne, Bacon's mother, is distressed about his devotion to plays and play-houses. In 1590 she had written to Anthony, complaining of his brother's irregular hours and poet-like habits:

> I verily think your brother's weak stomach to digest hath been much caused and confirmed by untimely going to bed, and then musing *nescio quid* when he should sleep, and then, in consequence, by late rising and long lying in bed, whereby his men are made slothful and himself sickly.[1]

In 1594 Bacon begins his *Promus of Formularies and Elegancies*, which has been so ably edited by Mrs. Pott, of London,[2] which fairly bristles with thoughts, expressions and quotations found in the Shakespeare Plays. It is clearly the work of a poet who is studying the *elegancies* of speech, with a view to increase his capacity for the expression of beautiful thoughts. It is not the kind of work in which a mere philosopher would engage.

In this year 1594 "Shakespeare's" *Comedy of Errors* appears (for the first time), at Bacon's law school, Gray's Inn. In the same year *Lucrece* is published. In the same year Bacon writes a *Device*, or mask, which Essex presents to her Majesty on the "Queen's Day," called *The Device of an Indian Prince*. In this year, also, Bacon is defeated by Cecil for the place of Attorney or Solicitor-General, and, as Dr. Delius thinks, the play of *Richard III.*, in which the hump-backed tyrant is held up to the detestation of mankind, appears the same year!

In 1604 Bacon writes to Sir Tobie Matthew, speaking of some important matter, that he cannot recall what passed, "my head being then wholly employed upon *invention*," a word which he uses for works of the imagination.

Here, then, we have the proof that the Plays appeared during Bacon's unemployed youth. No one pretends that he wrote plays while he was holding great and lucrative offices in the state.

XIX. SOME SECRET MEANS OF INCOME.

And we have evidences in Bacon's letters — although they seem to have been gone over carefully and excised and garbled — that he had some secret means of support.

In 1595 he writes Essex:

> I am purposed not to follow the practice of the law, and my reason is only because it drinketh too much time, which I have dedicated to better purposes.

---

[1] Lady Bacon to Anthony Bacon, May 24, 1590 — *Life and Works*, vol. 1, p. 114.
[2] *Bacon's Promus*, by Mrs. Henry Pott. Boston: Houghton, Mifflin & Co.

Mr. Spedding says:

> It is easier to understand why Bacon was resolved not to devote his life to the ordinary practice of a lawyer, than what plan he had to clear himself of the difficulties which were now accumulating upon him, and to obtain means of living and working. What course he betook himself to at the crisis which had now arrived, *I cannot possibly say.* I do not find any letter of his which can possibly be assigned to the winter of 1596, nor have I met among his brother's papers *with anything which indicates what he was about.*

And two years before, in April, 1593, we find Bacon writing to the Earl of Essex thus:

> I did almost conjecture, by your silence and countenance, a distaste in the course I imparted to your Lordship touching mine own fortune. . . . And for the free and loving advice your Lordship hath given me, I cannot correspond to the same with greater duty than by assuring your Lordship that I will not dispose of myself without your allowance. . . . But notwithstanding I know it will be pleasing to your good Lordship that I use my liberty of replying, and I do almost assure myself that your Lordship will rest persuaded by the answer of those reasons which your Lordship vouchsafed to open. They were two; the one that I should include. . . .

Mr. Spedding says:

> Here our light goes suddenly out, just as we are going to see how Bacon had resolved to dispose of himself at this juncture.[1]

Is it not very remarkable that this letter should be clipped off just at this point? We are forced to ask, first, what was the course which he intended to take "touching mine own fortune;" and secondly, if there was no mystery behind his life, why was this letter so emasculated?

And it seems he intimated to his mother that he had some secret means of obtaining money. Lady Bacon writes to Anthony at the same time, and in the same month and year:

> Besides, your brother told me before you twice, then, that he intended not to part with Markes [an estate], and the rather because Mr. Mylls would lend him £900; and, as I remember, I asked him how he was to come out of debt. His answer was that *means would be made without that.*[2]

Remember that it was not until January, 1598, that Bacon published the first of his acknowledged formal works, his *Essays*. And these were not the forty long essays we now have, but ten short, condensed compositions, which occupied but thirteen double pages of the original quarto edition. These, with a few brief papers, are the only acknowledged fruits we have to *represent the nineteen years*

---

[1] *Life and Works*, vol. i, p. 235.   [2] Ibid., p. 244.

between the date of his return from Paris, in 1579, and the publication of his ten brief essays in January, 1598.

What was that most fecund, prolific, laborious writer doing during these nearly twenty years? He was brimful of energy, industry, genius, mirth and humor: how did he expend it? What was that painful course of study and meditation which he underwent daily, as he told his uncle Burleigh?

Read what Hepworth Dixon says of him at the age of twenty-four:

How he appears in outward grace and aspect among these courtly and martial contemporaries, the miniature by Hilyard helps us to conceive. Slight in build, rosy and round in flesh, dight in sumptuous suit; the head well set, erect, and framed in a thick, starched fence of frill; a bloom of study and of travel on the fat, girlish face, which looks far younger than his years; the hat and feather tossed aside from the broad, white brow, over which crisps and curls a mane of dark, soft hair; an English nose — firm, open, straight; mouth delicate and small — a lady's or *a jester's mouth — a thousand pranks and humors, quibbles, whims and laughters lurking in its twinkling, tremulous lines*. Such is Francis Bacon at the age of twenty-four.[1]

Is this the description of a dry-as-dust philosopher? Is it not rather the picture of the youthful scholar, the gentleman, the wit, the poet, "fresh from academic studies," who wrote *The Two Gentlemen of Verona* and *Love's Labor Lost?*

In brief, the Shakespeare Plays are the fruits of Bacon's youth; for it is in youth he tells us that the imagination streams with divine felicity into the mind; while his philosophical works are the product of middle life. It is not until 1603, when Bacon was forty-two years of age, that he published the first of his scientific works, entitled *Valerius Terminus; or, the Interpretation of Nature: with the Annotations of Hermes Stella*. And who, we ask passingly, was "Hermes Stella"? Was Bacon, with his usual secretiveness, seeking another *mecd* — another Shakspere? Mrs. Pott says:

There is something so mysterious about this strange title, and in the obscurity of the text itself as well as in the meaning of the astronomical and astrological symbols written on the blank outside of the volume, that Mr. Ellis and Mr. Spedding comment upon them, but can throw no real light upon them.

XX. Another Mystery.

W. A. A. Watts, in a paper read before the Bacon Society of London while this work is going through the press,[2] calls attention to the striking fact that Ben Jonson, besides stating that Bacon

---

[1] Dixon's *Personal History of Lord Bacon*, p. 25.
[2] *Journal of the Baconian Society*, Aug., 1887, p. 130.

had "filled all numbers" and was "the mark and acme of our language," in a poem entitled "Underwoods," addressed to Bacon on is birthday, says:

> "In the midst,
> Thou stand'st as though *a mystery thou didst.*"

This is certainly extraordinary. What was the mystery? Was it in connection with those "numbers" which excelled anything in Greek or Roman dramatic literature, and which were "the mark and acme of our language?" If not, what did Ben mean?

XXI. COKE'S INSULTS.

We find all through that period of Bacon's life, between 1597 and his accession to the place of Lord Chancellor, that he was the subject of a great many slanders. But while he alludes to the slanders, he is careful not to tell us what they were. Did they refer to the Shakespeare Plays? Did they charge that he paid his debts with money taken in at the door of the play-house? For we may be sure that among the actors there were whisperings which it would be difficult to keep from spreading abroad; and

> Thus comes it that my name receives a brand,
> And almost thus my nature is subdued
> To what it works in, like the dyer's hand.

But there has come down to us a letter of Bacon which gives us some account of the insults he was subjected to. In it Bacon complains, in 1601, to his cousin, Lord Secretary Cecil, that his arch-enemy, Mr. Attorney-General Coke, had publicly insulted him in the Exchequer. He tells that he moved for the reseizure of the lands of one George Moore, a relapsed recusant, fugitive and traitor. He says:

Mr. Attorney kindled at it and said: "Mr. Bacon, if you have any tooth against me pluck it out, for it will do you more hurt than all the teeth in your head will do you good." I answered coldly, in these very words: "Mr. Attorney, I respect you; I fear you not; and the less you speak of your own greatness the more will I think of it."

He replied: "I think scorn to stand upon terms of greatness toward you, *who are less than little; less than the least;*" *and other such strange light terms he gave me,* with such insulting which cannot be expressed. Herewith I stirred, yet I said no more but this: "Mr. Attorney, do not depress me so far; for I have been your better, and may be again, when it please the Queen." With this he spake, neither I nor himself could tell what, as if he had been born Attorney-General; and in the end bade me not meddle with the Queen's business, but mine own. . . . *Then he said it were good to clap a capias utlegatum upon my back!* To which I only said he could not, and that he was at fault; *for he hunted upon an old scent.*

He gave me a *number of disgraceful words besides*, which I answered with silence.[1]

And Bacon writes Cecil, evidently with intent to have him silence Coke.

I will ask the reader to remember this letter when we come to the Cipher Narrative. It shows, it seems to me, that Cecil knew of something to Bacon's discredit, and that Coke, Cecil's follower, had heard of it and blurted it out in his rage in open court, and threatened Bacon with arrest; and Bacon writes to his cousin for protection against Coke's tongue. Spedding says the threat of the *capias utlegatum* may possibly have referred to a debt that Bacon owed in 1598; but what right would Coke have to arrest Bacon for a debt due to a third party, and which must have been paid three years before? And why should Bacon say "he was at fault." If Coke referred to the debt he was not "at fault," for Bacon certainly had owed it.

XXII. Conclusion.

In conclusion I would say that I have in the foregoing pages shown that, if we treat the real author of the Plays, and Francis Bacon, as two men, they belonged to the same station in society, to the same profession — the law; to the same political party and to the same faction in the state; that they held the same religious views, the same philosophical tenets and the same purposes in life. That each was a poet and a philosopher, a writer of dramatic compositions, and a play-goer. That Bacon had the genius, the opportunity, the time and the necessity to write the Plays, and ample reasons to conceal his authorship.

I proceed now to another branch of my argument. I shall attempt to show that these two men, if we may still call them such, pursued the same studies, read the same books, possessed the same tastes, enjoyed the same opinions, used the same expressions, employed the same unusual words, cited the same quotations and fell into the same errors

If all this does not bring the brain of the poet under the hat of the philosopher, what will you have?

---

[1] Spedding, *Life and Works*, vol. iii, p. 2. London: Longmans.

PART III.

PARALLELISMS.

CHAPTER I.

IDENTICAL EXPRESSIONS.

> As near as the extremest ends
> Of parallels.
> *Troilus and Cressida*, i, 3.

WHO does not remember that curious word used by Hamlet, to describe the coldness of the air, upon the platform where he awaits the Ghost:

> It is very cold.
> It is a nipping and an *eager* air.[1]

We turn to Bacon, and we find this very word used in the same sense:

> Whereby the cold becomes more *eager*.[2]

There is another strange word used by Shakespeare:

> *Light thickens*,
> And the crow makes wing to the rocky wood.[3]

We turn again to Bacon, and we find the origin of this singular expression:

> For the over-moisture of the brain doth *thicken* the spirits visual.[4]

In the same connection we have in Bacon this expression:

> The cause of dimness of sight is *the expense of spirits*.[5]

We turn to Shakespeare's sonnets, and we find precisely the same arrangement of words:

> *Th' expense of spirit* in a waste of shame.

---

[1] *Hamlet*, I, 4.   [3] *Macbeth*, iii, 2.   [5] Ibid.
[2] *Natural History*, § 688.   [4] *Natural History*, § 693.

One of the most striking parallelisms of thought and expression occurs in the following. Bacon says:

Some noises help sleep, as . . . soft *singing*. The cause is, for that they move in the *spirits* a gentle *attention*.[1]

In Shakespeare we have:

> I am never merry when I hear sweet music,
> The reason is, your *spirits* are *attentive*.[2]

Here we have *the same words applied in the same sense to the same thing*, the effect of music; and in each case the philosopher stops to give the reason — "the cause is," "the reason is."

∴

Both are very fond of the expressions, "parts inward" and "parts outward,' to describe the interior and exterior of the body.

Bacon says:

Mineral medicines have been extolled that they are safer for the *outward* than the *inward parts*.[3]

And again:

While the life-blood of Spain went *inward* to the heart, the *outward* limbs and members trembled and could not resist.[4]

Shakespeare has it:

> I see men's judgments are
> A parcel of their fortunes; and *things outward*
> Do draw the *inward* quality after them,
> To suffer all alike.[5]

Falstaff tells us:

But the sherris warms it and makes it course from the *inwards* to the *parts extreme*.[6]

∴

Bacon says:
> *Infinite variations*.[7]

Shakespeare says:
> Nor custom stale
> Her *infinite variety*.[8]

∴

The word *infinite* is a favorite with both writers.

Bacon has:

> Occasions are *infinite*.[9]
>
> *Infinite* honor.[10]
>
> The *infinite* flight of birds.[11]

---

[1] *Natural History*, § 745.
[2] *Merchant of Venice*, v, 1.
[3] *Advancement of Learning*, book ii.
[4] Speech in Parliament, 39 Elizabeth (1597-8) — *Life and Works*, vol. ii, p. 89.
[5] *Antony and Cleopatra*, iii, 2.
[6] 2d *Henry IV.*, iv, 3.
[7] *Advancement of Learning*, book ii.
[8] *Antony and Cleopatra*, ii, 2.
[9] *Wisdom of the Ancients — Acheloüs*.
[10] Speech.
[11] *New Atlantis*.

Shakespeare has:

> Conclusion *infinite* of easy ways to die.[1]
>
> Fellows of *infinite* tongue.[2]
>
> A fellow of *infinite* jest.[3]
>
> *Infinite* in faculties.[4]
>
> Nature's *infinite* book of secrecy.[5]

Bacon says:

Man in his mansion, sleep, exercise, passions, hath *infinite* variations; . . . the *faculties* of the soul.[6]

Shakespeare says:

> How *infinite* in *faculties*.[7]

Bacon speaks of

That gigantic state of mind which possesseth the *troublers of the world*, such as was Lucius Sylla.[8]

This is a very peculiar and unusual expression; we turn to Shakespeare, and we find Queen Margaret cursing the bloody Duke of Gloster, in the play of *Richard III.*, in these words:

> If heaven have any grievous plague in store,
> Exceeding those that I can wish upon thee,
> Oh, let them keep it, till thy sins be ripe,
> And then hurl down their indignation
> On thee, the *troubler of the* poor *world's* peace.[9]

In Shakespeare we find:

Which is to bring Signor Benedick and the Lady Beatrice into a *mountain of affection*, the one with the other.[10]

This was regarded as such a strange and unusual comparison that some of the commentators proposed to change it into "a mooting of affection." But we turn to Bacon and we find the same simile:

Perkin sought to corrupt the servants of the lieutenant of the Tower by *mountains of promises*.[11]

Bacon says:

To fall from a discord, or harsh accord, upon *a concord of sweet* accord.[12]

---

[1] *Antony and Cleopatra*, v, 2.
[2] *Henry V.*, v, 2.
[3] *Hamlet*, v, 1.
[4] Ibid., ii, 2.
[5] *Antony and Cleopatra*, i, 2.
[6] *Advancement of Learning*, book ii.
[7] *Hamlet*, ii, 2.
[8] *Advancement of Learning*.
[9] *Richard III.*, i, 3.
[10] *Much Ado about Nothing*, ii, 2.
[11] *History of Henry VII*.
[12] *Advancement of Learning*.

Shakespeare says:

> That is not moved with *concord of sweet* sounds.[1]

Here we have three words used in the same order and sense by both writers.

We find in Shakespeare this well-known but curious expression:

> There's a divinity that shapes our ends,
> *Rough-hew* them how we will.[2]

This word occurs only once in the Plays. George Stevens says:

> Dr. Farmer informs me that these words are merely technical. A woolman, butcher and dealer in *skewers* lately observed to him that his nephew (an idle lad) could only assist him in making them. "He could *rough-hew* them, but I was obliged to shape their ends." Whoever recollects the profession of Shakspere's father will admit that his son might be no stranger to such terms. *I have frequently seen packages of wool pinn'd up with skewers.*

This is the sort of proof we have had that Shakspere wrote the Plays. It is very evident that the sentence means, that while we may hew out roughly the outlines of our careers, the ends we reach are shaped by some all-controlling Providence. And when we turn to Bacon we find the very word used by him, to indicate carved out roughly:

> A *rough-hewn* seaman.[3]

And we find again in Shakespeare the same idea, that while we may shape our careers in part, the results to be attained are beyond our control:

> Our thoughts are ours, their *ends* none of our own.[4]

Bacon says:

> Instruct yourself in *all things between heaven and earth* which may tend to virtue, wisdom and honor.[5]

Shakespeare has:

> Crawling *between heaven and earth*.[6]

> There are more things *in heaven and earth*, Horatio,
> Than are dreamt of in your philosophy.[7]

Bacon refers to

> The particular remedies which learning doth *minister* to all *the diseases of the mind*.

Shakespeare says:

> Canst thou not *minister* to a *mind diseased*?[8]

---

[1] *Merchant of Venice*, v, 1.   [2] *Hamlet*, v, 2.   [3] *Apophthegms*.   [4] *Hamlet*, iii, 2.
[5] Bacon's Letter to the Earl of Rutland, written in the name of the Earl of Essex—*Life and Works*, vol. ii, p. 18.   [6] *Hamlet*, iii, 1.   [7] *Hamlet*, i, 5.   [8] *Macbeth*, v, 3.

Here the parallelism is complete. In each case it refers to remedies for mental disease, and in each case the word *minister* is used, and the "diseases of the mind" of the one finds its counterpart in "mind diseased" of the other, a change made necessary by the rhythm.

Surely the doctrine of accidental coincidences will not explain this.

Bacon says:

Men have their time, and *die many times*, in desire of some things which they principally take to heart.[1]

Shakespeare says:

Cowards *die many times* before their deaths.[2]

Bacon says:

The even carriage between two factions proceedeth not always of moderation, but of a *trueness to a man's self*, with end to make use of both.[3]

And again he says:

Be so *true* to *thyself* as thou be not *false to others*.[4]

Shakespeare says:

To *thine own self be true*
And it must follow, as the night the day,
Thou canst not then be *false* to any man.[5]

Bacon says:

The *ripeness* or unripeness of the occasion must ever be well weighed.[6]

Shakespeare says:

Ripeness is all.[7]

In Shakespeare we have this singular expression:

O Heaven! a beast, that wants *discourse of reason*,
Would have mourned longer.[8]

This expression "discourse of reason" is a very unusual one. Massinger has:

It adds to my calamity that I have
Discourse *and* reason.

Gifford thought that Shakespeare had written "discourse *and* reason," and that the *of* was a typographical error; but Knight, in discussing the question, refers to the lines in *Hamlet*:

[1] Essay *Of Friendship*. [3] Essay *Of Faction*. [5] *Hamlet*, i, 3. [7] *Lear*, v, 2.
[2] *Julius Cæsar*, ii, 2. [4] Essay *Of Wisdom*. [6] Essay *Of Delays*. [8] *Hamlet*, i, 2.

> Sure he that made us with such large discourse,
> Looking before and after, gave us not
> That capability and god-like reason
> To fust in us unused.[1]

But when we turn to Bacon we find this expression, which has puzzled the commentators, repeatedly used. For instance:

Martin Luther but in *discourse of reason*, finding, etc.[2]

Also:

God hath done great things by her [Queen Elizabeth] past *discourse of reason*.[3]

And again:

True fortitude is not given to man by nature, but must grow out of *discourse of reason*.[4]

Bacon has:

But men ... if they be not carried away with a *whirlwind* or *tempest* of ambition.[5]

Shakespeare has:

For in the very torrent, *tempest*, and, as I may say, the *whirlwind* of your passion.[6]

Here we have not only the figure of a wind-storm used to represent great mental emotions, but the same word, nay, the same words, *tempest* and *whirlwind*, used in the same metaphorical sense by both.

Mr. James T. Cobb calls my attention, while this work is going through the press, to the following parallelism.

Macbeth says:

> *Life's but a walking shadow.*[7]

Bacon writes to King James:

Let me live to serve you, else *life is but the shadow* of death to your Majesty's most devoted servant.

And, again, Mr. Cobb notes this.

Bacon says:

It is nothing else but words, which rather *sound than signify anything.*

---
[1] Act iv, scene 4.   [2] *Advancement of Learning*, book i.
[3] *History of Squires' Conspiracy—Life and Works*, vol. ii, p. 116.
[4] Bacon's Letter to the Earl of Rutland, written in the name of the Earl of Essex—*Life and Works*, vol. ii, p. 12.   [5] *Advancement of Learning*, book ii.   [6] *Hamlet*, iii, 2.   [7] *Macbeth*, v, 5.

IDENTICAL EXPRESSIONS.

Shakespeare makes Macbeth say of human life:

> 'Tis a tale
> Told by an idiot, full of *sound and fury*,
> *Signifying nothing*.[1]

A. J. Duffield, of Delaware Mine, Michigan, calls my attention to the following parallelism.

Shakespeare:

What a piece of work is a man! ... The paragon of animals; *the beauty of the world*.[2]

While Bacon has:

> The souls of the living are *the beauty of the world*.[3]

Both writers use the physical eye as a type or symbol of the intellectual faculty of perception.

Bacon says:

> The *eyes* of his *understanding*.[4]

> For everything depends on fixing the *mind's eye* steadily.[5]

> Illuminate the *eyes* of our *mind*.[6]

While in Shakespeare we have:

> *Hamlet.* My father,—methinks I see my father.
> *Horatio.* Oh, where, my lord?
> *Hamlet.* In my *mind's eye*, Horatio.

And again:

> Mine eye is my mind.[7]

Bacon says:

> Pirates and impostors ... are the *common enemies of mankind*.[8]

Shakespeare says:

> And mine eternal jewel
> Given to *the common enemy of man*
> To make them kings.[9]

Shakespeare also says:

> Consider, he's an *enemy* to *mankind*.[10]

> Thou *common* whore *of mankind*.[11]

Mrs. Pott[12] points out a very striking parallelism.

[1] Act v, scene 5.
[2] *Hamlet*, ii, 2.
[3] *Essay Pan*.
[4] *History of Squires' Conspiracy—Life and Works*, vol. ii, p. 113.
[5] Introduction to *Novum Organum*.
[6] *Prayer*.
[7] Sonnet.
[8] *History of Henry VII*.
[9] *Macbeth*, iii, 1.
[10] *Twelfth Night*, iii. 4.
[11] *Timon of Athens*, iv, 3.
[12] *Promus*, p. 24.

In Bacon's letter to King James, which accompanied the sending of a portion of *The History of Great Britain*, he says:

> This being but a leaf or two, I pray your pardon if I send it for your recreation, considering that *love must creep where it cannot go*.

We have the same thought in the same words in *The Two Gentlemen of Verona*, in this manner:

> Ay, gentle Thurio; for you know that *love*
> *Must creep in service where it cannot go*.[1]

∴

We have in Bacon the word *varnish* used as a synonym for *adorn*, precisely as in Shakespeare:

Bacon:

> But my intent is, without *varnish* or amplification, justly to weigh the dignity of knowledge.[2]

Shakespeare has:

> I will a round, *unvarnished* tale deliver.[3]
>
> And set a double *varnish* on the fame.[4]
>
> Beauty doth *varnish* age.[5]

∴

J. T. Cobb calls attention to the following parallelism. Bacon, in his letter of expostulation to Coke, says:

> The arising to honor is arduous, the *standing slippery*, the descent headlong.

Shakespeare says:

> Which, when they fall, as being *slippery standers*,
> The love that leaned on them as *slippery*, too.
> Do one pluck down another, and together
> Die in the fall.[6]

∴

The image of passion devouring the body of the man is common to both.

Bacon says:

> It causeth the spirit to *feed* upon the juices of the body.[7]
>
> Envy *feedeth* upon the spirits.[8]

Shakespeare says:

> If it will *feed* nothing else, it will *feed* my revenge.[9]
>
> The thing that *feeds* their fury.[10]

---

[1] Act iv, scene 2.
[2] *Advancement of Learning*, book i.
[3] *Othello*, i, 3.
[4] *Hamlet*, iv, 7.
[5] *Love's Labor Lost*, iv, 3.
[6] *Troilus and Cressida*, iii, 3.
[7] *History of Life and Death*.
[8] Ibid.
[9] *Merchant of Venice*, iii, 1.
[10] *Taming of the Shrew*, ii, 1.

> *Feed* fat the ancient grudge.[1]
>
> Advantage *feeds* him fat.[2]
>
> To *feed* contention in a lingering act.[3]

J. T. Cobb points out this parallelism.

Shakespeare:

> *Assume* a virtue if you have it not.[4]

Bacon says:

All wise men, to decline the envy of their own *virtues*, use to ascribe them to Providence and Fortune; for so they may the better *assume* them.[5]

Bacon speaks of

> The *accidents* of life.[6]
>
> The *accidents* of time.[7]

Shakespeare says:

> As place, riches, favor,
> Prizes of *accident* as oft as merit.[8]
>
> With mortal *accidents* opprest.[9]
>
> The shot of *accident*, the dart of chance.[10]

Bacon says:

And I do extremely desire there may be a full cry from *all sorts of people*.[11]

Macbeth says:

> And I have bought
> Golden opinions from *all sorts of people*.[12]

Here we have the same collocation of words.

Bacon says:

> Not only that it may be done, but that it may be well done.[13]

If that be done which I hope by this time is done, and that other matter shall be done which we wish may be done.[14]

Shakespeare says:

> If it were done when 'tis done, then 'twere well
> It were done quickly.[15]
>
> What's done cannot be undone.[16]

---

[1] *Merchant of Venice*, i, 3.
[2] *1st Henry IV.*, iii, 2.
[3] *2d Henry IV.*, i, 1.
[4] *Hamlet*, iii, 4.
[5] *Essay Of Fortune*.
[6] Letter to Sir R. Cecil.
[7] Letter to Villiers, June 3, 1616.
[8] *Troilus and Cressida*, iii, 3.
[9] *Cymbeline*, v, 4.
[10] *Othello*, iv, 1.
[11] Letter to Villiers, June 12, 1616.
[12] *Macbeth*, i, 7.
[13] Letter to Lord Chancellor.
[14] Letter to Sir John Stanhope—*Life and Works*, vol. ii, p. 90.
[15] *Macbeth*, i, 7.
[16] Ibid., v, 1.

Bacon says:

> But I will pray for you *to the last gasp*.[1]

Shakespeare says:

> I will follow thee
> *To the last gasp*.[2]
>
> Fight *till the last gasp*.[3]

Here is another identical collocation of words.

∴

Bacon says:

The new company and the old company are but the *sons of Adam* to me.[4]

Shakespeare says:

> *Adam's sons* are my brethren.[5]

∴

Bacon says:

> The common lot of mankind.[6]

Shakespeare has:

> The common curse of mankind.[7]

∴

Bacon:

> The *infirmity* of the human understanding.[8]

Shakespeare:

> The *infirmity* of sense.[9]
>
> A friend should bear his friend's *infirmities*.[10]

∴

And Mr. J. T. Cobb has called my attention to this parallelism.

Bacon says:

All those who have in some measure committed themselves to the waters of experience, seeing they were *infirm of purpose*, etc.[11]

While in Shakespeare we have:

> *Infirm of purpose*. Give me the daggers.[12]

∴

Bacon:

> Every tangible body contains an *invisible* and intangible *spirit*.[13]

Shakespeare:

> O, thou *invisible spirit* of wine.[14]

∴

[1] Letter to King James, 1621.
[2] *As You Like It*, ii, 3.
[3] *1st Henry VI.*, i, 1.
[4] Letter to Villiers.
[5] *Much Ado about Nothing*, ii, 1.
[6] Introduction to *Great Instauration*.
[7] *Troilus and Cressida*, ii, 3.
[8] *Novum Organum*, book ii.
[9] *Measure for Measure*, v, 1.
[10] *Julius Cæsar*, iv, 3.
[11] *The Interpretation of Nature*, Montagu ed., vol. ii, p. 550.
[12] *Macbeth*, ii, 2.
[13] *Novum Organum*, book ii.
[14] *Othello*, ii, 3.

Bacon:

> Flame, at the moment of its generation, is *mild and gentle*.[1]

Shakespeare:

> As *mild and gentle* as the cradled babe.[2]
>
> He was *gentle, mild* and virtuous.[3]
>
> I will be *mild and gentle* in my words.[4]

Bacon:

> Custom . . . an *ape of nature*.[5]

Shakespeare:

> This is the *ape of form*, monsieur the nice.[6]
>
> O sleep, thou *ape of death*.[7]

Bacon says:

Another precept of this knowledge is to *imitate nature*, which doth nothing in vain.[8]

In artificial works we should certainly prefer those which approach the nearest to an *imitation of nature*.[9]

We find the same expression in Shakespeare:

> I have thought some of Nature's journeymen had made men, and not made them well, they *imitated humanity* so abominably.[10]

And in the preface to the Folio of 1623, which was probably written by the author of the Plays, we read:

> He was a happy *imitator* of *nature*.

Bacon speaks of a

> Medicine . . . of secret *malignity* and disagreement toward man's body; . . . it worketh either by *corrosion* or by a secret *malignity* and *enmity* to nature.[11]

Shakespeare describes the drug which Hamlet's uncle poured into his father's ear as

> Holding such *enmity* with blood of man.

And again we have:

> A lingering dram, that should not work
> *Maliciously* like poison.[12]

> Though parting be a fretful *corrosive*,
> It is applied to a deathful wound.[13]

---

[1] *Novum Organum*, book ii.
[2] *Henry VI.*, iii, 2.
[3] *Richard III.*, i, 2.
[4] Ibid., iv, 4.
[5] *Advancement of Learning*, book ii
[6] *Love's Labor Lost*, v, 2.
[7] *Cymbeline*, ii, 2.
[8] *Advancement of Learning*, book ii.
[9] *Novum Organum*, book ii.
[10] *Hamlet*, iii, 2.
[11] *Natural History*, cent. i, § 36.
[12] *Winter's Tale*, i, 2.
[13] *2d Henry VI.*, iii, 2.

Bacon says:

Of all substances which nature has produced, man's body is the most extremely *npounded*.[1]

Shakespeare says:

> The brain of this foolish *compounded clay*, man.[2]

And Bacon, speaking of man, says:

Certain particles were taken from divers living creatures, and mixed and tempered with that *clayic* mass.[3]

Bacon says:

> The heavens turn about and . . . make an *excellent music*.

Shakespeare says:

And there is much *music, excellent* voice in this little organ; yet cannot you make it speak.[4]

Bacon says:

The nature of sounds in general hath been superficially observed. It is one of the subtilest *pieces of nature*.[5]

Shakespeare has this precise collocation of words:

> A ruined *piece of nature*.[6]

We also find:

> When *nature* framed this *piece*.[7]
> Thy mother was a *piece of virtue*.[8]
> As pretty a *piece of flesh*.[9]
> Oh, pardon me, thou bleeding *piece of earth*.[10]

Bacon also says:

> The *noblest piece* of justice.[11]

While Shakespeare says:

> What a *piece* of work is man;
> How *noble* in reason.[12]

Bacon says:

> A miracle of time.[13]

Shakespeare says:

> O miracle of men.[14]

---

[1] *Wisdom of the Ancients — Prometheus.*
[2] *2d Henry IV.*, i, 2.
[3] *Natural History*, cent. ii.
[4] Ibid.
[5] Ibid.
[6] *Lear*, iv, 6.
[7] *Pericles*, iv, 3.
[8] *Tempest*, i, 2.
[9] *Much Ado about Nothing*, iv, 2.
[10] *Julius Cæsar*, iii, 1.
[11] Charge against St. John.
[12] *Hamlet*, ii, 2.
[13] *Of a War with Spain.*
[14] *2d Henry IV.*, ii, 3.

Bacon:
> The fire maketh them *soft and tender*.[1]

Shakespeare:
> The *soft and tender* fork of a poor worm.[2]
>
> Beneath your *soft and tender* breeding.[3]
>
> As *soft and tender* flattery.[4]

Here again it is identity not alone of a word, but of a phrase.

Bacon says:

Where a rainbow seemeth to hang over or to touch, there *breatheth* forth a sweet smell.[5]

Shakespeare says:
> *Breathing* to his breathless excellence
> The *incense* of a vow.[6]
>
>   'Tis her *breathing*
> That *perfumes* the chamber thus.[7]

We find both Shakespeare and Bacon using the unusual word *disclose* for *hatch*.

Bacon says:

The ostrich layeth her eggs under the sand, where the heat of the sun *discloseth* them.[8]

Shakespeare:
> Anon, as patient as the female dove,
> When that her golden couplets are *disclosed*
> His silence will sit brooding.[9]

Bacon speaks of

The elements and their conjugations, the *influences* of heaven.[10]

While Shakespeare speaks of

> All the skiey *influences*.[11]

Bacon says:

For those smells do . . . rather *woo* the sense than satiate it.[12]

While Shakespeare says:

> The air smells *wooingly* here.[13]

---

[1] *Natural History*, §630.
[2] *Measure for Measure*, iii, 1.
[3] *Twelfth Night*, v, 1.
[4] *Pericles*, iv, 4.
[5] *Natural History*, §832.
[6] *King John*, iv, 3.
[7] *Cymbeline*, ii, 2.
[8] *Natural History*, §846.
[9] *Hamlet*, v, 1.
[10] *Natural History*, §835.
[11] *Measure for Measure*, iii, 1.
[12] *Natural History*, §833.
[13] *Macbeth*, i, 6.

Speaking of the smell where the rainbow rests, Bacon says:

> But none are so *delicate* as the dew of the rainbow.[1]

Shakespeare says:

> I have observed the air is *delicate*.[2]

We also have:

> A *delicate* odor.[3]
>
> *Delicate* Ariel.[4]

∴

Bacon speaks of

Shakespeare, of

> The *gentle dew*.[5]
>
> The *gentle rain*.[6]

∴

The word *fantastical* is a favorite with both.

Bacon says:

> Which showeth a *fantastical* spirit.[7]
>
> *Fantastical* learning.[8]

Shakespeare says:

> *High fantastical*.[9]
>
> A mad, *fantastical* trick.[10]
>
> A *fantastical* knave.[11]
>
> Telling her *fantastical* lies.[12]

∴

Bacon says:

> A *malign aspect* and influence.[13]

Shakespeare says:

> *Malevolent* to you in all *aspects*.[14]

∴

Bacon says:

So as your wit shall be whetted with conversing with many great wits, and you shall have the cream and *quintessence* of every one of theirs.[15]

Shakespeare says:

> What is this *quintessence* of dust?[16]
>
> The *quintessence* of every sprite.[17]

∴

---

[1] *Natural History*, §832.
[2] *Macbeth*, i, 6.
[3] *Pericles*, iii, 2.
[4] *Tempest*, i, 2.
[5] *Natural History*, §832.
[6] *Merchant of Venice*, iv, 1.
[7] *Civil Conv.*
[8] *Advancement of Learning*, book i.
[9] *Twelfth Night*, i, 1.
[10] *Measure for Measure*, iii, 2.
[11] *As You Like It*, iii, 3.
[12] *Othello*, ii, 1.
[13] *Advancement of Learning*, book ii.
[14] *1st Henry IV.*, i, 2.
[15] Bacon's Letter to the Earl of Rutland, written in the name of the Earl of Essex—*Life and Works*, vol. ii, p. 13.
[16] *Hamlet*, ii, 2.
[17] *As You Like It*, iii, 2.

Bacon says:

> I find envy *beating* so strongly upon me.[1]

This public envy seemeth to *beat* chiefly upon principal officers or ministers.[2]

Shakespeare says:

> Nor the tide of pomp
> That *beats* upon the high shore of this world.[3]

Bacon says:

To choose time is to save time; and an unseasonable motion is but *beating the air*.[4]

Shakespeare says:

> Didst thou *beat* heaven with blessings.[5]

Speaking of witchcrafts, *dreams* and divinations, Bacon says:

Your Majesty hath . . . with the two clear eyes of religion and natural philosophy looked deeply and wisely into these *shadows*.[6]

And again he says:

All whatsoever you have or can say in answer hereof are but *shadows*.[7]

While Shakespeare has:

A *dream* itself is but a *shadow*.[8]

To worship *shadows* and adore false shapes.[9]

Shadows to-night have struck more terror to the soul of Richard.[10]

Hence, horrible *shadow*.[11]

Life's but a walking *shadow*.[12]

Bacon enters in his commonplace-book:

The *Mineral* wytts, strong *poison* yf they be not corrected.[13]

Shakespeare has:

The thought doth, like a *poisonous mineral*, gnaw my inwards.[14]

Bacon says:

> Fullness and *swellings* of the heart.[15]

---

[1] Bacon to Queen Elizabeth — *Life and Works*, vol. ii, p. 160.
[2] Essay *Of Envy*.
[3] *Henry V.*, iv, 1.
[4] Essay *Of Despatch*.
[5] *2d Henry IV.*, i, 3.
[6] *Advancement of Learning*, book ii.
[7] Speech at Trial of Essex.
[8] *Hamlet*, ii, 2.
[9] *Two Gentlemen of Verona*, iv, 2.
[10] *Richard III.*, v, 3.
[11] *Macbeth*, iii, 4.
[12] Ibid., v, 5.
[13] *Promus*, § 140, p. 454.
[14] *Othello*, ii, 1.
[15] Essay *Of Friendship*.

Shakespeare says:

> Malice of thy *swelling heart*.[1]
>
> Their *swelling* griefs.[2]
>
> The *swelling* act of the imperial scene.[3]

Bacon says:

> The most *base, bloody* and envious persons.[4]

Shakespeare says:

> Of *base and bloody* insurrection.[5]

Bacon:

> Matters of no use or *moment*.[6]

Shakespeare:

> Enterprises of great pith and *moment*.[7]

In both we have the word *sovereign* applied to medicines.

Bacon:

> *Sovereign* medicines for the mind.[8]

Shakespeare:

> The *sovereign'st* thing on earth
> Was parmaceti for an inward bruise

In his letter of submission to Parliament, Bacon says:

> This is the beginning of a *golden* world.

Shakespeare, in *The Tempest*, says:

> I would with such perfection govern, sir,
> To excel the *golden* age.[10]
>
> In former *golden* days.[11]
>
> *Golden* times.[12]

Bacon says:

> This passion [love], which *loseth* not only other things, but *itself*.[13]

Shakespeare says:

> A loan oft *loseth* both *itself* and friend.[14]

Bacon:

> A *kindly* and pleasant sleep.[15]

Shakespeare:

> Frosty but *kindly*.[16]

[1] 1st Henry VI., iii, 1.
[2] 3d Henry VI., iv, 8.
[3] Macbeth, i, 3.
[4] Advancement of Learning, book i.
[5] 2d Henry IV., iv, 1.
[6] Advancement of Learning, book i.
[7] Hamlet, iii, 1.
[8] Advancement of Learning, book i.
[9] 1st Henry IV., i, 3.
[10] Act ii, scene 1.
[11] 3d Henry VI., iii, 3.
[12] 2d Henry IV., v, 3.
[13] Essay Of Love.
[14] Hamlet, i, 3.
[15] Advancement of Learning, book ii.
[16] As You Like It, ii, 3.

Bacon says:

    The *quality* of health and strength.[1]

Shakespeare says:

    The *quality* of mercy is not strained.[2]

    The *quality* of the flesh.[3]

    The *quality* of her passion.[4]

Bacon says:

    The states of Italy be like little *quillets* of freehold.[5]

And he speaks of

    A *quiddity* of the common law.[6]

Hamlet says:

    Where be his *quiddets* now, his *quillets*, his cases, his tenures.[7]

Bacon speaks of having one's mind

    Concentric with the orb of the universe.

Shakespeare says:

    His fame folds in this orb o' the earth.[8]

Bacon refers to

    The *top* of . . . workmanship.[9]

    The *top* of human desires.[10]

    The *top* of all worldly bliss.[11]

Shakespeare refers to

    The *top* of sovereignty.[12]

    The *top* of judgment.[13]

    The *top* of all design.[14]

On the other hand, Bacon says:

    He might have known the *bottom of his danger*.[15]

Shakespeare says:

    The *bottom of my place*.[16]

---

[1] Bacon's Letter to the Earl of Rutland, written in the name of the Earl of Essex — *Life and Works*, vol. ii, p. 15.
[2] *Merchant of Venice*, iv, 1.
[3] *Timon of Athens*, iv, 3.
[4] *Antony and Cleopatra*, v, 1.
[5] Discourse in Praise of the Queen — *Life and Works*.
[6] Arraignment.
[7] *Hamlet*, v, 1.
[8] *Coriolanus*, v, 5.
[9] Prayer.
[10] *Advancement of Learning*.
[11] *History of Henry VII*.
[12] *Macbeth*, iv, 1.
[13] *Measure for Measure*, ii, 2.
[14] *Antony and Cleopatra*, v, 1.
[15] *History of Henry VII*.
[16] *Measure for Measure*, i, 1.

The *bottom of your purpose*.[1]

The very *bottom of my soul*.[2]

Searches to the *bottom of the worst*.[3]

Bacon has:

Actions of great peril and motion.[4]

Shakespeare has:

Enterprises of great pith and moment.[5]

Bacon speaks of

The abuses of the times.[6]

Shakespeare speaks of

The poor *abuses of the times.*[7]

Here the identity is not in a word, but in a series of words.

Bacon says:

I will shoot my *fool's bolt* since you will have it so.[8]

Shakespeare says:

A *fool's bolt* is soon shot.[9]

According to the *fool's bolt*, sir.[10]

Bacon expresses the idea of the mind being in a state of rest or peace by the words, "The mind is *free*," as contradistinguished from "the mind is *agitated*."[11]

Shakespeare uses the same expression:

When the mind's *free*
The body's delicate.[12]

The doctor refers to Lady Macbeth's mental agony, expressed even in sleep, as "this slumbery *agitation*."

Bacon says:

In the midst of the greatest *wilderness of waters*.[13]

Shakespeare has:

Environed with a *wilderness of sea*.[14]

---

[1] *All's Well that Ends Well*, iii, 7.
[2] *Henry V.*, ii, 2.
[3] *Troilus and Cressida*, ii, 2.
[4] Speech in Parliament, 39 Elizabeth.
[5] *Hamlet*, iii, 1.
[6] Letter to the King.
[7] *1st Henry IV.*, i, 2.
[8] Letter to the Earl of Essex, 1598.
[9] *Henry V.*, iii, 7.
[10] *As You Like It*, v, 4.
[11] *Novum Organum*.
[12] *Lear*, iii, 4.
[13] *New Atlantis*.
[14] *Titus Andronicus*, iii, 1.

And again:

> A *wilderness of monkeys*.[1]
>
> A *wilderness of tigers*.[2]

Bacon says, in a speech in Parliament:

> This cloud still hangs over the House.[3]

Shakespeare has:

> And all the clouds that lowered upon our House.

Bacon speaks of,

> Any expert *minister* of nature.[4]

Shakespeare says:

> Angels and *ministers* of grace.[5]

That familiar but curious expression used by Marc Antony in his speech over the dead body of Cæsar can also be traced back to Bacon:

> Lend me your ears.[6]

Bacon, describing Orpheus' power over the wild beasts, paints them as

> Standing all at a gaze about him, and *lend their ears* to his music.[7]

Again Bacon says, referring to the power of music:

> Orpheus drew the woods and *moved the* very *stones* to come.[8]

Shakespeare, referring to the power of eloquence, says that it

> Should *move*
> The *stones* of Rome to rise and mutiny.[9]

Bacon says:

> The nature of the vulgar is always *swollen* and *malignant*.[10]

Shakespeare speaks of:

> The *malice* of my *swelling* heart.[11]

Bacon says:

> With an *undaunted* and bold *spirit*.[12]

Shakespeare speaks of an

> *Undaunted spirit* in a dying breast.[13]

---

[1] *Merchant of Venice*, iii, 1.
[2] *Titus Andronicus*, iii, 1.
[3] Speech about Undertakers.
[4] *Wisdom of the Ancients — Proteus*.
[5] *Hamlet*, i, 4.
[6] *Julius Cæsar*, iii, 2.
[7] *Wisdom of the Ancients*.
[8] Ibid.
[9] *Julius Cæsar*, iii, 2.
[10] *Wisdom of the Ancients*.
[11] *Titus Andronicus*, v, 3.
[12] *Wisdom of the Ancients — Sphinx*.
[13] *1st Henry VI.*, iii, 2.

The phrase "mortal men" is a favorite with both. Bacon says:

> Ravish and rap *mortal men*.[1]

Shakespeare says:

> Tush, man, *mortal men, mortal men*.[2]
> O momentary grace of *mortal men*.[3]

∴

Bacon says:

> *The state of man*.[4]

Shakespeare says:

> *The state of man*.[5]

∴

Bacon speaks of

> The *vapors* of ambition.[6]

Shakespeare speaks of

> The *vapor* of our valor.[7]
> The *vapor* of my glory.[8]

∴

Bacon says:

> She was most affectionate of her kindred, even *unto faction*.[9]

Shakespeare says:

> And drove great Mars *to faction*.[10]

∴

We find Bacon using the word *engine* for a device, a stratagem. Speaking of the Lambert Simnell conspiracy to dethrone King Henry VII., he says:

> And thus delivered of this so strange an *engine*, and new invention of fortune.[11]

Iago says to Roderigo:

> Take me from this world with treachery and devise *engines* for my life.[12]

∴

Bacon says:

> Whereupon the *meaner sort routed* together.[13]

Shakespeare says:

> Choked with ambition of the *meaner sort*.[14]
> Cheering a *rout* of rebels.[15]
> All is on the *rout*.[16]

∴

[1] *Wisdom of the Ancients—Sphynx.*
[2] *1st Henry IV.*, iv, 2.
[3] *Richard III.*, iii, 4.
[4] *Wisdom of the Ancients—Prom.*
[5] *Julius Cæsar*, ii, 1.
[6] *History of Henry VII.*
[7] *Henry V.*, iv, 2.
[8] *Richard III.*, iii, 7.
[9] *History of Henry VII.*
[10] *Troilus and Cressida*, iii, 3.
[11] *History of Henry VII.*
[12] *Othello*, iv, 2.
[13] *History of Henry VII.*
[14] *1st Henry VI.*, ii, 5.
[15] *2d Henry IV.*, iv, 2.
[16] *2d Henry VI.*, v, 2.

Bacon says:

And such superficial speculations they have; like *prospectives*, that show things inward, when they are but *paintings*.[1]

The same figure occurs in Shakespeare:

> Divides one thing entire to twenty objects,
> Like *perspectives*, which rightly gazed upon
> Show nothing but confusion; eyed awry
> Distinguish form.[2]

And Bacon, in describing a rebellion in Scotland against King James III., tells that the rebels captured the King's son — Prince James — and used him

To shadow their rebellion, and to be the titular and *painted* head of those arms.[3]

This is a very peculiar expression, and reminds us of Lady Macbeth's words:

> 'Tis the eye of childhood
> That fears a *painted* devil.[4]

And again Shakespeare says:

> Men are but gilded loam or *painted* clay.[5]

> Than is the deed to my most *painted* word.[6]

Bacon says:

He raised up the ghost of Richard . . . to *walk* and vex the King.[7]

Shakespeare says:

> Thy father's spirit,
> Doomed for a certain term to *walk* the night.[8]

> Spirits oft *walk* in death.[9]

Bacon says:

The news thereof came *blazing* and *thundering* over into England, that the Duke of York was sure alive.[10]

Shakespeare says:

> What act
> That roars so loud and *thunders* in the index?[11]

> He came in *thunder*; his celestial breath
> Was sulphurous to smell.[12]

> Hast thou not spoke like *thunder* on my side?[13]

[1] *Sylva Sylvarum.*
[2] *Richard II.*, ii, 2.
[3] *History of Henry VII.*
[4] *Macbeth,* ii, 2.
[5] *Richard II.*, i, 1.
[6] *Hamlet,* iii, 1.
[7] *History of Henry VII.*
[8] *Hamlet,* i, 5.
[9] *Ibid.*, i, 1.
[10] *History of Henry VII.*
[11] *Hamlet,* iii, 4.
[12] *Cymbeline,* v, 4.
[13] *King John,* iii, 1.

The fierce *blaze* of riot.[1]

The *blaze* of youth.[2]

Every *blazing* star.[3]

Bacon says:

A *spice* of madness.[4]

Shakespeare says:

This *spice* of your hypocrisy.[5]

Bacon speaks of

Our *sea-walls* and good shipping.[6]

Shakespeare describes England as

Our *sea-walled* garden.[7]

The word *pregnant*, signifying full of consequence or meaning, is a common one with both writers. Bacon says:

Many circumstances did feed the ambition of Charles with *pregnant* and apparent hopes of success.[8]

Shakespeare says:

Crook the *pregnant* hinges of the knee.[9]

Pregnant instruments of wealth.[10]

Were very *pregnant* and potential spurs.[11]

Bacon says:

His people were *hot* upon the *business*.[12]

Shakespeare says:

It is a *business* of some *heat*.[13]

Bacon says, speaking of old age:

He promised himself money, *honor*, *friends* and peace in the end.[14]

Shakespeare says:

And that which should accompany *old age*,
As *honor*, love, obedience, troops of *friends*,
I must not look to have.[15]

[1] *Richard II.*, ii, 1.
[2] *All's Well that Ends Well*, v, 3.
[3] Ibid., i, 3.
[4] *Of War with Spain*.
[5] *Henry VIII.*, ii, 3.
[6] Speech on Subsidy.
[7] *Richard II.*, iii, 4.
[8] *History of Henry VII*.
[9] *Hamlet*, iii, 2.
[10] *Pericles*, iv, Gower.
[11] *Lear*, ii, 1.
[12] *History of Henry VII*.
[13] *Othello*, i, 2.
[14] *History of Henry VII*.
[15] *Macbeth*, v, 3.

Bacon says:

> This bred a *decay* of people.[1]

Shakespeare speaks of

> *Decayed* men.[2]

∴

Bacon says:

> Divers things that were *predominant* in the King's *nature*.[3]

Macbeth says to the murderers:

> Do you find
> Your patience so *predominant* in your *nature?*[4]

∴

Bacon says:

> As if he had heard the news of some strange and fearful *prodigy*.[5]

Shakespeare says:

> A *prodigy* of fear and a portent
> Of broachèd mischief to the unborn times.[6]

> Now hath my soul brought forth her *prodigy*.[7]

∴

Bacon says:

> Turned law and justice into *wormwood*.[8]

Shakespeare says:

> Weed this *wormwood* from your fruitful brain.[9]

∴

Bacon says:

His ambition was so exorbitant and *unbounded*.[10]

And again:

Being a man of *stomach*, and hardened by his former troubles, he refused to pay a mite.[11]

God seeth that we have unbridled *stomachs*.[12]

While in Shakespeare we have the vastly ambitious Wolsey referred to as

> A man of *unbounded stomach*.[13]

∴

Bacon says:

As for her memory, it hath gotten such life, *in the mouths* and hearts *of men*, as that envy, being put out by her death, etc.[14]

---

[1] *History of Henry VII.*
[2] *Comedy of Errors*, iv, 3.
[3] *History of Henry VII.*
[4] *Macbeth*, iii, 1.
[5] *History of Henry VII.*
[6] *1st Henry IV.*, v, 1.
[7] *Richard II.*, ii, 2.
[8] *History of Henry VII.*
[9] *Love's Labor Lost*, v, 2.
[10] *History of Henry VII.*
[11] Ibid.
[12] Letter to Lord Coke.
[13] *Henry VIII.*, iv, 2.
[14] *Felic. Queen Elizabeth.*

Shakespeare says:

> So shalt thou live — such power hath my pen —
> Where breath most breathes, *even in the mouths of men*.[1]

Bacon says:

> *Vain pomp* and outward shows of power.[2]

Shakespeare says:

> *Vain pomp* and glory of this world, I hate ye.[3]

In both the thought of retirement is expressed in the word *cell* — referring to the monastic *cells*.

Bacon says:

> The *cells* of gross and solitary monks.[4]

Again:

> For it was time for me to go to a *cell*.[5]
>
> It were a pretty *cell* for my fortune.[6]

In Shakespeare we have:

> Nor that I am much better
> Than Prospero, master of a full poor *cell*,
> And thy no greater father.[7]
>
> O proud death!
> What feast is forward in thine eternal *cell*.[8]

Bacon says:

> The spark that first *kindled* such fire and *combustion*.[9]

And again he says:

> The King chose rather not to satisfy than to *kindle coals*.[10]

Shakespeare has:

> Your breath first *kindled* the dead *coal* of wars.[11]
>
> Constance would not cease
> Till she had *kindled* France and all the world.[12]
>
> For *kindling* such *combustion* in the state.[13]
>
> As dry *combustious* matter is to fire.[14]

Bacon says:

If the rules and maxims of law, in the first raising of tenures *in capite*, be weakened, *this nips the flower in the bud*.[15]

[1] *Sonnet.*
[2] *Char. Julius Cæsar.*
[3] *Henry VIII.*, iii, 2.
[4] *Advancement of Learning.*
[5] *Letter.*
[6] Ibid.
[7] *Tempest*, i, 2.
[8] *Hamlet*, v, 2.
[9] *History of Henry VII.*
[10] Ibid.
[11] *King John*, v, 2.
[12] Ibid., i, 1.
[13] *Henry VIII.*, v, 3.
[14] *Venus and Adonis.*
[15] Argument, Law's Case of Tenures.

Shakespeare says:

> *Nip* not the gaudy *blossoms* of your love.[1]

> *Nips* his root.[2]

Bacon, after his downfall, speaks of

> This *base court* of adversity, where scarce any will be seen stirring.

Shakespeare puts the same expression into the mouth of Richard II. after his downfall:

> In the *base court?* *Base court*, where kings grow base,
> To come at traitors' calls and do them grace.
> In the *base court*, come down.[3]

Bacon says:

> He *strikes terror*.[4]

Shakespeare says:

> And *strike such terror* to his enemies.[5]

> Have *struck more terror* to the soul of Richard.[6]

Bacon says:

> It is greatness in a man to be the care of the *higher powers*.[7]

In Shakespeare we have:

> Arming myself with patience
> To stay the providence of *some high powers*
> That govern us below.[8]

In his letter to Sir Humphrey May, 1625, speaking of his not having received his pardon, Bacon says:

> I deserve not to be the only *outcast*.

While Shakespeare has:

> I all alone bewail my *outcast* state.[9]

Bacon says:

And successions to great place will wax vile; and then his Majesty's prerogative goeth *down the wind*.[10]

[1] *Love's Labor Lost*, v, 2.
[2] *Henry VIII.*, iii, 2.
[3] *Richard II.*, iii, 3.
[4] Bacon's Letter to Sir Foulke Greville — *Life and Works*, vol. ii, p. 24.
[5] *1st Henry VI.*, ii, 3.
[6] *Richard III.*, v, 2.
[7] Essay *Of Fortune*.
[8] *Julius Cæsar*, v, 1.
[9] Sonnet.
[10] Letter relating to Lord Coke.

Othello says:

> If I do prove her haggard,
> Though that her jesses were my dear heart-strings,
> I'd whistle her off, and let her *down the wind*,
> To prey at fortune.[1]

And here we have a singular parallelism occurring in connection with the same sentence.

Bacon says:

For in consent, where tongue-strings and not *heart-strings* make the music that harmony may end in discord.

Shakespeare has:

> Though that her jesses were my dear *heart-strings*.[2]

Also:

> He grieves my very *heart-strings*.[3]

Shakespeare says:

> My love
> Was builded far from *accident*.[4]

Mr. J. T. Cobb points a similar expression in Bacon:

Another precept of this knowledge is not to engage a man's self too peremptorily in anything, though it seem not liable to *accident*.[5]

The wheel was, curiously enough, a favorite image with both.

Bacon says:

> My mind doth not move on the *wheels* of profit.[6]

> The *wheels* of his mind keep away with the *wheels* of his fortune.[7]

Shakespeare says:

> Then can I set the world on *wheels*.[8]

Let go thy hold, when a great *wheel* runs down a hill, lest it break thy neck with following it; but the great one that goes up the hill, let him draw thee after.[9]

Bacon says:

It is a rule, that whatsoever science is not consonant to presuppositions, must *pray in aid* of similitudes.[10]

Shakespeare says:

> A conqueror that will *pray in aid* for kindness,
> Where he for grace is kneeled to.[11]

---

[1] *Othello*, iii, 3.
[2] Ibid., iii, 2.
[3] *Two Gentlemen of Verona*, iv, 2.
[4] Sonnet cxxiv.
[5] *Advancement of Learning*.
[6] Letter.
[7] Essay *Of Fortune*.
[8] *Two Gentlemen of Verona*, iii, 1.
[9] *Lear*, ii, 4.
[10] *Advancement of Learning*.
[11] *Antony and Cleopatra*, v, 2.

Franklin Fiske Heard says:

Praying in aid is a law term, used for a petition made in a court of justice for the calling in of help from another, that hath an interest in the cause in question.[1]

How came the non-lawyer, Shakspere, to put this English law phrase into a Roman play?

J. T. Cobb draws attention to this parallelism.

Bacon says:

For *the poets feigned that Orpheus* . . . did call and assemble the beasts and birds . . . to stand about him, as in a theater; and soon after called likewise the *stones* and *woods* to remove.[2]

Shakespeare says:

> Therefore *the poet*
> Did *feign that Orpheus* drew *trees, stones* and floods.[3]

Bacon says:

Let him commend his inventions, not ambitiously or spitefully, but first in a manner most vivid and fresh, that is most fortified against *the injuries of time*.[4]

Shakespeare says, in one of the sonnets:

> *Injurious time*, blunt thou the lion's paws.

Bacon says:

> A man that hath no virtue in himself.[5]

Shakespeare says:

> The man that hath no music in his soul.[6]

Here the resemblance is not in the words, but in the rhythm and balance of the sentence.

Bacon speaks of

> *Justice* mixed with *mercy*.[7]

Says Shakespeare:

> Let *mercy* season *justice*.[8]

Bacon says:

> These *winds* of rumors could not be *commanded* down.[9]

Shakespeare says:

> Thou god of this great vast, rebuke these surges,
> Which wash both heaven and hell; and thou that hast
> Upon the *winds command*, bind them in brass.[10]

---

[1] *Shakespeare as a Lawyer*, p. 82.
[2] *The Plantation of Ireland*.
[3] *Merchant of Venice*, v, 1.
[4] *Interpretation of Nature*.
[5] *Essay Of Envy*.
[6] *Merchant of Venice*, v, 1.
[7] Proceedings York House.
[8] *Merchant of Venice*.
[9] Letter in name of Anthony Bacon to Essex, 1600.
[10] *Pericles*, iii, 1.

But it may be urged, by the unbeliever, that there is a vast body of the Shakespearean writings, and a still vaster body of Bacon's productions; and that it is easy for an ingenious mind, having these ample fields to range over, to find a multitude of similarities. In reply to this, I will cite a number of quotations from Bacon's essay *Of Death*, the shorter essay on that subject, not published until after his death, and which is found in the first volume of Basil Montagu's edition of *Bacon's Works*, on pages 131, 132 and 133. It is a small essay, comprising about two pages of large type, and does not exceed in all fifteen hundred words. And yet I find hundreds of instances, in this short space, where the expressions in this essay are paralleled in the Plays. Let me give you a few of the most striking examples.

Bacon, arguing that men should be content to die, says:

And as others have given place to us, so we must in the end give place to others.

Shakespeare says, speaking of death:

> Since I nor wax nor honey can bring home,
> I quickly were dissolvèd from my hive,
> *To give some laborers room.*[1]

We find a kindred thought in *Hamlet:*

> But, you must know, your father lost a father,
> That father lost, lost his, and the survivor bound,
> In filial obligation, for some term
> To do obsequious sorrow.[2]

Bacon says:

God sends men into this wretched *theater*, where being arrived, their first language is that of mourning.

This comparison of life and the world to a theater, and a melancholy theater, runs all through Shakespeare:

> This wide and universal *theater*
> Presents more *woeful* pageants.[3]

> I hold the world but as the world, Gratiano;
> A *stage* where every man must play his part,
> And mine a *sad* one.[4]

> All the world's a *stage*,
> And all the men and women merely players.[5]

[1] *All's Well that Ends Well*, i, 2.   [3] *As You Like It*, ii, 7.   [5] *As You Like It*, ii, 7.
[2] *Hamlet*, i, 2.   [4] *Merchant of Venice*, i, 1.

But let us look a little farther into this expression of Bacon.

God sends men headlong into this wretched theater, where being arrived, their first language is that of mourning.

In Shakespeare we have precisely the same thought:

> When we are born we *cry* that we are come
> To this great *stage* of fools.[1]

> Thou knowest the first time that we smell the air
> We wawl and *cry*.[2]

> We came *crying* hither.[3]

The word *wretched*, here applied by Bacon to the *theater*, is a favorite one with Shakespeare:

> A *wretched* soul bruised with adversity.[4]

> Art thou so bare and full of *wretchedness*,
> And fear'st to die?[5]

> To see *wretchedness* o'ercharged.[6]

Bacon says:

I compare men to the Indian fig-tree, which, being ripened to his full height, is said to decline his branches down to the earth.

Says Shakespeare:

> They are not kind:
> And nature, *as it grows again towards earth*,
> Is fashioned for the journey, dull and heavy.[7]

Bacon says:

> Man is made *ripe* for *death*.

We turn to Shakespeare and we have:

> So from hour to hour we *ripe* and *ripe*,
> And then from hour to hour we rot and rot.[8]

> Men must endure
> Their going hence, even as their coming hither;
> *Ripeness* is all.[9]

Bacon continues:

> He is sowed again in his *mother the earth*.

Shakespeare says:

Where is this young gallant that is so desirous to lie with his *mother earth*?[10]

[1] *Lear*, iv, 6.
[2] Ibid.
[3] Ibid.
[4] *Comedy of Errors*, ii, 1.
[5] *Romeo and Juliet*, v, 1.
[6] *Midsummer Night's Dream*, v, 1.
[7] *Titus Andronicus*, ii, 2.
[8] *As You Like It*, ii, 7.
[9] *Lear*, v, 2.
[10] *As You Like It*, i, 2.

Bacon says:

> So man, having derived his being from the earth, first lives the life of a tree, drawing his *nourishment* as a *plant*.

We have a kindred, but not identical, thought in Shakespeare:

> *Pericles.* How durst thy tongue move anger to our face?
> *Helicanus.* How dare the *plants* look up to heaven, from whence
> They have their *nourishment*?

The eighth paragraph of the essay *Of Death* is so beautiful, pathetic and poetical, and has withal so much of the true Shakespearean ring about it, that I quote it entire, notwithstanding the fact that I have made use of part of it heretofore:

> Death arrives gracious only to such as sit in darkness, or lie heavy-burdened with grief and irons; to the poor Christian that sits bound in the galley; to despairful widows, pensive prisoners and deposed kings; to them whose fortunes run back and whose spirits mutiny: unto such death is a redeemer, and the grave a place for retiredness and rest.
>
> These wait upon the shore of Death and waft unto him to draw near, wishing above all others to see his star, that they might be led to his place, wooing the remorseless sisters to wind down the watch of their life, and to break them off before the hour.

What a mass of metaphors is here! Fortune running backward, spirits mutinying; despairful widows and deposed kings waiting on the shores of death, beckoning to him, watching for his star, wooing the remorseless sisters to wind down the watch of their life, and break them off before the hour? And how many suggestions are in all this of Shakespeare? In the word *gracious* we are reminded of:

> There was not such a *gracious* creature born.[1]
>
> So hallowed and so *gracious* is the time.[2]

The association of sitting with sorrow is common in Shakespeare:

> Wise men ne'er *sit* and wail their loss,
> But cheerly seek how to redress their harms.[3]

> *Sitting* on a bank,
> Weeping against the king, my father's, loss.[4]

> Here can I *sit* alone, unseen of any,
> And to the nightingale's complaining notes
> Tune my distresses, and record my *woes*.[5]

> Let us *sit* upon the ground
> And tell *sad stories* of the death of kings —
> How some have been *deposed*, some slain in war.[6]

[1] *King John*, iii, 4.
[2] *Hamlet*, i, 1.
[3] *3d Henry VI.*, v, 4.
[4] *Tempest*, i, 2.
[5] *Two Gentlemen of Verona*, v, 4.
[6] *Richard II.*, iii, 2.

> *Sit* thee down, *sorrow.*[1]

> *Woe* doth the heavier *sit*
> Where it perceives it is but faintly borne.[2]

And when we find Queen Constance, in *King John*,

> Oppressed with wrongs, and therefore full of fears;
> A widow, husbandless, subject to fears;
> A woman naturally born to fears,[3]

crying out in her despair,

> Here I and sorrows *sit*:
> Here is my throne, let kings come bow to it,

we seem to read again the words of Bacon:

Death arrives gracious only to such as sit in darkness . . . to despairful widows, pensive prisoners and deposed kings.

And in Shakespeare we have another *deposed king* saying,

> Let's talk of graves, of worms and epitaphs,
> Make dust our paper, and with rainy eyes,
> Write sorrow on the bosom of the earth.[4]

And another, a deposed queen, *wafts* to Death to come and take her away, and cries out:

> Where art thou, Death?
> Come hither, come! come, come, and take a queen
> Worth many babes and beggars.[5]

Says Bacon:

> To them whose *fortunes run back*.

Shakespeare says:

> The fated sky
> Gives us free scope; only *doth backward pull*
> Our slow designs, when we ourselves are dull.[6]

> My *fortune runs* against the bias.[7]

Says Bacon:

> Whose spirits *mutiny*.

This peculiar metaphor is common in Shakespeare:

> Where will doth *mutiny* with wit's regard.[8]

> There is a *mutiny* in his mind.[9]

> That should move
> The stones of Rome to rise and *mutiny*.[10]

> My very hairs do *mutiny*.[11]

[1] *Love's Labor Lost*, i, 1.
[2] *Richard II.*, i, 3.
[3] *King John*, iii, 1.
[4] *Richard II.*, iii, 2.
[5] *Antony and Cleopa.*
[6] *Julius Cæsar*, i, 2.
[7] *Richard II.*, iii, 4.
[8] *Ibid.*, ii, 1.
[9] *Henry VIII.*, iii, 2.
[10] *Julius Cæsar*, iii, 2.
[11] *Antony and Cleopatra*, iii, 1.

Bacon says:

> Unto such death is a *redeemer*.

The sick King Edward IV., nigh unto death, says:

> I every day expect an embassage
> From my Redeemer to *redeem* me hence.[1]

Bacon says:

> And the grave a place of *retiredness* and *rest*.

Shakespeare says:

> That their souls
> May make a peaceful and a sweet *retire*.[2]

Again:

> His new kingdom of perpetual *rest*.[3]

> Oh, here
> Will I set up my everlasting *rest*.[4]

Says Bacon:

Wooing the remorseless sisters to wind down the watch of their life, and to break them off before the hour.

Wooing is a favorite word with Shakespeare, and applied, as here, in a peculiar sense.

> That *woo'd* the slimy bottom of the deep,
> And mocked the dead bones that lay scattered by.[5]

> More inconstant than the wind which *woos*
> Even now the frozen bosom of the north.[6]

> The heavens' breath
> Smells *wooingly* here.[7]

Says Bacon:

> To wind down the watch of their life.

Says Shakespeare:

> He is winding up the watch of his wit.[8]

This is indeed an odd comparison — the watch of his life, the watch of his wit.

Bacon says:

But death is a doleful messenger to a usurer, and fate untimely *cuts their thread*.

Shakespeare has:

> Let not Bardolph's *vital thread be cut*.[9]

---

[1] *Richard III.*, ii, 1. [4] *Romeo and Juliet*, v, 3. [7] *Macbeth*, i, 6.
[2] *Henry V.*, iv, 3. [5] Ibid., i, 4. [8] *Tempest*, ii, 1.
[3] *Richard III.*, ii, 2. [6] *Romeo and Juliet*, i, 4. [9] *Henry V.*, iii, 6.

> Had not churchmen prayed,
> His *thread of life* had not so soon decayed.[1]
>
> Till the destinies do *cut his thread* of life.[2]

In the same paragraph Bacon alludes to *the remorseless sisters*, and here we have:

> O fates! come, come,
> *Cut thread* and thrum ...
> Oh, *sisters three*,
> Come, come, to me,
> With hands as pale as milk;
> Lay them in gore,
> Since you have shore,
> With shears, his *thread* of silk.[3]

Here we not only have the three weird sisters of destiny alluded to by both writers, but in connection therewith the same expression, of cutting the thread of life.

Bacon says, speaking of death:

But I consent with Cæsar, that the suddenest passage is *easiest*.

We are reminded of Cleopatra's studies:

> She hath pursued conclusions infinite
> Of *easy* ways to die.[4]

Says Bacon:

Nothing more awakens our resolve and readiness to die than the *quieted conscience*.

We are reminded of Wolsey:

> I feel within me
> A peace above all earthly dignities,
> A still and *quiet conscience*.[5]

And again:

> O my Wolsey,
> The *quiet* of my wounded *conscience*.[6]

Says Bacon:

> Our *readiness* to die.

Hamlet associates the same word *readiness* with death:

> If it be not now, yet it will come: the *readiness* is all.[7]

Says Bacon:

> My ambition is not to foreflow the *tide*.

---

[1] *1st Henry VI.*, i. 1.
[2] *Pericles*, i. 2.
[3] *Midsummer Night's Dream*, v. 1.
[4] *Antony and Cleopatra*, v. 2.
[5] *Henry VIII.*, iii. 2.
[6] Ibid., ii. 2.
[7] *Hamlet*, v. 2.

Shakespeare says:

> For we must take the current when it serves,
> Or lose our ventures.[1]

Bacon says:

So much of our life as we have already discovered is already dead; ... for we *die daily*.

In Shakespeare we have:

> The Queen that bore thee,
> Oftener upon her knees than on her feet,
> *Died every day she lived.*[2]

Bacon says:

Until we return to our *grandmother, the earth*.

Shakespeare speaks of the earth in the same way:

> At your birth
> Our *grandam, earth*, having this distemperature,
> In passion shook.[3]

Bacon says:

> Art thou *drowned* in security?

Shakespeare says:

> He hath a sin that often *drowns* him.[4]

Bacon says:

There is nothing under heaven, saving a true friend, who cannot be counted within the number of *moveables*.

This is a strange phrase. We turn to Shakespeare, and we find a similar thought:

> *Katharine.* I knew you at the first,
> You were a *moveable*.
> *Petruchio.* Why, what's a *movable?*
> *Katharine.* A joint stool.[5]

And again:

> Love is not love
> Which alters where it alteration finds,
> Or bends with the remover to *remove*.[6]

Bacon says:

> They desired to be excused from *Death's banquet*.

---

[1] *Julius Cæsar*, iv, 3.   [3] *1st Henry IV.*, iii, 1.   [5] *Taming of the Shrew*, ii, 1
[2] *Macbeth*, iv, 3.   [4] *Timon of Athens*, iii, 5.   [6] Sonnet cxvi.

Shakespeare says:

> O proud *death*,
> What *feast* is forward in thine eternal cell?[1]

And again:

> O malignant and ill-boding stars!
> Now thou art come unto a *feast* of *death*.[2]

This is certainly an extraordinary thought — that Death devours and feasts upon the living.

Speaking of death, Bacon further says:

> Looking at the blessings, not the hand that *enlarged* them.

This is a peculiar expression — that death enlarges and liberates. We find precisely the same thought in Shakespeare:

> Just *death*, kind umpire of men's miseries,
> With sweet *enlargement* doth dismiss me hence.[3]

Bacon says:

> The soul having *shaken off* her flesh.

Shakespeare has it:

> O you mighty gods!
> This world I do renounce; and in your sights
> *Shake* patiently my great affliction *off*.[4]

And again:

> What dreams may come,
> When we have *shuffled off* this mortal coil.[5]

Bacon continues:

> The soul . . . shows what *finger* hath enforced her.

Here is a strange and unusual expression as applied to God. We turn to Shakespeare and we find it repeated:

> The *fingers* of *the powers above* do tune
> The harmony of this peace.[6]

And we find the word *finger* repeatedly used by Shakespeare in a figurative sense:

> How the devil luxury, with his potato *finger*, tickles these two together.[7]

> No man's pie is freed
> From his ambitious *finger*.[8]

[1] *Hamlet*, v, 2.
[2] *1st Henry VI.*, iv, 5.
[3] Ibid., ii, 5.
[4] *Lear*, iv, 6.
[5] *Hamlet*, iii, 1.
[6] *Cymbeline*, v, 5.
[7] *Troilus and Cressida*, v, 2.
[8] *Henry VIII.*, i, 1.

> They are not as a pipe for fortune's *finger*,
> To sound what stop she please.[1]

He shall not knit a knot in his fortunes with the *finger* of my substance.[2]

And the word *utter*, as applied to the putting out of music, is also found in the same scene:

> These cannot I command to any *utterance* of harmony:
> I have not the skill.[3]

Bacon says that the soul

Sometimes takes soil in an imperfect body, and so is slackened from showing her wonders; like an *excellent musician* which cannot *utter* himself upon a defective instrument.

This thought is very poetical. Shakespeare has a similar conception:

> How sour sweet music is
> When time is broke, and no proportion kept!
> *So is it in the music of our lives.*[4]

The comparison of a man to a musical instrument lies at the base of the great scene in *Hamlet*:

Why, look you now, how unworthy a thing you make of me. You would play upon me; you would seem to know my stops; you would pluck out the heart of my mystery; you would sound me from my lowest note to the top of my compass; and there is much music, *excellent* voice, in this little organ; yet cannot you make it speak. 'Sblood, do you think I am easier to be played upon than a pipe?[5]

Says Bacon

Nor desire any greater place than the *front* of good opinion.

Shakespeare has:

> The very head and *front* of my offending
> Hath this extent, no more.[6]

Says Bacon:

I should not be earnest to see the *evening* of my age; that extremity of itself being a disease, and a mere return unto infancy.

Speaking in sonnet lxxiii of his own age, Shakespeare says:

> In me thou seest the twilight of such day,
>   As after sunset fadeth in the west,
> Which by and by black night doth take away.

Bacon says:

The extremity of age.

---

[1] *Hamlet*, iii, 2. [3] *Hamlet*, iii, 2. [5] *Hamlet*, iii, 2.
[2] *Merry Wives of Windsor*, ii, 1. [4] *Richard II.*, v, 5. [6] *Othello*, i, 3.

Shakespeare has it, speaking of old age:

> Oh! time's *extremity*,
> Hast thou so cracked and splitted my poor tongue.[1]

And again he says:

The middle of youth thou never knowest, but the *extremity* of both ends.[2]

Says Bacon:

> A *mere* return unto infancy.

Shakespeare says:

> Last scene of all,
> That ends this strange, eventful history,
> Is second *childishness* and *mere* oblivion.[3]

Says Bacon:

> Mine *eyes* begin to discharge their *watch*.

Shakespeare says:

> Care keeps his *watch* in every old man's *eye*.[4]

Says Bacon:

> For a time of *perpetual rest*.

Says Shakespeare:

> Like obedient subjects, follow him
> To his new kingdom of *perpetual rest*.[5]

I. Conclusions.

This is certainly a most remarkable series of coincidences of thought and expressions; and, as I said before, they occur not in the ordinary words of our language, the common bases of speech, without which we cannot construct sentences or communicate with each other, but in unusual, metaphorical, poetical thoughts; or in ordinary words employed in extraordinary and figurative senses.

Thus it is nothing to find Bacon and Shakespeare using such words as *day* and *dead*, but it is very significant when we find both writers using them in connection with the same curious and abstruse thought, to-wit: that individuals metaphorically die daily. So the use of the word *blood* by both proves nothing, for they could scarcely have written for any length of time without employing it; but when we find it used by both authors in the sense of the

---

[1] *Comedy of Errors*, v, 1.
[2] *Timon of Athens*, iv, 3.
[3] *As You Like It*, ii, 7.
[4] *Romeo and Juliet*, ii, 3.
[5] *Richard III.*, ii, 2.

essential principle of a thing, as the *blood of virtue*, the *blood of malice*, it is more than a verbal coincidence: it proves an identity in the mode of thinking. So the occurrence in both of the words *death* and *banquet* means nothing; but the expression, *a banquet of death, a feast of death*, is a poetical conception of an unusual character. The words *soul* and *shake*, and even *shuffle*, might be found in the writings of all Bacon's contemporaries, but we will look in vain in any of them, except Shakespeare, for a description of death as *the shaking off of the flesh*, or *the shuffling off of the mortal coil*, to-wit, the flesh.

To my mind there is even more in these resemblances of modes of thought, which indicate the same construction and constitution of the mind, and the same way of receiving and digesting and putting forth a fact, not as a mere bare, dead fact, but enrobed and enfleshed in a vital metaphor, than in the similarity of thoughts, such as our crying when we come into the world, and the return of man in old age to mere infancy and second childishness; for these are things which, if once heard from the stage, might have been perpetuated in such a mind as that of Bacon.

This essay *Of Death* is entirely Shakespearean. There is the same interfusing of original and profound thought with fancy; the same welding together of the thing itself and the metaphor for it; the same affluence and crowding of ideas; the same compactness and condensation of expression; the same forcing of common words into new meanings; and above all, the same sense of beauty and poetry

Observe, for instance, that comparison of the soul shut up in an imperfect body, trying, like an excellent musician, to utter itself upon a defective instrument. What could be more beautiful? See the picture of the despairful widows, deposed kings and pensive prisoners, who sit in darkness, burdened with grief and irons, on the shore of Death, waving their hands to the grim tyrant to draw near, watching for the coming of his star, as the wise men looked for the coming of the star of Bethlehem, and wooing the remorseless sisters three to break them off before the hour. Or note the pathos of that comparison (bearing most melancholy application to Bacon's own fate) where he says:

Who can see worse days than he that, while yet living, doth follow at the funeral of his own reputation?

And in the craving for a period of "perpetual rest," which shows itself all through this essay, we catch a glimpse of the melancholy which overwhelmed the soul of him who cried out, through the mouth of Hamlet:

> Oh, that this too, too solid flesh would melt,
> Thaw and resolve itself into a dew!
> Or that the Everlasting had not fixed
> His canon 'gainst self-slaughter.

All through the essay it seems to be more than prose. From beginning to end it is a mass of imagery: it is poetry without rhythm. Like a great bird which as it starts to fly runs for a space along the ground, beating the air with its wings and the earth with its feet, so in this essay we seem to see the pinions of the poet constantly striving to lift him above the barren limitations of prose into the blue ether of untrammeled expression. It comes to us like the rude block out of which he had carved an exquisite statue full of life and grace, to be inserted perchance in some drama, even as we find another marvelous essay on death interjected into *Measure for Measure*.[1]

II. THE STYLE OF A BARREN MIND.

As a means of comparison and as an illustration of the wide difference between human brains, I insert the following letter from Lord Coke, who lived in the same age as Bacon, and was, like him, a lawyer, a statesman, a courtier and a politician.

Bacon's language overruns with flowers and verdure: it is literally buried, obscured and darkened by the very efflorescence of his fancy and his imagination. Coke speaks the same English tongue in the same period of development, but his thoughts are as bare, as hard, as soulless and as homely as an English work-house, in the midst of a squalid village-common, a mile distant from a flower or a blade of grass. When we read the utterances of the two men we are reminded of that amusing scene, depicted by the humorous pen of Mark Twain, where Scotty Briggs and the village parson carry on a conversation in which neither can understand a word the other says, though both speak the same tongue; illustrating that in the same language there may be many dialects

---

[1] Act iii, scene 1.

separated as widely from each other as French from German, and depending for their character on the mental constitution of the men who use them. The speech of an English "navvy" does not differ more from the language of Tennyson's *Morte d'Arthur* than do the writings of Coke from those of Bacon. It will puzzle our readers to find a single Shakespeareanism of thought or expression in a whole volume of Coke's productions.

THE HUMBLE AND DIRECT ANSWER TO THE LAST QUESTION ARISING UPON BAGG'S CASE.

It was resolved, that to this court of the King's bench belongeth authority not only to correct errors in judicial proceedings, but other errors and misdemeanors tending to the breach of the peace, or oppression of the subjects, or to the raising of faction or other misgovernment: so that no wrong or injury, either public or private, can be done, but it shall be reformed and punished by law.

Being commanded to explain myself concerning these words, and principally concerning this word, "misgovernment,"—

I answer that the subject-matter of that case concerned the misgovernment of the mayors and other the magistrates of Plymouth

And I intended for the persons the misgovernment of such inferior magistrates for the matters in committing wrong or injury, either public or private punishable by law, and therefore the last clause was added, "and so no wrong or injury, either public or private, can be done, but it shall be reformed and punished by law;" and the rule is: "*verba intelligenda sunt secundum subjectam materiam.*"

And that they and other corporations might know, that factions and other misgovernments amongst them, either by oppression, bribery, unjust disfranchisements, or other wrong or injury, public or private are to be redressed and punished by law, it was so reported.

But if any scruple remains to clear it, these words may be added, "by inferior magistrates," and so the sense shall be by faction or misgovernment of inferior magistrates, so as no wrong or injury, etc.

All which I most humbly submit to your Majesty's princely judgment.

EDW. COKE.

Now it may be objected that this paper is upon a dry and grave subject, and that Bacon would have written it in much the same style. But if the reader will look back at the quotations I have made from Bacon, in the foregoing pages, he will find that many of them are taken from his law papers and court charges, and his weighty philosophical writings, and yet they are fairly alive with fancy, metaphor and poetry.

CHAPTER II.

IDENTICAL METAPHORS.

> *Touchstone.* For all your writers do consent, that *ipse* is he;
> Now you are not *ipse*, for I am he.
> *William.* Which he, sir? — *As You Like It*, v, 1.

BOTH Bacon and Shakespeare reasoned by analogy. Whenever their thoughts encountered an abstruse subject, they compared it with one plain and familiar; whenever they sought to explain mental and spiritual phenomena, they paralleled them with physical phenomena; whenever they would render clear the lofty and great, they called up before the mind's vision the humble and the insignificant. All thoughts ran in parallel lines; no thought stood alone. Hence the writings of both are a mass of similes and comparisons.

I. HUMBLE AND BASE THINGS USED AS COMPARISONS.

We have seen that Bacon and his double were both philosophers, and especially *natural* philosophers, whose observation took in "the hyssop on the wall, as well as the cedar of Libanus;" and when we come to consider their identity of comparisons, we shall find in both a tendency to use humble and even disgusting things as a basis of metaphor.

We shall see that Bacon was always "puttering in physic," and we find Shakespeare constantly using medical terms and facts in his poetry.

We find, for instance, that both compared the driving-out of evil influences, in the state or mind, to the effect of purgative medicines.

Bacon says:

The King . . . thought . . . to proceed with severity against some of the principal conspirators here within the realm; thereby to *purge* the ill *humors* in England.[1]

And again:

Some of the garrison observing this, and having not their minds *purged* of the late ill blood of hostility.[2]

[1] *History of Henry VII.* [2] Ibid.

And again:

But as in bodies very corrupt the medicine rather stirreth and exasperateth the humor than *purgeth* it, so some turbulent spirits laid hold of this proceeding toward my lord, etc.[1]

While Shakespeare says:

> I
> Do come with words as medicinal as true;
> Honest as either; to *purge* him of that *humor*
> That presses him from sleep.[2]

And again:

> Blood hath been shed ere now, i' the olden time,
> Ere human statute *purged* the gentle weal.[3]

And again:

> Would *purge* the land of these drones.[4]

And again:

> And, for the day, confined to fast in fires,
> Till the foul crimes done in my days of nature,
> Are burnt and *purged* away.[5]

Bacon says:

> Sometimes opening the *obstructions*.[6]

Shakespeare says:

> Purge the *obstructions*.[7]

And the same thought occurs in different language.

Bacon says:

And so this traitor Essex made his color the *scouring* of some noblemen and counselors from her Majesty's favor.

In Shakespeare we have:

> What rhubarb, senna, or what *purgative drug*
> Will *scour* these English hence?[8]

The comparison of men and things to bodily sores is common in both — an unusual trait of expression in an elevated mind and a poet; but it was part of Bacon's philosophy "that most poor things point to rich ends."

Bacon says:

Augustus Cæsar, out of great indignation against his two daughters and Posthumus Agrippa, his grandchild, whereof the first two were infamous, and the last

---

[1] Report of Judicial Proceedings at York House.
[2] *Winter's Tale*, ii, 3.
[3] *Macbeth*, iv, 3.
[4] *Pericles*, ii, 1.
[5] *Hamlet*, i, 5.
[6] *History of Henry VII*.
[7] *2d Henry IV*, iv, 1.
[8] *Macbeth*, v, 3.

otherwise unworthy, would say "that they were not his seed, but some *imposthumes* that had broken from him."[1]

And again he says:

Should a man have them to be slain by his vassals, as the posthumus of Alexander the Great was? Or to call them his *imposthumes*, as Augustus Cæsar called his?[2]

While in Shakespeare we have:

> This is the *imposthume* of much wealth and peace,
> That *inward* breaks, and shows no cause without
> Why the man dies.[3]

And we find precisely the same thought in Bacon:

He that turneth the humors back and maketh the wound bleed *inwards*, ingendereth malign ulcers and pernicious *imposthumations*.[4]

We have a whole body of comparisons of things governmental to these ulcers, in their different stages of healing.

Bacon says:

We are here to search the wounds of the realm, not to *skin* them over.[5]

Spain having lately, with much difficulty, rather smoothed and *skinned over* than healed and extinguished the commotion of Aragon.[6]

Shakespeare says:

> A kind of medicine in itself
> That *skins* the vice o' the top.[7]
>
> Mother, for love of grace,
> Lay not that flattering unction to your soul,
> That not your trespass, but my madness speaks:
> It will but *skin* and film the *ulcerous place;*
> While rank corruption, *mining* all within,
> *Infects* unseen.[8]

And even this curious word *mining* we find in Bacon used in the same figurative sense:

To search and *mine* into that which is not revealed.[9]

And we find this same inward infection referred to in Bacon:

A profound kind of fallacies, . . . the force whereof is such as it . . . doth more generally and inwardly *infect* and corrupt.[10]

And then we have in both the use of the word *canker* or *cancer* as a source of comparison:

---

[1] *Apophthegms.*
[2] *Discourse in Praise of the Queen — Life and Works*, vol. i, p. 140.
[3] *Hamlet*, iv, 4.
[4] Essay *Of Sedition.*
[5] Speech in Parliament.
[6] *Observations on a Libel — Life and Works*, vol. i, p. 162.
[7] *Measure for Measure*, ii, 2.
[8] *Hamlet*, iii, 4.
[9] *Advancement of Learning*, book i.
[10] Ibid., book ii.

Bacon:
> The *canker* of epitomes.[1]

Shakespeare:
> The *cankers* of a calm world and a long peace.[2]
> Banish the *canker* of ambitious thoughts.[3]
> This *canker* of our nature.[4]
> This *canker*, Bolingbroke.[5]

∴

Out of this tendency to dwell upon physical ills, and the cure of them, we find both coining a new verb, *medicining*, or *to medicine*.

Bacon:
> The *medicining* of the mind.[6]

Again:

Let the balm distill everywhere, from your sovereign hands to the *medicining* of any part that complaineth.[7]

Shakespeare says:
> Great griefs, I see, *medicine* the less.[8]
>
> Not poppy, nor mandragora,
> Nor all the drowsy sirups of the world,
> Shall ever *medicine* thee to that sweet sleep,
> Which thou owedst yesterday.[9]

∴

We find the same tendency in both to compare physical ills with mental ills, the thing tangible with the thing intangible.

Bacon:

We know diseases of stoppings and suffocations are the most dangerous in the body; and it is not much otherwise in the mind: you may take sarsa to open the liver, steel to open the spleen, flour of sulphur for the lungs, castareum for the brain; but no receipt openeth the heart but a true friend, to whom you may impart griefs, joys, fears, hopes, suspicions, counsels and whatsoever *lieth upon the heart to oppress it*.[10]

You shall know what *disease* your *mind* is aptest to fall into.[11]

Good Lord, Madam, how wisely and aptly you can speak and discern of physic ministered to the body, and consider not that there is the like occasion of *physic ministered* to the *mind*.[12]

We turn to Shakespeare, and we find him indulging in the same kind of comparisons. In *Macbeth* we have:

---

[1] *Advancement of Learning*, book ii.
[2] *1st Henry IV.*, iv, 2.
[3] *2d Henry VI.*, i, 2.
[4] *Hamlet*, v, 2.
[5] *1st Henry IV.*, i, 3.
[6] *Advancement of Learning*, book ii.
[7] *Gesta Grayorum — Life and Works*, vol. i, p. 330.
[8] *Cymbeline*, iv, 2.
[9] *Othello*, iii, 3.
[10] Essay *Of Friendship*.
[11] Bacon's Letter to the Earl of Rutland, written in the name of the Earl of Essex — *Life and Works*, vol. ii, p. 9.
[12] *Apology*.

> *Macbeth.* How does your patient, doctor?
> *Doctor.* Not so sick, my lord,
> As she is troubled with thick-coming fancies
> That keep her from her rest.
>
> *Macbeth.* Cure her of that:
> Canst thou not minister to a *mind diseased*,
> Pluck from the memory a rooted sorrow,
> Raze out the written troubles of the brain;
> And, with some sweet oblivious antidote,
> Cleanse the stuffed bosom of that perilous stuff
> Which *weighs upon the heart?*
>
> *Doctor.* Therein the patient
> Must minister to himself.[1]

In both these extracts the stoppages and "suffocations" of the body are compared to the stuffed condition of the mind and heart; in both the heart is thus *oppressed* by that which *lies upon it;* in both we are told that there is no medicine that can relieve the overcharged spirit.

Malcolm says:

> Be comforted.
> Let's make us *med'cines* of our great revenge,
> To cure this deadly grief.[2]

II. THE ORGANS OF THE BODY USED AS A BASIS OF COMPARISON.

We turn to another class of comparisons. In both writers we find the organs of the body used as a basis of metaphor, just as we have seen the "medicining" of the body applied to the state of the mind.

Every reader of Shakespeare remembers that strange expression in *Richard III.*:

> Thus far into *the bowels of the land*
> Have we marched without impediment.[3]

We find the same comparison often repeated:

> Into the *bowels* of the battle.[4]
>
> The *bowels* of ungrateful Rome.[5]
>
> The fatal *bowels* of the deep.[6]

And we find Bacon employing the same strange metaphor:

> This fable is wise and seems to be taken out of the *bowels of morality.*[7]

---

[1] *Macbeth,* v. 3. [3] *Richard III.,* v. 2. [5] *Coriolanus,* iv. 5.
[2] Ibid., iv. 3. [4] *1st Henry VI.,* i. 1. [6] *Richard III.,* iii. 4.
[7] *Wisdom of the Ancients — Juno's Suitor.*

If any state be yet free from his factions, erected in the *bowels* thereof.[1]

Speaking of the fact that earthquakes affecting a small area reach but a short distance into the earth, Bacon observes that, where they agitate a wider area,

We are to suppose that their bases and primitive seats enter deeper into the *bowels of the earth*.[2]

This is precisely the expression used by Hotspur:

Villainous saltpeter dug out of the *bowels* of the harmless *earth*.[3]

And this comparison of the earth to the stomach, and of an earthquake to something which disturbs it, we find in Shakespeare:

> Diseasèd nature oftentimes breaks forth
> In strange eruptions: oft the teeming earth
> Is with a kind of colic pinched and vexed
> By the imprisoning of unruly wind
> Within her womb.[4]

And we find the processes of the stomach, in both sets of writings, applied to mental operations:

Shakespeare says:

> How shall we stretch our eye
> When capital crimes, *chewed, swallowed* and *digested*,
> Appear before us?[5]

Bacon says:

Some books are to be tasted, others to be *swallowed*, and some few to be *chewed* and *digested*.[6]

In both we find the human body compared to a musical instrument.

Bacon says:

The office of medicine is to tune this curious *harp* of man's body and reduce it to harmony.[7]

In Shakespeare, Pericles tells the Princess:

> You're a fair *viol*, and your sense the strings,
> Who, fingered to make man his lawful music,
> Would draw heaven down and all the gods to hearken.[8]

And the strings of the harp furnish another series of comparisons to both. Bacon says:

They did *strike upon a string* that was more dangerous.[9]

---

[1] Discourse in Praise of the Queen—*Life and Works*, vol. i, p. 137.
[2] *Nature of Things*.
[3] *1st Henry IV.*, i, 3.
[4] Ibid., iii, 1.
[5] *Henry V.*, ii, 2.
[6] Essay *Of Studies*.
[7] *Advancement of Learning*, book ii.
[8] *Pericles*, i, 1.
[9] *History of Henry VII*.

IDENTICAL METAPHORS.

And again:

The King was much moved, . . . because it struck upon that *string* which even he most *feared*.[1]

And Shakespeare says:

Harp not on that string, madam.[2]

And again:

I would 'twere something that would fret the *string*,
The master-cord on 's heart.[3]

And the word *harping* is a favorite with both. Bacon says:

This string you cannot *harp* upon too much.[4]

And again:

Harping upon that which should follow.[5]

And in Shakespeare we have:

Still *harping* on my daughter.[6]

Harping on what I am,
Not what he knew I was.[7]

Thou hast *harped* my *fear* aright.[8]

We have the disorders of the body of man also made a source of comparison for the disorders of the mind, in the following instance.

Bacon:

High conceits do sometimes come streaming into the minds and imaginations of base persons, especially when they are *drunk* with news, and talk of the people.[9]

Shakespeare:

Was the hope *drunk*
Wherein you dressed yourself?[10]

What! *drunk* with choler?[11]

Hath our intelligence been *drunk*?[12]

Here we have drunkenness applied to the affections and emotions — to the *mind* in the one case, to the intelligence in the other; to the imagination in the first instance, to the hope and the temper in the last.

We have the joints of the body used by both to express the condition of public affairs.

[1] *History of Henry VII.*
[2] *Richard III.*, iv, 4.
[3] *Henry VIII.*, iii, 2.
[4] Letter to Essex, Oct. 4, 1596.
[5] *Civil Conv.*
[6] *Hamlet*, ii, 2.
[7] *Antony and Cleopatra*, iii, 3.
[8] *Macbeth*, iv, 1.
[9] *History of Henry VII.*
[10] *Macbeth*, i, 7.
[11] *1st Henry IV.*, i, 3.
[12] *King John*, iv, 2.

Bacon says:

We do plainly see in the most countries of Christendom so unsound and shaken an estate, as desireth the help of some great person, to set together and join again the pieces asunder and *out of joint*.[1]

In Shakespeare we have Hamlet's exclamation, also applied to the condition of the country:

> The time is *out of joint*—Oh, cursed spite,
> That ever I was born to set it right.[2]

∴

We have the body of man made the basis of another comparison.

Bacon says:

The very springs and *sinews* of industry.[3]

We should intercept his [the King of Spain's] treasure, whereby we shall cut his *sinews*.[4]

While Shakespeare says:

> The portion and *sinew* of her fortune.[5]
>
> Nay, patience, or we break the *sinews* of our plot.[6]
>
> The noble *sinews* of our power.[7]

∴

We have the same comparison applied to the blood-vessels of the body.

Bacon:

He could not endure to have trade sick, nor any obstruction to continue in the *gate-vein* which disperseth that blood.[8]

Shakespeare:

> The natural *gates* and alleys of the body.[9]

∴

We have in both the comparison of the body of man to a tabernacle or temple in which the soul or mind dwells.

Bacon says:

Thus much for the body, which is but the *tabernacle* of the mind.[10]

Shakespeare says:

> Nothing vile can dwell in such a *temple*.[11]

---

[1] *Of the State of Europe.*
[2] *Hamlet*, i, 5.
[3] *Novum Organum*, book i.
[4] Letter to Essex, June, 1596.
[5] *Measure for Measure*, iii, 1.
[6] *Twelfth Night*, ii, 5.
[7] *Henry V.*, i, 2.
[8] *History of Henry VII.*
[9] *Hamlet*, i, 5.
[10] *Advancement of Learning*, book ii.
[11] *Tempest*, i, 2.

And again:

> For nature, crescent, does not grow alone
> In thews and bulk; but, as this *temple* waxes,
> The inward service of the mind and soul
> Grows wide withal.[1]

> Oh, that deceit should dwell
> In such a gorgeous *palace*.[2]

Even the clothing which covers the body becomes a medium of comparison in both.

Bacon:

Behavior seemeth to me as a *garment of the mind*.[3]

This curious idea, of robing the mind in something which shall cover or adorn it, is used by Shakespeare:

> With purpose to be *dressed in an opinion*
> Of wisdom.[4]

> And *dressed* myself in such *humility*.[5]

> Was the *hope* drunk wherein you *dressed* yourself?[6]

And the same thought occurs in the following:

> The *garment* of rebellion.[7]

> Dashing the *garment* of this peace.[8]

Part of the raiment of the body is used by both as a comparison for great things.

Bacon:

The motion of the air in great circles, such as are under *the girdle of the world*.[9]

Shakespeare says:

> *Puck.* I'll put a *girdle* round about the earth
> In forty minutes.[10]

We have said that both writers were prone to use humble and familiar things as a basis of comparison for immaterial and great things. We find some instances in the following extracts.

The blacksmith's shop was well known to both. Bacon says:

There is *shaped* a tale in London's *forge* that beateth apace at this time.[11]

---

[1] *Hamlet*, i, 3.
[2] *Romeo and Juliet*, iii, 2.
[3] *Advancement of Learning*, book ii.
[4] *Merchant of Venice*, i, 1.
[5] *1st Henry IV.*, iii, 2.
[6] *Macbeth*, i, 7.
[7] *1st Henry IV.*, v, 1.
[8] *Henry VIII*, i, 1.
[9] *Natural History*, § 398.
[10] *Midsummer Night's Dream*, ii, 2.
[11] Letter to Lord Howard.

Shakespeare:

Mrs. Page. Come, to the *forge* with it, then; *shape* it. I would not have things cool.[1]

Here we have in the one case a tale *shaped* in the *forge;* in the other a plan is to be *shaped* in the *forge.*

And again we have in Shakespeare:

> In the quick *forge* and working-house of *thought.*[2]
>
> I should make very *forges* of my cheeks,
> That would to cinders burn up modesty.[3]

Again we find in Bacon:

Though it be my fortune to be the anvil upon which these good effects are beaten and wrought.[4]

Speaking of Robert Cecil, Bacon says:

> He loved to have all business *under the hammer.*[5]

And this:

He stayed for a better hour till the *hammer* had wrought and beat the party of Britain more pliant.[6]

While in Shakespeare we have:

> I cannot do it, yet I'll *hammer* it out
> Of my brain.[7]
>
> Whereupon this month I have been *hammering.*[8]

.·.

The refuse left at the bottom of a wine-cask is used by both metaphorically.

Bacon:

That the [Scotch] King, being in amity with him, and noways provoked, should so burn in hatred towards him as to *drink* the *lees and dregs* of Perkin's intoxication, who was everywhere else detected and discarded.[9]

And again Bacon says:

The memory of King Richard lay like *lees* in the bottom of men's hearts; and if the vessel was but stirred it would come up.[10]

And Bacon speaks of

> The *dregs* of this age.[11]

We turn to Shakespeare and we find:

> He, like a puling cuckold, would *drink up*
> The *lees and dregs* of a flat, tamèd piece.[12]

---

[1] *Merry Wives of Windsor,* iv, 2.
[2] *Henry V.,* v, cho.
[3] *Othello,* iv, 2.
[4] Letter to the Lords.
[5] Letter to King James, 1612.
[6] *History of Henry VII.*
[7] *Richard II.,* v, 5.
[8] *Two Gentlemen of Verona,* i, 3.
[9] *History of Henry VII.*
[10] Ibid.
[11] Bacon to Queen Elizabeth—*Life and Works,* vol. ii, p. 160.
[12] *Troilus and Cressida,* iv, 1.

Again:

> All is but toys; renown and grace is dead;
> The wine of life is drawn, and the mere *lees*
> Is left this vault to brag of.[1]

Again:

> Some certain *dregs* of conscience.[2]

Again:

> The *dregs* of the storm be past.[3]

∴

And the floating refuse which rises to the top of a vessel is also used in the same sense by both.

Bacon speaks of

> The *scum* of the people.[4]

Again:

> A rabble and *scum* of desperate people.[5]

While Shakespeare says:

> A *scum* of Bretagnes and base knaves.[6]

Again:

> The filth and *scum* of Kent.[7]

Again:

> Froth and *scum*, thou liest.[8]

∴

Another instance of the use of humble and physical things as a basis of comparison in the treatment of things intellectual is found in the following curious metaphor:

Bacon:

He that seeketh victory over his nature, let him not set himself too great or too small tasks, . . . and at the first let him practice with helps, as *swimmers do with bladders*.[9]

While Shakespeare has:

> I have ventured,
> Like little wanton boys, *that swim on bladders*,
> This many summers in a sea of glory.[10]

∴

The people are compared by both to mastiffs.

Bacon:

The blood of so many innocents slain within their own harbors and nests by the scum of the people, who, like so many *mastiffs*, were let loose, and heartened and even set upon them by the state.[11]

---

[1] *Macbeth*, ii, 3.
[2] *Richard III*, i, 4.
[3] *Tempest*, ii, 2.
[4] *Felic. Queen Elizabeth.*
[5] *History of Henry VII.*
[6] *Richard III.*, v, 2.
[7] *2d Henry VI.*, iv, 2.
[8] *Merry Wives of Windsor*, i, 1.
[9] *Essay Of Nature in Men.*
[10] *Henry VIII.*, iii, 2.
[11] *Felic. Queen Elizabeth.*

While Shakespeare says:

The men do sympathize with their *mastiffs*, in robustious and rough coming-on.[1]

∴

We will see hereafter how much Bacon loved the pursuit of gardening.

He says:

He entered into due consideration how to *weed* out the partakers of the former rebellion.[2]

Again:

A man's nature runs either to herbs or weeds; therefore let him seasonably water the one and destroy the other.[3]

While Shakespeare has:

So one by one we'll *weed* them all at last.[4]

And again:

The caterpillars of the commonwealth,
Which I have sworn to *weed* and pluck away.[5]

The mirror is a favorite comparison in both sets of writings, as usual the thing familiar and physical illustrating the thing abstruse and intellectual.

Bacon says:

God hath framed the mind of man as a *mirror* or *glass* capable of the image of the universal world.[6]

Shakespeare:

Now all the youth of England are on fire, . . .
Following the *mirror* of all Christian kings.[7]

Bacon:

That which I have propounded to myself is . . . to *show* you your true shape in a *glass*.[8]

Shakespeare says of play-acting:

Whose end both at the first, and now, was and is, to hold, as 'twere, the *mirror* up to nature; to *show* virtue her own feature, scorn her own image, and the very age and body of the time his form and pressure.[9]

Bacon says:

If there be a *mirror* in the world worthy to hold men's eyes, it is that country.[10]

---

[1] *Henry V.*, iii, 7.
[2] *History of Henry VII.*
[3] *Essay Of Nature in Men.*
[4] *2d Henry VI.*, i, 3.
[5] *Richard II.*, ii, 3.
[6] *Advancement of Learning*, book i.
[7] *Henry V.*, ii, cho.
[8] *Letter to Coke.*
[9] *Hamlet*, iii, 2.
[10] *New Atlantis.*

Shakespeare says:
> The *mirror* of all courtesy.[1]

> He was, indeed, the *glass*
> Wherein the noble youth did dress themselves.[2]

Here is another humble comparison.

Bacon:

He thought it [the outbreak] but a *rag* or *remnant* of Bosworth-field.[3]

Shakespeare says:
> Away! thou *rag*, thou quantity, thou *remnant*.[4]

Here we have both words, *rag* and *remnant*, used figuratively, and used in the same order.

Again:
> Thou *rag* of honor.[5]

> Not a *rag* of money.[6]

Both writers use the humble habitation of the hog as a medium of comparison.

Bacon:

> *Styed* up in the schools and scholastic cells.[7]

Shakespeare:
> And here you *sty* me
> On this hard rock.[8]

Here is a comparison based on the same familiar facts.

Bacon speaks of

The wisdom of rats that will be sure to leave a house somewhat before it fall.[9]

Shakespeare says:
> A rotten carcass of a butt, not rigged,
> Nor tackle, sail, nor mast; the very rats
> Instinctively have quit it.[10]

The habits of birds are called into requisition by both writers.

Bacon says:

In her withdrawing-chamber the conspiracy against King Richard the Third had been *hatched*.[11]

Shakespeare says:
> Dire combustion and confused events
> New *hatched* to the woeful time.[12]

---

[1] *Henry VIII.*, ii, 1
[2] *2d Henry IV.*, ii, 3.
[3] *History of Henry VII.*
[4] *Taming of the Shrew*, iv, 3.
[5] *Richard III*, i, 3.
[6] *Comedy of Errors*, iv, 4.
[7] *Natural History.*
[8] *Tempest*, i, 2.
[9] Essay *Of Wisdom.*
[10] *Tempest*, i, 2.
[11] *History of Henry VII.*
[12] *Macbeth*, ii, 3.

And again:

> Such things become the *hatch* and brood of time.[1]

Bacon says:

Will you be as a *standing pool*, that spendeth and choketh his spring within itself?[2]

Shakespeare says:

> There are a sort of men whose visages
> Do cream and mantle like a *standing pond*.[3]

Even the humble wagon forms a basis of comparison.

Bacon says:

This is the *axle-tree* whereupon I have turned and shall turn.[4]

And again Bacon says:

The poles or *axle-tree* of *heaven*, upon which the conversion is accomplished.[5]

Shakespeare has:

> A bond of air strong as the *axle-tree*
> On which *heaven* rides.[6]

In the following another comparison is drawn from an humble source; and here, as in *rag* and *remnant*, not only is the same word used in both, but the same combination of words occurs.

Bacon says:

To reduce learning to certain empty and barren generalities; being but the very *husks* and *shells* of sciences.[7]

Shakespeare says:

> But the *shales* and *husks* of men.[8]
>
> Strewed with the *husks*
> And formless ruin of oblivion.[9]

Who can forget Hamlet's exquisite description of the heavens:

> This majestic *roof fretted* with golden fire.[10]

Few have stopped to ask themselves the meaning of the word *fretted*. We turn to the dictionary and we find no explanation that satisfies us. We go to Bacon, to the mind that conceived the thought, and we find that it means ornamented by fret-work.

---

[1] *2d Henry IV.*, iii, 1.
[2] *Gesta Grayorum—Life and Works*, vol. i, p. 339.
[3] *Merchant of Venice*, i, 1.
[4] Letter to Earl of Essex, 1600.
[5] *Advancement of Learning*, book ii.
[6] *Troilus and Cressida*, i, 3.
[7] *Advancement of Learning*, book ii.
[8] *Henry V.*, iv, 2.
[9] *Troilus and Cressida*, iv, 5.
[10] *Hamlet*, ii, 2.

For if that great Work-master had been of a human disposition, he would have cast the stars into some pleasant and beautiful works and orders, like the *frets* in the *roofs* of houses.[1]

Here we have a double identity: first, the heavens are compared to the roof of a house, or, more properly, the ceiling of a room; and secondly, the stars are compared to the fret-work which adorns such a ceiling.

It would be very surprising if all this came out of two separate minds.

In the following we have another instance of two words used together in the same comparison.

Bacon:

We set *stamps* and *seals of our own images* upon God's creatures and works.[2]

Shakespeare makes the nurse say to the black Aaron, bringing him his child:

> The empress sends it thee, thy *stamp*, thy *seal*,
> And bids thee christen it with thy dagger's point.[3]

And again:

> Nay, he is your brother by the surer side,
> Although my *seal* be *stamped* upon his face.[4]

Here we have precisely the same thought; Aaron had set "the stamp and seal of his own image" on his offspring.

We find in both the mind of man compared to a fountain.

Bacon says:

When the books of hearts shall be opened, I hope I shall not be found to have the *troubled fountain* of a *corrupt heart*.[5]

Again:

He [the King of Spain] hath by all means projected to *trouble the waters* here.[6]

And again:

One judicial and exemplar iniquity doth *trouble the fountains* of justice more than many particular injuries passed over by connivance.[7]

Pope Alexander . . . was desirous to *trouble the waters* in Italy.[8]

Shakespeare says:

> A woman moved is like a *fountain troubled*.[9]

---

[1] *Advancement of Learning*, book ii.
[2] *Exper. History.*
[3] *Titus Andronicus*, iv, 2.
[4] Ibid.
[5] Letter to the King.
[6] Report on Dr. Lopez' Treason — *Life and Works*, vol. i, p. 275.
[7] *Advancement of Learning*, book ii.
[8] *History of Henry VII.*
[9] *Taming of the Shrew*, v, 2.

> My mind is *troubled* like a *fountain* stirred.[1]
>
> But if he start,
> It is the flesh of a *corrupted heart*.[2]

In both we find the thoughts and emotions of a man compared to the coals which continue to live, although overwhelmed by misfortunes which cover them like ashes.

Bacon says:

Whilst I live my affection to do you service shall remain quick under the *ashes* of my fortune.[3]

And again:

So that the *sparks* of my affection shall ever rest quick, under the *ashes* of my fortune, to do you service.[4]

Shakespeare says:

> Pr'ythee go hence,
> Or I shall show the *cinders* of my spirits,
> Through the *ashes* of my chance.[5]

Again:

> The breath of heaven hath blown his spirit out,
> And strew'd repentant *ashes* on his head.[6]

Again:

> This late dissension, grown betwixt the peers,
> Burns under feigned *ashes* of forged love,
> And will at last break out into a *flame*.[7]

And the expression in the above quotation from Bacon:

> The *sparks* of my affection,

is paralleled in Shakespeare:

> *Sparks* of honor.[8]
>
> *Sparks* of life.[9]
>
> *Sparks* of nature.[10]

We find in both the state or kingdom compared to a ship, and the king or ruler to a steersman.

Bacon says:

Statesmen and such as *sit at the helms* of great kingdoms.[11]

In Shakespeare we find Suffolk promising Queen Margaret the control of the kingdom in these words:

---

[1] *Troilus and Cressida*, iii. 3.
[2] *Merry Wives of Windsor*, v. 5.
[3] Letter to the Earl of Bristol.
[4] Letter to Lord Viscount Falkland.
[5] *Antony and Cleopatra*, v. 2.
[6] *King John*, iv. 1.
[7] *1st Henry VI.*, iii. 1.
[8] *Richard II.*, v. 6.
[9] *Julius Cæsar*, i. 3.
[10] *Cymbeline*, iii. 3; *Lear*, iii. 7.
[11] *Felic. Queen Elizabeth.*

> So, one by one, we'll weed them all at last,
> And you yourself shall *steer the happy helm*.[1]

And again:

> God and King Henry govern England's *helm*.[2]

And again:

> A rarer spirit never
> Did *steer* humanity.[3]

We have seen Bacon speaking, in a speech in Parliament, of those "*viperous* natures" that would drive out the people from the lands and leave "nothing but a shepherd and his dog."

We find the same comparison, used in the same sense, in Shakespeare:

> Where is this *viper*
> That would depopulate the city,
> And be every man himself?[4]

The overwhelming influence of music on the soul is compared by both to a rape or ravishment.

Bacon says:

Melodious tunes, so fitting and delighting the ears that heard them, as that it *ravished* and betrayed all passengers. . . . Winged enticements to *ravish* and rape mortal men.[5]

While Shakespeare says:

> By this divine air, now is his soul *ravished*.[6]

And again:

> When we,
> Almost with *ravished* listening, could not find
> His hour of speech a minute.[7]

And again:

> One whom the music of his own vain tongue
> Doth *ravish* like enchanting harmony.[8]

We have in both the great power of circumstances compared to the rush of a flood of water.

Bacon:

> In this great *deluge* of danger.[9]

Shakespeare:

> Thy deed inhuman and unnatural
> Provokes this *deluge* most unnatural.[10]

---

[1] *2d Henry VI.*, i, 3.
[2] Ibid., ii, 3.
[3] *Antony and Cleopatra*, v, 1.
[4] *Coriolanus*, iii, 1.
[5] *Wisdom of the Ancients—The Sirens.*
[6] *Much Ado about Nothing*, ii, 5.
[7] *Henry VIII.*, i, 2.
[8] *Love's Labor Lost*, i, 1.
[9] *Felic. Queen Elizabeth.*
[10] *Richard III.*, i, 2.

Again:

> This *flood* of fortune.[1]

Again:

> And such a *flood* of greatness fell.[2]

Again:

> This great *flood* of visitors.[3]

∴

In their effort to express great quantity we have both referring to the ocean for their metaphors.

Bacon has:

> He came with such a *sea of multitude* upon Italy.[4]
>
> A *sea of air*.[5]

Shakespeare has precisely the same curious expression:

> A *sea of air*.[6]

Bacon also has:

> Vast *seas* of time.[7]
>
> A *sea* of quicksilver.[8]

Again Bacon says:

> Will turn a *sea of baser metal* into gold.[9]

In Shakespeare the same "large composition" of the mind drives him to seek in the greatest of terrestrial objects a means of comparison with the huge subjects which fill his thoughts:

> A *sea* of joys.[10]
>
> A *sea* of care.[11]
>
> Shed *seas* of tears.[12]
>
> A *sea* of glory.[13]
>
> That *sea* of blood.[14]
>
> A *sea* of woes.[15]

We also find in *Hamlet*:

> A *sea* of troubles.[16]

This word, thus employed, has been regarded as so peculiar and unusual that the commentators for a long time insisted that it was a misprint. Even Pope, himself a poet, altered it to read "a *siege* of troubles;" others would have it "*assail* of troubles." But we

---

[1] *Twelfth Night*, iv, 3.
[2] *1st Henry IV.*, v, 1.
[3] *Timon of Athens*, i, 1.
[4] *Apophthegms*.
[5] *Advancement of Learning*, book ii.
[6] *Timon of Athens*, iv, 2.
[7] *Advancement of Learning*, book i.
[8] Ibid., book ii.
[9] *Natural History*, § 326.
[10] *Pericles*, v, 1.
[11] *Henry VIII.*, iii, 2.
[12] *Rape of Lucrece*.
[13] *1st Henry VI.*, iv, 7.
[14] *3d Henry VI.*, ii, 3.
[15] *Timon of Athens*, i, 2.
[16] *Hamlet*, iii, 1.

see that it was a common expression with both Bacon and Shakespeare.

Bacon has also:

> The *ocean* of philosophy.[1]
>
> The *ocean* of history.[2]

Shakespeare has:

> An *ocean* of his tears.[3]
>
> An *ocean* of salt tears.[4]

In the same way the *tides* of the ocean became the source of numerous comparisons.

The most striking was pointed out some time since by Montagu and Judge Holmes. Not only is the tide used as a metaphor, but it enforces precisely the same idea.

Bacon:

In the third place, I set down reputation, because of the peremptory *tides* and *currents* it hath; which, if they be not *taken* in their due time, are seldom recovered.[5]

Shakespeare says:

> There is a *tide* in the affairs of men,
> Which, *taken* at the flood, leads on to fortune;
> Omitted, all the voyage of their life
> Is bound in shallows and in miseries.
> On such a full sea are we now afloat;
> And we must *take* the *current* when it serves,
> Or lose our ventures.[6]

Bacon and Shakespeare recur very often to this image of the *tides*:

My Lord Coke floweth according to his own *tides*, and not according to the tides of business.[7]

Here "tides of business" is the same thought as "tides of affairs" in the foregoing quotation from Shakespeare.

Bacon again says:

The *tide* of any opportunity, . . . the periods and *tides* of estates.[8]

And again:

Besides the open aids from the Duchess of Burgundy, there wanted not some secret *tides* from Maximilian and Charles.[9]

---

[1] *Exper. History.*
[2] *Great Instauration.*
[3] *Two Gentlemen of Verona*, ii, 7.
[4] *3d Henry VI.*, iii, 2.
[5] *History of Henry VII.*
[6] *Advancement of Learning*, book ii.
[7] *Julius Cæsar*, iv, 3.
[8] Letter to the King, February 25, 1615.
[9] Letter to Sir Robert Cecil.

And again:

> The *tides* and currents of received errors.[1]

Shakespeare says:

> The *tide* of blood in me
> Hath proudly flowed in vanity till now;
> Now doth it turn and ebb back to the sea;
> Where it shall mingle with the state of floods,
> And flow henceforth in formal majesty.[2]

And it will be observed that the curious fact is not that both should employ the word "*tide*," for that was of course a common word in the daily speech of all men, but that they should both employ it in a metaphorical sense; as the "tide of affairs," "the tide of business," "the tide of errors," "the tide of blood," etc.

And not only the ocean itself and the tides, but the swelling of the waters by distant storms is an image constantly in the minds of both.

Bacon says:

> There was an unusual *swelling* in the state, the forerunner of greater troubles.[3]

And again:

> Likewise it is everywhere taken notice of that *waters do somewhat swell and rise before tempests*.[4]

While in Shakespeare we have the same comparison applied in the same way:

> Before the days of change, still is it so;
> By a divine instinct, men's minds mistrust
> Ensuing danger; as, by proof, we see
> *The waters swell before a boisterous storm*.[5]

And here we have this precise thought in Bacon:

> As there are certain hollow blasts of wind and secret *swelling* of seas before a *tempest, so are there in states*.[6]

Can any man believe this exact repetition, not only of thought, but of the mode of representing it by a figure of speech, was accidental?

And from this rising of the water both coin an adjective.

Bacon says:

> Such a *swelling* season,[7]

meaning thereby one full of events and dangers.

---

[1] *Statutes of Uses.*
[2] *2d Henry IV.*, v, 2.
[3] *Folio. Queen Elizabeth.*
[4] *Natural History of Winds.*
[5] *Richard III.*, ii, 3.
[6] *Essay Of Sedition.*
[7] *History of Henry VII.*

While Shakespeare uses the adjective in the same peculiar sense:

> As happy prologues to the *swelling* act
> Of the imperial theme.[1]

Again:

> The *swelling* difference.[2]

Again:

> Behold the *swelling* scene[3]

Again:

> Noble, *swelling* spirits.[4]

The *clouds*, in both writers, furnish similes for overhanging troubles.

Bacon says:

Nevertheless, since I do perceive that this *cloud* hangs over the *House*.[5]

And again Bacon says:

The King, . . . willing to leave a *cloud* upon him, . . . produced him openly to plead his pardon.[6]

Shakespeare says:

> And all the *clouds* that lowered upon our *house*
> In the deep bosom of the ocean buried.[7]

And again Bacon says:

But the *cloud* of so great a rebellion *hanging* over his head, made him work sure.[8]

Shakespeare says:

> How is it that the *clouds* still *hang* on you?[9]

Bacon says:

The King had a careful eye where this wandering *cloud* would break.[10]

Shakespeare:

> Can such things be,
> And overcome us like a summer's *cloud*,
> Without our special wonder?[11]

Bacon says:

He had the *image and superscription* upon him of the Pope, in his honor of Cardinal.[12]

This thought is developed in Shakespeare into the well known comparison:

> A fellow by the hand of nature marked,
> Quoted and signed to do a deed of shame.[13]

[1] *Macbeth*, i, 3.
[2] *Richard II.*, i, 1.
[3] *Henry V.*, i, cho.
[4] *Othello*, ii, 3.
[5] Speech.
[6] *History of Henry VII.*
[7] *Richard III.*, i, 1.
[8] *History of Henry VII.*
[9] *Hamlet*, i, 2.
[10] *History of Henry VII.*
[11] *Macbeth*, iii, 4.
[12] *History of Henry VII.*
[13] *King John*, iv, 2.

In the one case the *superscription* of the Pope marks the Cardinal for honor; in the other the hand of nature has *signed* its signature upon the man to show that he is fit for a deed of shame.

And Bacon uses the word *signature* in the following:

Some immortal monument bearing a character and *signature* both of the power, etc.[1]

Bacon says:

Meaning thereby to *harrow* his people.[2]

Shakespeare says:

Let the Volsces
Plow Rome and *harrow* Italy.[3]

And again:

Whose lightest word would *harrow* up thy soul.[4]

Bacon says:

Intending the discretion of behavior is a great *thief of meditation*.[5]

Shakespeare says:

You *thief of love*.[6]

And again:

A very little *thief of occasion*.[7]

Bacon says:

It was not long but Perkin, who was make of *quicksilver*, which is hard to hold or imprison, began to stir.[8]

While Shakespeare says:

The rogue fled from me like *quicksilver*.[9]

And again:

That, swift as *quicksilver*, it courses through
The natural gates and alleys of the body.[10]

Here Perkin is compared to quicksilver by Bacon; and the volatile Pistol is compared to quicksilver by Shakespeare.

Bacon says:

They were executed ... at divers places upon the sea-coast of Kent, Sussex and Norfolk, for *sea-marks* or light-houses, to teach Perkin's people to avoid the coast.[11]

[1] *Advancement of Learning*, book i.
[2] *History of Henry VII*.
[3] *Coriolanus*, v, 3.
[4] *Hamlet*, i, 5.
[5] *Advancement of Learning*, book ii.
[6] *Midsummer Night's Dream*, iii, 2.
[7] *Coriolanus*, ii, 1.
[8] *History of Henry VII*.
[9] *Hamlet*, i, 5.
[10] 2d *Henry IV.*, ii, 4.
[11] *History of Henry VII*.

Shakespeare uses the same comparison:

> The very *sea-mark* of my utmost sail.[1]

In both cases the words are used in a figurative sense.

Bacon says:

The King being lost in a *wood* of suspicion, and not knowing whom to trust.[2]

Shakespeare:

> And I — like one lost in a thorny *wood*,
> That rents the thorns, and is rent with the thorns,
> Seeking a way, and straying from the way;
> Not knowing how to find the open air,
> But toiling desperately to find it out.[3]

Speaking of the Perkin Warbeck conspiracy, Bacon says:

This was a finer counterfeit *stone* than Lambert Simnel; being better done and worn upon greater hands; being graced after with the wearing of a King of France.[4]

And again:

Virtue is like a rich *stone*, best plain *set*.[5]

In Shakespeare, Richmond describes Richard III. as

> A base, foul *stone*, made precious by the foil
> Of England's chair, where he is falsely *set*.[6]

Here Bacon represents Warbeck as a "counterfeit stone;" Shakespeare represents Richard III. as "a foul stone." One is graced by a King's wearing; the other is made precious by being "set" in the royal chair of England.

Bacon says:

Neither the excellence of wit, however great, nor the *die* of experience, however frequently *cast*, can overcome such disadvantages.[7]

And again Bacon says:

Determined to put it to the *hazard*.[8]

Shakespeare says:

> I have set my life upon a *cast*,
> And I will stand the *hazard* of the *die*.[9]

The singular thought that ships are *walls* to the land occurs in Bacon:

---

[1] *Othello*, v, 2.
[2] *History of Henry VII.*
[3] *3d Henry VI.*, iii, 2.
[4] *History of Henry VII.*
[5] *Essay Of Beauty.*
[6] *Richard III.*, v, 3.
[7] Preface to *Great Instauration.*
[8] *Wisdom of the Ancients — Sphynx.*
[9] *Richard III.*, v, 4.

And for the timber of this realm ... it is the matter for our walls, *walls* not only for our houses, but *for our island*.¹

Shakespeare speaks of the sea itself as a wall:

> This precious *stone set* in a silver sea,
> Which serves it in the office of a *wall*.²

Here again we see Bacon's "Virtue is like a rich *stone*, best plain *set*."

And again Shakespeare says:

> When our *sea-walled* garden, the whole land,
> Is full of weeds.³

Bacon says:

> To speak and to *trumpet* out your commendations.⁴

Shakespeare says:

> Will plead like angels, *trumpet*-tongued.⁵

Bacon says:

This *lure* she cast abroad, thinking that this fame and belief ... would draw at one time or other some birds to strike upon it.⁶

Shakespeare employs the same comparison.

Petruchio says of Katharine:

> My falcon now is sharp and passing empty:
> And, till she stoop, she must not be full-gorged,
> For then she never looks upon her *lure*.⁷

Bacon has:

> Whose leisurely and *snail-like pace*.⁸

Shakespeare has:

> *Snail-paced* beggary.⁹

Bacon says:

But touching the reannexing of the duchy of Britain, ... the embassador bare aloof from it *as if it was a rock*.¹⁰

In the play of *Henry VIII.*, Norfolk sees Wolsey coming, and says to Buckingham:

> Lo, where comes that *rock*
> That I advise your shunning.¹¹

---

¹ *Case of Impeachment of Waste.*
² *Richard II.*, ii, 1.
³ *Ibid.*, iii, 4.
⁴ *Letter to Villiers, June 12, 1616.*
⁵ *Macbeth*, i, 7.
⁶ *History of Henry VII.*
⁷ *Taming of the Shrew*, iv, 1.
⁸ *History of Henry VII.*
⁹ *Richard III.*, iv, 3.
¹⁰ *History of Henry VII.*
¹¹ *Henry VIII.*, i, 1.

Both use the tempering of wax as a metaphor.

Bacon:

The King would not take his [Lambert's] life, taking him but as an image of *wax* that others had *tempered* and molded.[1]

Falstaff says:

There I will visit Master Robert Shallow, Esquire. I have him already *tempering* between my finger and my thumb, and shortly I will seal with him.[2]

Bacon says:

With long and continual counterfeiting, and with oft *telling* a *lie*, he was turned by habit almost into the thing he seemed to be; and from a liar to a believer.[3]

Shakespeare says:

> Like one
> Who having unto truth, by *telling* of it,
> Made such a sinner of his memory
> To *credit* his own *lie*.[4]

Bacon says:

Fortune is of a *woman's* nature, and will sooner follow by slighting than by too much wooing.[5]

Shakespeare:

Well, if *fortune* be a *woman*, she's a good wench for this gear.[6]

Bacon:

The Queen had endured a strange *eclipse* by the King's flight.[7]

Shakespeare:

> I take my leave of thee, fair son,
> Born to *eclipse* thy life this afternoon.[8]

Bacon says:

The King saw plainly that the kingdom must again be *put to the stake*, and that he must *fight* for it.[9]

Shakespeare says:

> They have tied me *to the stake*; I cannot fly,
> But, bear-like, I must *fight* the course.[10]

And again:

> Have you not set mine honor *at the stake*?[11]

Again:

> I am tied *to the stake*, and I must stand the course.[12]

---

[1] *History of Henry VII.*
[2] *2d Henry IV*, iv, 3.
[3] *History of Henry VII.*
[4] *Tempest*, i, 2.
[5] *Letter to Villiers*, 1616.
[6] *Merchant of Venice*, ii, 2.
[7] *History of Henry VII.*
[8] *1st Henry VI.*, iv, 5.
[9] *History of Henry VII.*
[10] *Twelfth Night*, iii, 1.
[11] *Macbeth*, v, 7.
[12] *Lear*, iii, 7.

Speaking of the rebellion of Lambert Simnell, Bacon says:

> But their *snow-ball* did not gather as it went.

Shakespeare says:

> If but a dozen French
> Were there in arms, they would be as a call
> To train ten thousand English to their side;
> Or, as a little *snow*, tumbled about,
> Anon becomes a mountain.[1]

∴

Both conceive of truth as something buried deep and only to be gotten out by digging.

Bacon says:

> As we can dig truth out of the mine.[2]

Shakespeare says:

> I will find
> Where truth is hid, though it were hid indeed
> Within the center.[3]

∴

Both compare human life to a pilgrimage.

Bacon:

In this progress and *pilgrimage* of human life.[4]

Shakespeare:

> How brief the life of man
> Runs his erring *pilgrimage*;
> That the stretching of a span
> Buckles in his sum of age.[5]

∴

Both use the comparison of *drowning* to express overwhelmed or lost.

Bacon:

> Truth *drowned* in the depths of obscurity.[6]

Shakespeare says:

> While heart is *drowned* in cares.[7]
>
> I *drowned* these news in tears.[8]

∴

Bacon says:

But men are wanting to themselves in laying this gift of the gods upon the back of a silly, slow-paced ass.[9]

---

[1] *King John*, iv. 4.
[2] *History of Henry VII.*
[3] *Hamlet*, i. 2.
[4] *Wisdom of the Ancients — Sphynx.*
[5] *As You Like It*, iii. 2.
[6] *Wisdom of the Ancients — Prometheus.*
[7] *3d Henry VI.*, iii. 1.
[8] *3d Henry VI.*, ii. 1.
[9] *Wisdom of the Ancients — Prometheus.*

IDENTICAL METAPHORS.

Shakespeare:

> If thou art rich thou art poor,
> For, like an ass, whose back with ingots bows,
> Thou bear'st thy heavy riches but a journey,
> And death unloads thee.[1]

In both we find the strange and unchristian thought that the heavenly powers use men as a means of amusement; and both express it with the same word, *sport*.

Bacon says:

As if it were a custom that no mortal man should be admitted to the table of the gods, but for *sport*.[2]

Shakespeare says:

> As flies to wanton boys are we to the gods:
> They kill us for their *sport*.[3]

Bacon says:

Your life is nothing but a continual *acting* on the *stage*.[4]

While Shakespeare has:

> All the world's a stage,
> And all the men and women merely players.[5]

We find Bacon making this comparison in the address of the Sixth Counselor to the Prince:

I assure your Excellency, their lessons were so cumbersome, as if they would make you a king in a play, who, when one would think he standeth in great majesty and felicity, is troubled to say his part.[6]

And we find Shakespeare making use of the same comparison in sonnet xxiii:

> As an imperfect actor on the stage,
> Who with his fear is put beside his part.

Bacon says:

The maintaining of the laws, which is the *hedge* and fence about the liberty of the subject.[7]

Shakespeare uses the same comparison:

> There's such divinity doth *hedge* a king.[8]

Bacon says:

The place I have in reversion, as it standeth now unto me, is like another

---

[1] *Measure for Measure*, iii, 1.
[2] *Wisdom of the Ancients — Nemesis*.
[3] *Lear*, iv, 1.
[4] Mask for Essex.
[5] *As You Like It*, ii, 7.
[6] *Gesta Grayorum — Life and Works*, vol. i, p. 340.
[7] Charge against St. John.
[8] *Hamlet*, iv, 5.

man's ground reaching upon my house, which may mend my prospect, but doth not fill my barn.[1]

While Shakespeare indulges in a parallel thought:

Falstaff. Of what quality was your love, then?
Ford. Like a fair house built on another man's ground; so that I have lost my edifice by mistaking the place where I erected it.[2]

Bacon says:

Duty, though my state lie buried in the sands, and my favors be cast upon the waters, and my honors be committed to the wind, yet *standeth* surely built upon *the rock*, and hath been and ever shall be unforced and unattempted.[3]

And Shakespeare says:

Yet my duty,
As does a *rock* against the chiding flood,
Should the approach of this wild river break
And *stand* unshaken yours.[4]

Bacon, speaking of popular prophecies, says:

My judgment is that they ought all to be despised and ought but to serve for *winter talk by the fireside*.[5]

Shakespeare says:

Oh, these flaws and starts
(Impostors to true fear) would well become
A woman's *story by a winter's* fire,
Authorized by her grandam.[6]

In the *Advertisement Touching an Holy War*, Bacon uses the comparison of a fan, separating the good from the bad by the wind thereof. Speaking of the extirpation of the Moors of Valentia, one of the parties to the dialogue, Zebedous, says:

Make not hasty judgment, Gamaliel, of that great action, which was as Christ's fan in those countries.

And in *Troilus and Cressida* we have the same comparison:

Distinction, with a broad and powerful fan,
Puffing at all, winnows the light away.[7]

Bacon says:

Though the deaf adder will not hear, yet is he charmed that he doth not hiss.

Shakespeare says in the sonnets:

My adder sense
To critic and to flatterer stoppèd is.

---

[1] *Letter to the Lord Keeper.*
[2] *Merry Wives of Windsor*, ii, 2.
[3] *Letter written for Essex.*
[4] *Henry VIII.*, iii, 2.
[5] *Essay Of Prophecies.*
[6] *Macbeth*, iii, 4.
[7] *Troilus and Cressida* i, 3.

Another very odd and unusual comparison is used by both:

Bacon, referring to the rebellion of Cornwall and the pretensions of Perkin Warbeck to the crown, says:

> But now these *bubbles* began to meet as they use to do upon the top of the water.[1]

And again:

> The action in Ireland was but a *bubble*.[2]

Shakespeare says, speaking of the witches in *Macbeth*:

> The earth hath *bubbles* as the *water* has,
> And these are of them.[3]

And again:

> Seeking the *bubble*, reputation,
> Even in the cannon's mouth.[4]

> And do but blow them to their trials, the *bubbles* are out.[5]

Bacon says:

> But it was ordained that this winding-*ivy* of a Plantagenet should kill the true tree itself.[6]

Shakespeare says:

> That now he was
> The *ivy* which had hid my princely trunk,
> And suck'd my virtue out on 't.[7]

Here it is not a reference merely to the ivy, but to the ivy as the destroyer of the tree, and in both cases applied metaphorically.

Bacon says:

> Upon the first grain of *incense* that was *sacrificed* upon the altar of peace at Bololgn, Perkin was smoked away.[8]

Shakespeare:

> Upon such *sacrifices*, my Cordelia,
> The gods themselves throw *incense*.[9]

Here is a curious parallelism:

Bacon:

> The last words of those that suffer death for religion, like the songs of *dying swans*, do wonderfully work upon the minds of men, and strike and remain a long time in their senses and memories.[10]

---

[1] *History of Henry VII.*
[2] Ibid.
[3] *Macbeth*, i, 3.
[4] *As You Like It*, ii, 7.
[5] *Hamlet*, v, 2.
[6] *History of Henry VII*
[7] *Tempest*, i, 2.
[8] *History of Henry VII.*
[9] *Lear*, v, 3.
[10] *Wisdom of the Ancients — Diomedes.*

Shakespeare says:

> The tongues of *dying* men
> Enforce attention like deep harmony.[1]

And again:

> Then if he lose, he makes a *swan*-like end,
> Fading in music.[2]

And again:

> 'Tis strange that *death* should sing.
> I am the cygnet to this pale, faint *swan*,
> Who chants a doleful hymn to his own *death*.[3]

Here we have in both not only the comparison of the words of dying men to the song of dying swans; but the fact is noted that the words of such men "enforce attention" and "strike and remain a long time" in the minds and memories of men.

In both, the *liming* of bushes to catch birds is used as a metaphor. Bacon says:

> Whatever service I do to her Majesty, it shall be thought to be but *servitium viscatum*, *lime-twigs* and *fetches* to place myself.[4]

Shakespeare says:

> They are *limed* with the *twigs*.[5]
>
> Myself have *limed* a bush for her.[6]
>
> O *limèd* soul, that, struggling to be free.[7]
>
> Like *lime-twigs* set.[8]
>
> Mere *fetches*, the images of revolt.[9]

In both, sickness and death are compared to an arrest by an officer.

Bacon says, alluding to his sickness at Huntingdon:

> This present *arrest* of me by his Divine Majesty.

Shakespeare says:

> This fell sergeant, Death,
> Is strict in his *arrest*.[10]

And in sonnet lxxiv Shakespeare says, speaking of his death:

> But be contented; when that fell *arrest*,
> Without all bail, shall carry me away.

---

[1] *Richard II.*, ii, 1.
[2] *Merchant of Venice*, iii, 2.
[3] *King John*, v, 7.
[4] Letter to F. Greville — *Life and Works*, vol. i, p. 299.
[5] *All's Well that Ends Well*, iii, 5.
[6] *2d Henry VI.*, i, 3.
[7] *Hamlet*, iii, 3.
[8] *2d Henry VI.*, iii, 3.
[9] *Lear*, ii, 4.
[10] *Hamlet*, v, 2.

Bacon speaks of

> The *hour-glass* of one man's *life*.[1]

Shakespeare says:

> Turning the accomplishment of many *years*
> Into an *hour-glass*.[2]

In Bacon we have the odor of flowers compared to music:

The breath of flowers is far sweeter in the air (where it comes and goes like the warbling of music) than in the hand.[3]

Shakespeare reverses the figure, and compares the sounds of music to the odor of flowers:

> That strain again;—it had a dying fall;
> Oh, it came o'er my soul like the sweet south,
> That breathes upon a bank of violets,
> Stealing and giving odor.[4]

Bacon says:

That repose of the mind which only rides *at anchor* upon hope.[5]

Shakespeare says:

> See, Posthumus *anchors* upon Imogen.[6]

> Whilst my invention, hearing not my tongue,
> *Anchors* on Isabel.[7]

Bacon says:

The desire of power in excess caused the *angels to fall*.[8]

Shakespeare says:

> I charge thee fling away ambition:
> By that sin *fell the angels*.[9]

We have in Bacon the following curious expression:

These things did he [King Henry] wisely foresee, . . . whereby all things *fell into his lap* as he desired.[10]

Shakespeare says:

> Now the time is come
> That France must veil her lofty plumèd crest,
> And let her head *fall into England's lap*.[11]

---

[1] *Advancement of Learning*, book ii.
[2] *Henry V.*, prologue.
[3] Essay *Of Gardens*.
[4] *Twelfth Night*, i, 1.
[5] *Med. Sacra—Of Earthly Hope*.
[6] *Cymbeline*, v, 5.
[7] *Measure for Measure*, ii, 4.
[8] Essay *Of Goodness*.
[9] *Henry VIII.*, iii, 2.
[10] *History of Henry VII*.
[11] *Henry VI.*, v, 2.

We all remember Keats' touching epitaph:

> Here lies one whose name was writ in water.

We find the original of this thought in Shakespeare:

> Noble madam,
> Men's evil manners live in brass; their virtues
> We write in water.[1]

And if we follow back the pedigree of the thought we find it in Bacon's

> High treason is not *written in ice*.[2]

And this reappears in Shakespeare thus:

> This weak impress of love is as a figure
> *Trench'd in ice*, which with an hour's heat
> *Dissolves to water*, and does lose his form.[3]

∴

Bacon:

Your *beadsman* therefore addresseth himself to your Majesty.[4]

Shakespeare:

> Commend thy grievance to my holy prayers,
> For I will be thy *beadsman*, Valentine.[5]

∴

In the following we have a striking parallelism. Bacon says:

> In this *theater* of man's life it is reserved, etc.[6]

Shakespeare says:

> This wide and universal *theater*
> Presents more woeful pageants than the scene
> Wherein we play.[7]

∴

And we have the same thought presented in another form. Bacon says:

> Your life is nothing but a continual *acting* upon a *stage*.[8]

Shakespeare says:

> All the world's a *stage*,
> And all the men and women merely players.[9]

∴

Bacon says:

For this giant *bestrideth the sea;* and I would take and snare him by the foot on this side.[10]

---

[1] *Henry VIII.*, iv, 2.
[2] *Coll. Sent.*
[3] *Two Gentlemen of Verona*, iii, 2.
[4] Letter to the King.
[5] *Two Gentlemen of Verona*, i, 1.
[6] *Advancement of Learning.*
[7] *As You Like It*, ii, 6.
[8] Mask.
[9] *As You Like It*, ii, 7.
[10] Duels.

Shakespeare says:

> His legs *bestrid the ocean*.[1]

And again:

> Why, man, he doth *bestride the narrow world*
> Like a Colossus.[2]

Bacon says:

Many were glad that these *fears* and uncertainties were *overblown*, and that the die was cast.[3]

Shakespeare says:

> The ague-fit of *fear* is *overblown*.[4]

Again:

> At 'scapes and perils *overblown*.[5]

Bacon says:

Religion, justice, counsel and treasure are the four *pillars* of *government*.[6]

Shakespeare says:

> Brave peers of England, *pillars* of the *state*.[7]

> The triple *pillar* of the world.[8]

> These shoulders, these ruined *pillars*.[9]

> I charge you by the law,
> Whereof you are a well-deserving *pillar*.[10]

The seeds of plants furnish a favorite subject of comparison with both writers.

Bacon speaks of ideas that

> Cast their *seeds* in the minds of others.[11]

He also refers to

> The secret *seeds* of diseases.[12]

Again he says:

There has been covered in my mind a long time a *seed* of affection and zeal toward your Lordship.[13]

Shakespeare says:

> There is a history in all men's lives
> Figuring the nature of the times deceased;

---

[1] *Antony and Cleopatra*, v. 2.
[2] *Julius Cæsar*, i. 2.
[3] Begin. *History of Great Britain*.
[4] *Richard II.*, iii. 2.
[5] *Taming of the Shrew*, v. 2.
[6] Essay *Of Seditions*.
[7] *2d Henry VI.*, i. 1.
[8] *Antony and Cleopatra*, i. 1.
[9] *Henry VIII.*, iii. 2.
[10] *Merchant of Venice*, iv. 1.
[11] *Advancement of Learning*, book I.
[12] Essay *Of Despatch*.
[13] Letter to Earl of Northumberland.

> The which observed, a man may prophesy,
> With a near aim, of the main chance of things
> As yet to come to life; which in their *seeds*
> And weak beginnings lie intreasured.[1]

He also speaks of

> The *seed* of honor.[2]
> The *seeds* of time.[3]

Bacon compares himself to a torch:

I shall, perhaps, before my death have rendered the age a light unto posterity, by kindling this new *torch* amid the darkness of philosophy.[4]

Again he says:

Matters should receive success by combat and emulation, and *not hang upon any one man's sparkling and shaking torch*.[5]

Shakespeare says:

> Heaven doth with us as we with *torches* do,
> Not light them for themselves; for if our virtues
> Did not go forth of us, 'twere all alike
> As if we had them not.[6]

Speaking of Fortune, Shakespeare says:

> The wise and fool, the artist and unread,
> The hard and soft, seem all affin'd and kin:
> But in the wind and tempest of her frown,
> Distinction, with a broad and powerful *fan*,
> Puffing at all, winnows the light away;
> And what hath mass or matter, by itself
> Lies, rich in virtue and *unmingled*.[7]

And in Bacon we have the same comparison of the winnowing fan separating the light from the heavy. He says, speaking of church matters:

And what are *mingled* but as the chaff and the corn, which need but a *fan* to sift and sever them.[8]

Shakespeare says:

> Be thou as *lightning* in the eyes of France.[9]

Bacon, describing Essex' expedition against Cadiz, said:

This journey was like *lightning*. For in the space of fourteen hours the King of Spain's navy was destroyed and the town of Cales taken.[10]

---

[1] *2d Henry IV.*, iii, 1.
[2] *Merchant of Venice*, ii, 9.
[3] *Macbeth*, i, 3.
[4] Letter to King James, prefaced to *Great Instauration*.
[5] *Wisdom of the Ancients — Prometheus.*
[6] *Measure for Measure*, i, 1.
[7] *Troilus and Cressida*, i, 3.
[8] *The Pacification of the Church.*
[9] *King John*, i, 1.
[10] *Consid. touching War with Spain.*

Bacon called one of his great philosophical works

The scaling-ladder of the intelligence.

Shakespeare has:

> Northumberland, thou *ladder*, wherewithal
> The mounting Bolingbroke ascends my throne.[1]

Bacon says:

It is the wisdom of *crocodiles* that *shed tears* when they would devour.[2]

Shakespeare says:

> Gloster's show
> Beguiles him, as the *mournful crocodile*
> With sorrow snares relenting passengers.[3]

Says Bacon:

> The axe should be put to the root of the tree.[4]

Says Shakespeare:

> We set the axe to thy usurping root.[5]

But the field of labor in this direction is simply boundless. One whose memory is stored with the expressions found in the two sets of writings cannot open either one without being vividly reminded of the other. Both writers, if we are to consider them, for the sake of argument, as two persons, thought in the same way; the cast of mind in each was figurative and metaphorical; both vivified the driest details with the electricity of the imagination, weaving it through them like lightning among the clouds; and each, as I have shown, was very much in the habit of repeating himself, and thus reiterated the same figures of speech time and again.

---

[1] *Richard II.*, v, 1.
[2] *2d Henry VI.*, iii, 1.
[3] Essay *Of Wisdom for a Man's Self.*
[4] Proceedings at York House.
[5] *3d Henry VI.*, ii, 2.

CHAPTER III.

IDENTICAL OPINIONS.

A plague of opinion! A man may wear it on both sides like a leather jerkin.
Troilus and Cressida, iii, 3.

WE come now to another group of parallelisms—those of thoughts, opinions or beliefs, where the identity is not in the expression, but in the underlying conception.

We find that both writers had great purposes or intentions of working for immortality; the one figuring his works as "banks or mounts," great earthworks, as it were; the other as great foundations or "bases" on which the future might build.

Bacon says:

I resolved to spend my time wholly in writing, and to put forth that poor talent or half talent, or what it is, that God hath given me, not, as heretofore, to particular exchanges, but to *banks or mounts of perpetuity*, which will not break.[1]

Shakespeare says:

> Were it aught to me I bore the canopy,
>   With my extern the outward honoring,
> Or *laid great bases for eternity*,
>   Which prove more short than waste or ruining.[2]

Here the same idea runs through both expressions—"banks of perpetuity" and "bases for eternity."

Both believed that a wise government should be omniscient.

Bacon says:

So unto princes and states, especially towards wise senators and councils, the natures and dispositions of the people, their conditions and necessities, their factions and combinations, their animosities and discontents, ought to be, in regard to the variety of their intelligence, the wisdom of their observations and the height of their station where they keep sentinel, in great part clear and transparent.[3]

Shakespeare says:

> The providence that's in a watchful state
> Knows almost every grain of Plutus' gold;
> Finds bottom in the uncomprehensive deeps;

[1] *Touching a Holy War.*   [2] *Sonnet cxxv.*   [3] *Advancement of Learning,* book ii.

> Keeps place with thought, and, almost like the gods,
> Does thoughts unveil in their dumb cradles.
> There is a mystery (with whom relation
> Durst never meddle) in the soul of state;
> Which hath an operation more divine
> Than breath, or pen, can give expression to.[1]

Both had noted that envy eats into the spirits and the very body of a man.

Bacon says:

Love and envy do make a man pine, which other affections do not, because they are not so continual.[2]

Such men in other men's calamities are, as it were, in season, and are ever on the loading part.[3]

Envy is the worst of all passions, and feedeth upon the spirits, and they again upon the body.[4]

Shakespeare says:

> Yond' Cassius has a lean and hungry look: . . .
> Such men as he be never at heart's ease
> Whiles they behold a greater than themselves.[5]

Both speak of hope as a medicine of the mind. Bacon says:

> To make *hope* the antidote of human diseases.[6]

And again:

And as Aristotle saith, "That young men may be happy but not otherwise but by *hope*."[7]

Shakespeare says:

> The miserable have no other medicine
> But only *hope*.[8]

Both had observed the shriveling of parchment in heat. Bacon says:

The parts of wood split and contract, *skins* become shriveled, and not only that, but if the spirit be emitted suddenly by the heat of the fire, become so hastily contracted as to twist and roll themselves up.[9]

Shakespeare uses the same fact as the basis of a striking comparison, as to King John, dying of poison:

> There is so hot a summer in my bosom,
> That all my bowels crumble up to dust:
> I am a scribbled form, drawn with a pen
> Upon a *parchment;* and against this fire
> Do I shrink up.[10]

---

[1] *Troilus and Cressida*, iii, 3.
[2] Essay *Of Envy*.
[3] Essay *Of Goodness*.
[4] *History of Life and Death*.
[5] *Julius Cæsar*, i, 2.
[6] *Med. Sacræ*.
[7] *Advancement of Learning*.
[8] *Measure for Measure*, iii, 1.
[9] *Novum Organum*, book ii.
[10] *King John*, v, 7.

We find both dwelling upon the fact that a shrewd mind will turn even disadvantages to use. Bacon says:

> *Excellent wits will make use of every little thing.*[1]

Falstaff says:

It is no matter if I do halt; I have the wars for my color, and my pension shall seem the more reasonable. *A good wit will make use of anything.* I will turn diseases to commodity.[2]

∴

Both had observed that sounds are heard better at night than by day. Bacon says:

Sounds are better heard, and farther off, in the evening or in the *night*, than at the noon or in the day. . . . But when the air is more thick, as in the night, the sound spendeth and spreadeth. As for the night, it is true also that the general *silence* helpeth.[3]

Shakespeare says:

> Soft *stillness* and the *night*
> Become the touches of sweet harmony.[4]

And again:

> *Nerissa.* It is your music, madam, of the house.
> *Portia.* Nothing is good, I see, without respect;
> Methinks it sounds much sweeter than by day.[5]

∴

In the following it appears that the same observation had occurred to both in another instance.

Bacon says:

Anger suppressed is also a kind of vexation, and causeth the spirit to feed upon the juices of the body; but let loose and breaking forth it helpeth.[6]

Shakespeare says:

> The grief that will not speak
> Whispers the o'erfraught heart and bids it break.[7]

And again:

> The heart hath treble wrong
> When it is barred the aidance of the tongue.[8]

∴

Both allude to the same curious belief. Bacon says:

The heavens turn about in a most rapid motion, without noise to us perceived; though in some dreams they have been said to make an excellent music.[9]

---

[1] Bacon's letter to Sir Foulke Greville, written in the name of the Earl of Essex— *Life and Works*, vol. ii, p. 23.
[2] 2d *Henry IV.*, i, 2.
[3] *Natural History*, cent. ii. § 143.
[4] *Merchant of Venice*, v, 1.
[5] Ibid.
[6] *History of Life and Death.*
[7] *Macbeth*, iv, 3.
[8] *Poems.*
[9] *Natural History* cent. ii.

Shakespeare idealizes dreams thus:

> There's not the smallest orb which thou beholdest
> But in his motion like an angel sings,
> Still quiring to the young-eyed cherubims.[1]

And here we find both drawing the same distinction between the approbation of the wise and the foolish.

Hamlet says to the players:

> Now this, overdone, or come tardy off, though it make the unskillful laugh, cannot but make the judicious grieve; the censure of the which one must, in your allowance, o'er-weigh a whole theater of others.[2]

Bacon says:

> So it may be said of ostentation, "Boldly sound your own praises, and some of it will stick." It will stick in the more ignorant and the populace, though men of wisdom may smile at it; and the reputation won with many will amply countervail the disdain of a few.[3]

This conclusion is, of course, ironical.

Bacon compares the earth to an ant-hill, with the men,

> Like ants, *crawling up and down*. Some carry corn and some carry their young, and some go empty, and all — to and fro — a little heap of *dust*.[4]

And we find the same thought in *Hamlet:*

> What should such fellows as I do *crawling* between earth and heaven.[5]

Here the word *crawling* expresses the thought of something vermin-like, insect-like, and the comparison of the whole ant-hill of the crawling world to "a little heap of *dust*" was in Bacon's mind when he wrote:

> What a piece of work is man! . . . And yet to me what is this quintessence of *dust?*

Both had noticed the servility of the creatures that fawn on power. Bacon says:

> Such instruments as are never failing about princes, which spy into their humors and conceits and second them; and not only second them, but in seconding increase them; yea, and many times without their knowledge pursue them farther than themselves would.[6]

Shakespeare puts these words into the mouth of King John:

> It is the curse of kings to be attended
> By slaves that take their humor for a warrant
> To break within the bloody house of life;

---

[1] *Merchant of Venice*, v, 1.
[2] *Hamlet*, iii, 2.
[3] *De Augmentis*, book viii, p. 281.
[4] *Advancement of Learning*, book 2.
[5] *Hamlet*, iii, 1.
[6] Letter to Essex, Oct. 4, 1596.

> And, on the winking of authority,
> To understand a law; to know the meaning
> Of dangerous majesty, when, perchance, it frowns
> More upon humor than advised respect.[1]

Here the same thought is followed out to the same afterthought: that the creature exceeds the purpose of the king, in his superserviceable zeal.

Bacon says:

He prays and labors for that which he knows he shall be no less happy without; ... he believes his prayers are heard, even when they are denied, and gives thanks for that which he prays against.[2]

Shakespeare says:

> We, ignorant of ourselves,
> Beg often our own harm, which the wise powers
> Deny us for our good; so find we profit
> By losing of our prayers.[3]

The Rev. H. L. Singleton, of Maryland, calls my attention to the following parallelism.

Bacon says:

And, therefore, it is no wonder that art hath not the power to conquer nature, and by pact or law of conquest to kill her; but on the contrary, it turns out that art becomes subject to nature, and yields obedience as wife to husband.[4]

And we find in Shakespeare the same philosophy that nature is superior to the very art which seeks to change her. He says:

> *Perdita.* For I have heard it said,
> There is an art which, in their piedness, shares
> With great creating nature.
> *Polixenes.* Say there be;
> Yet nature is made better by no mean
> But nature makes that mean; so, over that art
> Which, you say, adds to nature, is an art
> That nature makes.[5]

Again Shakespeare says:

> Nature's above art.[6]

Compare this with Bacon's expression, above:

> Art becomes subject to nature.

And Bacon says in *The New Atlantis:*

We make by art, in the same orchards and gardens, trees and flowers to come

---

[1] *King John,* iv, 2.
[2] *Character of a Believing Christian,* § 22.
[3] *Antony and Cleopatra.*
[4] *Atalanta or Gain.*
[5] *Winter's Tale,* iv, 3.
[6] *Lear,* iv, 6.

earlier or later than their seasons, and to come up and bear more speedily than by their natural course they do. We make them also by their art *greater than their nature*.[1]

This is the same thought that we find in the verses above quoted:

> That art
> Which, you say, *adds to nature*.

Mr. J. T. Cobb calls attention to the following parallelism of thought. In book ii, *Advancement of Learning*, Bacon says:

These *three*, as in the body so in the mind, seldom *meet* and commonly sever; . . . and sometimes two of them meet, and rarely all three.[2]

While in the Shakespeare sonnets we have:

> Three themes in one, which wondrous scope affords,
> Fair, kind and true, have often lived alone,
> Which *three*, till now, never did meet in one.[3]

Both regarded rather the fact than the expression of it.

Bacon says:

Here, therefore, is the first distemper of learning, when men study *words*, and not matter.[4]

We seem to hear Hamlet's mocking utterance:

> What read you, my lord?
> Words, words, words.[5]

Miss Delia Bacon noted that both held the same view as to the dependence of men on events.

Shakespeare says:

> So our virtues
> Lie in the *interpretation* of the *times*.[6]

While Bacon says:

> The *times*, in many cases, give great light to true *interpretations*.

Mrs. Pott calls attention to the following parallelism. In Bacon's *Promus*, No. 972, we have:

> Always *let losers* have their words.

And Shakespeare echoes this as follows:

> *Losers* will have *leave*
> To ease their stomachs with *their* bitter *words*.[7]

---

[1] *New Atlantis.*
[2] 1 Montagu, p. 28.
[3] Sonnet cv.
[4] *Advancement of Learning*, book i.
[5] *Hamlet*, ii, 2.
[6] *Coriolanus*, iv, 7.
[7] *Titus Andronicus*, iii, 1.

Also:
> And well such *losers* may have *leave* to speak.[1]

Bacon says:

> For protestations, and professions, and apologies, I never found them very fortunate; but they rather increase suspicion than clear it.[2]

In Shakespeare we have:

> *Hamlet.* Madam, how like you this play?
> *Queen.* The lady protests too much, methinks.[3]

Both even used and *believed in the same drug.*

Bacon says:

> For opening, I commend beads or pieces of *carduus benedictus*.[4]

In *Much Ado about Nothing* we have:

> Get you some of this distilled *carduus benedictus* and lay it to your heart, it is the only thing for a qualm.[5]

Both believed that murders were brought to light by the operation of God. Bacon speaks of the belief in the wounds of the murdered man bleeding afresh at the approach of the murderer, and says:

> It may be that this participateth of a miracle, by God's judgment, *who usually bringeth murders to light.*

Macbeth says:

> It will have blood; they say, blood will have blood;
> Stones have been known to move and trees to speak
> Augurs, and understood relations have
> By magot-pies, and choughs and rooks, brought forth
> The secretest man of blood.[6]

Bacon speaks of

> The instant occasion *flying away irreconcilably.*[7]

Shakespeare says:

> The *flighty* purpose *never is o'ertook*
> Unless the act go with it.[8]

Church speaks of Bacon's

> Great idea of the reality and boundless worth of knowledge . . . which had taken possession of his whole nature.[9]

---

[1] 2d *Henry VI.*, iii, 1.
[2] Speech about Undertakers.
[3] *Hamlet*, iii, 2.
[4] *Natural History*, cent. x, § 963.
[5] *Much Ado about Nothing*, iii, 4.
[6] *Macbeth*, iii, 4.
[7] Speech as Lord Chancellor.
[8] *Macbeth*, iv, 1.
[9] *Bacon*, p. 214.

Shakespeare says:

> There is no darkness but ignorance.[1]
>
> Oh, thou monster, ignorance![2]

Bacon says:

> There is no prison to the prison of the thoughts.[3]

Shakespeare has the same thought:

Hamlet. Denmark's a prison.
Rosencrautz. Then is the world one.
Ham. A goodly one; in which there are many confines, wards and dungeons; Denmark being one of the worst.
Ros. We think not so, my lord.
Ham. Why, then, 'tis none to you; for there is nothing either good or bad but thinking makes it so: to me it is a prison.[4]

As this book is going through the press Mr. James T. Cobb calls my attention to the following parallelism.

Bacon, in the *Novum Organum*, referring to the effect of opiates, says:

> The same opiates, when taken in moderation, do strengthen the spirits, render them more robust, and check the useless and *inflammatory* motion.[5]

Falstaff, describing the effect of wine on the system, says, speaking of the "demure boys," like Prince John:

> They are generally fools and cowards; which some of us should be, too, but for *inflammation*.[6]

This word *inflammation* is uncommon; this is the only occasion on which it appears in the Plays.

Shakespeare speaks of

> Sermons in stones and *good* in *everything*.

Bacon says:

> There is found in *every thing* a double nature of *good*.[7]

And here we have a curious parallelism. Bacon says:

> It is more than a philosopher morally can digest; but, without any such high conceit, I esteem it like the pulling out of an aching tooth, which I remember, when I was a child and had little *philosophy*, I was glad of when it was done.[8]

---

[1] *Twelfth Night*, iv, 2.
[2] *Love's Labor Lost*, iv, 2.
[3] Mask for Earl of Essex.
[4] *Hamlet*, ii, 2.
[5] *Novum Organum*, book ii.
[6] *2d Henry IV.*, iv, 2.
[7] *Advancement of Learning*, book ii.
[8] Letter to Essex.

While Shakespeare links the philosopher and the tooth-ache together thus:

> For there was never yet *philosopher*
> That could endure the *tooth-ache* patiently:
> However, they have writ the style of gods,
> And made a pish at chance and sufferance.[1]

The various modes in which fortunes are obtained had occurred to both writers. Bacon says:

Fortunes are not obtained without all this ado; for I know they come tumbling into some men's laps: and a number obtain good fortunes by diligence in a plain way.[2]

Shakespeare says:

Some men are born great; some achieve greatness; and some have greatness thrust upon them.[3]

That is to say, greatness "tumbles into their laps."

And to both had come the thought that while fortune gave with one hand she stinted with the other.

Bacon says:

It is easy to observe that many have strength of wit and courage, but have neither help from perturbations, nor any beauty or decency in their doings; some again have an elegancy and fineness of carriage, which have neither soundness of honesty nor substance of sufficiency; and some, again, have honest and reformed minds and can neither become themselves or manage business; and sometimes two of them meet, and rarely all three.[4]

Shakespeare says:

> Will fortune never come with both hands full? . . .
> She either gives a stomach and no food—
> Such are the poor in health; or else a feast,
> And takes away the stomach— such are the rich
> That have abundance and enjoy it not.[5]

Bacon says:

It is not good to look too long upon these turning wheels of vicissitude, lest we become giddy.[6]

Shakespeare has:

> *Fortune*, good-night; smile again,
> *Turn* thy *wheel*.[7]

Again:

> *Giddy Fortune's* furious fickle *wheel*.[8]

---

[1] *Much Ado about Nothing*, v. i.
[2] *Advancement of Learning*, book ii.
[3] *Twelfth Night*, iii. 5.
[4] *Advancement of Learning*, book ii.
[5] 2d *Henry IV.*, iv. 4.
[6] *History of Life and Death*.
[7] *Lear*, ii. 2.
[8] *Henry V*, iii. 6.

Again:

> Consider it not so deeply;
> That way madness lies.[1]

We find that both writers realized the wonderfully complex character of the human creature.

Bacon says:

> Of all things comprehended within the compass of the universe, man is a thing most mixed and compounded, insomuch that he was well termed by the ancients *a little world*. . . . It is furnished with most *admirable* virtues and *faculties*.[2]

And again:

> Of all the substances which nature hath produced, man's body is most extremely compounded: . . . in his mansion, sleep, exercise, passions, man hath *infinite variations*.[3]

The Plays were written, in part, to illustrate the characteristics of that wonderfully compounded creature, man. And in them we find:

> What a piece of work is man! How noble in reason! How *infinite* in *faculty*! In form and moving, how express and *admirable*! In action, how like an angel! In apprehension how like a god! The beauty of the world! The paragon of animals![4]

These are the *admirable faculties* referred to by Bacon; and "the little world" of the ancients, the *microcosm*, reappears in Shakespeare:

> If you see this in the map of my *microcosm*, follows it that I am known well enough too?[5]

And in the play of *Richard II.* we find the very expression, "little world," applied to the human being:

> My brain I'll prove the female to my soul;
> My soul the father: and these two beget
> A generation of still-breeding thoughts,
> And these same thoughts people *this little world*;
> In humors like the people of this world.[6]

Bacon has the following thought:

> No doubt in him, as in all men, and most of all in kings, his fortune wrought upon his nature, and his nature upon his fortune.[7]

The same thought occurs in Shakespeare:

> I grow to what I work in,
> Like the dyer's hand.[8]

[1] *Macbeth*, ii. ...
[2] *Wisdom of the Ancients — Prometheus*.
[3] *Advancement of Learning*, book ii.
[4] *Hamlet*, ii. 2.
[5] *Coriolanus*, ii. 1.
[6] *Richard II.*, v. 1.
[7] *History of Henry VII.*
[8] *Sonnet*.

And both concurred in another curious belief.

Bacon says:

And therefore whatsoever want a man hath, he must see that he pretend the virtue that shadoweth it.[1]

Shakespeare says:

> Assume a virtue if you have it not.[2]

∴

Bacon says:

> Envy makes greatness the mark and accusation the game.

Shakespeare says:

> That thou art blamed shall not be thy defect,
> For slander's mark was ever yet the fair;
> The ornament of beauty is suspect,
> A crow that flies in heaven's sweetest air.[3]

Something of the same thought is found in Bacon's *Promus*, No. 41:

Dat veniam corvis vexat censura columbas. (Censure pardons crows, but bears hard on doves.)

"Slander's mark was ever yet the fair." The beautiful dove falls readily under suspicion; but censure pardons "the crow that flies in heaven's sweetest air."

∴

Bacon says:

Health consisteth in an unmovable constancy and a freedom from passions, which are indeed *the sicknesses of the mind*.[4]

Macbeth asks the physician:

> Canst thou not minister to a *mind diseased?*[5]

∴

Bacon says:

> For reverence is that wherewith princes are girt from God.[6]

And again:

For God hath imprinted such a majesty in the face of a prince that no private man dare approach the person of his sovereign with a traitorous intent.[7]

Shakespeare surrounds the king with a hedge — a divine hedge — which girts him:

> There's such divinity doth hedge a king,
> That treason can but peep to what it would,
> Acts little of his will.[8]

∴

[1] *Advancement of Learning*, book ii.
[2] *Hamlet*, iii, 4.
[3] Sonnet lxx.
[4] Letter to Earl of Rutland, written in the name of the Earl of Essex.
[5] *Macbeth*, v, 3.
[6] Essay *Of Seditions*.
[7] Speech on the Trial of Essex.
[8] *Hamlet*, iv, 5.

Says Bacon:

> This princess having the spirit of a man and malice of a woman.[1]

Shakespeare has a similar antithesis:

> I have a man's mind, but a woman's might.[2]

The indestructibility of thought as compared with the temporary nature of material things had occurred to both. Bacon says:

> For have not the verses of Homer continued twenty-five hundred years, without the loss of a syllable or a letter, during which time infinite palaces, temples, castles, cities have been decayed and demolished.[3]

And Shakespeare, in a magnificent burst of egotism, possible only under a mask, cries out:

> Not marble,
> Nor the gilded monuments of princes,
> Shall outlive this powerful rhyme.[4]

Bacon has this thought:

> For opportunity makes the thief.[5]

Shakespeare says:

> And even thence thou wilt be stolen, I fear,
> For truth proves thievish for a prize so dear.[6]

And again:

> Rich preys make true men thieves.[7]

And again:

> How oft the sight of means to do ill deeds
> Makes ill deeds done.[8]

Bacon tells us that King Henry VII. sent his commissioners to inspect the Queen of Naples with a view to matrimony, and desired them

> To report as to her "complexion, favor, feature, stature, health, age, customs, behavior, condition and estate," as if he *meant to find all things in one woman*.[9]

And in Shakespeare we find Benedick soliloquizing:

> One woman is fair; yet I am well: another is wise; yet I am well: another virtuous; yet I am well; *but till all graces be in one woman*, one woman shall not come in my grace.[10]

---

[1] *History of Henry VII.*
[2] *Julius Cæsar*, ii, 4.
[3] *Advancement of Learning*, book i.
[4] Sonnet.
[5] Letter to Essex, 1598.
[6] Sonnet xlviii.
[7] *Venus and Adonis.*
[8] *King John*, iv, 2.
[9] *History of Henry VII.*
[10] *Much Ado about Nothing*, ii, 2.

Bacon says:

> The corruption of the best things is the worst.[1]

Shakespeare has the same thought:

> Lilies that fester smell far worse than weeds.[2]

∴

Bacon speaks of

The mind of man drawn over and clouded with the sable pavilion of the body.[3]

And Bacon also says:

So differing a *harmony* there is between the spirit of man and the spirit of nature.[4]

While Shakespeare says:

> Such *harmony* is in mortal souls;
> But, whilst this muddy vesture of decay
> Doth grossly close it in, we cannot hear it.[5]

∴

Bacon says:

> *A king is a* mortal *god* on *earth*.[6]

Shakespeare says:

> True hope is swift, and flies with swallow's wings,
> *Kings it makes gods*, and meaner creatures kings.[7]

Again:

> Kings are *earth's gods;* in vice their law's their will.[8]

Again:

> He is their god; he leads them like a thing
> Made by some other deity than Nature.[9]

∴

Bacon says:

> A beautiful face is a silent *commendation*.[10]

Shakespeare says:

> The beauty that is borne here in the face
> The bearer knows not, but *commends* itself
> To others' eyes.[11]

∴

We find a curious parallelism in the following. Bacon says:

For we die daily; and as others have given place to us, so we must in the end give way to others.[10]

---

[1] *History of Henry VII.*
[2] Sonnet.
[3] *Advancement of Learning*, book ii.
[4] *New Atlantis.*
[5] *Merchant of Venice*, v, 1.
[6] Essay *Of a King.*
[7] *Richard III.*, v, 2.
[10] Essay *Of Death.*
[8] *Pericles*, i, 1.
[9] *Coriolanus*, iv, 6.
[10] *Orna. Rati.*
[11] *Troilus and Cressida*, iii, 3.

Shakespeare puts into the mouth of Orlando these words:

Only in the world I fill up a place, which may be better supplied when I have made it empty.[1]

Bacon says:

The expectation [of death] brings terror, and that exceeds the evil.[2]

Shakespeare says:

Dost thou fear to die?
The sense of death is most in apprehension.[3]

Bacon says:

Art thou drowned in security? Then say thou art perfectly dead.

Shakespeare says:

You all know, security
Is mortal's chiefest enemy.[4]

Hamlet discusses the length of time a body will last in the earth. And Bacon had studied the same curious subject, and he notes the fact that

In churchyards where they bury much, the earth will consume the corpse in far shorter time than other earth will.[5]

Bacon says:

The green caterpillar breedeth in the inward parts of roses, especially not blown, where the dew sticketh.[6]

Shakespeare says:

But let concealment, like a worm i' the bud,
Feed on her damask cheek.[7]

H. L. Haydel, of St. Louis, calls my attention to the following parallelism noted by Rev. Henry N. Hudson, in his note upon a passage in *Hamlet*, i, 4.

Mr. Hudson gives the passage, in his edition of the Plays, as follows:

Their virtues else — be they as pure as grace,
As infinite as man may undergo —
Shall in the general censure take corruption
From that particular fault; the dram of leaven
Doth all the noble substance of 'em sour
To his own scandal.

Hudson says in his foot-note:

The meaning is that the dram of leaven sours all the noble substance of their

---

[1] *As You Like It*, i, . [4] *Macbeth*, iii, 5. [6] Ibid, § 728
[2] *Essay Of Death*. [5] *Natural History*, § 330. [7] *Twelfth Night*, ii, 4
[3] *Measure for Measure*, iii, 1.

virtues. . . . And so in Bacon's *History of Henry VII.*: "And as a little leaven of new distaste doth commonly sour the whole lump of former merits."

Here again we find the critics reading the obscure passages in Shakespeare by the light of Bacon's utterances.

∴

Both writers felt a profound contempt for the authority of books alone. In Shakespeare this was most remarkable. A mere poet, with no new philosophy to introduce, seeking in the writings of preceding ages only for the beautiful, could have had no motive for thus attacking existing opinions. And yet we find him saying:

> Study is like the heavens' glorious sun,
>   That will not be deep-searched with saucy looks;
> Small have continual plodders ever won,
>   Save *base authority*, from others' books.[1]

In Bacon we find the same opinion and the reason for it. His whole life was a protest against the accepted conclusions of his age; his system could only rise upon the overthrow of that of Aristotle. He protested against

> The first distemper of learning, when men study words and not matter.[2]

Again he says:

> In the universities of Europe men learn nothing but to believe; first to believe that others know that which they know not; and after, themselves to believe that they know that which they know not.[3]

And again:

> Are we richer by one poor invention by reason of all the learning that hath been these many hundred years.[4]

And again he says:

> Neither let him embrace the license of contradicting or *the servitude of authority*.[5]

This is the very expression of Shakespeare:

> Small have continual plodders ever won,
>   Save *base authority*.

And again Bacon says:

> To make judgment wholly by their rules [studies] is the humor of a scholar. Crafty men contemn them, simple men admire them, and wise men use them.

---

[1] *Love's Labor Lost*, i, 1.
[2] *Advancement of Learning*, book i.
[3] *In Praise of Knowledge*.
[4] Ibid.
[5] *Interpretation of Nature*.
[6] *Essay Of Studies*.

And Shakespeare says:

> Why universal plodding prisons up
> The nimble spirits in the arteries.[1]

And in this connection we have the following opinion of Bacon:

It seems to me that Pygmalion's frenzy is a good emblem or portraiture of this vanity, for *words* are but the images of matter; and, except they have life of reason and invention, to fall in love with them is all one to fall in love with a picture.

We hear the echo of this thought in Hamlet's contemptuous iteration:

> *Words, words, words.*

And Bacon's very thought is found again in the following:

> *Idle words*, servants to shallow fools,
> Unprofitable sounds, weak arbitrators!
> Busy yourselves in skull-contending schools;
> Debate, where leisure serves, with dull debaters.[2]

Both writers regarded the lusts or passions of the mind with contempt, and perceived their unsatisfying nature. Bacon says:

And they all know, who have paid dear for serving and obeying their lusts, that whether it be honor, or riches, or delight, or glory, or knowledge, or anything else which they seek after, yet are they but things cast off, and by divers men in all ages, after experience had utterly rejected and loathed.[3]

And we find the same thought in Shakespeare:

> The expense of spirit in a waste of shame
> Is lust in action; and till action, lust
> Is perjured, murderous, bloody, full of blame,
> Savage, extreme, rude, cruel, not to trust;
> Enjoyed no sooner but despisèd straight;
> Past reason hunted; and no sooner had,
> Past reason hated, as a swallowed bait,
> On purpose laid to make the taker mad:
> Mad in pursuit and in possession so;
> Had, having, and in quest to have, extreme;
> A bliss in proof — and proved a very woe;
> Before, a joy proposed; behind, a dream.[4]

And again:

If the balance of our lives had not one scale of reason to poise another of sensuality, the blood and baseness of our natures would conduct us to most preposterous conclusions.[5]

Both believed that the influences of evil were more persistent in the world than those of goodness.

---

[1] *Love's Labor Lost*, iv, 3. [2] *Poems.* [3] *Wisdom of the Ancients—Dionysius.*
[4] Sonnet cxxix. [5] *Othello*, i, 3.

Bacon says:

Those that bring honor into their family are commonly more worthy than most that succeed; ... for ill to man's nature (as it stands perverted) hath a natural motion *strongest in continuance*; but good, as a forced motion, strongest at first.[1]

Shakespeare says:

> The evil that men do lives after them,
> The good is oft interrèd with their bones.[2]

And again:

> Men's evil manners live in brass; their virtues
> We write in water.[3]

⁂

Neither writer assented to the belief of the age (since by scientific tests made a verity) that the condition of the patient's health was shown by the appearance of his urine.

Bacon says:

Those advertisements which your Lordship imputed to me I hold to be no more certain to make judgment upon than a patient's water to a physician.[4]

In Shakespeare we find the following:

Falstaff. Sirrah, you giant, what says the doctor to my water?
Page. He said, sir, the water itself was a good, healthy water; but for the party that owned it, he might have more diseases than he knew for.

⁂

Both believed that too long a continuance of peace caused the people to degenerate. Bacon argued that, as the body of man could not remain in health without exercise, the body of a state needed exercise also in the shape of foreign wars. He says:

If it seem strange that I account no state flourishing but that which hath neither civil wars nor too *long peace*, I answer that politic bodies are like our natural bodies, and must as well have some natural exercise to *spend their humors*, as to be kept from too violent or continual outrages which spend their best spirits.[5]

And we find the same thought, of the necessity of expelling the *humors* of the body by the exercise of war, in Shakespeare:

> This is the *imposthume* of much *wealth and peace*,
> That inward breaks, and shows no cause without
> Why the man dies.[6]

Again Bacon says:

This want of learning hath been in good countries ruined by civil wars, or in states corrupted through *wealth or too great length of peace*.[7]

---

[1] Essay.
[2] *Julius Cæsar*, iii, 2.
[3] *Henry VIII.*, iv, 2.
[4] Letter to Essex concerning Earl of Tyrone.
[5] Letter to the Earl of Rutland, written in the name of the Earl of Essex—*Life and Works*, vol. ii, p. 12.
[6] *Hamlet*, iv, 4.
[7] Letter to the Earl of Rutland, written in the name of the Earl of Essex—*Life and Works*, vol. ii, p. 12.

And in the foregoing we have the very collocation of *wealth* and *peace* used by Hamlet, and the same thought of *corruption* at work in both cases.

Shakespeare says:

This *peace* is nothing but to rust iron, increase tailors and breed balladmakers.[1]

And again:

Discarded, unjust servingmen, younger sons to younger brothers, revolted tapsters, and ostlers trade-fallen; the *cankers of a calm world and a long peace*.[2]

Both writers regarded the period of youth as one of great danger.

Bacon says:

For those persons which are of a turbulent nature or appetite do commonly pass their youth in many errors; and about their middle, and then and not before, they show forth their perfections.[3]

And again:

He passed that dangerous time of his youth in the highest fortune, and in a vigorous state of health.[4]

Shakespeare makes the same observation:

> Thou hast passed by the ambush of young days,
> Either not assailed, or victor, being charged.[5]

And this word *ambush*, then an unusual one, is also found in Bacon's writings: he speaks[6] of the Sphynx "lying in *ambush* for travelers."

We find a group of identities in reference to the use of intoxicating drinks. These I have already given in the chapter on "The Purposes of the Plays."

But while both condemned drunkenness they agreed in believing that, within reasonable limits, the use of intoxicating liquors strengthened and elevated the race.

Bacon says:

The use of wine in dry and consumed bodies is hurtful: *in moist and full bodies it is good*. The cause is, for that the spirits of the wine do prey upon the dew or radical moisture, as they call it, of the body, and so deceive the animal *spirits*. But where there is *moisture enough or superfluous*, there wine helpeth to digest, and *desiccate the moisture*.[7]

---

[1] *Coriolanus*, iv, 5.
[2] *1st Henry IV.*, iv, 2.
[3] *Civil Character of Augustus Cæsar*.
[4] *In Praise of Henry Prince of Wales*.
[5] Sonnet lxx.
[6] *Wisdom of the Ancients — Sphynx*.
[7] *Natural History*, ¶ 727.

And again:

I see France, Italy or Spain have not taken into use beer or ale; which, perhaps if they did, would *better both their healths and their complexions*.[1]

And Shakespeare puts into the mouth of Falstaff, who was "moist and full" enough, in a state of "constant dissolution and thaw," as he said himself, the same opinion:

A good sherris-sack hath a two-fold operation in it. It ascends me into the brain; *dries me there all the foolish and dull and crudy vapors* which environ it. . . . It illuminateth the face; which, as a beacon, gives warning to all the rest of this little kingdom, man, to arm; and then the vital commoners, the inland petty *spirits*, muster me all to their captain, the heart, who, great and puffed up with this retinue, doth any deed of courage.[2]

Here we have the same belief as to the virtues of wine, and the same reason, the drying or desiccating of the superfluous humors; and in both cases we have the belief that the *spirits* of the man are acted upon by the wine—a belief we shall touch upon hereafter. And in Bacon we will find another reference to this ascending of the spirits into the head. He says:

The *vapors* which were gathered by sitting fly more up into the head.[3]

But the identity of belief upon this point goes still farther. Each writer held to the opinion that the children of drunken men were more likely to be females than males. Bacon says:

It hath been observed by the ancients, and is yet believed, that the sperm of drunken men is unfruitful. The cause is, for that it is over-moistened and wanteth spissitude; and we have a merry saying, that they that go drunk to bed *get daughters*.[4]

Shakespeare says:

There's never any of these demure boys come to any proof; for their drink doth so overcool their blood, and making many fish-meals, that they fall into a kind of male green-sickness; and then, when they marry, they *get wenches*. . . . If I had a thousand sons, the first principle I would teach them should be, to forswear thin potations and to addict themselves to sack.[5]

And again:

He was gotten in drink. Is not the humor conceited?
His mind is not heroic, and there's the humor of it.[6]

And we find the same thought, that great vigor and vitality causes the offspring to be masculine in gender, in Macbeth's exclamation to Lady Macbeth:

[1] *Natural History*, § 705. [3] *Natural History*, § 734. [5] *2d Henry IV.*, iv, 3.
[2] *2d Henry IV.*, iv, 3. [4] Ibid., § 723. [6] *Merry Wives of Windsor*, i, 2.

> Bring forth men-children only,
> For thy undaunted mettle should compose
> Nothing but males.[1]

Both writers recognize the vast superiority of the intellectual forces over the bodily.

Bacon says:

> The *mind* is the man. . . . A man is but what he knoweth.[2]

Shakespeare has the same thought:

> In nature there's no blemish, but the *mind*.[3]
>
> 'Tis the *mind* that makes the body rich.[4]
>
> I saw Othello's visage in his *mind*.[5]

Bacon says:

> Pain and danger be great only by opinion.[6]

Shakespeare says:

> For there is nothing either good or bad but thinking makes it so.[7]

The discrimination which we find in Shakespeare between appetite and digestion, and their relations one to another, reappears in Bacon.

Macbeth says:

> Now good digestion wait on appetite,
> And health on both.[8]

Bacon speaks of

> Appetite, which is the spur of digestion.[9]

Both writers believed that the strict course of justice should be moderated by mercy.

Bacon says:

He [the King] must always resemble Him whose great name he beareth . . . in manifesting the sweet influence of his mercy on the severe stroke of his justice.[10]

And again:

In causes of life and death, judges ought (as far as the law permitteth) in justice to remember mercy, and to cast a severe eye upon the example, but a merciful eye upon the person.[11]

---

[1] *Macbeth*, i, 7.
[2] *Praise of Knowledge*.
[3] *Twelfth Night*, iii, 4.
[4] *Taming of the Shrew*, iv, 3.
[5] *Othello*, i, 3.
[6] Letter to the Earl of Rutland, written in the name of the Earl of Essex.
[7] *Hamlet*, ii, 2.
[8] *Macbeth*, iii, 4.
[9] *History of Life and Death*.
[10] Essay *Of a King*.
[11] Essay *Of Judicature*.

The same humane spirit is manifested in the Shakespeare writings:

> It is an attribute to God himself;
> And earthly power doth then show likest God's
> When mercy seasons justice.[1]

And again:

> Wilt thou draw near the nature of the gods?
> Draw near them, then, in being merciful.[2]

And again:

> Alas, alas!
> Why, all the souls that are were forfeit once;
> And He that might the vantage best have took
> Found out the remedy: How would you be,
> If He, which is the top of judgment, should
> But judge you as you are? Oh, think on that;
> And mercy then will breathe within your lips
> Like man new made.[3]

Both were keenly alive to the purity and sweetness of the atmosphere.

In his *History of Life and Death*[4] Bacon discusses "the healthfulness of the air" and the modes of testing its purity, as by exposing a lock of wool or a piece of flesh, etc.

He says in another place:

> At Gorhambury there is sweet air if any is.[5]

And again:

> The discovery of the disposition of the air is good . . . for the choice of places to dwell in; at the least for lodges and retiring-places for health.[6]

And in the same chapter in which he discusses the purity of the air in dwelling-houses and the mode of ascertaining it, he refers to *birds:*

> Which use to change countries at certain seasons, if they come earlier, do show the temperature of weather according to that country whence they came.[7]

> For prognostics of weather from living creatures, it is to be noted, that creatures that live in the open air, *sub dio*, must needs have a quicker impression from the air than men that live most within doors; and especially birds, that live in the air freest and clearest.[8]

And again he notes that

> Kites flying aloft show fair and dry weather, . . . for that they mount most into the air of that temper wherein they delight.[9]

---

[1] *Merchant of Venice*, iv, 1.
[2] *Titus Andronicus*, i, 2.
[3] *Measure for Measure*, ii, 2.
[4] § 19, etc.
[5] Letter to Buckingham, 1619.
[6] *Natural History*, § 808.
[7] Ibid., § 816.
[8] Ibid., § 822.
[9] Ibid., § 824.

And we have the same set of thoughts — the sweetness of the air in special places, and the delight of birds in pure air — in the famous words uttered by Duncan and Banquo:

> *Duncan.* This castle hath a pleasant seat: the air
> Nimbly and gently recommends itself
> Unto our senses.
>
> *Banquo.* This guest of summer,
> The temple-haunting martlet, does approve,
> By his loved mansionry, that the heaven's breath
> Smells wooingly here: no jutty, frieze,
> Buttress, nor coigne of vantage, but this bird
> Hath made his pendent bed and procreant cradle:
> Where they most breed and haunt, I have observed
> The air is delicate.[1]

Both refer to the effect of terror upon the rising of the hair.

Bacon says:

> The passions of the mind work upon the body the impressions following: fear causeth paleness, trembling, the *standing of the hair upright*, starting and *shrieking*.[2]

Shakespeare says:

> The time has been, my senses would have cooled
> To hear a night-*shriek;* and my fell of *hair*
> Would at a dismal treatise rouse, *and stir*
> As life were in 't.[3]

Both, while to some extent fatalists, believed that a man possesses to a large extent the control over his own fortune.

Bacon says:

> Chiefly the mould of a man's fortune is in his own hands.[4]

And again:

> It is not good to fetch fortune from the *stars*.[5]

While Shakespeare says:

> The fault, dear Brutus, is not in our *stars*,
> But in ourselves, that we are underlings.[6]

And curiously enough, both drew the same conclusions as to reading character by personal appearance, while they held that, as Shakespeare says:

> There's no art
> To read the mind's construction in the face.[7]

---

[1] *Macbeth*, i, 6.
[2] *Natural History*, § 713.
[3] *Macbeth*, v, 5.
[4] *Essay Of Fortune*.
[5] *History of Henry VII*.
[6] *Julius Cæsar*, i, 2.
[7] *Macbeth*, i, 2.

And again:

> No more can you distinguish of a man
> Than of his outward show, which, God he knows,
> Seldom, or never, jumpeth with the heart.[1]

And Bacon argued:

Neither let that be feared which is said, *Fronti nulla fides:* which is meant of a general outward behavior, and not of the private and subtle motions and labors of the countenance and gesture.[2]

And this distinction, between the revelations made by the mere cast or shape or controlled attitudes of the face, and the expressions of the face or motions of the body, appears in Shakespeare:

> There was speech in their dumbness, language in their very gestures.[3]

Again we find it in Ulysses' wonderful description of Cressida:

> Fie, fie upon her!
> There's language in her eye, her cheek, her lip,
> Nay, her foot speaks; her wanton spirits look out
> At every joint and motive [motion?] of her body.[4]

And we find Bacon observing:

For every passion doth cause, in the eyes, face and gesture, certain indecent and ill-seeming, apish and deformed motions.[5]

And again he says:

So in all physiognomy the lineaments of the body will discover those natural inclinations of the mind which dissimulation will conceal or discipline will suppress.[6]

And we find Shakespeare putting into the mouth of King John these words, descriptive of Hubert:

> Hadst thou not been by,
> A fellow by the hand of nature marked,
> Quoted and signed to do a deed of shame.[7]

And Bacon says:

For Aristotle hath very ingeniously and diligently handled the features of the body, but not the gestures of the body, which are no less comprehensible by art, and of greater use and advantage. For the lineaments of the body do disclose the disposition and inclination of the mind in general, but the motions of the countenance and parts do not only so, but do further disclose the present humor and state of the mind and will.[8]

And in this connection we find another parallelism. Bacon says:

It is necessary to use a steadfast countenance, not wavering with action, as it

---

[1] *Richard III.*, iii, 1.
[2] *Advancement of Learning*, book ii.
[3] *Winter's Tale*, v, 2.
[4] *Troilus and Cressida*, iv, 5.
[5] *Wisdom of the Ancients — Dionysus.*
[6] *Natural History*, cent. ix.
[7] *King John*, iv, 2.
[8] *Advancement of Learning*, book ii.

moving the head or *hand too much*, which showeth a fantastical, light and fickle spirit.[1]

And Hamlet, in his instructions to the players, says:

Nor do not saw the air *too much* — your *hand* thus; but use all gently.[2]

Both had the same high admiration for the capacity to bear misfortunes with patience and self-control.

Bacon says:

Yet it is a greater dignity of mind to *bear evils* by fortitude and judgment than by a kind of absenting and alienation of the mind from things present to things future, for that it is to hope. . . . I do judge a state of mind which in all doubtful expectations is settled and floateth not, and doth this out of good government and composition of the affections, to be one of the principal supporters of man's life; but that assurance and repose of the mind which *only rides at anchor upon hope*, I do reject as wavering and weak.[3]

Shakespeare says:

For thou hast been
As one, in suffering all, that suffers nothing;
A man that fortune's buffets and rewards
Has ta'en with equal thanks; and blessed are those
Whose blood and judgment are so well commingled
That they are not a pipe for fortune's finger
To sound what stop she please.[4]

And the expression of Bacon quoted above, "the mind which only rides at anchor upon hope," is paralleled in Shakespeare:

If eyes, corrupt by over-partial looks,
Be *anchored* in the bay where all men ride.[5]

Both believed in the universal presence and power of goodness. Bacon said:

The inclination to *goodness* is deeply implanted in the nature of man; insomuch, that if it issue not toward man it will take unto other living creatures.[6]

And again:

There is formed in everything a double nature of good.[7]

And again:

For the affections themselves carry ever an appetite to good, as reason doth.[8]

Shakespeare has:

There is some soul of goodness in things evil,
Would men observingly distill it out.[9]

---

[1] *Civil Conversations.*
[2] *Hamlet*, iii, 2.
[3] *Med. Sacra — Of Earthly Hope.*
[4] *Hamlet*, iii, 2.
[5] Sonnet cxxxvii.
[6] Essay *Of Goodness.*
[7] *Advancement of Learning*, book ii.
[8] Ibid.
[9] *Henry V.*, iv, 1.

And again:

> And this our life, exempt from public haunt,
> Finds tongues in trees, books in the running brooks,
> Sermons in stones, and *good in everything*.[1]

Bacon says:

> And we willingly place the history of arts among the species of natural history, because there have obtained a now inveterate mode of speaking and notion, as if art were something different from nature, so that things artificial ought to be discriminated from things natural, as if wholly and generically distinct. . . . And there has insinuated into men's minds a still subtler error, namely this, that art is conceived to be a sort of *addition to nature*, the proper effect of which is mere words and rhetorical ornament.[2]

Shakespeare has the following:

> *Perdita.* For I have heard it said,
> There is an art which in their piedness shares
> With great creating nature.
> *Polixenes.* Say there be;
> Yet nature is made better by no mean,
> But nature makes that mean; so o'er that art,
> Which *you say adds to nature*, is an art that nature makes.

Here we have, in the same words, a reference to an opinion, *held by others*, that *art* is an *addition* to nature, and a dissent from it by the writer, in each case.

And that other thought, that man's art shares with God the creative force and faculty, Judge Holmes shows had also occurred to Bacon:

> Art or man is added to the universe; and it must almost necessarily be concluded that the human soul is endowed with *providence*, not without the example, intention and authority of the greater providence.[3]

That is to say, that man is a sort of a deputy of God to carry forward the work of creation.

And we find Shakespeare alluding, in the same spirit, to "the *providence* that's in a watchful state,"[4] as if "the human soul," governing the state, "was endowed with providence."

And we find the same thought, that man is a species of lesser God, to whom the creative force has been delegated, expressed again in these lines:

> We, Hermia, *like two artificial gods*,
> Have with our needles *created* both one flower,
> Both on one sampler, sitting on one cushion.[5]

---

[1] *As You Like It*, ii, 1.
[2] *Intell. Globe*, chapter iii.
[3] *Authorship of Shak.*, p. 512.
[4] *Troilus and Cressida*, iii, 3.
[5] *Midsummer Night's Dream*, i, 2.

Both believed that sickness or weakness left the mind open to the influence of external spirits. Bacon says:

So much more in impressions from mind to mind, or from spirit to spirit, the impression taketh, but is encountered and overcome by the mind and spirit. . . . And, therefore, they work most upon *weak* minds and spirits, as those of women, sick persons, superstitious and fearful persons.[1]

Shakespeare makes Hamlet say:

> The spirit that I have seen
> May be the devil; and the devil hath power
> To assume a pleasing shape; yea, and, perhaps,
> Out of my *weakness* and my melancholy,
> (As he is very potent with such spirits),
> Abuses me to damn me.[2]

Here we have precisely the same idea.

∴

The author of *A New Study of Shakespeare*, Mr. W. F. C. Wigston, calls attention to the following parallelism.

Bacon says:

It is evident that the dullness of men is such, and so infelicitous, that when things are put before their feet, they *do not see them*, unless admonished, but pass on.

Shakespeare says:

> The jewel that we find we stoop and take it,
> *Because we see it;* but what we do not see
> We tread upon, and never think of it.[3]

∴

Both had observed the fear that men have of making their wills until the last moment.

Bacon says:

When their will is made they think themselves nearer the grave than before.[4]

In Shakespeare we find the following:

Slender. Now, good Mistress Anne.
Anne. What is your will?
Slender. My will? Ods-hart-lings, that's a pretty jest indeed. I ne'er made my will yet, I thank Heaven: I am not such a sickly creature, I give Heaven praise.[5]

∴

Mrs. Pott calls attention to the following parallelism.

Bacon has in his *Promus* this note:

It is in action as it is in ways: commonly the nearest is the foulest.[6]

---

[1] *Natural History*, § 901.
[2] *Hamlet*, II, 2.
[3] *Measure for Measure*, ii, 1.
[4] *Essay Of Death*.
[5] *Merry Wives of Windsor*, iii, 4.
[6] *Promus*, No. 532.

Shakespeare has it:

> [Your heart] is too full of the milk of human kindness
> To catch the nearest way.[1]

That is, the foul way of murder, which was the nearest way to the crown.

I might continue this chapter to greater length; but I think I have given enough to show that the same wonderful parallelism which exists between the forms of expression in the two sets of writings extends also to the opinions and beliefs set forth therein.

It will, of course, be easy for a dishonest mind to treat these parallelisms as Richard Grant White did those in Mrs. Pott's *Promus* — that is, ignore the strongest ones, and select the least striking and put them forth as the strongest. But in the long run truth is not to be arrested by such tricks, nor can a great argument be conducted by men who are mean enough to resort to them.

[1] *Macbeth*, i. 2.

CHAPTER IV.

IDENTICAL QUOTATIONS.

And these same thoughts people this little world.
Richard II., v, 5.

IF the two minds were one, if they thought the same thoughts, and employed the same comparisons and expressions, it might be that we would find them quoting the same things from the same books.

I remember a few instances of this kind, and many more might be found by a diligent examination of the two sets of writings.

Bacon says:

In this they fall into the error described in the ancient fable, in which the other parts of the body did suppose the stomach had been *idle*, because it neither performed the office of motion, as the limbs do, nor of sense, as the head doth; but yet, notwithstanding, it is the stomach that digesteth and distributeth to all the rest.[1]

In Shakespeare we have the following:

> There was a time when all the body's members
> Rebelled against the belly; thus accused it:
> That only like a gulf it did remain
> I' the midst o' the body, *idle* and unactive,
> Still cupboarding the viands, never bearing
> Like labor with the rest; where the other instruments
> Did see and hear, devise, instruct, walk, feel,
> And mutually participate; did minister
> Unto the appetite and affection common
> Of the whole body. The belly answered, . . .
> "True it is, my incorporate friends," quoth he,
> "That I receive the general food at first,
> Which you do live upon: and fit it is;
> Because I am the storehouse and the shop
> Of the whole body. But, if you do remember,
> I send it through the rivers of your blood
> Even to the court, the heart, to the seat o' the brain,
> And through the cranks and offices of man:
> The strongest nerves, and small inferior veins,
> From me receive that natural competency
> Whereby they live."[2]

---

[1] *Advancement of Learning*, book ii.   [2] *Coriolanus*, i, 1.

And here I would refer to the anecdote which Bacon tells in his *Apophthegms:*

Sir Nicholas Bacon, being appointed a judge for the northern circuit, . . . was, by one of the malefactors, mightily importuned to save his life, which, when nothing that he had said did avail, at length desired his mercy on the account of kindred. "Prythee," said my lord Judge, "how came that in?" "Why, if it please you, my lord, your name is Bacon and mine is Hog, and in all ages hog and bacon have been so near kindred that they are not to be separated." "Ay, but," replied Judge Bacon, "you and I cannot be kindred except you be hanged, for hog is not bacon until it be well hanged."

Shakespeare has this:

Evans. I pray you, have remembrance, child: *Accusativo*, hung, hang, hog.
Quickly. Hang hog is Latin for Bacon, I warrant you.[1]

Bacon says:

Such men in other men's calamities are, as it were, in season, and are ever on the loading part; not so good as the dogs that licked Lazarus' sores, but like flies that are still buzzing.[2]

Shakespeare says:

Ragged as Lazarus in the painted cloth; where the glutton's dogs licked his sores.[3]

Bacon says:

Philo Judæus saith that the sense is like the sun; for the sun seals up the globe of heaven [the stars] and opens the globe of earth; so the sense doth obscure heavenly things and reveals earthly things.[4]

When Lorenzo contemplates the heavens by night, thick "inlaid with patines of bright gold," he speaks of the music of the spheres, and adds:

> Such harmony is in immortal souls,
> But whilst this muddy vesture of decay
> Doth grossly close it in, we cannot hear it.[5]

Bacon says:

For of lions it is a received belief that their fury and fierceness ceaseth toward anything that yieldeth and prostrateth itself.[6]

Shakespeare has the following:

> Brother, you have a vice of mercy in you,
> Which better fits a lion than a man.[7]

And again:

> For 'tis the nature of that noble beast
> To prey on nothing that doth seem as dead.[8]

---

[1] *Merry Wives of Windsor*, iv, 1.
[2] *Essay Of Goodness.*
[3] *1st Henry IV.*, iv, 2.
[4] *Apophthegms.*
[5] *Merchant of Venice*, v, 1.
[6] *Med. Sacra—Exaltation of Charity.*
[7] *Troilus and Cressida*, v, 3.
[8] *As You Like It*, iv, 3.

Bacon says:

But these three are the true stages of knowledge, which, to those that are puffed up with their own knowledge and rebellious against God, are indeed no better than the giant's three hills:

> "*Ter sunt conati imponere Pelio Ossam,
> Scilicet atque Ossæ frondosum involvere Olympum.*"
> [Mountain on *mountain* thrice they strove to heap:
> *Olympus, Ossa*, piled on *Pelion's* steep.][1]

And we find Shakespeare employing the same quotation:

> Now pile your dust upon the quick and dead;
> Till of this flat a *mountain* you have made,
> To o'ertop old *Pelion*, or the skyish head
> Of old *Olympus*. . . .
>   Till our ground,
> Singeing his pate against the burning zone,
> Make *Ossa* like a wart.[2]

Here we have the three mountains named in the quotation — Olympus, Pelion, Ossa — and the comparison in both cases is that of piling one on top of the other.

·.·

Describing the chameleon, Bacon says:

He feedeth not only upon the air, though that be his principal sustenance.[3]

Again:

And so feed her [the Queen] with expectation.[4]

We turn to Shakespeare, and we find the following:

King. How fares our cousin Hamlet?
Ham. Excellent, i' faith; of the *chameleon's* dish: I *eat the air*, promise-crammed. You cannot feed capons so.[5]

·.·

Bacon says:

And therefore the poet doth elegantly call passions *tortures*, that urge men to confess their secrets.

Shakespeare says:

> Better be with the dead,
> Whom we, to gain our peace, have sent to peace,
> Than on the *torture* of the mind to lie
> In restless ecstacy.[6]

·.·

Bacon has the following:

It was both pleasantly and wisely said . . . by a Pope's nuncio, returning from a certain nation where he served as lieger; whose opinion being asked touch-

---

[1] *De Augmentis*, book iii.
[2] *Hamlet*, v, 1.
[3] *Natural History*, § 360.
[4] Letter to Essex, October 4, 1596.
[5] *Hamlet*, iii, 2.
[6] *Macbeth*, iii, 2.

ing the appointment of one to go in his place, he wished that in any case they did not send one that was too wise; because no very wise man would even imagine what they in that country were like to do.[1]

While Shakespeare puts the same quotation thus:

Hamlet. Ay, marry, why was he sent into England?
1st Clown. Why, because he was mad; he shall recover his wits there; or, if he do not, it is no great matter there.
Hamlet. Why?
1st Clown. 'Twill not be seen in him; there the men are as mad as he.[2]

In *The Wisdom of the Ancients* Bacon quotes the fable of Orpheus, and says:

So great was the power and alluring force of this harmony, that he drew the woods and moved the very stones to come and place themselves in an orderly and decent fashion about him.

Shakespeare says:

> Therefore, the poet
> Did feign that Orpheus drew trees, stones and floods;
> Since nought so stockish, hard and full of rage
> But music for a time doth change his nature.[3]
>
> For Orpheus' lute was strung with poets' sinews,
> Whose golden touch could soften steel and stones.[4]

Judge Holmes calls attention to the following instance.

In Plutarch's *Life of Antony* is told the story of Timon's tree. North's translation reads as follows:

Ye men of Athens, in a court-yard belonging to my house grows a large fig-tree, on which many an honest citizen has been pleased to hang himself: now, as I have thought of building upon that spot, I could not omit giving you this public notice, to the end that if any more among you have a mind to make the same use of my tree, they may do it speedily before it is destroyed.

Bacon alludes to this story as follows, in his essay *Of Goodness:*

Misanthropi that make it their practice to bring men to the bough, and yet have never a tree for the purpose in their gardens, as Timon had.

While Shakespeare, in the play of *Timon of Athens*,[5] says:

> *Timon.* I have a tree which grows here in my close,
> That mine own use invites me to cut down,
> And shortly must I sell it. Tell my friends,
> Tell Athens, in the sequence of degree,
> From high to low throughout, that whoso please
> To stop affliction, let him take his haste,
> Come hither, ere my tree hath felt the axe,
> And hang himself.

---

[1] *Advancement of Learning*, book ii.
[2] *Hamlet*, v, 1.
[3] *Merchant of Venice*, v, 1.
[4] *Two Gentlemen of Verona*, iii, 2.
[5] Act iv, scene 1.

Henry Lewis, in his *Essays of Bacon*, points out an instance where the two writers refer to the same incident. Bacon, in his essay *Of Prophecies*, says:

Henry VI. of England said of Henry VII., when he was a lad, and gave him water, "This is the *lad* shall enjoy the crown for which we strive."

In Shakespeare we find the same event thus alluded to:

> Come hither, England's hope. If secret powers
> Suggest but truth to my divining thoughts,
> This pretty *lad* will prove our country's bliss, . . .
> Likely, in time, to bless a regal throne.[1]

The same author also calls attention to this parallelism. In the same essay *Of Prophecies* Bacon refers to

A phantasm that appeared to M. Brutus in his tent, and said to him, *Philippus interum me videbis*—(Thou shalt see me again at Philippi).

Shakespeare, in *Julius Cæsar*, has:

> *Brutus.* Speak to me what thou art.
> *Ghost.* Thy evil spirit, Brutus.
> *Brutus.* Why comest thou?
> *Ghost.* To tell thee, thou shalt see me at Philippi.[2]

Aristotle says:

Usury is merely money *born* of money; so that of all means of money-making this is the most contrary to nature.

Bacon quotes this; he says:

> It is against nature for money to *beget* money.[3]

Shakespeare also quotes it:

> When did friendship take
> A *breed* of barren metal of his friend?[4]

Bacon says:

There is an observation among country people, that years of store of haws and hips do commonly portend cold winters; and they ascribe it to God's *providence*, that, as the Scripture saith, reacheth even to the *falling* of a *sparrow*.[5]

Shakespeare says:

> There's a special *providence* in the *fall* of a *sparrow*.[6]

And again:

> He that doth the ravens feed,
> Yea, providently caters for the sparrow.[7]

Bacon says:

The wisdom of crocodiles, that shed tears when they would devour.[8]

[1] *3d Henry VI.*, iv, 6.   [3] *Essay Of Usury.*   [5] *Natural History*, § 737.
[2] *Julius Cæsar*, iv, 3.   [4] *Merchant of Venice*, i, 3.   [6] *Hamlet*, v, 2.
[7] *As You Like It*, ii, 3.   [8] *Essay Of Wisdom.*

Shakespeare says:

> As the mournful crocodile
> With sorrow snares relenting passengers.[1]

...

Bacon, referring to a popular belief, says:

This was the end of this little *cockatrice* of a king [Perkin Warbeck], that was able to destroy those that did not espy him first.[2]

Shakespeare alludes to the same superstition:

> They will kill one another by the look, like *cockatrices*.[3]

> Shall poison more
> Than the death-darting eye of *cockatrice*.[4]

> A *cockatrice* hast thou hatched to the world,
> Whose unavoided eye is murtherous?[5]

...

Bacon says:

The parable of Pythagoras is dark but true. *Cor ne edito* — (eat not the heart).[6]

Shakespeare says:

> *I sup upon myself,*
> And so shall *starve* with *feeding*.[7]

> The canker *gnaw* thy *heart*.[8]

...

Bacon says:

Princes many times make themselves desires and set their hearts upon a toy, . . . as Nero for playing on the harp.[9]

Shakespeare says:

> Plantagenet, I will; and like thee, Nero,
> Play on the lute, beholding the towns burn.[10]

...

Bacon tells this story:

Periander, being consulted with how to preserve a tyranny newly usurped, bid the messenger attend and report what he saw him do; and went into his garden and topped all the highest flowers, signifying that it consisted in the cutting off and keeping low of the nobility and grandees.[11]

Shakespeare plainly alludes to the same story in the following:

> Go thou, and, like an executioner,
> Cut off the head of too-fast-growing sprays,
> That look too lofty in our commonwealth:
> All must be even in our government.[12]

...

[1] *2d Henry VI.*, iii, 1.
[2] *History of Henry VII.*
[3] *Twelfth Night*, iii. 4.
[4] *Romeo and Juliet*, iii, 2.
[5] *Richard III.*, iv, 1.
[6] *Essay Of Friendship.*
[7] *Coriolanus*, iv, 2.
[8] *Timon of Athens*, iv, 3.
[9] *Essay Of Empire.*
[10] *1st Henry VI.*, i, 4.
[11] *Advancement of Learning*, book ii.
[12] *Richard II.*, iii, 4.

Bacon quotes:

> It is not granted to man to love and be wise.[1]

And again:

Therefore it was well said "that it is impossible to love and be wise.[2]

Shakespeare says:

> To be wise and love, exceeds man's might.[3]

∴

Bacon says:

For, aspiring to be like God in power, the angels transgressed and fell.[4]

And again:

> For from the desire of power the angels fell.[5]

Shakespeare says:

> By that sin fell the angels.[6]

∴

Bacon uses this quotation:

Cardinal Wolsey said that if he had pleased God as he pleased the King, he had not been ruined.[7]

Shakespeare puts into the mouth of the same Cardinal Wolsey these words:

> O Cromwell, Cromwell,
> Had I but served my God with half the zeal
> I served my King, he would not in mine age
> Have left me naked to mine enemies.[8]

∴

Mr. R. M. Theobald, in the August, 1887, number of the *Journal of the Bacon Society of London*, page 157, gives us the following extraordinary parallelism, where both writers clearly refer to the same terrible story.

Bacon, in the *De Augmentis*, says:

What a proof of patience is displayed in the story told of Anaxarchus, who, when questioned under torture, *bit out his own tongue* (the only hope of information), *and spat it into the face of the tyrant*.

While in Shakespeare we find the same story alluded to. In *Richard II.*, i, 1, Bolingbroke, being invited by the King to reconcile himself to Mowbray, and throw down Mowbray's gage of battle which he had picked up, replies:

---

[1] *Advancement of Learning*, book ii.
[2] *Essay Of Love*.
[3] *Troilus and Cressida*, iii, 2.
[4] *Advancement of Learning*, book ii.
[5] Preface to *Great Instauration*.
[6] *Henry VIII.*, iii, 2.
[7] Letter to King James, September 5, 1621.
[8] *Henry VIII.*, iii, 4.

> O God, defend my soul from such foul sin!
> ... Ere my tongue
> Shall wound mine honor with such feeble wrong,
> Or sound so base a parle, *my teeth shall tear*
> The slavish motive of recanting fear,
> *And spit it bleeding*, in his high disgrace,
> Where shame doth harbor, *even in Mowbray's face.*

The play of *Richard II.* was published in 1597, and Bacon's *De Augmentis* in 1623; consequently Shakespeare did not borrow from Bacon. Mr. Theobald says:

> The story is derived from Diogenes Laertius; Bacon's version is taken from Pliny or Valerius Maximus. ... Where did Shakspere pick up the allusion? Perhaps Pliny and Valerius Maximus and Diogenes Laertius were text-books at the grammar school of Stratford-on-Avon!

Bacon, in his *Natural History*, says:

> There was an Egyptian soothsayer that made Antonius believe that his genius, which otherwise was brave and confident, was, in the presence of Octavius Cæsar, poor and cowardly; and therefore he advised him to absent himself as much as he could, and remove far from him. This soothsayer was thought to be suborned by Cleopatra, to make him live in Egypt and other remote places from home.[1]

And the same fact is referred to in Shakespeare. Macbeth says, speaking of Banquo:

> There is none but he
> Whose being I do fear: and under him
> My genius is rebuked; as, it is said,
> Mark Antony's was by Cæsar.

And in *Antony and Cleopatra* we have the very Egyptian soothsayer referred to:

> *Antony.* Say to me,
> Whose fortune shall rise higher, Cæsar's or mine?
> *Soothsayer.* Cæsar's.
> Therefore, O Antony, stay not by his side:
> Thy dæmon (that's thy *spirit* which keeps thee) is
> Noble, courageous, high, unmatchable,
> Where Cæsar's is not; but near him thy angel
> Becomes a Fear, as being overpowered; therefore
> Make space enough between you.[2]

Bacon says:

> What new hope hath made them return to their Sinon's note, in teaching Troy how to save itself.[3]

Shakespeare alludes to the same fact, thus:

> And, like a Sinon, take another Troy.[4]

---

[1] *Natural History*, cent. x, §910.
[2] *Antony and Cleopatra*, ii, 3.
[3] Speech in Parliament.
[4] *3d Henry VI.*, iii, 2.

Bacon says:

Aristotle dogmatically assigned the cause of generation to the sun.

Shakespeare has it:

If the sun breed maggots out of a dead dog. Have you a daughter? . . . Let her not walk in the sun. Conception is a blessing. Etc.[1]

Bacon speaks of

The ancient opinion that man was a *microcosmus*, an abstract or model of the world.[2]

And Shakespeare alludes to the same thing:

You will see it in the map of my *microcosm*.[3]

Bacon says:

Report has much prevailed of a stone bred in the head of an old and great toad.[4]

Shakespeare says:

Like the toad, ugly and venomous,
Bears yet a precious jewel in its head.[5]

Bacon speaks of taking the advantage of opportunity in the following words:

For occasion (as it is in the common verse) turneth a bald noddle after she has presented her locks in front, and no hold taken.[6]

Shakespeare says:

Let's take the instant by the forward top — for we are old.[7]

Bacon says:

For although Aristotle, as though he had been of the race of the Ottomans, thought he could not reign unless he killed off all his *brethren*.[8]

Shakespeare puts into the mouth of King Henry V. this address to his *brothers*:

This is the English, not the Turkish court;
Not Amurah an Amurah succeeds,
But Harry, Harry.[9]

Bacon in his *Apophthegms* tells this story:

The Queen of Henry IV. of France was great with child; Count Soissons, that

---

[1] *Hamlet*, ii, 2.
[2] *Advancement of Learning*, book ii.
[3] *Coriolanus*, ii, 1.
[4] *Inquisition of the Conversion of Bodies.*
[5] *As You Like It*, ii, 1.
[6] *Essay Of Delays.*
[7] *All's Well that Ends Well*, v, 3.
[8] *Advancement of Learning*, book ii.
[9] *2d Henry IV.*, v, 2.

had his expectation upon the crown, when it was twice or thrice thought that the Queen was with child before, said to some of his friends "that it was but with a pillow," etc.

Shakespeare must have had this story in his mind when, in describing Doll Tearsheet being taken to be whipped, he speaks as follows:

Hostess. Oh that Sir John were come, he would make this a bloody day to somebody. But I would the fruit of her womb might miscarry.
Officer. If it do, you shall have a dozen cushions; you have but eleven now.[1]

∴

Bacon says:

Question was asked of Demosthenes what was the chief part of an orator? He answered, Action. What next? *Action.* What next, again? Action. A strange thing that that part of an orator which is but superficial, and rather the virtue of a player, should be placed so high above those other noble parts of invention, *elocution*, and the rest; nay, almost alone, as if it were all in all. But the reason is plain. There is in human nature, generally, *more of the fool than the wise;* and therefore those faculties by which the foolish part of men's minds is taken are most potent.[2]

Shakespeare refers to the same story and gives the same explanation in the following:

> For in such business
> *Action* is *eloquence*, and the eyes of the ignorant
> More learnèd than their ears.[3]

∴

In *Henry V.* the Bishop of Exeter makes a comparison of government to the subordination and harmony of parts in music:

> For government, though high and *low* and lower,
> Put into parts, doth keep in one consent,
> Congruing in a full and natural close
> Like music.

Some have sought to find the origin of this simile in Cicero, *De Republica,* but that book was lost to literature and unknown, except by name, until Angelo Mai discovered it upon a palimpsest in the Vatican in 1822.

Its real source is in the apophthegm repeatedly quoted by Bacon as to Nero:

Vespasian asked of Apollonius what was the cause of Nero's ruin. Who answered: "Nero could tune the harp well, but in government he did always wind up the strings too high or let them down too *low.*"[4]

∴

[1] *2d Henry IV.*, v, 4.
[2] *Essay Of Boldness.*
[3] *Coriolanus*, iii, 2.
[4] Apophthegm 51.

Bacon has this story:

Queen Isabella of Spain used to say: "Whosoever hath a good presence and a good fashion *carries letters of recommendation*."[1]

Shakespeare says:

> The beauty that is borne here in the face
> The bearer knows not, but *commends itself*
> *To others' eyes.*[2]

Bacon has two anecdotes about the Salic law of France.[3] He says in one of them:

There was a French gentleman, speaking with an English of the law Salique: that women were excluded from inheriting the crown of France. The English said: "Yes; but that was meant of the women themselves, not of such males as claimed by women," etc.

And in the play of *Henry V.* we find Shakespeare discussing the same Salic law, at great length, and giving many instances to show that it did not exclude those who "claimed by women," one of which instances is:

> Besides their writers say
> King Pepin, which deposed Childerike,
> Did as their general, being descended
> Of Blithild, which was daughter to King Clothair,
> Make claim and title to the crown of France.[4]

The writer of the Plays had evidently studied the history of this law of another country in all its details;—a thing natural enough in a lawyer, extraordinary in a play-actor or stage manager.

Bacon refers to the story of Ulysses' wife thus:

Aristippus said: That those who studied particular sciences and neglected philosophy, were like Penelope's wooers, that made love to the waiting-women.[5]

Shakespeare also refers to Penelope:

You would be another Penelope; yet they say all the yarn she spun in Ulysses' absence did but fill Ithaca with moths.[6]

Bacon quotes the story of Icarus:

I was ever sorry that your Lordship should fly with waxen wings, doubting Icarus' fortune.[7]

Shakespeare has the following allusion to the same story:

> Then follow thou thy desperate sire of Crete,
> Thou Icarus.[8]

---

[1] Apophthegm 99.
[2] *Troilus and Cressida*, iii, 3.
[3] Apophthegms 184 and 185.
[4] *Henry V*, i, 1.
[5] Apophthegm 189.
[6] *Coriolanus*, i, 3.
[7] Letter to Essex, 1600.
[8] *1st Henry VI.*, iv, 6.

And again:

> And in that sea of blood my boy did drench
> His over-mounting spirit; and there died
> My Icarus, my blossom, in his pride.[1]

And again:

> I, Dædalus; my poor boy, Icarus;
> Thy father Minos, that denied our course;
> The sun that seared the wings of my sweet boy.[2]

Bacon says:

Frascatorius invented a remedy for apoplectic fits, by placing a heated pan at some distance around the head, for by this means the spirits that were suffocated and congealed in the cells of the brain, and oppressed by the humors, were dilated, excited and revived.[3]

And Falstaff seemed to hold the same view, that the disease was a torpidity that needed to be roused. He says:

This apoplexie is, as I take it, a kind of *lethargy*, a sleeping of the blood.[4]

And Bacon, in a letter to the King, at the time of his downfall, after describing a violent pain in the back of his head, says:

And then the little physic [medical learning] I had told me that it must either grow to a congelation, and so to a *lethargy*, and break, and so to a mortal fever or sudden death.

Bacon and Shakespeare both refer to the same fact in connection with the assassination of Julius Cæsar. Bacon says:

With Julius Cæsar, Decimus Brutus had obtained that interest, as he set him down in his testament for heir in remainder after his nephew; and this was the man that had power with him to draw him forth to his death: for when Cæsar would have discharged the Senate, in regard of some ill presages, and specially a dream of Calpurnia, this man lifted him gently by the arm out of his chair, telling him he hoped he would not dismiss the Senate till his wife had *dreamed a better dream*.

In Shakespeare we have Decimus Brutus saying to Cæsar:

> Besides, it were a mock
> Apt to be rendered, for some one to say:
> Break up the Senate, till another time,
> When Cæsar's wife shall meet with *better dreams*.

And is it not to the soldier Decimus Junius Brutus, and not to the great Marcus Junius Brutus, that the poet makes Mark Antony

---

[1] *1st Henry VI.*, iv, 7.
[2] *3d Henry VI.*, v, 6.
[3] *Historia Dens. et Rari.*
[4] *2d Henry IV*, i, 3.

allude (echoing Bacon's astonishment that the heir of Cæsar could have participated in his murder) in the following?

> Through this the well-beloved Brutus stabbed,
> And as he plucked his cursèd steel away,
> Mark how the blood of Cæsar followed it;
> As rushing out of doors, to be resolved
> If Brutus so unkindly knocked or no:
> For Brutus, as you know, was Cæsar's angel.
> Judge, O ye gods, how dearly Cæsar loved him.

∴

And we find in another historical instance the minds of both writers, if I may use the expression, dwelling on the same fact.

Bacon says, in a letter to King James, February 11, 1614:

> And I put the case of the Duke of Buckingham, who said that *if the King caused him to be arrested* of treason he *would stab him*.

The King here alluded to was Henry VIII., and we find the incident thus described in Shakespeare's play of that name. Buckingham's surveyor is giving testimony against his master. He says:

> *If* (quoth he) I for this had been *committed*,
> *As to the Tower*, I thought, I would have played
> The part my father meant to act upon
> The usurper Richard; who, being at Salisbury,
> Made suit to come in 's presence, which if granted,
> (As he made semblance of his duty), *would
> Have put his knife into him*.[1]

∴

Bacon makes this quotation:

> The kingdom of France . . . is now fallen into those calamities, that, as the prophet saith, *From the crown of the head to the sole of the foot* there is no whole place.[2]

Shakespeare uses the same quotation:

> *Don Pedro.* I will only be bold with Benedick for his company; for *from the crown of his head to the sole of his foot* he is all mirth.[3]

∴

I feel confident that, had I the time and did space permit, I could increase this list of identical quotations many-fold.

It is certain that these two writers not only held the same views, employed the same comparisons, used the same expressions,

---

[1] *Henry VIII.*, i, 2.
[2] Observations on a Libel — *Life and Works*, vol. i, p. 160.
[3] *Much Ado about Nothing*, iii, 2.

pursued the same studies and read the same books, but that their minds were constructed so exactly alike that the same things, out of their reading, lodged in them, and were reproduced for the same purposes.

And these mental twins — these intellectual identities — did not seem to know, or even to have ever heard of each other!

CHAPTER V.

IDENTICAL STUDIES.

> *Biron.* What is the end of study?
> *King.* Why, that to know, which else we should not know.
> *Biron.* Things hid and barred, you mean, from common sense?
> *King.* Ay, that is study's god-like recompense.
> *Love's Labor Lost,* i, 1.

MANY men *study* nothing. They are content with the stock of ideas, right or wrong, borrowed from others, with which they start into manhood. But of those who seek to penetrate beyond their preconceptions into knowledge, no two follow the same path and pursue the same subjects. The themes of study are as infinitely varied as the construction of human intellects. And herein, as in everything else, is manifested the wisdom of the great architect, who for every space in the edifice of life has carved a stone which fits it precisely. Many, it is true, are the mere rubble that fills up the interspaces; others are parts of the frieze ornamented with bass-reliefs of gnomes or angels; others, again, are the massive, hidden, humble foundation-blocks on which rests the weight of the whole structure. But in God's edifice nothing is little, and little can be said to be great.

And so in life: one man will devote his existence to a study of the motions of the heavenly bodies through their incalculable spaces; another will give up his whole life to a microscopic investigation of the wings and limbs of insects. One will soar on golden pinions through the magical realms of music; another will pursue the dry details of mathematics into their ultimate possibilities; a third will sail gloriously, like a painted nautilus, over the liquid and shining bosom of poetry; while still another will study

> The doubtful balance of rights and wrongs,
> With weary lawyers of endless tongues.

The purpose of life seems to be put upon the creature even before creation, and

> Necessity sits on humanity
> Like to the world on Atlas' neck.

And when we turn to consider what subjects were studied, at the same time, by the writer of the Shakespeare Plays and Francis Bacon, we shall find that identity which could not exist between two really distinct intellects.

In the first place, we are struck with the universality of thought, observation and study discoverable in both. Bacon "took all knowledge for his province," and the Shakespeare Plays embrace every theme of reflection possible to man: — religion, philosophy, science, history, human character, human passions and affections, music, poetry, medicine, law, statecraft, politics, worldly wisdom, wit, humor — everything. They are oceanic. Every year some new explorer drops his dredge a thousand fathoms deep into their unconsidered depths, and brings up strange and marvelous forms of life where we had looked only for silence and death.

And when we descend to particulars we find precise identity in almost everything.

I. Music.

Take the subject of music. This is a theme which comparatively few study, even to-day; and in that almost rude age of Elizabeth the number must have been greatly less. Neither does it necessarily follow that all great men love music and investigate it. In fact, the opinion of Shakespeare, that the man who "had no music in his soul" was not to be trusted, has provoked a perfect storm of adverse criticism.[1]

But Bacon's love of music was great. Sir John Hawkins says:

Lord Bacon, in his *Natural History*, has given a great variety of experiments touching music, that show him to have not been barely a philosopher, an inquirer into the phenomena of sound, but a master of the science of harmony, and very intimately acquainted with the precepts of musical education.[2]

And Sir John quotes the following from Bacon:

The sweetest and best harmony is when every part or instrument is not heard by itself, but a conflation of them all, which requireth to stand some distance off, even as it is in the mixtures of perfumes, or the taking of the smells of several flowers in the air.

On the other hand Richard Grant White says:

Shakespeare seems to have been a proficient in the art of music.[3]

---

[1] Knight's *Shak.*, note 7, act v, *Merchant of Venice.*
[2] *History of Music.* [3] *Life and Genius of Shak.*, p. 299.

The commentators say that Balthazar, a musician in the service of Prince John, in *Much Ado about Nothing*,[1] was probably thus named from the celebrated Balthazarini, an Italian performer on the violin, who was in great favor at the court of Henry II., of France, in 1577. In 1577 William Shakspere was probably going to the grammar school in Stratford, aged thirteen years. How could he know anything about a distinguished musician at the court of France, between which and Stratford there was then less intercourse than there is now between Moscow and Australia. But Francis Bacon was sent to Paris in 1576, and remained there for three years; and doubtless, for he was a lover of music, knew Balthazarini well, and sought in this way to perpetuate his memory. Or it may be that the cipher narrative in *Much Ado about Nothing* tells some story in which Balthazarini is referred to.

Bacon devoted many pages in his *Natural History*[2] to experiments in music. He noted that a musical note "*falling* from one tone to another" is "delightful," reminding us of

>That strain again! it hath a dying *fall*.[3]

And he further notes that "the division and quavering, which please so much in music, have an agreement with the glittering of light, as the moonbeams playing on a wave."[4]

Who can fail to believe that the same mind which originated this poetical image wrote the following?

>How sweet the moonlight sleeps upon this bank!
>Here will we sit, and let the sounds of music
>Creep in our ears; soft stillness and the night
>Become the touches of sweet harmony.[5]

And the following lines — giving the reason of things as a philosopher and scholar — are in the very vein of Bacon:

>The cause why music was ordained;
>Was it not to refresh the mind of man,
>*After his studies,* or his usual pain?
>Then *give me leave to read philosophy,*
>And, while I pause, serve in your harmony.[6]

Bacon says:

Voices or consorts of music do make a harmony by *mixture*. . . . The sweetest

---

[1] Act ii, scene 3.
[2] Century ii.
[3] *Twelfth Night*, I, 1.
[4] *Natural History*, cent. ii, § 113.
[5] *Merchant of Venice*, v, 1.
[6] *Taming of the Shrew*, III, 1.

and best harmony is, when every part or instrument is not heard by itself, but a conflation of them all. . . . But sounds do disturb and alter the one the other; sometimes the one drowning the other and making it not heard; sometimes the one jarring with the other and making a *confusion;* sometimes the one mingling with the other and making a harmony. . . . *Where echoes come from several parts at the same distance*, they must needs make, as it were, a *choir of echoes*. . . . There be many places where you shall hear a number of echoes one after another: and it is where there is a *variety of hills and woods*, some nearer, some farther off.[1]

Now turn to the following magnificent specimen of word-painting, from the *Midsummer Night's Dream:*

> We will, fair Queen, up to the mountain's top,
> And mark the musical *confusion*
> Of hounds and *echo* in conjunction.
> I was with Hercules and Cadmus once,
> When in a *wood* of Crete they bayed the bear,
> With hounds of Sparta: never did I hear
> Such gallant chiding; for, besides the *groves*,
> *The skies, the fountains*, every region near
> Seemed all one mutual cry: I never heard
> So musical a discord, such sweet thunder.[2]

It may, of course, be said that Bacon's statement of fact in the above is bare and barren, compared with the exquisite melody of the description given us in the play; but it must be remembered that the one is prose and the other poetry; and that the prose of the Plays is as much prose as is the prose of the *Natural History*. But no man, however perfect his perception of beauty may have been, could have given us the description in the *Midsummer Night's Dream* unless he had the analytic power to see that the delightful effects which his ear realized were caused by a "musical confusion" of the hounds and the echoes; the groves, skies, fountains and everything around flinging back echo upon echo, until the whole scene "seemed all one mutual cry," until, in fact, there was produced, as Bacon says, "a choir of echoes." And the very words, "a choir of echoes," are poetical; they picture the harmonious mingling of echoes, like the voices of singers, and remind us of the sonnet, where the poet speaks of the trees, deadened by the winter, as

> Bare, ruined *choirs*, where late the sweet birds sang.

It seems to me we have here the evidence not only that both writers loved music and had studied it, but that they had noted the same effects from the same cause; for surely Bacon's description of

---

[1] *Natural History*, cent. iii.
[2] *Midsummer Night's Dream*, iv. 1.

the "choir of echoes" from "a variety of hills and woods" must have been based on some such hunting scene as the poet gives us with such melodious detail.

II. Gardening.

Francis Bacon and the writer of the Plays both were filled with a great love for gardening.

Bacon calls it "the purest of all human pleasures."

Shakespeare, as Mrs. Pott has shown, refers to thirty-five different flowers:

Anemone, carnation, columbine, cornflower, cowslip, crown-imperial, crow-flower, daffodil, daisy, eglantine, flower-de-luce, fumitory, gilly-flower, hare-bell, honeysuckle, ladies' smocks, lavender, lilies, long purples, marigold, marjorum, myrtle, oxlips, pansies or love in idleness, peony, pimpernal, pink, primrose, rose "may," rose "must," rose "damask," rosemary, thyme, violet, woodbine.[1]

Mrs. Pott says:

These thirty-five flowers are all noted or studied by Bacon, with the exception of the columbine, pansy and long-purples. The hare-bell may be considered as included in the "bell-flowers," which he describes. *Twenty-one of these same thirty-five Shakespearean flowers are enumerated by Bacon in his essay* Of Gardens.

And this coincidence is the more remarkable when it is remembered that these flowers were but a small part of those well-known in the days of Shakespeare and Bacon. In all the notes on gardening, in Bacon's writings, there are only five flowers which are not named by Shakespeare, while of Ben Jonson's list of flowers only half are ever alluded to by Bacon.

Mrs. Pott points out that Bacon was the first writer that ever distinguished flowers by the season of their blooming; and Shakespeare follows this order precisely and never brings the flowers of one season into another, as Jonson and other poets do. In the midst of exquisite poetry he accurately associates the flower with the month to which it belongs. He says:

> Daffodils that come before the swallow dares
> And take the winds of *March* with beauty.[2]

Says Bacon:

For *March* there come violets, especially the single blue, which are the earliest.[3]

---

[1] *Shakespeariana*, May, 1885, p. 241. [2] *Winter's Tale*, iv, 3. [3] *Essay Of Gardens*.

And again:

> Thy banks with peonies and lilies brims,
> Which spongy *April* at thy hest betrims.[1]

And again the poet says:

> O rose of *May*, dear maid, kind sister.

In all this the poet shows the precision of the natural philosopher.

The whole article here quoted, from the pen of Mrs. Pott, can be read with advantage and pleasure.

Bacon studied gardening in all its details. His love for flowers was great. Even in his old age, when, broken in health and fortune, and oppressed with cares and debts, we find him writing the Lord Treasurer Cranfield that he proposes to visit him at Chiswick, he adds:

> I hope to wait on your Lordship and gather some violets in your garden.

He says in *The New Atlantis:*

> In these we practice likewise all conclusions of *grafting* and inoculating, as well of *wild* trees as fruit trees, which produceth many effects.

While Shakespeare says:

> You see, sweet maid,
> We *marry a gentle scion* to the *wildest* stock,
> And make conceive a bark of baser kind
> By bud of nobler race. This is an art
> Which does mend nature, change it rather; but
> The art itself is nature.[2]

And we find the same thought again:

> Our scions, put in *wild* and savage stocks,
> Spirt up so suddenly into the clouds.[3]

Shakespeare has that curious and strange comparison:

> If you can look into the seeds of time
> And say which grain will grow and which will not.[4]

And, in the same vein, we find Bacon devoting pages to the study of the nature of seeds, and of the mode of testing them, to see whether they will grow or not. He says:

> And therefore skillful gardeners make trial of the seeds before they buy them, whether they be good or no, by putting them into water gently boiled; and if they be good they will sprout within half an hour.[5]

---

[1] *Tempest*, iv, 1.   [2] *Winter's Tale*, iv, 3.   [3] *Henry V.*, iii, 5.
[4] *Macbeth*, i, 3.   [5] *Natural History*, § 500.

And again:

If any one investigate the vegetation of plants he should observe from the first sowing of any seed how and when the seed begins to swell and break, and be filled, as it were, with spirit.[1]

And here is a curious parallelism. Bacon says:

There be certain *corn-flowers*, which come seldom or never in other places unless they be set, but only amongst *corn*; as the blue-bottle, a kind of yellow marigold, wild poppy and *fumitory*. . . . So it would seem that it is the *corn* that qualifieth the earth and prepareth it for their growth.[2]

Shakespeare's attention had also been drawn to these humble corn-flowers, and he had reached the same conclusion, that the earth was prepared to receive these flowers by the presence of the corn. He describes Lear:

> Crowned with rank *fumitor*, and furrow weeds,
> With hardock, hemlocks, nettles, cuckoo-flowers,
> Darnel, and all the idle weeds that grow
> In our *sustaining corn*.[3]

Bacon writes an essay *Of Gardens*, and Shakespeare is full of comparisons and reflections based upon gardens. For instance:

Virtue? a fig! 'Tis in ourselves that we are thus or thus. *Our bodies are our gardens*, to the which our wills are gardeners: so that if we will plant nettles or sow lettuce; set hyssop, and weed up thyme; supply it with one gender of herbs or distract it with many; either to have it sterile with idleness, or manured with industry: why, the power and corrigible authority of this lies in our own wills.[4]

And again:

> Our sea-walled *garden*, the whole land,
> Is full of weeds, her fairest flowers choked up.[5]

And again:

> What rub, or what impediment there is,
> Why that the naked, poor and mangled peace,
> Dear nurse of arts, plenties and joyful births,
> Should not, in this best *garden* of the world,
> Our fertile France, put up her lovely visage? . . .
> The even mead, that erst brought sweetly forth
> The freckled cowslip, burnet, and green clover,
> Wanting the scythe, all uncorrected, rank,
> Conceives by idleness; and nothing teems
> But hateful docks, rough thistles, kecksies, burrs.[6]

And the closeness with which both studied the nature of plants

---

[1] *Novum Organum*, book ii. [3] *Lear*, iv, 4. [5] *Richard II.*, iii, 4.
[2] *Natural History*, § 482. [4] *Othello*, i, 3. [6] *Henry V.*, v, 2.

and their modes of growth is shown in the following remarkable parallel.

In that most curious and philosophical of the Plays, *Troilus and Cressida*, we find this singular comparison:

> Checks and disasters
> Grow in the veins of actions highest reared;
> As *knots*, by the conflux of meeting *sap*,
> Infect the sound pine, and divert his grain,
> Tortive and errant from his course of growth.[1]

And we find that Bacon had, in like manner, studied the effect of sap upon the growth of the tree:

> The cause whereof is, for that the *sap* ascendeth unequally, and doth, as it were, tire and stop by the way. And it seemeth they have some closeness and hardness in their stalk, which hindereth the sap from going up, until it hath *gathered into a knot*, and so is more urged to put forth.[2]

Here we find the poet setting forth that the knots are caused by "the conflux of the meeting sap," while the philosopher tells us that when the sap is arrested it "gathereth into a knot." And so it seems that both were studying the same subject and arriving at the same conclusions; and both thought that not only were the knots caused by the stoppage of the ascending sap, but that the knots produced the new branches: "so," says Bacon, "it is more urged to put forth." The knots, says Shakespeare, divert the grain from the straight, upright course of growth, to-wit, by making it put forth new branches. Can any man believe that Bacon and Shakspere were engaged at the same time in this same curious study, and reached independently these same remarkable conclusions?

And we see the gardener again in *Richard II.*:

> All superfluous branches
> We lop away, that bearing boughs may live.[3]

Again:

> A violet in the youth of primy Nature.[4]

The thoughts of both ran upon flowers. Bacon says:

> We commend the odor of plants growing, and not plucked, taken in the open air; the principal of that kind are violets, gilliflowers, pinks, bean-flowers, lime-tree blossoms, vine buds, honeysuckles, yellow wall-flowers, musk roses, strawberry leaves, etc. .... Therefore to walk or sit near the breath of these plants should not be neglected.[5]

---

[1] *Troilus and Cressida*, i, 3. [2] *Natural History*, § 589. [3] *Richard II.*, iii, 4.
[4] *Hamlet*, i, 3. [5] *History of Life and Death*.

And again he says:

> The daintiest smells of flowers are out of those plants whose leaves smell not as violets, roses, wall-flowers, gilliflowers, pinks, woodbines, vine-flowers, apple-blooms, bean-blossoms, etc.[1]

The same admiration for flowers is shown by Shakespeare. He speaks of

> Daffodils,
> That come before the swallow dares, and take
> The winds of March with beauty; violets, dim,
> But sweeter than the lids of Juno's eyes,
> Or Cytherea's breath; pale primroses,
> That die unmarried, ere they can behold
> Bright Phœbus in his strength, a malady
> Most incident to maids; bold oxlips, and
> The crown imperial; lilies of all kinds,
> The flower-de-luce being one.[2]

I might fill pages with further evidence that both Bacon and the writer of the Plays loved flowers and practiced gardening.

III. THE STUDY OF MEDICINE.

Bacon says of himself:

> I have been puddering in physic all my life.

Shakespeare says:

> 'Tis known I ever
> Have studied physic.[3]

∴

Bacon writes to Sir Robert Cecil:

> I ever liked the Galenists, that deal with good compositions, and not the Paracelsians, that deal with these fine separations.[4]

Shakespeare says:

> *Lafeau.* To be relinquished of the artists.
> *Parolles.* So I say, both of Galen and Paracelsus.
> *Lafeau.* Of all the learned and authentic fellows.

∴

Macaulay says, speaking of Bacon:

> Of all the sciences, that which he regarded with the greatest interest was the science which, in Plato's opinion, would not be tolerated in a well-regulated community. To make men perfect was no part of Bacon's plan. His humble aim was to make imperfect men comfortable. . . . He appealed to the example of Christ, and reminded his readers that the great Physician of the soul did not disdain to be also the physician of the body.[6]

---

[1] *Natural History*, § 389.　[2] *Pericles*, iii, 2.　[3] *All's Well that Ends Well*, ii, 3.
[2] *Winter's Tale*, iv, 3.　[4] Letter to Sir Robert Cecil.　[6] Essay *Bacon*, p. 276.

On the other hand, the celebrated surgeon Bell says:

> My readers will smile, perhaps, to see me quoting Shakespeare among physicians and theologians, but not one of all their tribe, populous though it be, could describe so exquisitely the marks of apoplexy, conspiring with the struggles for life, and the agonies o suffocation, to deform the countenance of the dead; so curiously does our poet present to our conception all the signs from which it might be inferred that the good Duke Humphrey had died a violent death.[1]

Dr. O. A. Kellogg, Assistant Professor of the State Lunatic Asylum at Utica, N. Y., says:

> The extent and accuracy of the medical, physiological and psychological knowledge displayed in the dramas of William Shakespeare, like the knowledge that is manifested on all matters upon which the rays of his mighty genius fell, have excited the wonder and astonishment of all men, who, since his time, have investigated those subjects upon which so much light is shed by the researches of modern science.

Speaking of Bacon, Osborne, his contemporary, said:

> I have heard him outcant a London chirurgeon,—

meaning thereby, excel him in the technical knowledge of his own profession.

∴

His marvelous delineations of the different shades of insanity in Lear, Ophelia, Hamlet, etc., are to be read in the light of the fact that Francis Bacon's mother died of insanity; and Bacon, with his knowledge of the hereditary transmissibility of disease, must have made the subject one of close and thorough study. There are instances in his biography which show that he was himself the victim of melancholy; and there are reasons to think, as will be shown hereafter, that he is the real author of a great medical work on that subject which passes now in the name of another.

He seems to have anticipated Harvey's discovery of the circulation of the blood. Harvey, in 1628, demonstrated that "the blood which passed out from the heart, by the arteries, returned to the heart by the veins."

But Shakespeare, long before that time, had said:

> As dear to me as are the ruddy drops
> That visit my sad heart,[2]—

indicating that he knew that the blood returned to the heart.

I find the following interesting passage in Disraeli's *Curiosities of Literature:*

---

[1] Bell's *Principles of Surgery*, 1815, vol. ii, p. 557.   [2] *Julius Cæsar*, ii, 2.

Dr. William Hunter has said that after the discovery of the valves in the veins, which Harvey learned while in Italy from his master, Fabricius ab Aquapendente, the remaining step might easily have been made by any person of common abilities. "This discovery," he observes, "set Harvey to work upon the *use* of the heart and vascular system in animals; and in the *course of some years* he was so happy as to discover, and to prove beyond all possibility of doubt, the circulation of the blood." He afterwards expresses his astonishment that this discovery should have been left for Harvey, though he acknowledges it occupied "a course of years;" adding that "Providence meant to reserve it for *him*, and would not let men *see what was before them nor understand what they read*. It is remarkable that when great discoveries are effected, their simplicity always seems to detract from their originality; on these occasions we are reminded of the egg of Columbus.[1]

But it seems that the author of the Shakespeare Plays, years before Harvey made his discovery, had also read of the observations of Fabricius ab Aquapendente, and understood that there were valves in the veins and arteries. And this he could only have done in the original Italian — certainly not in English. And he refers to these valves as "gates" in the following lines:

> And in the porches of mine ears did pour
> The leperous distilment; whose effect
> Holds such an enmity with *blood of man,*
> That swift as quicksilver *it courses through*
> *The natural gates and alleys of the body;*
> And with a sudden vigor it doth posset
> And curd, like aigre droppings into milk,
> The thin and wholesome blood.[2]

IV. Shakespeare's Physicians.

And it is a remarkable fact that, while the art of medicine was in that age at a very low ebb, and doctors were little better than quacks, Shakespeare represents, on two occasions, the physician in a light that would do no discredit to the profession in this advanced age. Let me give a few facts to show how reasonable and civilized was the medical treatment of the physicians in *Lear* and *Macbeth*, compared with that of the highest in skill in the sixteenth and seventeenth centuries.

Sir Theodore Mayern, Baron Aulbone, was born in France in 1573. He was the great doctor of his day. Among his patients were Henry IV. and Louis XIII., of France, and James I., Charles I. and Charles II., of England.

He administered calomel in scruple doses; he mixed sugar of

---

[1] Disraeli, *Curiosities of Literature*, p. 412.   [2] *Hamlet*, I, 5.

lead in his conserves; but his principal reliance was in pulverized human bones and "raspings of a human skull unburied." His sweetest compound was his *balsam of bats*, strongly recommended for hypochondriacal persons, into which entered adders, bats, sucking whelps, earth-worms, hogs' grease, the marrow of a stag and the thigh-bone of an ox! He died in 1655. He ought to have died earlier.

Another of these learned physicians of Elizabeth's time was Doctor William Bulleyn, who was of kin to the Queen. He died in 1576. His prescription for a child suffering from nervousness was "a smal yonge mouse, rosted."

And this state of ignorance continued for more than a century after Bacon's death. In 1739 the English Parliament passed an act to pay Joanna Stephens, a vulgar adventuress, £5,000, to induce her to make public her great remedy for all diseases. The medicines turned out to be, when revealed, a powder, a decoction and pills, made up principally of egg-shells, snails, soap, honey and swine-cresses!

∴

Now, bearing all this mountebank business in mind, let us turn to the scene where the Doctor appears in *Macbeth*. We read:

Doctor. I have two nights watched with you, but can perceive no truth in your reports. When was it she last walked?

Gentlewoman. Since his Majesty went into the field, I have seen her rise from her bed, throw her night-gown upon her, unlock her closet, take forth paper, fold it, write upon 't, read it, afterwards seal it, and again return to bed; yet all this while in a most fast sleep.

Doctor. A great perturbation in nature! to receive at once the benefit of sleep and do the effects of watching. In this slumbery agitation, besides her walking and other actual performances, what, at any time, have you heard her say?

Gentlewoman. That which I will not report after her.

Doctor. You may, to me; and 'tis most meet you should.

Gentlewoman. Neither to you nor any one; having no witness to confirm my speech.

Enter Lady Macbeth with taper.

Lady Macbeth. Wash your hands, put on your night-gown; look not so pale—I tell you yet again, Banquo's buried; he cannot come out on 's grave.

Doctor. Even so. . . . Will she go now to bed?

Gentlewoman. Directly.

Doctor. Foul whisperings are abroad. Unnatural deeds
Do breed unnatural troubles. Infected minds
To their deaf pillows will discharge their secrets.
More needs she the divine than the physician.
God, God, forgive us all! Look after her;

> Remove from her the means of all annoyance,
> And still keep eyes upon her: So, good night;
> My mind she has mated, and amazed my sight:
> I think, but dare not speak.

And farther on in the tragedy we have:

> *Macbeth.* How does your patient, doctor?
> *Doctor.* Not so sick, my lord,
> As she is troubled with thick-coming fancies,
> That keep her from her rest.
> *Macbeth.* Cure her of that:
> Canst thou not minister to a mind diseased,
> Pluck from the memory a rooted sorrow;
> Raze out the written troubles of the brain;
> And, with some sweet oblivious antidote
> Cleanse the stuffed bosom of that perilous stuff
> Which weighs upon the heart?
> *Doctor.* Therein the patient
> Must minister to himself.
> *Macbeth.* Throw physic to the dogs, I'll none of it.

How courteous and dignified and altogether modern is this physician? There is here nothing of the quack, the pretender, or the impostor. We hear nothing about recipes of human bones, or small roast mice, or snails, or swine-cresses.

And this declaration, of the inadequacy of drugs to relieve the heart, reminds us of what Bacon says:

> You may take sarsa to open the liver, steel to open the spleen, flower of sulphur for the lungs, castareum for the brain, but no receipt openeth the heart but a true friend.[1]

In *Lear* we have another doctor. He is called in to care for the poor insane King, and we have the following conversation:

> *Cordelia.* What can man's wisdom do
> In the restoring of his bereaved sense?
> He that helps him, take all my outward worth.
> *Physician.* There is means, madam;
> *Our foster-nurse of nature is repose,*
> The which he lacks; that to provoke in him,
> Are many simples operative, whose power
> Will close the eyes of anguish.
> *Cord.* All bless'd secrets,
> All you unpublished virtues of the earth,
> Spring with my tears! be aidant and remediate
> In the good man's distress.[2]

And how Baconian is this reference to the "unpublished virtues

---

[1] *Essay Of Friendship.* [2] *Lear* iv, 4.

of the earth"? It was the very essence of Bacon's philosophy to make those virtues known as "aidant and remediate" of the good of man. He sought, by a knowledge of the secrets of nature, to lift men out of their miseries and necessities.

And again, after the Doctor has, by his *simples operative*, produced sleep, and Lear is about to waken, we have the following:

> *Cordelia.* How does the King?
> *Physician.* Madam, he sleeps still.
>   . . . So please your Majesty,
> That we may wake the King? He hath slept long.
> *Cord.* Be governed by your knowledge and proceed,
> I' the sway of your own will.
> *Phys.* Be by, good madam, when we do awake him;
> I doubt not of his temperance.
> *Cord.*   Very well.
> *Phys.* Please you, draw near.— Louder the music there. . . .
> *Cord.* He wakes; speak to him.
> *Phys.* Madam, do you; 'tis fittest.
> *Cord.* How does my royal Lord? How fares your Majesty?
> *Lear.* You do me wrong to take me out o' the grave. . . .
> *Cord.*   Sir, do you know me?
> *Lear.* You are a spirit, I know. When did you die?
> *Cord.* Still, still, far wide.
> *Phys.* He's scarce awake: let him alone a while.[1]

Surely there is nothing here, either in the mode of treatment or the manner of speech, that the modern physician could improve upon. The passage contains Bacon's forecasting of what the doctor should be — of what he has come to be in these latter times.

V. THE MEDICINAL VIRTUES OF SLEEP.

And how well did both Bacon and the writer of the Plays know the virtue of those

> Simples operative, whose power
> Will close the eyes of anguish.

Bacon in his *Natural History*, §738, discussing all the drugs that "inebriate and provoke sleep," speaks of "the tear of *poppy*," of "*henbane-seed*" and of "*mandrake*."

While Shakespeare is familiar with the same medicines. He says:

> Not *poppy*, nor *mandragora*,
> Nor all the drowsy syrups of the world,
> Shall ever minister thee to that sweet sleep
> Which thou ow'dst once.[2]

---

[1] *Lear*, iv, 4.   [2] *Othello*, iii, 3.

And again:

>With juice of cursed *hebenon* in a vial.[1]

And when the doctor in *Lear* says that "the foster-nurse of nature is repose," he speaks a great truth, but faintly recognized in that age, and not even fully understood in this. And yet in that unscientific, crude era both Bacon and the writer of the Plays clearly perceived the curative power of sleep.

Shakespeare calls it

>Great nature's second course,
>Chief *nourisher* in life's feast.[2]

And this curious idea of the *nourishing* power of sleep is often found in Bacon. He says:

Sleep doth supply somewhat to *nourishment*.[3]

Sleep *nourisheth*, or, at least, preserveth bodies a long time without other *nourishment*.[4]

Sleep doth *nourish* much, for the spirits do less spend the *nourishment* in sleep than when living creatures are awake.[5]

And Shakespeare says:

>The innocent sleep:
>Sleep, that knits up the ravel'd sleeve of care;
>The death of each day's life, sore labor's bath,
>Balm of hurt minds.[6]

And again:

>O sleep, O gentle sleep,
>Nature's soft nurse.[7]

And Bacon has something of that same idea of knitting up the raveled sleeve of care. He says:

I have compounded an ointment: . . the use of it should be between sleeps, for in the latter sleep the parts *assimilate chiefly*.[8]

That is, they become *knitted* together. Bacon and the writer of the Plays seem both to have perceived that the wear of life frayed the nervous fiber.

Shakespeare says of sleep:

>Please you, sir,
>Do not omit the heavy offer of it:
>It seldom visits sorrow; when it doth
>It is a comforter.[9]

---

[1] *Hamlet*, i, 5.
[2] *Macbeth*, ii, 2.
[3] *History of Life and Death*.
[4] *Natural History*, § 746.
[5] Ibid., cent. i, § 57.
[6] *Macbeth*, ii, 2.
[7] 2d *Henry IV.*, iii, 1.
[8] *Natural History*, cent. 1, § 59.
[9] *Tempest*, ii, 1.

Bacon says:

Such is the force of sleep to restrain all vital consumption.[1]

And again:

Sleep is nothing else but a reception and retirement of the living spirit into itself.[2]

∴

It would almost seem as if spirit was so incompatible with its enfoldment of matter that the union could only continue at the price of periods of oblivion, or semi-death; during which the conscious spirit, half-parted from its tenement, sinks back into the abyss of God, and returns rejuvenated, and freshly charged with vital force for the duties of life. But for centuries after Bacon's time there were thousands, even among the most enlightened of their age, who regarded sleep as the enemy of man, to be curtailed by all possible means. It is therefore a striking proof of identity when two writers, of that period, are found united in anticipating the conclusions of modern thought on this important subject. In the medicinal science of to-day sleep is indeed "sore labor's bath," and above all "the balm of hurt minds."

VI. Use of Medical Terms.

But the Shakespeare writings bubble over with evidences that the writer was, like Bacon, a student of medicine.

Bacon says:

For opening, I commend beads or pieces of the roots of *carduus benedictus*.[3]

And Shakespeare says:

Get you some of this distilled *carduus benedictus;* . . . it is the only thing for a qualm.[4]

It would be extraordinary indeed if two distinct men not only used the same expressions, thought the same thoughts, cited the same quotations and pursued the same studies, but *even recommended the same medicines!*

∴

Bacon says:

Extreme *bitter as* in *coloquintida*.[5]

Shakespeare says:

The food that to him now is as luscious as locusts, shall be to him shortly as *bitter as coloquintida*.[6]

---

[1] *History of Life and Death.*
[2] Ibid.
[3] *Natural History,* § 963.
[4] *Much Ado about Nothing,* iii, 4.
[5] *Natural History,* cent. i, § 36.
[6] *Othello,* i, 3.

Here we have the writer of the Plays and Francis Bacon dwelling upon another medicine, and describing it in the same terms.

Shakespeare speaks in *Lear* of "the *hysterica passio*." He also knew about the vascular membrane lining the brain:

These are begot in the ventricle of memory, nourished in the womb of *pia mater*, and delivered upon the mellowing of occasion.[1]

He also says:

> What rhubarb, senna, or what purgative drug
> Will scour these English hence.[2]

Again:

> Dangerous conceits are, in their natures, poisons,
> Which at first are scarce found to distaste;
> But with a little act upon the blood,
> Burn like the mines of sulphur.[3]

And again:

> And nothing is at a like goodness still;
> For goodness, growing to a *pleurisy*,
> Dies in his own too-much.[4]

And again:

> And I will through and through
> Cleanse the foul body of the infected world,
> If they will *patiently receive my medicine*.[5]

No wonder some have argued that the writer of the Plays was a physician.

In *1st Henry IV.*[6] he refers to the *midriff*; in *2d Henry IV.* and *Othello* and *Macbeth* he describes accurately the effect of intoxicating liquor on the system; in *2d Henry IV.*[7] he refers to *aconite*; in *The Merry Wives of Windsor* he drags in the name of *Esculapius*. In *King John* he says:

> Before the curing of a strong disease,
> Even in the instant of repair and health,
> The fit is strongest; evils that take leave,
> On their departure most of all show evil.[8]

In *Coriolanus* he says:

> Sir, these cold ways,
> That seem like prudent helps, are very poisonous
> Where the disease is violent.[9]

In *Lear* he says:

> Crack nature's moulds, all *germens* spill at once
> That make ungrateful man.[10]

---

[1] *Love's Labor Lost*, iv, 2.
[2] *Macbeth*, v, 3.
[3] *Othello*, iii, 3.
[4] *Hamlet*, iv, 7.
[5] *As You Like It*.
[6] Act iii, scene 3.
[7] Act iv, scene 4.
[8] *King John*, iii, 4.
[9] *Coriolanus* iii, 1.
[10] *Lear*, iii, 2.

In *Julius Cæsar*[1] he describes correctly the symptoms of epilepsy. In *Timon of Athens*[2] he gives us the mode of treatment of a still more formidable disease.

In *Henry V.* he furnishes us with a minute description of Falstaff's death:

> A' parted even just between twelve and one, e'en at the turning of the tide, for after I saw him fumble with the sheets, and play with flowers, and smile upon his finger-ends, I knew there was but one way, for his nose was as sharp as a pen, and a' babbled of green fields. . . . So he bade me lay more clothes on his feet. I put my hand into the bed, and felt them, and they were as cold as any stone.[3]

And it is a curious fact that Francis Bacon studied the signs of death, as he studied everything else, with the utmost particularity and minuteness, and he has put them on record. He says:

> The immediate preceding signs of death are, great unquietness and tossing in the bed, *fumbling* with the hands ["I saw him *fumble* with the sheets," says Dame Quickly], catching and grasping hard, gnashing with the teeth, speaking hollow, trembling of the nether lip, paleness of the face, the memory confused ["a babbled of green fields," says Dame Quickly], speechless, cold sweats, the body shooting in length, lifting up the white of the eye, changing of the whole visage, as *the nose sharp* ["his *nose was as sharp* as a pen," says Dame Quickly], eyes hollow, cheeks fallen, contraction and doubling of the *coldness in the extreme parts of the body* ["his feet were as *cold as any stone*," says Dame Quickly].[4]

Here we have the same symptoms, *and in the same order.* Who is there can believe that these descriptions of death came out of two different minds?

VII. THE SAME HISTORICAL STUDIES.

Shakespeare wrote a group of historical plays extending from Richard II. to Henry VIII., with a single break — the reign of Henry VII. *And Bacon completed the series by writing a history of Henry VII.!*

Shakespeare wrote a play turning upon Scotch history — *Macbeth.* Bacon had studied the history of Scotland. He says:

> The kingdom of Scotland hath passed through no small troubles, and remaineth full of boiling and swelling tumors.[5]

Shakespeare wrote a play concerning Danish history — *Hamlet.* Bacon had carefully studied Scandinavian history. He says:

---

[1] Act i, scene 2.
[2] Act iv, scene 3.
[3] *Henry V.*, ii, 3.
[4] *History of Life and Death*, div. 2, § 30.
[5] Observations on a Libel — *Life and Works*, vol. I, p. 162.

The kingdom of Swedeland, besides their foreign wars upon their confines, the Muscovites and the Danes, hath also been subject to divers intestine tumults and mutations, *as their stories do record*.[1]

Shakespeare wrote a play of *Julius Cæsar*; Bacon wrote a biography or character of *Julius Cæsar*.

Shakespeare wrote a play, *Antony and Cleopatra*, in which Augustus Cæsar is a principal character. Bacon wrote a biography of *Augustus Cæsar*. And he discusses, in his essay *Of Love*, Mark Antony, "the half-partner of the empire of Rome, a voluptuous man and inordinate, whose great business did not keep out love." And this is the very element of the great Roman's character on which the play of *Antony and Cleopatra* turns.

Shakespeare wrote a play of *Timon of Athens*, the misanthrope. Bacon speaks of "misanthropi, that make it their practice to bring men to the bough, and yet have never a tree in their garden for the purpose, as Timon had."[2]

VIII. Julius Cæsar in the Plays.

Shakespeare manifests the highest admiration for Julius Cæsar. He calls him "the foremost man of all this world."

In *Cymbeline* he says:

There is no more such Cæsars; other of them may have crooked noses; but to own such straight arms, none.[3]

In *Hamlet* he refers to him as "the mighty Julius." He says:

> A little ere the mighty Julius fell,
> The graves stood tenantless, and the sheeted dead
> Did squeak and gibber in the Roman streets.[4]

In *2d Henry VI.* he says:

> For Brutus' bastard hand stabbed Julius Cæsar.[5]

On the other hand, Bacon shows a like admiration for Cæsar. He says:

Machiavel says if Cæsar had been overthrown "he would have been more odious than ever was Catiline;" as if there had been no difference, but in fortune, between a very fury of lust and blood and the *most excellent spirit* (his ambition reserved) *of the world*.[6]

---

[1] Observations on a Libel—*Life and Works*, vol. i, p. 162.
[2] Essay *Of Goodness*.
[3] *Cymbeline*, iii, 1.
[4] *Hamlet*, i, 1.
[5] *2d Henry IV.*, iv, 1.
[6] *Advancement of Learning*, book ii.

This is but another way of saying: "The foremost man of all this world." He also refers to Cæsar's letters and apophthegms, "which excel all men's else."[1]

Shakespeare says:

> Kent, in the commentaries Cæsar writ,
> Is termed the civil'st place of all this isle.[2]

Bacon refers to Cæsar's *Commentaries*, and pronounces them "the best history of the world."[3]

In the play of *Julius Cæsar* we see the conspirators coming together at the house of Brutus. In *The Advancement of Learning*, book ii, we find Bacon describing the supper given by M. Brutus and Cassius to "certain whose opinions they meant to feel whether they were fit to be made their associates" in the killing of Cæsar.

Bacon says of Julius Cæsar:

> He referred all things to himself, and was the true and perfect center of all his actions. By which means, being so fast tied to his ends, he was still prosperous and prevailed in his purposes, insomuch that neither country, nor religion, nor good turns done him, nor kindred, nor friendship diverted his appetite nor bridled him from pursuing his own ends.[4]

In the play we find the same characteristic brought into view. Just before the assassination Cassius falls at Cæsar's feet to beg the enfranchisement of Publius Cimber. Cæsar replies:

> I could be well moved if I were as you;
> If I could pray to move, prayers would move me.
> But I am constant as the northern star
> Of whose true-fixed and resting quality
> There is no fellow in the firmament.
> The skies are painted with unnumbered sparks,
> They are all fire, and every one doth shine;
> But there is one in all doth hold his place:
> So, in the world: 'tis furnished well with men,
> And men are flesh and blood and apprehensive;
> Yet, in the number, I do know but one
> That unassailable holds on his rank,
> Unshaked of motion, and that I am he
> Let me a little show it.[5]

Here we see the same man described by Bacon, whom "neither country, nor good turns done him, nor kindred, nor friendship diverted . . . from pursuing his own ends."

---

[1] *Advancement of Learning*, book ii.
[2] *2d Henry VI.*, iv, 7.
[3] *Advancement of Learning*, book ii.
[4] *Character of Julius Cæsar*.
[5] *Julius Cæsar*, iii, 1.

In *Julius Cæsar* we find Shakespeare suggesting the different temperaments and mental states that accompany particular conditions of the body:

> Let me have men about me that are *fat:*
> Sleek-headed men and such as sleep o' nights.
> Yond' Cassius hath a *lean* and hungry look;
> He thinks too much: such men are dangerous.[1]

And in Bacon's *Catalogue of Particular Histories*, to be studied, we find this:

> 52. A history of different habits of body, of fat and lean, of complexions (as they are called), etc.

IX. Studies of Mortality.

Shakespeare tells us that Cleopatra had pursued

> Conclusions infinite
> Of easy ways to die.

And she speaks of the *asp* as the "baby at my breast that sucks the nurse to sleep."

Bacon had made the same subject a matter of study. He says:

> The death that is *most without pain* hath been noted to be upon the taking of the potion of hemlock, which in humanity was the form of execution of capital offenders in Athens. The poison of the *asp, that Cleopatra used, hath some affinity with it.*[2]

Marvelous! marvelous! how the heads of these two men — if you will insist on calling them such — were stored with the same facts and gave birth to the same thoughts!

Both had studied the condition of the human body after death.

Bacon says:

> I find in Plutarch and others that when Augustus Cæsar visited the sepulcher of Alexander the Great in Alexandria, he found the body to keep its dimensions, but withal, that notwithstanding all the embalming, which no doubt was the best, the body was so tender, as Cæsar touching but the nose defaced it.[3]

And, on the other hand, we find Shakespeare's mind dwelling upon the dust of this same Alexander, and tracing it, in his imagination, through many transmutations, until he finds it "stopping the bung-hole of a beer-barrel."[4]

We observe the mind of the poet pursuing some very curious and ghastly, not to say unpoetical, inquiries. In *Hamlet* we have:

---

[1] *Julius Cæsar*, i, 2. [2] *Natural History*, § 643. [3] Ibid., § 771. [4] *Hamlet*, v, 1.

Hamlet. How long will a man lie i' the earth ere he rot?

Clown. Faith, if he be not rotten before he die (as we have many pocky corses now-a-days, that will scarce hold the laying in), he will last you some eight year, or nine year: a tanner will last you nine year.

Hamlet. Why he more than another?

Clown. Why, sir, his hide is so tanned with his trade that he will keep out water a great while; and your water is a sore decayer of your whoreson dead body.[1]

And Bacon's mind had turned to similar studies. He says:

It is strange, and well to be noted, how long carcasses have continued uncorrupt, and in their former dimensions, as appeareth in the mummies of Egypt; having lasted, as is conceived, some of them three thousand years.[2]

X. ORATORY.

Both Bacon and the writer of the Shakespeare Plays were practical orators and students of oratory.

As to the first, we have Ben Jonson's testimony:

There happened in my time one noble speaker, who was full of gravity in his speaking. His language, where he could spare or pass by a jest, was nobly censorious. No man ever spake more neatly, more pressly, more weightily, or suffered less emptiness, less idleness, in what he uttered. No member of his speech but consisted of his own graces. His hearers could not cough or look aside from him without loss. He commanded where he spoke and had his judges angry and pleased at his devotion. No man had their affections more in his power. The fear of every man who heard him was lest he should make an end.

Howell, another contemporary, says of him: "He was the eloquentest man that was born in this island."[3]

Let us turn now to the great oration which Shakespeare puts into the mouth of Mark Antony, as delivered over the dead body of Julius Cæsar.

Well did Archbishop Whately say of Shakespeare:

The first of dramatists, he might easily have been the first of orators.

Only an orator, accustomed to public speech, and holding "the affections of his hearers in his power," and capable of working upon the passions of men, and making them "angry or pleased" as he chose, could have conceived that great oration. It is climactic in its construction. Mark Antony begins in all humility and deep sorrow, asking only pity and sympathy for the poor bleeding corpse:

I come to bury Cæsar, not to praise him.

---

[1] *Hamlet*, v, 1. [2] *Natural History*, § 771. [3] Holmes, *Authorship of Shak.*, vol. ii, p. 600.

He is most deferential to "the honorable men" who had assassinated Cæsar:

> Here, under leave of Brutus, and the rest,
> (For Brutus is an honorable man,—
> So are they all, all honorable men),
> Come I to speak in Cæsar's funeral.

And he gives the humble reason:

> He was my friend, faithful and just to *me*.

And then how cunningly he interjects appeals to the feelings of the mob:

> He hath brought many captives home to Rome,
> Whose ransoms did the general coffers fill.

And how adroitly, and with an *ad captandum vulgus* argument, he answers the charge that Cæsar was ambitious:

> You all did see that on the Lupercal
> I thrice presented him a kingly crown,
> Which he did thrice refuse. Was this ambition?
>
> When that the poor have cried, Cæsar hath wept:
> Ambition should be made of sterner stuff.

And then, protesting that he will not read Cæsar's will, he permits the multitude to know that they are his heirs.

And what a world of admiration, in the writer, for Cæsar himself, lies behind these words:

> Let but the commons hear this testament,
> (Which, pardon me, I do not mean to read),
> And they would go and kiss dead Cæsar's wounds,
> And dip their napkins in his sacred blood;
> Yea, beg a hair of him for memory,
> And dying, mention it within their wills,
> Bequeathing it, as a rich legacy,
> Unto their issue.

Then he pretends to draw back.

Citizens. Read the will; we'll hear it, Antony; you shall read us the will—Cæsar's will.

Antony. Will you be patient? Will you stay a while? I have o'ershot myself to tell you of it.

And then, at last, encouraged by the voices and cries of the multitude, he snarls out:

> I fear I wrong the *honorable men*
> *Whose daggers have stabbed Cæsar.*

But before reading the will he descends to uncover the dead body of the great commander; the multitude pressing, with fiery Italian eyes, around him, and glaring over each others' shoulders at the corpse.

But first he brings back the memory of Cæsar's magnificent victories:

> You all do know this mantle: I remember
> The first time ever Cæsar put it on;
> 'Twas on a summer's evening, in his tent,
> *That day he overcame the Nervii.*

Then he plucks away the garment and reveals the hacked and mangled corpse,

> Marred, as you see, by traitors.

And thereupon he gives the details of the assassination, points out and identifies each wound, "poor, poor dumb mouths"; and at last reads the will, and sends the mob forth, raging for revenge, to let slip the dogs of war.

Beside this funeral oration all other efforts of human speech are weak, feeble, poverty-stricken and commonplace. Call up your Demosthenes, your Cicero, your Burke, your Chatham, your Grattan, your Webster,—and what are their noblest and loftiest utterances compared with this magnificent production? It is the most consummate eloquence, wedded to the highest poetry, breathing the profoundest philosophy, and sweeping the whole register of the human heart, as if it were the strings of some grand musical instrument, capable of giving forth all forms of sound, from the sob of pity to the howl of fury. It lifts the head of human possibility a whole shoulder-height above the range of ordinary human achievement.

We find Bacon writing a letter, in 1608–9, to Sir Tobie Matthew, in which he refers back to the time of the death of Elizabeth (1603), and, alluding to a rough draft of his essay, *The Felicity of Queen Elizabeth*, which Bacon had shown to Sir Tobie, he says:

> At that time methought you were more willing to hear *Julius Cæsar* than Elizabeth commended.

Bacon, it is known, submitted his acknowledged writings to the criticism of his friend, Sir Tobie; and we can imagine him reading to Sir Tobie, in secret, this grand oration, with all the heat and fervor with which it came from his own mind. And we can imagine

Sir Tobie's delight, touched upon and referred to cunningly in the foregoing playful allusion.

What a picture for a great artist that would make: Bacon and Sir Tobie alone in the chamber of Gray's Inn, with the door locked; and Bacon reading, with flashing eyes, to his enraptured auditor, Mark Antony's oration over the dead body of Julius Cæsar.

XI. OTHER STUDIES.

But, in whatever direction we turn, we find the writer of the Plays and Francis Bacon devoting themselves to the same pursuits.

Bacon in *The New Atlantis* discusses the possibility of there being discovered in the future "some perpetual motions"—a curious thought and a curious study for that age.

Shakespeare makes Falstaff say to the Chief Justice:

I were better to be eaten to death with rust, than to be scoured to nothing with *perpetual motion*.[1]

Bacon says:

Snow-water is held unwholesome; inasmuch as the people that dwell at the foot of the snow mountains, or otherwise upon the ascent, especially the women, by drinking snow-water have great bags hanging under their throats.[2]

Shakespeare says:

> When we were boys,
> Who would believe that there were mountaineers
> Dew-lapped like bulls, whose throats had hanging at them
> Wallets of flesh?[3]

Shakespeare was familiar with the works of Machiavel, and alludes to him in *The Merry Wives of Windsor*, in *1st Henry VI.* and in *3d Henry VI.*

Bacon had studied his writings, and refers to him in *The Advancement of Learning*, book ii, and in many other places.

Shakespeare was a great observer of the purity of the air. He says in *Macbeth*:

> This castle hath a pleasant seat; the air
> Nimbly and sweetly recommends itself
> Unto our gentle senses.

And Bacon says:

I would wish you to observe the climate and the temperature of the air; for so you shall judge of the healthfulness of the place.[4]

---

[1] *2d Henry IV.*, i, 2. [2] *Natural History*, § 396. [3] *Tempest*, iii, 4.
[4] Letter to the Earl of Rutland, written in the name of the Earl of Essex — *Life and Works*, vol. ii, p. 19.

Bacon also says:

The heart receiveth benefit or harm most from the air we breathe, from vapors and from the affections.[1]

One has only to read the works of Francis Bacon to see that they abound in quotations from and references to the Bible. He had evidently made the Scriptures the subject of close and thorough study.

On the other hand, the Rev. Charles Wordsworth says:

Take the entire range of English literature, put together our best authors who have written upon subjects professedly not religious or theological, and we shall not find, I believe, in all united, so much evidence of the Bible having been read and used as we have found in Shakespeare alone.

We have already seen that both the author of the Plays and Francis Bacon had studied law, and had read even the obscure law-reports of Plowden, printed in the still more obscure black-letter and Norman French.

In fact, I might swell this chapter beyond all reasonable bounds by citing instance after instance, to show that the writer of the Plays studied precisely the same books that Francis Bacon did; and, in the chapter on *Identical Quotations*, I have shown that he took out of those books exactly the same particular facts and thoughts which had adhered to the memory of Francis Bacon. It is difficult in this world to find two men who agree in devoting themselves not to one, but to a multitude of the same studies; and rarer still to find two men who will be impressed alike with the same particulars in those studies.

But let us move forward a step farther in the argument.

[1] *History of Life and Death.*

CHAPTER VI.

IDENTICAL ERRORS.

Lend thy serious hearing to what I shall unfold.
Hamlet, i, 5.

THE list of coincident errors must necessarily be brief. We can not include the errors common to all men in that age, for those would prove nothing. And the mistakes of so accurate and profound a man as Francis Bacon are necessarily few in number. But if we find *any* errors peculiar to Francis Bacon repeated in Shakespeare, it will go far to settle the question of identity. For different men may read the same books and think the same thoughts, but it is unusual, in fact, extraordinary, if they fall into the same mistakes.

I. BOTH MISQUOTE ARISTOTLE.

Mr. Spedding noticed the fact that Bacon in *The Advancement of Learning* had erroneously quoted Aristotle as saying "that *young men* are no fit auditors of *moral* philosophy," because "they are not settled from the boiling heat of their affections, nor attempered with time and experience"; while, in truth, Aristotle speaks, in the passage referred to by Bacon, of "*political* philosophy."

Mr. Spedding further noted that this precise error of confounding *moral* with *political* philosophy *had been followed by Shakespeare*. In *Troilus and Cressida* the two "young men," Paris and Troilus, had given their opinion that the Trojans should keep possession of the fair Helen. To which Hector replies:

> Paris and Troilus, you have both said well;
> And on the cause and question now in hand
> Have glozed — but superficially; not much
> Unlike *young men* whom *Aristotle* thought
> Unfit to hear *moral* philosophy.[1]

And what reason did Bacon give why young men were not fit to hear moral philosophy? Because "they are not settled from the

---

[1] *Troilus and Cressida*, ii, 2.

boiling heat of their affections, nor attempered with time and experience." And why does Hector think young men are "unfit to hear moral philosophy"? Because:

> The reason you allege do more conduce
> To the hot passions of *distempered blood*,
> Than to make up a free determination
> 'Twixt right and wrong; for pleasure and revenge
> Have ears more deaf than adders, to the voice
> Of any true decision.

II. AN ERROR IN NATURAL PHILOSOPHY.

Shakespeare had a curious theory about fire: it was that each fire was an entity, as much so as a stick of wood; and that one flame could push aside or drive out another flame, just as one stick might push aside or expel another. This of course was an error. He says:

> Even as *one heat another heat expels*,
> Or as *one nail by strength drives out another*,
> So the remembrance of my former love
> Is by a newer object quite forgotten.[1]

And the same thought is repeated in *Coriolanus:*

> *One fire drives out another; one nail, one nail.*[2]

We turn to Bacon's *Promus of Formularies and Elegancies*, now preserved in the British Museum, and, in his own handwriting, we have, as one of the entries:

> *Clavum clavo pellere*—(To *drive out a nail with a nail*).

This is precisely the expression given above:

> *One nail* by strength *drives out another.*

> One fire *drives out* another; *one nail, one nail.*

But behind this was a peculiar and erroneous theory held by Bacon, concerning heat, which he records in the *Sylva Sylvarum*.[3] He held that heat was a substance; some of his favorite fallacies were that "one flame within another quencheth not," and that "flame doth not mingle with flame, but remaineth contiguous." He speaks of one heat being "mixed with another," of its being "pushed farther,"—as if so much matter. This is precisely the erroneous theory which was held by the writer of the Plays.

---

[1] *Two Gentlemen of Verona*, ii, 4.   [2] *Coriolanus*, iv, 7.   [3] Vol. i, p. 32.

Mrs. Pott says:

Knowing, as we now do, that these theories were *as mistaken as they appear to have been original*, it seems almost past belief that any two men should, at precisely the same period, have independently conceived the same theories and made the same mistakes.[1]

III. Spirits of Animate and Inanimate Nature.

Bacon had another peculiar theory which the world has refused to accept, at least in its broad significance.

He believed that there is a living spirit, or life principle, in every thing in the created universe, which conserves its substance and holds it together; and thus that, in some sense, the stones and the clods of the earth possess souls; that without some such spiritual force, differing in kinds, there could be no difference in substances. For why should the arrangement of the molecules of foam, for instance, differ from that of the molecules of iron, if some external force has not been imposed upon them to hold them in their peculiar relation to each other, and thus constitute the difference between the light froth and the dense metal?

This theory is akin to the expression which Shakespeare puts into the mouth of the Duke, in *As You Like It:*

> And this our life, exempt from public haunt,
> Finds tongues in trees, books in the running brooks,
> Sermons in stones, and good in everything.[2]

And Prince Arthur says:

My uncle's spirit is in these stones.[3]

Bacon says:

All tangible bodies contain a spirit enveloped with the grosser body. There is no known body in the upper part of the earth without its spirit. The spirit which exists in all living bodies keeps all the parts in due subjection; when it escapes the body decomposes, or the similar parts unite — as metals rust, fluids turn sour.

And Bacon sees a relationship between the spirit within the animal and the spirit of the objects, even inanimate, which act upon the senses of the animal; and he strikes out the curious thought that

There might be as many senses in animals as there are points of agreement with inanimate bodies if the animated body were *perforated*, so as to allow the spirit to have access to the limb properly disposed for action, as a fit organ.[4]

That is to say, the spirit of the universe pervades all created

---

[1] *Promus*, p. 33. [2] *As You Like It*, ii, 1. [3] *King John*, iv, 3. [4] *Novum Organum*, book ii.

things, animate and inanimate, but the intelligence of man and animal only takes cognizance of the spirits of other things around them through the *perforations of the senses;* the eyes, ears, touch, taste and smell being, as it were, *holes,* through which the external universal vitality reaches into our vitality and stirs it to recognition. A solemn thought, doubtless true, and which should teach us modesty; for it would follow that we see not all God's works, but only those limited areas which come within the range of the peep-holes of our few senses. In other words, the space around us may be filled with forms, animate and inanimate, which hold "no points of agreement" with our senses, and of which, therefore, we can have no knowledge. And thus the dream of the schoolman of old may be true, that the space around us is filled as thick with spirits as the snow-storm is filled with snow-flakes.

This doctrine of *spirits* runs through all Bacon's writings. He says in one place:

All bodies have spirits and pneumatical parts within them. . . . But the spirits of things inanimate are shut in and cut off by the tangible parts.[1]

That is to say, they have no holes of the senses, through which the spirit of the inanimate object can communicate with us; any more than we could communicate with a human spirit, locked up in a body devoid of all the senses.

Again he says:

Spirits are nothing else but a natural body rarified to a proportion, and included in the tangible parts of bodies as in an integument; . . . and they are in all tangible bodies whatsoever, more or less.[2]

And again, speaking of the superstition of "the evil eye," he says:

Besides, at such times [times of glory and triumph], the spirits of the persons envied do come forth most into the outward parts, and so meet the blow.[3]

Bacon does not speak, as we would, of *the spirit* in a man, but of *the spirits,* as if there were a multitude of them in each individual, occupying every part of the body. For instance:

Great joys attenuate the *spirits;* familiar cheerfulness strengthens the *spirits* by calling them forth.[4]

Again:

In bashfulness the *spirits* do a little go and come.[5]

[1] *Natural History,* § 601.
[2] Ibid., § 98.
[3] *Essay Of Envy.*
[4] *History of Life and Death.*
[5] *Essay Of Goodness.*

IDENTICAL ERRORS.

And again:

> The *spirits* of the wine oppress the *spirits animal.*[1]

And in Shakespeare we find this same theory of *the spirits.* He says:

> Fair daughter! you do draw my *spirits* from me,
> With new lamenting ancient oversights.[2]

And again:

> Forth at your eyes your *spirits* wildly peep.[3]

And again:

> I am never merry when I hear sweet music.
> The reason is, your *spirits* are attentive.[4]

And again:

> Your *spirits* shine through you.[5]
>
> Young gentleman, your *spirits* are too bold for your years.[6]
>
> My *spirits*, as in a dream, are all bound up.[7]
>
> My *spirits* are nimble.[8]
>
> Heaven give your *spirits* comfort.[9]
>
> Summon up your dearest *spirits.*[10]
>
> The nimble *spirits* in the arteries.[11]
>
> Their great guilt,
> Like poison given to work a great time after,
> Now 'gins to bite the *spirits.*[12]
>
> *Spirits* are not finely touched but to fine issues.[13]

Thus in the Shakespeare Plays we find the reflection of one of Bacon's most peculiar philosophical beliefs.

IV. Spontaneous Generation.

Bacon fell into another error in natural philosophy which reappears in the Plays. This was a belief, which continued down to our own times, in *spontaneous generation;* that is to say, that life could come out of non-life. We now realize that that marvelous and inexplicable thing we call life ascends by an unbroken pedigree, through all time, back to the central Source of Force in the universe, by whatever name we may call it. But Bacon believed that life could come out of conditions of inorganic matter. He says:

---

[1] *Natural History,* § 726.
[2] *2d Henry IV.,* ii, 3.
[3] *Hamlet,* iii, 4.
[4] *Merchant of Venice,* v, 1.
[5] *Macbeth,* iii, 1.
[6] *As You Like It,* i, 2.
[7] *Tempest,* i, 2.
[8] *Ibid.,* ii, 1.
[9] *Measure for Measure,* iv, 2.
[10] *Love's Labor Lost,* ii, 1.
[11] *Ibid.,* iv, 3.
[12] *Tempest,* iii, 3.
[13] *Measure for Measure,* i, 1.

The first beginnings and rudiments or effects of life in animalculæ spring from putrefaction, as in the eggs of ants, worms, mosses, frogs after rain, etc.[1]

Again he says:

The *excrements* of living creatures do not only *breed* insecta when they are exerned, but also while they are in the body.[2]

We find that the poet Shakespeare had thought much upon this same very unpoetical subject. He says:

> And, as the sleeping soldiers in the alarm,
> Your bedded hair, *like life in excrements*,
> Starts up and stands on end.[3]

Bacon says:

For all putrefaction, if it dissolve not in arefaction, will in the end issue into plants, or living creatures *bred* of putrefaction.[4]

And again he speaks of

Living creatures *bred* of putrefaction.[5]

And in Shakespeare we have Hamlet saying:

For if the sun *breed* maggots in a dead dog, being a god kissing carrion.[6]

And in all this we see, also, the natural philosopher, who believed that " most *base things* tend to rich ends."

V. Other Errors.

Both believed that there was a precious stone in the head of a toad. Bacon says:

Query. If the stone taken out of a toad's head be not of the like virtue; for the toad loveth shade and coolness.[7]

Shakespeare says:

> Sweet are the uses of adversity;
> Which, like the toad, ugly und venomous,
> Wears yet a precious jewel in his head.[8]

Both thought the liver was the seat of sensuality. Bacon in *The Advancement of Learning*, book ii, refers to Plato's opinion to that effect. And in Shakespeare we have:

> This is the liver vein, which makes flesh a deity;
> A green goose, a goddess.[9]

---

[1] *Novum Organum*, book ii.
[2] *Natural History*, § 696.
[3] *Hamlet*, iii, 4.
[4] *Natural History*, § 605.
[5] Ibid., § 328.
[6] *Hamlet*, ii, 2.
[7] *Natural History*, cent. 2, § 967.
[8] *As You Like It*, ii, 1.
[9] *Love's Labor Lost*, iv, 3.

Both believed, despite the discoveries of Galileo, that the earth was the center of the universe, and that the heavens revolved around it. Later in his life Bacon seemed to accept the new theories, but at the time the Plays were written he repudiated them. He says:

> Who would not smile at the astronomers, I mean not these new carmen *which drive the earth about*.[1]

Again he says:

> It is a poor center of a man's actions, himself. It is right earth, for that only stands fast upon his own center; whereas all things that have affinity with the heavens move upon the center of another, which they benefit.[2]

While Shakespeare also rejected the new theories. He says in *Hamlet*:

> Doubt thou the stars are fire,
> *Doubt that the sun doth move*.[3]

Again he says:

> The heavens themselves, the planets *and this center*,
> Observe degree, priority and place.[4]

And in the same play he says:

> But the strong base and building of my love
> Is as the very center of the earth,
> Drawing all things to it.[5]

---

[1] Essay *In Praise of Knowledge*, 1590
— *Life and Works*, vol. i, p. 124.
[2] Essay *Of Wisdom*.
[3] *Hamlet*, ii, 2.
[4] *Troilus and Cressida*, i, 3.
[5] Ibid., iv, 2.

CHAPTER VII.

THE IDENTICAL USE OF UNUSUAL WORDS.

> Letter for letter! Why, this is the very same: the very hand: the very words.
> *Merry Wives of Windsor, ii, 1.*

I HAVE already shown, in the first chapter of Book I., the tendency manifested in the Plays to use unusual words, especially those derived from or constructed out of the Latin. I may add to the list already given the following instances:

> And all things rare
> That heaven's air in this huge *rondure* hems.[1]

> Cowards and men *cautelous*.[2]

> No soil or *cautel*.[3]

> Through all the world's *vastidity*.[4]

> Such *exsufflicate* and blown surmises.[5]

> His pendant bed and *procreant* cradle.[6]

> Thou *vinew'dst* leaven.[7]

> Rend and *deracinate*.[8]

> Thou *cacodæmon*.[9]

We have a very crowding of words, unusual in poetry, into the following lines:

> As knots, by the *conflux* of meeting sap,
> *Infect* the sound pine and *divert* his grain
> *Tortive* and *errant* from his course of growth.[10]

All these things bespeak the scholar, overflowing with Roman learning and eager to enrich his mother-tongue by the coinage of new words. It is not too much to say that Bacon has doubled the capacity of the English language. He was aware of this fact himself, and in his *Discourse in Praise of Queen Elizabeth* he says that the tongue of England "has been infinitely polished since her happy times."

---

[1] Sonnet xxi.
[2] *Julius Cæsar*, ii, 1.
[3] *Hamlet*, i, 3.
[4] *Measure for Measure*, iii, 2.
[5] *Othello*, iii, 3.
[6] *Macbeth*, i, 6.
[7] *Troilus and Cressida*, ii, 1.
[8] *Ibid.*, i, 3.
[9] *Richard III.*, i, 3.
[10] *Troilus and Cressida*, i, 3.

We find in Bacon's prose works the same tendency to coin or transfer words bodily from the Latin. I give a few examples:

"Coarctation," "percutient," "mordication," "carnosities," "the ingurgitation of wine," "incomprehensions," "arefaction," "flexuous courses of nature," "exulcerations," "reluctation," "embarred," "digladiation," "vermiculate questions," "morigeration," "redargution," "maniable," "ventosity."

But we will also find, in both sets of writings, a disposition to use quaint, odd and unusual words, borrowed, many of them, from that part of common speech which rarely finds its way into print,—the colloquialisms of the shop and the street,—and we will find many of them that are used in the same sense by both Bacon and Shakespeare.

Macbeth says:

> I *pull* in resolution, and begin
> To doubt the equivocation of the fiend,
> That lies like truth.[1]

The commentators have been puzzled with this word, but we have it also in Bacon:

> Those smells are all strong, and do *pull* and vellicate the sense.[2]

To *vellicate* is to twitch convulsively.

We find in *Hamlet* the strange word *pall:*

> Our indiscretion sometimes serves us well
> When our dear plots do *pall*.[3]

We turn to Bacon and we find him using the same word:

> The beer or wine hath not been *palled* or deaded at all.[4]

And again:

> The refreshing or quickening of drink *palled* or dead.[5]

In Bacon we have:

> For if they go *forth right* to a place, they must needs have sight.[6]

Shakespeare says:

> Step aside from the direct *forth right*.[7]

> Through *forth rights* and meanders.[8]

Bacon says:

> I have been *puddering* in physic all my life.

---

[1] *Macbeth*, v, 4.
[2] *Natural History*, §835.
[3] *Hamlet*, v, 1.
[4] *Natural History*, §385.
[5] Ibid., §314.
[6] Ibid., §698.
[7] *Troilus and Cressida*, iii, 3.
[8] *Tempest*, iii, 3.

Shakespeare says:

> The gods that keep such a *pudder* o'er our heads.[1]

This word occurs but on this occasion in the Plays. It means *bother*.

There is a word in *Henry V.*[2] — *imbar* — which has excited considerable controversy among the commentators. It occurs in the discussion of the Salic law of France:

> So that as clear as is the summer's sun,
> King Pepin's title, and Hugh Capet's claim,
> King Lewis his satisfaction, all appear
> To hold in right and title of the female;
> So do the kings of France unto this day:
> Howbeit they would hold up this Salic law,
> To bar your Highness claiming from the female;
> And rather choose to hide them in a net,
> Than amply to *imbar* their crooked titles
> Usurped from you and your progenitors.

I quote Knight's foot-note upon this word:

Imbar. The Folio gives this word *imbarre*, which modern editors, upon the authority of Theobald, have changed into *imbars*. Rowe, somewhat more boldly, reads *make bare*. There can be no doubt, we think, that *imbar* is the right word. It might be taken as placed in opposition to *bar*. To *bar* is to obstruct; to *imbar* is to bar in, to secure. They would hold up the Salic law "to bar your Highness," hiding "their crooked titles" in a net rather than amply defending them. But it has been suggested to us that *imbar* is here used for "to set at the bar" — to place their crooked titles before a proper tribunal. This is ingenious and plausible.

I quote these comments to show that the word is a rare and obscure one. The two words, *bar* and *imbar*, seem to me to mean substantially the same thing; as we find *plead* and *implead*, *personate* and *impersonate*, *plant* and *implant*. If there is any difference, it consists in the fact that *bar* means, as suggested by Knight, to shut out, and *imbar* to shut in. In the sentence under consideration it seems that both the title of the reigning French King and the claim of King Henry V. came through the female line, and the Archbishop of Canterbury shows that the French, while their King holds in contravention of the Salic law, yet set it up as a *bar* to the claim of the English King, also holding through the female line, and thus involve themselves in a *net* or tangle of contradictions, instead of amply, fully, and on other and substantial grounds, *imbarring* their titles, inclosing them and defending them from the world.

And here again, where we would find the explanation of obscure words in Shakespeare, we are driven to Bacon.

In his *History of Henry VII*. he says:

> The King forthwith banished all Flemings . . . out of his kingdom; commanding his subjects likewise, and by name his merchants adventurers, which had a reisance in Antwerp, to return; translating the mart, which commonly followed the English cloth, unto Calais; and *embarred* also all further trade for the future.

Here we get at the meaning of the word. He not only drove the Flemish merchants out of his country and recalled his own merchants resident in Flanders, and changed the foreign mart, but he *also* embarred all further trade — that is, denied the Flemish commerce access to his people.

And it is a curious fact that in our great American dictionary (*Webster's Unabridged*) the two words, *embarred* and *imbare*, are given — the first with the above quotation from Bacon, and the other with the example of the word from *Henry V.*, with a meaning attached, created to suit the emergency, "to lay bare, to uncover, to expose." So that, to attempt to read Shakespeare without Bacon, the commentators are driven to coin new words "which never were, and no man ever saw."

We read in Shakespeare:

> How cam'st thou to be the siege of this *mooncalf?*[1]

J. O. Halliwell says in a foot-note upon this passage:

> A *mooncalf* is an imperfectly-developed fœtus, here metaphorically applied to a misshapen monster.

But we turn to Bacon, and there we find the real explanation:

> It may be that children and *young cattle* that are brought forth in the full of the moon are stronger and *larger* than those which are brought forth in the wane; and those, also, which are begotten in the full of the moon [are stronger and larger].[2]

So that the term was applied to Caliban with reference to his gross proportions.

The curious word *starting-hole* occurs but once in the Plays, in Falstaff's interview with the Prince,[3] after the robbery on Gads-hill; and it is so rare that it is made the foundation of a foot-

---

[1] *Tempest*, ii, 2.   [2] *Natural History*, § 897.   [3] *1st Henry IV.*, ii, 4.

note. We turn to Bacon, and we find it used by him in the same sense:

> He [Lopez] thought to provide himself with as many *starting-holes* and evasions as he could devise.[1]

Bacon says:

> So with *marvelous* consent and applause.[2]

Shakespeare says:

> The rogues are *marvelous* poor.[3]
>
> *Marvelous* foul linen.[4]

Bacon speaks of

> *Incredible* affection.[5]

This word is found but once in the Plays:

> I tell you, 'tis *incredible* to believe
> How much she loves me.[6]

Bacon says:

> The people entertained this airy body or *phantasm*.[7]

Shakespeare says:

> A fanatical *phantasm*.[8]

This is a rare word; it occurs but twice in the Plays; the word *phantasma* once.

Bacon says:

> It [Ireland] was a *ticklish* and unsettled state.[9]

Shakespeare says:

> And wide unclasp the tables of their thoughts
> To every *ticklish* reader.[10]

This word occurs but once in the Plays, the instance given.

Bacon says:

> The embassador did so magnify the King and Queen, as was enough to *glut* the hearers.[11]

This odd word occurs only once in the Plays, in *The Tempest*, and is considered so unusual as to be the subject of a foot-note:

---

[1] *The Lopez Conspiracy — Life and Works*, vol. i, p. 283.
[2] *History of Henry VII*.
[3] *All's Well that Ends Well*, iv, 3.
[4] *2d Henry IV*, v, 2.
[5] *History of Henry VII*.
[6] *Taming of the Shrew*, ii, 1.
[7] *History of Henry VII*.
[8] *Love's Labor Lost*, v, 1.
[9] *History of Henry II*.
[10] *Troilus and Cressida*, iv, 5.
[11] *History of Henry VII*.

THE IDENTICAL USE OF UNUSUAL WORDS.

> Though every drop of water swear against it
> And gape at widest to *glut* him.[1]

We find the word *inoculate* but once in the Plays:

> For virtue cannot so *inoculate* our old stock but we shall relish of it.[2]

Bacon uses the same rare word:

> Grafting and *inoculating* wild trees.[3]

Imogen says to the entranced Ioachimo:

> What, dear sir,
> Thus *raps* you? Are you well?[4]

And Knight has a foot-note:

Raps you — transports you. We are familiar with the participle *rapt*, but this form of the verb *is uncommon*.

We turn to Bacon and we find him using the same uncommon form:

> Winged enticements that ravish and *rap* mortal men.[5]

We find in the Plays a very curious expression. Ajax calls Thersites:

> A vinew'dst *leaven*.[6]

We turn to Bacon and we find him applying the same word to human beings:

> A *leaven* of men.[7]

Bacon says:

> A *core* of people.[8]

Shakespeare:

> Thou *core* of envy.[9]

Bacon:

> *Dregs* of the northern people.[10]

Shakespeare:

> *Dregs* of the storm.[11]
>
> *Dregs* of conscience.[12]

Bacon says:

I doubt not but in the university you shall find choice of many excellent wits, and in things wherein they have *waded* many of good understanding.[13]

---

[1] *Tempest*, i, 1.
[2] *Hamlet*, iii, 1.
[3] *New Atlantis*.
[4] *Cymbeline*, i, 7.
[5] *Wisdom of the Ancients — Sphynx*.
[6] *Troilus and Cressida*, ii, 1.
[7] *History of Henry VII*.
[8] Ibid.
[9] *Troilus and Cressida*, v, 1.
[10] *History of Henry VII*.
[11] *Tempest*, ii, 2.
[12] *Richard III.*, i, 4.
[13] Letter to Sir Foulke Greville — *Life and Works*, vol. ii, p. 25.

And again:

> But if I should *wade* further into this Queen's praises.[1]

Shakespeare says:

> For their joy *waded* in tears.[2]
>
>   I am in blood
> Stepped in so far, that should I *wade* no more,
> Returning were as tedious as go o'er.[3]

Bacon says:

> He was wholly *compounded* of frauds and deceits.[4]

Shakespeare says:

> This foolish *compounded* clay, man.[5]
>
> In the large *composition* of this man.[6]
>
> We might *compound* a boy, half French, half English.[7]
>
>   And she, of all *compounded*,
> Outsells them all.[8]

The word *slobber* is referred to by the commentators as a strange and unusual word. It is probably the same word as *slubber*.[9] It is used in *The Merchant of Venice*, ii, 8:

> *Slubber* not on the business for my sake, Bassanio.

Bacon[10] speaks of "*slubbering* on the lute," to illustrate his "cautioning exercise, as to beware lest by evil doing, as all beginners do weakly, a man grow to be *inveterate* in a bad habit." Slubbering on the lute means, therefore, practicing in a slovenly manner.

And this word *inveterate* is a favorite one with Shakespeare:

> The *inveterate* canker.[11]
>
> *Inveterate* malice.[12]
>
> *Inveterate* hate.[13]

In Shakespeare we find:

> Yea, all which it inherit shall dissolve;
> And, like this unsubstantial pageant faded,
> Leave not a *rack* behind.

[1] *Felic. Queen Elizabeth.*
[2] *Winter's Tale*, v. 2.
[3] *Macbeth*, iii, 4.
[4] *Character of Julius Cæsar.*
[5] *2d Henry IV.*, i, 2.
[6] *King John*, i, 2.
[7] *Henry V.*, v, 2.
[8] *Cymbeline*, iii, 5.
[9] *Shakespeariana*, May, 1884, p. 185 — Article by J. Lauglin.
[10] *Discourse Concerning Help for the Intellectual Powers.*
[11] *King John*, v, 2.
[12] *Richard II.*, i, 1.
[13] *Coriolanus*, ii, 3.

This word *rack* has led to great controversy, and as an emendation the word *wreck* was suggested, but the true explanation was found in Bacon.[1] He says:

> The winds in the upper regions, which move the clouds above, which we call *the rack*, and are not perceived below, pass without noise.[2]

Hence the *rack* evidently means the light, fleecy, upper clouds, a fine image for unsubstantiality.

And we have another curious instance wherein Shakespeare is only to be explained by Bacon. In *2d Henry IV.*, ii, 2, Poins says of Falstaff, speaking to Bardolph:

> And how doth the *Martlemas*, your master.

The commentators explain this as meaning the feast of St. Martin, the 11th of November.

> Poins calls Falstaff the Martlemas because his year of life is running out.[3]

But we turn to Bacon's *Natural History*. We find

> That that is dry is unapt to putrefy; and therefore smoke preserveth flesh, as we see in bacon, and neat's tongues and *Martlemas beef*, etc.[4]

This is a much more natural explanation. Poins refers to the aged but gross Falstaff as a beef, dried and smoked by time.

Bacon says:

> The breath in man's *microcosmos* and in other animals do very well agree.[5]

Shakespeare says:

> If you see this in the map of my *microcosm*, follows it I am known well enough too.[6]

Bacon says:

> But sure it could not be that *pelting* matter.[7]

Shakespeare says:

> Every *pelting*, petty officer.[8]
>
> Poor *pelting* villages, sheep-cotes.[9]

Shakespeare says:

> Do cream and *mantle* like a standing pool.[10]

---

[1] Knight's *Shak.*, note B, vol. ii, p. 429.
[2] *Natural History*, cent. ii, § 115.
[3] Knight.
[4] *Natural History*, cent. iv.
[5] *Natural History of Winds*.
[6] *Coriolanus*, ii, 1.
[7] Letter to Buckingham.
[8] *Measure for Measure*, ii, 2.
[9] *Lear*, ii, 3.
[10] *Merchant of Venice*, i, 1.

> Their rising senses
> Begin to chase the ignorant fumes that *mantle*
> Their clearer reason.[1]

Bacon says:

> It [the beer] drinketh fresh, flowereth and *mantleth* exceedingly.[2]

∴

Bacon says:

> If there be any biting or *nibbling* at my name.[3]

Shakespeare says:

> And as pigeons bill, so wedlock would be *nibbling*.[4]

∴

Bacon says:

> I have lived hitherto upon the *scraps* of my former fortunes.[5]

Shakespeare says:

> He hath been at a feast of languages
> And stolen the *scraps*.[6]
>
> Those *scraps* are good deeds past.[7]

∴

We find the rare word *graveled* in both sets of writings. I can recall only one other instance, in all our literature, where this strange word has been employed; that is in John Hay's *Banty Tim*.

Bacon says:

Her Majesty was somewhat *graveled* upon the offense she took at my speech in Parliament.[8]

Shakespeare says:

> O *gravel* heart.[9]

And when you were *graveled* for lack of matter, you might take occasion to kiss.[10]

∴

The word *perturbation* was a favorite with both.

Bacon has:

The Epicurians placed felicity in serenity of mind and freedom from *perturbation*.[11]

And they be the clouds of error which descend in the storms of passions and *perturbations*.[12]

Is it not knowledge that doth alone clear the mind of all *perturbations?* . . . These be the clouds of error that turn into the storms of *perturbation*.[13]

---

[1] *Tempest*, v, 1.
[2] *Natural History*, cent. i, § 46.
[3] Letter to Mr. Davis.
[4] *As You Like It*, iii, 2.
[5] Letter to Buckingham, Sept. 5, 1621.
[6] *Love's Labor Lost*, v, 1.
[7] *Troilus and Cressida*, iii, 3.
[8] Letter to Lord Burleigh, June, 1595.
[9] *Measure for Measure*, iv, 3.
[10] *As You Like It*, iv, 1.
[11] *Advancement of Learning*, book ii.
[12] Ibid., book i.
[13] *In Praise of Knowledge*.

THE IDENTICAL USE OF UNUSUAL WORDS. 453

Shakespeare has:

> O polished *perturbation!* golden care.[1]
>
> *A great perturbation in nature.*[2]
>
> From much grief, from study and *perturbation* of the brain.[3]

Bacon says:

She had no *props*, or supports of her government, but those that were of her own making.[4]

Shakespeare says:

> The boy was the very staff of my age, my very *prop*.[5]
>
> See where his Grace stands 'tween two clergymen.
> Two *props* of virtue for a Christian prince.[6]

Bacon also says:

There was also made a shoaring or *underpropping* act for the benevolence.[7]

Shakespeare says:

> What penny hath Rome borne,
> What men provided, what munition sent,
> To *underprop* this action?[8]
>
> Here am I left to *underprop* his land.[9]

Extirpate occurs but once in the Plays. Prospero says his brother proposed "to *extirpate* me and mine." Bacon uses this then unusual word in the same sense:

But for *extirpating* of the roots and cause of the like commotions.[10]

Bacon says:

This depressing of the house of York did *rankle* and *fester* the affections of his people.[11]

Shakespeare says:

> His venom tooth will *rankle* to the death.[12]
>
> They *fester* 'gainst ingratitude.[13]

Bacon says:

He saith that towards his latter time that closeness did impair and a little *perish* his understanding.[14]

[1] 2d *Henry IV.*, iv, 5.
[2] *Macbeth*, v, 1.
[3] 2d *Henry IV.*, i, 2.
[4] *Felic. Queen Elizabeth.*
[5] *Merchant of Venice*, ii, 2.
[6] *Richard III.*, iii, 7.
[7] *History of Henry VII.*
[8] *King John*, v, 2.
[9] *Richard II.*, ii, 2.
[10] *History of Henry VII.*
[11] Ibid.
[12] *Richard III.*, i, 3.
[13] *Coriolanus*, i, 9.
[14] Essay *Of Friendship.*

Henry Lewis says:

> The use of the verb thus as transitive is rare.[1]

But rare as it is, we find it in Shakespeare:

> Because thy flinty heart, more hard than they,
> Might in thy palace *perish* Margaret.[2]

Bacon says:

I do esteem whatsoever I have or may have in this world but as *trash* in comparison.[3]

And again:

> It shows he weighs men's minds and not their *trash*.[4]

Shakespeare says:

> Who steals my purse steals *trash*.[5]
>
> Wrung
> From the hard hands of peasants their vile *trash*.[6]

Bacon speaks of

> A shrunken and *wooden* posture.[7]

Shakespeare speaks of

> The *wooden* dialogue.[8]

Bacon says:

> Young men *puffed up* with the glittering show of vanity.[9]

Shakespeare says:

> The sea *puffed up* with winds.[10]
>
> The heart, *puffed up* with this retinue, doth any deed of courage.[11]
>
> Led by a delicate and tender prince,
> Whose spirit, by divine ambition *puffed*,
> Makes mouths at the invisible event.[12]

Bacon says:

> To make hope the *antidote* of human diseases.[13]

Shakespeare says:

> And with some sweet oblivious *antidote*
> Cleanse the stuffed bosom.[14]

---

[1] Essay, *Bacon*, p. 161.
[2] 2d *Henry VI.*, iii, 2.
[3] Letter to the Earl of Salisbury.
[4] Essay *Of Goodness*.
[5] *Othello*, iii, 2.
[6] *Julius Cæsar*, iv, 3.
[7] Essay *Of Boldness*.
[8] *Troilus and Cressida*, i, 3.
[9] *Wisdom of the Ancients — Memnon*.
[10] *Taming of the Shrew*, i, 2.
[11] 2d *Henry IV.*, iv, 3.
[12] *Hamlet*, iv, 4.
[13] *Med. Sacra*.
[14] *Macbeth*, v, 3.

THE IDENTICAL USE OF UNUSUAL WORDS. 455

> Trust not the physician: his *antidotes* are poisons.[1]

The word was an unusual one, and occurs but twice in the Plays.

Bacon, in his essay *Of Masks*, speaking of the decorations of the stage, refers to "oes or spangs," meaning, as I should take it, round, shining spots or spangles, like eyes, which, "as they are of no great cost, so are they of most glory." And in Shakespeare this figure repeatedly appears:

> All you fiery *oes* and eyes of light.[2]

And he speaks in the prologue to *Henry V.* of the play-house as "this wooden O."

And he uses the same root in another odd word, *œiliads* — glances of the eye:

> Judicious *œiliads*.[3]
>
> She gave strange *œiliads*.[4]

Bacon says:

> *Pyonner* in the myne of truth.[5]
>
> A *pioneer* in the mine of truth.[6]

Shakespeare says:

> Canst work in the earth so fast;
> A worthy *pioneer*.[7]
>
> The general camp, *pioneers* and all.[8]

This rare word occurs but three times in the Plays.

And in Shakespeare we have, as a parallel to Bacon's "*mine of truth*":

> O, Antony, thou *mine of bounty*.[9]

Bacon speaks of

Such natural philosophy as shall not vanish in the *fume* of subtle and delectable speculation.[10]

While in Shakespeare we have:

> Love is a smoke raised with the *fume* of sighs.[11]

Bacon says:

Neither did they observe so much as the *half-face* of justice, in proceeding by indictment.[12]

---

[1] *Timon of Athens*, iv, 3.
[2] *Midsummer Night's Dream*, iii, 2.
[3] *Merry Wives of Windsor*, i, 3.
[4] *Lear*, iv, 5.
[5] *Promus*, § 1395, p. 451.
[6] Letter to Burleigh.
[7] *Hamlet*, i, 5.
[8] *Othello*, iii, 3.
[9] *Antony and Cleopatra*, iv, 6.
[10] *Advancement of Learning*, book ii.
[11] *Romeo and Juliet*, i, 1.
[12] *History of Henry VII*.

Shakespeare says:

> Out upon this *half-faced* fellowship.[1]
>
> This same *half-faced* fellow, Shadow.[2]
>
> Because he hath a *half-face*, like my father,
> With that *half-face* would he have all my land.[3]

They both use another very rare word.

Bacon says:

Seditions and wars arise: in the midst of which *hurly-burlies* laws are silent.[4]

Shakespeare says:

> When the *hurly-burly's* done.[5]
>
> The news of *hurly-burly* innovation.[6]

This word occurs but twice in the Plays. We will see hereafter that the last syllable is the cipher synonym for *Burleigh*,— the Lord Treasurer,— Bacon's uncle.

Bacon speaks of

> This *jumping* or flying to generalities.[7]

Shakespeare says:

> We'd *jump* the life to come.[8]
>
> In some sort it *jumps* with my humor.[9]
>
> *Jumping* o'er times,
> Turning the accomplishment of many years
> Into an hour-glass.[10]

We remember the use of a peculiar word in the mouth of *Othello*, when he makes his confession to the Venetian senate:

> Nothing *extenuate*, nor set down aught in malice.

We find the same word in Bacon:

> Disgracing your actions, *extenuating* and blasting of your merit.[11]

Also:

> How far a defense might *extenuate* the offense.[12]

Also:

> In excusing, *extenuating* or ingenious *confession*.[13]

It is a favorite word with both; it occurs eight times in the Plays.

---

[1] *1st Henry IV.*, i, 3.
[2] *2d Henry IV*, iii, 2.
[3] *King John*, i, 1.
[4] *Wisdom of the Ancients — Orpheus.*
[5] *Macbeth*, I, 1.
[6] *1st Henry IV.*, v, 1.
[7] *Novum Organum.*
[8] *Macbeth*, i, 7.
[9] *1st Henry IV.*, i, 2.
[10] *Henry V.*, i, cho.
[11] Letter to Essex, Oct. 4, 1596.
[12] Letter to the Lords.
[13] Letter to the King.

We recall another very peculiar word in *Lear:*

> Oh, how this *mother* swells up toward my heart.[1]

We turn to Bacon and we read:

The stench of feathers, or the like, they cure the rising of the *mother.*[2]

In Bacon we find:

> The *skirts* of my living in Hertfordshire.[3]

In Shakespeare:

> Here, in the *skirts* of the forest.[4]

> The *skirts* of this wild wood.[5]

> Young Fortinbras
> Hath in the *skirts* of Norway, here and there,
> Sharked up a list of landless resolutes.[6]

Bacon says:

> Folds and *knots* of nature.[7]

Shakespeare says:

> This *knot* intrinsicate of life untie.[8]

> Motives, those strong *knots* of love.[9]

> This *knot* of amity.[10]

Bacon says:

> Then there *budded forth* some probable *hopes* of succession.[11]

Shakespeare says:

> This is the state of man: to-day he puts *forth*
> The *tender leaves* of *hope;* to-morrow blossoms.[12]

And again:

> *Buckingham.* Every man,
> . . . Not consulting, broke
> Into a general prophecy, that this tempest,
> Dashing the garment of this peace, aboded
> The sudden breach on't.
> *Norfolk.* Which is *budded out.*[13]

Bacon:

> And after he had not a little *bemoaned* himself.[14]

[1] *Lear,* ii, 4.
[2] *Natural History,* cent. i, §63.
[3] Letter to Robert Cecil, 1603.
[4] *As You Like It,* iii, 2.
[5] Ibid., v, 4.
[6] *Hamlet,* i, 1.
[7] Preface to *Great Instauration.*
[8] *Antony and Cleopatra,* v, 2.
[9] *Macbeth,* iv, 3.
[10] *1st Henry VI.*
[11] *Felic. Queen Elizabeth.*
[12] *Henry VIII.,* iii, 2.
[13] Ibid., i, 1.
[14] *History of Henry VII.*

Shakespeare:

> I all alone *bemoan* my outcast state.[1]

> He so *bemoaned* his son.[2]

This word occurs only twice in the Plays.

∴

Bacon speaks of

> The meeting-point and *rendezvous* of all my thoughts.[3]

Shakespeare has:

> A comfort of retirement lives in this,
> A *rendezvous*, a home to fly unto.[4]

And again:

And when I cannot live any longer I will do as I may; that is my rest, that is the *rendezvous* of it.[5]

∴

Bacon speaks of

> A *compacted* strength.[6]

Shakespeare says:

> Of imagination all *compact*.[7]

> My heart is now *compact* of flint.[8]

∴

Bacon says:

> Suspicions that the mind itself gathers are but *busses*.[9]

Shakespeare says:

> Each *bus*, each fancy, each complaint.[10]

> I hear a *bussing* of a separation.[11]

∴

Bacon:

> There is a lively, *jocund*, and, as I may say, a dancing age.[12]

Shakespeare:

> The *jocund* day
> Stands tiptoe on the misty mountain top.[13]

The quotation from Bacon gives us the complete image that was in the mind of the poet:—the dawn was *dancing* on the mountain top.

∴

Bacon says:

For it is a dull thing to tire, and, as we say, to *jade* anything too far.[14]

---

[1] Sonnet.
[2] *3d Henry VI.*, ii, 5.
[3] Letter to Lord Burleigh, 1580.
[4] *1st Henry IV.*, iv, 1.
[5] *Henry V.*, ii, 1.
[6] *Advancement of Learning*, book ii.
[7] *Midsummer Night's Dream*, v, 1.
[8] *Titus Andronicus*, v, 3.
[9] Essay *Of Suspicion*.
[10] *Lear*, i, 4.
[11] *Henry VIII.*, ii, 1.
[12] *Wisdom of the Ancients—Pan*.
[13] *Romeo and Juliet*, iii, 5.
[14] Essay *Of Discourse*.

Shakespeare says:

> To let imagination *jade* me.[1]

Speaking of a young man overthrown and dying, Bacon says:

> The *flower* of virtue *cropped* with sudden chance.[2]

Shakespeare speaks of

> A fresh, un*cropped* *flower*.[3]

Comparing her son to the violets that "strew the green lap of the spring," the Duchess says to him:

> Well, bear you well in this new spring of time,
> Lest you be *cropped* before you come to prime.[4]

Speaking of the history of an event, Bacon says:

> The King hath so *muffled* it.[5]

Shakespeare says:

> *Muffle* your false love.[6]
>
> Love whose view is *muffled* still.[7]

Bacon says:

The King resolved to make this business of Naples as a *wrench* and means of peace.[8]

Shakespeare says:

> A noble nature
> May catch a *wrench*.[9]
>
> *Wrenching* the true cause the false way.[10]

Bacon says:

The corruption and ambition of the times did *prick* him forward.[11]

Our fear of Spain, which hath been the *spur* to this rigor.[12]

Shakespeare says:

> I have no *spur*
> To *prick* the sides of my intent.[13]
>
> My duty *pricks* me on.[14]

Honor *pricks* me on. Yea, but how if honor *prick* me off when I come on.[15]

---

[1] *Twelfth Night*, ii, 5.
[2] *Wisdom of the Ancients — Memnon.*
[3] *All's Well that Ends Well*, v, 3.
[4] *Richard II.*, v, 1.
[5] *History of Henry VII.*
[6] *Comedy of Errors*, ii, 2.
[7] *Romeo and Juliet*, i, 1.
[8] *History of Henry VII.*
[9] *Timon of Athens*, ii, 2.
[10] *2d Henry IV.*, ii, 1.
[11] *Character of Julius Cæsar.*
[12] *Felic. Queen Elizabeth.*
[13] *Macbeth*, i, 7.
[14] *Two Gentlemen of Verona*, iii, 1.
[15] *1st Henry IV.*, v, 1.

Falstaff complains on the battle-field that his bowels are "as hot as *molten* lead." Bacon, speaking of the horror of Essex when he found that the city would not sustain his attempted insurrection, graphically says:

So, as being extremely appalled, as divers that happened to see him then might visibly perceive in his face and countenance, and almost *molten* with sweat, though without any cause of bodily labor, but only by the perplexity and horror of his mind.[1]

What a dramatical command of language does this sentence exhibit!

∴

While my book is being printed, Mr. J. G. Bronson, of Chicago, calls my attention to the following parallelism.

In a letter of "Sir Francis Walsingham, Secretary, to Monsieur Critoy, Secretary of France," said by Mr. Spedding to have been written by Bacon, we find:

But contrariwise her Majesty, not liking to *make windows into men's hearts and secret thoughts*, except the abundance of them did overflow into overt and express acts or affirmations, etc.

While in the Shakespeare sonnets we have this precisely parallel thought:

> For through the painter must you see his skill,
>   To find where your true image pictur'd lies,
> Which in my bosom's shop is hanging still,
>   *That hath his windows glazed with thine eyes.*
> Now, see what good turns eyes for eyes have done:
>   Mine eyes have drawn thy shape, and thine for me
> *Are windows to my breast,* wherethrough the sun
>   Delights to peep, to gaze therein on thee:
>   Yet eyes this cunning want to grace their art;
>   They draw but what they see, know not the heart.[2]

Here we have not only the same thought, but the same conclusion: that the heart can only be read by its acts.

∴

Bacon says:

And there used to *shuffle* up a summary proceeding, by examination.[3]
Whatsoever singularity, chance and the *shuffle* of things has produced.[4]

Shakespeare says:

> I am fain to *shuffle*, to hedge and to lurch.[5]
>
>   'Tis not so above:
> There is no *shuffling*.[6]

---

[1] *A Declaration of the Treasons.*
[2] Sonnet xxiv.
[3] *History of Henry VII.*
[4] *Gesta Grayorum* — *Life and Works*, vol. i, p. 335.
[5] *Merry Wives of Windsor*, ii, 2.
[6] *Hamlet*, iii, 3.

> Your life, good master,
> Must *shuffle* for itself.[1]
>
> When we have *shuffled* off this mortal coil.[2]
>
> *Shuffle* her away.[3]

And here, as illustrating the scholarly acquirements of the writer of the Plays, and his tendency to enrich the English language by the creation of new words, I would refer to two instances, which,—although I have observed no parallels for them in Bacon's writings,—are curious enough to be noted here:

> Dost thou *infamonize* me among potentates.[4]
>
> As he had been *incorpsed* and *demi-natured*.[5]

And here we have a very unusual word used by both — used only once, I think, by either of them.

Bacon:
> To win fame and to *eternize* your name.[6]

Shakespeare:
> *Eternized* in all ages.[7]

Bacon:
> The vain and *indign* comprehensions of heresy.[8]

Shakespeare:
> All *indign* and base adversities.[9]

I could give many more instances of this use in the two bodies of writings of the same quaint and unusual words, did I not fear to offend the patience of the reader and extend this book beyond all reasonable proportions.

I regret that I am not where I could have access to authorities which would show how many of these strange words appeared for the first time, in the history of our language, in the Bacon and Shakespeare writings. But this will constitute a work for scholars hereafter.

---

[1] *Cymbeline*, v, 5.
[2] *Hamlet*, iii, 1.
[3] *Merry Wives of Windsor*, ii, 2.
[4] *Love's Labor Lost*, v, 2.
[5] *Hamlet*, iv, 7.
[6] *Gesta Grayorum — Life and Works*, vol. i, p. 336.
[7] *2d Henry VI.*, v, 3.
[8] Letter to the King, 1612.
[9] *Othello*, i, 3.

CHAPTER VIII.

IDENTITIES OF CHARACTER.

> I saw Othello's visage in his mind.
> *Othello*, i, 3.

CHARACTER, after all, constitutes the man. I do not mean thereby reputation,— for that concerns the opinions of others, and they may or may not be deserved; but those infinite shades of disposition which separate one man from all other men. And as there were never in the world two men who possessed heads of precisely the same shape, so there cannot be two men having precisely the same character. The Creator has a thousand elements which go to make *man*, and he never puts all of them in any one man; nor does he ever mix a part of them, in his alembic, in the same proportions, for any two men. "In the catalogue we all go for men." Anything, with the human osseous system and flesh on it, is, perforce, a man; but the difference between one man and another may be as wide as that between the primordial cell and the regenerated soul.

The writer of the Plays had thought this thought, as he seems to have thought all other thoughts, and he exclaims:

> Oh, the difference of man and man![1]

When we seek, however, to institute a comparison between Francis Bacon and the writer of the Plays, we are met by this difficulty: We know, accurately enough, what was the character of Francis Bacon — his life reveals it; — but if we turn to the author of certain dramatic compositions, we are at a loss to know when the man himself speaks and when the character he has created speaks. We are more apt to see the inner nature of the writer in the general frame, moral and purpose of the piece, and in those utterances which burst from him unawares, and which have no necessary connection with the plot or the characters of the play, than in the acts performed in the course of the drama, or in the

[1] *Lear*, iv, 2.

sentiments put into the mouths of the men who perform them, and which are parts of the acts and parcel of the plots.

But, notwithstanding these difficulties, we can perceive clearly enough that the writer of the Plays possessed essentially the same traits of character which we know to have belonged to Francis Bacon.

The reader has seen already that both personages, if we may call them such, possessed the philosophical and poetical cast of mind; that they were persons of unequaled genius, command of language, elevation of mind and loftiness of moral purpose. Let us go a step farther.

I. INDUSTRY.

I have shown on page 92, *ante*, that the writer of the Plays was a man of vast industry, and that he elaborated his work with the utmost skill and pains. Knight says:

The whole of this scene,[1] in the Folio, exhibits the greatest care in remodeling the text of the quarto.

But let us turn to another play.

A comparison of that part of the text of *The Merry Wives of Windsor* which embraces the scene at Hernes' oak, in the edition of 1602, with the text of the Folio of 1623, will show how elaborately the writer revised and improved his text. I place the new parts of the Folio in italics, and where it repeats the words of the edition of 1602 they are given in quotation marks. In this way the changes are made more conspicuous.

In the edition of 1602 we have:

> *Quickly.* You fairies that do haunt these shady groves,
> Look round about the woods if you espy
> A mortal that doth haunt our sacred round:
> If such a one you can espy, give him his due,
> And leave not till you pinch him black and blue.
> Give them their charge, Puck, ere they part away.

In the Folio of 1623 we have this thus amplified:

> *Quickly.* "Fairies," *black, gray, green and white,*
> *You moonshine revelers and shades of night,*
> *You orphan heirs of fixèd destiny,*
> *Attend your office and your quality.*
> *Crier Hobgoblin, make the fairy oyes.*

[1] *Henry V.*, ii, 1.

Here there is only one word—*fairies*—repeated from the parallel passage in the edition of 1602.

The 1602 version continues:

> *Sir Hugh.* Come hither, Pead, go to the country houses,
> And when you find a slut that lies asleep,
> And all her dishes foul and room unswept,
> With your long nails pinch her till she cry
> And swear to mend her sluttish housewifery.

In the Folio this speech is put in the mouth of Pistol, but greatly changed in language:

> *Pistol. Elves, list your names; silence, you airy toys.*
> *Cricket, to Windsor chimneys shalt thou leap:*
> *Where fires thou find'st unraked, and hearths* "unswept,"
> *There* "pinch" *the maids as blue as bilberry:*
> *Our radiant queen hates* "sluts" *and sluttery.*

Here there are but *three* words that occur in the edition of 1602. In the 1602 copy there is added after this speech:

> *Fairy.* I warrant you I will perform your will.

This line is lacking in the Folio, and instead of it Falstaff says:

> They are fairies; he that speaks to them shall die:
> I'll wink and couch: no man their works must eye.

The 1602 edition gives the next speech as follows:

> *Sir Hugh.* Where is Pead? Go you and see where brokers sleep,
> And fox-eyed serjeants, with their mace,
> Go lay the proctors in the street,
> And pinch the lousy serjeant's face:
> Spare none of these when they are a-bed,
> But such whose nose looks plue and red.

In the Folio we have this speech rendered as follows:

> *Evans.* "Where's Bead? Go you, and" *where you find a maid,*
> *That, ere she sleep, has thrice her prayers said,*
> *Rein up the organs of her fantasy,*
> *Sleep she as sound as careless infancy;*
> *But those as* "sleep" *and think not on their sins,*
> "Pinch" *them, arms, legs, backs, shoulders, sides and shins.*

But I have given enough to prove that the play, as it appears in the Folio of 1623, was practically re-written, and I might add that in every case the changes were for the better. For instance, in the 1602 edition we have:

> Go straight, and do as I command,
> And take a taper in your hand,
> And set it to his finger ends,
> And if you see it him offends,

And that he starteth at the flame,
Then he is mortal, know his name;
If with an F it doth begin,
Why, then, be sure, he's full of sin.

This doggerel is transformed in the Folio into the following:

With trial-fire touch me his finger end:
If he be chaste, the flame will back descend
And turn him to no pain; but if he start,
It is the flesh of a corrupted heart.

Speaking of *King Henry V., Romeo and Juliet, The Merry Wives of Windsor* and *Hamlet*, Swinburne says:

Of these four plays the two tragedies at least were thoroughly re-cast and re-written from end to end, the pirated editions giving us a transcript, more or less perfect or imperfect, accurate or corrupt, of the text as it first came from the poet's hand, *a text to be afterwards indefinitely modified and incalculably improved*. . . . But *King Henry V.*, we may fairly say, is hardly less than transformed. Not that it has been re-cast after the fashion of *Hamlet*, or even re-written after the fashion of *Romeo and Juliet;* but the corruptions and imperfections of the pirated text are here more flagrant than in any other instance, while the general revision of style, by which it is at once purified and fortified, extends to every nook and corner of the restored and renovated building. Even had we, however, a perfect and trustworthy transcript of Shakespeare's original sketch for this play, there can be little doubt that the rough draft would still prove almost as different from the final masterpiece as is the soiled and ragged canvas now before us, on which we trace the outline of figures so strangely disfigured, made subject to such rude extremities of defacement and defeature.[1]

Is it reasonable to suppose that the author who took such pains to perfect his work would have made no provision for its preservation, but would die and leave one-half of the great Plays in manuscript?

He knew that the work of his youth was not equal to the work of his manhood, and he labored conscientiously to improve his crude designs. Dowden says:

It is the opinion of Dyce, of Grant White and of others that Shakespeare began to work upon *Romeo and Juliet* not later than about 1591, that is, almost at the moment when he began to write for the stage, and, that having occupied him for a series of years, the tragedy assumed its present form about 1595-7. If this be the case, and if, as there is reason to believe, Shakespeare was also during many years interested in the subject of *Hamlet*, we discover that he accepted the knowledge that his powers were undeveloped and acted upon it, and waited until he believed himself competent to do justice to his conceptions.[2]

De Quincey says of the Plays:

The further on we press in our discoveries, the more we shall see proofs of design and self-supporting arrangement, where the careless eye has seen nothing but accident.

---

[1] *A Study of Shak.*, p. 104.   [2] Dowden, *Shak. Mind and Art.* p. 51.

Swinburne illustrates this question of the industry of Shakespeare by the following excellent remarks:

That priceless waif of piratical salvage, which we owe to the happy rapacity of a hungry publisher, is, of course, more accurately definable as the first play of *Hamlet* than as the first edition of the play. . . . The deeper complexities of the subject are merely indicated; simple and trenchant outlines of character are yet to be supplanted by features of subtler suggestion and infinite interfusion. Hamlet himself is almost more of a satirist than a philosopher. . . . The Queen, whose finished figure is now something of a riddle, stands out simply enough in the first sketch as confidant of Horatio, if not as accomplice of Hamlet. . . . This minor transformation of style in the inner play, made solely with the evident view of marking the distinction between its duly artificial forms of speech and the natural forms of speech passing between the spectators, is but one among innumerable indications, which only a purblind perversity of prepossession can overlook, of the especial store set by Shakespeare himself on this favorite work; and the exceptional pains taken by him to *preserve it for aftertime* in such fullness of finished form as might make it *worthiest of profound and perpetual study* by the light of far other lamps than illuminate the stage.

Of all vulgar errors, the most wanton, the most willful, and the most resolutely tenacious of life, is that belief bequeathed from the days of Pope, in which it was pardonable, to the days of Mr. Carlyle, in which it is not excusable, to the effect that Shakespeare threw off *Hamlet* as an eagle may moult a feather or a fool may break a jest; that he dropped his work as a bird may drop an egg, or a sophist a fallacy; that he wrote "for gain, not glory," or that, having written *Hamlet*, he thought it nothing very wonderful to have written. For himself to have written, he possibly, nay, probably, did not think it anything miraculous; but that he was in the fullest degree conscious of its wonderful positive worth to all men for all time, we have the best evidence possible — his own; and that not by mere word of mouth, but by actual stroke of hand. . . . Scene by scene, line for line, stroke upon stroke and touch after touch, he went over all the old labored ground again; and not only to insure success in his own day, and fill his pockets with contemporary pence, but merely and wholly with a purpose to make it worthy of himself *and his future students*. . . .

Every change in the text of *Hamlet* has impaired its fitness for the stage, and increased its value for the closet, in exact and perfect proportion. . . . Even in Shakespeare's time the actors threw out his additions; they throw out these very same additions in our time. The one especial speech, if any one such especial speech there be, in which the personal genius of Shakespeare soars up to the very highest of its height, and strikes down to the very deepest of its depth, is passed over by modern actors; it was cut away by Heminge and Condell.[1]

It seems to me that in the face of these facts there can be no question that the writer of the Plays was a man of intense and enormous industry.

We turn to Francis Bacon, and we find, as I have suggested heretofore, that he was, perhaps, the most laborious man that ever lived on the planet. Church says of him:

---

[1] Swinburne, *A Study of Shak.*, p. 164.

In all these things he was as industrious, as laborious, as calmly persevering and tenacious as he was in his pursuit of his philosophical speculations.[1]

He re-wrote the *Essays*, we are told, thirty times. His chaplain tells us that he had " twelve times transcribed the *Novum Organum* with his own hand."

Bacon himself says:

My great work goeth forward, and, after my manner, I alter even when I add, so that nothing is finished until all is finished.[2]

Bacon's *Promus of Formularies and Elegancies* takes us into the workshop of the great artist. There we see him with his blouse on, among his pots and brushes. We see him studying the quality of his canvas and grinding his own paints. These daubs upon the wall are part of his experiments in the contrasts of colors; these rude lines, traced here and there, with charcoal or chalk, are his first crude conceptions of figures and faces and attitudes which are to reappear hereafter, perfected in his immortal works.

Here we can trace the genesis of thought, the pedigree of ideas, the ancestry of expressions. We look around us and realize that genius is neither more nor less than great powers conjoined with extraordinary industry.

It is better, for humanity's future, that the statue at Stratford-upon-Avon should be taken down from its pedestal. It represents a fraud and a delusion:—a fraud in authorship, and a delusion in philosophy, still more destructive, to-wit: that ignorance, idleness and dissipation can achieve results which mankind will worship through all ages; that anything worth having can come out of nothing.

For, in truth, the universe is industry. We are appalled when we think of the intense, persistent, laborious, incalculable, awful force, constantly exerted, to keep the vast whole in motion—from the suns to to the bacilli. God might be fitly described as the Great Worker:—a worker without a task-master—who never pauses, never wearies, and never sleeps.

No man should shrink from labor. Energy is God's glorious stamp set on his creatures. He who has it not is a drone in the hive, and unworthy the notice of his Great Master. And it has

---

[1] *Bacon*, p. 57. [2] Letter to Tobie Matthew, 1610.

been a shameful and poisonous thing, to the human mind, that all these hundreds of years the world has been taught that the most marvelous of human works were produced by accident, without effort, by a slouching, shiftless, lazy, indifferent creature, who had not even force enough to provide for their perpetuation.

Let it be known hereafter, and for all time to come, that the greatest of men was the most industrious of men.

The notes in the *Promus* show that Bacon was studying the *elegancies*, the niceties of language, especially of colloquial expression, noting down not only thoughts, but peculiar and strong phrases and odd and forcible words. And surely there was no necessity for all this in his philosophical works. He makes a study not only of courteous salutations, but of the continuances of speech. Take, for instance:

> It is like, sir, etc., (putting a man agayne into his tale interrupted).[1]

Or:

> The rather bycause (contynuing another's speech).[2]

Or:

> To the end, saving that, whereas, yet, (contynuances of all kynds).[3]

Would one who contemplated works of philosophy alone, which were to be translated into the Latin language, for the use of posterity, devote such study to the refinements of *dialogue?* And where do we find any of these *elegancies* of *speech* in Bacon's acknowledged writings?

II. Commonplace-Books.

Both writers possessed that characteristic habit of studious and industrious men, the noting down of thoughts and quotations in commonplace-books. The *Promus* is one of these. Bacon repeatedly recommends the use of such helps to composition. He says:

> I hold the entry of commonplaces to be a matter of great use and essence in studying, as that which assureth "copia" of invention and contracteth judgment to a strength.[4]

And again — discussing how to "procure the ready use of knowledge" — he says:

---

[1] *Promus*, § 1385, p. 449.
[2] Ibid., § 1378, p. 447.
[3] Ibid., § 1379, p. 447.
[4] *Advancement of Learning*, book ii.

The other part of invention, which I term suggestion, doth assign and direct us to certain marks or places, which may excite our mind to return and produce such knowledge as it hath formerly collected, to the end we may make use thereof.[1]

And again he says:

It is of great service in studies to bestow diligence in setting down commonplaces.[2]

On the other hand, we turn to the writer of the Plays, and we find him, as I have shown on page 78, *ante*, recommending the use of commonplace-books in very much the same language. He says, in the 76th sonnet:

> Look, what thy memory cannot contain
> Commit to these waste blanks, and thou shalt find
> These children nursed, delivered of thy brain,
> To take a new acquaintance of thy mind.

This is in the very spirit of Bacon's

Certain marks or places, which may excite our mind to return and produce such knowledge as it hath formerly collected.

And we think we can see the personal habits of the writer of the Plays reflected in the words of his *alter ego*, Hamlet:

> My tables:—meet it is I set it down,
> That one may smile and smile and be a villain.[3]

And again, in *The Merry Wives:*

> I will make a brief of it in my note-book.[4]

III. A Thorough Student.

Not only was the writer of the Plays, like Francis Bacon, vastly industrious, but it was the industry of a scholar: he was a student. He combined a life of retirement and contemplation with knowledge of affairs, as Bacon did. He realized Goethe's axiom:

> *Es bildet ein Talent sich in der Stille,*
> *Sich ein Charakter in dem Strom der Welt.*

The early plays all bespeak the student; they breathe the atmosphere of the university.

Proteus complains:

> Thou, Julia, hast metamorphosed me;
> Made me neglect my studies, lose my time.

---

[1] *Advancement of Learning,* book ii.
[2] Ibid.
[3] *Hamlet,* i, 5.
[4] *Merry Wives of Windsor,* i, 1.

Love's Labor Lost is full of allusions to studies:

> *Biron.* What is the end of study?
> *King.* Why, that to know which else we should not know.
> *Biron.* Things hid and barred, you mean, from common sense?
> *King.* Ay, that is *study's god-like recompense*.[1]

And, like Bacon, the writer of the Plays believed that books were a means, not an end; and that original thought was a thousand times to be preferred to the repetition of the ideas of other men. He says:

> Study is like the heavens' glorious sun,
> That will not be deep-searched with saucy looks;
> Small have continual plodders ever won,
> Save base authority, from others' books.[2]

We seem to hear in this the voice of Bacon. In his essay *Of Studies* he says:

> To spend too much time in studies, is sloth; to use them too much for ornament, is affectation; to make judgment *wholly by their rules, is the humor of a scholar*.

And how Baconian are these utterances:

> *Mi perdonate*, gentle master mine,
> I am in all affected as yourself;
> Glad that you thus continue your resolve,
> To *suck the sweets of sweet philosophy*.
> Only, good master, while we do admire
> This virtue, and this moral discipline,
> Let's be no stoicks, nor no stocks, I pray:
> Or so devote to *Aristotle's checks*,
> As Ovid be an outcast quite abjured:
> Balk logic with acquaintance that you have,
> And practice rhetoric with your common talk:
> Music and poetry use to quicken you;
> The mathematics, and the metaphysics,
> Fall to them, as you find your stomach serves you:
> No profit grows where is no pleasure ta'en;
> In short, sir, study what you most affect.[3]

Here we find allusions to Bacon's love of philosophy, his dislike for Aristotle, his contempt for logic, and his studies of music and poetry. And we note, also, the didactic and educational tone of the essay, natural to the man who was always laboring to instruct and improve his fellow-men.

---

[1] *Love's Labor Lost*, i, 1.   [2] *Ibid.*   [3] *Taming of the Shrew*, i, 1.

IV. His Wisdom.

We know it is conceded that Bacon was the wisest man of his time, or of all time. And wisdom is not knowledge merely of things. It means an accurate acquaintance with the springs of human nature, and a capacity to adapt actions to events. And the same trait has been many times noted in the writer of the Plays. Henry Hallam says:

> The philosophy of Shakespeare—his intimate searching out of the human heart, whether in the gnomic form of sentence or in the dramatic exhibition of character—is a gift peculiarly his own.

Henry Giles says of Shakespeare's genius:

> It has the power of practical intellect. Under a careless guise it implies serious judgment, and in the vesture of motley it pronounces many a recondite decision. . . . Out from its mockeries and waggeries there could be collected a philosophy of common sense by which the gravest might be instructed.

I have already quoted (page 150, *ante*) the expression of Emerson, applied to Shakespeare:

> He was inconceivably *wise;* the others conceivably.

And of Landor:

> The *wisest* of men, as well as the greatest of poets.

V. The Universality of his Mind.

We know that Bacon's mind ranged through all created nature, and his learning levied tribute on everything underneath the sun. He had "taken all knowledge for his province."

Osborne, a contemporary, called Bacon

> The most *universal genius* I have ever seen or was like to see.

While, on the other hand, De Quincey says:

> Shakespeare thought more finely and more *extensively* than all the other poets combined.

Professor Dowden says of Shakespeare:

> This vast and varied mass of information he assimilated and made his own. . . . He was a center for the drifting capital of knowledge. His whole power of thought increased steadily as the years went by, both in sure grasp of the known and in brooding intensity of gaze upon the unknown.[1]

And the same writer continues:

> Now, what does extraordinary growth imply? It implies capacity for obtaining the materials of growth; in this case materials for the growth of intellect, of imagination, of the will, of the emotions. It means, therefore, capacity for seeing

---

[1] *Shak. Mind and Art*, p. 39.

many facts, of meditating, of feeling deeply, and of controlling such feeling. . . . It implies a power in the organism to fit its movements to meet numerous external coexistences and sequences. In a word, it brings us back once again to Shakespeare's *resolute fidelity to the fact*.[1]

And surely "resolute fidelity to the fact" was the distinguishing trait of Bacon's philosophy.

VI. Powers of Observation.

Macaulay says of Bacon:

In keenness of observation he has been equaled, though perhaps never surpassed. But the largeness of his mind was all his own.[2]

And the great Scotsman makes this fine comparison touching Bacon's mind:

With great minuteness of observation he had an amplitude of comprehension, such as has never yet been vouchsafed to any other person. The small, fine mind of Labruyère had not a more delicate tact than the large intellect of Bacon. . . . His understanding resembled the tent which the fairy Parabanon gave to Prince Ahmed. Fold it, and it seemed a toy for the hand of a lady; spread it, and the armies of powerful sultans might repose beneath its shade.[3]

While, on the other hand, Sir William Hamilton calls Shakespeare

The greatest known observer of human nature.

And Richard Grant White calls him

The most observant of men.

VII. His Secretiveness.

We have seen Bacon admitting that he was "a *concealed* poet."

Spedding concedes that a letter written in the name of the Earl of Essex to Sir Foulke Greville, about the year 1596, was written by Bacon.[4]

There has been attributed to Bacon a work called *An Historical Account of the Alienation Office*, published in 1590, in the name of William Lambarde.

Spedding finds[5] that the letters which purported to have been written by the Earl of Essex to the Earl of Rutland, who was about to travel on the continent, containing advice as to his course of studies, were unquestionably the work of Bacon.

---

[1] *Shak. Mind and Art*, p. 41.
[2] Macaulay's *Essays — Bacon*, p. 284.
[3] Ibid.
[4] See vol. 2, *Life and Works*, p. 21.
[5] *Letters and Life of Bacon*, vol. ii, p. 5.

Mr. Spedding says:

> At another time he [Bacon] tries to disguise himself under a style of *assumed superiority*, quite unlike his natural style; as in the *Temporis Partus Masculus*, where again the very same argument is set forth in a spirit of scornful invective, poured out upon all the popular reputations in the annals of philosophy.[1]

We have seen him writing letters to Essex as from his brother Anthony, in which Anthony is made to refer back to himself, and then writing a reply from Essex, the whole to be shown to the Queen.

We have seen Ben Jonson alluding to him in some birthday verses:

> As if a *mystery* thou didst.

And in all this we see the man who under a mask could put forth the Plays to the world; and who, inside the Plays, could, in turn, conceal a cipher.

VIII. Splendid Tastes.

Emerson says of Shakespeare:

> What trait of his private mind has he hidden in his dramas? One can discern in his ample pictures of the gentleman and the king what forms and humanities pleased him; his delight in troops of friends, in large hospitality, in cheerful giving. Let Timon, let Warwick, let Antonio the merchant, answer for his great heart.

When we read this the magnificence of Bacon occurs to our remembrance — his splendid marriage, his princely residence at St. Albans, his noble presents.

Hepworth Dixon thus describes his wedding:

> Feathers and lace light up the rooms in the Strand. Cecil has been warmly urged to come over from Salisbury House. Three of his gentlemen, Sir Walter Cope, Sir Baptist Hicks and Sir Hugh Beeston, hard drinkers and men about town, strut over in his stead, flaunting in their swords and plumes; yet the prodigal bridegroom, *sumptuous in his tastes as in his genius*, clad in a suit of Genoese velvet, purple from cap to shoe, outbraves them all. The bride, too, is richly dight, her whole dowry seeming to be piled up on her in cloth of silver and ornaments of gold.[2]

The author of *Aulicus Coquinariæ*, speaking of Bacon after his downfall, says:

> And let me give this light to his better character, from an observation of the late King, then Prince. Returning from hunting, he espied a coach attended with a goodly troop of horsemen, who, it seems, were gathered together to wait upon the Chancellor to his house at Gorhambury, at the time of his declension. At

---

[1] Preface to part iii, vol. iii, *Works*, p. 171. [2] *Personal History of Lord Bacon*, p. 181.

which the Prince smiled: "Well, do we what we can," said he, "this man scorns to go out like a snuff."

Nay, master King! And he will not go out like a snuff;—not till the civilization of the world is snuffed out. And the time will come when even thou,—O King,—wilt be remembered simply because thou didst live in the same age with him.

IX. HIS SPLENDID EGOTISM.

There was about Bacon a magnificent self-assertion.

Dean Church says:

> He [Bacon] never affected to conceal from himself his superiority to other men, in his aims and in the grasp of his intelligence.[1]

He recognized his own greatness, in an impersonal sort of way, as he might have perceived the magnitude of a mountain. Hence we find him beginning one of his great works in the following lordly manner:

> *Francis of Verulam thought thus*, and such is the method which he within himself pursued, which he thought *it concerned both the living and posterity to become acquainted with*.[2]

And again he says:

> *Francis Bacon thought in this manner.*[3]

We turn to Shakespeare, and we find him, in the sonnets, indulging in the same bold and extraordinary, although justifiable, egotism. He says:

> Not marble,
> Nor the gilded monuments of princes
> Shall outlive this powerful rhyme.

And again:

> Nor shall Death brag thou wanderest in his shade,
> When in *eternal lines to time thou goest:*
> So long as men can breathe or eyes can see,
> So long lives this, and this gives life to thee.[4]

And again he says:

> Oh, 'tis the first; 'tis flattery in my seeing,
> And *my great mind most kingly drinks it up*.[5]

If these were the utterances of the man of Stratford, why did he not assert himself, as Bacon did, in the affairs of his age? Would

---

[1] *Bacon*, p. 58.
[2] Introduction to *Great Instauration*.
[3] *Filum Labyrinthi*.
[4] Sonnet xviii.
[5] Sonnet cxiv.

a man with this consciousness of supreme greatness crawl away to Stratford, to brew beer and lend money? No; he would have fought for recognition, as Bacon did, to the last gasp.

X. His Toleration.

I have already shown that Bacon and the writer of the Plays were tolerant in the midst of the religious passions of the time.

William Henry Smith says:

> In an age of bigotry and religious persecution we find Bacon and Shakespeare expressing a toleration of all creeds and religions.[1]

Hepworth Dixon says, alluding to the appropriations for war expenses:

> James takes this money, not without joy and wonder; but when they ask him to banish recusants from London, to put down masses in embassadors' houses, to disarm all the Papists, to prevent priests and Jesuits from going abroad, he will not do it. In this resistance to a new persecution, his tolerant Chancellor stands at his back and bears the odium of his refusal. Bacon, who thinks the penal laws too harsh already, will not consent to inflame the country, at such a time, by a new proclamation; the penalties are strong, and in the hands of the magistrates; he sees no need to spur their zeal by royal proclamations or the enactment of more savage laws. Here is a chance for Coke. Raving for gibbets and pillories in a style to quicken the pulse of Brownists, men who are wild with news from Heidelberg or Prague believe in his sincerity and partake of his heat. To be mild now, many good men think, is to be weak. In a state of war, philosophy and tolerance go to the wall; when guns are pounding in the gates, even justice can be only done at the drumhead.[2]

Bacon's downfall, as we shall see hereafter, was largely due to this refusal to persecute the helpless at the bidding of the fanatical, led on by the brutal and sordid Coke.

XI. His Benevolence.

And in the same spirit he at all times preached mercy and generosity, in both his acknowledged works and in the Plays.

Bacon, in his essay *Of Discourse*, enumerates, among the things which ought to be privileged from jest, "religion, matters of state, and *any case that deserveth pity.*"

While Carlyle says of Shakespeare:

> His laughter seems to pour forth in floods. . . . Not at mere weakness — *at misery or poverty never.*

Bacon says:

> The state and bread of the poor have always been dear to my heart.

[1] *Bacon and Shak.*, p. 88. [2] *Personal History of Lord Bacon*, p. 325.

He labors

> To lift men out of their necessities and miseries.

He seeks, "in a despised weed, the good of all men."

Bacon describes one of the fathers of "Solomon's House," in *The New Atlantis*, and says:

> He had an aspect *as if he pitied men.*

We turn to Shakespeare and we find the same great traits of character.

Charles Knight speaks of

Shakespeare's unvarying kindness toward wretched and oppressed humanity, in however low a shape.

Gerald Massey says:

He has infinite pity for the suffering and struggling and wounded by the way. The most powerful and pathetic pleadings on behalf of Christian charity, out of the New Testament, have been spoken by Shakespeare. He takes to his large, warm heart much that the world usually casts out to perish in the cold. There is nothing too poor or mean to be embraced within the circle of his sympathies.[1]

Barry Cornwall refers to "the extensive charity which Shakespeare inculcates."

Birch says:

He has, more than any other author, exalted the love of humanity. However he may indulge in invective against the artificial systems of religion, and be found even speaking against Christianity, yet in his material and natural speculations he endeavors to give philosophical consolation to mankind, to inculcate submission to inevitable circumstances *and encourage scientific investigation into the nature of things.*[2]

The reader will probably pause to see whether I have not misplaced this quotation, so completely does it fit the character and purposes of Francis Bacon. But no; it was written by an English clergyman, in an essay upon the religion of Shakespeare; and the author probably never heard of the theory that Bacon wrote the Plays.

I append a few illustrative extracts from the Plays, in corroboration of these opinions:

> 'Tis a cruelty
> To load a falling man.[3]

> Neither in our hearts nor outward eyes,
> Envy the great nor do the low despise.[4]

---

[1] *Sonnets of Shak.*, p. 549.
[2] *Philosophy and Religion of Shak.*, p. 10.
[3] *Henry VIII.*, v, 2.
[4] *Pericles*, ii, 3.

> There is a soul of goodness in things evil,
> Would men observingly distill it out.[1]

> Oh, I have ta'en
> Too little care of this! Take physic, pomp;
> Expose thyself to feel what wretches feel;
> That thou mayst shake the superflux to them
> And show the heavens more just.[2]

XII. HIS COMMAND OVER THE EMOTIONS.

Ben Jonson says of Bacon:

He commanded where he spoke, and had his judges angry or pleased at his devotion. No man had their affections [passions] more in his power.

Pope says of Shakespeare:

The power over our passions was never possessed in a more eminent degree, or displayed in so different instances. . . . We are surprised the moment we weep, and yet, upon reflection, find the passion so just, that we should be surprised if we had not wept, and wept at that very moment.[3]

XIII. HIS WIT.

Basil Montagu says of Bacon:

His wit was brilliant, and when it flashed upon any subject it was never with ill-nature, which, like the crackling of thorns, ending in sudden darkness, is only fit for the fool's laughter. The sparkling of his wit was that of the precious diamond, valuable for its worth and weight, denoting the riches of the mine.[4]

And Macaulay, a severe critic, and in many things, so far as Bacon was concerned, an unjust one, says of his wit:

The best jest-book in the world is that which he dictated from memory, without referring to any book, on a day on which illness had rendered him incapable of serious study.[5]

And again he says:

But it occasionally happened that, when he was engaged in grave and profound investigations, his wit obtained the mastery over all his other faculties, and led him into absurdities into which no dull man could possibly have fallen.[6]

And again Macaulay says:

In wit, if by wit be meant the power of perceiving analogies between things which appear to have nothing in common, he never had an equal — not even Cowley, not even the author of *Hudibras*. Indeed he possessed this faculty, or this faculty possessed him, to a morbid degree. When he abandoned himself to it, without reserve, as he did in the *Sapientia Veterum*, and at the end of the second book of the *De Augmentis*, the feats which he performed were not merely admirable but portentous and almost shocking. On those occasions we marvel at him as clowns on a fair day marvel at a juggler, and can hardly help thinking that the devil must be in him.[7]

---

[1] *Henry V.*, iv, 1.
[2] *Lear*, iii, 4.
[3] William H. Smith, *Bacon and Shak.*, p. 6.
[4] *Works of Lord Bacon*, vol. i, p. 116.
[5] Macaulay's *Essays—Bacon*, p. 280.
[6] Ibid., p. 285.
[7] Ibid., p. 285.

And Ben Jonson says of Bacon:

His language, *where he could spare or pass by a jest*, was nobly censorious.

I need not cite many authorities to prove that the writer of the Shakespeare Plays was not only a great wit, but that his wit sometimes overmastered his judgment.

Hudson says of Falstaff:

I must add that, with Shallow and Silence for his theme, Falstaff's wit fairly grows gigantic, and this, too, without any abatement of its frolicsome agility. The strain of humorous exaggeration with which he pursues the theme is indeed almost sublime. Yet in some of his reflections thereon, we have a clear though brief view of *the profound philosopher underlying the profligate humorist and makesport*, for he there discovers a *breadth and sharpness of observation* and a *depth of practical sagacity* such as might have placed him [Shakespeare] in *the front rank of statesmen and sages*.[1]

XIV. Great Aims.

We know the grand objects Bacon kept continually before his mind's eye.

The writer of the Plays declares, in sonnet cxxv, that he had

Laid great bases for eternity.

What were they? What "great bases for eternity" had the Stratford man built or attempted to build?

Francis Bacon wrote *The New Atlantis*, an attempt to show to what perfections of civilization developed mankind might attain in a new land, an island; and we find Shakespeare also planning an improved commonwealth upon another island — the island that was the scene of *The Tempest*. And we find him borrowing therein from Montaigne.

Gonzalo says in the play:

> Had I plantation of this isle, my lord, . . .
> I' the commonwealth, I would by contraries
> Execute all things; for no kind of traffic
> Would I admit; no name of magistrate;
> Letters should not be known; riches, poverty,
> And use of service none; contract, succession,
> Bourn, bound of land, tilth, vineyard, none:
> No use of metal, corn, or wine or oil:
> No occupation; all men idle, all —
> And women, too; but innocent and pure.
> No sovereignty:
> All things in common nature should produce
> Without sweat or endeavor; treason, felony,

---

[1] *Shak. Life and Art*, vol. ii, p. 94.

> Sword, pike, knife, gun or need of any engine,
> Would I not have, but nature should bring forth,
> Of its own kind, all foison, all abundance,
> To feed my innocent people.[1]

Here, as in *The New Atlantis*, we see the philosopher-poet devising schemes to lift men out of their miseries — to "feed the innocent people."

XV. His Goodness.

Coleridge says:

> Observe the fine humanity of Shakespeare, in that his sneerers are all villains.

Gerald Massey says of Shakespeare:

> There is nothing rotten at the root, nothing insidious in the suggestion. Vice never walks abroad in the mental twilight wearing the garb of virtue.[2]

Coleridge says:

> There is not one really vicious passage in all Shakespeare.

We know that Bacon, in his acknowledged works, said nothing that could impair the power of goodness in the world.

XVI. Another Curious Fact.

While the last pages of this work are going through the press, my friend Professor Thomas Davidson sends me a letter addressed to him by a correspondent (M. Le B. G.), in which occur these words:

> Please look at the 6th chapter of Peter Bayne's new *Life of Luther*, if you have not already read it. It is called *The Century of Luther and Shakespeare*. It is a glorification of Shakespeare, but, curiously enough, quotes from Brewer, about the correspondence in altitude between Bacon and Luther; and then goes on to show that Shakespeare was perfectly familiar not only with the Bible but with Luther's thought, and with special incidents of his history.
>
> Bayne says that all the main points in the theology of the Reformation could be pieced together from the dramas of Shakespeare. One would not naturally look in a Life of Luther for any testimony on the "Baconian Theory," so please (if it seems worth while to you) to call Mr. Donnelly's attention to this rather curious chapter.

I quote this with pleasure, although a little out of place in this chapter, as another case where the indentations of the Baconian theory fit into all other related facts and, as an additional evidence that the Plays were not pumped out of ignorance by the handle of genius, under the pressure of a play-actor's necessities, but were the works of a broadly-learned man, who was fully abreast of all

---

[1] *Tempest*, ii, 2. [2] *Sonnets of Shakespeare*, p. 549.

the affairs of his day, and who had read everything that was accessible in that age, in every field of thought.

In short, each new addition to our information requires us to widen the shelves of the library of the man who wrote the Plays.

XVII. Conclusions.

When, therefore, we institute a comparison between the personal character and mental disposition of Francis Bacon and that of the man who wrote the Plays, we find that:

1. Both were poetical.
2. Both were philosophical.
3. Both were vastly industrious.
4. Both were students.
5. Both were profoundly wise.
6. Both possessed a universal grasp of knowledge.
7. Both had splendid tastes.
8. Both were tolerant of religious differences of opinion.
9. Both were benevolent.
10. Both were wits.
11. Both were possessed of great aims for the good of man.
12. Both were morally admirable.

I cannot better conclude this chapter than with a comparison extracted from the work of Mr. William Henry Smith, the patriarch of the Baconian discussion in England. Mr. Smith quotes Archbishop Whately as follows:

> There is an ingenious and philosophical toy called "a thaumatrope," in which two objects painted on opposite sides of a card — for instance, a man and a horse, a bird and a cage, etc. — are, by a quick rotary motion, made so to impress the eye in combination as to form one picture — of the man on the horse's back, the bird in the cage, etc. As soon as the card is allowed to remain at rest, the figures, of course, appear as they really are, separate and on opposite sides.[1]

Mr. Smith continues:

> Bacon and Shakespeare we know to be distinct individuals, occupying positions as opposite as the man and the horse, the bird and the cage; yet, when we come to agitate the question, the poet appears so combined with the philosopher, and the philosopher with the poet, we cannot but believe them to be identical.

[1] *Bacon and Shak.*, p. 89.

CHAPTER IX.

IDENTITIES OF STYLE.

I replied, "Nay, Madam, rack him not; . . . rack his style."—*Bacon.*

WE come now to an interesting branch of our subject, to-wit: Is there any resemblance between the style of Francis Bacon and that of the writer of the Plays?

I. THE GENIUS OF SHAKESPEARE.

And first let us ask ourselves, what are the distinguishing features of the writings which go by the name of Shakespeare? In other words, what is his style?

It might be described as the excess of every great faculty of the soul. Reason, the widest and most profound; imagination, the most florid and tropical; vivacity, the most sprightly and untiring; passion, the most burning and vehement; feeling, the most earnest and intense.

In other words, it is a human intellect, multiplied many hundred-fold beyond the natural standard. Behind the style and the works we see the man:—a marvelous, many-sided, gigantic soul; a monster among thinkers;—standing with one foot upon the bare rocks of reason, and the other buried ankle-deep in the flowers of the imagination; spanning time and accomplishing immortality.

Behind the tremendous works is a tremendous personality.

Not from a weak or shallow thought
His mighty Jove young Phidias wrought.

His was a ponderous, comprehensive, extraordinary intelligence, inflamed as never man's was, before or since, by genius; and filled with instincts and purposes which we cannot but regard as divine. Every part of his mind was at white heat—it *flamed*. He has left all mankind to repeat his expressions, because never before did any one so captivate and capture words, or crush them into subjection, as he did. The operations of his mind—its greed, its spring, its grasp, its domination—were, so to speak, *ferocious*. It is no wonder that his body showed the marks of premature age; it is a surprise that this immense, vehement and bounding spirit did not tear the flesh into disorganization long before his allotted time.

And yet, high aloft in the charioteer's seat, above the plunging, rebellious, furious Passions, sat the magnificent Reason of the man; curbing, with iron muscles, their vehemence into measured pace, their motion into orderly progression.

Hear what the great Frenchman, H. A. Taine, says of Shakespeare:

I am about to describe an extraordinary species of mind, perplexing to all the French modes of analysis and reasoning, all-powerful, excessive, master of the sublime as well as of the base; the most creative mind that ever engaged in the exact copy of the details of actual existence, in the dazzling caprice of fancy, in the profound complications of superhuman passions; a nature poetical, immortal, inspired, superior to reason by the sudden revelations of its seer's madness; so extreme in joy and grief, so abrupt of gait, so agitated and impetuous in its transports, that this great age alone could have cradled such a child.[1]

And, speaking of the imagination of the great poet, Taine says:

Shakespeare imagines with copiousness and excess; he scatters metaphors profusely over all he writes; every instant abstract ideas are changed into images; it is a series of paintings which is unfolded in his mind.[2]

And the same writer says:

This exuberant fecundity intensifies qualities already in excess, and multiplies a hundred-fold the luxuriance of metaphor, the incoherence of style, and the unbridled vehemence of expression.[3]

And Richard Grant White speaks to much the same purpose:

Akin to this power in Shakespeare is that of pushing hyperbole to the verge of absurdity; of mingling heterogeneous metaphors and similes which, coldly examined, seem discordant; in short, of apparently setting at naught the rules of rhetoric.[4]

And again White says:

Never did intellectual wealth equal in degree the boundless riches of Shakespeare's fancy. He compelled all nature and all art, all that God had revealed, and all that man had discovered, to contribute materials to enrich his style and enforce his thought; so that the entire range of human knowledge must be laid under contribution to illustrate his writings. This inexhaustible mine of fancy, furnishing metaphor, comparison, illustration, impersonation, in ceaseless alternation, often intermingled, so that the one cannot be severed from the other, . . . is the great distinctive intellectual trait of Shakespeare's style. In his use of simile, imagery and impersonation he exhibits a power to which that of any other

[1] Taine's *History of English Literature*, pp. 204 and seq.
[2] Ibid., p. 212.
[3] Ibid., p. 213.
[4] *Life and Genius of Shak.*, p. 229.

poet in this respect cannot be compared, even in the way of derogation, for it is not only superior to but unlike any other.[1]

When we turn to Bacon, we find the formal, decorous, world-respecting side of the man's character. Under the disguise of the player of Stratford he could give free vent to all the passions and enormities of his soul. In the first capacity he was a philosopher, courtier and statesman; in the latter he was simply a poet and play-writer. In the one he was forced to maintain appearances before court, bar and society; in the other, behind his mask, he was utterly irresponsible and could turn out his very soul, with none to question him.

Hence we must look for the characteristics of the poet in a modified form in those of the philosopher. He is "off the tripod." But even then we shall find the traces of the constitution of the mind which distinguished Shakespeare.

I have just cited Taine's description of Shakespeare; let us see what he has to say of Bacon:

> In this band of scholars, dreamers and inquirers, appears the most comprehensive, sensible, originative of the minds of the age, Francis Bacon; a great and luminous intellect, one of *the finest of this poetic progeny*, who, like his predecessors, was naturally disposed to clothe his ideas in the most splendid dress: in this age a thought did not seem complete until it had assumed form and color. But what distinguishes him from the others is, that with him an image only serves to concentrate meditation. He reflected long, stamped on his mind all the parts and relations of his subject; he is master of it, and then, instead of exposing this complete idea in a graduated chain of reasoning, he embodies it in a comparison so expressive, exact, lucid, that behind the figure we perceive all the details of the idea, like liquor in a fine crystal vase.[2]

And a writer in the *Encyclopædia Britannica*, speaking of Bacon, says:

> A sentence from the *Essays* can rarely be mistaken for the production of any other writer. The short, pithy sayings,
>
> > Jewels, five words long,
> > That on the stretched forefinger of all time
> > Sparkle forever,
>
> have become popular mottoes and household words. The style is quaint, original, *abounding in allusions and witticisms*, and *rich, even to gorgeousness, with piled-up analogies and metaphors.*

Alexander Smith says of Bacon's *Essays:*

> He seems to have written his *Essays with the pen of Shakespeare.*

---

[1] *Life and Genius of Shak.*, p. 252.   [2] *Taine's History of English Literature*, p. 153.

E. P. Whipple says of them:

They combine the greatest brevity with the greatest beauty of expression.

A. F. Blaisdell says:

Notice, also, the poetry of his style. So far as is known, he wrote but one poem, but all his literary works are instinct with poetry, in the wider sense of the word. Sometimes it is seen in a beautiful simile or a felicitous phrase; sometimes in a touch of pathos, more often in the rhythmical cadence of a sentence which clings to the memory as only poetry can.

Even the *passion* and *vehemence* which we have found to be such distinguishing traits of Shakespeare's genius are found in Bacon.

The laborious, but incredulous, Spedding remarks:

Bacon's mind, with its fullness and eagerness of thought, was at all times apt to outrun his powers of grammatical expression, but also of the history of the English language, then gradually finding its powers and settling, but not settled, into form.[1]

This outrunning the powers of grammatical expression is the very trait which has been observed in Shakespeare; — as when he makes Mark Antony say of the wound inflicted upon Cæsar by the dagger of Brutus:

This was the most unkindest cut of all.[2]

And here we are reminded of Bacon's theory that the English grammar should be reorganized; that he thought of making a grammar for himself.

And Spedding says of the *Natural History*, a most dry subject:

The addresses to the reader are full of weighty thought and passionate eloquence.[3]

But there was one man who knew Francis Bacon better than any and all others of his age; that was his "other self," Sir Tobie Matthew. He was in the heart of all Bacon's secrets; he knew just what Bacon had written, because his compositions were all submitted to him in the first instance, hot from the mint of the author's great mind. He knew Bacon's acknowledged writings, and he knew, also, those "concealed" writings which constituted him, in his judgment, "the greatest wit of our country, . . . though he be known by another name." And Sir Tobie was a scholar and an author, and an eminently conscientious and righteous man; who had suffered exile from his native land, and had sacrificed all the victories of life for his religious convictions;

---

[1] *Life and Works*, vol. I, p. 245.
[2] *Julius Cæsar*, III, 2.
[3] *Life and Works*, vol. VII, p. 381.

and the man who does that, whatever may be his creed or his dogmas, is worthy of all praise and honor. And Sir Tobie, with all this knowledge of Bacon, spoke of him, long after his death, in terms which are extravagant if applied to Bacon's acknowledged writings, but which fit precisely into the characteristics of the Shakespeare Plays. He said:

... A man so rare in knowledge, of so many several kinds, endued with the facility and *felicity of expressing it all* in so elegant, significant, so *abundant*, and yet so *choice and ravishing a way of words, of metaphors, of allusions*, as perhaps the world hath not seen since it was a world.[1]

II. A Startling Revelation.

And even as this book is being printed, a writer in the Chicago *Tribune* calls attention to the surprising fact that the *New English Dictionary*, now being published in England, on a magnificent scale, and in which is given the time when and the place where each English word made its first appearance, proves that in the first two hundred pages of the work there are *one hundred and forty-six words*, now in common use, which were invented, or formed out of the raw material of his own and other languages, by the man who wrote the Shakespeare Plays. And the writer shows that, at this rate, our total indebtedness to the man we call Shakespeare, for additions to the vocabulary of the English tongue, cannot be less than *five thousand words*. I quote:

Rome owed only one word to Julius Cæsar. The nature of our debt will be more apparent if we examine some of these hundred and a half of Shakespearean words, all so near the beginning of the alphabet that the last one of them is *air*. We owe the poet the first use of the word *air* itself in one of its senses as a noun, and in three as a verb or participle. He first said *air-drawn* and *airless*. He added a new signification to *airy* and *aerial*. Nobody before him had written *aired*, and more than a tithe of the verbal gifts now in view were such perfect participles. Well-nigh as many were adverbs. In no previous writer have Dr. Murray's argus eyes detected *accidentally*, nor any of the following: *Abjectly, acutely, admiringly, adoptedly, adversely*. How our fathers could exist so long without some of these vocables must move our special wonder. To *absolutely, accordingly, actively* and *affectionately* Shakespeare added a new sense. It is not a little surprising that the word *abreast* was never printed before the couplet:

My soul shall thine keep company to heaven:
Tarry, sweet soul, for mine, then fly *abreast*.

Of the 146 words and meanings first given us by Shakespeare at least two-thirds are of classical origin.... The strangest thing seems to be that so few of Shake-

---

[1] *Address to the Reader*, prefixed to *Collection of English Letters*, 1660.

speare's innovations — not so much as one-fifth — have become obsolete. He gave them not only life, but immortality.

Is anybody shallow enough to believe that the play-actor of Stratford — selling malt and suing his neighbors — had the brain, the capacity or the purpose to thus create a language?

I say a language, for it is to be remembered that the ordinary peasant or *navvy* of England has but about three hundred words in his vocabulary. And here was one man who, we are told, added to the English tongue *probably seventeen times the number of words used by the inhabitants of Stratford in that age.*

And when we turn to Bacon's *Promus*, or storehouse of suggestions for *elegancies* of speech, we find him in the very work of manufacturing words to enrich the English tongue. We see him, in *Promus* notes 1214 and 1215, playing on the words "*Abedd — ro*(u)*se you — owt bed*": and then we find him developing this into *uprouse*, a word never seen before in the world; and, as Mrs. Pott has shown, this reappears in the play of *Romeo and Juliet* in connection with *golden sleep* (which is also found in the *Promus* notes[1]) thus:

> But where unbruised youth with unstuffed brain
> Doth couch his limbs, there *golden sleep* doth reign:
> Therefore thy earliness doth me assure
> Thou art *uproused* by some distemperature.[2]

And, close at hand, in these *Promus* notes, we find the word *rome*, which may have been a hint jotted down for the name of Romeo. And we find that Bacon, in these *Promus* notes, coined and used for the first time *barajar* (for *shuffle*), *real, brazed, peradventure*, etc.

In other words, we learn now that the writer of the Plays added five thousand new words to the English language. We look into Bacon's work-shop and we find the great artist at work manufacturing words. We peep into the kitchen of New Place, Stratford, and we see the occupant brewing beer! Who wrote the plays?

And Bacon notes that the English language has been greatly enriched during Elizabeth's reign!

More than this, Mrs. Pott has shown in her great work[3] that Bacon, anxious to humanize his race and civilize his age, created and introduced into our speech those pleasant conventionalities

---

[1] *Promus*, note 1209.   [2] *Romeo and Juliet*, ii, 3.   [3] *Promus*, p. 62.

and sweet courtesies with which we now salute each other; as "good-morrow," "good-night," etc.; and that he is found jotting them down in his *Promus* notes, from which they reappear in the Shakespeare Plays, for the first time in English literature. And all this goes to confirm my view, hereinbefore expressed, of the great *purposes* which lie behind the Plays: for in it all, with the creation of the five thousand new words, we see the soul of the philanthropist, who, "in a despised weed, had procured the good of all men." Mighty soul! We are but beginning to catch glimpses of thy vast proportions! Shame on the purblind ages that have failed to recognize thy light.

And in connection with all this we must remember Bacon's modest remark, that during the reign of Elizabeth the powers of the English language had been vastly increased.

Why, this man overshadows the world! He has not only revolutionized our philosophy, delighted our eyes, enraptured our ears and educated our hearts, but he has even armed our tongues with new resources and fitted our English speech to become, as it will in time, the universal language of the globe.

III. Other Details of Style.

The great Scotch essayist, Mackintosh, said of Bacon:

No man ever united a more poetical style to a less poetical philosophy. One great end of his discipline is to prevent mysticism and fanaticism from obstructing the pursuit of truth. With a less *brilliant fancy* he would have had a mind less qualified for philosophical inquiry. His fancy gave him that power of illustrative metaphor, by which he seemed to have *invented again the part of language* which respects philosophy; and it rendered new truths more distinctly visible even to his own eye, *in their bright clothing of imagery*.[1]

And, again, the same writer says:

But that in which he most excelled all other men was the range and compass of his intellectual view, and the power of contemplating many and distant objects together without indistinctness or confusion, which he himself has called the "discursive" or "comprehensive" understanding. This wide-ranging intellect was *illuminated by the brightest fancy that ever contented itself with the office of only ministering to Reason:* and from this singular relation of the two grand faculties of man it has resulted that his philosophy, though illustrated still more than adorned by *the utmost splendor of imagery*, continues still subject to the undivided supremacy of Intellect. In the midst of all the prodigality of *an imagination which, had it been independent, would have been poetical*, his opinions remained severely rational.[2]

---

[1] *The Modern British Essayists — Mackintosh*, p. 18.   [2] Ibid., p. 17.

And, on the other hand, as matching this utterance, Mr. T. B. Shaw finds in both Bacon and Shakespeare the same combination of reason and imagination. He says, speaking of Bacon:

> In his style there is the same quality *which is applauded in Shakespeare*, a combination of the intellectual and the imaginative, the *closest reasoning in the boldest metaphor*.

And Taine says of Bacon:

> *Like the poets*, he peoples nature with instincts and desires; attributes to bodies an actual voracity; to the atmosphere a thirst for light, sounds, odors, vapors, which it drinks in; to metals a sort of haste to be incorporated with acids.[1]

The same trait of impersonation is found in Shakespeare carried to the greatest excess. The echo becomes

> The babbling gossip of the air.[2]

The wind becomes "the wanton wind;" "the bawdy wind, that kisses all it meets;" "the scolding wind;" "the posting wind," etc. In short, every quality of nature becomes a living individuality.

> He puts a spirit of life in everything,
> Till wanton nature laughs and leaps with him.

IV. PLEONASMS.

Speaking of the affluence and superabundance of Shakespeare's genius, Taine says:

> These vehement expressions, so natural in their upwelling, instead of following one after the other slowly and with effort, are hurled out by hundreds with an impetuous ease and abundance like the bubbling waves from a welling spring, which are heaped together, rise one above another, and find nowhere room enough to spread and exhaust themselves? You may find in *Romeo and Juliet* a score of examples of this inexhaustible inspiration. The two lovers pile up an infinite mass of metaphors, impassioned exaggerations, clenches, contorted phrases, amorous extravagances.[3]

This trait leads in both writers to that use of redundant words known in rhetoric as *pleonasm*. It marks a trait of mind which cannot be satisfied with a bare statement of fact, but in its prodigal richness heaps adjective on adjective and phrase on phrase.

Take this instance from Bacon:

> Everything has been abandoned either to the mists of tradition, the *whirl and confusion* of argument, or the *waves and mazes* of chance, and *desultory, ill-combined* experiments.[4]

---

[1] Taine's *History of English Literature*, p. 155.
[2] *Twelfth Night*, I, 5.
[3] Taine's *History of English Literature*, p. 213.
[4] *Novum Organum*, book I.

Again he says:

> Those acts which are *permanent and perpetual*.[1]

And here we see the piling-on of adjectives often observed in Shakespeare, what Swinburne calls "an effusion or effervescence of words":

> It is the property of *good and sound* knowledge to *putrefy and dissolve* into a number of *subtle, idle, unwholesome*, and, I may term them, *vermiculate* questions.[2]

And again he speaks of

> The *flowing and watery* vein of Osorius, the Portugal bishop.

And again:

> Was *esteemed and accounted* a more pernicious engine.[3]

> All things dissolve into *anarchy and confusion*.[4]

> The *emulation and provocation* of their example have much *quickened and strengthened* the state of learning.[5]

And again:

> All things may be *endowed and adorned* with speeches, but knowledge itself is more beautiful than any apparel of words that can be put upon it.[6]

We turn to Shakespeare, and we find Grant White noting the same tendency. He says:

> Shakespeare mingles words of native and foreign origin which are synonymous so closely as to subject him to the charge of pleonasm; . . . he has, for instance, in *King John*, "*infinite and boundless* reach;" in *Measure for Measure*, "*rebate and blunt* his natural edge;" and in *Othello*, "to such *exsufficate and blown* surmises."[7]

Let me give some further examples of this inherent tendency of Shakespeare to pour words in superabundance over thoughts:

> I am one
> Whom the vile *blows and buffets* of the world
> Have so incensed.[8]

> *Hugged and embraced* by the strumpet wind.[9]

> Into the *harsh and boisterous* tongue of war.[10]

> Of *hinds and peasants, rude and merciless*.[11]

> That it may *grow and sprout* as high as heaven.[12]

> Hath given them *heart and courage* to proceed.[13]

---

[1] *Advancement of Learning*, book i.
[2] Ibid.
[3] Ibid.
[4] Ibid.
[5] Ibid.
[6] *In Praise of Knowledge*.
[7] *Life and Genius of Shak.*, p. 219.
[8] *Macbeth*, iii, 1.
[9] *Merchant of Venice*, ii, 6.
[10] *2d Henry IV.*, iv, 1.
[11] *2d Henry VI.*, iv, 4.
[12] *2d Henry IV.*, ii, 3.
[13] *2d Henry VI.*, iv, 2.

Within the *book and volume* of my brain.[1]

If that rebellion
Came like itself in *base and abject* routs.[2]

To *fleer and scorn* at our solemnity.[3]

As *broad and general* as the casing air.[4]

Luxurious, avaricious, *false, deceitful*.[5]

What *trash* is Rome,
What *rubbish and what offal*.[6]

Led by a *delicate and tender* prince.[7]

Tortive and errant from his course of growth.[8]

Things *base and vile*, holding no quantity.[9]

Hast thou so *cracked and splitted* my poor tongue.[10]

And I will *stoop and humble* my intents.[11]

An *unlessoned girl, unschooled*, unpracticed.[12]

Garnished and decked in modest compliment.[13]

Divert and crack, rend and deracinate
The *unity and married calm of states*
Quite from their fixture.[14]

I might heap up many more examples to demonstrate the unity of style in the two sets of writings in this particular, but it seems to me that it is not necessary. I will close this branch of the subject with a quotation from Mark Antony's speech over the dead body of Cæsar:

Oh, pardon me, thou bleeding piece of earth,
That I am *meek and gentle* with these butchers!

. . .

Which like dumb mouths do ope their ruby lips,
To beg the *voice and utterance* of my tongue!
A curse shall light upon the limbs of men;
Domestic fury and *fierce civil strife*
Shall cumber all the parts of Italy;
Blood and destruction shall be so in use.[15]

[1] *Hamlet*, i, 5.
[2] *2d Henry IV.*, iv, 1.
[3] *Cymbeline*, i, 4.
[4] *Macbeth*, iii, 4.
[5] Ibid., iv, 3.
[6] *Julius Cæsar*, i, 3.
[7] *Hamlet*, iv, 4.
[8] *Troilus and Cressida*, i, 3.
[9] *Midsummer Night's Dream*, i, 2.
[10] *Comedy of Errors*, v, 1.
[11] *2d Henry IV.*, v, 2.
[12] *Merchant of Venice*, iii, 2.
[13] *Henry V.*, ii, 2.
[14] *Troilus and Cressida*, i, 3.
[15] *Julius Cæsar*, iii, 1.

It is no wonder that the precise and single-minded Hume thought that both Bacon and Shakespeare showed

A want of simplicity and purity of diction, with defective taste and elegance.

Certainly no other men in the world ever wasted such an affluence of words, thoughts, images and metaphors in their writings.

V. Condensation of Style.

Another marked feature of the style of both sets of writings is their marvelous compactness and condensation. Macaulay says of Bacon:

He had a wonderful faculty for packing thought close and rendering it portable.[1]

We need only turn to Bacon's *Essays* to find ample confirmation of this statement.

Take one instance, from one of his letters, which might serve to pass into a proverb:

A timorous man is everybody's, and a covetous man is his own.[2]

Neither is it necessary to use any argument to demonstrate that Shakespeare possessed in an exceptional degree this faculty of "packing thought close and rendering it portable." Take an example:

> Who steals my purse steals trash;
> '*Twas mine*, '*tis his*, and has been slave to thousands.

Here is an essay stated in two lines. And here we have another:

> Let the end try the man.[3]

Again:
> Let proof speak.[4]

Again:
> Things won are done; joy's soul lies in the doing.[5]

Take this instance:

We defy augury; there is a special providence in the fall of a sparrow. If it be now, 'tis not to come; if it be not to come, it will be now; if it be not now, yet it will come; the readiness is all.[6]

It requires an analytical mind to follow the thought here through the closely-packed and compressed sentences.

But the faculty is the same in both. Taine says of Bacon:

Shakespeare and the seers do not contain more vigorous or *expressive condensations of thought*, more resembling inspiration; and in Bacon they are to be found everywhere.[7]

---

[1] *Essays — Bacon*, p. 285.
[2] Letter to the Lord Keeper, April 5, 1594.
[3] 2d *Henry IV.*, ii, 2.
[4] *Cymbeline*, iii, 1.
[5] *Troilus and Cressida*, i, 2.
[6] *Hamlet*, v, 2.
[7] *History of English Literature*, p. 154.

VI. The Tendency to Aphorisms.

One of the most marked characteristics of both sets of writings is the tendency to rise from particulars to principles; to see in a mass of facts simply the foundation for a generalization; to indulge in aphorisms.

Taine says of Bacon:

> On the whole, his process is not that of the creators: it is intuition, not reasoning. When he has laid up his store of facts, the greatest possible, on some vast subject, on some entire province of the mind, on the whole anterior philosophy, on the general condition of the sciences, on the power and limits of human reason, he casts over all this a comprehensive view, as it were, a great net, brings up a universal idea, *condenses his idea into a maxim*, and hands it to us with the words, "Verify and profit by it." . . . Nothing more; no proof, no effort to convince: he affirms, and does nothing more; *he has thought in the manner of artists and poets, and he speaks after the manner of prophets and seers.* Cogitata et Visa, this title of one of his books might be the title of all. The most admirable, the *Novum Organum*, is *a string of aphorisms* — a collection, as it were, of scientific decrees, as of an oracle, who foresees the future and reveals the truth. And to make the resemblance complete he expresses them by poetical figures, by enigmatic abbreviations, almost in Sibyllene verses. *Idola specûs, Idola tribûs, Idola fori, Idola theatri;* every one will recall these strange names by which he signifies the four kinds of illusions to which man is subject.[1]

The words which Taine applies to Bacon's *Novum Organum*, "a string of aphorisms," might with equal appropriateness be used to describe the Shakespeare Plays. We can hardly quote from them an elevated passage which does not enunciate some general principle. Hence his utterances cling to the tongues of men like proverbs. He takes a mass of facts, as the chemist takes the crude bark of the Peruvian tree, and distills out of it, in the marvelous alembic of his mind, a concentrated essence, which, while it holds an infinitesimal relation to the quantity of the original substance, yet contains all its essential virtues.

Let me give a few instances of this trait. Shakespeare says:

> His rash, fierce blaze of riot cannot last,
> (1) For violent showers soon burn out themselves;
> (2) Small showers last long, but sudden storms are short;
> (3) He tires betimes that spurs too fast betimes;
> (4) With eager feeding food doth choke the feeder;
> (5) Like vanity, insatiate cormorant,
> Consuming means, soon preys upon itself.[2]

One would scarcely believe that these five aphorisms, contained in seven lines, stood in this connected order in the play. It would

---

[1] *Taine's History of English Literature*, p. 134.   [2] *Richard II.*, ii, 1.

naturally be thought that they had been selected from a wide range. The tendency to form generalizations might almost be called a disease of style in both writers.

Shakespeare can hardly touch a particular fact without rising from it to a principle. He says:

> Take up this mangled matter at the best;
> Men do their broken weapons rather use
> Than their bare hands.[1]

Again:

> (1) Our indiscretions sometimes serve us well,
> When our deep plots do pall; and that should teach us,
> (2) There's a divinity that shapes our ends,
> Rough-hew them how we will.[2]

Again:

> They say best men are molded out of faults.[3]

Again:

> (1) The evil that men do lives after them;
> (2) The good is oft interrèd with their bones.[4]

Again:

> (1) Men's evil manners live in brass; (2) their virtues
> We *write in water*.[5]

This last sentence reminds one of Bacon's "but *limns the water* and but *writes* in dust."

And again:

> Thieves for their robbery have authority
> When judges steal themselves.

We turn to Bacon, and we might fill pages with similar aphorisms. Here are a few examples:

Extreme self-lovers will set a man's house afire to roast their own eggs.

The best part of beauty is that which a picture cannot express.

Riches are the baggage of virtue; they cannot be spared nor left behind, but they hinder the march.

That envy is most malignant which is like Cain's, who envied his brother because his sacrifice was better accepted — when there was nobody but God to look on.

Discretion in speech is more than eloquence.

This reminds us of Shakespeare's parallel thought:

> The better part of valor is discretion.

---

[1] *Othello*, i, 3.   [3] *Measure for Measure*, v, 1.   [5] *Henry VIII.*, iv, 2.
[2] *Hamlet*, v, 2.   [4] *Julius Cæsar*, iii, 2.

And again Bacon says:

> Fortune is like a market, where, many times, if you stay a little, the price will fall.
>
> A faculty of wise interrogating is half a knowledge.

Observe, too, how Bacon, like Shakespeare, always reasons by analogy — the great by the small, the mind by the body. He says, speaking of natural philosophy:

> Do not imagine that such inquiries question the immortality of the soul, or derogate from its sovereignty over the body. The infant in its mother's womb partakes of the accidents to its mother, but is separable in due season.

What a thought is this! The body carries the soul in it as the mother's womb carries the child; but the child is separable at birth and becomes a distinct entity — so does the soul at death. To care for the mother does not derogate from the child; justice to the conditions of the body, growing out of knowledge, cannot be injurious to the tenant of the body, or detract from its dignity.

What a mind, that can thus pack comprehensive theories in a paragraph!

VII. THE TENDENCY TO TRIPLE FORMS.

We find in Bacon a disposition, growing out of his sense of harmony, to run his sentences into triplicate forms, and we will observe the same characteristic in Shakespeare.

Compare, for instance, the two following sentences. I mark the triplicate form by inserting numbers.

Shakespeare says, in Maria's letter to Malvolio:

> (1) Some are born great, (2) some achieve greatness, and (3) some have greatness thrust upon them.[1]

Bacon says, in his essay *Of Studies:*

> (1) Some books are to be tasted, (2) others are to be swallowed, (3) and some few to be chewed and digested.

Can any man doubt that these utterances came out of the same mind? There is the same condensation; the same packing of thought into close space; the same original and profound way of looking into things; and the same rhythmical balance into triplicate forms.

But, lest the reader may think that I have selected two phrases accidentally alike, I give the sentences in which they are found.

[1] *Twelfth Night*, ii, 5.

Maria says to Malvolio:

Be not afraid of greatness. (1) Some are born great, (2) some achieve greatness, and (3) some have greatness thrust upon them. . . . (1) Be opposite with a kinsman, surly with servants; (2) let thy tongue tang arguments of state; (3) put thyself into the trick of singularity. . . . If not, let me see thee (1) a steward still, (2) the fellow of servants, and (3) not worthy to touch Fortune's fingers.

And here is a larger extract from Bacon's essay *Of Studies:*

Studies serve (1) for delight, (2) for ornament, and (3) for ability. . . . (1) To spend too much time in them is sloth; (2) to use them too much for ornament is affectation; (3) to make judgment wholly by their rules is the humor of a scholar. . . . (1) Crafty men contemn them, (2) simple men admire them, (3) and wise men use them. . . . (1) Read not to contradict and confute, (2) nor to believe and take for granted, (3) nor to find talk and discourse; but to weigh and consider. (1) Some books are to be tasted, (2) others to be swallowed, (3) and some few to be chewed and digested. . . . (1) Reading maketh a full man, (2) conference a ready man, (3) and writing an exact man. And therefore (1) if a man write little he had need to have a great memory; (2) if he confer little, he had need have a present wit; (3) and if he read little, he had need have much cunning, to seem to know that he doth not.[1]

We find this triplicate form all through Bacon's writings. He says:

He can disclose and bring forward, therefore, things which neither (1) the vicissitudes of nature, (2) nor the industry of experiment, (3) nor chance itself would ever have brought about, and which would forever have escaped man's thoughts.[2]

And again:

What is (1) constant, (2) eternal and (3) universal in nature?[3]

And again:

Every interpretation of nature sets out from the senses, and leads by a (1) regular, (2) fixed and (3) well-established road.[4]

And again:

Letters are good (1) when a man would draw an answer by letter back again; (2) or when it may serve for a man's justification afterward, or (3) where there may be danger to be interrupted or heard by pieces.[5]

And again:

A (1) brief, (2) bare and (3) simple enumeration.[6]

And again:

Nature is (1) often hidden, (2) sometimes overcome, (3) seldom extinguished.[7]

And again:

The (1) crudities, (2) impurities and (3) leprosities of metals.[8]

[1] Essay *Of Studies.*
[2] *Novum Organum,* book ii.
[3] Ibid.
[4] Ibid., book i.
[5] Essay *Of Negotiating.*
[6] *Novum Organum,* book i.
[7] Essay *Of Nature in Men.*
[8] *Natural History,* § 326.

And again:

Whether it be (1) honor, or (2) riches, or (3) delight, or (1) glory, or (2) knowledge, or (3) anything else which they seek after.[1]

And again:

To (1) assail, (2) sap, and (3) work into the constancy of Sir Robert Clifford.[2]

We turn to Shakespeare, and we find the same tendency. How precisely in the style of Bacon's *Essays* are the disquisitions of Falstaff:

Yea, but how if honor prick me off when I come on; how then? (1) Can honor set a leg? No. (2) Or an arm? No. (3) Or take away the grief of a wound? No. Honor has no skill in surgery, then? No. (1) What is honor? A word. (2) What is that word? Honor. (3) What is that honor? Air. A trim reckoning. Who hath it? He that died Wednesday. (1) Doth he feel it? No. (2) Doth he hear it? No. (3) Is it insensible, then? Yea, to the dead. But will it not live with the living? No. Detraction will not suffer it.[3]

And, speaking of the effect of good wine, Falstaff says:

It ascends me into the brain; dries me there all the (1) foolish, (2) and dull, (3) and crudy vapors which environ it: makes it (1) apprehensive, (2) quick, (3) forgetive; full of (1) nimble, (2) fiery and (3) delectable shapes. . . . The cold blood he did naturally inherit from his father, he hath, like (1) lean, (2) sterile and (3) bare land, (1) manured, (2) husbanded and (3) tilled.[4]

But this trait is not confined to the utterances of Falstaff. We find it all through the Plays. Take the following instances:

> For I have neither (1) wit, (2) nor words, (3) nor worth,
> (1) Action, (2) nor utterance, (3) nor the power of speech,
> To stir men's blood.[5]

Again:

(1) Romans, (2) countrymen and (3) lovers. . . . (1) As Cæsar loved me, I weep for him; (2) as he was fortunate, I rejoice at it; (3) as he was valiant, I honor him; but, as he was ambitious, I slew him. . . . (1) Who is here so base that would be a bondman? If any, speak; for him have I offended. (2) Who is here so rude that would not be a Roman? If any, speak; for him have I offended. (3) Who is here so vile that will not love his country? If any, speak; for him have I offended. I pause for a reply.[6]

Again:

> (1) Thou art most rich being poor;
> (2) Most choice, forsaken; (3) and most loved, despised.[7]

Again:

Alas, poor Romeo! he is already dead; (1) stabbed with a white wench's black eye; (2) shot through the ear with a love-song; (3) the very pin of his heart cleft with the blind bow-boy's butt-shaft.[8]

---

[1] *Wisdom of the Ancients — Dionysus.*
[2] *History of Henry VII.*
[3] *1st Henry IV.*, v, 1.
[4] *2d Henry IV.*, iv, 3.
[5] *Julius Cæsar*, iii, 2.
[6] Ibid.
[7] *Lear*, i, 1.
[8] *Romeo and Juliet*, ii, 4.

IDENTITIES OF STYLE.

Again:

> Oh, what a noble mind is here o'erthrown!
> (1) The courtier's, (2) soldier's, (3) scholar's (1) eye, (2) tongue, (3) sword.

Again:

I am myself indifferent honest: but yet I could accuse me of such things, that it were better my mother had not borne me: I am very (1) proud, (2) revengeful, (3) ambitious; with more offenses at my beck than I have (1) thoughts to put them in, (2) imagination to give them shape, or (3) time to act them in.[1]

Again:

> 'Tis slander,
> (1) Whose edge is sharper than the sword; (2) whose tongue
> Outvenoms all the worms of Nile; (3) whose breath
> Rides on the posting winds, and doth belie
> All corners of the world: (1) kings, (2) queens and (3) states,
> (1) Maids, (2) matrons, nay, (3) the secrets of the grave,
> This viperous slander enters.[2]

Again:

This peace is nothing but (1) to rust iron, (2) increase tailors and (3) breed ballad-makers.[3]

Again:

> Live loathed and long,
> Most (1) smiling, (2) smooth, (3) detested parasites,
> (1) Courteous destroyers, (2) affable wolves, (3) meek bears,
> (1) You fools of fortune, (2) trencher fiends, (3) time's flies,
> (1) Cap-and-knee slaves, (2) vapors, and (3) minute jacks.[4]

Again:

> Must I needs forego
> (1) So good, (2) so noble and (3) so true a master.[5]

And again:

> (1) Her father loved me; (2) oft invited me;
> (3) Still questioned me the story of my life,
> From year to year; the (1) battles, (2) sieges, (3) fortunes
> That I have passed.[6]

Again:

It would be (1) argument for a week, (2) laughter for a month, and (3) a good jest forever.[7]

Again:

(1) Wooing, (2) wedding and (3) repenting are as (1) a Scotch jig, (2) a measure, and (3) a cinque pace: (1) the first suit is hot and hasty, like a Scotch jig, and full as fantastical; (2) the wedding mannerly, modest, as a measure full of state and ancientry; and (3) then comes repentance, and, with his bad legs, falls into the cinque pace faster and faster, until he sinks into his grave.[8]

[1] *Hamlet*, iii, 1.
[2] *Cymbeline*, iii, 4.
[3] *Coriolanus*, iv, 5.
[4] *Titus Andronicus*, ii, 6.
[5] *Henry VIII.*, ii, 2.
[6] *Othello*, i, 3.
[7] *1st Henry IV.*, ii, 2.
[8] *Much Ado about Nothing*, iii, 1.

Again:

> Oh, that I were a god, to shoot forth thunder
> Upon these (1) paltry, (2) servile, (3) abject drudges.[1]

Again:

Not only, Mistress Ford, in the simple office of love, but in all (1) accoutrement, (2) complement (3) and ceremony of it.[2]

Again:

> How could (1) communities,
> (2) Degrees in schools and (3) brotherhood in cities,
> (1) Peaceful commerce from divided shores,
> (2) The primogeniture and due of birth,
> (3) Prerogative of age, (1) crowns, (2) scepters, (3) laurels,
> But by degree, stand in authentic place?[3]

Again:

But (1) manhood is melted into courtesies, (2) valor into compliment, and (3) men are turned into tongues, and trim ones, too.[4]

Again:

> For she is (1) lumpish, (2) heavy, (3) melancholy.[5]

Again:

> Say that upon the altar of her beauty
> You sacrifice (1) your tears, (2) your sighs, (3) your heart.[6]

Again:

> Had I power I should
> (1) Pour the sweet milk of concord into hell,
> (2) Uproar the universal peace, (3) confound
> All unity on earth.[7]

Again:

> To be directed
> As from her (1) lord, (2) her governor, (3) her king.[8]

Again:

> To wound (1) thy lord, (2) thy king, (3) thy governor.[9]

Again:

> Is fit for (1) treasons, (2) stratagems and (3) spoils.[10]

I might continue these examples at much greater length, but I think I have given enough to prove that both Bacon and the writer of the Plays possessed, as a characteristic of style, a tendency to balance their sentences in triplicate forms. This trait grew out of the sense of harmony in the ear; it was an unconscious arrangement of thoughts in obedience to a peculiar inward instinct, and it goes far to establish identity.

---

[1] *2d Henry VI.*, iv, 1.
[2] *Merry Wives of Windsor*, iv, 2.
[3] *Troilus and Cressida*, i, 3.
[4] *Much Ado about Nothing*, iv, 1.
[5] *Two Gentlemen of Verona*, iii, 2.
[6] Ibid.
[7] *Macbeth*, iv, 3.
[8] *Merchant of Venice*, iii, 2.
[9] *Taming of the Shrew*, v, 2.
[10] *Merchant of Venice*, v, 1.

VIII. Catalogues of Words.

The man who thinks in concrete forms solidifies words into ideas. He who has trained himself to observe as a natural philosopher, builds in numerical order bases for his thought. He erects the poem on a foundation of facts. He collects materials before he builds.

This trait is very marked in Bacon. He was the most observant of men. No point or fact escaped him. Hence he runs to the habit of stringing together catalogues of words.

For instance, he says in *The Experimental History:*

There are doubtless in Europe many capable, free, sublimed, subtile, solid constant wits.

Again he speaks of

Servile, blind, dull, vague and abrupt experiments.[1]

Again he says:

Let anti-masques not be long; they have been commonly of fools, satyrs, baboons, wild men, antics, beasts, spirits, witches, Ethiopes, pigmies, turquets, nymphs, rustics, cupids, statues moving, and the like.[2]

Bacon also says:

Such are gold in weight, iron in hardness, the whale in size, the dog in smell, the flame of gunpowder in rapid expansion, and others of like nature.[3]

We turn to *Lear*, and we hear the same voice speaking of

False of heart, light of ear, bloody of hand; hog in sloth, fox in stealth, wolf in greediness, dog in madness, lion in prey.[4]

Again Shakespeare says:

As honor, love, obedience, troops of friends.[5]

And here is another instance of the tendency to make catalogues of words:

Beauty, wit,
High birth, vigor of bone, desert in service,
Love, friendship, charity, are subjects all
To envious and calumniating time.[6]

Again we have, in the same play — the most philosophical of all the Plays — these lines:

All our abilities, gifts, natures, shapes,
Severals and generals of grace exact,
Achievements, plots, orders, preventions,
Excitements to the field, or speech for truce,

---

[1] *Great Instauration.* [3] *Novum Organum*, book ii. [5] *Macbeth*, v. 2.
[2] *Essay Of Masks.* [4] *Lear*, iii, 4. [6] *Troilus and Cressida*, iii, 3.

> Success or loss, what is, or what is not, serves
> As stuff for these two to make paradoxes.[1]

And in the famous description of the horse, in *Venus and Adonis*, we see the same closely-observing eye of the naturalist:

> Round-hoofed, short-jointed, fetlocks shag and long,
>   Broad breast, full eye, small head, and nostril wide,
> High crest, short ears, straight legs and passing strong,
>   Thin mane, thick tail, broad buttock, tender hide.

Prof. Dowden says:

> This passage has been much admired; but is it poetry or a paragraph from an advertisement of a horse-sale?[2]

And here, in a more poetical passage, we observe the same tendency to the enumeration of facts:

> My hounds are bred out of the Spartan kind,
> So flew'd, so sanded, and their heads are hung
> With ears that sweep away the morning dew;
> Crook-kneed and dew-lapped, like Thessalian bulls;
> Slow in pursuit, but matched in mouth-like bells,
> Each under each.[3]

And in the same vein of close and accurate observation of details, "the contracting of the eye of the mind," as Bacon calls it, is the following description of a murdered man:

> But see, his face is black and full of blood;
> His eye-balls further out than when he lived,
> Staring full-ghastly like a strangled man;
> His hair upreared, his nostrils stretched with struggling;
> His hands abroad displayed, as one that grasped
> And tugged for life, and was by strength subdued.
> Look, on the sheets his hair, you see, is sticking;
> His well-proportioned beard made rough and rugged,
> Like to the summer's corn by tempests lodged.[4]

IX. THE EUPHONIC TEST.

In Mr. Wilkes' book, *Shakespeare from an American Point of View*, there is contained an essay (p. 430) by Professor J. W. Taverner, of New York, in which he attempts to show that Bacon could not have written the Shakespeare Plays, because of the *Euphonic Test*. And yet he says:

> Upon examination of the limited poetry which we have from the pen of Bacon, I find nothing to criticise. Like unto Shakespeare, he takes good note of any deficiency of syllabic pulsation, and imparts the value of but one syllable to the

---

[1] *Troilus and Cressida*, i, 3.
[2] *Shak. Mind and Art*, p. 45.
[3] *Midsummer Night's Dream*, iv, 1.
[4] *2d Henry VI.*, iii, 2.

dissyllables *heaven, wearest, many, even, goeth;* and to *glittering* and *chariot* but the value of two, *precisely as Shakespeare would.*

But he tries to show that Bacon could not have written the Plays because it was his custom to run his sentences, as I have shown, into triplets. He says:

> Bacon, in this feature of the rhythmical adjustment of clauses, attaches to those sentences of his which are composed of *triple clauses of equal dimensions*, and which possess such regularity which he never seeks to disturb, etc.

And he gives in addition to the instances I have quoted from Bacon the following, among others:

> A man cannot speak (1) to his son but as a father, (2) to his wife but as a husband, and (3) to his enemy but upon terms.

> Judges ought to be (1) more learned than witty, (2) more reverent than plausible, and (3) more advised than confident.

And he argues that Shakespeare

> Does not object to four or more clauses, but he does to three.

And therefore Bacon did not write the Plays. Such arguments are fully answered by the pages of examples I have just given from the Shakespeare Plays, showing that the poet is even more prone to fall into the triple form of expression than Bacon—more prone, because there is more tendency to harmonious and balanced expressions in poetry than in prose.

But the Professor admits that there "is a kind of melody of speech that belongs to Bacon," and that his ear is exact, "and counts its seconds like the pendulum of a clock."

In truth, if any man would take the pains to print the prose disquisitions and monologues of Shakespeare, intermixed with extracts from as nearly similar productions of Bacon as may be, the ordinary reader would scarcely be able to tell which was which.

If such a reader was handed this passage, and asked to name the author, I think the probabilities are great that he would say it was from the pen of Francis Bacon:

> Novelty is only in request; and it is dangerous to be aged in any kind of course, as it is virtuous to be constant in any undertaking. There is scarce truth enough alive to make societies secure, but security enough to make fellowship accursed: much upon this riddle runs the wisdom of the world.

We have here the same condensed, pithy sentences which mark the great philosopher, together with the same antithetical way of balancing thought against thought.

Yet this is from Shakespeare. It will be found in *Measure for Measure.*[1]

And we can conceive that the following passage might have been written by Shakespeare — the very extravagance of hyperbole sounds like him:

<blockquote>Contrary is it with hypocrites and impostors, for they, in the church and before the people, *set themselves on fire*, and are *carried*, as it were, *out of themselves*, and, becoming as *men inspired with holy furies*, they *set heaven and earth together.*[2]</blockquote>

There is not a great stride from this to the poet's eye in a fine phrensy rolling from earth to heaven, from heaven to earth; and the madman seeing more devils than vast hell could hold.

In short, the resemblance between the two bodies of compositions is as close as could be reasonably expected, where one is almost exclusively prose, and the greatness of the other consists in the elevated flights of poetry. In the one case it is the lammergeyer sitting among the stones; in the other it is the great bird balanced on majestic pinions in the blue vault of heaven, far above the mountain-top and the emulous shafts of man.

[1] Act, iii, scene 2.   [2] *Meditationes Sacræ — Of Impostors.*

A000009791626